W9-COI-362

LANGENSCHEIDT'S
POCKET
DICTIONARIES

LANGENSCHEIDT'S POCKET HEBREW DICTIONARY

TO THE OLD TESTAMENT

HEBREW-ENGLISH

By

DR. KARL FEYERABEND

LANGENSCHEIDT

PREFACE

This Pocket Hebrew Dictionary contains the whole vocabulary of the Hebrew Old Testament, and will be useful even to advanced students.

The transcription gives the Sephardic pronunciation of Hebrew, and the Langenscheidt phonetic system is used to convey the sounds.

It is a handy and reliable pocket dictionary in an easy-to-read type. No user should have difficulties in finding the information he wants with complete ease and confidence.

TRANSCRIPTION

A. Vowels

	Hebrew characters		
1	◌ָ	ā	long } = a in *father*
2	◌ַ	ă	short } = a in *father*
3	◌ֲ	a	volatilized
4	◌ֵ	ē	long and narrow
5	◌ֶ	ĕ	short and open = a in *bad*
6	◌ֱ	e	volatilized = e in *happen*
7	◌ִ, ִי	ī	long = ee in *bee*
8	◌ִ	ĭ	short = i in *sin*
9	◌ֹ, וֹ	ō	long and narrow
10	◌ָ	ŏ	short and open = o in *god*
11	◌ֳ	o	volatilized, a very short open o
12	וּ, ◌ֻ	ū	long = o in *move*
13	◌ֻ	ŭ	short = u in *full*
14	◌ְ	e	(Shva mobile) shortest **e**

B. Consonants

15	א	'	denoting consonant Alef = the Greek soft breathing or h in French *homme*
16	ב	ḇ	} aspirated
17	ג	ḡ	} aspirated
18	ד	ḏ	} aspirated
19	בּ	b	
20	גּ	g	in *get*
21	דּ	d	
22	ה	h	
23	ו	v	nearly = English *w*

	Hebrew characters		
24	ז	z	in *zeal*
25	ח	𝖈𝖍	= ch in Scottish *loch*
26	ט	𝖙	very hard or emphatic
27	י	y	in *yes*
28	ך כ	𝔠𝔥	= ch in German *ich*
29	כּ	k	= k in *kind*
30	ל	l	
31	ם מ	m	
32	ן נ	n	
33	ס	ß	= s in *sin*
34	ף פ	f	
35	פּ	p	
36	ע	•	a guttural peculiar to the Semitic languages
37	ץ צ	**ß**	= s in *sin*, very hard or emphatic (also pronounced as ts)
38	ק	**k**	hard or emphatic
39	ר	r	mostly guttural
40	שׂ	ß	= s in *sin*
41	שׁ	š	= sh in *wish*
42	ת	ϑ	= th in *thing*
43	תּ	𝔱	

LIST OF ABBREVIATIONS

abs. = absolute
adj. = adjective
adv. = adverb
art. = article
c. = construct
Chald. = Chaldee (Aramæan)
cohort. = cohortative
coll. = collective
conj. = conjunction
def. = definite
dem. = demonstrative
denom. = denominative
dimin. = diminutive
du. = dual
e. g. = exempli gratia, for example
f = feminine
fut. = future
gent. = gentilic
Hi. = Hiphil
Hith. = Hithpael
Hithpalp. = Hithpalpel
Hithpo. = Hithpolel
Ho. = Hophal
Hoth. = Hothpael
i.e. = id est, that is
imp. = imperative
inf. = infinitive
interj. = interjection
interr. = interrogative
intr. = intransitive
i.p. = in pause
loc. = local
m = masculine
n. = noun
Ni. = Niphal
Nithp. = Nithpael
num. = numeral,number
opp. = opposed
p. = pause
patr. = patronymic
perf., *pf.* = perfect
Pers. = Persian
pers. = person, personal
Pi. = Piel
Pil. = Pilel
Pilp. = Pilpel
pl. = plural
Po. = Poel, Poal
prep. = preposition
pr. n. = proper name
pron. = pronoun
prop. = properly
pt. = participle
pt. p. = passive participle
Pu. = Pual
Pul. = Pulal
Q. = Qal (Kal)
quadril. = quadriliteral
refl. = reflexive
rel. = relative
s. = suffix
sg., *sing.* = singular
st. abs. = *status absolutus*
subst. = substantive
Tiph. = Tiphel
tr. = transitive
w. art. = with article
w. loc. ה = with local ה
w. s. = with suffix

א

א the first letter of the alphabet, called אָלֶף (ā'lĕf) [= אֶלֶף ox, cattle]; as a numeral = 1 or 1000.

אָב (āb) *m*, *c.* אֲבִי, *w.s.* אָבִי, *pl.* אָבוֹת (ābō'th), *c.* אֲבוֹת, father, begetter, parent, ancestor, forefather; creator, lord, master; counsellor, adviser; benefactor, teacher.

אֵב (ēb) [root אָבַב] *m*, *w.s.* אִבּוֹ, *pl. c.* אִבֵּי, young shoot, sprout; greenness, verdure, fresh grass.

אֲבַגְתָא (abăgthā') *pr.n.m.* [Persian].

אָבַד (ābă'd) *fut.* יֹאבֵד, יֹאבַד, to wander about, to be lost, perish, cease; *pt.* אֹבֵד being lost. — *Pi.* אִבֵּד (ĭbbē'd) to lead astray, scatter, destroy, annihilate. — *Hi.* הֶאֱבִיד (hĕebī'd), *fut.* 1. *sg.* אֹבִיד, אֹבִידָה the same as *Pi.*

אֹבֵד (ōbē'd) *m* destruction, ruin.

אֲבֵדָה (abēdā') *f* anything lost, loss.

אֲבַדֹּה and **אֲבַדּוֹן** (abăddō') *m* destruction, place of perdition, abyss, nether world.

אַבְדָן (ăbdā'n) and **אָבְדָן** (ābedā'n) *m*, *c.* אָבְדַן, destruction.

אָבָה (ābā'), *fut.* יֹאבֶה to be willing, to desire, consent, obey.

אֵבֶה (ēbĕ') *m* reed, cane; אֳנִיּוֹת א swift sailing ships, made of reed.

אָבוֹא = אָבוֹ [from אָבָה].

אֲבוֹי (abō'y) [neediness, poverty] *interj.* = אוֹי woe to.

אֵבוּס (ēbū's) *m*, *c.* אֵבוּס, *pl.* אֲבוּסִים, place of feeding, crib, manger.

אֵבוֹשׁ see בּוֹשׁ.

אִבְחָה (ĭbḥā') *f*, *c.* אִבְחַת, threat; אִבְחַת חֶרֶב the threat of the sword, the threatening sword.

אֲבַטִּיחַ (ᵃḇăttī'ᵃḥ) *m*, only *pl.* אֲבַטִּיחִים pumpkin, melon.

אֲבִי (ᵃḇī') *pr.n.f.* = אֲבִיָּה.

אָבִי[1] (āḇī') *interj.* oh that, I wish that

אָבִי[2] = אָבִיא, see בּוֹא *Hi.*

אֲבִיאֵל (ᵃḇī'ē'l) *pr.n.m.*

אֲבִיאָסָף (ᵃḇī''ăsā'f) *pr.n.m.*

אָבִיב (āḇī'ḇ) *m* ear [*coll.*], ears of barley; month of the ears, first month in the spring; see also תֵּל.

אֲבִיגַיִל, אֲבִיגַל (ᵃḇīgă'yīl) *pr.n.f.*

אֲבִידָן (ᵃḇīdā'n) *pr.n.m.*

אֲבִידָע (ᵃḇīdā'ᵉ) *pr.n.m.*

אֲבִיָּה (ᵃḇīyyā'), אֲבִיָּהוּ (ᵃḇīyyā'hū). אֲבִיָּם *pr.n.m.*

אֲבִיהוּא (ᵃḇīhū') *pr.n.m.*

אֲבִיהוּד (ᵃḇīhū'd) *pr.n.m.*

אֲבִיהַיִל (ᵃḇīhă'yīl) *pr.n.f.*

אֶבְיוֹן (ĕḇyō'n) *adj.*, *w.s.* אֶבְיֹנְךָ, *pl.* אֶבְיוֹנִים, needy, poor, miserable, wretched.

אֲבִיּוֹנָה (ᵃḇīyyōnā') *f* caper, berry of the caper-bush.

אֲבִיחַיִל (ᵃḇīḥă'yīl) *pr.n.f.*

אֲבִיטוּב (ᵃḇītū'ḇ) *pr.n.m.*

אֲבִיטַל (ᵃḇītă'l) *pr.n.f.*

אֲבִיָּם see אֲבִיָּה.

אֲבִימָאֵל (ᵃḇīmā'ē'l) *pr.n.m.*

אֲבִימֶלֶךְ (ᵃḇīmĕ'lĕḵ) *pr.n.m*

אֲבִינָדָב (ᵃḇīnādā'ḇ) *pr.n.m.*

אֲבִינֹעַם (ᵃḇīnō''ăm) *pr.n.m*

אֲבִינֵר see אַבְנֵר.

אֶבְיָסָף see אֲבִיאָסָף.

אֲבִיעֶזֶר (ᵃḇī'ĕ'zĕr) *pr.n.m.*

אֲבִיעַלְבוֹן (ᵃḇī'ălḇō'n) *pr.n.m.*

אָבִיר (āḇī'r) *m*, *c.* אֲבִיר vigorous man, hero, protector.

אַבִּיר (ăbbī'r) *adj.*, *pl.* אַבִּירִים, *c.* אַבִּירֵי, strong, manly, courageous, powerful, distinguished, noble; also applied to oxen and horses.

אֲבִירָם (ᵃḇīrā'm) *pr.n.m.*

אֲבִישַׁג (ᵃḇīšă'g) *pr.n.f.*

אֲבִישׁוּעַ (ᵃḇīšū'aᵉ) *pr.n.m.*

אֲבִישׁוּר (ᵃḇīšū'r) *pr.n.m.*

אֲבִישַׁי (ᵃḇīšă'y) *pr.n.m.* [also אַבְשַׁי].

אֲבִישָׁלוֹם (ᵃḇīšālō'm) *pr.n.m.* [also אַבְשָׁלוֹם].

אֶבְיָתָר (ĕḇyāṯā'r) *pr.n.m.*

אָבַךְ (āḇă'ḵ), *Hith. fut.*

יִתְאַבֵּךְ to wind oneself upward, to rise in rotation.

אָבַל (ā̱ḇă'l) to fade, languish, pine, mourn. — *Hi.* הֶאֱבִיל, *fut.* יַאֲבִל־ to cause to mourn. — *Hith.* הִתְאַבֵּל to mourn, lament.

אָבֵל[1] (ā̱ḇē'l) *adj.*, *c.* אֲבֵל. *pl.* אֲבֵלִים, *c.* אֲבֵלֵי, *f.* אֲבֵלוֹת mourning, desolate.

אָבֵל[2] (ā̱ḇē'l) *f* meadow, grassy place, pasture, plain. — In proper names: אָבֵל בֵּית־מַעֲכָה town in Naphtali; אָ׳ הַשִּׁטִּים place in Moab; אָ׳ כְּרָמִים a village of the Ammonites; אָ׳ מְחוֹלָה town in Issachar; אָ׳ מִצְרַיִם place east of the Jordan.

אֵבֶל (ē'ḇĕl) *m*, *w.s.* אֶבְלִי, mourning, lament.

אוּבָל, אֻבָל (ūḇā'l) *m*, *c.* אוּבַל, river, stream.

אֶבֶן (ĕ'ḇĕn) *f*, *i.p.* אָבֶן, *w.s.* אַבְנוֹ, *pl.* אֲבָנִים, c. אַבְנֵי, stone, precious stone, gem; rock, ore, weighing stone, weight, plummet.

אֹבֶן *m*, only *du.* **אָבְנַיִם** (ŏḇnă'yĭm) potter's wheel; chair of delivery, midwife-stool [others: vagina, or the two sexes]

אֲבָנָה = אֲמָנָה.

אַבְנֵט (ăḇnē't) *m*, *w.s.* אַבְנֵטְךָ, *pl.* אַבְנֵטִים girdle, sash, belt (of a priest).

אַבְנֵר (ăḇnē'r) *pr.n.m.*

אָבַס (ā̱ḇă's), *pt. p.* אָבוּס, *pl.* אֲבוּסִים to feed, fatten.

אֲבַעְבֻּעָה (aḇă'bū'ā') *f*, only *pl.* אֲבַעְבֻּעֹת, blister, pustule, ulcer.

אֶבֶץ (ĕ'ḇĕs) *pr.n.* of a town in Issachar.

אִבְצָן (Iḇsā'n) *pr.n.m.*

אָבַק (ā̱ḇă'k), only *Ni. inf. w.s.* בְּהֵאָבְקוֹ, fut. יֵאָבֵק to wrestle.

אָבָק (ā̱ḇā'k) *m*, *c.* אֲבַק, *w.s.* אֲבָקָם dust.

אֲבָקָה (aḇāķā') *f*, *c.* אַבְקַת dust, powder, powdered spice.

אָבַר (ā̱ḇă'r), only *Hi. fut.* יַאֲבֶר to fly up, soar.

אֵבֶר (ē'ḇĕr) *m* and **אֶבְרָה** (ĕḇrā') *f*, *c.* אֶבְרַת, *pl. w.s.* אֶבְרוֹתֶיהָ, wing, pinion.

אַבְרָהָם (ăḇrāhā'm) and **אַבְרָם** (ăḇrā'm) *pr.n.m.*

אַבְרֵךְ (ăḇrē'ch) an Egyptian word, probably with the meaning of an imperative:

kneel, bend your heads, prostrate yourself.

אַבְשַׁי see אֲבִישַׁי.

אַבְשָׁלוֹם = אֲבִישָׁלוֹם.

אָגֵא (āgē') *pr.n.m.*

אֲגָג (ᵃgā'g) and אֲגַג *pr.n.m.* of Amalekite kings.

אֲגָגִי (ᵃgāgī') *m*, surname of Haman, the Agagite [= Amalekite].

אֲגֻדָּה (ᵃgŭddā') *f, pl.* אֲגֻדּוֹת connection, knot, bundle; band, troop; celestial vault.

אֱגוֹז (ᵉgō'z) *m* nut, nut-tree [Persian].

אָגוּר (āgū'r) *pr.n.m.*

אֲגוֹרָה (ᵃgōrā') *f, c.* אֲגוֹרַת, [berry], small coin, mite.

אֶגֶל (ĕ'gĕl) or **אֵגֶל** (ē'gĕl) *m*, only *pl.c.* אֶגְלֵי, drops.

אֶגְלַיִם (ĕglă'yĭm) *pr.n.* of a place in Moab.

אֲגַם (ᵃgă'm) *m, c.* אֲגַם, *pl.* אֲגַמִּים, *c.* אַגְמֵי pool, pond; reed; bulrush.

אָגֵם (āgē'm) *adj.*, only *pl.c.* אַגְמֵי, sad, grieved.

אַגְמוֹן (ăgmō'n) *m, c.* אַגְמֹן reed, bulrush; cord made of rushes; caldron.

אַגָּן (ăggā'n) *m, c.* אַגַּן, *pl.* אַגָּנוֹת basin, bowl, round vessel.

אֲגַף (ᵃgă'f) *m*, only *pl.* אֲגַפִּים, *w.s.* אֲגַפָּיו army, troops.

אָגַר (āgă'r), *fut.* יֶאֱגֹר to collect, gather.

אֶגְרֹף, **אֶגְרוֹף** (ĕgrō'f) *m* fist.

אֲגַרְטָל (ᵃgărtā'l) *m*, only *pl. c.* אֲגַרְטְלֵי basin, bowl, charger.

אִגֶּרֶת (ĭggĕ'rĕϑ) *f, pl.* אִגְּרוֹת, official letter, writ, edict.

אֵד (ēḍ) *m, w.s.* אֵדוֹ, mist, vapour.

אָדַב (āḍă'ḅ), only *Hi. inf.* לַאֲדִיב [for לְהַאֲדִיב] to cause to languish, to grieve.

אַדְבְּאֵל (ăḍbᵉē'l) *pr.n.m.*

אֲדַד (ᵃḍă'ḍ) *pr.n.m.*

אֶדַּדֶּה and **אֶדַּדֵּם** see דָּדָה *Hith.*

אֹדָה see אוֹדָה.

אִדּוֹ (ĭddō') *pr.n.m.*

אֱדוֹם see אֱדֹם.

אָדוֹן (āḍō'n) *m, c.* אֲדוֹן, *w.s.* אֲדוֹנִי, *pl.* אֲדוֹנִים, *c.* אֲדוֹנֵי commander, lord, master; the *pl.* is also applied to single persons; אֲדוֹנָי my Lord, the Lord God [יהוה]; hence Adonis.

אַדּוֹן see אֶדֶן.

אֲדוֹרַיִם (ᵃḏōrā'yīm) *pr.n.* of a town in Judah.

אֲדוֹרָם see אֲדֹנִירָם.

אֹדוֹת see אוּד.

אַדִּיר (ăddī'r) *adj.*, *w.s.* אַדִּירוֹ, *f* אַדֶּרֶת (ăddĕ'rĕϑ), *pl.* אַדִּירִים, *c.* אַדִּירֵי great, powerful, mighty, majestic, splendid, distinguished, glorious, noble.

אֲדַלְיָה (ᵃḏălyā') *pr.n.m.*

אָדֵם (āḏē'm) or **אָדֹם** (āḏō'm), *pl.* אָדְמוּ (āḏᵉmū') to be red. — *Pu. pt.* מְאָדָּם (mᵉŏddā'm) for מְאֻדָּם to be red-coloured. — *Hi. fut.* יַאְדִּימוּ to be red. — *Hith. fut. i.p.* יִתְאַדָּם to become red, to be erubescent.

אָדָם¹ (āḏā'm) *m* man, *coll.* men, some one; בְּנֵי א׳ serves as a *pl.*: the sons of man, mortals; *pr.n.m.* the first man created.

אָדָם² (āḏā'm) *pr.n.* of a town on the Jordan.

אָדֹם (āḏō'm) *adj.*, *f.* אֲדֻמָּה, *pl.* אֲדֻמִּים red, red-cheeked; a red thing, red colour.

אֹדֶם (ō'ḏĕm) *f* a red precious stone, carneol.

אֱדוֹם (ᵉḏō'm) *pr.n.m.* = Esau, Edom; the tribe and land of the Edomites.

אֲדָמָה (ᵃḏāmā') *f*, *c.* אַדְמַת, *w.s.* אַדְמָתִי, *pl.* אֲדָמוֹת, humus, arable land, earth, soil; country.

אֲדַמְדַּם (ᵃḏămdă'm) *adj.*, *f* אֲדַמְדֶּמֶת, *pl.* אֲדַמְדַּמּוֹת, reddish.

אֶדַּמֶּה see דָּמָה *Hith.*

אַדְמָה (ăḏmā') *pr.n.* of a town in the vale of Siddim.

אַדְמֹנִי, אַדְמוֹנִי (ăḏmōnī') *adj.* reddish, red-haired, of a red complexion.

אֲדָמִי (ᵃḏāmī') *pr.n.* of a town in Naphtali.

אֲדֹמִי (ᵃḏōmī') *pr.n. adj.*, *f* אֲדֹמִית, *pl. m* אֲדֹמִים, *f* אֲדֹמִיּוֹת, אֲדֹמִיֹּת, Edomitish, Edomite.

אֲדֻמִּים (ᵃḏŭmmī'm) *pr.n.* of a district between the Jordan and Gilgal.

אַדְמָתָא (ăḏmāϑā') *pr.n.m.* [Persian].

אֶדֶן (ĕ'ḏĕn) *m*, *i.p.* אָדֶן, *pl.* אֲדָנִים, *c.* אַדְנֵי foundation, basis, pedestal, socket of a column.

אַדָּן (ăddā'n) *pr.n.* of a place in Babylonia.

אֲדֹנִי־בֶזֶק (ᵃdō'nī-bĕ'zĕk) *pr.n.m.*

אֲדֹנִיָּה (ᵃdōnīyyā'), **אֲדֹנִיָּהוּ** (ᵃdōnīyyā'hū) [אֲדֹנִיקָם] *pr.n.m.*

אֲדֹנִי־צֶדֶק (ᵃdō'nī ẓĕ'dĕk) *pr.n.m.*

אֲדֹנִירָם (ᵃdōnīrā'm), **אֲדוֹרָם** (ᵃdōrā'm) *pr.n.m.*

אָדַר (ādā'r) *Ni.* נֶאְדַּר (nĕ'dā'r), *pt.* נֶאְדָּרִי [=נֶאְדָּר with connecting ־ִי] to show oneself glorious, splendid. — *Hi. fut.* יַאְדִּיר to glorify.

אֲדָר (ᵃdā'r) *m* twelfth month of the Hebrew year, corresponding to March and April.

אֶדֶר (ĕ'dĕr) *m* garment, mantle; splendour, magnificence.

אַדָּר (ăddā'r) *pr.n.* of a place in Judah; *pr.n.m.*

אֲדַרְכּוֹן (ᵃdărkō'n) *m*, *pl.* אֲדַרְכֹּנִים, Persian gold-coin [not connected with Darius].

אַדְרַמֶּלֶךְ (ădrămmĕ'lĕch) *pr.n.m.* of an Assyrian deity and of an Assyrian king [son of Sennacherib].

אֶדְרֶעִי (ĕdrᵉ'ī) *pr.n.* of the chief-town of Bashan; of a town in Naphtali.

אַדֶּרֶת (ăddĕ'rĕth) *f* a wide garment, mantle; glory, magnificence; see also אַדִּיר.

אָדַשׁ (ādă's) *inf.* אָדוֹשׁ — דּוּשׁ to thrash.

אָהֵב (āhē'b), **אָהַב** (āhă'b), *inf.* אֱהֹב, אַהֲבָה, *imp.* אֱהַב, *fut.* יֶאֱהַב, 1. *sg.* אֹהַב and אֵהַב, *pt.* אֹהֵב, *f* אֹהֶבֶת [friend], to love, to like, to be fond of; to desire, covet. — *Ni. pt.* נֶאֱהָב to be beloved, amiable. — *Pi. pt.* מְאַהֵב, *pl.* מְאַהֲבִים to be a passionate lover or paramour.

אַהַב (ă'hăb) *m*, only *pl.* אֲהָבִים love-affair, intrigue; charm, loveliness.

אֹהַב (ō'hăb) *m*, *w.s.* אֳהָבָם (ŏhᵒbā'm), *pl.* אֳהָבִים (ohābī'm) love, love-intrigue; lover.

אַהֲבָה (ăhᵃbā') *f* [also *inf.* of אָהַב] love, affection, tender friendship.

אֹהַד (ō'hăd) *pr.n.m.*

אֲהָהּ (ᵃhā'h) *interj.* [expressing sorrow] woe, alas, ah, oh.

אַהֲוָא (ăhavā') *pr.n.* of a river in Media.

אֵהוּד (ēhū'd) *pr.n.m.*

אֲהוֹדֶנּוּ see יָדָה *Hi.*

אֱהִי [1] (ehī') *adv.* [interrogative] = אֵי how? where?

אֱהִי [2] see הָיָה.

אָהַל [1] (ăhă'l) *Hi. fut.* יַאֲהִיל to shine, to be bright.

אָהַל [2] (ăhă'l) [*denom.* of אֹהֶל], *fut.* יֶאֱהַל to pitch tents, to wander.— *Pi. fut.* יַהֵל [for יְאַהֵל] the same as *Q.*

אֹהֶל [1] (ō'hĕl) *m, ws.* אָהֳלִי (ŏholī'), *w.* loc. ה אֹהֱלָה, *pl.* אֳהָלִים (ohălī'm), אֹהָלִים, *c.* אָהֳלֵי (ŏholē'), *w.s.* אֹהָלַי, tent, hut, habitation, family; א׳ מוֹעֵד tent of congregation, tabernacle, also א׳ הָעֵדוּת tent of the law.

אֹהֶל [2] (ō'hĕl) *pr.n.m.*

אָהָל (ăhă'l) *m,* only *pl.* אֲהָלִים and אֲהָלוֹת aromatic wood, aloe-wood.

אָהֳלָה (ŏholā') *pr.n.f.* [a woman symbolizing Samaria].

אָהֳלִיאָב (ŏholī'ā'b) *pr.n.m.*

אָהֳלִיבָה (ŏholībā') *pr.n.f.* [a lewd woman, symbolically denoting Jerusalem].

אָהֳלִיבָמָה (ŏholībāmā') *pr. n.f.*

אֲהֵמְיָה = אֶהֱמֶה, see הָמָה.

אַהֲרֹן (ăharō'n) *pr.n.m.* Aaron.

אוֹ (ō) *conj.* or [Lat. vel and aut]; אוֹ—אוֹ either—or; or if, or perhaps.

אוּאֵל (ū'ē'l) *pr.n.m.*

אוֹב (ōb) *m, pl.* אוֹבוֹת, skin, leather bag; spectre, conjuring ghost; necromancer, sorcerer.

אוֹבֹת (ōbō'th) *pr.n.* of a camping station.

אוֹבִיל (ōbī'l) *pr.n.m.*

אוּבָל see אֻבָל.

אוֹד (ōd) *m,* only *pl.* אוֹדוֹת, אֹדוֹת, circumstance, cause, occasion, concern; עַל אֹדוֹת because of, on account of, concerning.

אוּד (ūd) *m, pl.* אוּדִים, firebrand, fire-stick, poker.

אָוָה [1] *Pi.* אִוָּה (ivvā'), *fut.* יְאַוֶּה to desire eagerly, to covet. — *Hith.* הִתְאַוָּה, *fut.* יִתְאָו (yith'ā'v) to desire, want, lust after.

אָוָה[2] only *Hith.* הִתְאַוָּה, 2. *pl. m* הִתְאַוִּיתֶם to measure off, to mark for oneself.

אַוָּה (ăvvā') *f* desire, longing, lust.

אוּזַי (ūză'y) *pr.n.m.*

אוּזָל (ūzā'l) *pr.n.m.* [Arabian tribe and its capital, Zanaa in Yemen].

אֱוִי (ᵉvī') *pr.n.m.*

אוֹי (ŏy) and אוֹיָה (ŏ'yā) *interj.* woe, alas, ah.

אוֹיֵב see אֹיֵב.

אֱוִיל (ᵉvī'l) *adj.*, *pl.* אֱוִלִים foolish, silly; impious.

אֱוִילִי, אֱוִלִי — אֱוִיל.

אֱוִיל מְרֹדַךְ (ᵉvī'l mᵉrŏdă'ch) *pr.n.m.* [king of Babylon].

אוּל[1] (ūl) *m*, *w.s.* אוּלָם belly, body; strength.

אוּל[2] (ūl) *m*, *pl. c.* אוּלֵי, a mighty, powerful person [see אַיִל *pl.*].

אוּלַי[1] (ūlă'y) *pr.n.* of a river in Persia [Eulæus].

אוּלַי[2] (ūlă'y) *conj.* and *adv.* if not, whether not, if perhaps; perhaps.

אוּלָם[1] (ūlā'm), אֻלָם (ŭllā'm) *m*, *pl. c.* אֻלַמֵּי vestibule, hall, portico [of the temple].

אוּלָם[2] (ūlā'm) *adv.* but however, yet, nevertheless.

אוּלָם[3] *pr.n.m.*

אִוֶּלֶת (ĭvvĕ'lĕth) *f*, *w.s.* אִוַּלְתִּי folly, foolishness; ungodliness, wickedness.

אוֹמָר (ŏmā'r) *pr.n.m.*

אָוֶן (ā'vĕn) *m*, *c.* אוֹן (ŏn), *w.s.* אוֹנְךָ, *pl.* אוֹנִים breath, vainness, nothingness; idolatry, idol; falsehood, wickedness, sin; distress, hardship, toil.

אוֹן[1] (ŏn) *m*, *pl.* אוֹנִים, substance, wealth; power, strength.

אוֹן[2], אֹן (ŏn) *pr.n.* of a city in lower Egypt (Heliopolis).

אוֹנוֹ (ŏnŏ') *pr.n.* of a town in Benjamin.

אוֹנִיּוֹת see אֳנִיָּה.

אוֹנָם (ŏnā'm) *pr.n.m.*

אוֹנָן (ŏnā'n) *pr.n.m.*

אוּפָז (ūfā'z) *pr.n.* of an unknown country rich in gold.

אוֹפָן, אֹפָן (ŏfā'n) *m*, *c.* אוֹפַן, *pl.* אוֹפַנִּים, wheel [of a chariot, of a thrashing-sledge].

אוֹפִיר, אוֹפִר, אֹפִיר (ōfī'r) *pr.n.m.* a son of Joktan; the gold-country Ophir, probably in Southern Arabia [acc. to others in India or East Africa].

אוּץ (ūß), *pt.* אָץ to press; to be pressed or narrow; to hasten. — *Hi. fut.* יָאִיץ to press, urge, impel.

אוֹצָר, אֹצָר (ōßā'r) *m, c.* אוֹצַר, *pl.* אוֹצָרוֹת, *c.* אוֹצְרוֹת, store, stock, provision, supply; store-house, treasury.

אוֹר¹ (ōr), *fut.* יָאוֹר, יָאֹר, to be or become bright, to dawn, to become clear, to shine. — *Ni.* נָאוֹר, *fut.* יֵאוֹר, *inf.* לֵאוֹר [for לְהֵאוֹר] to become lighted, to dawn; *pt.* נָאוֹר bright, splendid, glorious. — *Hi.* הֵאִיר, *fut.* יָאִיר, וַיָּאֶר to lighten, to fill with light, to make clear; to enlighten, instruct, teach; to enliven, to comfort; *intr.* to be light.

אוֹר² (ōr) *m, pl.* אוֹרִים, light, brightness, daylight, sunlight, lightning; illumination, enlightenment; happiness, cheerfulness.

אוּר¹ (ūr) *m* — אוֹר², *pl.* אוּרִים, אֻרִים lighted country, land of the sunrise, the east; fire, flame; enlightenment, revelation; אוּרִים וְתֻמִּים light and truth, the oracle on the breastplate of the high priest.

אוּר² (ūr) *pr.n.* of a town in Chaldea, south of Babylon [אוּר כַּשְׂדִּים].

אוֹרָה¹ *f* (ōrā') — אוֹר².

אוֹרָה² (ōrā') *f*, only *pl.* אוֹרוֹת, אֹרוֹת, green herbs, vegetables.

אוּרוֹת see אֻרְוָה.

אוּרִי (ūrī'), **אוּרִיאֵל** (ūrī'ēl), **אוּרִיָּה** (ūrīyyā'), **אוּרִיָּהוּ** (ūrīyyā'hū) *pr.n.m.*

אוֹת, אֹת (ōϑ) *m* and *f*, *pl.* אוֹתוֹת, אֹתֹת, sign, mark, token, badge, standard, monument, memorial, warning, omen, prodigy, symbol.

אוּת (ūϑ), **אוֹת** (ōϑ), only *Ni. fut.* יֵאוֹת, *cohort.* נֵאוֹתָה to consent, agree, yield.

אָז (āz) *adv.* then, at that time; therefore; מֵאָז [— מִן אָז] formerly, heretofore, of old; *prep.* since.

אֶזְבַּי (ĕzbă'y) *pr.n.m.*

אֵזוֹב (ēzō'b) *m* an aromatic plant, hyssop.

אֵזוֹר (ēzō'r) *m* girdle, belt; fetter.

אֲזַי (ᵃză'y) *adv.* = אָז then.

אַזְכָּרָה (ăzkără') *f* memorial; that part of an offering which was destined to bring the sacrifice to the remembrance of God.

אָזַל (āză'l), *fut.* תֵּזְלִי for תֶּאֱזְלִי to go away, to go out; to fail, cease, vanish. — *Pu. pt.* מְאוּזָּל what is spun, yarn, thread [perh. miswritten for מֵאוּזָל, see אוּזָל].

אֶזֶל (ĕ'zĕl) in אֶבֶן הָאֶזֶל stone of departure [a memorial stone].

אָזַן[1] (āză'n) *Q.* not used. — *Hi.* [*denom.* of אֹזֶן] הֶאֱזִין, *imp.* הַאֲזִין, *fut.* יַאֲזִין [אָזִין for אַאֲזִין], *pt.* מַאֲזִין = מֵזִין, to turn or lend an ear to, to listen, hearken, attend; to answer [a prayer]; to obey.

אָזַן[2] only *Pi.* אִזֵּן (ĭzzē'n) to weigh, to prove.

אֹזֶן (ō'zĕn) *f*, *du.* אָזְנַיִם (ŏznă'yĭm) ear [organ of hearing].

אֻזֵּן שֶׁאֱרָה (ŭzzē'n šĕᵉrā') *pr.n.* of a town in Naphtali.

אָזְנִי (ŏznī') *pr.n.m.*

אֲזַנְיָה (ᵃzănyā') *pr.n.m.*

אֲזִקִּים (ᵃzĭkkī'm) only *pl.* [from אֵזֶק], *w. art.* הָאזִקִּים, chains, fetters, handcuffs.

אָזַר (āză'r) *fut.* יֶאְזֹר, *w.s.* יַאַזְרֵנִי to bind, gird, put on. — *Ni. pt.* נֶאְזָר to be girded. — *Pi. pt.* יְאַזֵּר, *pt* מְאַזֵּר to gird, to arm with. — *Hith.* הִתְאַזֵּר, *i.p.* הִתְאַזָּר to gird or equip oneself.

אֶזְרוֹעַ see זְרוֹעַ.

אֶזְרָח (ĕzrā'ḥ) *m*, *c.* אֶזְרַח a tree not transplanted; native, indigene.

אֶזְרָחִי (ĕzrāḥī') *pr.n. patr.*, Ezrahite, son of one אֶזְרָח.

אָח[1] (āḥ) *m*, *c.* אֲחִי, *w.s.* אָחִי, אָחִיךָ, אָחִיו, אֲחִיכֶם. *pl.* אַחִים, *w.s.* אַחַי, אֶחָיו. *c.* אֲחֵי, brother, near relation, cousin, countryman, fellow-man, friend; אָח-אִישׁ the one — the other.

אָח[2] (āḥ) *f* fire-pot, coal-pan.

אָח[3] (āḥ) *interj.* woe! alas!

אֹחַ (ō'aḥ) *m*, only *pl.* אֹחִים a howling animal, bird with lamenting voice, owl, scops.

אַחְאָב (ăḥ'ā'b) *pr.n.m.* [once אֶחָב].

אַחְבָּן (ăḥbā'n) *pr.n.m.*

אֶחָד (ĕḥā'd) *num.*, *c.* אַחַד, *f.* אַחַת [for אַחֶדֶת], *i.p.* אֶחָת, one, some one, the same, a single one, the first; *pl.* אֲחָדִים some few, the same. — בְּאַחַת once, at once; כְּאֶחָד like one, jointly, in a body, together.

אָחַד (āḥă'd) only *Hith.* [denom. of אֶחָד] הִתְאַחֵד to unite oneself, to collect one's strength or faculties.

אָחוּ (ā'ḥū) *m* reed, Nile-grass.

אֵחוּד (ēḥū'd) *pr.n.m.*

אַחְוָה (ăḥvā') *f* declaration, explanation.

אַחֲוָה (ăḥavā') *f* brotherhood.

אֲחוֹחַ (aḥō'aḥ) *pr.n.m.*

אֲחוּמַי (aḥūmă'y) *pr.n.m.*

אָחוֹר (āḥō'r) *m* back, backside; *adv.* back, backward, behind; west, west side, westward, westerly; future.

אָחוֹת (āḥō'th) *f*, *c.* אֲחוֹת, *w.s.* אֲחוֹתִי, *pl.* [אֲחָיוֹת], *c.* *w.s.* אַחְיוֹתָיו, אֲחוֹתַי, sister, female relation, friend; after אִשָּׁה = the other [compare אָח].

אָחַז (āḥă'z) *fut.* יֹאחַז, יֶאֱחֹז, to seize, take, grasp, lay hold of; to lock up, bolt, fasten, connect. — *Ni.* נֶאֱחַז to get caught, to be held fast. — *Ni.* [denom.] נֹאחַז, *fut.* יֵאָחֵז to take possession of. — *Pi. pt.* מְאַחֵז to hold back, to lock up, to hide. — *Ho. pt.* מָאֳחָז to be attached or fastened.

אָחָז (āḥā'z) *pr.n.m.*

אֲחֻזָּה (aḥŭzzā') *f*, *c.* אֲחֻזַּת, occupation, possession, property.

אַחְזַי (ăḥză'y); אֲחַזְיָה (aḥăzyā'), אֲחַזְיָהוּ (aḥăzyā'hū); אֲחֻזָּם (aḥŭzzā'm); אֲחֻזַּת (aḥŭzză'th) *pr.n.m.*

אֲחֻחִי *pr.n.m.*, *patr.* of אֲחוֹחַ.

אַחַטְּנָה = אֲחַטְאֶנָּה, see חָטָא *Pi.*

אֵחִי (ēḥī') *pr.n.m.* = אֵחוּד.

אֲחִי (aḥī') *pr.n.m.* = אֲחִיָּה.

אֲחִיאָם (aḥī'ā'm); אֲחִיָּה (aḥīyyā'); אֲחִיָּהוּ (aḥīyyā'hū); אֲחִיהוּד (aḥībū'd); אַחְיוֹ

(ăchyō'); אֲחִיטוּב (achītū'ḅ); אֲחִילוּד (achīlū'ḏ); אֲחִימוֹת (achīmō'ϑ); אֲחִימֶלֶךְ (achīmĕ'lĕch); אֲחִימַן (achīmă'n); אֲחִימַעַץ (achīmă''ăß); אֲחִינָדָב (achīnāḏā'ḅ) *pr.n.m.*

אֲחִינֹעַם (achīnō''ăm) *pr.n.f.*

אֲחִיסָמָךְ (achīßāmā'ch); אֲחִיעֶזֶר (achī'ĕ'zĕr); אֲחִיקָם (achīkā'm); אֲחִירָם (achīrā'm) [חוּרָם]; אֲחִירַע (achīră''); אֲחִישַׁחַר (achīšă'chăr); אֲחִישָׁר (achīšā'r); אֲחִיתֹפֶל (achīϑō'fĕl) *pr.n.m.*

אַחְלָב (ăchlā'ḅ) *pr.n.* of a place in North Palestine.

אַחֲלַי (ăchală'y), **אַחֲלֵי** (ăchalē') particle of wishing: oh that! might it be that.

אַחְלַי (ăchlă'y) *pr.n.m.*

אַחְלָמָה (ăchlā'mā) *f* a precious stone, amethyst.

אַחְמְתָא (ăchmeϑā') *pr.n.* of the capital of Media, Egbatana.

אֲחַסְבַּי (achăzbă'y) *pr.n.m.*

אָחַר (āchă'r), *fut.* 1. *sg.* אֵחַר to be behind, to remain behind, to tarry.—*Pi.* אִחֵר, *fut.* יְאַחֵר *intr.* to tarry, stay; *tr.* to delay, detain, procrastinate.

אַחֵר (ăchē'r) *adj.*, *f* אַחֶרֶת, *pl.* אֲחֵרִים, אֲחֵרוֹת the following, second, other, later; foreign, strange.

אַחַר (ăchă'r) *m*, *pl.* [אֲחָרִים] *c.* אַחֲרֵי, *w.s.* אַחֲרַי, אַחֲרָיו the hind-part, back-part; *adv.* and *prep.* behind, after, afterward; אַחֲרֵי כֵן after that, thereupon; מֵאַחֲרֵי from after, from behind.

אֶחֱרוּ – אַחֲרוּ, see אָחַר *Pi.*

אַחֲרוֹן (ăcharō'n) *adj.*, *f* אַחֲרוֹנָה, *pl* אַחֲרוֹנִים, hinder, following, later, latter, last, posterior, western; *f. adv.* for the last time, lastly.

אַחְרַח (ăchră'ch); **אֲחַרְחֵל** (achărchē'l) *pr.n.m.*

אַחֲרִית (ăcharī'ϑ) *f* hindest, latest part, future, end, posterity.

אֲחֹרַנִּית (achōrănnī'ϑ) *adv.* backwards.

אֲחַשְׁדַּרְפְּנִים (achăšdărpenī'm) *m.pl.* [*sing.* ~פַּן] Persian governors, satraps.

אֲחַשְׁוֵרוֹשׁ (achăšvērō'š), **אֲחַשְׁרֹשׁ** (achăšrō'š) *pr.n.m.* of Persian kings, Ahasuerus [= Xerxes, Cambyses, Astyages].

אֲחַשְׁתָּרִי (ᵃḥăštārī') *pr.n.m.* [Persian].

אֲחַשְׁתְּרָנִים (ᵃḥăštᵉrānī'm) *m.pl.* [*sing.* ־תָּרָן] *adj.* one being of the royal service [others: mules].

אַחַת see אֶחָד.

אַט (ăt) *m* whisper, low, noiseless speaking; אִטִּים whisperers, sorcerers, necromancers; *adv.* אַט, לְאַט, לְאִט noiselessly, in a whisper, secretly, slowly, by degrees.

אָטָד (ātā'd) *m* thorn-bush [Christ's thorn].

אֵטוּן (ētū'n) *m* thread, yarn.

אָטַם (ātă'm) *pt.p.* אָטוּם, *pl.* אֲטוּמִים to shut, close; to grate up, to lattice.— *Hi. fut.* יַאְטֵם to close.

אָטַר (ātă'r), *fut.* יֶאְטַר to shut, close.

אָטֵר (ātē'r) *pr.n.m.*

אִטֵּר (ĭttē'r) *adj.* bound, hampered; אִ׳ יַד יְמִינוֹ left-handed.

אַי (ăy) *adv.*, *c.* אֵי, *w.s.* אַיֶּכָּה, אַיּוֹ, אַיָּם where? [where art thou? &c.]; אֵי זֶה which one? who?; אֵי מִזֶּה wherefrom?; אֵי לָזֹאת why?

אִי[1] (ī) *m* and *f*, *pl.* אִיִּים, coast-land, island; foreign, transmarine parts round the Mediterranean and in India.

אִי[2] (ī) *m*, only *pl.* אִיִּים, howler, jackal.

אִי[3] (ī) = אוֹי *interj.* woe to.

אִי[4] (ī) [= אֵין from אַיִן] *adv.* denoting negation [equal to the prefixes in-, un-]; אִי־כָבוֹד without honour, inglorious.

אָיַב (āyă'b) to hate, to treat as an enemy; *pt.* אֹיֵב, אוֹיֵב, *w.s.* אֹיִבְךָ, *f* אוֹיֶבֶת, *pl.* אֹיְבִים, *c.* אֹיְבֵי, enemy, hater.

אֵיבָה (ēbā') *f*, *c.* אֵיבַת enmity, hostility.

אֵיד (ēd) *m* burden, oppression, misfortune, misery, distress.

אַיָּה[1] (ăyyā') *f* vulture, kite.

אַיָּה[2] (ăyyā') *pr.n.m.*

אַיֵּה (ăyyē') = אֵי *adv.* where, wherever.

אִיּוֹב (ĭyyō'b) *pr.n.m.* Job.

אִיזֶבֶל (īzĕ'bĕl) *pr.n.f.*

אֵיזֶה (ēzĕ') *adv.* where?

אֵיךְ, אֵיכָה (ēḉ, ēḉā') *adv.* and *interj.* how? where? alas!

אֵיכֹה, אֵיכוֹ (ēḉō') *adv.* where.

אֵיכָכָה (ēḉā'ḉā) *adv.* how?

אֱיָל (ᵉyā'l) *m* power, strength.

אַיִל (ă'yĭl) *m, c.* אֵיל, *pl.* אֵילִים, אֵלִים, *c.* אֵילֵי [strength] a ram; pilaster, projection [in architecture], socle; strong tree, oak, terebinth; *pl.* mighty, powerful people, the nobles.

אַיָּל (ăyyā'l) *m, pl.* אַיָּלִים buck, stag, hart.

אַיָּלָה (ăyyālā') *f, c.* אַיֶּלֶת, *pl.* אַיָּלוֹת, *c.* אַיְלוֹת a hind; אַיֶּלֶת הַשַּׁחַר hind of the dawn.

אַיָּלוֹן (ăyyālō'n) *pr.n.* of towns in Dan and Zebulon.

אֵילֹן, אֵילוֹן (ēlō'n) *pr.n.m.*; *pr.n.* of a town in Dan.

אֱיָלוּת (ăyyālū'ϑ) *f* strength, power.

אֵילוֹת see אֵילַת.

אֵילָם (ēlā'm) *m, pl.* אֵילַמִּים, אֵילַמּוֹת, projection [in architecture], moulding.

אֵילִם (ēlī'm) *pr.n.* of a station in the desert.

אֵילַת (ēlă'ϑ), **אֵילוֹת** (ēlō'ϑ) *pr.n.* of an Edomitish seaport on the Red Sea [now Akaba].

אָיֹם (āyō'm) *adj.*, *f* אֲיֻמָּה terrible, formidable.

אֵימָה (ēmā') *f, c.* אֵימַת, *w. loc.* ה אֵימָתָה, *pl.* אֵימוֹת terror, fear.

אֵימִים (ēmī'm) *pl.m.* terrors, horrors; idols; giants, original inhabitants of the Moabite country.

אַיִן[1] (ă'yĭn) *m, c.* אֵין, nonentity, nothingness, nonexistence; *adv.* not, not existing, without; *w.s.* אֵינֶנִּי [I am not there]; אֵינֵימוֹ, אֵינֶנּוּ, אֵינְךָ [= אֵינָם]; אֵין לִי I have not [there is not to me].— בְּאֵין without, when there was not, before being; כְּאַיִן almost, nearly; לְאֵין = לַאֲשֶׁר אֵין to him to whom not; מֵאֵין because not, so that not.

אַיִן[2] (ă'yĭn) *adv.* where?; מֵאַיִן [= מִן אַיִן] from where, whence.

אִין (īn) *adv. interr.* [is there] not?

אִיעֶזֶר (īᵉĕ'zĕr) = אֲבִיעֶזֶר.

אֵיפָה, אֵפָה, אֵיפָה (ēfā') *f*, *c.* אֵיפַת a corn measure, equal to 1,08 bushel.

אֵיפֹה (ēfō') *adv.* where? how?

אֵיפוֹא see אֵפוֹא.

אִישׁ (īš) *m*, *w.s.* אִישִׁי, *pl.* אֲנָשִׁים, אִישִׁים, *c.* אַנְשֵׁי a man [as opposed to beast and woman and God], a mortal, husband, possessor, inhabitant, follower, attendant; some one, any one, every one, each; with אָח or רֵעַ the one — the other.

אִישׁ־בֹּשֶׁת (īš-bō'šeϑ) *pr.n.m.*

אִישְׁהוֹד (īšhō'd) *pr.n.m.*

אִישׁוֹן (īšō'n) *m* [dimin. of אִישׁ little man] the pupil of the eye, eye-ball, centre.

אִישׁ־חַיִל (īš hă'yīl) *m* valiant man, perh. *pr.n.m.*

אִישׁ־טוֹב (īš tō'b) *pr.n.* of a town or district in Syria.

אִישַׁי see יִשַׁי.

אִיתוֹן (īϑō'n) *m* entrance.

אִיתַי (īϑă'y) *pr.n.m.*

אִיתִיאֵל (īϑī'ē'l) *pr.n.m.* [for אִתִּי אֵל God with me].

אֵיתָם[1] see אֵתָם.

אֵיתָם[2] = אִתָּם, אִתָּם, see תָּמַם.

אִיתָמָר (īϑāmā'r) *pr.n.m.*

אֵתָן, אֵיתָן (ēϑā'n) *pr.n.m.*

אַךְ (ăch) *adv.* certainly, yea; only, but, however, yet; hardly, no sooner than.

אַכַּד (ăkkă'd) *pr.n.* of a town built by Nimrod.

אַכְזָב (ăchzā'b) *m* deceiving brook [without water].

אַכְזִיב (ăchzī'b) *pr.n.* of towns in Asher [Ecdippa] and in Judah.

אַכְזָר (ăchzā'r) *adj.* bold, cruel, merciless, destructive, deadly.

אַכְזָרִי (ăchzārī') *adj.* hard, harsh, cruel, terrible.

אַכְזְרִיּוּת (ăchzⁱrīyyū'ϑ) *f* cruelty, fierceness.

אֲכִילָה (ªchīlā') *f* eating, food.

אָכִישׁ (āchī'š) *pr.n.m.*

אָכַל (āchă'l) *inf.* אֱכֹל, *w.s.* אָכְלוֹ (ŏchlō'), *fut.* יֹאכַל, *i.p.* יֹאכֵל, 1. *sing.* אֹכַל, to eat, enjoy, devour, consume, take away, destroy — *Ni.* נֶאֱכַל, *fut.* יֵאָכֵל to be eaten, consumed. — *Pu.* אֻכַּל to be consumed, destroyed. — *Hi.* הֶאֱכִיל, *fut.*

יַאֲכִיל to make eat, to give to eat.

אֹכֶל (ō'chĕl) *m*, *w.s.* אָכְלוֹ (ŏchlō') [act and material of] eating, food, meat.

אֻכָל (ūchā'l), **אֻכָּל** (ŭkkā'l) *pr.n.m.* [or to be derived from כָּלָה].

אָכְלָה (ŏchlā') *f* = אֹכֶל.

אֲכַלֶּךָּ = אֲכַלְּךָ, see כָּלָה *Pi.*

אָכֵן (āchē'n) *adv.* certainly, surely, even so; but, yet.

אָכַף (āchă'f) to burden, weigh on, press, drive on.

אֶכֶף (ĕ'chĕf) *m*, *w.s.* אַכְפִּי, burden, load, pressure.

אִכָּר (ĭkkā'r) *m*, *pl.* אִכָּרִים, ploughman, tiller, husbandman.

אַכְשָׁף (ăchsā'f) *pr.n.* of a town in Asher.

אַל[1] (ăl) a negation corresponding to Greek μή, applied in prohibitions and wishes: that not, lest, may not, let not.

אַל[2] [אֶל] the Arabic definite article, occurring in אַלְקוּם, אַלְמֻגִּים, אַלְגָּבִישׁ.

אֵל[1] (ēl) *m*, *w.s.* אֵלִי, *pl.* אֵלִים, a strong, mighty one, a hero, a god; הָאֵל the true God; אֵל שַׁדַּי almighty God; אֵל עֶלְיוֹן God the most high; strength, power, might; יֵשׁ לְאֵל יָדִי it is in the power of my hand, I am able. [אֵלִים once for אֵילִים rams].

אֵל[2] (ēl), הָאֵל *pron. dem. pl.* = אֵלֶּה these.

אֶל־ (ĕl) *prep.* to, towards, in the direction of, according to, in addition to, with regard to, against, into, among, near, with.

אֵלָא (ēlā') *pr.n.m.*

אֶלְגָּבִישׁ (ĕlgābī's) *m* hail, ice.

אַלְגּוּמִּים see אַלְמֻגִּים.

אֶלְדָּד (ĕldā'd) *pr.n.m.*

אֶלְדָּעָה (ĕldā'ā') *pr.n.m.*

אָלָה[1] (ālā') to confirm by an oath, to swear, forswear.— *Hi.inf.* הַאֲלוֹת, *fut.* וַיֹּאֶל to confirm, to cause to swear, to swear.

אָלָה[2] (ālā') *f*, *w.s.* אָלָתִי, *pl.* אָלוֹת swearing, oath; curse; agreement by oath, sworn covenant.

אַלָּה (ăllā') *f* oak.

אֵלָה[1] (ēlā') *f* oak, terebinth.

אֵלָה² (ēlā') *pr.n.m.*

אֵלֶּה (ē'llĕ) ***pron. dem. pl.*** these, those.

אִלּוּ (ĭllū') *conj.* [אִם לוּ] if.

אֱלוֹהַּ (elō'ah) *m, sing.* mostly in poetry: a god, God; *pl.* אֱלֹהִים, *c.* אֱלֹהֵי, *ws.* אֱלֹהֵינוּ God, the one, true God [הָאֱ']; אִישׁ אֱ', בֶּן אֱלֹהִים angel, Israelitic king, prophet; heathen gods, higher and godlike beings.

אֱלוּל (elū'l) *m* the sixth month of the Hebrew year, corresponding to September and October; *adj.* = אֱלִיל.

אֵלוֹן¹ (ēlō'n), **אַלּוֹן** (ăllō'n) *m, pl.* אֵלוֹנִים, אַלּוֹנִים, *c.* ~נֵי, oak, terebinth.

אֵלוֹן² (ēlō'n) *pr.n.m,; patr.* אֵלוֹנִי.

אַלּוּף (ăllū'f) *m* and *adj., pl.* אַלֻּפִים tame beast, lamb, ox, cow; attached friend, companion, husband; head of a family, of a tribe [אָלַף].

אֵלוֹת see אֵילוֹת.

אָלוּשׁ (ālū's) *pr.n.* of a station in the desert.

אֶלְזָבָד (ĕlzābā'd) *pr.n.m.*

אָלַח (ālă'ȟ) only *Ni.* נֶאֱלַח to be corrupt, to get spoiled.

אֶלְחָנָן (ĕlȟānā'n) *pr.n.m.*

אֱלִיאָב (elī'ā'b); **אֱלִיאֵל** (elī'ē'l); **אֱלִיאָתָה** (elī'ā'θā); **אֱלִידָד** (elīdā'd) [אֶלְדָּד]; **אֶלְיָדָע** (ĕlyādā'ᵉ) *pr.n.m.*

אַלְיָה (ălyā') *f* fat tail of oriental sheep.

אֵלִיָּה (ēlĭyyā') and **אֵלִיָּהוּ** (ēlĭyyā'hū); **אֱלִיהוּ** and **אֱלִיהוּא** (elīhū'); **אֶלְיְהוֹעֵינַי** (ĕlyᵉhō'ᵉēnă'y); **אֶלְיוֹעֵינַי** (ĕlyō'ᵉēnă'y); **אֶלְיַחְבָּא** (ĕlyăȟbā'); **אֱלִיחֹרֶף** (elīȟō'rĕf) *pr.n.m.*

אֱלִיל (elī'l) *adj.* null, vain, nought; nothingness, feebleness; *pl.* אֱלִילִים idols.

אֱלִימֶלֶךְ (elīmĕ'lĕȟ); **אֶלְיָסָף** (ĕlyāsā'f); **אֱלִיעֶזֶר** (elīᵉĕ'zĕr); **אֱלִיעֵינַי** (elī'ᵉēnă'y); **אֱלִיעָם** (elīᵉā'm); **אֱלִיפַז** (elīfă'z); **אֱלִיפָל** (elīfā'l); **אֱלִיפְלֵהוּ** (elīfᵉlē'hū); **אֱלִיפֶלֶט** (elīfĕ'lĕt); **אֱלִיצוּר** (elīẞū'r); **אֱלִיצָפָן** (elī'ẞāfā'n); **אֱלִיקָא** (elīkā'); **אֶלְיָקִים** (ĕlyākī'm) *pr.n.m.*

אֱלִישֶׁבַע (elīšĕ'băᵉ) *pr.n.f.* [Elizabeth].

אֱלִישָׁה (elīšā') *pr.n.m.* [Greek

tribe in the Peloponnesus or in Sicily].

אֱלִישׁוּעַ (elīšū'a'); **אֶלְיָשִׁיב** (ĕlyāšī'b); **אֱלִישָׁמָע** (elī'šāmā'); **אֱלִישָׁע** (elīšā'); **אֱלִישָׁפָט** (elī'šāfā't); **אֱלִיָּתָה** [= **אֱלִיאָתָה**] *pr.n.m.*

אַלְלַי (ăl-lă'y) *interj.* alas, woe to!

אָלַם (ālă'm), *Ni.* נֶאֱלַם, *fut.* יֵאָלֵם to be bound in the tongue, to be dumb, mute. — *Pi. pt.* מְאַלֵּם to bind, to make up in sheaves.

אֵלֶם (ē'lĕm) *m* the growing dumb, dumbness, silence.

אִלֵּם (ĭllē'm) *adj., pl.* אִלְּמִים, dumb, mute.

אִלָּם (ŭllă'm) see אוּלָם.

אַלְמֻגִּים (ălmŭggī'm) *m*, only *pl.*, a precious wood, red or white sandal-wood.

אֲלֻמָּה (alŭmmā') *f, pl.* אֲלֻמִּים, אֲלֻמּוֹת, bundle, sheef.

אַלְמוֹדָד (ălmōdā'd) *pr.n.m.* [Arabian tribe in Yemen].

אַלַּמֶּלֶךְ (ăllămmĕ'lĕch) *pr.n.* of a town in Asher.

אַלְמָן (ălmā'n) *adj.* widowed.

אַלְמֹן (ălmō'n) *m* widowhood, interregnum.

אַלְמָנָה (ălmānā') *f, pl.* אַלְמָנוֹת, *c* אַלְ׳ מְנוֹת widow, a widowed state [without a ruler]

אַרְמְנוֹת (ălmānō'ϑ) *f/pl.* [perh. for אַרְמָנוֹת] palaces.

אַלְמָנוּת (ălmānū'ϑ) *f, c.* אַלְמְנוּת, *pl.* אַלְמְנוּתִים, widowhood; destitution [exile].

אַלְמֹנִי (ălmōnī') *m*, with preceding פְּלֹנִי, a certain one, one not named.

אֶלְנַעַם (ĕlnă'ăm); **אֶלְנָתָן** (ĕlnāϑā'n) *pr.n.m.*

אֶלָּסָר (ĕllāsā'r) *pr.n.* of town and district in Mesopotamia.

אֶלְעָד (ĕl'ā'd), **אֶלְעָדָה** (ĕl'ādā'); **אֶלְעוּזַי** (ĕl'ūză'y); **אֶלְעָזָר** (ĕl'āzā'r) *pr.n.m.*

אֶלְעָלֵא, **אֶלְעָלֵה** (ĕl'ālē') *pr.n.* of a town near Hesbon [in Reuben].

אֶלְעָשָׂה (ĕl'āsā') *pr.n.m.*

אָלַף (ālă'f), *fut.* יֶאֱלַף to learn. — *Pi. fut.* יְאַלֵּף, *pt.* מַלֵּף [for מְאַלֵּף] to teach. — *Hi. pt.* מַאֲלִיף, *pl. f* מַאֲלִיפוֹת to make thousands, to bring forth thousands [denom. of אֶלֶף].

אֶלֶף[1] (ĕ'lĕf) *m*, *i.p.* אָלֶף, *w.s.* אַלְפִּי, *du.* אַלְפַּיִם, *pl.* אֲלָפִים, *c.* אַלְפֵי 1. only *pl.* domesticated beasts, oxen, cows, cattle. 2. a thousand, *du.* two thousands, *pl.* thousands. 3. a community, family, part of a tribe.

אֶלֶף[2] (ĕ'lĕf) *pr.n.* of a town in Benjamin.

אֶלְפֶּלֶט [אֱלִיפֶּלֶט] (ĕlpĕ'lĕt); **אֶלְפַּעַל** (ĕlpă''ăl) *pr.n.m.*

אָלַץ (ālă'ts) *Pi. fut.* יְאַלֵּץ to drive, press, urge.

אֶלְצָפָן (ĕltsāfā'n) = אֱלִיצָפָן.

אַלְקוּם (ălkū'm) *m* no resistance; מֶלֶךְ א׳ a king against whom there is no rising up [others: people, militia].

אֶלְקָנָה (ĕlkānā') *pr.n.m.*

אֶלְקשִׁי (ĕlkōshī') *pr.n.m.*, a native of אֶלְקשׁ [a village in Galilee].

אֶלְתּוֹלַד [תּוֹלַד] (ĕltōlă'd) *pr.n.* of a town in Simeon.

אֶלְתְּקֵא, אֶלְתְּקֵה (ĕlt'kē') *pr.n.* of a town in Dan.

אֶלְתְּקוֹן (ĕlt'kō'n) *pr.n.* of a town in Judah.

אֵם (ēm) *f*, *w.s.* אִמִּי, *pl.* אִמּוֹת, mother, grandmother, ancestress; benefactress; metropolis, mother-country, people; אֵם הַדֶּרֶךְ parting-way.

אִם (ĭm) *conj.* [in direct and indirect questions] if, whether; הֲ—אִם whether—or; in conditional sentences: if, when, אִם לֹא if not; in sentences of wishing and asseveration: oh that [Lat. utinam], certainly not, אִם לֹא certainly.

אֹם *m*, only *pl.* אֻמִּים (ŭmmī'm), people, nation.

אָמָה (āmā') *f*, *w.s.* אֲמָתִי, *pl.* אֲמָהוֹת, *c.* אַמְהוֹת, maid-servant, female slave.

אַמָּה[1] (ămmā') *f*, *c.* אַמַּת, *du.* אַמָּתַיִם, *pl.* אַמּוֹת, fore-arm; ell, cubit; in architecture: foundation; metropolis

אַמָּה[2] (ămmā') *pr.n.* of a hill near Gibeon.

אֵמָה see אֵימָה.

אֻמָּה (ŭmmā') *f*, only *pl.* אֻמּוֹת people, nation, tribe.

אֲמָהוֹת see אָמָה.

אָמוֹן[1] (āmō'n) *m* builder, architect.

אָמוֹן[2] (āmō'n) *pr.n.m.*; also the Egyptian god Ammon.

אָמוֹן[3] see הָמוֹן.

אֵמוּן (ēmū'n), אֵמֻן *adj.*, *pl.* אֱמוּנִים fastened, faithful; *pl.* fidelity, trustiness.

אֱמוּנָה (emūnā') *f*, *w.s.* אֱמֻנָתִי, *pl.* אֱמוּנוֹת firmness, security, fidelity, honesty, conscientiousness, faith.

אָמוֹץ (āmō'ẞ) *pr.n.m.*

אֵמִים see אֵימִים.

אֲמִינוֹן see אַמְנוֹן.

אַמִּיץ (ămmī'ẞ) *adj.* firm, strong, valiant.

אָמִיר (āmī'r) *m* top of a tree, summit of a mountain.

אָמַל (āmă'l) [אָמֵל] *pt. p.f.* אֻמְלָלָה to fade, languish. — *Pul.* אֻמְלַל, *pt.* אֻמְלָל [for מְאֻמְלָל] to fade, droop, wither; to be sorrowful, to mourn.

אֲמֵלָל (amēlā'l) *adj.*, only *pl.* אֲמֵלָלִים weak, feeble.

אֲמָם (amā'm) *pr.n.* of a town in Judah.

אָמַן (āmă'n) *intr.* to be firm; *tr.* to make firm, fasten, bring up, nurse; *pt.* אֹמֵן guardian, fosterer, *f* אֹמֶנֶת nurse. — *Ni.* נֶאֱמַן, *fut.* יֵאָמֵן to be fastened, to be firm, constant, faithful, honest; to last, continue; to be nursed, supported; *pt.* נֶאֱמָן firm, faithful, constant, lasting. — *Hi.* הֶאֱמִין, *fut.* יַאֲמִין, יַאֲמֵן to hold fast by, to believe firmly, to trust; to stand still, to stop.

אָמָן (āmā'n) *m* workmaster, artist.

אָמֵן (āmē'n) *adj.* firm, true, faithful; *m* faithfulness; *adv.* certainly, truly, so be it!

אֹמֶן (ō'mĕn) *m* truth, fidelity.

אֲמָנָה[1] (amānā') *f* firm covenant; fixed wages.

אֲמָנָה[2] (amānā') *pr.n.* of a river flowing through Damascus [and of that part of the Antilibanus from which it comes].

אֹמְנָה (ōmenā') *f*, only *pl.* אֹמְנוֹת, pilaster, column.

אָמְנָה (ŏmnā') *f* the bringing up, nursing; *adv.* in truth truly.

אַמְנוֹן (ămnō'n) *pr.n.m.*

אָמְנָם (ŏmnā'm), אֻמְנָם *adv.* in truth, truly, verily.

אָמֵץ (āmē'ß) *fut.* יֶאֱמַץ to be strong, vigorous; to be stronger, to prevail. — *Pi.* אִמֵּץ, *fut.* יְאַמֵּץ to make strong, to strengthen, harden; to select. — *Hi.* *fut.* יַאֲמֵץ to display strength, to act courageously. — *Hith.* הִתְאַמֵּץ to collect one's strength, to show oneself vigorous, bold or quick; to be firmly resolved.

אָמֹץ (āmō'ß) *adj.*, only *pl.* אֲמֻצִּים strong; others: reddish, bay [horse].

אֹמֶץ (ō'mĕß) *m* strength, vigour.

אַמְצָה (ămßā') *f* strength.

אַמְצִי (ămßī'), אֲמַצְיָה (ᵃmăßyā') *pr.n.m.*

אָמַר (āmă'r) *inf.* אָמוֹר, אֱמֹר, with לְ לֵאמֹר [in the way of saying], *w.s.* אָמְרִי (ŏmrī'), *fut.* יֹאמַר, וַיֹּאמַר, וַיֹּאמֶר, 1. *sing.* אֹמַר, to say, name, call, admonish, promise, praise; to say to oneself, to think, intend; to command. — *Ni.* נֶאֱמַר, *fut.* יֵאָמֵר to be said, to be named; it is said. — *Hi.* הֶאֱמִיר to make say, to promise. — *Hith.* הִתְאַמֵּר to boast, to be over-proud, imperious.

אֵמֶר (ē'mĕr) *m*, *w.s.* אִמְרוֹ, *pl.* אֲמָרִים, *c.* אִמְרֵי a saying, word, utterance, command, promise.

אִמֵּר (Ĭmmē'r) *pr.n.m.*

אֹמֶר (ō'mĕr) *m* word, saying, song, praise, promise; thing [like דָּבָר].

אִמְרָה (Ĭmrā'), אֶמְרָה (ĕmrā') *f*, *c.* אִמְרַת, *pl.* אֲמָרוֹת, *c.* אִמְרוֹת word, utterance, song.

אֱמֹרִי (ᵉmōrī') *pr.n.m.* Amorite, chief tribe of the Canaanites.

אִמְרִי (Ĭmră'y); אֲמַרְיָה (ᵃmăryā'), אֲמַרְיָהוּ (ᵃmăryā'hū) *pr.n.m.*

אַמְרָפֶל (ămrāfĕ'l) *pr.n.m.* [king of Shinar, Hammurabi].

אֶמֶשׁ (ĕ'mĕš) *m* and *adv.* yesterday, last night.

אֱמֶת (ᵉmĕ'ϑ) [from אֱמֶנֶת] *f*, *w.s.* אֲמִתִּי firmness, duration, certainty, security, faithfulness, faith, truth, honesty.

אַמְתַּחַת (ămtă'ḥăϑ) *f*, *w.s.*

אַמְתַּחְתּוֹ, *pl. c.* אַמְתְּחוֹת bag, sack.

אֲמִתַּי (ᵃmĭttă'y) *pr.n.m.*

אָן (ān) [comp. אַיִן] *adv.* where? whither?; מֵאָן whence?; עַד־אָן till when? how long? — *w. loc.* ה אָנָה [also אָנָה] whither? where? how long?; אָנָה וְאָנָה hither and thither.

אֹן see אוֹן.

אָנָּא, אָנָּה (ā'nnā) *interj.* I pray! pray thee!

אָנֶה see אָן.

אָנָה[1] (ānā') to sigh, lament.

אָנָה[2] (ānā') *Pi.* אִנָּה to cause to meet. — *Pu.* אֻנָּה to befall, happen. — *Hith.* הִתְאַנָּה to seek opportunity [for a quarrel].

אֲנוּ see אֲנַחְנוּ.

אֱנוֹשׁ[1] (ᵉnō'š) *m* man, human being, mankind.

אֱנוֹשׁ[2] (ᵉnō'š) *pr.n.m.*

אָנַח (ānă'ḥ), only *Ni.* נֶאֱנַח to sigh, lament, mourn.

אֲנָחָה (ᵃnāḥā') *f, pl.* אֲנָחוֹת, lament, sighing.

אֲנַחְנוּ (ᵃnă'ḥnū) *pron. pers.* 1. *pl., i.p.* אֲנָחְנוּ, once אֲנוּ, abbreviated נַחְנוּ we, ourselves.

אֲנָחֲרַת (ᵃnā'ḥᵃrā'ϑ) *pr.n.* of a town in Issachar.

אֲנִי (ᵃnī') *pron. pers.* 1. *sing.* I, I myself = אָנֹכִי.

אֳנִי (ᵒnī') *m* and *f coll.* ships, a fleet.

אֳנִיָּה (ᵒnĭyyā') *f, pl.* אֳנִיּוֹת, ship.

אֲנִיָּה (ᵃnĭyyā') *f* lamentation, mourning.

אֲנִיעָם (ᵃnī'ā'm) *pr.n.m.*

אֲנָךְ (ᵃnā'ḵ) *m* the metal lead; plummet, plumb-line.

אָנֹכִי (ā'nōḵī') *pron. pers.* 1. *sing., i.p.* אָנֹכִי I, myself.

אָנַן (ānă'n), only *Hith.* הִתְאֹנֵן to complain, to murmur.

אָנַס (ānă's), *pt.* אֹנֵס to urge, compel.

אָנַף (ānă'f) *fut.* יֶאֱנַף to breathe heavily, to be angry. — *Hith.* הִתְאַנַּף to be angry.

אֲנָפָה (ᵃnāfā') *f* an unclean bird, parrot, sandpiper, or heron.

אָנַק (ānă'k) *fut.* יֶאֱנֹק, to groan, sigh. — *Ni. imp.* הֵאָנֵק, *pt.* נֶאֱנָק the same as *Q.*

אֲנָקָה (ᵃnākā') *f, c.* אֶנְקַת, sighing, complaint, moaning.

אָנַשׁ (ānă'š) *pt. p.* אָנוּשׁ to sicken, to make incurable; *pt. p.* ill, sick, incurable; melancholy, sorrowful; bad, wicked. — *Ni. fut.* יֵאָנֵשׁ to be sick to death.

אָסָא (āsā') *pr.n.m.*

אָסוּךְ (āsū'ɸ) *m* oil-flask.

אָסוֹן (āsō'n) *m* damage, hurt.

אֵסוּר (ēsū'r) *m, pl.* אֲסוּרִים, cord, fetter, bond.

אָסִיף (āsī'f) *m* harvest, ingathering time.

אָסִיר (āsī'r) *m*, also אַסִּיר[1] (ăssī'r), *pl.* אֲסִירִים, prisoner, captive, exile.

אַסִּיר[2] (ăssī'r) *pr.n.m.*

אָסָם (āsā'm) *m*, only *pl.* אֲסָמִים store house, granary.

אַסְנָה (ăsnā') *pr.n.m.*

אָסְנַפַּר (ŏsnăppă'r) *pr.n.m.* [an Assyrian king or a dignitary].

אָסְנַת (āsᵉnă'ϑ) *pr.n.f.*

אָסַף (āsă'f) *fut.* יֶאֱסֹף, יֹאסֵף, *w.s.* יַאַסְפֵנִי, אֹסִפְךָ [*fut.* 1. *sing. w.s.* and also *pt.* אֹסֵף *w.s.*] to gather, collect, to draw together, to receive, to take under protection; to draw up [feet]; to withdraw, to take away; to close a march, bring up the rear. — *Ni.* נֶאֱסַף to assemble, to be gathered [to one's forefathers, i. e. to die]; to be received, withdrawn, to disappear. — *Pi.* אִסֵּף to gather diligently, to receive, to close. — *Pu.* אֻסַּף to be gathered. — *Hith.* הִתְאַסֵּף to be gathered together.

אָסָף (āsā'f) *pr.n.m.*

אָסֹף (āsō'f) *m*, only *pl.* אֲסֻפִּים, gathered-in provisions, store.

אֹסֶף (ō'sĕf) *m, pl. c.* אָסְפֵּי (ŏsfē') ingathering, harvest.

אֲסֵפָה (ᵃsēfā') *f* assemblage; seizure, imprisonment.

אֲסֻפָּה (ᵃsŭppā') *f*, only *pl.* אֲסֻפּוֹת assembly [of wise men].

אֲסַפְסֻף (ᵃsăfsŭ'f) *m, w. art.* הָסַ~, mixed multitude, rabble.

אַסְפָּתָא (ăspā'ϑā) *pr.n.m.* [Persian].

אָסַר (āsă'r) *fut.* יֶאֱסֹר, יֶאְסֹר, *w.s.* יַאַסְרֻהוּ, *inf.* אֱסֹר, *pt. p.* אָסוּר to bind, fetter; to seize, to put in prison; to put to harness or in yoke; to begin, join [battle]; to charge oneself with, to engage; *pt. p.* captive, prisoner.—*Ni. fut.* יֵאָסֵר to be fettered, to be held captive. — *Pu.* אֻסַּר to be taken captive.

אִסָּר (ĭssā'r), **אֱסָר** (essā'r) *m*, *w.s.* אֱסָרָהּ, *pl. ws.* אֱסָרֶיהָ, vow of abstinence, renunciation.

אֵסַר־חַדֹּן (ēsărhăddō'n) *pr.n. m* [king of Assyria].

אֶסְתֵּר (ĕstē'r) *pr.n.f.* Esther [Persian: star, bliss].

אַף¹ (ăf) *conj.* [denoting addition, climax or emphasis], also, too, and yet, and even, even more; אַף—אַף as well as; אַף כִּי even more; in questions: is it so? really?

אַף² (ăf) [from אָנַף] *m, i.p.* אָף, *w.s.* אַפִּי heavy breathing, anger, wrath; nose.— *du.* אַפַּיִם, *c.* אַפֵּי the nostrils, nose, face; anger, wrath; two persons.

אַפְּאֵיהֶם see פָּאָה *Hi.*

אָפַד (āfă'd) *fut.* יֶאְפֹּד to surround, gird, put on.

אֲפֻדָּה (afŭddā') *f*, *c.* אֲפֻדַּת the act of girding round; a covering, coat of a statue.

אַפֶּדֶן (ăppĕ'dĕn) *m*, *w.s.* אַפַּדְנוֹ, palace.

אָפָה (āfā') *fut.* יֹאפֶה, יֹפֶה to bake; *pt.* אֹפֶה, *pl.* אֹפִים baker, *f* אֹפָה, *pl.* אֹפוֹת female baker or cook. — *Ni. fut.* יֵאָפֶה to be baked.

אֵפוֹ, אֵפוֹא (ēfō') *adv.* now, then, consequently.

אֵפוֹד¹, אֵפֹד (ēfō'd) *m* the ephod or official garment of priests, especially of the high-priest, a bipartite covering.

אֵפוֹד² (ēfō'd) *pr.n.m.*

אֲפִיחַ (afī'aḥ) *pr.n.m.*

אָפִיל (āfī'l) *adj.*, *f/pl.* אֲפִילוֹת, late in ripening.

אַפַּיִם (ăppă'yĭm) *pr.n.m.*

אָפִיק¹ (āfī'k) *m*, *c.* אֲפִיק, *pl.* אֲפִיקִים, *c.* אֲפִיקֵי, river-bed, bottom, channel, stream, brook, river.

אָפִיק² (āfī'k) *adj.* strong, powerful.

אֲפִיק see אָפֵק.

אֹפֶל (ō'fĕl) darkness, concealment; misfortune.

אָפֵל (āfē'l) *adj.* dark.

אֲפֵלָה (ᵃfēlā′) *f*, *pl.* אֲפֵלוֹת deep darkness.

אֶפְלָל (ĕflā′l) *pr.n.m.*

אֹפֶן (ō′fĕn) *m*, only *pl. w.s.* אָפְנָיו (ŏfnā′v) circumstance, turn, due time.

אֹפֶן see אוֹפָן.

אָפֵס (āfē′ß) to end, cease, disappear.

אֶפֶס (ĕ′fĕß) *m*, *du.* אַפְסַיִם, *pl. c.* אַפְסֵי, end, extremity; *du.* soles of the feet; *adv.* at an end, no more, not, except, only; בְּאֶפֶס without; אֶפֶס כִּי only that, however.

אֶפֶס דַּמִּים (ĕ′fĕß dămmī′m) *pr.n.* of a place in Judah.

אַפְסִי (ăfßī′) *adv.* except, nothing besides.

אֶפַע (ĕ′fă*) *m*, *i.p.* אָפַע, breath, nothingness.

אֶפְעֶה (ĕf*ĕ′) *m* and *f* adder, viper, basilisk.

אָפַף (āfă′f) [not contracted, e.g. אֲפָפוּ] to involve, to surround.

אָפַק (āfă′k) only *Hith.* הִתְאַפֵּק to control or restrain oneself.

אֲפֵק (ᵃfē′k) *pr.n.* of towns in northern Palestine.

אֲפֵקָה (ᵃfēkā′) *pr.n.* of a town in Judah.

אֵפֶר (ē′fĕr) *m* ashes, dust, nothingness.

אֲפֵר (ᵃfē′r) *m* head-cover, tiara.

אֶפְרֹחַ (ĕfrō′ᵃḥ) *m*, only *pl.* אֶפְרֹחִים, young bird, nestling.

אֶפְרַיִם (ĕfră′yĭm) *pr.n.m.*

אֶפְרָת (ĕfrā′ϑ), *w. loc.* ה אֶפְרָתָה *pr.n.*, older name for Bethlehem; also equivalent to אֶפְרַיִם.

אֶפְרָתִי (ĕfrāϑī′) *pr.n.m.*, a Bethlehemite; an Ephraimite.

אֶצְבֹּון (ĕßbō′n) *pr.n.m.*

אֶצְבַּע (ĕßbă′*) *f*, *w.s.* אֶצְבָּעִי, *pl.* אֶצְבָּעוֹת, *c.* אֶצְבְּעוֹת, finger, index, toe; fingerbreadth.

אָצִיל (āßī′l) *m*, *pl. c.* אֲצִילֵי extremity, remote corner. *adj.* noble, chief person.

אַצִּיל (ăßßī′l) *m*, *pl. c.* אַצִּילֵי, joint [knuckle, elbow].

אָצַל (āßă′l) [derived from אֵצֶל] to put aside, to take away, withdraw, refuse. — *Ni.* נֶאֱצַל to be taken away, to be reduced. — *Hi. fut.* וַיָּאצֶל to take away.

אֵצֶל (ē'Bĕl) *m, w.s.* אֶצְלִי, side, region; *prep.* at the side of, beside, close to, near.

אָצֵל (āBē'l) *pr.n.m.* [*i.p.* אָצַל]; *pr.n.* of a place.

אֲצַלְיָהוּ (ᵃBălyā'hū) *pr.n.m.*

אֹצֶם (ō'Bĕm) *pr.n.m.*

אֶצְעָדָה (ĕB'ādā') *f* bracelet, step-chain.

אָצַר (āBă'r) *pt.* אֹצֵר to heap up, store up. — *Ni. fut.* יֵאָצֵר to be stored up. — *Hi. fut.* 1. *sing.* וָאוֹצְרָה to appoint one treasurer.

אֹצָר see אוֹצָר.

אֵצֶר (ē'Bĕr) *pr.n.m.*

אֶצֹּר see יָצַר and נָצַר.

אֶקְדָּח (ĕkdā'ḥ) *m* a sparkling precious stone, carbuncle.

אַקּוֹ (ăkkō') *m* roe [or wild goat].

אֶקַּח, אֶקְחָה see לָקַח.

אֶקְרָאֶה [for אֶקְרָא] see קָרָא.

אֹר see אוֹר.

אֲרָא (ᵃrā') *pr.n.m.*

אַרְאִיל see אֲרִיאֵל.

אֶרְאֵל (ĕr'ē'l) *m*, only *pl.w.s.* אֶרְאֶלָּם their heroes.

אַרְאֵלִי (ăr'ēlī') *pr.n.m.*

אָרַב (āră'b) *fut.* יֶאֱרֹב to weave plots, to lie in ambush, to lurk; *pt.* אֹרֵב, אוֹרֵב lurking, lurker; *coll.* ambush. — *Pi. pt. pl.* מְאָרְבִים lurkers, liers in wait. — *Hi. fut.* וַיָּאֶרֶב [for וַיַּאֲרֵב] to form an ambush.

אֲרָב (ᵃrā'b) *pr.n.* of a town in Judah.

אֶרֶב (ĕ'rĕb) *m* ambush, lurking-place.

אֹרֶב (ō'rĕb) *m, w.s.* אָרְבּוֹ (ŏrbō') ambush, plot, cunning, deceit.

אַרְבְּאֵל (ărbē'l) *pr.n.* [בֵּית אַ׳] of a place in Naphtali.

אָרְבָּה (ŏrbā') *f*, only *pl. c.* אָרְבּוֹת, intrigue, plot.

אַרְבֶּה (ărbĕ') *m* locust, migratory locust.

אֲרֻבָּה (ᵃrŭbbā') *f*, *pl.* אֲרֻבּוֹת lattice, window, dove-cote, latticed outlet for the smoke.

אֲרֻבּוֹת (ᵃrŭbbō'th) *pr.n.* of a place in Judah near Sochoh.

אַרְבִּי (ărbī') *pr.n.m.*, inhabitant of אֲרָב.

אַרְבַּע[1] (ărbă'') *num. f, m* אַרְבָּעָה, *c.* אַרְבַּעַת, four; *du.* אַרְבַּעְתַּיִם fourfold; *pl.* אַרְבָּעִים forty.

אַרְבַּע[2] (ărbă'') *pr.n.m.* [an Anakite giant].

אָרַג (ārā'g) *fut.* יֶאֱרֹג, יַאֲרֹג, to plait, weave; *pt.* אֹרֵג, *f.* אֹרְגָה weaver.

אֶרֶג (ĕ'rĕg) *m* plait, texture; weaver's shuttle.

אַרְגֹּב (ărgō'b) *pr.n.* of a region in Bashan.

אַרְגְּוָן (ărgᵉvā'n) see אַרְגָּמָן.

אַרְגָּז (ărgā'z) *m* chest, box.

אַרְגָּמָן (ărgāmā'n) *m* purple, purple cloth.

אַרְדְּ (ărd) *pr.n.m.*

אַרְדּוֹן (ărdō'n) *pr.n.m.*

אָרָה[1] (ārā') to pull, pluck off, collect.

אָרָה[2] [אָרָה־לִּי] see אָבַר.

אֲרוֹד [אֲרוֹדִי] (ᵃrō'd) *pr.n.m.*

אַרְוַד (ărvă'd) *pr.n.* of a Phenician city, Arvad or Aradus; אַרְוָדִי the inhabitant.

אֻרְוָה (ŭrvā') *f*, only *pl.* [אֻרָוֺת] *c.* אֻרְוֹת (ŭrvō'th) and אֻרְיוֹת, crib, manger, stable, set of horses.

אָרוּז (ārū'z) *adj.*, only *pl.* אֲרֻזִים, cedrine, firm like cedar-wood.

אֲרוּכָה (ᵃrūchā'), אֲרֻכָה *f* healing, recovery, convalescence.

אֲרוּמָה (ᵃrūmā') *pr.n.* of a place near Sichem.

אֲרוֹמִים miswritten for אֱדוֹמִים Edomites.

אֲרוֹמֵם [for אֶתְרוֹמֵם] see רום *Hith.*

אָרוֹן (ārō'n) *f* and *m*, *c.* אֲרוֹן chest, box, coffin [for a mummy]; אֲ׳ הַבְּרִית ark of the covenant; אֲ׳ הָעֵדוּת ark of the testimony; אֲ׳ אֱלֹהִים ark of God, the sacred ark containing the tables of the law.

אֲרַוְנָה (ᵃrăvnā') *pr.n.m.*

אֶרֶז (ĕ'rĕz) *m, i.p.* אָרֶז, *pl.* אֲרָזִים, *c.* אַרְזֵי cedar; panel of cedar-wood.

אַרְזָה (ărzā') *f* cedar-work.

אָרַח[1] (āră'ch) to wander, travel; *pt.* אֹרֵחַ (ōrē'ᵃch), *pl.* אֹרְחִים wanderer, traveller.

אָרַח[2] (āră'ch) *pr.n.m.*

אֹרַח (ō'răch) *f* and *m*, *w.s.*

אָרְחוֹ (ŏrḥō'), *pl.* אֳרָחוֹת (orāḥō'th), *c.* אָרְחוֹת (ŏrḥō'th), אֹרְחוֹת, path, way, manner of life, manner, condition, lot; wanderer, caravan.

אֹרְחָה (ōreḥā') *f, pl.* אֹרְחוֹת, travelling company, caravan.

אֲרֻחָה (arūḥā') *f* portion, allowance; אֲרֻחַת יָרָק dish of greens.

אֲרִי (arī') *m, pl.* אֲרָיִים, אֲרָיוֹת, lion.

אֲרִיאֵל (arī'ēl) *m* lion of God, hero; the heroic city, Jerusalem; the hearth of God, altar.

אֲרִידַי (arīdă'y), אֲרִידָתָא (arīdāthā') *pr.n.m.* [Persian = Aridaeus].

אַרְיֵה[1] (ăryē') *m* and *f* lion, lioness.

אַרְיֵה[2] (ăryē') *pr.n.m.*

אֹרְיָה see אֹרְוָה.

אַרְיוֹךְ (ăryō'ḥ) *pr.n.m.*

אֲרַיֶּוְךָ [for אֲרַוֶּיךָ] see רָוָה *Pi.*

אֲרִיסַי (arīsă'y) *pr.n.m.* [Persian].

אָרַךְ (āră'ḥ) *fut.* יֶאֱרַךְ, יַאֲרֹךְ to stretch, to be long, to wear on. — *Hi.* הֶאֱרִיךְ, *fut.* יַאֲרִיךְ to make long, to lengthen, prolong, extend, delay; *intr.* to be long, to abide, sojourn.

אָרֵךְ (ārē'ḥ) *adj.*, only *c.* אֶרֶךְ long, patient; אֶרֶךְ אַפַּיִם forbearing.

אָרֹךְ (ārō'ḥ) *adj.*, *f* אֲרֻכָּה, long, enduring.

אֶרֶךְ[1] (ĕ'rĕḥ) *m* length, delay [see also אָרֵךְ].

אֶרֶךְ[2] (ĕ'rĕḥ) *pr.n.* of a city in Babylonia.

אֹרֶךְ (ō'rĕḥ) *m, w.s.* אָרְכּוֹ (ŏrkō'), length, duration, patience.

אֲרֻכָה *f* see אֲרוּכָה.

אַרְכִּי (ărkī') *pr.n.m*, inhabitant of אֶרֶךְ, a town in Palestine.

אֲרָם (arā'm) *pr.n.*, *c.* אֲרַם [mountain-land] Aramæa, Syria, and people therein, descended from Aram, the grandson of Nahor; אֲרַם נַהֲרַיִם Aramæa of the two rivers, Mesopotamia.

אַרְמוֹן (ărmō'n) *m, pl. c.* אַרְמְנוֹת, palace, castle, citadel.

אֲרַמִּי (arămmī') *pr.n.m.*, *pl.* אֲרַמִּים, *f* אֲרַמִּיָּה, Aramæan, Syrian, Mesopotamian.

אֲרָמִית (ᵃrāmī'ϑ) *adv.* [*f* from אֲרַמִּי Aramæan], in the Aramæan or Syrian language.

אַרְמֹנִי (ărmōnī') *pr.n.m.*

אֲרָן (ᵃrā'n) *pr.n.m.*

אֹרֶן[1] (ō'rĕn) *m* a cedar or pine [perh. miswritten for אֶרֶז].

אֹרֶן[2] (ō'rĕn) *pr.n.m.*

אַרְנֶבֶת (ărnĕ'ḇĕϑ) *f* a hare.

אַרְנוֹן (ărnō'n) *pr.n.* of a river between Moab and Ammon.

אֲרַנְיָה (ᵃrănyā') and אָרְנָן (ŏrnā'n) *pr.n.m.* = אֲרַוְנָה.

אַרְנָן (ărnā'n) *pr.n.m.*

אַרְפָּד (ărpā'ḏ) *pr.n.* of a city in Syria near Hamath.

אַרְפַּכְשַׁד (ărpăchsă'ḏ) *pr.n.m.*, a son of Shem, father of the Chaldeans or Northern Shemites.

אֶרֶץ (ĕ'rĕß) *f* and *m*, *w. art.* הָאָרֶץ, *i.p.* אָרֶץ, *w. loc.* אַרְצָה ה, *w.s.* אַרְצִי, *pl.* אֲרָצוֹת, *c.* אַרְצוֹת the earth [as a body of the universe], the earth [opposed to heaven]; land, ground, soil, country, fatherland, territory.

אַרְצָא (ărßā'') *pr.n.m.*

אָרַר (ārā'r) *imp.* אֹר, אָרָה־לִּי (ŏ'rrā-llī), *pl.* אֹרוּ, אוֹרוּ, *fut.* יָאֹר, *pt.* אֹרֵר, *pt.p.* אָרוּר, to curse, execrate. — *Ni. pt.* נֵאָר to be cursed. — *Pi.* אֵרֵר to curse, to cause a curse. — *Ho. fut. i.p.* יוּאָר to be cursed.

אֲרָרָט (ᵃrārā't) *pr.n.* of a district and high mountain in Armenia; all Armenia.

אֲרָרִי (ᵃrārī') *pr.n.m.*

אָרַשׂ (ārā's) *Pi.* אֵרַשׂ [with אִשָּׁה] to take a wife, to espouse. — *Pu.* אֹרַשׂ, *pt. f* מְאֹרָשָׂה to be engaged, betrothed.

אֲרֶשֶׁת (ᵃrĕ'sĕϑ) *f* desire, wish.

אַרְתַּחְשַׁשְׁתָּא (ărtăchsă'stā), אַרְתַּחְשַׁסְתְּא, אַרְתַּחְשַׁסְתָּא, *pr.n.m.*, Artaxerxes I. Longimanus, king of Persia.

אֲשַׂרְאֵל (ᵃsăr'ē'l) *pr.n.m.*

אַשְׂרִיאֵל (ăsrī'ē'l) *pr.n.m.*

אֵשׁ (ēs) *f* and *m*, *w.s.* אִשִּׁי, אֶשְׁכֶם fire, heat; lightning; flame of war; wrath; radiance, glitter.

אִשׁ (ĭs) = יֵשׁ there is.

אֶשְׁבֵּל (ĕsbē'l); אֶשְׁבָּן

(ĕšbā'n); אַשְׁבֵּעַ (ăšbē'a'); אֶשְׁבַּעַל (ĕšbă''ăl) *pr.n.m.*

אֶשֶׁד (ĕ'šĕd) *m* the flowing out, discharge of water, watered place.

אֲשֵׁדָה (ᵃšēdā') *f, pl.* אֲשֵׁדוֹת, *c.* אַשְׁדּוֹת outpouring; declivity where mountain waters flow together.

אַשְׁדּוֹד (ăšdō'd) *pr.n.*, one of the five Philistine cities, Azotus, Ashdod.

אֵשְׁדָּת — אֲשֵׁדָה or — אֵשׁ דָּת [see דָּת].

אִשָּׁה (ĭššā') *f, c.* אֵשֶׁת, *w.s.* אִשְׁתִּי, *pl.* נָשִׁים, *c.* נְשֵׁי, woman, wife, female; with אָחוֹת or רְעוּת the one — the other; every one, each [*f*].

אִשֶּׁה (ĭššĕ') *m, c.* אִשֵּׁה, *pl. c.* אִשֵּׁי, a burning, burnt-offering, holocaust, sacrifice.

אֲשׁוּיָה see אָשְׁיָה.

אֱשׁוּן *m*, only *c.* אֱשׁוּן perh. — אִישׁוֹן.

אָשׁוּר (ăšū'r) *m, pl.* אֲשֻׁרִים, *c.* אֲשֻׁרֵי step, gait; — תְּאַשּׁוּר a kind of cedar [sherbîn].

אַשּׁוּר[1] (ăššū'r) — אָשׁוּר.

אַשּׁוּר[2] (ăššū'r) *pr.n.* Assyria [in some passages including Syria, Babylonia, Persia] *pl.* אַשּׁוּרִים an Arabian tribe, descended from Dedan.

אֲשׁוּרִי (ᵃšūrī') *pr.n.*, a native of אֲשׁוּר [a district in Asher].

אַשְׁחוּר (ăšḥū'r) *pr.n.m.*

אָשְׁיָה (ŏšyā') *f, pl. w.s.* אָשְׁיוֹתֶיהָ, support, prop.

אֲשִׁימָא (ᵃšīmā') *pr.n.* of an idol in Hamath.

אֲשֵׁירָה see אֲשֵׁרָה.

אָשִׁישׁ (ăšī's) *m*, only *pl. c.* אֲשִׁישֵׁי foundations, ruined remains.

אֲשִׁישָׁה (ᵃšīšā') *f, pl.* אֲשִׁישׁוֹת and אֲשִׁישִׁים, cake, pancake.

אֶשֶׁךְ (ĕ'šĕḵ) *m, i.p.* אָשֶׁךְ, testicle.

אַשְׁכִּים see שָׁכַם *Hi.*

אֶשְׁכֹּל[1] (ĕškō'l) *m, pl.* אֶשְׁכְּלוֹת, *c.* אַשְׁכְּלוֹת, cluster of grapes, grape, raceme.

אֶשְׁכֹּל[2] (ĕškō'l) *pr.n.m.* of an Amorite; *pr.n.* of a valley near Hebron.

אַשְׁכְּנַז (ăškᵉnă'z) *pr.n.m.* of a Japhetite, son of Gomer, and his race [Armenia;

according to the Rabbins: Germany].

אֶשְׁכָּר (ĕškā'r) *m* barter, ware; gift, tribute.

אֵשֶׁל (ē'šĕl) *m* tamarisk, grove, wood.

אָשֵׁם[1] (āšē'm) and **אָשַׁם** (āšă'm) *fut.* יֶאְשַׁם, יֶאְשָׁם to be guilty, to trespass; to atone; to lie waste. — *Ni.* נֶאְשַׁם to suffer for, to be destroyed. — *Hi. imp.* הַאֲשִׁים to punish, destroy.

אָשָׁם (āšā'm) *m, w.s.* אֲשָׁמוֹ, *pl.* אֲשָׁמִים, fault, guilt, trespass; trespass-offering.

אָשֵׁם[2] (āšē'm) *adj.* guilty, bound to atone.

אַשְׁמָה (ăšmā') *f, c.* אַשְׁמַת, *pl.* אֲשָׁמוֹת, *c.* אַשְׁמוֹת fault, trespass, guilt; idol, as worshipped sinfully; trespass-offering.

אַשְׁמַן (ăšmă'n) *m,* only *pl.* אַשְׁמַנִּים, darkness, desolate place [others: fat, healthy].

אַשְׁמוּרָה.אַשְׁמֻרָה (ăšmūrā') and **אַשְׁמֹרֶת** (ăšmō'rĕϑ) *f, c.* אַשְׁמֹרֶת, *pl.* אַשְׁמוּרוֹת, night-watch [third part of the night].

אֶשְׁנָב (ĕšnā'b) *m, w.s.* אֶשְׁנַבִּי, lattice, window.

אַשְׁנָה (ăšnā') *pr.n.* of two towns in Judah.

אֶשְׁעָן (ĕšʼā'n) *pr.n.* of a town in Judah.

אַשָּׁף (ăššā'f) *m,* only *pl.* אַשָּׁפִים, enchanter, magician.

אַשְׁפָּה[1] (ăšpā') *f* quiver.

אַשְׁפָּה[2] (ăšpā') *f,* only *pl.* אַשְׁפֹּת [which is also taken as a *sing. m*] dirt, dunghill.

אַשְׁפְּנַז (ăšpᵉnă'z) *pr.n.m.* [Persian].

אֶשְׁפָּר (ĕšpā'r) *m* a measure for fluids, cup, portion.

אַשְׁפָּת (ăšpā'ϑ) *f,* only *pl.* אַשְׁפַּתּוֹת, dunghill.

אַשְׁקְלוֹן (ăškᵉlō'n) *pr.n.,* one of the five Philistine cities, Askalon; אַשְׁקְלוֹנִי the inhabitant.

אָשַׁר (āšā'r) to walk straight. — *Pi.* אִשֵּׁר to go, lead, direct the right way; to make happy, to pronounce happy. — *Pu.* אֻשַּׁר to be made happy.

אָשֵׁר (āšē'r) *pr.n.m.*; *pr.n.* of a town east of Shechem.

אֲשֶׁר (ᵃšĕ'r) particle denoting relation, corresponding to our *pron. rel.* in all genders and numbers: who, which, that; also opening dependent sentences: that, how, because, when; אֲשֶׁר־שָׁם where; אֲשֶׁר־מִשָּׁם whence; בַּאֲשֶׁר where, because, since; כַּאֲשֶׁר as, in so far as; מֵאֲשֶׁר from where, since.

אֶשֶׁר (ĕ'šĕr) *m*, only *pl. c.* אַשְׁרֵי, happiness, bliss; אַ׳ הָאִישׁ happiness of the man, i. e. happy is the man; אַשְׁרֶיךָ hail to thee, happy art thou.

אֹשֶׁר (ō'šĕr) *m*, *w.s.* אָשְׁרִי (ŏšrī'), happiness.

אָשֻׁר, אַשֻּׁר see אָשׁוּר, אַשּׁוּר.

אֲשַׂרְאֵל (ᵃsăr'ē'l), אֲשַׂרְאֵלָה (ᵃsăr'ēlā') *pr.n.m.*

אֲשֵׁרָה, אֲשֵׁירָה (ᵃšērā') *f*, *pl.* אֲשֵׁרִים, אֲשֵׁרוֹת a Phenician goddess of prosperity [sometimes identified with עַשְׁתֹּרֶת]; image or pillar of the goddess.

אָשַׁשׁ (āšă'š) *Hithpo.* הִתְאשֵׁשׁ (hĭϑ'ōšē's) to show oneself strong, firm.

אֵשֶׁת see אִשָּׁה

אֶשְׁתָּאֹל (ĕštā'ō'l) *pr.n.* of a town in Dan; *gent.* אֶשְׁתָּאֻלִי.

אֶשְׁתּוֹן (ĕštō'n) *pr.n.m.*

אֶשְׁתְּמֹה (ĕštᵉmō') and אֶשְׁתְּמוֹעַ (ĕštᵉmō'aᵉ) *pr.n.* of a town in Judah.

אַתְּ, אַתְּ see אַתָּה.

אֵת[1] (ēϑ) *m*, *w.s.* אִתּוֹ, *pl.* אִתִּים and אֵתִים, an agricultural tool: mattock, hoe or plough-share.

אֵת[2] (ēϑ), אֶת־ (ĕϑ), *w.s.* אֹתִי, אֹתְךָ, אֶתְכֶם [properly *m* existence, substance] particle denoting the determined accusative.

אֵת[3] (ēϑ), אֶת־ (ĕϑ) *prep.*, *w.s.* אִתִּי, אִתְּכֶם [also אֹתִי, &c.], with, at, near; מֵאֵת from, away from.

אֹת see אוֹת, and אֵת[3].

אֶתְבַּעַל (ĕϑbă'ᵉăl) *pr.n.m.* [a king of Sidon].

אָתָה (āϑā') [אָתָא] *pf.* 1. *pl.* אָתָנוּ, *imp. pl.* אֵתָיוּ, *fut.* יֶאֱתֶה, תֵּאתֶה [for תֶּאֱתֶה], וַיֵּתֶא, וַיֵּאת [for וַיֶּאֱת] to come, to come to pass, to impend, to pass away; *pt. pl. f* אֹתִיּוֹת future things, coming events. — *Hi.* הֵתָה [for הֶאֱתָה], *pl.* הֵתָיוּ [or *imp. pl.*], to bring.

אַתָּה (ăttā'), אַתָּ *m*, אַתְּ (ătt) *f.*, *pron. pers.* 2. *sing.* thou, thyself.

אֶתְוַדַּע – אֶתְיַדַּע, see יָדַע *Hith.*

אָתוֹן (āϑō'n) *f*, *c.* אֲתוֹן, *pl.* אֲתֹנוֹת, she-ass.

אַתִּי (ăttī') = אַתְּ thou [*f*].

אַתִּיק (ăttī'k) [also אַתּוּק] *m*, *pl.* אַתִּיקִים, portico, gallery.

אַתֶּם (ăttĕ'm) *m*, אַתֵּנָה [אַתֵּנָּה] (ăttē'nā) and אַתֵּן (ăttĕ'n) *f*, *pron. pers.* 2. *pl.* you, yourselves.

אֵתָם (ēϑā'm) *pr.n.* of an encampment on the border of the Arabian desert.

אֶתְמוֹל (ĕϑmō'l), אִתְּמוֹל (ĭtmō'l), אֶתְמוּל (ĕϑmū'l) *adv.* formerly, of old, yesterday.

אַתֵּנָה see אַתֶּם.

אֶתְנָה (ĕϑnā') *f* reward.

אֶתְנִי (ĕϑnī') *pr.n.m.*

אֶתְנַן (ĕϑnă'n) *m*, *i.p.* אֶתְנָן, *w.s.* אֶתְנַנָּהּ, *pl.* אֶתְנַנִּים, reward, harlot's hire.

אֲתָרִים (aϑārī'm) *pr.n.* of a place in southern Palestine.

ב

ב the second letter of the alphabet, called בֵּית (bēϑ) = בַּיִת tent; as a numeral = 2 or 2000.

בְּ (bᵉ) prefix or inseparable *prep.*; combined with the def. *art.* בַּ, בָּ, בֶּ, *ws.* בִּי, בְּךָ, בָּךְ, בּוֹ, בָּהּ &c., in, at, to, on, among, with, towards; according to, by, because of.

בִּאָה (bī'ā') *f* entrance.

בֵּאֵר (bē'ē'r) *Pi.* בֵּאֵר, *imp.* בָּאֵר to engrave, to explain.

בְּאֵר[1] (bᵉ'ē'r) *f*, *pl.* בְּאֵרוֹת, *c.* בְּאֵרֹת [once בְּאֵרוֹת], pit, well.

בְּאֵר[2] (bᵉ'ē'r) *pr.n.* of several places.

בְּאֵר אֵלִים (bᵉ'ē'r ēlī'm) *pr.n.* of a place on the border of Moab [well of the heroes].

בְּאֵר לַחַי רֹאִי (bᵉ'ē'r lăḥă'y rō'ī') *pr.n.* of a well in the desert [*prop.* well of the living, i. e. God, looking upon me].

בְּאֵר שֶׁבַע (b'ē'r šĕ'bă') *pr.n.* of a well and place on the southern frontier of Palestine [*prop.* well of the oath].

באר see בּוֹר.

בְּאֵרָא, בְּאֵרָה (b'ērā') *pr.n.m.*

בְּאֵרוֹת (b'ērō'ϑ) *pr.n.* of a town in Benjamin; *gent.* בְּרֹתִי, בְּאֵרֹתִי.

בְּאֵרוֹת בְּנֵי־יַעֲקָן (b'ērō'ϑ b'nē' yă'akā'n) *pr.n.* of an encampment in the desert.

בְּאֵרִי (b'ērī') *pr.n.m.*

בָּאַשׁ (bā'ă's) to be foul or loathsome, to stink. — *Ni.* נִבְאַשׁ to make oneself stinking, i. e. hated. — *Hi.* הִבְאִישׁ, *fut.* יַבְאִישׁ to make stinking, loathsome, hated, defamed. — *Hith.* הִתְבָּאֵשׁ to become odious.

בְּאשׁ (b'ō's) *m*, *w.s.* בָּאְשָׁם (bŏ'šā'm) stench, stink.

בְּאֹשׁ (bā'ō's) *m*, only *pl.* בְּאֻשִׁים unripe, useless grapes.

בָּאְשָׁה (bŏ'šā') *f* foul plant, weed.

בָּבָה (bābā') *f*, *c.* בָּבַת, apple [of the eye], pupil.

בֵּבַי (bēbă'y) *pr.n.m.*

בָּבֶל (bābĕ'l) *pr.n.f.*, *w. loc.* ה בָּבֶלָה, Babylon; Babylonia including Persia [*prop.* gate of God].

בַּג (băg) *m* food [or booty].

בָּגַד (bāgă'd) *fut.* יִבְגֹּד, יִבְגַּד to act secretly, to deceive, cheat, betray, forsake, fall off; *pt. pl.* בֹּגְדִים the recreant, impious.

בֶּגֶד (bĕ'gĕd) *m*, *w.s.* בִּגְדִי [without dagesh], *pl.* בְּגָדִים, once בְּגָדֹת, *c.* בִּגְדֵי, covering, garment, dress, robe, cloth; concealment, malignity, robbery.

בֹּגְדוֹת (bō'g'dō'ϑ) *f/pl.* faithlessness, treachery.

בָּגוֹד (bāgō'd) *adj.*, only *f* בָּגוֹדָה, faithless, treacherous.

בִּגְוַי (bĭgvă'y) *pr.n.m.* [Persian].

בִּגְלַל see גָּלָל.

בִּגְתָא (bĭgϑā') *pr.n.m.* [Persian]; also בִּגְתָן.

בַּד[1] (băd) [from בָּדַד] *m*, *pl.* בַּדִּים, *c.* בַּדֵּי, separation, separable part [בַּד בְּבַד part by part, at equal parts]; *pl.* parts of the body, limbs; parts of a tree, branches, poles, bars; לְבַד *adv.* separately, apart, besides, except, alone; לְבַדִּי I alone, by myself.

בַּד[2] (bắḍ) *m*, *pl.* בַּדִּים, white linen, linen clothes.

בַּד[3] (bắḍ) *m*, only *pl.* בַּדִּים, idle talk, prattle; prater, braggart, liar.

בָּדָא (bāḍā') *pt.* *w.s.* בֹּדָאם for בֹּדְאָם, to invent [in an evil sense], to lie.

בָּדַד (bāḍă'ḍ) *pt.* בּוֹדֵד to be separated, to be lonely, solitary.

בָּדָד (bāḍā'ḍ) *m* separation; *adv.* [also לְבָדָד] separately, alone.

בְּדַד (bᵉḍă'ḍ) *pr.n.m.*

בְּדֵי see דַּי.

בֵּדְיָה (bēḍᵉyā') *pr.n.m.*

בְּדִיל (bᵉḍī'l) *m*, *pl.* בְּדִילִים, lead-alloy [mixed with silver], tin.

בָּדַל (bāḍă'l) *Ni.* נִבְדַּל, *fut.* יִבָּדֵל, to separate oneself, to be separated or selected. — *Hi.* הִבְדִּיל, *fut.* יַבְדִּיל, וַיַּבְדֵּל, *pt.* מַבְדִּיל, to sever, separate, divide, discern, select, distinguish, shut out.

בָּדָל (bāḍā'l) *m*, only *c.* בְּדַל, part, flap [of the ear].

בְּדֹלַח (bᵉḍō'lăḥ) *m* bdellium, an aromatic resin [according to the Rabbins: pearls].

בְּדָן (bᵉḍā'n) *pr.n.m.* [for עַבְדּוֹן – עַבְדָן, or בָּרָק, שִׁמְשׁוֹן – בֶּן־דָּן].

בָּדַק (bāḍă'k) *inf.* בְּדוֹק, to repair, rebuild.

בֶּדֶק (bĕ'ḍĕk) *m*, *i.p.* בָּדֶק, *w.s.* בִּדְקֵךְ, rent, cleft, gap, dilapidation.

בִּדְקַר (bĭḍkă'r) *pr.n.m.*

בֹּהוּ (bō'hū) *m* [always preceded by תֹּהוּ], emptiness, chaos.

בַּהַט (bă'hăṭ) *m* a marble-like stone, alabaster.

בָּהִיר (bāhī'r) *adj.* shining, bright.

בָּהַל (bāhă'l) *Ni.* נִבְהַל, *fut.* יִבָּהֵל, to be terrified, frightened, perplexed; to be quick, overhasty; to flee; *pt.* *f* נִבְהָלָה sudden destruction. — *Pi.* בִּהֵל, *inf.* בַּהֵל, *fut.* יְבַהֵל to frighten, confound, perplex; to accelerate, to do in haste. — *Pu.* בֹּהַל to be hastened, *pt.* מְבֹהָל gotten in haste.

—*Hi.* הִבְהִיל, *fut.* יַבְהִיל to frighten, to scare away.

בֶּהָלָה (bĕhālā') *f, pl.* בֶּהָלוֹת, fright, terror, sudden destruction.

בְּהֵמָה (bʼhēmā') *f, c.* בֶּהֱמַת, *w.s.* בְּהֶמְתְּךָ, בְּהֶמְתּוֹ, *pl.* בְּהֵמוֹת, *c.* בַּהֲמוֹת beast, brute, mammal, tame or wild animal.

בְּהֵמוֹת (bʼhēmō'ϑ) *m* [used as a *sing.*], *c.* בַּהֲמוֹת hippopotamus, Nile-horse.

בֹּהֶן (bō'hĕn) *f, pl.* בְּהֹנוֹת [from בְּהוֹן] thumb, big toe.

בֹּהַן (bō'hăn) *pr.n.m.*; *pr.n.* of a place in Benjamin.

בֹּהַק (bō'hăk) *m* a whitish breaking-out on the skin.

בַּהֶרֶת (băhĕ'rĕϑ) *f, pl.* בֶּהָרוֹת, white spot on the skin.

בְּהִשַּׁמָּה — בְּהָשַׁמָּה, see שָׁמַם *Ho.*

בּוֹא (bō) *pf.* and *pt.* בָּא [1. *pl.* also בָּנוּ for בָּאנוּ], *inf.* בּוֹא, בֹּא, *imp.* בּוֹא [בֹּא], בֹּאִי, בֹּאוּ, *fut.* יָבֹא, יָבוֹא, יָבֹו, to go in, step in, to enter, to turn in, to alight, to set [of the sun]; to come, arrive; עַד בֹּאֲךָ [*inf. w.s.*] till thy coming, till one comes; to come to pass; to go, to travel. — *Hi.* הֵבִיא, הֵבֵאתָ, *w.s.* הֲבִיאֹתַנִי, *inf.* הָבֵא and הָבִיא, *imp.* הָבֵא and הָבִיא, הָבִיאִי and הָבִי, *fut.* יָבִיא, וַיָּבֵא, *pt.* מֵבִיא to cause to come in, to lead in, to bring in, to put in; to lead; to offer, to bring on. — *Ho.* הוּבָא, 3. *sing. f* הֻבָאת, *pt.* מוּבָא to be led in, to be brought, to be put in.

בּוּז[1] (būz) *pf.* and *pt.* בָּז [בַּז], *fut.* יָבוּז to despise, disdain, treat with contempt.

בּוּז[2] (būz) *m* contempt, scorn, derision.

בּוּז[3] (būz) *pr.n.m.*, an Arabian tribe; *gent.* בּוּזִי [also *pr.n.m.*].

בּוּזָה (būzā') *f* object of contempt.

בַּוַּי (băvvă'y) *pr.n.m.* [perh. Persian].

בּוּךְ (būḉ) *Ni.* נָבוֹךְ, *pt.* נָבֹךְ, *pl.* נְבֻכִים, to be confused, bewildered, to go astray.

בּוּל[1] (būl) *m* produce, fruit; branch, bough.

בּוּל[2] (bûl) *m* eighth month of the old Hebrew year [November to December].

בּוּן see בִּין.

בּוּנָה (bûnā') *pr.n.m.*

בּוּנִּי (bûnnî') *pr.n.m.*

בּוּס (bûs) *fut.* יָבוּס, *pt. pl.* בּוֹסִים [for בָּסִים] to tread down, to crush. — *Pil.* בּוֹסֵס to tread down, trample on, profane. — *Ho. pt.* מוּבָס to be crushed under foot. — *Hith. pt. f* מִתְבּוֹסֶסֶת to be trodden down, to be abandoned to kicks.

בּוּץ (bûẞ) *m* byssus, a fine white cotton or linen texture.

בּוֹצֵץ (bōẞē'ẞ) *pr.n.* of a rock.

בּוּקָה (bûkā') *f* devastation, desolation.

בּוֹקֵר (bōkē'r) *m* herdsman, shepherd.

בּוֹר (bōr) *m, pl.* בֹּרוֹת pit, hole; cistern, well; dungeon, grave.

בּוֹשׁ (bōš) *pf.* בֹּשׁ, בּוֹשׁ, *inf.* and *imp.* בּוֹשׁ, בֹּשׁ, *fut.* יֵבוֹשׁ, אֵבוֹשׁ to be or feel ashamed, to be confounded, to be disappointed; עַד בּוֹשׁ till they were disappointed in waiting. — *Pil.* בּוֹשֵׁשׁ to make ashamed, to disappoint expectation, to keep waiting. — *Hi.* הֵבִישׁ, הוֹבִאישׁ, הוֹבִישׁ, הֹבִישׁ, 2. *sing. m* הֳבִישׁוֹתָ (hºbîšō'θā), *fut.* יָבִישׁ, *pt.* מֵבִישׁ to confound, deceive, disappoint; to act shamefully; *intr.* to be ashamed, disappointed. — *Hith.* הִתְבֹּשֵׁשׁ to be ashamed.

בּוּשָׁה (bûšā') *f* shame, disgrace.

בַּז (bāz) *m, w.s.* בִּזָּהּ (bîzzā'h), booty, prey.

בָּזָא (bāzā') to cut through, flow through.

בָּזָה (bāzā') *fut.* יִבְזֶה, נִבְזֶה, *pt.* בֹּזֶה, *pl. w.s.* בֹּזַי, *pt. p.* בָּזוּי to despise; *intr.* to be contemptible. — *Ni. pt.* נִבְזֶה to be despised. — *Hi. inf.* הַבְזוֹת to make contemptible.

בָּזֹה (bāzō') *adj.*, only *c.* בְּזֹה despised.

בִּזָּה (bîzzā') *f* booty, prey, spoil.

בָּזַז (bāzā'z) *inf.* בֹּז, *fut.* יָבֹז, *pt.* בּוֹזֵז, *pt. p.* בָּזוּז, to plunder, spoil, rob, get as booty. — *Ni.* נָבֹז, *inf.* הִבּוֹז,

fut. יִבּוֹז to be plundered. — *Pu.* בֻּזַּז to be robbed.

בִּזָּיוֹן (bĭzzāyō'n) *m* contempt.

בִּזְיוֹתְיָה (bĭzyō'ϑᵉyā') *pr.n.* of a place in Judah.

בָּזָק (bāzā'k) *m* lightning.

בֶּזֶק (bĕ'zĕk) *pr.n.* of a town in northern Palestine.

בָּזַר (bāză'r) *fut.* יִבְזוֹר and *Pi.* בִּזֵּר to scatter.

בִּזְּתָא (bĭzϑā') *pr.n.m.* [Persian].

בָּחוֹן (bāḥō'n) *m* [*adj.*] trier of metals.

בַּחוּן (băḥū'n) *m, pl. w.s.* בַּחוּנָיו, watch-tower.

בָּחוּר [for בַּחוּר] (bāḥū'r) *m, pl.* בַּחוּרִים, *c.* בַּחוּרֵי, youth, young man, adult fit to bear arms, young warrior.

בְּחוּרִים (bᵉḥūrī'm) *m/pl.* and בְּחוּרוֹת (bᵉḥūrō'ϑ) *f/pl.* age of youth.

בַּחִין — בַּחוּן.

בָּחִיר (bāḥī'r) *adj.*, *c.* בְּחִיר, chosen, elect.

בָּחַן (bāḥă'n) *imp.* בְּחַן, *fut.* יִבְחַן to try, prove, test, examine, purify. — *Ni.* נִבְחַן to be tried. — *Pu.* בֹּחַן the test is made.

בַּחַן (bă'ḥăn) *m* watch-tower.

בֹּחַן (bō'ḥăn) *m* trial, proof [see also בָּחַן *Pu.*]; אֶבֶן בֹּחַן tried stone, head-stone, corner-stone.

בָּחַר (bāḥă'r) *imp.* בְּחַר, *fut.* יִבְחַר, *pt. p.* בָּחוּר, *pl. c.* בְּחוּרֵי to prove, try, choose, select, distinguish, prefer, like, love. — *Ni.* נִבְחַר to be chosen, preferred, to be pleasing. — *Pu.* בֻּחַר to be chosen.

בְּחֻרִים see בְּחוּרִים.

בַּחֻרִים (băḥūrī'm) *pr.n.* of a town between Jerusalem and Jericho; *gent.* בַּחֲרוּמִי, בַּרְחֻמִי.

בָּטָא (bātā') *Pi.* בִּטֵּא, *fut.* יְבַטֵּא to talk idly.

בָּטַח (bātă'ḥ) *imp.* בְּטַח, *fut.* יִבְטַח, *pt.* בֹּטֵחַ, *f* בֹּטְחָה, *pt. p.* בָּטוּחַ, to attach oneself, to trust, to confide in [בְּ, עַל, אֶל]; to feel secure, to be careless. — *Hi.* הִבְטִיחַ, *fut.* יַבְטַח, *pt.* מַבְטִיחַ to make secure and fearless, to inspire with confidence.

בֶּטַח[1] (bĕ'tăḥ) *m, i.p.* בָּטַח security, safety, confidence;

לָבֶטַח and בֶּטַח *adv.* securely, carelessly.

בֶּטַח² (bĕ'ṭăḥ) *pr.n.* of an Aramæan town.

בִּטְחָה (biṭḥā') *f* and בִּטָּחוֹן (biṭṭāḥō'n) *m* confidence, hope.

בַּטֻּחוֹת (băṭṭūḥō'ϑ) *f/pl.* security [see also טֻחוֹת].

בָּטַל (bāṭă'l) to cease, to rest.

בֶּטֶן (bĕ'ṭĕn) *f*, *i.p.* בָּטֶן, *w.s.* בִּטְנוֹ, belly, womb, the inmost part, bottom of the heart; belly-shaped protuberance on pillars.

בָּטְנָה (bŏṭnā') *m*, only *pl.* בָּטְנִים (bŏṭnī'm) pistacia-nut.

בְּטֹנִים (bᵉṭōnī'm) *pr.n.* of a town in Gad.

בִּי (bī) particle of entreaty: I pray; בִּי אֲדֹנָי pray, my Lord!

בִּין [בּוּן] (bīn) *imp.* בִּין, *fut.* יָבִין, וַיָּבֶן to discern, perceive, observe, pay attention, understand, know.— *Ni.* נָבוֹן, 1. *sing.* נְבֻנוֹתִי, *pt.* נָבוֹן to be intelligent, knowing. — *Pil.* בּוֹנֵן to heed.—*Hi.* הֵבִין, *inf.* הָבִין, הָבֵן, *imp.* הָבֵן, הָבִינוּ [בִּינוּ or Q.], *fut.* יָבִין, וַיָּבֶן [or Q.], *pt.* מֵבִין to make intelligent; to make understood; to instruct, teach; like Q. to perceive, mark, understand, know. — *Hith.* הִתְבּוֹנֵן to perceive, mark, to attend to; to be sensible.

בַּיִן (bă'yĭn) *m* [*st. abs.* not used], *c.* בֵּין (bēn), *du.* בֵּינַיִם, *pl.* בֵּינוֹת, *w.s.* בֵּינִי, בֵּינֵיהֶם, בֵּינוֹתֵנוּ, interstice, space between; אִישׁ בֵּינַיִם mediator, champion; *c.* בֵּין *adv.* between, among; מִבֵּין from between.

בִּינָה (bīnā') *f*, *c.* בִּינַת, *pl.* בִּינוֹת, understanding, insight, prudence.

בֵּיצָה (bēẞā') *f*, only *pl.* בֵּיצִים, egg.

בַּיִר (bă'yĭr) = בְּאֵר.

בִּירָה (bīrā') *f* castle, citadel, fortress; palace, temple; chief city.

בִּירָנִית (bī'rānī'ϑ) *f*, only *pl.* בִּירָנִיּוֹת, castle, fortress.

בַּיִת (bă'yĭϑ) *m*, *i.p.* בָּיִת, *c.* בֵּית, *w. loc.* ה בַּיְתָה and בֵּיתָה, *pl.* בָּתִּים (bātī'm or bāttī'm), *c.* בָּתֵּי (bātē') tent, hut, house, mansion; palace, temple; dwelling-place; receptacle, place where things are found; interior [*opp.* חוּץ]; בַּיְתָה towards the inside, within; מִבַּיִת from within; — family, household, race, descendants.

בֵּית in compound proper names of places: ב׳ אָוֶן in Benjamin; בֵּיתְאֵל, בֵּית־אֵל on the border of Benjamin and Ephraim; ב׳ בַּעַל מְעוֹן in Reuben; ב׳ בִּרְאִי in Simeon; ב׳ בָּרָה [perh. for ב׳ עֲבָרָה] place of passage, ford on the Jordan; ב׳ גָּדֵר in Judah; ב׳ גָּמוּל in Moab; ב׳ דָּגוֹן in Judah and in Asher; ב׳ הַיְשִׁימוֹת in Moab [Reuben]; ב׳ הַכֶּרֶם in Judah; ב׳ הַמֶּרְחָק near Jerusalem; ב׳ הַמַּרְכָּבוֹת in Simeon; ב׳ חָנָן in Judah or Dan; ב׳ חוֹרוֹן in Ephraim; ב׳ לֶחֶם near Mizpah; ב׳ כַּר in Judah, Bethlehem, *gent.* בֵּית הַלַּחְמִי; ב׳ מִלּוֹא citadel of Shechem [see מִלּוֹא]; ב׳ מַעֲכָה at the foot of Hermon; ב׳ עֶדֶן on mount Lebanon; ב׳ עֲנוֹת in Judah; ב׳ עֲנָת in Naphtali; ב׳ עֵקֶד הָרֹעִים between Jezreel and Samaria; ב׳ פְּעוֹר in Moab; ב׳ צוּר in the mountains of Judah; ב׳ שְׁאָן, ב׳ שָׁן in Manasseh, in the valley of the Jordan, afterwards Scythopolis; ב׳ שֶׁמֶשׁ on the border of Judah and Dan, *gent.* בֵּית־הַשִּׁמְשִׁי, also in Naphtali and in Issachar [see אוֹן]; ב׳ תַּפּוּחַ in Judah.

בִּיתָן (bĭϑā'n) *m*, *c.* בִּיתַן house, palace.

בָּכָא (bāɸā') *m*, *pl.* בְּכָאִים, a species of tree, balm-tree [others: mulberry-tree]; עֵמֶק הַבָּכָא [for בָּכָה] valley of weeping.

בָּכָה (bāɸā') *inf.* בָּכֹה, בָּכוֹ, בְּכוֹת, *fut.* יִבְכֶּה, וַיֵּבְךְּ, *pt. pl.* בֹּכִים to weep, to shed tears. — *Pi. pt. f* מְבַכָּה to bewail.

בֶּכֶה (bĕ'ɸĕ) *m* weeping.

בְּכֹר, **בְּכוֹר** (bᵉɸō'r) *adj.* first-born [of men and beasts], eldest son.

בִּכּוּר (bĭkkū'r) *m*, only *pl.* בִּכֻּרִים, בִּכּוּרִים, *c.* בִּכּוּרֵי first-fruits, firstlings, early grapes or corn.

בִּכּוּרָה (bĭkkūrā'), בַּכּוּרָה (bākkūrā') *f* early fig.

בְּכוֹרַת (bᵉᶁōrăʹϑ) *pr.n.m.*
בָּכוּת (bāᶁūʹϑ) *f* weeping.
בְּכִי (bᵉᶁīʹ) *m*, *i.p.* בֶּכִי, *w.s.* בִּכְיִי weeping, lamentation; dripping [of water in a mine].
בֹּכִים (bōᶁīʹm) *pr.n.* of a place near Gilgal.
בָּכִיר (bāᶁīʹr) *adj.*, only *f* בְּכִירָה, first-born.
בְּכִית (bᵉᶁīʹϑ) *f* = בְּכִי.
בֵּכֶר (bēʹᶁĕr) *m*, *pl.* *c.* בִּכְרֵי young male camel.
בֶּכֶר (bĕʹᶁĕr); בֹּכְרוּ (bōᶁᵉrūʹ); בִּכְרִי (bĭᶁrīʹ) *pr.n.m.*
בִּכְרָה (bĭᶁrāʹ) *f* young female camel.
בְּכוֹרָה, בְּכֹרָה (bᵉᶁōrāʹ) *f*, *pl.* בְּכֹרוֹת, first-birth, primogeniture.
בַּל (băl) particle of negation: not, not yet, hardly, that not.
בֵּל (bēl) *m* Belus, the highest god of the Babylonians [from בַּעַל Lord].
בַּלְאֲדָן (bălʹᵃdāʹn) *pr.n.m.*, a Babylonian king.
בֵּלְאשַׁצַּר see בֵּלְשַׁאצַּר.
בָּלַג (bālăʹg) *Hi.* *fut.* יַבְלִיג, *pt.* מַבְלִיג to cause to flash up, to spread; *intr.* to burst forth in splendour.
בִּלְגָּה (bĭlgāʹ), בִּלְגַּי (bĭlgăʹy) *pr.n.m.*
בִּלְדַּד (bĭldăʹd) *pr.n.m.*
בָּלָה (bālāʹ) *inf.* בְּלֹת, *fut.* יִבְלֶה to be worn out, wasted, rotten; to decay. — *Pi.* בִּלָּה, *inf.* בַּלּוֹת, *fut.* יְבַלֶּה to consume, wear out, use, waste.
בָּלֶה (bālĕʹ) *adj.*, *f* בָּלָה, *pl.* בָּלִים, בָּלוֹת old, worn out, consumed.
בָּלַהּ (bālăʹh) *Pi.* *pt.* *pl.* *m* מְבַלְּהִים to terrify, frighten.
בַּלָּהָה (băllāhāʹ) *f*, *pl.* בַּלָּהוֹת, *c.* בַּלְהוֹת, fright, sudden terror, death.
בִּלְהָה (bĭlhāʹ) *pr.n.f.*
בִּלְהָן (bĭlhāʹn) *pr.n.m.*
בְּלוֹיִם [בְּלוֹאִים] (bᵉlōyīʹm) *m/pl.*, only *c.* בְּלוֹאֵי, בְּלוֹיֵ, rags, worn out clothes.
בֵּלְטְשַׁאצַּר (bēltšăššăʹr) *pr.n.m.* [Chaldean surname of Daniel].
בְּלִי (bᵉlīʹ) *m* annihilation, perdition, nothingness; used as a particle of negation: no, not, without,

un-; לִבְלִי without; מִבְּלִי because not; עַד בְּלִי till not; עַל בְּלִי because not.

בְּלִיל (b'lī'l) *m* farrago, mixed fodder.

בְּלִימָה (b'līmā') *f* [from בְּלִי and מָה] nothing.

בְּלִיַּעַל (b'līyyă''ăl) *m* worthlessness, good-for-nothingness, wickedness; perdition; wicked man; destroyer.

בָּלַל (bālă'l) *fut.* וַיָּבָל (văyyā'-bŏl), 1. *pl.* נָבְלָה [for נָבֹל, נְבֻלָּה], *pt. p.* בָּלוּל, to flow, to be moistened; *tr.* to pour over, to mix, to confound; to give fodder [בְּלִיל].—*Hith. fut.* יִתְבּוֹלָל to mix oneself.

בָּלַם (bālă'm) *inf.* בָּלוֹם to bind, bridle, check.

בָּלַס (bālă's) *pt.* בּוֹלֵס to cultivate sycamore-figs by nipping.

בָּלַע (bālă'') *fut.* יִבְלַע, to swallow, devour, eat up.—*Ni.* נִבְלַע to be destroyed or overcome. — *Pi.* בִּלַּע, *imp.* בַּלַּע, *fut.* יְבַלַּע to swallow up, devour; to destroy; כְּבַלַּע like a swallowing, i. e. for a moment. — *Pu.* בֻּלַּע, *fut.* יְבֻלַּע and *Hith. fut.* יִתְבַּלַּע to be destroyed.

בֶּלַע[1] (bĕ'lă') *m*, *i.p.* בָּלַע, *w.s.* בִּלְעִי something swallowed; a swallowing, destruction.

בֶּלַע[2] (bĕ'lă') *pr.n.m.*, *patron.* בַּלְעִי; *pr.n.* of a town, afterwards called Zoar [צֹעַר].

בַּלְעֲד (băl'ă'd), בִּלְעֲד (bĭl'ă'd), only *pl. c.* בִּלְעֲדֵי, בַּלְעֲדֵי, *w.s.* בִּלְעָדַי, בַּלְעָדַי, *prep.* without, except; מִבַּלְעָדַי apart from me, without my being concerned, besides me.

בִּלְעָם (bĭl'ā'm) *pr.n.m.*; *pr.n.* of a town in Manasseh.

בָּלַק (bālă'k) *pt.* בּוֹלֵק to destroy, to waste.—*Pu. pt.* מְבֻלָּק to be laid waste.

בָּלָק (bālā'k) *pr.n.m.* [king of the Moabites].

בִּלְתִּי [*c.* of a not used בֶּלֶת] (bĭltī') *adv.* not; *prep.* without, besides, except; *conj.* besides that, unless. — לְבִלְתִּי with *inf.* not to, so that not; מִבִּלְתִּי because not; עַד־בִּלְתִּי till not.

בָּמָה (bāmā') *f, pl.* בָּמוֹת, *c.* בָּמוֹת and בָּמוֹתֵי, *w.s.* בָּמוֹתַי, height, hill, elevation; stronghold; height destined for unlawful worship; grave-mound, tomb-hill.

בִּמְהָל (bĭmhā'l) *pr.n.m.*

בָּמוֹת (bāmō'ϑ) *f/pl., pr.n.* of a place in Moab [identical with בָּמוֹת בַּעַל].

בֵּן[1] (bēn) *m, c.* בֶּן, בֶּן־, בְּנוֹ, בִּנְךָ, בְּנֵהוּ בְּנִי *w.s.* בְּנִי, בְּנֵנוּ, *pl.* בָּנִים, *c.* בְּנֵי, son, child, boy, young one [בְּנֵי אָדָם used as *pl.* of אָדָם, children of man, mankind]; grandson, grandchild, descendant; pupil; subject, disciple, favourite. — בֵּן with following subst. noun supplies the place of adjectives: בֶּן חָמֵשׁ שָׁנִים five years old; בֶּן שֶׁמֶן fat, stout.

בֵּן[2] (bēn) *pr.n.m.*

בֶּן־אוֹנִי [=בִּנְיָמִין] (bĕn-ōnī'); בֶּן־הֲדַד (bĕn-hadă'd); בֶּן־חַיִל (bĕn-ḥă'yĭl); בֶּן־חָנָן (bĕn-ḥānā'n); בֶּן־יְמִין [בִּנְיָמִין] (bĕn-yāmī'n), *patron.* בֶּן־הַיְמִינִי, *pr.n.m.*

בָּנָה (bānā') *inf.* בְּנוֹת, בָּנֹה, *fut.* יִבְנֶה, וַיִּבֶן, *pt.* בֹּנֶה, *pt. p.* בָּנוּי, *f.* בְּנוּיָה, to build, form, develop, erect; to cover with buildings; to repair, to rebuild; to edify [to make prosperous].—*Ni.* נִבְנָה, *inf.* הִבָּנוֹת, *fut.* יִבָּנֶה to be built, restored; to get issue.

בָּנוּ = בָּאנוּ, see בּוֹא.

בִּנּוּי (bĭnnū'y); **בָּנִי** (bānī'); **בֻּנִּי** (bŭnnī') *pr.n.m.*

בְּנֵי־בְרַק (b^enē'-b^era'k) *pr.n.* of a place in Dan.

בְּנָיָה (b^enāyā'), **בְּנָיָהוּ** (b^enāyā'hū) *pr.n.m.*

בִּנְיָה (bĭnyā') *f* building.

בִּנְיָן (bĭnyā'n) *m* building.

בְּנִינוּ (b^enī'nū) *pr.n.m.*

בִּנְעָא or **בִּנְעָה** (bĭn'ā'); **בְּסוֹדְיָה** (b^esō'd^eyā'); **בֵּסַי** (bēsă'y) *pr.n.m.*

בֶּסֶר (bē'sĕr) and **בֹּסֶר** (bō'sĕr) *m, coll.* unripe grapes.

בַּעַד (bă''ăd) *m, c.* בְּעַד, *w.s.* בַּעֲדִי, בַּעַדְךָ, interval, distance; *prep.* behind, after, through, around, among; in favour of, for.

בְּעֹד see עוֹד.

בָּעָה (bā'ā') *imp.* בְּעָיוּ, *fut.* יִבְעֶה to make bubble up, to boil; to desire, covet, demand, ask. — *Ni.* נִבְעָה, *pt.* נִבְעֶה to swell [to a bulge], to project; to be searched.

בְּעוֹר (b'ō'r) *pr.n.m.*

בִּעוּתִים (bi'ūthī'm) *m/pl.* terror, anguish.

בֹּעַז (bō'az) *pr.n.m.*; name of a bronze pillar in front of the temple.

בָּעַט (bā'ā't) *fut.* יִבְעַט, to tread down, to kick, jerk.

בְּעִי (b'ī') *m* prayer.

בְּעִיר (b'ī'r) *m coll.* cattle.

בָּעַל (bā'ā'l) *fut.* יִבְעַל, *pt.* בֹּעֵל, *pt. p. f* בְּעוּלָה to be master, to rule, possess, marry. — *Ni. fut.* תִּבָּעֵל to be married, to be taken to wife.

בַּעַל (bā'al) *m*, *i.p.* בָּעַל, *w.s.* בַּעְלִי, *pl.* בְּעָלִים, *c.* בַּעֲלֵי, master, lord, possessor, owner, husband, citizen, burgess, inhabitant; as *pr.n.m.* the supreme Syro-Phenician deity [*pl.* the different appearances of the god]; בַּעַל בְּרִית Baal of the Covenant, ב׳ זְבוּב B. of the Flies [keeping off vermin], ב׳ פְּעוֹר B. of Denudation. — In *pr.n.* of places: ב׳ צְפוֹן, ב׳ פְּרָצִים, ב׳ חֶרְמוֹן, ב׳ שָׁלִשָׁה, &c.

בַּעֲלָה (bā'alā') *f*, *c.* בַּעֲלַת, mistress, owner; *pr.n.* of some places.

בְּעָלוֹת (b'ālō'th) *f/pl.*, *pr.n.* of a town in Judah.

בְּעֶלְיָדָע (b'elyādā'); **בְּעַלְיָה** (b'alyā'); **בַּעֲלִים** (bā'alī's) *pr.n.m.*

בַּעֲלַת (bā'alā'th) *pr.n.* of a town in Dan.

בְּעֹן *pr.n.* = מְעוֹן.

בַּעֲנָא, **בַּעֲנָה** (bā'anā') *pr.n.m.*

בָּעַר[1] (bā'ā'r) *fut.* יִבְעַר, *pt.* בֹּעֵר, *f* בֹּעֲרָה, בְּעֵרָה, בֹּעֶרֶת, *tr.* to burn; *intr.* to burn, to be on fire, to be consumed by fire. — *Pi.* בִּעֵר, *fut.* יְבַעֵר, to kindle, burn, consume, destroy. — *Pu. pt.* מְבֹעָר to be kindled. — *Hi.* הִבְעִיר, *fut.* וַיַּבְעֵר, *pt.* מַבְעִיר, to kindle, burn, consume, destroy.

בָּעַר[2] (bā'ā'r) *fut.* יִבְעַר, *pt*

בֹּעֵר, to be stupid, brutish. — *Ni. pt.* נִבְעָר to become stupid or bad.

בַּעַר (bă'ăr) *m* stupidity; *adj.* stupid, brutish.

בַּעֲרָא (bă'ărā') *pr.n.f.*

בְּעֵרָה (b'ērā') *f* fire, burning.

בַּעְשָׂא (bă'sā') *pr.n.m.*

בְּעֶשְׁתְּרָה (b'ĕsht'rā') *pr.n.* of a town in Manasseh.

בָּעַת (bā'ă'th) *Ni.* נִבְעַת to be frightened. — *Pi.* בִּעֵת, *fut.* יְבַעֵת, *pt. f w.s.* מְבַעֶתְךָ [מְבַעֶתֶת] to overtake, frighten, strike with fear.

בְּעָתָה (b'āthā') *f* terror.

בֹּץ (bōts) *m* mud, mire.

בִּצָּה (bĭtstsā') *f, pl. w.s.* בִּצֹּאתָיו [for בִּצּוֹתָיו], swamp.

בָּצוּר (bātsū'r) *adj., f* בְּצוּרָה, cut off, steep, inaccessible, impregnable.

בְּצוּר (b'tsū'r) *m,* perh. = בֶּצֶר [or from צוּר].

בֵּצַי (bētsă'y) *pr.n.m.*

בָּצִיר (bātsī'r) *m, c.* בְּצִיר, cutting of grapes, vintage.

בֶּצֶל (bĕ'tsĕl) *m,* only *pl.* בְּצָלִים, onion.

בְּצַלְאֵל (b'tsăl'ē'l); **בַּצְלוּת** (bătslū'th) *pr.n.m.*

בָּצַע (bātsă'') *inf.* בְּצֹעַ, *fut.* יִבְצַע, *pt.* בֹּצֵעַ to cut off, to break; to get unrighteous gain, to overreach. — *Pi. fut.* יְבַצַּע to cut off, rob; to complete, finish.

בֶּצַע (bĕ'tsă') *m, w.s.* בִּצְעוֹ, curtailment, unjust gain, profit, lucre, covetousness.

בָּצֵק[1] (bātsē'k) to swell up.

בָּצֵק[2] (bātsē'k) *m, w.s.* בְּצֵקוֹ, dough.

בָּצְקַת (bŏtskă'th) *pr.n.* of a town in the plain of Judah.

בָּצַר (bātsă'r) *fut.* יִבְצֹר, to cut off; to gather grapes [*pt.* בּוֹצֵר vintager]; to diminish, shorten; see also בָּצוּר. — *Ni. fut.* יִבָּצֵר to be cut off, prohibited. — *Pi. inf.* בַּצֵּר to make steep, to fortify.

בֶּצֶר[1] (bĕ'tsĕr) and בְּצָר (b'tsā'r) *m, pl.* בְּצָרִים, ore of gold and silver.

בֶּצֶר[2] (bĕ'tsĕr) *pr.n.* of a town in Reuben.

בָּצְרָה[1] (bŏtsrā') *f* fold, fence.

בָּצְרָה[2] (bŏßrā') *pr.n.* of the chief town of the Edomites [Bostra].

בַּצָּרָה (băßßārā') and בַּצֹּרֶת (băßßō'rĕϑ) *f, pl.* בַּצָּרוֹת, deficiency, want, lack of rain, drought.

בִּצָּרוֹן (bĭßßārō'n) *m* fortress, stronghold.

בַּקְבֻּק, בַּקְבּוּק (băkbū'k) *m* bottle.

בַּקְבֻּקְיָה (băkbŭkyā'); בַּקְבַּקַּר (băkbăkkă'r); בֻּקִּי (bŭkkī'); בֻּקִּיָּהוּ (bŭkkĭyyā'hū) *pr.n.m.*

בָּקִיעַ (bākī'ă') *m*, only *pl.* בְּקִיעִים, *c.* בְּקִיעֵי, cleft, rent, breach.

בָּקַע (bākă'') *fut.* יִבְקַע, *pt.* בֹּקֵעַ, to cleave, sever, burst open; to invade; to split in brooding. — *Ni.* נִבְקַע, *fut.* יִבָּקַע, to be cloven, torn, broken, opened; to burst forth; to be hatched [break the shell]; to be taken by storm. — *Pi.* בִּקַּע [3. *pl.* בִּקְּעוּ], *fut.* יְבַקַּע to cleave, split, rend, open, hatch. — *Pu.* *pt.* מְבֻקָּע to be rent, to be stormed. — *Hi. inf.* הַבְקִיעַ, *fut. pl.* נַבְקִעֶנָּה, to open [a town, to storm]; to break through, to force one's way. — *Hith.* הִתְבַּקַּע to be cleft, rent.

בֶּקַע (bĕ'kă') *m* half, half-shekel.

בִּקְעָה (bĭk'ā') *f, pl.* בְּקָעוֹת, fissure, wide valley, plain.

בָּקַק (bākă'k) *pt.* בּוֹקֵק, to empty, unpeople, deprive; to grow luxuriantly. — *Ni.* נָבַק, *inf.* הִבּוֹק, *fut.* יִבּוֹק to be emptied out, to be poured out. — *Po.* בּוֹקֵק to depopulate.

בָּקַר (bākă'r) *Pi.* בִּקֵּר, *inf.* בַּקֵּר, *fut.* יְבַקֵּר to examine, to look after, to consider with pleasure; to judge, punish.

בָּקָר (bākā'r) *m* [and *f*], *c.* בְּקַר, *pl.* [rare] בְּקָרִים, *coll.* plough-cattle, horned cattle, oxen, cows; בֶּן בָּקָר calf, heifer.

בֹּקֵר see בּוֹקֵר.

בֹּקֶר (bō'kĕr) *m, pl.* בְּקָרִים, morning, morning-time, dawn; the next morning; *adv.* to-morrow, early, soon.

בַּקָּרָה (băkkārā') *f* care, superintendence.

בִּקֹּרֶת (bĭkkō'rĕϑ) *f* judicial inquiry, punishment.

בִּקֵּשׁ (bākkā'š) *Pi.* בִּקֵּשׁ, *fut.* יְבַקֵּשׁ, *pt.* מְבַקֵּשׁ to seek, to search for, to investigate; to aim at; to require, demand, ask. — *Pu.* בֻּקַּשׁ, *fut.* יְבֻקַּשׁ to be sought.

בַּקָּשָׁה (bākkāšā') *f* request.

בַּר[1] (băr) and בָּר (bār) *m* corn, grain; cornfield.

בַּר[2] (băr) *m, w.s.* בְּרִי, son.

בַּר[3] (băr) *adj., i.p.* בָּר, *f* בָּרָה, chosen, pure, clear, sincere; empty.

בֹּר[1] see בּוֹר.

בֹּר[2] [once בּוֹר] (bōr) *m* purity, innocence; salt of lye, alkali.

בָּרָא[1] (bārā') *inf.* בְּרֹא, *imp.* בְּרָא, *fut.* יִבְרָא, *pt.* בֹּרֵא to create, form, make, produce. — *Ni.* נִבְרָא, *inf.* הִבָּרֵא to be created, to be made. — *Pi.* בֵּרֵא to cut, cut down; to engrave, carve.

בָּרָא[2] (bārā') *Hi. inf.* הַבְרִיא to fatten.

בְּרֹאדַךְ see מְרֹדַךְ.

בְּרָאיָה (b'rāyā') *pr.n.m.*

בַּרְבֻּר (bărbū'r) *m*, only *pl.* בַּרְבֻּרִים, fat bird, fowl [capon or goose].

בָּרַד (bārā'd) to hail.

בָּרָד (bārā'd) *m* hail, hailstone.

בָּרֹד (bārō'd) *adj., pl.* בְּרֻדִּים, spotted, pied.

בֶּרֶד (bĕ'rĕd) *pr.n.* of a place in the desert of Shur.

בָּרָה[1] (bārā') *imp. pl.* בְּרוּ, to decide, choose, select.

בָּרָה[2] (bārā') *fut.* יִבְרֶה, to eat, to feed. — *Pi. inf.* בָּרוֹת to eat. — *Hi. inf.* הַבְרוֹת, *fut.* יַבְרֶה to give to eat.

בָּרוּךְ (bārū'ḵ) *pr.n.m.* [blessed].

בְּרוֹם (b'rō'm) *m, pl.* בְּרוֹמִים, party-coloured cloth, damask.

בְּרוֹשׁ (b'rō'š) *m, pl.* בְּרוֹשִׁים, cypress, pine; spear of cypress wood; musical instrument.

בְּרוֹת (b'rō'θ) = בְּרוֹשׁ.

בָּרוּת (bārū'θ) *f* food, nourishment.

בֵּרוֹתָה (bē'rōθā') *pr.n.* of a town in Syria [perh. Berytus].

בִּרְזוֹת (bĭrzō'θ) or בִּרְזָיִת (bĭrză'yĭθ) *pr.n.f.*

בַּרְזֶל (bărzĕ'l) *m* iron, iron tool, fetter.

בַּרְזִלַּי (bărzĭllă'y) *pr.n.m.*

בָּרַח (bāră'ḥ) *inf.* בְּרֹחַ, *imp.* בְּרַח, *fut.* יִבְרַח to flee, to run away, to escape; to go through. — *Hi.* הִבְרִיחַ, *pt.* מַבְרִיחַ to put to flight, to drive away; to make [a bolt] go through.

בָּרִחַ (bārē'aḥ) [בָּרִיחַ] *adj.*, *pl.* בְּרִיחִים, swift, fleeing, fugitive.

בַּרְחֻמִי (bărḥūmī') = בַּחֲרוּמִי, a native of בַּחֻרִים.

בֵּרִי (bērī') *pr.n.m.*

בְּרִי[1] (b'rī') *adj.*, *f* בְּרִיָּה [בְּרִיָּה] see בָּרִיא.

בְּרִי[2] see רִי.

בָּרִיא (bārī') *adj.*, *f* בְּרִיאָה [בְּרִיָּה = בְּרִיָּה], *pl.* בְּרִיאִים, *f* בְּרִיאוֹת, fat, fattened, thick, stout.

בְּרִיאָה (b'rī'ā') *f* a thing created, a novelty.

בִּרְיָה (bĭryā') *f* food.

בָּרִיחַ (bārī'aḥ) *m*, see בָּרִחַ.

בְּרִיחַ (b'rī'aḥ) *m*, *pl.* בְּרִיחִים, *c.* בְּרִיחֵי, bar, bolt.

בֵּרִים (bērī'm) *pr.n.* of a place.

בְּרִיעָה (b'rī'ā') *pr.n.m.*; *patron.* בְּרִיעִי.

בְּרִית (b'rī'ϑ) *f* determination, stipulation, covenant.

בֹּרִית (bōrī'ϑ) *f* salt of lye, vegetable alkali.

בָּרַךְ (bāră'ḥ) *fut.* יִבְרַךְ to bend the knee, to kneel down; to bless, praise; *pt. p.* בָּרוּךְ blessed, praised. — *Ni.* נִבְרַךְ to be blessed. — *Pi.* בֵּרֵךְ, *inf.* בָּרֵךְ, *fut.* יְבָרֵךְ, *pt.* מְבָרֵךְ to bless, to praise; to pray to, to invoke, to ask a blessing; to greet; to curse. — *Pu.* בֹּרַךְ, *pt.* מְבֹרָךְ to be blessed, praised. — *Hi. fut.* וַיַּבְרֵךְ to make kneel down. — *Hith.* הִתְבָּרֵךְ to be blessed, to bless oneself.

בֶּרֶךְ (bĕ'rĕḥ) *f*, *du.* [denoting also *pl.*] בִּרְכַּיִם, *c.* בִּרְכֵּי, בִּרְכֵי, knee, lap.

בְּרַכְאֵל (b'răḥ'ēl) *pr.n.m.*

בְּרָכָה[1] (b'rāḥā') *f*, *c.* בִּרְכַּת, *pl.* בְּרָכוֹת, *c.* בִּרְכוֹת, blessing, benediction, benefit, favour, peace; a happy or blessed man.

בְּרָכָה[2] (b'rāḥā') *pr.n.m.*

בְּרֵכָה (b'rēḥā') *f*, *c.* בְּרֵכַת, *pl.* בְּרֵכוֹת, pond, pool.

בֶּרֶכְיָה (bĕ'rĕɕyā') and בֶּרֶכְיָהוּ (bĕ'rĕɕyā'hū) *pr.n.m.*

בַּרְנֵעַ see קָדֵשׁ.

בֶּרַע (bĕ'rā') *pr.n.m.*

בָּרַק (bārā'**k**) *inf.* בְּרוֹק to send forth lightning.

בָּרָק[1] (bārā'**k**) *m* splendour, flash of lightning.

בָּרָק[2] (bārā'**k**) *pr.n.m.*

בַּרְקוֹס (bărkō'ß) *pr.n.m.*

בַּרְקָן (bărkā'n) *m*, only *pl.* בַּרְקָנִים thorns; threshing-sledge.

בָּרֶקֶת (bārĕ'kĕϑ) and בָּרְקַת (bārᵉkā'ϑ) *f* a precious stone, emerald.

בָּרַר (bārā'r) *inf.* בַּר, *w.s.* לְבָרָם, *pt*, *p.* בָּרוּר to separate, secrete, single out, choose; to cleanse, purify, polish; to prove. — *Ni.* נָבַר, *imp.* הִבָּרוּ, *fut.* יִבַּר, *pt.* נָבָר, to keep oneself pure. — *Pi. inf.* בָּרֵר to purify.— *Hi. inf. i.p.* הָבַר, *imp.* הָבֵר, to clean, polish. — *Hith.* הִתְבָּרֵר, *fut.* יִתְבָּרַר and יִתַּבַּר, *i.p.* יִתָּבָר to purify oneself, to show oneself pure.

בִּרְשַׁע (bĭrshā'') *pr.n.m.*

בֵּרֹתַי (bēʹrōϑă'y) *pr.n.* of a city in Syria = בֵּרוֹתָה

בְּשׂוֹר (bᵉßō'r) *pr.n.* of a brook near Gaza.

בְּשׂוֹרָה see בְּשֹׂרָה.

בָּשָׂם (bāßā'm) *m* balsam-shrub.

בֶּשֶׂם (bĕ'ßĕm) and בֹּשֶׂם (bō'ßĕm) *m*, *pl.* בְּשָׂמִים sweet scent, fragrance, balsam-scent; aromatic spice; also = בָּשָׂם.

בָּשְׂמַת (bā'ßᵉmă'ϑ) *pr.n.f.*

בָּשַׂר (bāßă'r) *Pi.* בִּשֵּׂר, *pt.* מְבַשֵּׂר, *f* מְבַשֶּׂרֶת to announce, esp. to bring good news, to tell glad tidings. — *Hith.* הִתְבַּשֵּׂר to receive good tidings, to be told good news.

בָּשָׂר (bāßā'r) *m*, *c.* בְּשַׂר, *pl.* בְּשָׂרִים flesh [of men and beasts], body, living creature; man, mankind; blood-relation; skin, pudenda.

בְּשֹׂרָה (bᵉßōrā') *f* glad tidings, message of good; reward for good news.

בָּשַׁל (bāshă'l) *intr.* to boil, seethe, ripen. — *Pi.* בִּשֵּׁל, *fut.* יְבַשֵּׁל *tr.* to boil, cook, roast. — *Pu. pt.* מְבֻשָּׁל to be boiled.—*Hi.* הִבְשִׁיל to make ripe.

בָּשֵׁל (bāšē'l) *adj.*, *f* בְּשֵׁלָה, boiled, cooked.

בְּשֶׁלְּמִי, בְּשֶׁלִּי, בְּשֶׁל see שֶׁל.

בִּשְׁלָם (bĭšlā'm) *pr.n.m.*

בָּשָׁן (bāšā'n) *pr.n.* of a fertile country on the eastern side of the Jordan, Bashan or Batanæa.

בָּשְׁנָה (bŏšnā') *f* shame.

בֹּשֶׁת (bō'šĕϑ) *f*, *w.s.* בָּשְׁתִּי (bŏštī') shame, disgrace; a [scandalous] idol.

בַּת[1] (băϑ) [from בֶּנֶת] *f*, *w.s.* בִּתִּי, *pl.* בָּנוֹת, *c.* בְּנוֹת, daughter, grand-daughter, girl, maid, pupil; בַּת צִיּוֹן or בְּנוֹת women of Jerusalem. — בַּת with following subst. noun supplies the place of adjectives; with cities it denotes the villages and environs belonging to them.

בַּת[2] (băϑ) *m*, *pl.* בַּתִּים, a measure for liquids, tenth part of a חֹמֶר.

בָּתָה (bāϑā') and **בַּתָּה** (băttā') *f*, *pl.* בַּתּוֹת, something cut off, precipice, cliff; end, ruin, desolation.

בְּתוּאֵל (b'ϑū'ēl) *pr.n.m.*

בְּתוּלָה (b'ϑūlā') *f*, *c.* בְּתוּלַת, *pl.* בְּתוּלוֹת, chaste maiden, virgin, bride.

בְּתוּלִים (b'ϑūlī'm) *m/pl.*, *c.* בְּתוּלֵי, virginity, maidenhood.

בִּתְיָה (bĭϑyā') *pr.n.f.*

בָּתַר (bāϑă'r) *Q.* and *Pi.* *fut.* יְבַתֵּר to cut into pieces, to divide.

בֶּתֶר (bĕ'ϑĕr) *m*, *w.s.* בִּתְרוֹ, piece, portion; disruption, cleft.

בַּת־רַבִּים (băϑ-răbbī'm) *pr.n.* of a gate of Heshbon.

בִּתְרוֹן (bĭϑrō'n) *m* ravine; *pr.n.* of a defile on the eastern side of the Jordan.

בַּת־שֶׁבַע (băϑ-šĕ'bă') *pr.n.f.*

ג

ג the third letter of the alphabet, called גִּמֶל or גִּימֶל [= גָּמָל camel]; as a numeral = 3 or 3000.

גֵּא (gē) *adj.* proud, haughty.

גָּאָה (gā'ā') *inf.* גָּאֹה, *fut.* יִגְאֶה to rise, grow up; to be high, elevated, majestic.

גֵּאָה (gē'ā') *f* pride, haughtiness.

גֵּאֶה (gē'ě') *adj., pl.* גֵּאִים, high, exalted, proud, presumptious.

גְּאוּאֵל (g'ū'ē'l) *pr.n.m.*

גַּאֲוָה (gă'avā') *f, c.* גַּאֲוַת elevation, majesty, magnificence, pride, insolence.

גְּאוּלִים (g'ūlī'm) *m/pl.* redemption, release.

גָּאוֹן (gā'ō'n) *m, c.* גְּאוֹן, swelling, highness, excellence, majesty; splendour, glory, pride, haughtiness.

גֵּאוּת (gē'ū'ϑ) *f* = גָּאוֹן.

גַּאֲיוֹן (gă'ayō'n) *adj.* proud. insolent.

גֵּאָיוֹת (gē''āyō'ϑ) *f,* only *pl.* valley [perh. for גֵּאָיוֹת, גֵּיאוֹת].

גָּאַל[1] (gā'ă'l) *imp.* גְּאַל, *fut.* יִגְאַל, *pt.* גּוֹאֵל, *pl.* גּוֹאֲלִים, *pt. p.* גָּאוּל to redeem, to ransom, release, deliver; to fulfil the duties of relationship, to marry the childless widow of an elder brother; גּוֹאֵל revenger, kinsman-helper. — *Ni.* נִגְאַל to be redeemed, to be brought back, to ransom oneself.

גָּאַל[2] (gā'ă'l) *Ni. pf. pl.* נְגֹאֲלוּ [for נִגְאֲלוּ or *Pu.*], *fut.* יִגָּאֵל, to be polluted, defiled, stained. — *Pi.* גֵּאֵל to defile, profane. — *Pu.* גֹּאַל, *pt.* מְגֹאָל to be polluted, profaned, to be rejected as unclean. — *Hi. pf.i.p.* אֶגְאָלְתִּי [for הִגְאַלְתִּי], to soil, to make unclean. — *Hith. fut.* יִתְגָּאַל to defile oneself.

גֹּאַל (gō'ăl) *m,* only *pl.* גָּאֳלֵי (gŏolē'), pollution, profanation.

גְּאֻלָּה (g'ŭllā') *f* redemption, release, repurchase, duty of relationship [as a גּוֹאֵל, see גָּאַל[1]].

גַּב (găb) *m, i.p.* גָּב, *w.s.* גַּבִּי, *pl.* גַּבִּים and גַּבּוֹת, elevation, top, back, hunch, hump, boss; arch, vault, brothel; rim of a wheel.

גָּב see גּוּב.

גֵּב[1] (gēb) *m,* only *pl.* גֵּבִים, pit, water-hole, cistern; a cut piece of wood, board.

גֵּב² (gēḇ) *m*, only *pl.* גֵּבִים, locust.

גֹּב (gōḇ) *pr.n.* of a place.

גֵּבִים – יְגֵבִים or יְגֵבִים.

גֶּבֶא (gĕ'ḇĕ) *m* cistern, pool, lagoon.

גַּבָּה see גַּב.

גָּבַהּ (gāḇă'h) *inf.* גְּבֹהַּ, *fut.* יִגְבַּהּ to be high, elevated, exalted, high-minded, proud, haughty.— *Hi. inf.* הַגְבֵּהַּ, *fut.* יַגְבִּיהַּ, *pt.* מַגְבִּיהַּ to make high, to raise.

גָּבֹהַּ (gāḇō'ah) *adj.*, *c.* גְּבַהּ and גְּבֹהַּ, *f* גְּבֹהָה, *pl.* גְּבֹהִים, גְּבֹהוֹת, high, tall, elevated; proud, haughty.

גֹּבַהּ (gō'ḇăh) *m*, *w.s.* גָּבְהוֹ (gŏḇhō'), *pl. c.* גָּבְהֵי (gŏḇhē') height; highness, majesty, pride, insolence.

גַּבְהוּת (găḇhū'ϑ) *f* pride, haughtiness.

גְּבוּל and גְּבֻל (gᵉḇū'l) *m*, *pl.* גְּבוּלִים, extremity, border, edge, boundary, territory.

גְּבוּלָה (gᵉḇūlā') *f*, mostly *pl.* גְּבוּלוֹת, גְּבֻלוֹת, border, margin, territory.

גִּבּוֹר, גִּבֹּר (gĭbbō'r) *adj.* and *m* strong, mighty, valiant, powerful, violent, rich; hero, warrior, leader; גִּ׳ חַיִל a warlike hero; tyrant.

גְּבוּרָה (gᵉḇūrā') *f*, *pl.* גְּבוּרוֹת strength, power, force, valour, courage, victory.

גִּבֵּחַ (gĭbbē'ach) *m* a bald-headed man [of the forehead].

גַּבַּחַת (găbbă'chăϑ) *f* baldness.

גַּבַּי (găbbă'y) *pr.n.m.*

גֵּבִים (gēḇī'm) [cisterns or locusts; see גֵּב] *pr.n.* of a place.

גְּבִינָה, גְּבִנָה (gᵉḇīnā') *f* hard curds, cheese.

גָּבִיעַ (gāḇī'aʿ) *m*, *c.* גְּבִיעַ, cup, bell of a flower.

גְּבִיר (gᵉḇī'r) *m* lord, master.

גְּבִירָה (gᵉḇīrā') *f*, *c.* גְּבֶרֶת, *w.s.* גְּבִרְתִּי, mistress, queen.

גָּבִישׁ (gāḇī'š) *m* ice, hail, crystal.

גָּבַל (gāḇă'l) *fut.* יִגְבֹּל to confine, to draw a boundary; to border upon. — *Hi.* הִגְבִּיל to bound, confine.

גְּבַל (gᵉḇă'l) *pr.n.* of a town in Phenicia [Byblos]; *gent* גִּבְלִי, *pl.* גִּבְלִים.

גְּבָל (gᵉḅā'l) *pr.n.* of a mountainous country, south of the Dead Sea, belonging to the Edomites.

גְּבֻל see גְּבוּל.

גַּבְלֻת (găḅlŭ'ϑ) [for גַּבְלוּת] *f* compactness, twisted work.

גִּבֵּן (gĭbbē'n) *adj.* gibbous, hunch-backed.

גִּבְנָה see גְּבִינָה.

גַּבְנֹן (găḅnō'n) *adj.*, only *pl.* גַּבְנֻנִּים, peaked mountains.

גֶּבַע (gĕ'ḅă') *pr.n.* of a town in Benjamin [confounded also with גִּבְעָה² and גִּבְעוֹן].

גִּבְעָה¹ (gĭḅᵉā') *f*, *pl.* גְּבָעוֹת, *c.* גִּבְעוֹת, height, hill.

גִּבְעָה² (gĭḅᵉā') *pr.n.* of several towns in Benjamin and Judah; *gent.* גִּבְעָתִי.

גִּבְעוֹן (gĭḅᵉō'n) *pr.n.* of a town in Benjamin; *gent.* גִּבְעֹנִי.

גִּבְעֹל (gĭḅᵉō'l) *m* cup, bell of flowers [or perh. capsule].

גִּבְעַת (gĭḅᵉă'ϑ) *pr.n.* of a place.

גָּבַר (gāḅă'r) [גָּבֵר] *fut.* יִגְבַּר to be or become strong and mighty, to grow, swell, prevail, overcome. — *Pi.* גִּבֵּר, *fut.* יְגַבֵּר to make strong. — ***Hi.*** הִגְבִּיר, *fut.* יַגְבִּיר to make strong, to exert strength. — ***Hith.*** *fut. i.p.* יִתְגַּבָּר to show oneself strong, to prevail.

גֶּבֶר¹ (gĕ'ḅĕr) *m*, *i.p.* גָּבֶר, *c.* גֶּבֶר and גְּבַר, *pl.* גְּבָרִים, man, valiant man, male person, boy, husband, warrior; every one [= אִישׁ].

גֶּבֶר² (gĕ'ḅĕr) *pr.n.m.*

גִּבָּר (gĭbbā'r) *pr.n.* of a place.

גַּבְרִיאֵל (găḅrī'ē'l) *pr.n.m.* [an archangel].

גְּבֶרֶת see גְּבִירָה.

גִּבְּתוֹן (gĭbbᵉϑō'n) *pr.n.* of a town in Dan.

גָּג (gāg) *m*, *c.* גַּג, *w.s.* גַּגּוֹ, *w. loc.* ה גָּגָה, *pl.* גַּגּוֹת, flat roof, cover of an altar.

גָּד¹ (gāḍ) *m* fortune, good luck; בְּגָד fortunately.

גָּד² (gāḍ) *pr.n.m.*; *gent.* גָּדִי.

גַּד¹ (găḍ) *m* coriander.

גַּד² (găḍ) *pr.n.m.*, Babylonian god of fortune [Baal or Jupiter].

גִּדְגָּד (gĭdgā'd) or **גֻּדְגֹּד** (gŭdgō'd), *w. loc.* ה **גֻּדְגֹּדָה**, *pr.n.* of a place.

גָּדַד (gādā'd) *fut. pl.* יָגֹדּוּ to cut; to break in, to fall upon. — *Hith.* הִתְגּוֹדֵד to make cuts; to collect in a crowd.

גָּדָה (gādā') *f*, only *pl. c.* גִּדְוֹת, bank of a river.

גַּדָּה (gāddā') *f* goddess of fortune, only in *pr.n.* חֲצַר גַּדָּה.

גְּדוּד (g'dū'd) *m*, *pl.* גְּדוּדִים, *c.* גְּדוּדֵי, cut, furrow; collection of warriors, troop of soldiers, plunderers, scouring party, attack.

גְּדוּדָה (g'dūdā') *f*, only *pl.* גְּדוּדוֹת, incision, cut in the skin.

גָּדוֹל, גָּדֹל (gādō'l) *adj.*, *c.* גְּדוֹל, *f* גְּדוֹלָה, *pl.* גְּדֹלִים, גְּדֹלוֹת, great, large, tall, high, mighty, old, elder; גְּדֹלִים the great, noble, proud; גְּדֹלוֹת great things, great deeds.

גְּדֻלָּה, גְּדוּלָה, גְּדוּלָּה (g'dūlā'), (g'dŭllā') *f* greatness, majesty; great deeds.

גִּדּוּף (gĭddū'f) *m*, only *pl.* גִּדּוּפִים and גִּדּוּפוֹת, scorn, reproach.

גְּדוּפָה = גִּדּוּף.

גָּדִי and **גַּדִּי** (gādī', gāddī') *pr.n.m.*

גְּדִי (g'dī') *m*, *pl.* גְּדָיִים, *c.* גְּדָיֵי, young goat, kid [mostly with following עִזִּים].

גַּדִּיאֵל (gāddī'ē'l) *pr.n.m.*

גְּדָיָה (g'dāyā') *f*, only *pl. c.* גִּדְיוֹת = גָּדָה.

גְּדִיָּה (g'dĭyyā') *f*, only *pl.* גְּדִיֹּת, little goat, kid.

גָּדִיל (gādī'l) *m*, only *pl.* גְּדִלִים twisted threads, tassels; festoons.

גָּדִישׁ (gādī's) *m* pile of corn, heap of sheaves; tomb-hill.

גָּדַל (gādā'l), **גָּדֵל** (gādē'l) *fut.* יִגְדַּל, *pt.* גָּדֵל, to be or become great, to grow up; to be mighty, rich, important, precious. — *Pi.* גִּדַּל, גִּדֵּל, *inf.* גַּדֵּל, to make great or strong, to bring up; to make distinguished, mighty, powerful; to praise, extol. — *Pu. pt.* מְגֻדָּל to be brought up. — *Hi.*

הִגְדִּיל, *fut.* יַגְדִּיל, the same as *Pi*; to do great, proud things. — *Hith.* הִתְגַּדֵּל to show oneself great or proud.

גָּדֵל (gādē'l) *adj.*, *pl. c.* גִּדְלֵי, becoming great, growing strong.

גָּדֵל see גָּדִיל.

גִּדֵּל (gĭddē'l) *pr.n.m.*

גֹּדֶל (gō'dĕl) *m*, *w.s.* גָּדְלוֹ (gŏdlō') and גָּדְלוֹ greatness, tallness, power, might, dignity, majesty; arrogance, pride.

גְּדֻלָּה see גְּדוּלָּה.

גְּדַלְיָה (gᵉdălyā') and גְּדַלְיָהוּ (gᵉdălyā'hū) *pr.n.m.*

גִּדַּלְתִּי (gĭddă'ltī) *pr.n.m.*

גָּדַע (gādă'ᵉ) *fut.* יִגְדַּע, *pt. p.* גָּדוּעַ, *pl.* גְּדֻעִים, to hew down, to fell; to cut, to shave off, to destroy. — *Ni.* נִגְדַּע [נִגְדָּע] and *Pu.* גֻּדַּע to be cut down, to be broken, to be destroyed. —*Pi.* גִּדַּע and גִּדֵּעַ, *fut.* יְגַדַּע, *i.p.* יְגַדֵּעַ to break to pieces.

גִּדְעוֹן (gĭdᵉō'n) *pr.n.m.*

גִּדְעֹם (gĭdᵉō'm) *pr.n.* of a place.

גִּדְעֹנִי (gĭdᵉōnī') *pr.n.m.*

גָּדַף (gādă'f) only *Pi.* גִּדֵּף, *pt.* מְגַדֵּף, to revile, blaspheme.

גָּדַר (gādă'r) *fut.* יִגְדֹּר, to enclose, hedge in, wall up, to surround with a wall; *pt. pl.* גֹּדְרִים masons.

גָּדֵר (gādē'r) *m*, *c.* גֶּדֶר, *w.s.* גְּדֵרוֹ, *pl.* גְּדֵרִים, wall, enclosure, fence; walled place.

גֶּדֶר (gĕ'dĕr) *pr.n.* of a place; *gent.* גְּדֵרִי.

גְּדֹר, גְּדוֹר (gᵉdō'r) *pr.n.m.*; *pr.n.* of two places.

גְּדֵרָה[1] (gᵉdērā') *f*, *pl* גְּדֵרוֹת, *c.* גִּדְרוֹת, wall, hedge, fence; fold, hurdle.

גְּדֵרָה[2] (gᵉdērā') and גְּדֵרוֹת (gᵉdērō'ϑ) *pr.n.* of places.

גְּדֵרוֹתַיִם (gᵉdērōϑă'yĭm) *pr.n.* of a town in Judah.

גֵּה miswritten for זֶה [or — גֵּא plain, valley].

גָּהָה (gāhā') *fut.* יִגְהֶה to be removed [the bandage of a wound], to heal.

גֵּהָה (gēhā') *f* healing.

גָּהַר (gāhă'r) *fut.* יִגְהַר, to bow down, to prostrate oneself.

גַּו (găv) *m*, *w.s.* גֵּוְךָ, גֵּוָם the back.

גֵּו (gēv) *m*, *w.s.* גֵּוִי, גֵּוְךָ, the back; the middle, interior, circle.

גּוּב (gūḇ) to plough; only *pt. pl.* גֹּבִים ploughmen, husbandmen.

גּוֹב[1] (gōḇ), גּוֹבַי (gōḇā'y) *m coll.* locusts; גּוֹב גּוֹבַי locusts upon locusts.

גּוֹב[2] (gōḇ) *pr.n.* of a place.

גּוֹג (gōg) *pr.n.m.*, Gog, prince of the people of Magog.

גּוּד (gūḏ) *fut.* יָגֻד, יָגוּד, *w.s.* יְגוּדֶנּוּ [*pl.* יָגוֹדּוּ, belongs to גָּדַד] to break in, to fall upon, to attack.

גֵּוָה (gēvā') *f* body; lifting up, elevation; pride.

גֹּוֶה (gōvě') *m*, only *pl. w.s.* גֹּוַיִךְ see גּוֹי.

גּוּז (gūz) *pf.* גָּז, *fut.* וַיָּגָז (văyyā'gŏz) to fly away, to pass rapidly; *tr.* to drive on.

גּוֹז (gōz) *m*, *w.s.* גּוֹזִי refuge [or from גָּזָה].

גּוֹזָל (gōzā'l) *m*, *pl.* גּוֹזָלִים, young bird, young dove.

גּוֹזָן (gōzā'n) *pr.n.* of an Assyrian district in Mesopotamia.

גּוּחַ (gū'aḥ), גִּיחַ (gī'aḥ) *imp. f* גֹּחִי to send forth, to bring forth, to bear.—*Hi.* הֵגִיחַ [*inf.* גִּיחַ = הָגִיחַ], *fut.* יָגִיחַ, וַתָּגַח to break or burst forth, to sally.

גּוֹי, גֹּי (gōy) *m*, *w.s.* גּוֹיִ, *pl.* גּוֹיִם, *c.* גּוֹיֵי, *w.s.* גּוֹיֶךָ, person, inhabitant, populace, people, tribe, nation; *pl.* non-Israelitic or heathen peoples.

גְּוִיָּה (gᵉvīyyā') *f*, *c.* גְּוִיַּת, *pl.* גְּוִיּוֹת, body, corpse.

גּוּל see גִּיל.

גּוֹלָה, גֹּלָה (gōlā') *f* emigration, evacuation, exile, banishment; exiles, captives.

גּוֹלָן (gōlā'n) *pr.n.* of a town in Manasseh.

גּוּמָּץ (gūmā'ṣ) *m* pit.

גּוּנִי (gūnī') *pr.n.m.*; *patron.* גּוּנִי.

גָּוַע (gāvă'') *inf.* גְּוֹעַ and גְּוֹעַ (gᵉvō'ă'), *pt.* גֹּוֵעַ, to expire, pine away, die away.

גּוּף (gūf) only *Hi. fut.* יָגִיף, to shut.

גּוּפָה (gūfā') *f* body, corpse.

גּוּר[1] (gūr) *pf.* גָּר, *inf.* גּוֹר and גּוּר, *imp.* גּוּר, *fut.* יָגוּר, וַיָּגָר (văyyā'gŏr), *pt.* גָּר, *pl.* גָּרִים, *c.* גָּרֵי, to take up one's abode, to dwell [as a stranger], to lodge, sojourn; to fear, to be afraid or anxious, to revere; to crowd together, to meet; to stir, to excite. —*Hith.* הִתְגּוֹרֵר, *fut.* יִתְגּוֹרֵר to settle, dwell, sojourn; to assemble, to gather together.

גּוּר[2] (gūr) and **גּוֹר** (gọr) *m*, *pl.* גּוּרִים, גֻּרִים, גּוֹרוֹת, young animal, whelp.

גּוּר[3] (gūr) *pr.n.* of a place; גּוּר בַּעַל dwelling of Baal [town in Arabia].

גּוֹרָל (gọrā'l) *m*, *c.* גּוֹרַל, *pl.* גּוֹרָלוֹת, voting-stone, lot, portion, share.

גּוֹרֶן see גֹּרֶן.

גּוּשׁ (gūš) *m* clod, lump of earth.

גֵּז (gẹz) *m*, *pl. c.* גִּזֵּי fleece, clip, shearing, mowing.

גִּזְבָּר (gĭzbā'r) *m* treasurer.

גָּזָה (gāzā') *pt. w.s.* גּוֹזִי [or perh. from גזז] to deliver [from the mother's womb].

גִּזָּה (gĭzzā') *f* shearing, fleece.

גָּזַז (gāză'z) *inf.* גְּזוֹז and גֹּז, *imp.* גֹּזִּי, *i.p.* גֹּזִּי, *fut.* יָגֹז, וַיָּגָז (văyyā'gọz), *pt.* גֹּזֵז, *pl.* גֹּזְזִים, *c.* גֹּזְזֵי, to cut off, to shear, mow. — *Ni.* נָגוֹז to be cut off, to be extirpated.

גָּזֵז (gāzẹ'z) *pr.n.m.*

גָּזִית (gāzī'ϑ) *f* cutting or hewing of stones, hewn stone, square-stone.

גָּזַל (gāză'l) *fut.* יִגְזֹל, *pt.* גֹּזֵל, *pt. p.* גָּזוּל to tear, pull, take away, to seize, rob, plunder; to flay. — *Ni.* נִגְזַל to be robbed.

גָּזֵל (gāzẹ'l), **גֵּזֶל** (gẹ'zĕl) *m* and **גְּזֵלָה** (g^ezẹlā') *f* robbed things, spoil, plunder.

גָּזָם (gāzā'm) *m* locust [not yet winged].

גַּזָּם (găzzā'm) *pr.n.m.*

גִּזוֹנִי (gĭ'zọnī') *m*, *gent.* of גִּזֹה or גִּזוֹן [an unknown place].

גֶּזַע (gĕ'ză') *m*, *w.s.* גִּזְעָם, trunk or stem of a tree.

גָּזַר (gāză'r) *imp.* גְּזֹר, *fut.* יִגְזֹר, יִגְזַר, *pt.* גֹּזֵר, to cut, to fell, to divide; to eat, consume; to decide; *intr.* to be cut off, to be gone. — *Ni.* נִגְזַר to be separated, excluded; to be undone or lost; to be decreed.

גֶּזֶר[1] (gĕ'zĕr) *m*, *pl.* גְּזָרִים, piece, part.

גֶּזֶר[2] (gĕ'zĕr) *pr.n.* of a Levitic town.

גִּזְרָה (gⁱzĕrā') *f* outline of the body, figure, frame; sequestered place [part of the temple buildings, hall or court].

גִּזְרִי (gīzrī') *pr.n.m.* of a people in the south of Palestine.

גָּחוֹן (gāḥō'n) *m*, *c.* גְּחוֹן, belly.

גֵּחֲזִי (gēḥᵃzī') *pr.n.m.*

גַּחֶלֶת (gāḥĕ'lĕth) *f*, *w.s.* גַּחַלְתִּי, *pl.* גֶּחָלִים, *c.* גַּחֲלֵי [as from גֶּחָל] burning coal, lightning.

גַּחַם (gā'ḥăm) *pr.n.m.*

גַּחַר (gă'ḥăr) *pr.n.m.*

גַּי, גַּיְא (găy), גֵּיא, גֵּי (gē), גֶּיא (gĕ) *m* and *f*, *c.* גֵּי, גֵּיא, *pl.* גֵּיאוֹת and גֵּאָיוֹת, depression, lowland, valley; גֵּיא [בְנֵי] בֶן הִנֹּם valley of the sons of Hinnom, south of Jerusalem [Geenna]; גֵּי מֶלַח salt-valley, near the Dead Sea; other compounds denoting geographical names: גֵּ׳ הַחֲרָשִׁים, גֵּ׳ הַצְּבֹעִים, גֵּ׳ יִפְתַּח־אֵל, &c.

גִּי see גּוֹי.

גִּיד (gīd) *m* sinew, muscle; chain, band.

גִּיחַ (gī'ᵃḥ) *pr.n.* of a place in Benjamin.

גִּחוֹן, גִּיחוֹן (gīḥō'n) *pr.n.* of a river in Paradise; of a fountain west of Jerusalem; a name of the Nile.

גֵּיחֲזִי see גֵּחֲזִי.

גִּיל[1] [גּוּל] (gīl) *pf.* גַּל, גַּלְתִּי, *inf.* גִּיל, *imp.* גִּילוּ, *fut.* יָגִיל, יָגֵל, וַיָּגֶל, to turn oneself round; to rejoice, to exult; to tremble; to shake with fear.

גִּיל[2] (gīl) *m* generation, age; exultation, joy.

גִּילָה (gīlā') *f* exultation.

גִּילֹנִי see גִּלֹה.

גִּינַת (gīnă'th) *pr.n.m.*

גִּיר, גִּר (gīr) *m* lime.

גֵּישָׁן (gēšā'n) *pr.n.m.*

גַּל[1] (găl) *m*, *i.p.* גָּל, *pl.* גַּלִּים, heap of stones, ruins; well, fountain, wave.

גַּל[2] (găl) — גַּלֵּה, see גָּלָה *Pi.*

גֵּל (gēl) *m*, *w.s.* גֶּלְלוֹ, *pl. c.* גֶּלְלֵי, dung, excrements.

גֹּל (gōl) *m* oil-vessel.

גַּלָּב (gállā'b) *m* barber.

גִּלְבֹּעַ (gilbō'ā') *pr.n.* of a mountain in Issachar.

גַּלְגַּל (gálgā'l) *m*, *pl.* גַּלְגַּלִּים, wheel, water-wheel; whirlwind, whirling dust or chaff.

גִּלְגָּל[1] (gilgā'l) *m*, *c.* גִּלְגַּל, wheel.

גִּלְגָּל[2] (gilgā'l) *pr.n.* of three different towns, one near Jericho.

גֻּלְגֹּלֶת (gŭlgō'lĕth) *f*, *w.s.* גֻּלְגָּלְתּוֹ, *pl.* גֻּלְגְּלוֹת, skull, head.

גֶּלֶד (gĕ'lĕd) *m*, *w.s.* גִּלְדִּי, skin, hide.

גָּלָה (gālā') *inf.* גְּלוֹת, גָּלֹה, *imp.* גְּלֵה, גְּלֵה, *fut.* יִגְלֶה, וַיִּגֶל, *pt.* גֹּלֶה, *f* גֹּלָה, *pt. p.* גָּלוּי, to bare, denudate, strip, unveil, disclose, reveal; to evacuate a country, to emigrate, to go into exile. — *Ni.* נִגְלָה, *inf.* הִגָּלוֹת, נִגְלוֹת, נִגְלֹה, *fut.* יִגָּלֶה, תִּגָּל to be uncovered, unveiled, revealed; to appear, to show, reveal or bare oneself; to be led away. — *Pi.* גִּלָּה, *imp.* גַּל = גַּלֵּה, *fut.* יְגַלֶּה, וַיְגַל, to uncover, to open, reveal, show. — *Pu.* גֻּלָּה to be removed [or to be stript]. — *Hi.* הִגְלָה, הֶגְלָה, *fut.* יַגְלֶה, וַיֶּגֶל to lead into exile. — *Ho.* הָגְלָה (hŏglā') to be driven into exile. — *Hith. fut.* יִתְגַּל to uncover oneself, to reveal oneself.

גִּלֹה (gilō') *pr.n.* of a town; *gent.* גִּילֹנִי.

גֹּלָה (gōlā') see גּוֹלָה.

גֻּלָּה (gŭllā') *f*, *c.* גֻּלַּת, *pl.* גֻּלּוֹת, well, spring; oil-vessel; rounded part of a capital.

גִּלּוּל (gillū'l) *m*, only *pl.* גִּלֻּלִים, גִּלּוּלִים, roller, log, idol.

גְּלוֹם (gᵉlō'm) *m* large covering, mantle.

גָּלוּת (gālū'th) *f*, *c.* גָּלוּת, *w.s.* גָּלוּתִי, deportation, captivity, exile; captives, exiles.

גָּלַח (gālā'ḥ) *Pi.* גִּלַּח, *inf.* גַּלַּח, *fut.* יְגַלַּח to make bald, to shear, shave. — *Pu.* גֻּלַּח to be shorn. —

Hith. הִתְגַּלַּח to shave oneself.

גִּלָּיוֹן (gĭllāyō'n) *m*, *pl.* גִּלְיֹנִים, table, polished plate, mirror.

גָּלִיל (gālī'l) *m*, *c.* גְּלִיל, *pl.* גְּלִילִים, *c.* גְּלִילֵי, turning-door, folding-door; roller, cylinder; circuit, district, country; גְּלִיל הַגּוֹיִם Galilee.

גְּלִילָה (gᵉlīlā') *f*, *pl.* גְּלִילוֹת, circuit, territory, country.

גַּלִּים (găllī'm) *pr.n.* of a place in Benjamin.

גָּלְיַת (gŏlyă'ϑ) *pr.n.m.*

גָּלַל (gālă'l) *inf.* גֹּל, גּוֹל, *imp.* גֹּל, גּוֹל, גַּל, *pl.* גֹּלּוּ, *pt.* גֹּלֵל, to whirl, to roll, turn, drive away. — *Ni.* נָגוֹל, *fut.* וְיִגַּל, to be rolled together, to roll oneself on. — *Pilp.* גִּלְגֵּל to roll. — *Po. pt.* מְגוֹלָל to be rolled [in blood], to be dyed red. — *Hi. fut.* וַיָּגֶל to roll away. — *Hith.* הִתְגֹּלֵל and הִתְגַּלְגֵּל to roll oneself upon.

גָּלָל[1] (gālā'l) *m* dung, excrement.

גָּלָל[2] (gālā'l) *m*, *c.* גְּלַל, turn, occasion, circumstance, concern; בִּגְלַל for the sake of, on account of.

גִּלֲלַי (gĭ'lᵃlă'y) *pr.n.m.*

גָּלַם (gālă'm) *fut.* יִגְלֹם, to wrap together.

גֹּלֶם (gō'lĕm) *m*, *w.s.* גָּלְמִי (gŏlmī') something wrapt together, a mass not yet formed, fetus.

גַּלְמוּד (gălmū'd) *adj.*, *f* גַּלְמוּדָה, unfruitful, sterile, barren; desolate, famished.

גָּלַע (gālă'') *Hith.* הִתְגַּלַּע to quarrel [to show one's teeth].

גִּלְעָד (gĭl'ā'd) *pr.n.m.*; *patron.* גִּלְעָדִי; a country east of the Jordan.

גַּלְעֵד (găl'ē'd) *pr.n.* of a hill.

גָּלַשׁ (gālă's) to lie down.

גַּם (găm) *adv.* and *conj.* together, also, too, even; גַּם—גַּם as well as; גַּם כִּי even when, although.

גָּמָא (gāmā') *Pi. fut.* יְגַמֶּא to drink in, to carry along. — *Hi. imp.* הַגְמִיאִי, to give to drink, to water.

גֹּמֶא (gō'mĕ) *m* papyrus-plant, papyrus-reed.

גַּמָּד (gămmā'd) *m*, only *pl.* גַּמָּדִים, warrior.

גֹּמֶד (gō'mĕd) *m* a measure, ell or span.

גָּמוּל (gāmū'l) *pr.n.m.* [see also גָּמַל].

גְּמוּל (gᵉmū'l) *m*, *w.s.* גְּמֻלְכֶם, *pl.* גְּמוּלִים, deed, action, benefit; recompense, desert; עַל ג׳, לִגְמוּל, בִּגְמוּל in return of.

גְּמוּלָה (gᵉmūlā') *f*, *pl.* גְּמוּלוֹת, recompense, retaliation.

גִּמְזוֹ (gĭmzō') *pr.n.* of a place in Judah

גָּמַל (gāmă'l) *inf. w.s.* גָּמְלֵךְ (gŏmlē'ḏ), *fut.* יִגְמֹל, *pt.* גֹּמֵל, *pt. p.* גָּמוּל, גְּמֻל, *intr.* to become ripe; *tr.* to make ripe; to wean; to do, perform, accomplish; to deal with, to do [good or evil], to requite.

גָּמָל (gāmā'l) *m* and *f*, *pl.* גְּמַלִּים, *c.* גְּמַלֵּי camel.

גְּמַלִּי (gᵉmăllī') *pr.n.m.*

גַּמְלִיאֵל (gămlī'ē'l) *pr.n.m.*

גָּמַר (gāmă'r) *fut.* יִגְמֹר, *pt.* גֹּמֵר, to cease, disappear, vanish; *tr.* to finish, accomplish.

גֹּמֶר[1] (gō'mĕr) *pr.n.f.*

גֹּמֶר[2] (gō'mĕr) *pr.n.m.*, son of Japhet and people descended from him [Cappadocians or Cimmerians].

גְּמַרְיָה (gᵉmăryā'); **גְּמַרְיָהוּ** (gᵉmăryā'hū) *pr.n.m.*

גַּן (găn) *m* and *f*, *i.p.* גָּן, *w.s.* גַּנִּי, *pl.* גַּנִּים, garden, orchard, park.

גָּנַב (gānă'ḇ) *inf.* גָּנֹב, *fut.* יִגְנֹב, *pt.* גֹּנֵב, *pt. p.* גָּנוּב, *pl.* גְּנוּבִים, *f c.* גְּנֻבְתִי [for גְּנֻבַת] to purloin, abstract, steal, deceive. — *Ni. fut.* יִגָּנֵב to be stolen. — *Pi. fut.* יְגַנֵּב to steal or deceive by habit. — *Pu.* גֻּנַּב, *fut.* יְגֻנַּב, *inf.* גֻּנֹּב, to be stolen, to be imparted by stealth. — *Hith.* הִתְגַּנֵּב to steal oneself away, to withdraw by stealth.

גַּנָּב (gănnā'ḇ) *m*, *pl.* גַּנָּבִים, thief [by habit].

גְּנֵבָה (gᵉnēḇā') *f* theft. something stolen.

גְּנֻבַת (gᵉnūḇă'ϑ) *pr.n.m.*

גַּנָּה (gănnā') *f*, *w.s.* גַּנָּתוֹ, *pl.* גַּנּוֹת, garden, grove.

גִּנָּה (gĭnnā') *f* — גַּנָּה.

גֶּנֶז (gē'nĕz) *m*, only *pl. c.* גִּנְזֵי treasures, coffers.

גַּנְזַךְ (gănză'ꝺ) *m*, only *pl.* גַּנְזַכִּים, treasure-house, treasury.

גָּנַן (gānă'n) *inf.* גָּנוֹן, to cover, protect, guard. — *Ni. fut.* יָגֵן the same as *Q.*

גִּנְּתוֹן (gĭnϑō'n) *pr.n.m.* [גִּנְּתוֹי].

גַּע, **גַּעַת** see נָגַע.

גָּעָה (gā'ā') *inf.* גְּעוֹ, *fut.* יִגְעֶה to roar, to low.

גֹּעָה (gō'ā') *pr.n.* of a place near Jerusalem.

גָּעַל (gā'ă'l) *fut.* יִגְעַל, to abhor, detest, reject. — *Ni.* נִגְעַל to be rejected, to be thrown away. — *Hi.* הִגְעִיל to cast away, to waste.

גַּעַל (gă''ăl) *pr.n.m.*

גֹּעַל (gō''ăl) *m* rejection, reprobation.

גָּעַר (gā'ă'r) *inf.* גְּעֹר, *imp.* גְּעַר, *fut.* יִגְעַר to address harshly, to cry at, scold, rebuke, threaten.

גְּעָרָה (g''ārā') *f*, *c.* גַּעֲרַת, scolding, threatening, rebuke.

גָּעַשׁ (gā'ă's) *fut.* יִגְעַשׁ, to quake, tremble, shake. — *Pu. fut.* יְגֹעֲשׁ to be shaken. — *Hith.* הִתְגָּעֵשׁ, הִתְגַּעַשׁ to be shaken, to stagger or reel.

גַּעַשׁ (gă''ăs) *pr.n.* of a mountain in Ephraim.

גַּעְתָּם (gă'tā'm) *pr.n.m.*

גַּף (găf) *m*, *w.s.* גַּפּוֹ, *pl. c.* גַּפֵּי, back, top; body, person.

גֶּפֶן (gĕ'fĕn) *f* [twice *m*], *w.s.* גַּפְנוֹ, *pl.* גְּפָנִים, vine, vine-plant; shoot, tendril.

גֹּפֶר (gō'fĕr) *m* a resinous tree, cypress, cedar or fir.

גָּפְרִית (gŏfrī'ϑ) *f* brimstone.

גָּר (gār) *adj.* [*pt.* of גּוּר], *pl. c.* גָּרֵי, *f* גָּרָה, dwelling, abiding; with בַּיִת: inmate, servant.

גֵּר (gēr) *m*, *w.s.* גֵּרְךָ, *pl.* גֵּרִים, *c.* גֵּרֵי, stranger, foreigner, pilgrim, guest, visitor.

גִּר (gĭr) *m* lime.

גֹּר = גּוּר[2].

גֵּרָא (gērā') *pr.n.m.*

גָּרָב (gārā'ḃ) *m* itch, scurvy [leprosy].

גָּרֵב (gārē'ḃ) *pr.n.m.* [scabby, leper].

גַּרְגַּר (gărgă'r) *m*, *pl.* גַּרְגְּרִים, berry.

גַּרְגֶּרֶת (gărgĕ'rĕθ) *f*, only *pl. c.* גַּרְגְּרוֹת, throat, neck.

גִּרְגָּשִׁי (gĭrgāšī') *pr.n.* of a Canaanitic people, Girgasites.

גָּרַד (gārā'd) *Hith.* הִתְגָּרֵד to scratch oneself.

גָּרָה (gārā') *Pi. fut.* יְגָרֶה, to kindle, provoke, stir. — *Hith. imp.* הִתְגָּר, *fut.* יִתְגָּרֶה, יִתְגָּר to grow angry or enraged; to make war upon, to infest,

גֵּרָה (gērā') *f* chewed cud; grain, berry, 20th part of a shekel [smallest weight of the Hebrews].

גָּרוֹן (gārō'n) *m*, *w.s.* גְּרוֹנִי, throat, voice, neck.

גֵּרוּת (gērū'θ) *f* harbour, shelter, inn.

גָּרַז (gārā'z) *Ni.* נִגְרַז to be cut off.

גְּרִזִּי (g^e^rĭzzī') and גִּרְזִי (gĭrzī') *pr.n.* of a people in southern Palestine.

גְּרִזִּים (g^e^rĭzzī'm) *pr.n.* of a mountain in Ephraim.

גַּרְזֶן (gărzĕ'n) *m* hatchet, axe.

גָּרֹל (gārō'l) *adj.*, *c.* גְּרָל־ (g^e^rŏ'l), rough, harsh [perh. for גָּדוֹל].

גֹּרָל see גּוֹרָל.

גָּרַם (gārā'm) to skin, flay; to let remain. — *Pi. fut.* יְגָרֵם to skin, to gnaw.

גֶּרֶם (gĕ'rĕm) *m*, *i.p.* גָּרֶם, *pl.* גְּרָמִים, bone; body, person, self [= עֶצֶם].

גַּרְמִי (gărmī') *pr.n.m.*

גֹּרֶן (gō'rĕn) *f*, *w.s.* גָּרְנִי (gŏrnī'), *pl.* גְּרָנוֹת, *c.* גָּרְנוֹת (gŏrnō'θ), thrashing-floor; open place before the gate of a town.

גָּרַס (gārā's) to be crushed. — *Hi. fut.* יַגְרֵס to crush.

גָּרַע (gārā'^a^) *fut.* יִגְרַע to cut off, remove, withdraw, diminish; to shear, shave. — *Ni. fut.* יִגָּרַע, *pt.* נִגְרָע to be withdrawn, diminished, lessened. — *Pi. fut.* יְגָרַע to draw in, to swallow.

גָּרַף (gārā'f) to sweep away, to snatch away.

גָּרַר (gārā'r) *fut.* יָגֹר to draw, collect, snatch away; *fut.* יִגַּר to draw up, to chew the cud. — *Pu. pt.* *f/pl.* מְגוֹרָרוֹת to be sawed asunder. — *Hith.* הִתְגּוֹרֵר to whirl [see also גּוּר].

גְּרָר (g'rā'r) *pr.n.* of a town of the Philistines.

גֶּרֶשׂ (gĕ'rĕs) *m* something pounded or crushed.

גָּרַשׁ (gārā'š) *fut. pl.* יִגְרְשׁוּ, *pt.* גֹּרֵשׁ, *pt. p. f* גְּרוּשָׁה to drive away, to expel; to divorce [a wife]; to empty, pillage. — *Ni.* נִגְרַשׁ, *pt.* נִגְרָשׁ, to be cast out, to be stirred up. — *Pi.* גֵּרֵשׁ, *inf.* גָּרֵשׁ, *imp.* גָּרֵשׁ, *fut.* יְגָרֵשׁ to drive away, expel. — *Pu.* גֹּרַשׁ to be expelled.

גֶּרֶשׁ (gĕ'rĕš) *m* fruit, produce.

גְּרֻשָׁה (g'rūšā') *f* expulsion.

גֵּרְשׁוֹן (gē'r'šō'n) *pr.n.m.*

גֵּרְשֹׁם (gēr'šō'm) *pr.n.m.*

גְּשׁוּר (g'šū'r) *pr.n.* of a district between Hermon and Bashan; *gent.* גְּשׁוּרִי.

גָּשַׁם (gāšā'm), only *Hi.* הִגְשִׁים to cause to rain.

גֶּשֶׁם (gĕ'šĕm) *m, i.p.* גָּשֶׁם, *pl.* גְּשָׁמִים, *c.* גִּשְׁמֵי, heavy rain, shower.

גֹּשֶׁם (gō'šĕm) *m, w.s.* גֻּשְׁמָהּ = גֶּשֶׁם.

גֹּשֶׁן (gō'šĕn) *pr.n.* of a district in eastern Egypt; of a town in Judah.

גִּשְׁפָּא (gĭšpā') *pr.n.m.*

גָּשַׁשׁ (gāšā'š) *Pi. fut.* יְגַשֵּׁשׁ, to grope, fumble.

גֶּשֶׁת see נָגַשׁ.

גַּת[1] (gāϑ) *f, pl.* גִּתּוֹת, wine-press.

גַּת[2] (gāϑ) *pr.n.* of a city of the Philistines; *gent.* גִּתִּי.

גִּתַּיִם (gĭttă'yĭm) *du, pr.n.* of a town in Benjamin.

גִּתִּית (gĭttī'ϑ) *f* name of a tune, or of a musical instrument.

גֶּתֶר (gĕ'ϑĕr) *pr.n.* of an Aramæan people.

ד

ד the fourth letter of the alphabet, called דָּלֶת [door]; as a numeral = 4.

דָּאַב (dā'ăb) *inf.* דַּאֲבָה, to languish, pine, faint.

דְּאָבָה (d'ābā') *f* fear, anguish.

דְּאָבוֹן (d'ābō'n) *m, c.* דַּאֲבוֹן, faintness, pining.

דָּאג see דָּג.

דָּאַג (dā'ă'g) *fut.* יִדְאַג, to be anxious or troubled, to fear.

דֹּאֵג (dō''ēg) *pr.n.m.*

דְּאָגָה (dᵉ'āgā') *f* fear, apprehension.

דָּאָה[1] (dā'ā') *fut.* יִדְאֶה, וַיֵּדֶא, to fly, soar.

דָּאָה[2] (dā'ā') *f* bird of prey, vulture or kite.

דֹּאר see דּוֹר.

דֹּב, דּוֹב (dōḇ) *m* and *f*, *pl.* דֻּבִּים bear, she-bear.

דֹּבֶא (dō'ḇĕ) *m*, *w.s.* דָּבְאֶךָ (dŏḇ'ē'ḵ) well-being, comfort, affluence.

דָּבַב (dāḇă'ḇ) *pt.* דּוֹבֵב to cause to speak.

דִּבָּה (dĭbbā') *f* talk, report, slander, calumny.

דְּבוֹרָה[1] (dᵉḇōrā') *f*, *pl.* דְּבֹרִים bee.

דְּבוֹרָה[2] (dᵉḇōrā') *pr.n.f.*

דִּבְיוֹן (dĭḇyō'n) *m*, only *pl.* דִּבְיוֹנִים dung, excrements of doves.

דְּבִיר[1] (dᵉḇī'r) *m* hinder or western part of the temple, the inner sanctuary, the holy of holies.

דְּבִיר[2] (dᵉḇī'r) *pr.n.m.*; *pr.n.* of towns.

דְּבֵלָה (dᵉḇēlā') *f*, *c.* דְּבֶלֶת, *pl.* דְּבֵלִים, cake of figs.

דִּבְלָה (dĭḇlā') miswritten for רִבְלָה.

דִּבְלַיִם (dĭḇlă'yĭm) *pr.n.m.*

דָּבַק (dāḇă'k), **דָּבֵק** (dāḇē'k) *inf.* דָּבְקָה (dŏḇkā'), *fut.* יִדְבַּק to stick, cling, adhere, to be attached to, to pursue. — *Pu.* דֻּבַּק to cleave fast together. — *Hi.* הִדְבִּיק, *fut.* יַדְבֵּק to cause to cleave, to pursue, to catch. — *Ho. pt.* מֻדְבָּק to cleave, to be attached.

דָּבֵק (dāḇē'k) *adj.*, *pl.* דְּבֵקִים, *f* דְּבֵקָה, cleaving, attached to.

דֶּבֶק (dĕ'ḇĕk) *m*, *pl.* דְּבָקִים, welding of metals, solder; joint in a coat of mail.

דָּבַר (dāḇă'r) *inf. w.s.* דָּבְרְךָ (dŏḇrĕ'ḵā), *pt.* דֹּבֵר, *pl.* דֹּבְרִים, *f* דֹּבְרוֹת, *pt. p.* דָּבֻר, the same as *Pi.* — *Pi.* דִּבֵּר, *i.p.* דִּבֶּר, *inf.* דַּבֵּר, דַּבֶּר, דַּבֶּר־, *imp.* דַּבֵּר, דַּבֶּר, *fut.* יְדַבֵּר, *pt.* מְדַבֵּר, *f* מְדַבֶּרֶת to speak, to accost; to say [with *acc.*], to promise, command, exhort, [to destroy]. — *Pu.* *fut.* יְדֻבַּר, *pt.* מְדֻבָּר to be spoken; to be wooed. — *Ni.* נִדְבַּר to speak to one another, to consult. — *Hi. fut.* יַדְבֵּר to drive, subdue. — *Hith. pt.* מִדַּבֵּר [for מִתְדַּבֵּר] to converse.

דָּבָר (dāḇā'r) *m*, *c.* דְּבַר, *pl.* דְּבָרִים, *c.* דִּבְרֵי, word, saying, speach, news, command, promise; thing, incident, occurrence, history, concern, cause, question, law-suit.

דֶּבֶר (dĕ'ḇĕr) *m*, *i.p.* דָּבֶר, *pl.* דְּבָרִים, destruction, pestilence, plague.

דֹּבֶר (dō'ḇĕr) *m* pasture, steppe, desert.

דִּבְרָה (dĭḇrā') *f*, *w.s.* דִּבְרָתִי, manner, fashion, cause; עַל דִּבְרַת on account of, in order that.

דְּבֹרָה (dᵉḇōrā') see דְּבוֹרָה.

דִּבְרִי (dĭḇrī') *pr.n.m.*

דֹּבְרֹת (dōḇĕ'rĕϑ) *f*, only *pl.* דֹּבְרוֹת, raft, float.

דָּבְרַת (dā'ḇᵉră'ϑ) *pr.n.* of a Levitical town.

דְּבַשׁ (dᵉḇă'š) *m*, *i.p.* דְּבָשׁ, *w.s.* דִּבְשִׁי, honey, sirup of grapes.

דַּבֶּשֶׁת¹ (dăbbĕ'šĕϑ) *f* lump of fat, hump of a camel.

דַּבֶּשֶׁת² (dăbbĕ'šĕϑ) *pr.n.* of a place.

דָּג (dāg) *m*, *pl.* דָּגִים, *c.* דְּגֵי fish.

דָּגָה¹ (dāgā') *f*, *c.* דְּגַת, *w.s.* דְּגָתָם, *coll.* fish.

דָּגָה² (dāgā') *fut.* יִדְגֶּה to increase, multiply.

דָּגוֹן (dāgō'n) *pr.n.m.*, the national god of the Philistines.

דָּגַל (dāgă'l) *fut.* יִדְגֹּל, *pt. p.* דָּגוּל to set up a banner; *pt. p.* distinguished. — *Ni.* נִדְגַּל to be provided with banners.

דֶּגֶל (dĕ'gĕl) *m*, *w.s.* דִּגְלִי, *pl.* דְּגָלִים, *c.* דִּגְלֵי banner, flag.

דָּגָן (dāgā'n) *m*, *c.* דְּגַן, *w.s.* דְּגָנִי corn, grain, bread, nourishment.

דָּגַר (dāgă'r) to gather, to hatch.

דַּד (dăḍ) *m*, only *du.* דַּדַּיִם, breast, teat.

דֹּד see דּוֹד.

דָּדָה (dāḍā') only *Hith.* הִדַּדָּה, *fut.* אֶדַּדֶּה to walk slowly, to go in a procession.

דְּדָן (dᵉdā'n) *pr.n.m.* of an Ethiopian tribe; *gent.* דְּדָנִי, *pl.* דְּדָנִים.

דֹּדָנִים (dō'dānī'm) *pr.n.m.* of a Japhetic people [Rhodians, Dardanians or Dodonæans].

דָּהַם (dāhă'm) *Ni. pt.* נִדְהָם to be perplexed, terrified.

דָּהַר (dāhă'r) *pt.* דֹּהֵר to run, to galop.

דַּהֲרָה (dă'hᵃrā') *f*, only *pl. c.* דַּהֲרוֹת, course, run.

דּוּב (dūb) *Hi. pt.* מַדִיב, to cause to pine.

דַּוָּג (dăvvā'g) *m* fisher.

דּוּגָה (dūgā') *f* fishing, fishery.

דּוֹד, דֹּד (dōd) *m*, *w.s.* דּוֹדִי, *pl.* דּוֹדִים, love; one beloved, friend; relation, cousin, uncle.

דּוּד (dūd) *m*, *pl.* דּוּדִים and דְּוָדִים, pot, kettle; basket.

דָּוִד, דָּוִיד (dāvī'd, dāvī'd) *pr.n.m.*

דּוֹדָה (dōdā') *f* aunt.

דּוֹדוֹ (dōdō'); דֹּדָוָהוּ (dōdāvā'hū); דּוֹדַי (dōdă'y) *pr.n.m.*

דּוּדַי (dūdă'y) *m*, only *pl.* דּוּדָאִים, = דּוּד basket; mandragora, love-apple.

דָּוָה (dāvā') *inf.* דְּוֹת, to be sick [of monthly courses], to be ill.

דָּוֶה (dāvĕ') *adj.*, *f* דָּוָה sick, unwell, unclean; sad, wretched.

דּוּחַ (dū'ᵃḥ) *Hi.* הֵדִיחַ, *fut.* יָדִיחַ, to expel, cast out; to wash off, cleanse.

דְּוַי (dᵉvă'y) *m*, *i.p.* דְּוָי, *c.* דְּוֵי, sickness; something unclean and loathsome.

דַּוָּי (dăvvā'y) *adj.* severely ill.

דּוֹיֵג = דֹּאֵג.

דּוּךְ (dūḥ) *pf.* דָּךְ, to pound [in a mortar].

דּוּכִיפַת (dū'ḥīfă'ϑ) *f* an unclean bird [hoopoe or mountain-cock].

דּוּמָה[1] (dūmā') *f* stillness, realm of death.

דּוּמָה[2] (dūmā') *pr.n.* of an Arabian tribe; of towns in Edom and Judah.

דֻּמִיָּה, דּוּמִיָּה (dū'mīyyā') *f* stillness, silence, trust, submission [*f* of דּוּמִי *adj.* silent, still].

דּוּמָם (dūmā'm) *adv.* silently, still; *m* silence, dumbness.

דּוּמֶשֶׂק see דַּמֶּשֶׂק.

דּוּן (dūn), דּוֹן (dōn) *fut.* יָדוֹן to prevail, rule, remain.

דּוֹנַג (dōnă'g) *m*, *i.p.* דּוֹנָג, wax.

דּוּץ (dūẞ) *fut.* יָדוּץ to leap, jump.

דּוּק see דָּקַק.

דּוֹר[1], דֹּר (dōr) *m*, *w.s.* דּוֹרִי, *pl.* דּוֹרוֹת and דּוֹרִים, period of a man's life, generation, age; race, class of men, contemporaries.

דּוֹר[2] (dōr) *m* habitation, dwelling; דּוֹר and דֹּאר *pr.n.* of a sea-town near mount Carmel.

דּוּר[1] (dūr) *inf.* דּוּר, to sojourn, to dwell.

דּוּר[2] (dūr) *m* circle, ball; pile of wood.

דּוּשׁ (dūš) *pf.* דָּשׁ, *inf.* דּוּשׁ, דּוֹשׁ, *fut.* יָדוּשׁ, *w.s.* יְדוּשֶׁנּוּ, *pt.* דָּשׁ to tread out, to thrash; to tread down, to crush. — *Ni.* נָדוֹשׁ, *inf.* הִדּוֹשׁ and *Ho. fut.* יוּדַשׁ to be trodden out, to be thrashed.

דָּחָה (dāḥā') *inf.* דְּחֹה, דְּחוֹת, *pt.* דֹּחֶה, *pt. p. f* דְּחוּיָה, to push, to thrust down, to overthrow. — *Ni. fut.* יִדָּחֶה, *pt. pl. c.* נִדְחֵי [or from נָדַח] to be thrust down, to be driven away. — *Pu.* דֹּחָה to be overthrown.

דָּחַח (dāḥă'ḥ) *Ni. fut. pl.* יִדַּחוּ, the same as דָּחָה *Ni.*

דְּחִי (d'ḥī') *m*, *i.p.* דֶּחִי, overthrow, downfall, destruction.

דֹּחַן (dō'ḥăn) *m* millet.

דָּחַף (dāḥă'f) to drive, to impel; *pt. p.* דָּחוּף dispatched, at full speed. — *Ni.* נִדְחַף to hasten.

דָּחַק (dāḥă'k) *fut.* יִדְחַק, *pt.* דֹּחֵק to press, oppress.

דַּי (dăy) *m*, *i.p.* דָּי, *c.* דֵּי, *w.s.* דַּיֶּךָ, דַּיְךְ, דַּיָּם the requisite, necessary supply, sufficency, plenty; *adv.* enough; בְּדֵי in proportion to, as often as, as soon as; כְּדֵי according to need, corresponding to; מִדֵּי as often as.

דִּי זָהָב (dī zāhā'b) *pr.n.* of a place near Mount Sinai.

דִּיבוֹן (dībō'n) *pr.n.* of two towns, in Moab and in Judah.

דַּיָּג (dăyyā'g) *m*, *pl.* דַּיָּגִים fisher.

דַּיָּה (dăyyā') *f*, *pl.* דַּיּוֹת, a bird of prey, vulture.

דְּיוֹ (dᵉyō') *m* colour for writing, ink.

דִּין[1] (dīn) *pf.* דָּן, *inf.* and *imp.* דִּין, *fut.* יָדִין, *pt.* דָּן to rule, sway; to judge, defend, punish; to litigate. — *Ni. pt.* נָדוֹן to contend at law, to quarrel.

דִּין[2] (dīn) *m* judgment, sentence, law-suit, cause, quarrel.

דַּיָּן (dăyyā'n) *m* judge.

דִּינָה (dīnā') *pr.n.f.*

דִּיפַת (dīfă'ϑ) *pr.n.m.* = רִיפַת.

דָּיֵק (dāyē'k) *m* watch-tower, bulwark.

דַּיִשׁ (dă'yĭš) *m* thrashing time.

דִּישׁוֹן[1] (dīšō'n) *m* antelope, mountain-goat.

דִּישׁוֹן[2] (dīšō'n), דִּישָׁן (dīšā'n) *pr.n.m.*

דַּךְ (dăch) *adj.*, *i.p.* דָּךְ, *pl. w.s.* דַּכָּיו, crushed, oppressed, wretched.

דָּכָא (dāchā') *Ni. pt.* נִדְכָּא, to be cast down, humbled. — *Pi.* דִּכָּא, *inf. w.s.* דַּכְּאוֹ to break, crush, oppress, humble, tread down. — *Pu. pt.* מְדֻכָּא, *pl.* מְדֻכָּאִים to be broken, crushed, humbled, afflicted. — *Hith. fut.* יִדַּכֵּא to be crushed, humbled.

דַּכָּא[1] (dăkkā') *m* something bruised, dust.

דַּכָּא[2] (dăkkā') *adj.*, *pl. c.* דַּכְּאֵי bruised, humbled, discouraged.

דָּכָה (dāchā') *fut.* יִדְכֶּה to be bowed, to cower. — *Ni. pf.* נִדְכֵּיתִי, *pt.* נִדְכֶּה to be bruised, crushed. — *Pi.* דִּכָּה to bruise, dash.

דַּכָּה (dăkkā') *f* bruising, castration.

דֳּכִי (dᵒchī') *m* surging waves, billows, surf.

דַּל[1] (dăl) *m* = דֶּלֶת.

דַּל[2] (dăl) *adj.*, *i.p.* דָּל, *pl.* דַּלִּים, *f* דַּלָּה, *pl.* דַּלּוֹת, tottering, weak, humble, wretched, poor.

דָּלַג (dālă'g) to leap, jump. — *Pi. fut.* יְדַלֵּג to leap over.

דָּלָה (dālā') *pf. pl.* דַּלְיוּ [for דָּלוּ], דָּלְיוּ, *inf.*

דָּלָה, *fut.* יִדְלֶה, to draw [water], to draw out. — *Pi.* דִּלָּה to draw out, to deliver.

דַּלָּה[1] (dållā') *f*, *c.* דַּלַּת, *pl.* דַּלּוֹת lowliness, poverty; דַּלַּת עָם the low, the poor.

דַּלָּה[2] (dållā') *f* threadwork [of the weaver], thrum.

דָּלַח (dālă'ḥ) *fut.* יִדְלַח to trouble, to make muddy [by treading].

דְּלִי (dolī'), דְּלִי (dᵉlī') *m*, *w.s.* דָּלְיוֹ (dŏlyō'), *du. w.s.* דָּלְיָו (dā'lᵉyā'v), basket, leather-bag.

דְּלָיָה (dᵉlāyā'), דְּלָיָהוּ (dᵉlā-yā'hū) *pr.n.m.*

דְּלִילָה (dᵉlīlā') *pr.n.f.* [— languishing, tender].

דָּלִית (dālī'ϑ) *f*, only *pl.* דָּלִיּוֹת, branch, tendril.

דָּלַל (dālă'l) *pf. pl.* דַּלּוּ and דָּלְלוּ, 1. *pl.* דַּלּוֹנוּ, *fut.* יִדַּל [or *Ni.*] to totter, wave, hang loose; to be poor, humble, wretched; to languish, to be dry. — *Ni. fut.* יִדַּל to be weak, wretched

דִּלְעָן (dĭlᵉā'n) *pr.n.* of a town in Judah.

דָּלַף (dālă'f) *fut.* יִדְלֹף to flow slowly, to drop, trickle; to weep, to shed tears.

דֶּלֶף (dĕ'lĕf) *m* a dropping, eaves.

דַּלְפוֹן (dålfō'n) *pr.n.m.*

דָּלַק (dālă'k) *inf.* דְּלֹק, *fut.* יִדְלֹק, *pt.* דֹּלֵק to burn, to glow, to be passionate; to be anxious; דָּלַק אַחֲרֵי to pursue hotly. — *Hi.* הִדְלִיק, *fut.* יַדְלִיק to heat, to kindle.

דַּלֶּקֶת (dållĕ'kĕϑ) *f* hot fever.

דֶּלֶת (dĕ'lĕϑ) *f*, *i.p.* דָּלֶת, *w.s.* דַּלְתֵּךְ and דַּלְתּוֹ, *du.* דְּלָתַיִם, *c.* דַּלְתֵי, *w.s.* דְּלָתַי, *pl.* דְּלָתוֹת, *c.* דַּלְתוֹת, door, folding-door, gate, opening; column or page of a manuscript.

דָּם[1] (dām) *m*, *c.* דַּם, *w.s.* דָּמִי, דִּמְכֶם, *pl.* דָּמִים, *c.* דְּמֵי, blood, bloody deed, blood-guiltiness; juice, sap, red wine.

דָּם[2] (dām) *m*, perh. = דְּמוּת likeness.

דָּמָה[1] (dāmā') *imp.* דְּמֵה, *fut.* יִדְמֶה, to be like, to resemble; to make like. — *Ni.* נִדְמָה to be made like, to resemble. — *Pi.* דִּמָּה, *fut.* יְדַמֶּה to compare, to speak in similitudes; to imagine, think, remember; to intend, to purpose. — *Hith. fut.* 1. *sg.* אֶדַּמֶּה to make oneself like.

דָּמָה² (dāmā') *fut.* יִדְמֶה, to cease, to rest, to be silent; to destroy. — *Ni.* נִדְמָה to be destroyed, to perish.

דֻּמָּה (dŭmmā') *f* stillness, desolation.

דְּמוּת (dᵉmū'ϑ) *f* likeness, resemblance; image, model, shape; *adv.* like.

דֳּמִי (dᵒmī'), דְּמִי (dᵉmī') *m* silence, rest.

דִּמְיוֹן (dĭmyō'n) *m*, *w.s.* דִּמְיֹנוֹ, resemblance, image.

דָּמַם (dāmă'm) *imp.* דּוֹם, דֹּמּוּ, *fut.* יִדֹּם [יִדַּם] to cease, to be silent or dumb, to rest. — *Ni.* נָדַם, *fut. pl.* יִדַּמּוּ, *i.p.* יִדָּמּוּ, to be destroyed, to perish; to be silent, to rest. — *Po.* דּוֹמֵם to silence. — *Hi.* הֵדֵם, *w.s.* הֲדִמָּנוּ, to destroy.

דְּמָמָה (dᵉmāmā') *f* silence, stillness, calm, whisper.

דֹּמֶן (dō'mĕn) *m* dung, excrements.

דִּמְנָה (dĭmnā') *pr.n.* of a town in Zebulon.

דָּמַע (dāmă'ᵉ) *inf.* דְּמֹעַ, *fut.* יִדְמַע to weep, to shed tears.

דֶּמַע (dĕ'măᵉ) *m*, *w.s.* דִּמְעֲךָ, tear; juice of grapes and olives.

דִּמְעָה (dĭmᵉā') *f*, *c.* דִּמְעַת, *pl.* דְּמָעוֹת, tear, tears.

דַּמֶּשֶׂק (dămmĕ'ßĕk), also דּוּמֶּשֶׂק and דַּרְמֶשֶׂק, *pr.n.*, Damascus.

דְּמֶשֶׁק (dᵉmĕ'ßĕk) *m* silken damask.

דָּן (dān) *pr.n.m.*, *gent.* דָּנִי; *pr.n.* of a town near mount Hermon = לַיִשׁ.

דַּנָּה (dănnā') *pr.n.* of a town in Judah.

דִּנְהָבָה (dĭnhābā') *pr.n.* of a town of the Edomites.

דָּנִיֵּאל (dā'nī'ē'l) *pr.n.m.*

דַּעַת, דְּעוּ, דַּע see יָדַע.

דֵּעַ (dē'ăᵉ) *m* and דֵּעָה (dēᵉā') *f*, *pl.* דֵּעוֹת, knowledge, wisdom.

דְּעוּאֵל (dᵉʼūʼēʼl) *pr.n.m.*

דָּעַךְ (dāʻăʼḏ) *fut.* יִדְעַךְ to be extinguished, to be quenched. — *Ni.* נִדְעַךְ to be dried up. — *Pu.* דֹּעַךְ to be destroyed, to become extinct.

דַּעַת (dăʻʻăth) *f*, *i.p.* דָּעַת, knowledge, insight.

דֳּפִי (dᵒfīʼ) *m*, *i.p.* דֹּפִי, scorn, insult.

דָּפַק (dāfăʼk) *pt.* דּוֹפֵק, to strike, to knock; to drive on. — *Hith. pt.* מִתְדַּפֵּק to knock.

דָּפְקָה (dŏfkāʼ) *pr.n.* of a station in the wilderness.

דַּק (dăk) *adj.*, *f* דַּקָּה, *pl.* דַּקּוֹת, crushed, fine, thin, lean, low; *m* dust.

דִּקְלָה (dĭklāʼ) *pr.n.m.* of an Arabian tribe.

דָּקַק (dākăʼk) *fut.* יָדֹק to crush, pound, grind, thrash; *intr* to be crushed, to be pulverised. — *Hi.* הֵדַק, *inf.* הָדֵק, *fut.* וַיָּדֶק. 1. *sg. w.s.* אֲדִקֵּם to crush, to bruise, to destroy; *inf. adv.* fine, dustlike. — *Ho. fut. i.p.* יוּדַק to be beaten out, to be crushed.

דָּקַר (dākăʼr) *fut.* יִדְקֹר, to pierce. — *Ni. fut.* יִדָּקֵר to be pierced, stabbed. — *Pu. pt.* מְדֻקָּר to be stabbed or slain, to perish.

דֶּקֶר (dĕʼkĕr) *pr.n.m.*

דַּר (dăr) *m* pearl, mother-of-pearl.

דֹּר see דּוֹר.

דֵּרָאוֹן (dērāʼōʼn) *m*, *c.* דִּרְאוֹן, aversion, object of aversion.

דָּרְבָן (dāʼrᵉbāʼn) and דָּרְבוֹן (dāʼrᵒbōʼn) *m*, *pl.* דָּרְבֹנוֹת, prick, goad.

דַּרְדַּע (dărdăʻʼ) *pr.n.m.*

דַּרְדַּר (dărdăʼr) *m* a prickly plant, thorn or thistle.

דָּרוֹם (dārōʼm) *m* south, southern region.

דְּרוֹר (dᵉrōʼr) *f* swallow; *m* freedom, delivery, release from servitude.

דָּרְיָוֶשׁ (dāʼrᵉyāʼvĕš) *pr.n.m.*, Darius [i.e. Cyaxares II., Darius I., son of Hystaspes, and Darius II. Nothus].

דָּרַךְ (dārăʼḏ) *fut.* יִדְרֹךְ, *pt.* דֹּרֵךְ, *pt. p.* דָּרוּךְ, *f*

דְּרוֹכָה to tread, to walk, to go; to step forth, to wander; to tread down, to trample on; to bend [a bow]. — *Hi.* הִדְרִיךְ, *imp.* *w.s.* הַדְרִיכֵנִי, *fut.* יַדְרִיךְ, יַדְרֵךְ, *pt.* מַדְרִיךְ to cause to tread or walk, to lead; *intr.* to tread; to bend; to catch, to reach.

דֶּרֶךְ (dě'rěch) *m* and *f*, *i.p.* דָּרֶךְ, *w.s.* דַּרְכִּי, *pl.* דְּרָכִים, *c.* דַּרְכֵי, a going, walk, journey; way, path, road; mode, manner, course, way of life, lot; worship.

דַּרְכְּמוֹן (dărkᵉmō'n) see אֲדַרְכּוֹן.

דַּרְמֶשֶׂק see דַּמֶּשֶׂק.

דָּרַע (dě'răᵉ) *pr.n.m.*

דַּרְקוֹן (dărkō'n) *pr.n.m.*

דָּרַשׁ (dără's) *fut.* יִדְרֹשׁ, *pt.* דֹּרֵשׁ, *pt.* *p.* דָּרוּשׁ, *f* דְּרוּשָׁה to seek, to examine, to investigate, inquire; to demand, desire, ask; to visit. — *Ni.* נִדְרַשׁ, *inf.* אִדָּרֵשׁ, *fut.* יִדָּרֵשׁ, *pt.* נִדְרָשׁ to be sought, explored; to allow oneself to be sought. — *Pi.* *inf.* דַּרְיוֹשׁ for דַּרּוֹשׁ [but probably written for דְּרוֹשׁ *Q.* *inf.*], to investigate.

דָּשָׁא (dāsā') to shoot, sprout. — *Hi.* *fut.* יַדְשֵׁא to cause to sprout, to bring forth.

דֶּשֶׁא (dě'sě) *m* green herbage, fresh grass.

דָּשֵׁן[1] (dāsē'n) to become fat. — *Pi.* דִּשֵּׁן, *inf.* *w.s.* דַּשְּׁנוֹ, *fut.* יְדַשֵּׁן and יְדַשְּׁנֶה to make fat, strong or oily; to anoint; to accept as fat or pleasing; to cleanse from ashes. — *Pu.* *fut.* *i.p.* יְדֻשָּׁן to be made fat, to be well fed. - *Hoth.* הֻדַּשַּׁן to be oiled, greased.

דָּשֵׁן[2] (dāsē'n) *adj.*, *pl.* דְּשֵׁנִים, *c.* דִּשְׁנֵי, fat, juicy, well fed; rich, mighty.

דֶּשֶׁן (dě'sěn) *m*, *i.p.* דָּשֶׁן, *w.s.* דִּשְׁנִי, fatness, oil; abundance, affluence; fat ashes [from the altar].

דָּת (dāϑ) *f*, *pl.* דָּתִים, *c.* דָּתֵי royal command, prescription, law.

דָּתָן (dāϑā'n) *pr.n.m.*

דֹּתָן (dōϑā'n) and דֹּתַיִן (dō-ϑă'yīn) *pr.n.* of a place in Samaria.

ה

ה the fifth letter of the alphabet, called הֵא [air-hole]; as a numeral = 5.

הַ־ [with dagesh following], הָ, הֶ the definite article, used for all numbers and genders; originally a *pron. demon.*, הַיּוֹם this day, to-day.

הֲ־ *interrog.* particle in direct and indirect questions [*Lat.* ne, num]; הֲלֹא = *Lat.* nonne; הֲ־—אִם in disjunctive questions: whether—or.

הֵא (hē) *interj.* lo! behold!

הֶאֱזְנִיחוּ see זָנַח *Hi.*

הֶאָח (hĕ'ā'ch) *interj.* [exclamation of joy or mockery], aha! haha!

הַב, הָבָה, הָבוּ see יָהַב.

הִבְאִישׁ see בּוֹשׁ.

הַבְהַב (hăbhă'b) *m*, only *pl.* הַבְהָבִים, offering, sacrifice, gift.

הִבֹּק see בָּקַק *Ni.*

הָבַל (hābă'l) *fut.* יֶהְבַּל to breathe out; to be vain, to act foolishly, to hope vainly. — *Hi. pt.* מַהְבִּל to befool.

הֶבֶל[1] (hĕ'bĕl) *m*, *i.p.* הָבֶל, *c.* הֲבֵל, *w.s.* הֶבְלִי, *pl.* הֲבָלִים, *c.* הַבְלֵי, breath, breeze, nothingness, transitoriness, vanity, show; idol; *adv.* in vain, uselessly.

הֶבֶל[2] (hĕ'bĕl) *pr.n.m.*, Abel.

הָבְנִי (hŏbnī') *adj.*, only *pl.* הָבְנִים, made of ebony [הָבֶן].

הָבַר[1] (hābă'r) *pt.* הֹבֵר to cut, to divide [the heavens in astrology].

הָבַר[2] (hābă'r) see בָּרַר *Hi.*

הֵגֵא (hēgē') and הֵגַי (hēgă'y) *pr.n.m.*

הָגָה[1] (hāgā') *inf.* הָגֹה, *fut.* יֶהְגֶּה to murmur, mutter, growl, coo, sigh, moan, roar; to meditate, muse, speak, praise. — *Po. inf.* הֹגוֹ to speak. — *Hi. pt. pl.* מַהְגִּים to murmur, whisper, speak.

הָגָה[2] (hāgā') *inf.* הָגוֹ to separate, divide, remove.

הֶגֶה (hĕ'gĕ) *m* murmur, sighing, meditation, thought

הֹגוֹ see הָגָה¹.

הָגוּת (hāgū'ϑ) *f* meditation.

הָגִיג (hāgī'g) *m, w.s.* הֲגִיגִי sighing, musing.

הִגָּיוֹן (higgāyō'n) *m, c.* הֶגְיוֹן, murmur, gentle sound, musical accompaniment; pause; meditation, plot.

הָגִין (hāgī'n) *adj., f* הֲגִינָה, convenient, suitable.

הָגָר (hāgā'r) *pr.n.f.*

הַגְרִי (hăgrī') *pr.n.m., pl.* הַגְרִים a tribe of Arabian nomads.

הֵד (hēḏ) *m* shout of joy, exultation.

הֲדַד (haḏă'ḏ) *pr.n.m.*; also name of a Syrian deity.

הֲדַדְעֶזֶר (haḏăḏʿĕ'zĕr) *pr.n.m.*

הֲדַדְרִמּוֹן (haḏăḏrĭmmō'n) *pr.n.* of a place in the plain of Megiddo.

הָדָה (hāḏā') to stretch out [the hand].

הֹדּוּ (hō'ḏū) *pr.n.*, India.

הָדוּר (hāḏū'r) *m, pl.* הֲדוּרִים hill.

הֲדוֹרָם (haḏōrā'm) *pr.n.* of an Arabian tribe.

הִדַּי (hĭddā'y) *pr.n.m.*

הֲדֹךְ (hăḏă'ᵭ) *imp.* הֲדֹךְ to pull down.

הֲדֹם (hăḏō'm) *m. c.* הֲדֹם foot-stool.

הֲדַס (haḏă's) *m, pl.* הֲדַסִּים myrtle.

הֲדַסָּה (haḏăssā') *pr.n.f.* = Esther.

הָדַף (hāḏă'f) *inf. w.s.* הָדְפָהּ (hŏḏfā'h), *fut.* יֶהְדֹּף to push, thrust, expel, repulse.

הָדַר (hāḏă'r) *fut.* יֶהְדַּר, to adorn, to honour. — *Ni.* נֶהְדַּר to be esteemed, honoured. — *Hith. fut.* יִתְהַדַּר to boast.

הָדָר (hāḏā'r) *m, c.* הֲדַר, *w.s.* הֲדָרִי, *pl. c.* הַדְרֵי elevation, pride, highness, splendour, glory.

הֶדֶר (hĕ'ḏĕr) *m* ornament, splendour.

הֲדָרָה (haḏārā') *f, c.* הַדְרַת = הָדָר.

הֲדֹרָם (haḏōrā'm) *pr.n.m.* = אֲדֹנִירָם and אֲדֹרָם.

הֲדַרְעֶזֶר = הֲדַדְעֶזֶר.

הֲדַשְׁנָה see דָּשֵׁן *Hoth.*

הָהּ (hāh) *interj.* ah! alas!

הוֹ = הוֹי.

הוּא (hū) *pron. pers.* 3. *sg m* he, himself.

הוֹד, הֹד (hōḍ) *m* splendour, majesty, renown, ornament.

הוֹדַוְיָה (hō'ḍăvyā'); הוֹדַוְיָהוּ (hō'ḍăvyā'hū); הוֹדִיָּה (hō'ḍĭyyā'); הוֹדִיָה (hō'ḍᵉyā') *pr.n.m.*

הָוָה (hāvā') *imp.* הֱוֵה, הֱוִי, *pt.* הֹוֶה = הָיָה.

הַוָּה (hăvvā') *f, c.* הַוַּת, *w.s.* הַוָּתִי, *pl.* הַוּוֹת, passion, eagerness; destruction, corruption, wickedness.

הֹוָה (hōvā') *f* = הַוָּה.

הוֹהָם (hōhā'm) *pr.n.m.*

הוֹי (hōy) *interj.* alas! woe!

הוֹלֵלוֹת (hō'lēlō'ϑ) *f/pl.* and הוֹלֵלוּת (hō'lēlū'ϑ) *f* folly, madness.

הוֹלֶם (hō'lĕm), הֹלֶם *m* stroke of a hammer [perh. for הֹלֵם, see הָלַם].

הוּם (hūm) *pf.* הַם, *w.s.* הָמָם, to perplex, confound. — *Ni. fut.* יֵהֹם to be agitated, excited. — *Hi. fut.* יָהִים to sigh, moan, to be noisy.

הוֹמָם (hōmā'm) *pr.n.m.*

הוֹן (hōn) *m* wealth, riches, affluence; *adv.* enough, sufficiently; בְּלֹא־הוֹן for nothing.

הוּן (hūn) *Hi. fut.* יָהִין to act lightly, to make light of.

הוֹר, הֹר (hōr) *m* mountain; *pr.n.* of two mountains.

הַשִּׁיבוֹתִים — הוֹשַׁבוֹתִים, see יָשַׁב.

הוֹשָׁמָע (hō'šāmā'ᵉ); הוֹשֵׁעַ (hōšē'aᵉ), הוֹשַׁעְיָה (hō'šă'yā') *pr.n.m.*

הוּת (hūϑ) *Pil. fut.* יְהוֹתֵת to assail, rush upon.

הוֹתִיר (hōϑī'r) *pr.n.m.*

הוּתַל see תָּלַל *Ho.*

הָזָה (hāzā') *pt. pl.* הֹזִים, to be sleepy, to dream.

הֶחְבָּאתָה see חָבָא *Hi.*

הֶחֱטִי see חָטָא *Hi.*

הַט see נָטָה *Hi.*

הִי (hī) *m* lamentation.

הִיא (hī) *pron. pers.* 3. *sg. f* she, herself.

הֵידָד (hēḍā'ḍ) *m* shout of joy [in the vintage].

הֻיְּדָה (hŭyyᵉḍā') *f,* only *pl.* הֻיְּדוֹת [also הֻיְּדוּת] songs of praise, choruses.

הָיָה (hāyā') *inf.* הָיֹה, הָיוֹ, הֱיוֹת, *imp.* הֱיֵה, הֱיִי, הֱיוּ, *fut.* יִהְיֶה, וַיְהִי, יְהִי, *pt. f* הוֹיָה, to be, to exist; to become, to come to pass. — *Ni.* נִהְיָה to become, to be done, to be finished, to happen.

הַיָּה = הַוָּה.

הַיּוֹם see יוֹם.

הֵיךְ (hēḉ) *interj.* = אֵיךְ.

הֵיכָל (hēḉā'l) *m* and *f*, *c.* הֵיכַל, *pl.* הֵיכָלִים and הֵיכָלוֹת, *c.* הֵיכְלֵי, great house, palace, citadel; temple, tabernacle, sanctuary.

הֵילֵל (hēlē'l) *m* brightness, brilliant star, morning-star.

הֵימָן (hēmā'n) *pr.n.m.*

הִין (hīn) *m* a measure for liquids, $^1/_{60}$ of a חֹמֶר, or $^1/_{10}$ of a בַּת.

הִכְּךָ, הַכּוֹת, הַכֵּה, הַךְ, הִכָּנִי see נָכָה *Hi.*

הָכַר (hāḉă'r) *Hi. fut.* תַּהְכְּרוּ [for תַּהְכִּירוּ] to trouble, to do an injury.

הַכָּרָה (hăkkārā') *f*, *c.* הַכָּרַת, sight, appearance.

הַל (hăl) original form of the defin. article; as an *interrog.* part. = הֲ.

הָלָא (hālā') only *Ni. pt. f* נַהֲלָאָה, to be removed far off.

הָלְאָה (hā'lᵉā) *adv.* thither, yonderward, farther, back; further, forward.

הַלָּאוֹת see לָאָה *Hi.*

הִלּוּלִים (hĭllūlī'm) *m/pl.* rejoicings, harvest-festival, feast of thanksgiving.

הַלָּז (hăllā'z) and הַלָּזֶה (hăllāzĕ') *m* and *f* [also הַלֵּזוּ *f*] *pron. dem.* this, that.

הָלִיךְ (hālī'ḉ) *m*, only *pl.* הֲלִיכִים, step.

הֲלִיכָה (hᵃlīḉā') *f*, only *pl.* הֲלִיכוֹת, procession, march; way, caravan.

הָלַךְ (hālă'ḉ) *inf.* הָלוֹךְ, לֶכֶת, *imp.* לֵךְ, *fut.* יֵלֵךְ and יְהָלֵךְ to go, walk, come, wander, travel; to live; to go off, to disappear; to continue; הָלוֹךְ *inf.* as an *adv.* continually. — *Ni.* נֶהֱלַךְ to be gone, to vanish. — *Pi.* הִלֵּךְ, *fut.* יְהַלֵּךְ, *pt.* מְהַלֵּךְ to go about, to walk swiftly; to live. — *Hi.* הוֹלִיךְ and הֵילִיךְ, *pt. pl.* מַהְלְכִים, to cause to go, to lead, to carry away, to destroy. — *Hith.* הִתְהַלֵּךְ to go about, to walk, to lead a life.

הֵלֶךְ (hē'lĕch) *m* way, course, stream; traveller.

הָלַל¹ (hālă'l) *fut.* יָהֵל to be bright, to shine; to be splendid; to boast. — *Pi.* הִלֵּל, *imp.* הַלֵּל, הַלְלִי, הַלְלוּ [הַלְלוּ־אֵל, הַלְלוּ־יָהּ praise the Lord!] to praise, celebrate, glorify. — *Pu.* הֻלַּל, *pl. i.p.* הֻלָּלוּ, *fut.* יְהֻלַּל, *pt.* מְהֻלָּל to be praised, to be famous. — *Hi. fut. pl.* יָהֵלּוּ to cause to shine, to make bright, to give light. — *Hith. fut.* יִתְהַלֵּל to deserve praise, to be praised; to boast.

הָלַל² (hālă'l) *pt. pl.* הוֹלְלִים to be insolent, foolish, mad. — *Poel fut.* יְהוֹלֵל to befool, confound. — *Poal pt.* מְהוֹלָל to be mad, to rave. — *Hith. fut.* יִתְהוֹלֵל to be mad, to feign madness.

הִלֵּל (hĭllē'l) *pr.n.m.*

הָלַם (hālă'm) *inf.* הֲלֹם, *fut.* יַהֲלֹם, *w.s.* יֶהֶלְמֵנִי, *pt. p.* הָלוּם to strike, smite, stamp; to beat to pieces; to disperse.

הֲלֹם (hᵃlō'm) *adv.* hither, here.

הֵלֶם (hē'lĕm) *pr.n.m.*

הַלְמוּת (hălmū'ϑ) *f* hammer.

הָם (hām) or הַם (hăm) *pr.n.* of a country near the Ammonites.

הֵם¹ (hēm) or הָמֶה (hāmĕ') *m*, only *pl. w.s.* הֱמֵהֶם, bustle, multitude [= הָמוֹן].

הֵם² (hēm), הֵמָּה (hē'mmā) *pron. pers.* 3. *pl. m* [and *f*] they, themselves.

הַמְּדָתָא (hămmᵉdā'ϑā) *pr.n. m.* [Persian].

הָמָה (hāmā') *inf.* הֲמוֹת, *fut.* יֶהֱמֶה, 3. *pl.* יֶהֱמָיוּן, *cohort.* אֶהֱמָיָה, *pt. f* הֹמָה, הֹמִיָּה, *pl.* הֹמוֹת and הֹמִיּוֹת, to sound, hum, gnarl, growl, bark, coo, rustle, roar, shout; to be agitated and noisy.

הָמוֹן (hāmō'n) *m*, *c.* הֲמוֹן. *pl.* הֲמֹנִים, bustle, tumult, noise, agitation, commotion; crowd, plenty.

הֲמוֹנָה (hᵃmōnā') *pr.n.* of a town.

הֶמְיָה (hĕmyā') *f* sound.

הֵמִין = הֵימִין, see יָמַן *Hi.*

הֵמִית see מוּת.

הֲמֻלָּה (hᵃmŭllā') and הֲמוּלָּה (hᵃmūlā') *f* noise.

הָמַם (hāmă'm) [= הוּם] *fut.* יָהֹם, *w.s.* יְהֻמֵּם, to drive, agitate, trouble, confound, disturb, disperse; to undo.

הָמָן (hāmā'n) *pr.n.m.*

הָמָס (hāmā's) *m*, only *pl.* הֲמָסִים, brushwood.

הִמֵּס see מָסַס *Ni.*

הֵן[1] (hēn) *pron.*, see הֵנָּה.

הֵן[2] (hēn) *adv.* lo! behold!; *conj.* whether, if.

הֵנָּה[1] (hē'nnā) [הֵן] *pron. pers.* 3. *pl.* *f* they, themselves.

הֵנָּה[2] (hē'nnā) *adv.* hither, here.

הִנֵּה (hĭnnē') *interj.* lo! see!; *w.s.* הִנְנִי, *i.p.* הִנֵּנִי behold me! = here I am.

הֵנִיחַ, הִנִּיחַ, הֵנַח see נוּחַ *Hi.*

הֲנָחָה (hanāchā') *f* permission of rest, ease.

הִנֹּם see גַּי.

הֵנַע (hēnă'") *pr.n.* of a town in Mesopotamia.

הֲנָפָה (hanāfā') *f* a shaking; sieve.

הַס (hăs) *interj.* hist! hush! silence!

הָסָה (hāsā') *Hi. fut.* וַיַּהַס, to silence, to still.

הֵסִתָּה see סוּת *Hi.*

הֶעֱלָה, הַעַל see עָלָה *Hi.*

הֲפוּגָה (hafūgā') *f* cessation.

הָפַךְ (hāfă'ch) *inf.* הֲפֹךְ, הָפוֹךְ, *fut.* יַהֲפֹךְ, *pt.* הֹפֵךְ, *pt. p.* הָפוּךְ *tr.* and *intr.* to turn, to turn over or about, to turn back; to change, to pervert; to overturn, distroy. — *Ni.* נֶהְפַּךְ, *fut.* יֵהָפֵךְ, *pt.* נֶהְפָּךְ, to turn oneself, to be changed, perverted, overturned, destroyed. — *Ho.* הָהְפַּךְ (hŏhpă'ch) to be turned against. — *Hith. pt.* מִתְהַפֵּךְ to turn oneself, to be changed, to roll oneself.

הֶפֶךְ (hĕ'fĕch) and הֵפֶךְ (hē'fĕch) *m* the reverse, the contrary.

הֹפֶךְ (hō'fĕch) *m*, *w.s.* הָפְכְּכֶם (hŏfk'chĕ'm), perversity.

הֲפֵכָה (hafēchā') *f* overthrow, destruction.

הֲפַכְפַּךְ (hafăchpă'ch) *adj.* turned, crooked, tortuous.

הַצָּלָה (hăssālā') *f* deliverance.

הֹצֶן (hō'sĕn) *m* a weapon.

הַר (hăr) *m*, *w. loc.* ה הָרָה, הַהָרָה, *w.s.* הֲרָרִי, *pl.* הָרִים,

w. art. הֶהָרִים, *c.* הָרֵי and הַרְרֵי, mountain, hill, hilly country.

הֹר see הוֹר.

הָרָא (hārā') *pr.n.* of a district in Assyria.

הַרְאֵל (hăr'ē'l) *m* hearth, altar.

הָרֶב, הַרְבָּה, הַרְבֵּה, הַרְבּוֹת see רָבָה *Hi.*

הָרַג (hāră'g) *fut.* יַהֲרֹג, *pt.* הֹרֵג, *pt. p.* הָרוּג to kill, to murder, to slay. — *Ni. inf.* בֵּהָרֵג [for בְּהֵהָרֵג] *fut.* יֵהָרֵג to be killed. — ***Pu.*** הֹרַג to be slain.

הֶרֶג (hĕ'rĕg) *m* murder, slaughter.

הָרָה (hārā') *inf.* הָרֹה, הָרוֹ, *fut.* וַתַּהַר, תַּהֲרוֹ, *pt. f* הוֹרָה, הָרָה, *pl.* הוֹרוֹת, הָרוֹת, to conceive, to be pregnant; הוֹרִים parents. — ***Pu.*** הֹרָה to be conceived; to conceive [in mind].

הָרֶה (hārĕ') *adj.*, only *f* הָרָה [also הָרִיָּה], *c.* הָרַת, *pl.* הָרוֹת pregnant.

הֵרוֹן (hērō'n) and הֵרָיוֹן (hē'rāyō'n) *m* conception, pregnancy.

הֲרִיסָה (h^{a}rīsā') *f* a thing torn down, ruin.

הֲרִיסוּת (h^{a}rīsū'ϑ) *f* destruction.

הָרֻם (hārū'm); הֹרָם (hōrā'm) *pr.n.m.*

הַרְמוֹן (hărmō'n) = אַרְמוֹן citadel, tower [others: Hermon or Armenia].

הָרָן (hārā'n) *pr.n.m.*

הָרַס (hāră's) *imp.* הֲרָס־ (h^{a}rŏ's), *w.s.* הָרְסָה (hŏrsā'h), *fut.* יֶהֱרֹס, יַהֲרֹס, *pt.* הֹרֵס, *pt. p. w. art.* הֶהָרוּס, to pull down, to tear, break, destroy. — ***Ni.*** *fut.* יֵהָרֵס to be pulled down, to be destroyed. — ***Pi.*** *inf.* הָרֵס, *fut.* יְהָרֵס, *pt.* מְהָרֵס to tear down.

הֶרֶס (hĕ'rĕs) *m* destruction [others: lion; or = חֶרֶס sun].

הֶרֶף see רָפָה *Hi.*

הָרָר see הַר.

הֲרָרִי (h^{a}rārī'), הָרָרִי (hā'rārī') *m* mountaineer.

הָשֵׁב see שׁוּב *Hi.*

הָשֵׁם (hāsē'm) *pr.n.m.* [= יָשֵׁן].

הַשְׁמָעוּת (hăšmā'ū'ϑ) *f* announcement.

הָשַׁע see שָׁעָה Hi.
הִשְׁתַּחֲוָה see שָׁחָה Hith.
הִתְחַבְּרוּת see חָבַר Hith.
הִתְחַל see חָלָה Hith.
הֵתָיוּ see אָתָה Hi.
הֲתִימֹךְ see תָּמַם Hi.
הָתַל (hāθă'l) *Pi. fut.* יְהַתֵּל to mock, to deride.
הֵתֶל, הֵתֵל see תָּלַל Hi.
הָתֹל (hāθō'l) *m*, only *pl.* הֲתֻלִּים mockery, derision.

ו

ו the sixth letter of the alphabet, called וָו [nail, hook]; as a numeral = 6.
וְ, וַ, וָ, וּ *conj.* and, and therefore, also, then, yet.
וְדָן (vᵉḏā'n) *pr.n.* of a place in Arabia [Aden?].
וָהֵב (vāhē'ḇ) *pr.n.* of a town near the river Arnon.
וָו (vāv) *m*, only *pl.* וָוִים, *c.* וָוֵי, nail, hook.
וָזָר (vāzā'r) *m* guilt [or *adj.* guilty].
וַיְזָתָא (văyzā'θā) *pr.n.m.* [Persian].
וָלָד (vālā'ḏ) and וָלֶד (vĕ'lĕḏ) *m* child [= יֶלֶד].
וַנְיָה (vănyā'); וָפְסִי (vŏfsī'); וַשְׁנִי (văšnī') *pr.n.m.*
וַשְׁתִּי (văštī') *pr.n.f.* [Persian].

ז

ז the seventh letter of the alphabet, called זַיִן [weapon]; as a numeral = 7.
זְאֵב[1] (zᵉ'ē'ḇ) *m*, *pl.* זְאֵבִים, wolf.
זְאֵב[2] (zᵉ'ē'ḇ) *pr.n.m.*
זֹאת (zōθ) *pron. dem. f* this, that; once זֹאתָה.
זָבַד (zāḇă'ḏ) to present with.
זָבָד (zāḇā'ḏ) *pr.n.m.*
זֶבֶד (zĕ'ḇĕḏ) *m* present, gift.
זַבְדִּי (zăḇdī'); זַבְדִּיאֵל (zăḇdī'ē'l); זְבַדְיָה (zᵉḇăḏyā'), זְבַדְיָהוּ (zᵉḇăḏyā'hū) *pr.n.m.*
זְבוּב (zᵉḇū'ḇ) *m*, *pl. c.* זְבוּבֵי, fly, musquito; בַּעַל זְבוּב Lord of the flies, Beelzebub.

זָבוּד (zāḇū'ḏ) and **זַבּוּד** (zăbbū'ḏ) *pr.n.m.*

זְבוּדָה (zᵉḇūḏā') *pr.n.f.*

זְבוּל, זְבֻל (zᵉḇū'l) *m* habitation, dwelling-place.

זְבֻלוּן, זְבוּלוּן, זְבוּלֻן (zᵉḇūlū'n) *pr.n.m.* Zebulon.

זָבַח (zāḇă'ḥ) *inf.* זְבֹחַ, *imp.* זְבַח, *fut.* יִזְבַּח, *pt.* זֹבֵחַ, *pl.* זֹבְחִים to slaughter, kill, sacrifice. — *Pi.* זִבַּח, *inf.* זַבֵּחַ, *fut.* יְזַבֵּחַ, *pt.* מְזַבֵּחַ, to sacrifice [repeatedly].

זֶבַח[1] (zĕ'ḇăḥ) *m, i.p.* זָבַח, *w.s.* זִבְחִי, *pl.* זְבָחִים, *c.* זִבְחֵי [once זִבְחוֹת] slaughtering, sacrifice, victim; meal, repast.

זֶבַח[2] (zĕ'ḇăḥ) *pr.n.m.*

זַבַּי (zăbbă'y) *pr.n.m.*

זְבִידָה see זְבוּדָה.

זְבִינָא (zᵉḇīnā') *pr.n.f.*

זָבַל (zāḇă'l) *fut. w.s.* יִזְבְּלֵנִי to dwell or lie with.

זְבֻל[1] see זְבוּל.

זְבֻל[2] (zᵉḇū'l) *pr.n.m.*

זָג (zăg) *m* skin of grapes.

זֵד (zēḏ) *adj.* [or *pt.* of זוּד], *pl.* זֵדִים, proud, insolent, wanton, wicked.

זָדוֹן (zāḏō'n) *m, c* זְדוֹן, pride.

זֶה[1] (zĕ) *pron. dem. m, w. art.* הַזֶּה, this, that, such; *pron. rel. m* who, which; *adv.* here, there; מִזֶּה hence; בָּזֶה here.

זֶה[2] = שֶׂה.

זֹה (zō) = זֹאת.

זָהָב (zāhā'ḇ) *m, c.* זְהַב gold, shekel of gold; gold-coloured oil.

זָהַם (zāhă'm) *Pi.* זִהֵם to make loathsome.

זַהַם (ză'hăm) *pr.n.m.*

זָהַר (zāhă'r) *Ni.* נִזְהַר, *pt.* נִזְהָר to be enlightened or taught, to take warning — *Hi.* הִזְהִיר to enlighten, to teach, to warn; to shine.

זֹהַר (zō'hăr) *m* brightness.

זִו, זִיו (zīv) *m* brightness of flowers; month of flowers [May].

זוֹ = זֹה, זֹאת.

זוּ (zū) *pron. dem.* and *rel. m* and *f* = זֶה and זֹאת.

זוּב (zūḇ) *pf.* and *pt.* זָב, *f* זָבָה, *c.* זָבַת, *fut.* יָזוּב to flow, to flow abundantly;

to have a flux of blood; to melt, to pine away.

זוֹב (zōb) *m* monthly courses; gonorrhœa.

זוּד (zūd) [זִיד] to seethe; to be proud, arrogant. — *Hi.* הֵזִיד, *fut.* יָזִיד, וַיָּזֶד to cause to boil, to cook; to act proudly, wickedly.

זוּזִים (zūzī'm) *pr.n.m. pl.* tribe of gigantic aborigines in Palestine.

זוֹחֵת (zōḥē'θ) *pr.n.m.*

זָוִית (zāvī'θ) *f,* only *pl.* זָוִיּוֹת corner [of an altar], corner-pillar.

זוּל (zūl) *pt.* זָל to pour out, to lavish.

זוּלָה (zūlā') *f, c.* זוּלַת, *w.s.* זוּלָתִי removal; *prep.* besides, except.

זוּן (zūn) *Ho. pt.* מוּזָן to be well fed.

זוֹנָה — זֹנָה see זָנָה.

זוּעַ (zū'a) to move oneself, to tremble. — *Pi. pt.* מְזַעְזֵעַ to agitate, to vex.

זְוָעָה (zᵉvā'ā') *f* terror, vexation.

זוּר (zūr) *pf.* זָר, *pl.* זָרוּ and זֹרוּ [or from זָרַר], *fut.* יָזוּר, יָזֻר, *pt. p. f* זוּרָה [for זוּרָה] to press together, to press out, to bind up, to crush, to squeeze; to recede, to retreat, to turn away; *pt.* זָר strange, stranger, foreigner, adulterous. — *Ni.* נָזוֹר to turn away. — *Ho. pt.* מוּזָר to be estranged.

זוּרֶה (zūrĕ') *adj. f* crushed [see זוּר].

זָזָא (zāzā') *pr.n.m.*

זָחַח (zāḥă'ḥ) *Ni. fut.* יִזַּח to be displaced.

זָחַל (zāḥă'l) *pt.* זֹחֵל, *pi. c.* זֹחֲלֵי, to creep, crawl; to steal off timidly.

זֹחֶלֶת (zōḥĕ'lĕθ) *f* serpent, reptile [in the *pr.n.* אֶבֶן הַזֹּחֶלֶת].

זֵידוֹן (zēdō'n) *adj.* seething, swelling, raging.

זִיז (zīz) *m* fulness; what moves and lives, animal.

זִיזָא, זִיזָה (zīzā'); זִינָה (zīnā'); זִיעַ (zī'a); זִיף[1] (zīf) *pr.n.m.*

זִיף[2] (zīf) *pr.n.* of a town in Judah; *gent.* זִיפִי.

זִיפָה (zīfā') *pr.n.m.*

זִיקוֹת, זִיקִים see זֵק.

זַיִת (ză'yīθ) *m, i.p.* זָיִת, *c.*

זַיִת, *pl.* זֵיתִים, olive-tree, olive, olive-branch, olive-oil; הַר הַזֵּיתִים the Mount of Olives.

זֵיתָן (zē̦ϑā'n) *pr.n.m.*

זַךְ (zăφ) *adj.*, *i.p.* זָךְ, *f* זַכָּה, transparent, clear, pure, innocent.

זָכָה (zāφā') *fut.* יִזְכֶּה to be transparent, clear, pure, innocent. — *Pi.* זִכָּה, *fut.* יְזַכֶּה to cleanse, purify. — *Hith.* הִזַּכָּה to cleanse oneself.

זְכוּכִית (zᵉφūφī'ϑ) *f* glass, crystal.

זָכוּר (zāφū'r) *adj.*, *w.s.* זְכוּרְךָ, born as a male, *coll.* males.

זַכּוּר (zăkkū'r); זַכַּי (zăkkă'y) *pr.n.m.*

זָכַךְ (zāφă'φ) to shine, to be bright, pure. — *Hi.* הֵזַךְ to cleanse.

זָכַר (zāφă'r) *inf.* זָכֹר, זְכֹר, *imp.* זְכֹר, *fut.* יִזְכֹּר to pierce; to impress [on the memory], to remember, recollect, mention. — *Ni.* נִזְכַּר, *fut.* יִזָּכֵר to be remembered, mentioned; to be born as a male [from זָכָר]. — *Hi.* הִזְכִּיר, *inf.* הַזְכִּיר, *fut.* יַזְכִּיר, *pt.* מַזְכִּיר to bring to remembrance, to mention, to record [*pt.* historiographer]; to praise, to offer praise, to burn incense.

זָכָר (zāφā'r) *m*, *pl.* זְכָרִים, a male [of men and animals], man.

זֵכֶר (zē̦'φĕr), זֶכֶר[1] (zĕ'φĕr) *m*, *w.s.* זִכְרִי, remembrance, memory; memorial, fame, praise.

זֶכֶר[2] (zĕ'φĕr) *pr.n.m.*

זִכָּרוֹן (zĭkkārō̦'n) *m*, *c.* זִכְרוֹן, *w.s.* זִכְרוֹנְךָ, *pl.* זִכְרֹנִים and זִכְרֹנוֹת, memorial, remembrance, record, account; memorable saying; celebration.

זִכְרִי (zĭφrī') *pr.n.m*

זְכַרְיָה (zᵉφăryā') and זְכַרְיָהוּ (zᵉφăryā'hū) *pr.n.m.*

זֻלּוּת (zŭllū'ϑ) *f* baseness.

זַלְזַל (zălză'l) *m*, only *pl.* זַלְזַלִּים, shoot, twig.

זָלַל (zālă'l) *pt.* זוֹלֵל to be a glutton, to squander, to debauch; to be mean, miserable, despised. — *Ni.* נָזֹל to be shaken, to quake. — *Hi.* הֵזִיל to despise.

זַלְעָפָה (zăl'ăfā') *f, pl.* זַלְעָפוֹת, *c.* זַלְעֲפוֹת, hot wind, heat.

זִלְפָּה (zĭlpā') *pr.n.f.*

זִמָּה (zĭmmā') *f, c.* זִמַּת, plan, counsel; evil deed, lewdness, incest, apostasy.

זְמוֹרָה (zᵉmōrā') *f, c.* זְמֹרַת, *pl.* זְמֹרִים, vine-twig, shoot, branch.

זַמּוֹתִי see זָמַם.

זַמְזֹם (zămzō'm) *pr.n.*, only *pl.* זַמְזֻמִּים, a tribe of gigantic aborigines in the country of the Ammonites.

זָמִיר (zāmī'r) *m* vine-cutting.

זְמִיר (zᵉmī'r) *m, pl.* זְמִרוֹת, song, hymn, song of praise or triumph.

זְמִירָה (zᵉmīrā') *pr.n.m.*

זָמַם (zāmă'm) *pf.* 1. *sg.* זַמֹּתִי and זַמֹּתִי, *inf.* זַמּוֹת, *fut.* יָזֹם, *pl.* יָזְמוּ [for יָזֹמּוּ], *pt.* זֹמֵם, to muse, meditate, think, devise, resolve, plot.

זָמָם (zāmā'm) *m, w.s.* זְמָמוֹ plan, plot.

זָמַן (zāmă'n) *Pu. pt.* מְזֻמָּן to be appointed, determined.

זְמָן (zᵉmā'n) *m, pl.* זְמַנִּים, determined time.

זָמַר (zāmă'r) to cut off, to pinch off [vines]. — *Ni. fut.* יִזָּמֵר to be pruned. — *Pi.* זִמֵּר, *inf.* and *imp.* זַמֵּר, *fut.* יְזַמֵּר, to harp on chords, to play, sing, praise, celebrate.

זֶמֶר (zĕ'mĕr) *m* an unknown animal, wild goat, gazelle or antelope.

זִמְרָה (zĭmrā') and זִמְרָת (zĭmrā'ϑ) *f, c.* זִמְרַת, *pl.* זְמִרוֹת, music, song, praise, object of praise, choice things.

זִמְרִי (zĭmrī'); זִמְרָן (zĭmrā'n) *pr.n.m.*

זַן (zăn) *m, pl.* זְנִים, species, sort, kind.

זָנַב (zānă'b) *Pi.* זִנֵּב [from זָנָב] to beat or destroy the rear.

זָנָב (zānā'b) *m, w.s.* זְנָבוֹ, *pl.* זְנָבוֹת, *c.* זַנְבוֹת, tail, end, stump; something mean.

זָנָה (zānā') *inf.* זָנֹה, זְנוֹת, *fut. f* תִּזְנֶה, וַתִּזֶן, *pt.* זֹנֶה, *f* זֹנָה, *pl.* זֹנִים, זֹנוֹת, to fornicate, to whore, to commit adultery; *pt. f* זֹנָה, זוֹנָה harlot; to apostatise, to commit idolatry, to have intercourse with false gods or foreigners. — *Pu.* זוּנָּה whoring is committed. — *Hi.* הִזְנָה, *inf. w.s.* לְהַזְנוֹתָהּ, to seduce to whoredom, to commit fornication.

זָנוֹחַ (zānō'ah) *pr.n.* of two places.

זְנוּנִים (zenūnī'm) *m/pl.* whoredom, idolatry, intercourse with foreigners.

זְנוּת (zenū'th) *f, pl.* זְנוּתִים, idolatry, apostasy, unfaithfulness.

זָנַח (zānă'ḥ) *fut.* יִזְנַח to reject. — *Hi.* הִזְנִיחַ, הֶאֱזְנִיחַ to reject, profane; to cause or produce stench; to be dried up [a river].

זִנֵּק (zānă'k) *Pi. fut.* יְזַנֵּק to leap forth.

זֵעָה (zēʿā') *f, c.* זֵעַת sweat.

זַעֲוָה (zăʿavā') *f* [for זְוָעָה] terror, vexation.

זַעֲוָן (zăʿavā'n) *pr.n.m.*

זְעֵיר (zeʿē'r) *m* a little, a trifle; *adv.* a little while.

זָעַךְ (zāʿă'kh) *Ni.* נִזְעַךְ to be extinguished.

זָעַם (zāʿă'm) *imp.* זָעֲמָה, זָעֳמָה (zŏʿomā'), *fut.* יִזְעֹם, *pt.* זֹעֵם to be irritated or angry; to punish, to curse. — *Ni. pt.* נִזְעָם to be angry, black-browed.

זַעַם (zăʿă'm) *m, i.p.* זָעַם, *w.s.* זַעְמִי, anger, wrath, rage.

זָעַף (zāʿă'f) *pt. pl.* זֹעֲפִים, to be angry, to look sorrowful or sullen.

זָעֵף (zāʿē'f) *adj.* angry, irritated.

זַעַף (zăʿă'f) *m, w.s.* זַעְפּוֹ anger, rage, raging [of the sea].

זָעַק (zāʿă'k) *inf.* זְעֹק, *imp.* זְעַק, *fut.* יִזְעַק, to cry, lament, implore. — *Ni.* נִזְעַק, *fut.* יִזָּעֵק to be called together, to assemble. — *Hi. inf.* הַזְעִיק, *imp.* הַזְעֵק, *fut.* יַזְעֵק to cry; to call together.

זַעַק (zăʿă'k) *m* and **זְעָקָה** (zeʿākā') *f, c.* זַעֲקַת outcry, complaint, lamentation.

זִפְרוֹן (zifrō'n) *pr.n.* of a town in northern Palestine.

זֶפֶת (zĕ'fĕth) *f, i.p.* זָפֶת, pitch.

זֵק (zē'k) *m*, only *pl.* זִקִּים and זִיקוֹת, fetter, chain; burning dart, fiery arrow

זָקָן (zăkā'n) *m* and *f*, *c.* זְקַן, *w.s.* זְקָנוֹ chin, beard.

זָקֵן[1] (zăkē'n) *fut.* יִזְקַן, to be or grow old. — *Hi. fut.* יַזְקִין to grow old.

זָקֵן[2] (zăkē'n) *adj.*, *c.* זְקַן, *pl.* זְקֵנִים, *c.* זִקְנֵי, old, aged; *m* old man, elder, senator.

זֹקֶן (zō'kĕn) *m* old age.

זִקְנָה (zĭknā') *f* and זְקֻנִים *m/pl.* old age.

זָקַף (zăkă'f) *pt.* זֹקֵף to lift up, to raise.

זָקַק (zăkă'k) *Pi.* זִקֵּק to purify, refine. — *Pu.* זֻקַּק, *pt.* מְזֻקָּק to be purified, refined.

זָר (zăr) *adj.* [*pt.* of זוּר], *f* זָרָה, *pl.* זָרִים, strange, alien, foreign.

זֵר (zēr) *m* border, ledge, edge.

זָרָא (zărā') *m* something loathsome.

זָרַב (zără'b) *Pu.* *fut.* יְזֹרֲבוּ to be made to flow [others: to be heated].

זְרֻבָּבֶל (zᵉrŭbbābĕ'l) *pr.n.m.*

זֶרֶד (zĕ'rĕd) *pr.n.*, *i.p.* זָרֶד, brook or valley in Moab.

זָרָה (zărā') *inf.* זְרוֹת, *imp.* זְרֵה, *fut.* יִזְרֶה, וַיִּזֶר, *pt.* זֹרֶה to scatter, to winnow. — *Ni. inf.* הִזָּרוֹת to be scattered. — *Pi.* זֵרָה, *inf.* זָרוֹת, *fut.* יְזָרֶה, *pt.* מְזָרֶה to scatter, disperse; to winnow, sift. — *Pu.* זֹרָה, *pt.* זֹרֶה [for מְזֹרֶה] to be strawn, to be spread out.

זְרֹעַ, **זְרוֹעַ** (zᵉrō'aᵉ) *f* and *m*, *w.s.* זְרֹעִי, *pl.* זְרֹעִים, זְרֹעוֹת, *c.* זְרֹעֵי the arm, the lower arm, shoulder [of animals]; strength, power, might, army; violence; help.

זֵרוּעַ (zērō'aᵉ) and זֵרוּעַ (zērū'aᵉ) *m*, *pl.* זֵרֹעִים, זֵרוּעִים, things sown, garden herbs.

זַרְזִיף (zărzī'f) *m* heavy shower.

זַרְזִיר (zărzī'r) *m* girded.

זָרַח (zără'ḥ) *inf.* זְרֹחַ, *fut.* יִזְרַח to flash up, to shine forth, to rise [of the sun]; to break out, to grow up, to bloom.

זֶרַח[1] (zĕ'răḥ) *m*, *w.s.* זַרְחֵךְ, sun-rise.

זֶרַח[2] (zĕ'răḥ) *pr.n.m.*; *patron.* זַרְחִי.

זְרַחְיָה (zᵉrăḥyā') *pr.n.m.*

זָרַם (zārā'm) to wash away. — *Po.* זֹרַם to pour out.

זֶרֶם (zĕ'rĕm) *m, i.p.* זָרֶם, shower of rain, flood, hail-storm.

זִרְמָה (zĭrmā') *f* emission [of seed].

זָרַע (zārā'') *inf.* זְרֹעַ, *imp.* זְרַע, *fut.* יִזְרַע, *pt.* זֹרֵעַ, *pt. p.* זָרוּעַ to scatter, to strew seed, to sow, to plant. — *Ni.* נִזְרַע, *fut.* יִזָּרַע to be sown, to be scattered, to be propagated. — *Pu.* זֹרַע to be sown. — *Hi. fut.* יַזְרִיעַ, *pt.* מַזְרִיעַ to yield seed; to conceive seed.

זֶרַע (zĕ'rā') *m, i.p.* זָרַע, *c.* זֶרַע and זְרַע, *w.s.* זַרְעִי, *pl. w.s.* זַרְעֵיכֶם sowing; seed, corn, crop; issue, progeny, posterity, family, race.

זֵרָעוֹן (zē'rā'ō'n) *m*, only *pl.* זֵרְעֹנִים, vegetables.

זָרַק (zārā'k) *fut.* יִזְרֹק to scatter, strew, sprinkle; *intr.* to be sprinkled. — *Pu.* זֹרַק to be sprinkled.

זָרַר[1] (zārā'r) *Po. fut.* יְזוֹרֵר to sneeze.

זָרַר[2] (zārā'r) *pf. pl.* זֹרוּ [or from זור] to be pressed out.

זֶרֶשׁ (zĕ'rĕš) *pr.n.f.* [Persian].

זֶרֶת (zĕ'rĕϑ) *f* span [others: the little finger].

זַתּוּא (zāttū'); **זֵתָם** (zēϑā'm); **זֵתַר** [Persian] (zēϑā'r) *pr.n.m.*

ח

ח the eighth letter of the alphabet, called חֵית [fence]; as a numeral = 8.

חֹב (ḥōḇ) *m, w.s.* חֻבִּי bosom.

חָבָא (ḥāḇā') and חָבָה, *imp. m* חֲבִי [for חֲבֵה] to hide oneself. — *Ni.* נֶחְבָּא, 2. *sg. m* נַחְבֵּאתָ, *inf.* הֵחָבֵה, *fut.* יֵחָבֵא, *pt. pl.* נֶחְבְּאִים to conceal oneself, to be hidden; to step back. — *Pu.* חֻבָּא to hide oneself. — *Hi.* הֶחְבִּיא, *fut.* וַיַּחְבִּא, to hide, conceal. — *Ho.* הָחְבָּא (hŏḥbā') to be hidden. — *Hith.* הִתְחַבֵּא to hide or conceal oneself.

חָבַב (ḥāḇā'ḇ) *pt.* חֹבֵב to love, to cherish.

חֹבָב (ḥōḇā'ḇ) *pr.n.m.*

חָבָה see חָבָא.

חָבוֹר (ḥāḇō'r) *pr.n.* of a tributary of the Euphrates.

חַבּוּרָה (ḥᵃḇūrā') and חַבּוּרָה (ḥăbbūrā') *f* stripe, wound.

חָבַט (ḥāḇă'ṭ) *fut.* יַחְבֹּט, *pt.* חֹבֵט to knock, to strike, to beat out. — *Ni. fut.* יֵחָבֵט to be beaten out.

חֲבָיָה (ḥᵃḇāyā') *pr.n.m.*

חֶבְיוֹן (ḥĕḇyō'n) *m* a hiding, covering, tent, hut.

חָבַל[1] (ḥāḇă'l) *fut.* יַחְבֹּל, יַחְבֹּל, *pt. p.* חָבוּל, to bind, to pledge. — *Ni. fut.* יֵחָבֵל to be pledged. — *Pi.* חִבֵּל, *fut.* יְחַבֵּל to labour in childbirth, to bring forth with pain.

חָבַל[2] (ḥāḇă'l) *inf.* חֲבֹל, *fut.* יַחְבֹּל to act perversely. — *Ni. fut.* יֵחָבֵל to be injured, destroyed. — *Pi. inf.* חַבֵּל, *fut.* יְחַבֵּל to injure, ravage, destroy. — *Pu.* חֻבַּל to be broken, to be diminished.

חֵבֶל (ḥē'ḇĕl) *m, pl.* חֲבָלִים, *c.* חֶבְלֵי pain, pains of birth.

חֶבֶל (ḥĕ'ḇĕl) *m* [once *f*], *pl* חֲבָלִים, *c.* חַבְלֵי and חֶבְלֵי, cord, rope, line, snare; measuring-line, portion of land, district; troop, band of men.

חֲבֹל (ḥᵃḇō'l) *m* and **חֲבֹלָה** (ḥᵃḇōlā') *f* a pledge.

חִבֵּל (ḥĭbbē'l) *m* rope, cable [others: mast or helm].

חֹבֵל (ḥōḇē'l) *m, pl. c.* חֹבְלֵי, sailor, shipman, *coll.* crew.

חֲבַצֶּלֶת (ḥᵃḇăṣṣĕ'lĕṯ) *f* a flower, lily, daffodil, crocus or meadow-saffron.

חֲבַצִּנְיָה (ḥᵃḇăṣṣĭnyā') *pr. n.m.*

חָבַק (ḥāḇă'k) *pt. f* חֹבֶקֶת, to embrace. — *Pi. inf.* חַבֵּק, *fut.* יְחַבֵּק to embrace, clasp, hug.

חִבֻּק (ḥĭbbū'k) *m* folding of the hands.

חֲבַקּוּק (ḥᵃḇăkkū'k) *pr.n.m.*

חָבַר (ḥāḇă'r) *pt.* חֹבֵר, *pt. p.* חָבוּר to be bound together, to be united; to conjure, charm, fascinate. — *Pi.* חִבֵּר, *inf.* חַבֵּר, *fut.* יְחַבֵּר to bind, unite. — *Pu.* חֻבַּר, *fut.* יְחֻבַּר, *w.s.* יְחָבְרְךָ (yᵉḥŏbrᵉḵā') [or for *Q.* יַחְבָרְךָ], to be joined, to be bound together. — *Hi.* הֶחְבִּיר to string together, to compose. — *Hith.* הִתְחַבֵּר [once אֶתְחַבַּר] to unite oneself.

חָבָר (ḥāḇā'r) *m*, *pl.* חֲבָרִים, conjurer, sorcerer.

חַבָּר (ḥăbbā'r) *m*, *pl.* חַבָּרִים, an associate.

חָבֵר (ḥāḇē'r) *adj.*, *pl.* חֲבֵרִים, *c.* חַבְרֵי, *f* חֲבֵרָה, *c.* חֲבֶרֶת joined, united; associate, companion, friend.

חֶבֶר[1] (ḥĕ'ḇĕr) *m*, *pl.* חֲבָרִים, community, company, society; spell, charm, enchantment.

חֶבֶר[2] (ḥĕ'ḇĕr) [חֵבֶר] *pr.n.m.*; *patr.* חֶבְרִי.

חֲבַרְבֻּרָה (ḥaḇărbūrā') *f*, only *pl.* חֲבַרְבֻּרוֹת, stripe, streak.

חֶבְרָה (ḥĕḇrā') *f* society, company.

חֲבֻרָה see חַבּוּרָה.

חֶבְרוֹן (ḥĕḇrō'n) *pr.n.* of a town in Judah; also *pr.n.m.*, *patr.* חֶבְרוֹנִי.

חֲבֶרֶת (ḥaḇĕ'rĕϑ) *f*, see חָבֵר.

חֹבֶרֶת (ḥōḇĕ'rĕϑ) *f* joining, junction.

חָבַשׁ (ḥāḇă's) *inf.* חֲבֹשׁ, *imp.* חֲבוֹשׁ, *fut.* יַחֲבֹשׁ and יֶחְבַּשׁ, *pt.* חֹבֵשׁ, *pt. p.* חָבוּשׁ to bind on, to wrap round; to bind up [a wound], חֹבֵשׁ surgeon; to saddle; to cover, envelop, enclose; to govern, rule. — *Pi.* חִבֵּשׁ, *pt.* מְחַבֵּשׁ to bind up, to restrain. — *Pu.* חֻבַּשׁ to be bound up.

חָבֵת (ḥāḇē'ϑ) *m*, only *pl.* חֲבִתִּים, baked things, pastry.

חָג (ḥāg), חַג (ḥăg) *m*, *c.* חַג, *w. art.* הֶחָג, *w.s.* חַגִּי, *pl.* חַגִּים, *c.* חַגֵּי, festival, feast.

חָגָּא (ḥŏggā') [for חָגָּה] *f* fear, trembling.

חָגָב[1] (ḥāgā'ḇ) *m*, *pl.* חֲגָבִים [eatable] locust.

חָגָב[2] (ḥāgā'ḇ) *pr.n.m.*

חֲגָבָא, חֲגָבָה (ḥagāḇā') *pr.n.m.*

חָגַג (ḥāgă'g) *inf.* חֹג, *imp.* *f* חָגִּי (ḥŏggī') *fut.* יָחֹג, *pl.* יָחוֹגּוּ, *pt.* חוֹגֵג to dance, to move in a procession, to keep a festival; to reel, to be giddy.

חֲגָו (ḥagā'v), חָגוּ (ḥāgū') *m*, only *pl.* חַגְוֵי, ravine, cleft.

חָגוֹר (ḥāgō'r) *adj.*, *pl. c.* חֲגוֹרֵי, girded.

חֲגוֹר (ḥᵃgō'r) *m* girdle.

חֲגוֹרָה (ḥᵃgōrā') *f*, *w.s.* חֲגוֹרָתִי, *pl.* חֲגֹרֹת, girdle. apron.

חַגַּי (ḥăggă'y); חַגִּי (ḥăggī'); חַגִּיָּה (ḥăggīyyā') *pr.n.m.*

חַגִּית (ḥăggī'ϑ) *pr.n.f.*

חָגְלָה (ḥŏglā') *pr.n.f.*

חָגַר (ḥāgă'r) *inf.* חֲגֹר, *imp.* חֲגוֹר, חִגְרוּ, *fut.* יַחְגֹּר, יַחְגֹר, *pt.* חֹגֵר, *pt. p.* חָגוּר, *w. art.* הֶחָגוּר, to bind about, to gird, to put on.

חַד (ḥăd) *adj.*, *f* חַדָּה, sharp.

חָדַד (ḥādă'd) *fut.* יַחַד to be sharp; to be quick. — *Hi. fut.* יַחַד to sharpen. — *Ho.* הוּחַד to be sharpened.

חֲדַד (ḥᵃdă'd) *pr.n.m.*

חָדָה (ḥādā') *fut.* וַיִּחַדְּ to be glad, to rejoice. — *Pi. fut.* יְחַדֶּה to gladden, to cheer.

חַדּוּד (ḥăddū'd) *m*, only *pl.* חַדּוּדִים, sharp point.

חֶדְוָה (ḥĕdvā') *f* joy.

חָדִיד (ḥādī'd) *pr.n.* of a town in Benjamin.

חָדַל (ḥādă'l), חָדֵל[1] (ḥādē'l), *w. interrog.* ה הֶחֳדַלְתִּי, *inf.* חֲדֹל, *imp.* חֲדַל, *pl.* חִדְלוּ, *fut.* יֶחְדַּל, *pl.* יַחְדְּלוּ, to cease, to leave off; to abstain, refrain, desist; to quiet, resign; to rest.

חָדֵל[2] (ḥādē'l) *adj.*, *c.* חֲדַל, ceasing, failing, forsaken, forbearing.

חֶדֶל (ḥĕ'dĕl) *m*, *i.p.* חָדֶל, resting-place of the dead, grave.

חַדְלַי (ḥădlă'y) *pr.n.m.*

חֵדֶק (ḥē'dĕ**k**), חֶדֶק (ḥĕ'dĕ**k**) *m* a thorn, thorn-bush.

חִדֶּקֶל (ḥĭddĕ'**k**ĕl) *pr.n.*, the river Tigris.

חָדַר (ḥādă'r) *pt. f* חֹדֶרֶת, to enclose, to assault.

חֶדֶר (ḥĕ'dĕr) *m*, *i.p.* חָדֶר, *w. loc.* ה חַדְרָה, *w. art. i.p.* הֶחָדְרָה, *c.* חֲדַר, *pl.* חֲדָרִים, *c.* חַדְרֵי appartment, chamber, sleeping-room, bride-chamber; recess, inmost part.

חַדְרָךְ (ḥădrā'ḵ) *pr.n.*, either a Syrian king, or a town and district near Damascus.

חָדַשׁ (ḥādă's) *Pi.* חִדֵּשׁ, *imp.* חַדֵּשׁ, *fut.* יְחַדֵּשׁ, to renew, restore. — *Hith.* הִתְחַדֵּשׁ to renew oneself, to make oneself young again.

חָדָשׁ (ḥādā'š) *adj.*, *w. art.* הֶחָדָשׁ, *f* חֲדָשָׁה, *pl.* חֲדָשִׁים, חֲדָשׁוֹת, new, fresh, young, renewed, unusual; unheard of news; new sword.

חֹדֶשׁ (ḥō'dĕš) *m* [once *f*], *w.s.* חָדְשׁוֹ (ḥŏdšō'), *pl.* חֳדָשִׁים (ḥodāšī'm), *w. art.* הֶחֳדָשִׁים, *c.* חָדְשֵׁי (ḥŏdšē'), new moon, day of the new moon; month.

חָדְשִׁי (ḥŏdšī') *pr.n.* of a district near Lake Gennezaret.

חוּב (ḥūb) *Pi.* חִיֵּב to make guilty.

חוֹב (ḥōb) *m* debt.

חוֹבָה (ḥōbā') *pr.n.* of a place north of Damascus.

חוּג[1] (ḥūg) *pf.* חָג, to describe a circle, to enclose.

חוּג[2] (ḥūg) *m* circle, horizon, the vault of heaven.

חוּד (ḥūd) *pf.* חָד, *imp.* חוּדָה, *fut.* יָחוּד, to propose a riddle or a parable.

חָוָה (ḥāvā') *Pi. fut.* יְחַוֶּה, to announce, relate.

חַוָּה[1] (ḥăvvā') *f*, *pl.* חַוֹּת (ḥăvvō'th), tent, village of nomads.

חַוָּה[2] (ḥăvvā') *pr.n.f.* of the first woman, Eve [= life].

חוֹזַי (ḥōză'y) *pr.n.m.*

חוֹחַ (ḥō'aḥ) *m*, *pl.* חוֹחִים and חֲוָחִים, hook; thorn, thorn-bush; fissure, cleft.

חוּט (ḥūṭ) *m* thread, measuring-line, cord.

חִוִּי (ḥĭvvī') *pr.n.m.* of a Canaanitic tribe, Hivites.

חֲוִילָה (ḥavīlā') *pr.n.* of a country in northern Arabia.

חוּל[1] (ḥūl), חִיל (ḥīl) *pf.* חָל, *inf.* חוּל, *imp.* חוּלִי, חִילוּ, *fut.* יָחוּל, יָחֹל, יָחִיל, וַיָּחֶל, to turn in a circle, to whirl, twist, writhe; to be in labour [of child-birth]; to be afraid, to tremble, to reel; to wait, hope; to revolve, to rage, to assault, to be strong or pithy. — *Pi.* חוֹלֵל, *fut.* יְחוֹלֵל, *pt.* מְחוֹלֵל to dance in a circle; to bear a child, to produce; to cause to bring forth; to hope, wait. — *Pu.* חוֹלַל to be born. — *Hi.* הֵחִיל, *fut.* יָחִיל to cause to tremble; to twist, shake, tremble; to wait anxiously; to be in labour. — *Ho. fut.* יוּחַל

to be born.—*Hith.* הִתְחוֹלֵל to writhe with pain; to whirl oneself; to wait, hope. — *Hithpalp. fut.* יִתְחַלְחַל to be terrified, grieved.

חוּל[2] (ḥūl) *pr.n.* of an Aramæan district.

חוֹל (ḥōl) *m* sand.

חוּם (ḥūm) *adj.* sunburnt, black.

חוֹמָה (ḥōmā') [חֹמָה] *f,* c. חוֹמַת, *pl.* חוֹמוֹת, *du.* חֹומוֹתַיִם, enclosure, wall; chaste maiden.

חוּס (ḥūs) *pt.* חָס, *imp.* חוּסָה, *fut.* יָחוּס, יָחֹס, וַיָּחָס (văyyā'ḥŏs) to commiserate, to pity, to spare.

חוֹף [חֹף] (ḥōf) *m* coast, shore.

חוּפָם (ḥūfā'm) [חוּפִּים] *pr. n.m.*; *patr.* חוּפָמִי.

חוּץ (ḥūs) *m, w. loc.* ה חוּצָה, הַחוּצָה, *pl.* חוּצוֹת, חֻצוֹת outside, exterior, street, lane, field; *adv.* without, outside; מִחוּץ from without [opp. מִבַּיִת]; except.

חוֹק (ḥōk) *m* bosom.

חָוַר (ḥāvă'r) *fut. i.p.* יֶחֱוָרוּ, to be white, to grow pale.

חוֹר, חוֹרִי see חֹר, חֹרִי.

חוּר[1], חֻר (ḥūr) *m* fine white linen or cotton, white cloth, byssus.

חוּר[2] (ḥūr) *m* hole, prison.

חוּר[3] (ḥūr) *pr.n.m.*

חוּרָי = חוּר[1].

חוּרִי (ḥūrī') *pr.n.m.*

חוּרָם (ḥūrā'm) *pr.n.m.* = חִירָם, חִירֹם.

חַוְרָן (ḥăvrā'n) *pr.n.* of a district south of Damascus, Auranitis.

חוּשׁ (ḥūš) [חִישׁ] *pf.* חָשׁ, *inf.* חוּשׁ, *imp.* חוּשָׁה, *fut.* יָחוּשׁ, וַתָּחַשׁ, to make haste, to flee, to hasten to, *pt. p.* חוּשׁ hasty; to feel, to be affected.—*Hi. fut.* יָחִישׁ to cause to haste, to haste, to flee, to do quickly.

חוּשָׁה (ḥūšā'); חוּשַׁי (ḥūšă'y); חוּשִׁים (ḥūšī'm); חוּשָׁם (ḥūšā'm) *pr.n.m.*

חוֹתָם[1], חֹתָם (ḥōϑā'm) *m* seal, signet-ring.

חוֹתָם[2] (ḥōϑā'm) *pr.n.m.*

חֲזָהאֵל, חֲזָאֵל (ḥᵃzā'ēl) *pr.n.m.* of a king of Syria.

חָזָה (ḥāzā') *inf.* חֲזוֹת, *imp.* חֲזֵה, *fut.* יֶחֱזֶה, וַיִּחַז, *pt.*

חָזָה, *pl.* חֹזִים to split, divide; to see, look, behold, observe, gaze; to select; to prophesy.

חָזֶה (ḥāzĕ') *m*, *c.* חֲזֵה, *pl.* חָזוֹת, middle part or breast of animals.

חֹזֶה (ḥōzĕ') *m* [*pt.* of חָזָה], *c.* חֹזֵה, a seer, prophet, astrologer; covenant.

חֲזוֹ (ḥᵃzō') *pr.n.m.*

חָזוֹן (ḥāzō'n) *m*, *c.* חֲזוֹן, vision, revelation, prophecy.

חָזוֹת (ḥāzō'ϑ) *f*, *c.* חֲזוֹת, vision, revelation.

חָזוּת (ḥāzū'ϑ) *f* appearance, conspicuousness; vision, revelation; covenant.

חָזִיז (ḥāzī'z) *m*, *c.* חֲזִיז, bolt, flash of lightning.

חֲזִיר (ḥᵃzī'r) *m* swine, boar.

חֵזִיר (ḥēzī'r) *pr.n.m.*

חָזַק (ḥāză'k) *inf.* חָזְקָה (ḥŏzkā'), *imp.* חֲזַק, חִזְקוּ, *fut.* יֶחֱזַק, יֶחְזַק to be bound fast, to be attached; to make firm, to support, preserve; to be firm, strong, courageous; to conquer, to hold fast. — *Pi.* חַזֵּק, *inf.* and *imp.* חַזֵּק, *fut.* יְחַזֵּק to bind fast, to gird; to make firm, to encourage; to strengthen, support; to harden, obdurate. — *Hi.* הֶחֱזִיק, *inf.* הַחֲזִיק, בְּהַחֲזִיק, *fut.* יַחֲזִיק, *pt.* מַחֲזִיק to make firm, to strengthen; to hold fast, to seize, to retain, to keep; to be strong, firm; to be attached. — *Hith.* הִתְחַזֵּק to be confirmed; to prove courageous, valiant, helpful.

חָזָק (ḥāzā'k) *adj.*, *w. art.* הֶחָזָק, *pl.* חֲזָקִים, *c.* חִזְקֵי, *f* חֲזָקָה strong, firm, valiant; sound, powerful, violent, hard.

חָזֵק (ḥāzē'k) *adj.* = חָזָק.

חֵזֶק (ḥē'zĕk) *m*, *w.s.* חִזְקִי, strength, might, help.

חֹזֶק (ḥō'zĕk) *m* = חֵזֶק.

חֶזְקָה (ḥĕzkā') *f*, *c.* חֶזְקַת, the growing strong, strength, the overcoming.

חָזְקָה (ḥŏzkā') *f* a strengthening, repairing; force, violence, severity; בְּחָזְקָה violently.

חִזְקִי (ḥīzkī'); חִזְקִיָּה (ḥīzkīyyā') and חִזְקִיָּהוּ (ḥīzkīyyā'hū) [Hezekiah] *pr.n.m.*

חָח (ḥāḥ) *m, w.s.* חַחִי, *pl.* חַחִים, *c.* חַחֵי [= חוֹחַ] hook, brooch, ring.

חֲחִי (ḥaḥi') *m*, only *pl.* חֲחִיִּם = חָח.

חָטָא (ḥāṭā') *inf.* חֲטֹא, חֲטוֹ, *fut.* יֶחֱטָא, *pt.* חֹטֵא, חֹטֶא, *pl.* חֹטְאִים, *f* חֹטֵאת to fail, to miss; to sin, to forfeit; to endanger. — *Pi.* חִטֵּא, *fut.* יְחַטֵּא to atone for, to expiate, to clear from sin. — *Hi.* הֶחֱטִיא, *inf.* בַּחֲטִיא, *fut.* יַחֲטִיא, וַיַּחֲטֵא, *pt.* מַחֲטִיא to miss, fail; to cause to sin, to seduce, to make guilty, to condemn. — *Hith.* הִתְחַטָּא to miss one's way [from terror]; to free oneself from sin.

חַטָּא (ḥăttā') *m, pl.* חַטָּאִים, *f* חַטָּאָה, sinner, penitent.

חֵטְא (ḥēt) *m, w.s.* חֶטְאוֹ, חֲטָאוֹ, *pl.* חֲטָאִים, *c.* חֲטָאֵי, sin, transgression, fault; punishment of sin.

חֲטָאָה (ḥaṭā'ā') *f* sin; sacrifice for sins.

חַטָּאָה (ḥăttā'ā') *f* sin, guilt, punishment.

חַטָּאת (ḥăttā'θ) *f, c.* חַטַּאת, *w.s.* חַטָּאתִי, *pl.* חַטָּאוֹת, *c.* חַטֹּאת, sin, transgression; sin-offering, atonement.

חָטַב (ḥāṭă'ḇ) *fut.* יַחְטֹב, *pt.* חֹטֵב, *pl. c.* חֹטְבֵי, to cut wood, to split. — *Pu. pt.* מְחֻטָּב to be hewn, sculptured.

חֲטֻבָה (ḥaṭūḇā') *f*, only *pl.* חֲטֻבוֹת, party-coloured texture, tapestry.

חִטָּה (ḥĭttā') *f, pl.* חִטִּים, wheat, grain of wheat.

חֲטוֹ see חָטָא.

חַטּוּשׁ (ḥăttū's); **חֲטִיטָא** (ḥaṭītā'); **חַטִּיל** (ḥăttī'l); **חֲטִיפָא** (ḥaṭīfā') *pr.n.m.*

חָטַם (ḥāṭă'm) *fut.* 1. *sg.* אֶחֱטָם־ (ĕḥṭŏ'm), to limit, restrain.

חָטַף (ḥāṭă'f) *inf.* חֲטוֹף, *fut.* יַחְטֹף, to snatch away, to rob.

חֹטֶר (ḥō'ṭĕr) *m* shoot, twig, rod.

חַטָּת see חַטָּאת.

חַי (ḥăy) *adj. i.p.* חָי, *w. art.* הַחַי, *c.* חֵי, *pl.* חַיִּים, *c.* חַיֵּי, *f* חַיָּה, *c.* חַיַּת, *w.s.* חַיָּתִי, *pl.* חַיּוֹת, living, alive, vigorous, fresh, raw, running [water]; in exclamations and oaths חַי — by the life of, as one lives; *subst. pl.* life, livelihood, refreshment.

חִיאֵל (ḥīʼēʹl) *pr.n.m.*

חִידָה (ḥīdāʹ) *f, w.s.* חִידָתִי, *pl.* חִידוֹת, riddle, parable, proverb, oracle; song; intrigue.

חָיָה (ḥāyāʹ) *pf.* 3. *sg.* also חַי, *inf.* חָיֹה, חֲיוֹת, *imp.* חְיֵה, *fut.* יִחְיֶה, יְחִי, וַיְחִי, *i.p.* וַיֶּחִי, to live, to exist, to enjoy life; to live anew, to recover, to be well. — *Pi.* חִיָּה, *inf.* חַיּוֹת, *imp.* חַיֵּה, *fut.* יְחַיֶּה, *pt.* מְחַיֶּה, to make alive, to enliven, to animate, to quicken; to preserve, to refresh, to rebuild. — *Hi.* הֶחֱיָה, *inf.* הַחֲיוֹת, הַחֲיֵה, to preserve in life, to restore to life.

חָיֶה (ḥāyēʹ) *adj., f/pl.* חָיוֹת, living, vigorous.

חַיָּה[1] (ḥăyyāʹ) *f, c.* חַיַּת and חַיְתוֹ, *w.s.* חַיָּתִי, *pl.* חַיּוֹת, living being, animal, beast; life.

חַיָּה[2] (ḥăyyāʹ) *f* crowd, band, troop.

חַיּוּת (ḥăyyūʹθ) *f* life, lifetime.

חִיל[1] see חוּל.

חִיל[2] (ḥīl) *m* pain, pang, trembling.

חַיִל (ḥăʹyīl) *m, i.p.* חָיִל, *c.* חֵיל, חֵל, *w.s.* חֵילוֹ, *pl.* חֲיָלִים, *c.* חֵילֵי, power, strength, valour; military force, army; wealth; **virtue**, honesty.

חֵיל see חֵל.

חִילָה (ḥīlāʹ) *f* = חִיל[2]

חֵילָם (ḥēlāʹm) *pr.n.* of a town in Syria.

חִילֵן (ḥīlēʹn) *pr.n.* of a town in Judah.

חִין (ḥīn) *m* beauty, grace.

חַיִץ (ḥăʹyīẞ) *m* wall.

חִיצוֹן (ḥīẞōʹn) *adj., f* חִיצוֹנָה, outer, exterior, civil [opp. sacred].

חֵיק, חֵק (ḥēk) *m* bosom, lap; inside, hollow, enclosed part.

חִירָה (ḥīrāʹ) *pr.n.m.*

חִירָם (ḥīrāʹm), חִירוֹם (ḥīrōʹm), חוּרָם (ḥūrāʹm) *pr.n.m.* of a king of Tyre.

חִישׁ[1] (ḥīš) = חוּשׁ, *imp.* חִישָׁה, to hasten.

חִישׁ[2] (ḥīš) *m* haste; *adv.* hastily, swiftly.

חַיְתוֹ see חַיָּה[1].

חֵךְ (ḥēḥ) *m, w.s.* חִכִּי, *pl. c.* חִכֵּי, palate, cavity of the mouth.

חָכָה (ḥāḥā') *pt.* חוֹכֶה, *pl. c.* חוֹכֵי, to wait for, to hope. — *Pi.* חִכָּה, *fut.* יְחַכֶּה, *pt.* מְחַכֶּה to wait for, to hope, to expect, to long for, to tarry.

חַכָּה (ḥăkkā') *f* hook, angle.

חֲכִילָה (ḥᵃḥīlā') *pr.n.* of a hill near the desert of Siph.

חֲכַלְיָה (ḥᵃḥălyā') *pr.n.m.*

חַכְלִיל (ḥăḥlī'l) *adj.*, *c.* חַכְלִילֵי, darkling, dim.

חַכְלִילוּת (ḥăḥlīlū'ϑ) *f* darkening [of the eye], drunkenness.

חָכַם (ḥāḥă'm) *imp.* חֲכַם, *fut.* יֶחְכַּם, to be wise, intelligent, prudent; to become wise. — *Pi. fut.* יְחַכֵּם to make wise, to teach. — *Pu. pt.* מְחֻכָּם to be cunning, clever. — *Hi. pt.* מַחְכִּים to make wise. — *Hith.* הִתְחַכֵּם to think oneself wise, to show oneself wise.

חָכָם (ḥāḥā'm) *adj.*, *c.* חֲכַם, *pl.* חֲכָמִים, *c.* חַכְמֵי, *f* חֲכָמָה, *c.* חַכְמַת, *pl* חֲכָמוֹת, *c.* חַכְמוֹת, wise, intelligent, prudent, experienced, clever; *subst.* a wise man, philosopher, magician.

חָכְמָה (ḥŏḥmā') *f, c.* חָכְמַת, wisdom, knowledge, experience, intelligence, insight, judgment.

חַכְמוֹנִי (ḥăḥmōnī') *pr.n.m.*

חָכְמוֹת (ḥŏḥmō'ϑ) and **חַכְמוֹת** (ḥăḥmō'ϑ) *f* [*sg.*] wisdom.

חֵל, חֵיל (ḥēl) *m* outer fortification, bulwark, wall, rampart.

חֹל (ḥōl) *adj.* profane, unholy.

חֶלְאָה[1] (ḥĕl'ā') *f* rust.

חֶלְאָה[2] (ḥĕl'ā') *pr.n.f.*

חָלָב (ḥālā'b) *m, w. art.* הֶחָלָב, *c.* חֲלֵב, milk.

חֵלֶב (ḥē'lĕb) and **חֶלֶב** (ḥĕ'lĕb) *m, w.s.* חֶלְבּוֹ, חֶלְבָּמוֹ, *pl.* חֲלָבִים, *c.* חֶלְבֵי, fat, marrow, best part.

חֶלְבָּה (ḥĕlbā') *pr.n.* of a town in Asher.

חֶלְבּוֹן (ḥĕlbō'n) *pr.n.* of a place near Damascus.

חֶלְבְּנָה (ḥĕlbᵉnā') *f* a strong-smelling resin.

חֵלֶד (ḥē'lĕd) *pr.n.m*

חֶלֶד (ḥĕ'lĕd) *m*, *i.p.* חָלֶד, *w.s.* חֶלְדִּי, life, lifetime; world, worldliness.

חֹלֶד (ḥō'lĕd) *m* mole [others: weazel].

חֻלְדָּה (ḥŭldā') *pr.n.f.*

חֶלְדַּי (ḥĕldă'y) *pr.n.m.*

חָלָה (ḥālā') *inf.* חֲלוֹת, *fut.* יֶחֱלֶה, וַיַּחַל, *pt.* חֹלֶה, *f* חֹלָה, to be languid, weak, ill, to be sick, to suffer, to be pained. — *Ni.* נֶחֱלָה, *pt. f* נַחְלָה to become sick, to be incurable, to be grieved. — *Pi.* חִלָּה, *inf.* חַלּוֹת, *imp.* חַל־, *fut.* וַיְחַל, to make ill or sick; to flatter, to implore. — *Pu.* חֻלָּה to become weak or sick. — *Hi.* הֶחֱלִי [for הֶחֱלָה, or for הֶחֱלִיא from חָלָא] to make sick, to show sickness. — *Ho.* הָחֳלָה (hŏ'ḥolā') to be wounded. — *Hith. inf.* הִתְחַלּוֹת, *imp.* הִתְחַל, *fut.* וַיִּתְחַל, to become sick, to feign oneself sick.

חַלָּה (ḥallā') *f*, *c.* חַלַּת, *pl.* חַלֹּת, cake [for offering].

חֲלוֹם (ḥalō'm) *m*, *pl.* חֲלֹמוֹת, dream.

חַלּוֹן (ḥallō'n) *m* and *f*, *pl.* חַלּוֹנִים and חַלּוֹנוֹת, *c.* חַלּוֹנֵי, hole, window.

חֹלוֹן (ḥōlō'n) *pr.n.* of towns.

חֵלוֹן (ḥēlō'n) *pr.n.m.*

חַלּוֹנַי (ḥallōnă'y) *m* window-work [others: *adj.* with many windows].

חֲלוֹף (ḥalō'f) *m* destitution, orphanage.

חַלּוּק (ḥallū'k) *adj.*, *pl. c.* חַלֻּקֵי, smooth.

חֲלוּשָׁה (ḥalūšā') *f* defeat.

חַלּוֹתִי see חָלַל[1].

חֲלַח (ḥală'ḥ) *pr.n.* of a place or district in Mesopotamia.

חַלְחוּל (ḥalḥū'l) *pr.n* of a town in Judah.

חַלְחָלָה (ḥalḥalā') *f* trembling, anguish, pain.

חָלַט (ḥală't) *Hi. fut.* וַיַּחְלְטוּ, to ascertain, to take for an omen.

חֲלִי[1] (ḥalī') *m*, *pl.* חֲלָאִים, and חֶלְיָה (ḥĕlyā') *f* necklace, ornament.

חֲלִי[2] (ḥalī') *pr.n.* of a town in Asher.

חֳלִי (ḥolī') *m*, *w. art.* הָחֳלִי, *i.p.* חֹלִי, *w.s.* חָלְיוֹ (ḥŏlyō'), *pl.* חֳלָיִים, *w.s.* חֳלָיֵנוּ, sickness, illness, suffering.

חָלִיל[1] (ḥālī'l) *m, pl.* חֲלִלִים, something hollowed out, pipe, flute.

חָלִיל[2] (ḥālī'l) *adj.* profane; *adv.* חָלִילָה, חָלִלָה far be it! God forbid!

חֲלִיפָה (ḥălīfā') *f, pl.* חֲלִיפוֹת, חֲלִפוֹת, change, alteration; garment for changing, festal dress; exchange of soldiers, relief.

חֲלִיצָה, חֲלִצָה (ḥălīṣā') *f, pl.* חֲלִיצוֹת, spoils, armour.

חֵלְכָה (ḥē'lĕkā') *adj., i.p.* חֵלֵכָה, *pl.* חֵלְכָּאִים [from חֵלְכַּי] unfortunate, wretched.

חָלַל[1] (ḥālă'l) *inf. w.s.* חֲלוֹתִי, to be pierced, perforated. — *Po. pt. f* מְחוֹלֶלֶת to pierce, wound. — *Pi. pt. pl.* מְחַלְּלִים [from [1]חָלִיל] to play on the flute. — *Pu. pt.* מְחֻלָּל and מְחוֹלָל to be pierced, perforated.

חָלַל[2] (ḥālă'l) *Ni.* נִחַל, *fut. i.p.* יֵחָל to be profaned, to be defiled. — *Pi.* חִלֵּל, *inf.* חַלֵּל. *w.s.* חַלְּלוֹ, *fut.* יְחַלֵּל to profane, defile, pollute, prostitute; to make common. — *Hi. fut.* יַחֵל to loose, break, profane.

חָלַל[3] (ḥālă'l) *Hi.* הֵחֵל, 1. *sg.* הַחִלּוֹתִי, 3. *pl.* הֵחֵלּוּ, *inf.* הָחֵל, *w.s.* הַחִלָּם, *fut.* יָחֵל, וַיָּחֶל, to begin, to open.

חָלָל (ḥālā'l) *m* [or *adj.*], *w. art.* הֶחָלָל, *c.* חֲלַל, *pl.* חֲלָלִים, *c.* חַלְלֵי, pierced, killed, slain; *f* חֲלָלָה prostitute.

חָלַם (ḥālă'm) *fut.* יַחֲלֹם, *pt.* חֹלֵם, to be strong; to dream. — *Hi. fut.* יַחֲלִים, *pt. pl.* מַחְלְמִים, to make sound or strong; to cause to dream.

חֵלֶם (ḥē'lĕm) *pr.n.m.*

חַלָּמוּת (ḥăllāmū'th) *f* the white of an egg, insipid food.

חַלָּמִישׁ (ḥăllāmī'sh) *m, c.* חַלְמִישׁ, hard stone, flint.

חָלַף (ḥālă'f) *inf.* חֲלוֹף, *fut.* יַחֲלֹף, to glide along, to move past, to pass away, to hasten past, to pass on; to transgress; to pass through, to pierce; to change; to shoot forth, to grow up. — *Pi. fut.* יְחַלֵּף to change [clothes]. — *Hi.* הֶחֱלִיף, *fut.* יַחֲלִיף, וַיַּחֲלֵף, to change, exchange, alter, substitute, renew.

חֵלֶף (ḥē'lĕf) *m* exchange; *adv.* instead of.

חֵלֶף (ḥĕ'lĕf) *pr.n.* of a town in Naphtali.

חָלַץ[1] (ḥālă'ṣ) *fut.* יַחֲלֹץ, *pt. p.* חָלוּץ, to draw off, to draw out, to withdraw. — *Ni. fut.* יֵחָלֵץ to be drawn out, to be delivered. — *Pi.* חִלֵּץ, *imp.* חַלְּצָה, *fut.* יְחַלֵּץ to draw out, to extricate or deliver; to rob.

חָלַץ[2] (ḥālă'ṣ) *fut.* יַחֲלֹץ to equip, to make ready for battle; *pt. p.* חָלוּץ warrior. — *Ni. fut.* יֵחָלֵץ to be equipped, to arm oneself. — *Hi. fut.* יַחֲלִיץ, to arm, to make strong.

חֵלֶץ (ḥē'lĕṣ) and **חֶלֶץ** (ḥĕ'lĕṣ) *pr.n.m.*

חֲלָצַיִם (ḥalāṣă'yĭm) *f du.* loins, hips.

חָלַק[1] (ḥālă'k) to be smooth; to be hypocritical. — *Hi.* הֶחֱלִיק, *fut.* יַחֲלִיק, *pt.* מַחֲלִיק to make smooth, to make the tongue smooth, to flatter.

חָלַק[2] (ḥālă'k) *fut.* יַחֲלֹק to spoil, plunder; to divide, distribute; to divide into shares. — *Ni. fut.* יֵחָלֵק to be divided, to be parted; to be allotted; to be formed into divisions. — *Pi.* חִלֵּק, *inf.* חַלֵּק, *w.s.* חַלְּקָם, *fut.* יְחַלֵּק to divide, distribute, allot; to scatter. — *Pu.* חֻלַּק to be divided out. — *Hi. inf.* לַחֲלֹק [for לְהַחֲלִיק] to take one's share. — *Hith.* הִתְחַלֵּק to divide among themselves.

חָלָק (ḥālā'k) *adj.*, *w. art.* הֶחָלָק, smooth, bald, bare; hypocritical, lying; *f/pl.* חֲלָקוֹת flattering words, hypocrisy.

חֵלֶק[1] (ḥē'lĕk) *m*, *w.s.* חֶלְקִי, *pl.* חֲלָקִים, *c.* חֶלְקֵי share, portion, lot, inheritance, piece of land.

חֵלֶק[2] (ḥē'lĕk) *m* smoothness, flattery.

חֶלְקָה[1] (ḥĕlkā') *f* = חֵלֶק[2].

חֶלְקָה[2] (ḥĕlkā') *f*, *c.* חֶלְקַת, share, piece of land.

חֲלָקָה (ḥalākā') and **חֲלַקָּה** (ḥalăkkā') *f*, *pl.* חֲלָקוֹת and חֲלַקּוֹת, flattery, promise.

חֶלְקִי (ḥĕlkī') *pr.n.m.*

חִלְקִיָּה (ḥĭlkĭyyā'), **חִלְקִיָּהוּ** (ḥĭlkĭyyā'hū) *pr.n.m.*

חֲלַקְלַק (ḥalăklă'k) *adj.*, *f/pl.*

חֲלַקְלַקּוֹת, slippery places, flattering speech, cunning.

חֶלְקַת (ḥĕlkā'ϑ) or חֶלְקַת (ḥĕlkā'ϑ) *pr.n.* of a town in Asher.

חָלַשׁ (ḥālă's) *fut. intr.* יֶחֱלַשׁ, *tr.* יַחֲלֹשׁ to be weak, feeble; to prostrate, to overthrow.

חַלָּשׁ (ḥăllā's) *m* weak, feeble.

חָם[1] (ḥām) *m*, *w.s.* חָמִיךְ, father-in-law.

חָם[2] (ḥām) *adj.* warm, hot.

חָם[3] (ḥām) *pr.n.m.* of a son of Noah; Egyptians and Ethiopians.

חֹם (ḥōm) *m* warmth, heat.

חֵמָא see חֵמָה.

חֶמְאָה (ḥĕm'ā') *f*, *c.* חֶמְאַת, curds, cream, butter.

חָמַד (ḥāmă'd), *fut.* יַחְמֹד, נֶחְמֹד, *pt. p.* חָמוּד, to desire, covet, long for, *pt. p.* desirable, costly. — *Ni. pt.* נֶחְמָד, *pl.* נֶחֱמָדִים to be desirable, costly, precious. — *Pi.* חִמֵּד to feel delight.

חֶמֶד (ḥĕ'mĕd) *m* pleasantness, loveliness.

חֶמְדָּה (ḥĕmdā') *f*, *c.* חֶמְדַּת desire, wish, longing; object of desire; loveliness, delight.

חֲמֻדוֹת see חָמַד *pt. p.*

חֶמְדָּן (ḥĕmdā'n) *pr.n.m.*

חַמָּה (ḥămmā') *f*, *w.s.* חַמָּתוֹ, warmth, heat; sun.

חֵמָה[1] (ḥēmā') *f*, *c.* חֲמַת, *w.s.* חֲמָתִי, *pl.* חֵמוֹת, חֵמֹת, warmth, heat, anger, wrath; prison.

חֵמָה[2] = חֶמְאָה.

חַמּוּאֵל (ḥămmū'ē'l); חֲמוּטַל (ḥamūṭă'l); חָמוּל (ḥāmū'l) *pr.n.m.*

חָמוֹץ (ḥāmō'ṣ) *adj.* violent; robber.

חָמוּץ (ḥāmū'ṣ) *adj.* [*pt. p.* of חָמֵץ], *c.* חֲמוּץ, deep red, purple.

חֲמוֹר[1] (ḥamō'r) [חֲמֹר] *m*, *pl.* חֲמֹרִים, [male] ass; heap, load = חֹמֶר.

חֲמוֹר[2] (ḥamō'r) *pr.n.m.*

חֲמוֹרָה (ḥamōrā') *f* = חֹמֶר heap.

חָמוֹת (ḥāmō'ϑ) *f*, *w.s.* חֲמוֹתֵךְ, mother-in-law.

חֹמֶט (ḥō'mĕṭ) *m* lizard.

חֻמְטָה (ḥŭmṭā') *pr.n.* of a place in Judah.

חָמִיץ (ḥāmī'ß) *adj.* salted; בְּלִיל חָמִיץ salted provender.

חֲמִישִׁי (ḥᵃmīšī'), חֲמִשִּׁי (ḥᵃmīššī') *m*, *f* חֲמִישִׁית, חֲמִשִּׁית, *num.* the fifth, the fifth part.

חָמַל (ḥāmă'l) *fut.* יַחְמֹל, to be mild, compassionate, to pity; to spare, forbear.

חֶמְלָה (ḥĕmlā') *f*, *c.* חֶמְלַת, pity, compassion.

חָמַם (ḥāmă'm), *pf.* חַם, *inf.* חֹם, חֲמֹם, חֻמָּם, חֻם, *fut.* יָחֹם, וַיִּחַם (văyyā'ḥŏm), יֵחַם [*pl.* וַיֵּחֲמוּ, perh. from יָחַם], to burn, to glow. — *Pi. fut.* יְחַמֵּם to warm, to hatch. — *Hith. fut.* יִתְחַמֵּם to warm oneself.

חַמָּן (ḥămmā'n) *m*, only *pl.* חַמָּנִים sun-pillars, idols of Baal.

חָמַס (ḥāmă's) *fut.* יַחְמֹס to oppress, to be bold, violent, to hurt, to overthrow, to tear down. — *Ni.* נֶחְמַס to be treated violently, to be disgraced.

חָמָס (ḥāmā's) *m*, *c.* חֲמַס, *pl.* חֲמָסִים violence, oppression, wickedness, wrong; unrighteous gain.

חָמֵץ[1] (ḥāmē'ß) *inf.* חֶמְצָה, *fut.* יֶחְמַץ, *pt.* חוֹמֵץ, *pt. p.* חָמוּץ to be sharp, sour, salted, to be leavened; to be deep red or purple; to be violent. — *Hith. fut.* יִתְחַמֵּץ to be excited, to be bitterly moved.

חָמֵץ[2] (ḥāmē'ß) *m* anything fermented or leavened [ill-gotten wealth].

חֹמֶץ (ḥō'mĕß) *m* vinegar.

חָמַק (ḥāmă'k) to turn about, to go away. — *Hith. fut.* 2. *f/pl.* תִּתְחַמָּקִין to go about, to rove about.

חָמַר[1] (ḥāmă'r) *fut.* יֶחְמַר to ferment, seethe, foam, boil up, swell. — *Poalal* חֳמַרְמַר to bubble up, to burn.

חָמַר[2] (ḥāmă'r) *fut. w.s.* תַּחְמְרָה to pitch, to cover with bitumen.

חֵמָר (ḥēmā'r) *m* bitumen, asphalt.

חֶמֶר (ḥĕ'mĕr) *m* wine.

חֹמֶר (ḥō'mĕr) *m* heap; a dry measure = 10 בַּת or אֵיפָה; clay, loam, mortar.

חֲמֹרָה (ḥᵃmōrā') *f*, *du.* חֲמֹרָתַיִם, see חֲמוֹרָה.

חָמַשׁ (ḥāmă'š) to gird the loins, to make ready for battle; *pt. p. pl.* חֲמֻשִׁים equipped, well armed, warriors.

חָמֵשׁ (ḥāmē'š) *num. f, c.* חֲמֵשׁ, five. — *denom. Pi.* חִמֵּשׁ to fifth, to take the fifth part.

חֹמֶשׁ[1] (ḥō'mĕš) *m* the fifth part as a tax or tribute.

חֹמֶשׁ[2] (ḥō'mĕš) *m* abdomen, paunch.

חֲמִשָּׁה (ḥᵃmĭššā') *num. m, c.* חֲמֵשֶׁת, five.

חֲמִשִּׁי (ḥᵃmĭššī') or חֲמִישִׁי (ḥᵃmĭšī') *num. m, f* חֲמִשִּׁית, חֲמִישִׁית the fifth; *f* the fifth part.

חֲמִשִּׁים (ḥᵃmĭššī'm) *num. pl., c.* חֲמִשֵּׁי, fifty.

חֵמֶת (ḥē'mĕṯ) *m, c.* חֵמַת, leather-bag, skin-bottle.

חֲמָת (ḥᵃmā'ṯ) *pr.n.* of a city in Syria; *gent.* חֲמָתִי.

חַמַּת (ḥămmă'ṯ) and חַמּוֹת (ḥămmō'ṯ) *pr.n.* of a town in Naphtali.

חֵן (ḥēn) *m, w.s.* חִנּוֹ favour, kindness, grace, loveliness, charm, preciousness.

חֵנָדָד (ḥē'nādā'd) *pr.n.m.*

חָנָה (ḥānā') *inf.* חֲנוֹת, *imp.* חֲנֵה, *fut.* יַחֲנֶה, וַיִּחַן, *pt.* חֹנֶה, *w.s.* חֹנְךָ, *pl.* חֹנִים, *f* חֹנָה to bend down, to incline; to encamp, settle, dwell; to encamp against, to besiege, to defend.

חַנָּה[1] (ḥănnā') *f*, only *pl.* חַנּוֹת compassion, grace.

חַנָּה[2] (ḥănnā') *pr.n.f.*

חֲנוֹךְ (ḥᵃnō'ḵ); חָנוּן (ḥānū'n) *pr.n.m.*

חַנּוּן (ḥănnū'n) *adj.* gracious, merciful.

חָנוּת (ḥānū'ṯ) *f*, only *pl.* חֲנֻיוֹת, vault, cell, prison.

חָנַט (ḥānă'ṭ) *inf.* חֲנוֹט, *fut.* יַחֲנֹט, to spice, to ripen; to embalm.

חֲנֻטִים (ḥᵃnūṭī'm) *m/pl.* act of embalming.

חַנִּיאֵל (ḥănnī'ē'l) *pr.n.m.*

חָנִיךְ (ḥānī'ḵ) *adj.* initiated, trained, skilled.

חֲנִינָה (ḥᵃnīnā') *f* mercy, favour.

חֲנִית (ḥᵃnī'ṯ) *f, pl.* חֲנִיתוֹת and חֲנִיתִים, spear, lance.

חָנַךְ (ḥānă'ḵ) *imp.* חֲנֹךְ, *fut.* יַחֲנֹךְ, to initiate, teach; to dedicate, consecrate.

חֲנֻכָּה (ḥᵃnŭkkā') *f* dedication.

חִנָּם (ḥĭnnā'm) *adv.* gratuitously; in vain; without cause.

חֲנַמְאֵל (ḥᵃnăm'ē'l) *pr.n.m.*

חֲנָמַל (ḥᵃnāmă'l) *m*, *i.p.* חֲנָמָל, hail, hailstones.

חָנַן (ḥānă'n) *inf.* חָנוֹן, חַנּוֹת, *w.s.* חֶנְנָהּ, *imp. w.s.* חָנֵּנִי (ḥŏnnē'nī), *fut.* יָחֹן, וַיָּחָן (văyyā'ḥŏn), *w.s.* יְחָנֵּנוּ, יְחָנְךָ (yŏḥnᵉḥā'), יְחָנֵּנוּ, to be inclined, favourable, kind, gracious, to pity, to have mercy, to bestow. — *Ni.* נֵחַן to be pitied, to complain. — *Pi.* חוֹנֵן, *fut.* יְחוֹנֵן to be favourable, to pity; חִנֵּן, *fut.* יְחַנֵּן to make lovely.— *Ho.* הֻחַן, *fut.* יֻחַן to be pitied, to be favoured. — *Hith. pf.* and *inf.* הִתְחַנֵּן to implore, to seek mercy.

חָנָן (ḥānā'n); חֲנַנְאֵל (ḥᵃnăn'ē'l); חֲנָנִי (ḥᵃnānī'); חֲנַנְיָה (ḥᵃnănyā'); חֲנַנְיָהוּ (ḥᵃnănyā'hū) *pr.n.m.*

חָנֵס (ḥānē's) *pr.n.* of a city in middle Egypt [Heracleopolis].

חָנַף (ḥānă'f), חָנֵף¹ (ḥānē'f) *fut.* יֶחֱנַף, to be wicked, to sin; to be desecrated, unclean; *tr.* to profane, to pollute. — *Hi.* הֶחֱנִיף, *fut.* יַחֲנִיף to profane, pollute; to seduce.

חָנֵף² (ḥānē'f) *m* [*adj.*], *pl. c.* חַנְפֵי, profane, wicked, hypocrite.

חֹנֶף (ḥō'nĕf) *m* and חֲנֻפָּה (ḥᵃnŭfā') *f*, impiety, godlessness.

חָנַק (ḥānă'k) *Ni. fut.* יֵחָנֵק, to strangle or hang oneself.—*Pi.* חִנֵּק to strangle.

חַנָּתֹון (ḥᵃnnāthō'n) *pr.n.* of a town in Zebulon.

חָסַד¹ (ḥāsă'd) *Pi.* חִסֵּד to insult, reproach.

חָסַד² (ḥāsă'd) *Hith. fut.* יִתְחַסָּד to show oneself kind.

חֶסֶד¹ (ḥĕ'sĕd) *m*, *i.p.* חָסֶד, *w.s.* חַסְדּוֹ, *pl.* חֲסָדִים, *c.* חַסְדֵי, love, kindness, benevolence, good-will, favour, benefit, mercy, grace, piety; beauty.

חֶסֶד² (ḥĕ'sĕd) *m* reproach, shame, disgrace.

חֲסַדְיָה (ḥᵃsădyā') *pr.n.m.*

חָסָה (𝔥āsā') *inf.* חֲסוֹת, *imp. pl.* חֲסוּ, *fut.* יֶחְסֶה, *pt.* חֹסֶה, *pl.* חֹסִים, to flee, to take refuge; to trust.

חֹסָה (𝔥ōsā') *pr.n.m.*

חָסוֹן or חָסֹן (𝔥āsō'n) *adj.* strong, mighty.

חָסוּת (𝔥āsū'ϑ) *f* refuge, refuge-seeking.

חָסִיד (𝔥āsī'd) *adj., pl.* חֲסִידִים, kind, benevolent, gracious; pious, good.

חֲסִידָה (𝔥ᵃsīdā') *f* stork.

חָסִיל (𝔥āsī'l) *m, w. art.* הֶחָסִיל, a species of locust.

חָסִין (𝔥āsī'n) *adj.* mighty.

חָסַל (𝔥āsă'l) *fut. w.s.* יַחְסְלֶנּוּ, to eat off.

חָסַם (𝔥āsă'm) *fut.* יַחְסֹם, to bar, stop; to muzzle.

חָסַן (𝔥āsă'n) *Ni. fut.* יֵחָסֵן, to be laid up.

חָסֹן see חָסוֹן.

חֹסֶן (𝔥ō'sĕn) *m* treasure, wealth, riches, might.

חָסַף (𝔥āsă'f) *Pu. pt.* מְחֻסְפָּס to be made scaly, to be scaly [fine].

חָסֵר[1] (𝔥āsē'r) *inf.* חָסוֹר, *fut.* יֶחְסַר, *pl.* יַחְסְרוּ, to decrease, to be diminished, to fail; to want, lack. — *Pi. fut.* יְחַסֵּר to make less, to cause to want. — *Hi.* הֶחְסִיר, *fut.* יַחְסִיר, to cause to fail; to want, to suffer.

חָסֵר[2] (𝔥āsē'r) *adj., c.* חֲסַר deficient, wanting, lacking; *m* lack of understanding.

חֶסֶר (𝔥ĕ'sĕr) *m* want, poverty.

חֹסֶר (𝔥ō'sĕr) = חֶסֶר.

חַסְרָה (𝔥ăsrā') *pr.n.m.*

חֶסְרוֹן (𝔥ĕsrō'n) *m* deficiency, want.

חַף (𝔥ăf) *adj.* pure, innocent.

חֹף see חוֹף.

חָפָא (𝔥āfā') *Pi. fut.* יְחַפֵּא to do secretly.

חָפָה (𝔥āfā') *pt. p.* חָפוּי to cover, to veil.— *Ni.* נֶחְפָּה to be covered. — *Pi.* חִפָּה, *fut.* וַיְחַף to overlay.—*Pu.* חֻפָּה to be protected.

חֻפָּה[1] (𝔥ŭppā') *f* covering, tent, canopy, bride-chamber.

חֻפָּה[2] (𝔥ŭppā') *pr.n.m.*

חָפַז (𝔥āfă'z) *inf. w.s.* חָפְזִי (𝔥ŏfzī'), *fut.* יַחְפֹּז, to leap, to start, to be startled. — *Ni.* נֶחְפַּז, *inf.* הֵחָפֵז, *fut.*

יֵחָפֵז, pt. נֶחְפָּז to be afraid, to be anxious, to flee.

חִפָּזוֹן (ḥĭppāzō'n) m hasty flight,

חֻפִּים (ḥŭppī'm) pr.n.m.

חֹפֶן (ḥō'fĕn) m, only du. חָפְנַיִם (ḥŏfnă'yĭm), w.s. חָפְנֵיכֶם, fist.

חָפְנִי (ḥŏfnī') pr.n.m.

חָפַף (ḥāfă'f) pt. חֹפֵף, to cover, to protect.

חָפֵץ[1] (ḥāfē'ß) inf. חָפֹץ, fut. יַחְפֹּץ, יֶחְפַּץ to find pleasure in, to have an affection to, to delight in, to desire, to choose; tr. to bend, to bow.

חָפֵץ[2] (ḥāfē'ß) adj., pl. חֲפֵצִים, c. חֲפֵצֵי, f חֲפֵצָה, taking pleasure in, liking, willing.

חֵפֶץ (ḥē'fĕß) m, w.s. חֶפְצִי, pl. חֲפָצִים, c. חֶפְצֵי, pleasure, delight, wish, desire; matter, business, pursuit.

חֶפְצִי־בָהּ (ḥĕfßī'-bā'h) pr.n.f.

חָפַר (ḥāfă'r) inf. חָפֹר, fut. יַחְפֹּר to dig, to dig into; to paw; to search out, explore, spy.

חָפֵר (ḥāfē'r) fut. יֶחְפַּר, יַחְפַּר, to turn red, to blush, to be ashamed, to be disappointed. — Hi. הֶחְפִּיר, fut. יַחְפִּיר, to be ashamed; to cause shame.

חֵפֶר (ḥē'fĕr) pr.n. of a town in southern Palestine; pr.n.m.

חֲפָרַיִם (ḥᵃfāră'yĭm) pr.n. of a place in Issachar.

חָפְרַע (ḥŏfră'ᵒ) pr.n.m. of an Egyptian king.

חֲפַרְפֶּרֶת (ḥᵃfărpĕ'rĕϑ) f, only pl. חֲפַרְפָּרוֹת [to be read for לַחְפֹּר פֵּרוֹת], rat, mole.

חָפַשׂ (ḥāfă's) fut. יַחְפֹּשׂ, to search, scrutinize, devise. — Ni. נֶחְפַּשׂ to be searched out. — Pi. חִפֵּשׂ, fut. יְחַפֵּשׂ, to search, examine, seek out. — Pu. pt. מְחֻפָּשׂ to be devised; to be concealed — Hith. הִתְחַפֵּשׂ to disguise oneself.

חֵפֶשׂ (ḥē'fĕs) m device, plan.

חָפַשׁ (ḥāfă'š) Pu. חֻפַּשׁ to be set free.

חֹפֶשׁ (ḥō'fĕš) m, w.s. חָפְשִׁי (ḥŏfšī') couch.

חֻפְשָׁה (ḥŭfšā') f freedom, release.

חָפְשׁוּת (ḥŏfšū'ϑ), חָפְשִׁית

(ḥŏfsī'ϑ) *f* sickness; בֵּית ח' hospital.

חָפְשִׁי (ḥŏfšī') *adj.*, *pl.* חָפְשִׁים, released, freed, free, exempt from taxes.

חֵץ (ḥēß) *m*, *w.s.* חִצִּי, *pl.* חִצִּים, *c.* חִצֵּי, arrow, lightning; punishment, plague, wound; point of a spear.

חָצַב (ḥāßă'b), חָצֵב (ḥāßē'b), *fut.* יַחְצֹב, *pt.* חֹצֵב, חוֹצֵב, *pl.* חֹצְבִים, to cut, hew, split; to slay, kill. — *Ni.* נֶחְצַב to be engraven. — *Pu.* חֻצַּב to be hewn out. — *Hi. pt. f* מַחֲצֶבֶת to slay, to destroy.

חָצָה (ḥāßā') *fut.* יֶחֱצֶה, וַיַּחַץ to split, divide, to halve. — *Ni. fut.* יֵחָצֶה to be divided, halved.

חָצוֹר (ḥāßō'r) *pr.n.* of Canaanitish towns.

חָצוֹת (ḥāßō'ϑ) *f*, *c.* חֲצוֹת middle, half.

חֲצִי (ḥaßī') *m*, *i.p.* חֵצִי, *w.s.* חֶצְיוֹ, middle, half; arrow [= חֵץ].

חֲצִי הַמְּנֻחוֹת (ḥaßī' hămnūḥō'ϑ) *pr.n.* of a place.

חָצִיר[1] = חָצֵר.

חָצִיר[2] (ḥāßī'r) *m*, *c.* חֲצִיר, grass; leek.

חֵצֶן (ḥē'ßĕn) *m*, *c.* חִצְנוֹ, and **חֹצֶן** (ḥō'ßĕn) *m*, *w.s.* חָצְנִי (ḥŏßnī') bosom, lap; battle-axe.

חָצַץ (ḥāßă'ß) *pt.* חוֹצֵץ to divide, to form into ranks or bands. — *Pi. pt.* מְחַצֵּץ to divide booty or to shoot arrows. — *Pu.* חֻצַּץ to be cut off, shortened.

חָצָץ (ḥāßā'ß) *m* fragment, small stone, gravel [*pl. w.s.* חֲצָצֶיךָ = חִצֶּיךָ see חֵץ].

חַצְצוֹן־תָּמָר (ḥă'ßaßō'n tāmā'r) *pr.n.* of a place in Judah [afterwards עֵין גֶּדִי].

חֲצֹצְרָה (ḥaßō'ßerā') *f*, *pl.* חֲצֹצְרוֹת, trumpet.

חָצַר (ḥāßă'r) *Pi. pt.* מְחַצֵּר to blow the trumpet.

חָצֵר (ḥāßē'r) *m* and *f*, *w. art.* הֶחָצֵר, *c.* חֲצַר, *pl.* חֲצֵרִים, *c.* חַצְרֵי and חֲצֵרוֹת, *c.* חַצְרוֹת, enclosure, fence, enclosed camp, village; court, yard; many geographical names are compounded with חֲצַר.

חֶצְרוֹן (ḥĕßrō'n) *pr.n.* of a town; *pr.n.m.*

חֲצֵרוֹת (ḥªẞērō'ϑ) *pr.n.* of a station in the desert.

חֶצְרַי (ḥĕẞrā'y) *pr.n.m.*

חֲצַרְמָוֶת (ḥªẞărmā'vĕϑ) *pr.n.* of an Arabian tribe and district [Hadramaut].

חֵק see חֵיק.

חֹק (ḥōk) *m*, *c.* חָק־ (ḥŏk), *w.s.* חֻקִּי, חָקְכֶם (ḥŏkḥĕ'm), *pl.* חֻקִּים, *c.* חֻקֵּי, חֻקְקֵי, statute, regulation, law, custom; decree; share, task, term, limit, boundary.

חָקָה (ḥākā') *Pu. pt.* מְחֻקֶּה to be engraved, carved.— *Hith. fut.* יִתְחַקֶּה to set limits.

חֻקָּה (ḥŭkkā') *f*, *c.* חֻקַּת, *pl.* חֻקּוֹת, law, statute, custom.

חֲקוּפָא (ḥªkūfā') *pr.n.m.*

חָקַק (ḥākă'k) *imp. w.s.* חָקֵהוּ, *pt.* חֹקֵק, חוֹקֵק to cut, to engrave, to inscribe, trace; to establish, ordain, prescribe. — *Pi. pt.* מְחֹקֵק, *pl. c.* חֹקְקֵי, to decree, ordain; *pt.* leader, ruler, lawgiver; sceptre. — *Pu. pt.* מְחֻקָּק what is ordained, law. — *Ho. fut.* יֻחַק to be engraved.

חֻקֹּק (ḥŭkkō'k) *pr.n.* of a town in Naphtali.

חָקַר (ḥākă'r) *inf.* חֲקֹר, *imp. w.s.* חָקְרֵנִי (ḥŏkrē'nī), *fut.* יַחְקֹר to search out, explore, examine, spy out. — *Ni.* נֶחְקַר to be searched out, to be ascertained. — *Pi.* חִקֵּר to find out.

חֵקֶר (ḥē'kĕr) *m*, *pl. c.* חִקְרֵי, searching out, examination, meditation, deliberation; אֵין חֵקֶר unsearchable, unfathomable, mystery.

חֹר[1] (ḥōr) *m*, only *pl.* חֹרִים, חוֹרִים the free, the noble.

חֹר[2], **חוֹר** [also חָר] (ḥōr) *m* hole, opening, breach.

חֶרֶא (ḥĕ'rĕ) *m*, only *pl. c.* חֲרָאֵי excrements, dung.

חָרֵב[1] (ḥārē'ḅ) *imp.* חָרְבִי, *fut.* יֶחֱרַב to dry up, to become or be dry; to be stupefied. — *Pu.* חֹרַב to be dried.— *Hi.* הֶחֱרִיב, *pt. f* מַחֲרֶבֶת to dry up.

חָרֵב[2] (ḥārē'ḅ) *inf.* חָרֹב, *fut.* יֶחֱרַב, to be devastated, to be desolate or waste; *tr.* to destroy, to lay waste. — *Ni.* נֶחֱרַב to be laid waste; to fight with one another.— *Hi.* הֶחֱרִיב, *fut.*

יַחֲרִיב, *pt.* מַחֲרִיב to lay waste, to destroy. — *Ho.* הָחֳרַב (hŏ'ḥºrā'b) to be desolated, destroyed.

חָרֵב[3] (ḥārē'b) *adj.*, *f* חֲרֵבָה, dry.

חָרֵב[4] (ḥārē'b) *adj.*, *f/pl.* חֲרֵבוֹת, waste, desolated.

חֶרֶב (ḥĕ'rĕb) *f*, *i.p.* חָרֶב, *w.s.* חַרְבִּי, *pl.* חֲרָבוֹת, *c.* חַרְבוֹת sword, knife.

חֹרֶב[1] (ḥō'rĕb) *m* dryness, drought.

חֹרֶב[2] (ḥō'rĕb) *m* desolation, destruction.

חֹרֵב (ḥōrē'b) *pr.n.* of a top of Sinai.

חָרְבָּה[1] (ḥŏrbā') *f*, *pl.* חֳרָבוֹת, dry country, desert.

חָרְבָּה[2] (ḥŏrbā') *f*, *pl.* חֳרָבוֹת, *c.* חָרְבוֹת desolation, ruin.

חָרָבָה (ḥā'rābā') *f* dryness, dry land.

חֲרָבוֹן (ḥªrābō'n) *m*, *pl. c.* חַרְבוֹנֵי, heat, drought.

חַרְבוֹנָא (ḥărbōnā') *pr.n.m.* [Persian].

חָרַג (ḥārā'g) *fut.* יַחְרֹג, to tremble, to flee trembling.

חַרְגֹּל (ḥărgō'l) *m* a species of locust.

חָרַד (ḥārā'd) *fut.* יֶחֱרַד to tremble, to be afraid, to be anxious, to come with trepidation. — *Hi.* הֶחֱרִיד, *pt.* מַחֲרִיד to frighten, terrify.

חָרֵד (ḥārē'd) *adj.*, *pl.* חֲרֵדִים, trembling, fearful, anxious, reverent.

חֲרֹד, חֲרוֹד (ḥªrō'd) *pr.n.* of a fountain and place near Jezreel; *gent.* חֲרֹדִי.

חֲרָדָה[1] (ḥªrādā') *f*, *c.* חֶרְדַּת, *pl.* חֲרָדוֹת terror, fear, consternation, care, careful service.

חֲרָדָה[2] (ḥªrādā') *pr.n.* of a station in the wilderness.

חָרָה (ḥārā') *inf.* חָרֹה, חֲרוֹת, *fut.* יֶחֱרֶה, יִחַר, וַיִּחַר to burn, to glow with anger. — *Ni. pt. pl.* נֶחֱרִים to be angry, incensed. — *Tiph.* [*Pi.*] יְתַחֲרֶה to be zealous, to rival. — *Hi.* הֶחֱרָה, *fut.* וַיַּחַר to cause to burn, to kindle anger; to act zealously. — *Hith. fut.* יִתְחַר to grow indignant.

חַרְהֲיָה (ḥărhªyā') *pr.n.m.*

חֲרוֹד see חֲרֹד.

חֲרוּזִים (ḥªrūzī'm) *m/pl.* string of pearls or corals.

חָרוּל (ḥārū'l) *m, pl.* חֲרֻלִּים thorn, nettle.

חֲרוּמַף (ḥarūmă'f) *pr.n.m.*

חָרוֹן (ḥārō'n) *m, c.* חֲרוֹן, *pl.* חֲרוֹנִים, heat, anger; a combustible or burning thing [dry wood].

חֹרֹון (ḥōrō'n) *pr.n.* of a place; *gent.* חֹרֹנִי.

חֹרוֹנַיִם (ḥō'rōnă'yĭm) *pr.n.* of a town in Moab.

חָרוּץ[1] (ḥārū'ṣ) *adj.* sharp, pointed, zealous, industrious; *m* thrashing-sledge.

חָרוּץ[2] (ḥārū'ṣ) *m* ditch, incision; decision, judgment.

חָרוּץ[3] (ḥārū'ṣ) *m* gold.

חָרוּץ[4] (ḥārū'ṣ) *pr.n.m.*

חַרְחוּר (ḥărḥū'r) *pr.n.m.*

חַרְחַס (ḥărḥă's) *pr.n.m.*

חַרְחֻר (ḥărḥŭ'r) *m* inflammation, fever.

חֶרֶט (ḥĕ'rĕt) *m* chisel, style [for engraving], character.

חַרְטֹם (ḥărtō'm) *m, only pl.* חַרְטֻמִּים, *c.* חַרְטֻמֵּי scribe, writer of hieroglyphics, Egyptian sage.

חָרֵי see חָרָא.

חֳרִי (ḥorī') *m* heat, anger.

חֹרִי[1] (ḥōrī') *m* white or fine bread.

חֹרִי[2] (ḥōrī') *pr.n., pl.* חֹרִים [troglodyte] a people in Mount Seir.

חָרִיט (ḥārī't) *m, pl.* חֲרִיטִים, pocket, bag, purse.

חָרִיף (ḥārī'f) *pr.n.m.*; *patr.* חֲרִיפִי.

חָרִיץ (ḥārī'ṣ) *m*, only *pl. c.* חֲרִיצֵי, slice, piece; thrashing-sledge.

חָרִישׁ (ḥārī's) *m* act and time of ploughing.

חֲרִישִׁי (ḥarīšī') *adj., f* חֲרִישִׁית silent, still, sultry.

חָרַךְ (ḥāră'ḥ) *fut.* יַחֲרֹךְ, to roast [others: to scare up].

חֲרַכִּים (ḥarăkkī'm) *m/pl.* lattice, window-lattice.

חָרֹל see חָרוּל.

חָרַם[1] (ḥāră'm) *Hi.* הֶחֱרִים, *inf.* הַחֲרֵם, הַחֲרִים, *fut.* יַחֲרִים, וַיַּחֲרֵם to dedicate, devote, curse, destroy. — *Ho. fut.* יָחֳרַם (yŏ'ḥoră'm) to be doomed, exterminated.

חָרַם[2] (ḥără'm) to cut, to split; *pt. p.* חָרוּם, חָרֻם

flat-nosed [others: with a split or pierced nose].

חֳרֵם (ḥārē'm) *pr.n.* of a town in Naphtali.

חָרִים (ḥārī'm) *pr.n.m.*

חֵרֶם (ḥe'rĕm) [once חֶרֶם], *w.s.* חֶרְמִי, *pl.* חֲרָמִים, curse, extermination, a thing or person devoted to destruction; net, enticement.

חָרְמָה (ḥŏrmā') *pr.n.* of a Canaanitish town.

חֶרְמוֹן (ḥĕrmō'n) *pr.n.* of a mountain in Antilibanus.

חֶרְמֵשׁ (ḥĕrmē's) *m* a sickle.

חָרָן (ḥārā'n) *pr.n.* of a town in Mesopotamia, Carrhae; also *pr.n.m.*

חַרְנֶפֶר (ḥărnĕ'fĕr) *pr.n.m.*

חֶרֶס[1] (ḥĕ'rĕs) *m*, *i.p.* חָרֶס itch, scab.

חֶרֶס[2] (ḥĕ'rĕs) *m* [also חַרְסָה], *i.p.* חָרֶס, the sun; עִיר הַחֶרֶס Heliopolis in Egypt.

חֶרֶס[3] (ḥĕ'rĕs) *pr.n.* of a place near סֻכּוֹת.

חַרְסוּת (ḥărsū'ϑ) *f* pottery.

חָרַף[1] (ḥāră'f) *inf.* חֲרֹף, *fut.* יֶחֱרַף, *pt.* חֹרֵף, to scorn, reproach, insult. — *Ni.* נֶחֱרַף to be betrothed. — *Pi.* חֵרֵף, *inf.* חָרֵף, *fut.* יְחָרֵף, *pt.* מְחָרֵף to reproach, scorn, despise; to expose [life].

חָרַף[2] (ḥāră'f) *fut.* יֶחֱרַף, to pass the autumn or winter.

חָרֵף (ḥārē'f) *pr.n.m.*

חֹרֶף (ḥō'rĕf) *m*, *w.s.* חָרְפִּי (ḥŏrpī') harvest-time, autumn [and winter].

חֶרְפָּה (ḥĕrpā') *f*, *c.* חֶרְפַּת, *pl.* חֲרָפוֹת, *c.* חֶרְפּוֹת reproach, shame, object of reproach; pudenda.

חָרַץ (ḥāră'ß) *fut.* יֶחֱרַץ, to cut, sharpen, point, wound; to decide, to be sharp, zealous, quick. — *Ni. pt.* נֶחֱרָץ to be decided, decreed.

חַרְצֻבּוֹת (ḥărßŭbbō'ϑ) *f/pl.* fetters; tortures.

חַרְצָן (ḥărßā'n) *m*, only *pl.* חַרְצַנִּים kernels of grapes [others: sour grapes].

חָרַק (ḥāră'k) *fut.* יַחֲרֹק, *pt.* חֹרֵק, to gnash, to grind the teeth.

חָרַר (ḥără'r) *pf. pl.* חָרוּ, to burn, to glow; to be parched. — *Ni.* נָחַר, נִחַר, *fut.* יֵחַר to be heated, burnt, scorched, dried up. — *Pilp.* *inf.* חַרְחַר to kindle.

חָרֵר (ḥārē'r) *m*, only *pl.* חֲרֵרִים sunburnt, dry country.

חֶרֶשׂ (ḥĕ'rĕs) *m*, *pl.* חֲרָשִׂים, *c.* חַרְשֵׂי clay, pottery, earthen ware, potsherd.

חָרַשׁ (ḥāră'š) *inf.* חֲרֹשׁ, *fut.* יַחֲרֹשׁ, *pt.* חֹרֵשׁ, *pt. p.* חָרוּשׁ to cut, to engrave, to forge; to devise; to plough.— *Ni.* נֶחֱרַשׁ to be ploughed.— *Hi.* *pt.* מַחֲרִישׁ to contrive, devise.

חָרֵשׁ (ḥārē'š) *fut.* יֶחֱרַשׁ to be deaf, dumb, silent, still. — *Hi.* הֶחֱרִישׁ, *imp.* 2. *sg.* *f* הַחֲרִישִׁי, *fut.* יַחֲרִישׁ, *pt.* מַחֲרִישׁ to be deaf, silent; to silence; to keep quiet; to conceal; to go away in silence. — *Hith.* הִתְחָרֵשׁ to keep oneself quiet.

חָרָשׁ (ḥārā'š) *m*, *c.* חָרַשׁ, *pl.* חָרָשִׁים, *c.* חָרָשֵׁי, a cutter in wood, metal, stone; smith, workman, artisan, artificer, artist.

חֵרֵשׁ (ḥērē'š) *adj.*, *pl.* חֵרְשִׁים, deaf, deaf and dumb.

חֶרֶשׁ[1] (ḥĕ'rĕš) *m*, only *pl.* חֲרָשִׁים, artificial work, artifice.

חֶרֶשׁ[2] (ḥĕ'rĕš) *m* silence; *adv.* silently.

חֹרֵשׁ (ḥōrē'š) *m* cutting-tool; *pt.* worker.

חֹרֶשׁ (ḥō'rĕš) *m*, *w. loc.* ה חֹרְשָׁה, *pl.* חֳרָשִׁים (ḥorāšī'm), thicket, forest.

חַרְשָׁא (ḥăršā') *pr.n.m.*

חֲרֹשֶׁת (ḥarō'šĕth) *pr.n.* of a place in northern Palestine, חֲרֹשֶׁת הַגּוֹיִם.

חָרַת (ḥāră'th) *pt. p.* חָרוּת [= חָרוּשׁ] to cut, engrave.

חֶרֶת (ḥĕ'rĕth) *pr.n.* of a forest in Judah.

חֲשׂוּפָא (ḥasūfā') *pr.n.m.*

חָשִׂיף (ḥāsī'f) *m*, only *pl. c.* חֲשִׂפֵי, a separate flock.

חָשַׂךְ (ḥāsă'ch) *imp.* חֲשֹׂךְ, *fut.* יַחְשֹׂךְ, *pt.* חוֹשֵׂךְ, to hold back, to keep off, to preserve; to refuse, withold, deny, check, stop; to spare, to save. — *Ni.* נֶחֱשַׂךְ, *fut.* יֵחָשֵׂךְ to be checked; to be reserved.

חָשַׂף (ḥāsă'f) *inf.* חֲשֹׂף, לַחְשֹׂף, *imp.* *f* חֶשְׂפִּי, *fut.* יֶחֱשֹׂף, *pt. p.* חָשׂוּף to bare, uncover, defoliate; to draw, to take off [water].

חָשַׁב (ḥāšă'ḇ) *inf.* חֲשֹׁב, חְשֹׁב, *fut.* יַחְשֹׁב, יַחֲשֹׁב, to count, to count for, to impute, to esteem, to reckon; to think, combine, devise, invent; *pt.* חֹשֵׁב artificial worker, weaver. — *Ni.* נֶחְשַׁב, *fut.* יֵחָשֵׁב, *pt.* נֶחְשָׁב, to be counted, reckoned, esteemed. — *Pi.* חִשֵּׁב, *fut.* יְחַשֵּׁב to think, meditate, count, reckon devise; to be about. — *Hith.* הִתְחַשֵּׁב to count oneself among.

חֵשֶׁב (ḥē'šĕḇ) *m* girdle, belt [of a priest].

חַשְׁבַּדָּנָה (ḥăšbăddā'nā); חֲשֻׁבָה (ḥašūḇā') *pr.n.m.*

חֶשְׁבּוֹן¹ (ḥĕšbō'n) *m* computation, account, reasoning.

חֶשְׁבּוֹן² (ḥĕšbō'n) *pr.n.* of the chief-town of the Amorites.

חִשָּׁבוֹן (ḥĭššāḇō'n) *m*, only *pl.* חִשְּׁבוֹנוֹת, device, invention, war-engine.

חֲשַׁבְיָה (ḥašăḇyā'), חֲשַׁבְיָהוּ (ḥašăḇyā'hū); חֲשַׁבְנָה (ḥašăḇnā'); חֲשַׁבְנְיָה (ḥašăḇnᵉyā') *pr.n.m.*

חָשָׁה (ḥāšā') *inf.* חֲשׁוֹת, *fut.* יֶחֱשֶׁה to be quiet, inactive, silent. — *Hi.* הֶחֱשָׁה, *imp. pl.* הַחֲשׁוּ, *pt.* מַחְשֶׁה to keep silence, to be quiet, to rest; to silence.

חַשּׁוּב (ḥăššū'ḇ) *pr.n.m.*

חָשַׁךְ (ḥāšă'ḵ) *fut.* יֶחְשַׁךְ to be or grow dark, to be obscured. — *Hi.* הֶחְשִׁיךְ, *fut.* יַחְשִׁיךְ to make dark, to darken; to spread darkness.

חָשֹׁךְ (ḥāšō'ḵ) *adj.*, only *pl.* חֲשֻׁכִּים, dark, obscure, low.

חֹשֶׁךְ (ḥō'šĕḵ) *m*, *w.s.* חָשְׁכִּי (ḥŏškī') darkness; misery, ignorance, falsehood.

חֲשֵׁכָה or חֲשֵׁיכָה (ḥašēḵā') *f*, *c.* חֶשְׁכַת [also חָשְׁכָה (ḥŏšḵā')], *pl.* חֲשֵׁכִים the same as חֹשֶׁךְ.

חָשַׁל (ḥāšă'l) *Ni.* *pt.* נֶחֱשָׁל to be enfeebled, tired.

חֻשָׁם (ḥāšū'm) *pr.n.m.*

חֶשְׁמוֹן (ḥĕšmō'n) *pr.n.* of a place in Judah.

חַשְׁמֹנָה (ḥăšmōnā') *pr.n.* of a station in the desert.

חַשְׁמַל (ḥăšmă'l) *m*, *w. loc.*

חַשְׁמַלָּה ה, shining metal [electrum, or pyropus].

חַשְׁמַן (chăsmă'n) *adj.*, only *pl.* חַשְׁמַנִּים, noble, distinguished, rich.

חֹשֶׁן (chō'sĕn) *m* ornament, breast-plate of the High Priest.

חָשַׁק (chāsă'k) to be attached to, to love, to have pleasure or delight in. — *Pi.* חִשֵּׁק to fasten together. — *Pu. pt.* מְחֻשָּׁק to be bound together.

חֵשֶׁק (chē'sĕk) *m*, *w.s.* חִשְׁקִי delight, desire.

חָשׁוּק (chāsū'k) *m*, only *pl.* חֲשֻׁקִים attachment, junction-rod.

חִשּׁוּק (chĭssū'k) *m*, only *pl.* חִשֻּׁקִים, spoke of a wheel.

חַשְׁרָה (chăsrā') *f*, *c.* חַשְׁרַת a gathering.

חִשּׁוּר (chĭssū'r) *m*, only *pl.* חִשֻּׁרִים the nave of a wheel.

חֲשַׁשׁ (chᵃsă's) *m* hay, dry grass, stubble.

חַת (chăth) *adj.*, *pl.* חַתִּים, broken, terrified; *m*, *w.s.* חִתְּכֶם fear, dread.

חָתָה (chāthā') *inf.* לַחְתּוֹת, *fut.* יַחְתֶּה, *w.s.* יַחְתְּךָ, to take, to seize.

חִתָּה (chĭttā') *f*, *c.* חִתַּת, fear, terror.

חִתּוּל (chĭttū'l) *m* bandage.

חַתְחַת (chăthchă'th) *m*, only *pl.* חַתְחַתִּים terrors.

חִתִּי (chĭttī') *pr.n.*, *pl.* חִתִּים, *f* חִתִּית[1], *pl.* חִתִּיֹּת, descendant of חֵת, Hittite.

חִתִּית[2] (chĭttī'th) *f* terror.

חָתַךְ (chāthă'ch) *Ni.* נֶחְתַּךְ to be determined.

חָתַל (chāthă'l) *Pu.* חֻתַּל and *Ho.* הָחְתַּל (hŏchtă'l) to be swathed, swaddled.

חֲתֻלָּה (chᵃthŭllā') *f* swaddling cloth, bandage.

חֶתְלֹן (chĕthlō'n) *pr.n.* of a place in Syria.

חָתַם (chāthă'm) *inf.* חֲתֹם, *fut.* יַחְתֹּם, *pt. p.* חָתוּם, to shut, close, seal; to hide, to reveal as a secret. — *Ni. inf.* נַחְתּוֹם to be sealed. — *Pi.* חִתֵּם to close, to shut up. — *Hi.* הֶחְתִּים to stop, to shut up.

חֹתָם see חוֹתָם.

חֹתֶמֶת (chōthĕ'mĕth) *f* seal.

חָתַן (chāthă'n) *Hith.* הִתְחַתֵּן,

to contract affinity by marriage.

חָתָן (ḥāthā'n) *m* bridegroom; son-in-law; relative by marriage.

חֹתֵן (ḥōthē'n) *m*, *w.s.* חֹתֶנְךָ, חֹתְנוֹ father-in-law.

חֹתֶנֶת (ḥōthĕ'nĕth) *f* mother-in-law.

חֲתֻנָּה (ḥathŭnnā') *f* nuptials.

חָתַף (ḥāthă'f) *fut.* יַחְתֹּף to catch, seize.

חֶתֶף (ḥĕ'thĕf) *m* robber.

חָתַר (ḥāthă'r) *fut.* יַחְתֹּר to break through, to break into; to beat, to row.

חָתַת (ḥāthă'th) *imp. pl.* חֹתּוּ to be dismayed, confounded. — *Ni.* נִחַת, *fut.* יֵחַת, יֵחַתּוּ to be broken, crushed, terrified, dismayed, alarmed, to be in fear, to be in despair. — *Pi.* חִתַּת to be broken; to terrify. — *Hi.* הֵחַת, הַחְתֹּתָ, הַחְתַּתִּי, *fut.* יָחֵת to break; to terrify.

חֲתַת[1] (ḥathă'th) *m* terror, dismay.

חֲתַת[2] (ḥathă'th) *pr.n.m.*

ט

ט the ninth letter of the alphabet, called טֵית [a coiling, twisting]; as a numeral = 9 [טו = 15].

טָא, טָאטָא (tātā') *Pi.* טֵאטֵא to sweep away.

טָבְאֵל (tā'bĕ'ē'l) *pr.n.m.*

טָבוּל (tābū'l) *m*, only *pl.* טְבוּלִים turban.

טַבּוּר (tăbbū'r) *m* navel, height, summit.

טָבַח (tābă'ḥ) *inf.* and *imp.* טְבֹחַ, *pt. p.* טָבוּחַ to slaughter, to kill; to cook, to dress.

טַבָּח (tăbbā'ḥ) *m*, *pl.* טַבָּחִים butcher, cook; executioner, guardsman.

טֶבַח[1] (tĕ'băḥ) *m*, *i.p.* טָבַח, *w.s.* טִבְחָהּ, killing, slaughter, massacre; killed beast, meal of meat.

טֶבַח[2] (tĕ'băḥ) *pr.n.m.*; also *pr.n.* of a town.

טַבָּחָה (tăbbāḥā') *f*, *pl.* טַבָּחוֹת, female cook.

טִבְחָה (tĭbḥā') *f*, *w.s.* טִבְחָתִי = טֶבַח[1].

טִבְחַת (tĭbḥă'th) *pr.n.* of a town.

טָבַל (tāḇă'l) *fut.* יִטְבֹּל, *pt.* טֹבֵל to dip, to immerse. — *Ni.* נִטְבַּל to be immersed, moistened.

טְבַלְיָהוּ (tᵉḇălyā'hū) *pr.n.m.*

טָבַע (tāḇă'') *fut.* יִטְבַּע, 1. *sg.* אֶטְבָּעָה to sink, to sink down. — *Pu.* טֻבַּע to be sunk. — *Ho.* הָטְבַּע to be sunk, to be laid deep.

טַבַּעַת (tăbbă''ăϑ) *f, w.s.* טַבַּעְתּוֹ, *pl.* טַבָּעוֹת, *c.* טַבְּעוֹת, seal, signet-ring, ring.

טַבָּעוֹת (tăbbā'ō'ϑ) *pr.n.m.*

טַבְרִמּוֹן (tăḇrĭmmō'n) *pr.n.m.*

טַבָּת (tăbbā'ϑ) *pr.n.* of a place.

טֵבֵת (tēḇē'ϑ) *m* name of the tenth Hebrew month [January or February].

טָהוֹר, טָהֹר (tāhō'r) *adj.*, *c.* טְהֹר, *pl.* טְהֹרִים, *f* טְהוֹרָה, *pl.* טְהֹרוֹת, pure, clean, purified, unalloyed.

טָהֵר (tāhē'r) *imp.* טְהַר, *fut.* יִטְהַר, to be clean, pure, innocent, righteous. — *Pi.* טִהַר, *imp. w.s.* טַהֲרֵנִי, *fut.* יְטַהֵר, יְטַהֵר, to make clean, to purify.—*Pu. pt.* מְטֹהָר to be cleansed. — *Hith.* הִטַּהֵר, הִטַּהַר to purify oneself.

טֹהַר (tō'hăr) *m, w.s.* טָהֳרוֹ, splendour, brightness, purity, purification.

טָהֳרָה (tŏ'hºrā') *f, w.s.* טָהֳרָתוֹ, purity, purification.

טוֹב¹ (tōḇ) to be good, well, pleasing, lovely, cheerful,comfortable,happy. — *Hi.* הֵטִיב to make good; to do well; to do good; to adorn, to cheer, to please.

טוֹב² (tōḇ) *adj., pl.* טוֹבִים, טֹבִים, *f* טוֹבָה, *c.* טוֹבַת, *pl.* טוֹבוֹת, טֹבוֹת, טֹבֹת, beautiful, good, excellent, pleasant, lovely, convenient, fruitful, sound, cheerful, kind; *subst. m* the good, the right, virtue, happiness, pleasantness; *adv.* well.

טוֹב³ (tōḇ) *pr.n.* of a district east of the Jordan.

טוּב (tūḇ) *m* goodness, beauty, excellence, cheerfulness, well-being; good things, the best things.

טוֹב אֲדוֹנִיָּהוּ (tōḇ ªdō'nĭyyā'-hū) *pr.n.m.*

טוֹבָה (tōḇā') *f* = טוֹב.

טוֹבִיָּה (tō'ḇīyyā'), טוֹבִיָּהוּ (tō'ḇīyyā'hū) *pr.n.m.*

טָוָה (tāvā') *pf.* 3. *pl.* טָווּ, to spin, to weave.

טוּחַ (tū'aḥ) *pf.* טָח, טַח, to smear, to daub, to plaster, to whitewash. — *Ni.* נָטוֹחַ, *inf.* הִטּוֹחַ to be plastered.

טוֹטֶפֶת (tōtĕ'fĕṯ) *f*, only *pl.* טוֹטָפוֹת, band about the forehead, before or above the eyes, round the arm, prayer-fillet.

טוּל (tūl) *Hi.* הֵטִיל, *fut.* וַיָּטֶל, יָטִיל to throw, to cast forth. — *Ho. fut.* יוּטַל, יֻטַל to be cast, to be prostrated. — *Pilp.* טִלְטֵל to throw or fling about.

טוּר (tūr) *m*, *pl.* טוּרִים, טֻרִים, *c.* טוּרֵי, row, series, range; [hearth, enclosure?]

טוּשׂ (tūs) *fut.* יָטוּשׂ to fly, to dash.

טָחָה (tāḥā') *Pi. pt. pl. c.* מְטַחֲוֵי to bend a bow, to shoot.

טֻחָה (tūḥā') *f*, only *pl.* טֻחוֹת, reins, kidneys; the inmost part.

טְחוֹן (tᵉḥō'n) *m* mill, hand-mill.

טָחַן (tāḥă'n) *inf.* טָחוֹן, *imp. f* טַחֲנִי, *fut.* יִטְחַן, *pt.* טוֹחֵן to crush, grind; to turn the hand-mill as a slave; to oppress; *pt. f/pl.* הַטֹּחֲנוֹת the grinders, i. e. the teeth.

טַחֲנָה (tă'ḥanā') *f* a mill.

טְחֹר (tᵉḥō'r) *m*, only *pl.* טְחֹרִים, *c.* טְחֹרֵי, swellings, carbuncles, ulcers.

טִיחַ (tī'aḥ) *m* plaster on a wall.

טִיט (tīt) *m* loam, clay, mud.

טִירָה (tīrā') *f* habitation, tent, encampment, village; a row of bricks, pinnacle of a wall.

טַל (tăl) *m*, *i.p.* טָל, *w.s.* טַלֶּךָ, dew.

טָלָא (tālā') *pt. p.* טָלוּא to be spotted, variegated. — *Pu. pt.* מְטֻלָּא to be patched, to be mended.

טָלֶה (tālĕ') *m*, *c.* טְלֵה, a young lamb.

טַלְטֵלָה (tăltēlā') *f* a throwing or hurling down.

טְלִי (tᵉlī') *m*, only *pl.* טְלָאִים, lamb.

טָלַל (tālă'l) *Pi* טִלֵּל to cover with beams or rafters.

טֶלֶם (tĕ'lĕm) *pr.n.* of a town

in Judah [also called טְלָאִים].

טַלְמוֹן (tălmō'n) *pr.n.m.*

טָמֵא[1] (tāmē') *inf.* טָמְאָה (tŏm'ā'), *fut.* יִטְמָא to be unclean [ritually and morally]. — *Ni.* נִטְמָא to defile oneself, to be profaned. — *Pi.* טִמֵּא, *fut.* יְטַמֵּא to make unclean, to profane, to desecrate, to pronounce unclean. — *Hothp.* הֻטַּמָּא to be defiled.

טָמֵא[2] (tāmē') *adj., c.* טְמֵא, *pl.* טְמֵאִים, *f* טְמֵאָה unclean [ritually and morally].

טָמְאָה (tŏm'ā') and טֻמְאָה (tŭm'ā') *f* uncleanness, impurity.

טָמָה (tāmā') *Ni.* נִטְמָה to be unclean.

טָמַן (tāmă'n) *inf.* טְמֹן, *fut.* יִטְמֹן, *pt. p.* טָמוּן, *pl.* טְמֻנִים, *f* טְמוּנָה, to hide, to conceal, to bury; to keep, to preserve; to lay a snare. — *Ni. imp.* הִטָּמֵן to hide oneself. — *Hi. fut.* יַטְמִין to hide, preserve.

טֶנֶא (tĕ'nĕ) *m, w.s.* טַנְאֲךָ basket.

טָנַף (tānă'f) only *Pi. fut.* יְטַנֵּף to sully.

טָעָה (tā'ā') *Hi.* הִטְעָה to lead astray.

טָעַם (tā'ă'm) *inf.* טְעֹם. *imp. pl.* טַעֲמוּ, *fut.* יִטְעַם to taste, to try, to perceive, to understand.

טַעַם (tă''ăm) *m, w.s.* טַעְמוֹ taste, flavour; feeling, understanding, judgment; royal decree.

טָעַן[1] (tā'ă'n) *Pu.* טֹעַן to be pierced.

טָעַן[2] (tā'ă'n) *imp. pl.* טַעֲנוּ to load, burden.

טַף (tăf) *m, i.p.* טָף, *w.s.* טַפְּכֶם, טַפֵּנוּ *coll.* children, little ones.

טָפַח (tāfă'ḥ) *Pi.* טִפַּח, to spread out, to stretch out; to bring up, to nurse.

טֶפַח (tĕ'făḥ) *m, pl.* טְפָחוֹת palm, flat hand, handbreadth; console, corbel.

טִפֻּחַ (tĭppū'aḥ) *m,* only *pl.* טִפֻּחִים nursing [of children].

טֹפַח (tō'făḥ) *m* handbreadth.

טָפַל (tāfă'l) *fut.* יִטְפֹּל to paste, to besmear, to impute.

טִפְסַר (tĭfsă'r) *m, pl.* טַפְסְרִים,

Assyrian dignitary, commander, captain.

טָפַף (tāfă'f) *inf.* טָפוֹף to mince one's steps, to walk coquettishly.

טָפַשׁ (tāfă's) to be dull, stupid.

טָפַת (tāfă'ϑ) *pr.n.f.*

טָרַד (tāră'd) *pt.* טֹרֵד to push, to persist, to drop continually.

טְרוֹם = טֶרֶם.

טָרַח (tāră'ḥ) *Hi. fut.* יַטְרִיחַ to load, burden.

טֹרַח (tō'răḥ) *m* burden, hardship, encumbrance.

טָרִי (tārī') *adj.*, only *f* טְרִיָּה moist, fresh.

טֶרֶם (tĕ'rĕm) [expectation] *adv.* and *conj.* before, not yet; בְּטֶרֶם, מִטֶּרֶם before.

טָרַף (tāră'f) *inf.* טְרֹף, טָרֹף, *fut.* יִטְרֹף, יִטְרַף, *pt.* טֹרֵף to tear in pieces; to pluck off. — *Ni.* נִטְרַף to be torn in pieces. — *Pu.* טֹרַף, *i.p.* טֹרָף to be torn in pieces. — *Hi. imp. w.s.* הַטְרִיפֵנִי to cause to eat, to feed.

טָרָף (tārā'f) *adj.* newly plucked off, fresh.

טֶרֶף (tĕ'rĕf) *m*, *w.s.* טַרְפּוֹ, fresh leaf; prey [torn beast]; food, nourishment.

טְרֵפָה (tᵉrēfā') *f* cattle torn by wild beasts; booty.

י

י the tenth letter of the alphabet, called יוֹד [= יָד hand]; as a numeral = 10.

יָאַב (yā'ă'b) to long for, to desire.

יָאָה (yā'ā') to be becoming, to suit.

יְאוֹר see יְאֹר.

יַאֲזַנְיָה (yă''ăzănyā') *pr.n.m.* [יַאֲזַנְיָהוּ].

יָאִיר (yā'ī'r) *pr.n.m.*

יָאַל[1] (yā'ă'l) *Ni.* נוֹאַל to be foolish, to act or appear as a fool.

יָאַל[2] (yā'ă'l) *Hi.* הוֹאִיל, *imp.* הוֹאֵל, *fut.* וַיּוֹאֶל, to be willing, to undertake, begin, venture; to be pleased, to be content.

יֹאֶל see אָלָה *Hi.*

יְאֹר, יְאוֹר (yᵉō'r) *m*, *pl.* יְאֹרִים, *c.* יְאֹרֵי, river; as a *pr.n.* the Nile.

יָאַשׁ (yā'ă's) *Ni.* נוֹאַשׁ, *pt.* נוֹאָשׁ to desist from, to despair. — *Pi. inf.* יָאֵשׁ to cause to despair, to abandon.

יְאשִׁיָּה (yō'šĭyyā') [יְאשִׁיָּהוּ] *pr.n.m.*

יַאת see אָתָה.

יְאַתְרַי (yᵉăθrā'y) *pr.n.m.*

יָבַב (yābă'b) *Pi. fut.* תְּיַבֵּב to cry out, to call aloud.

יָבוֹ see בּוֹא.

יְבוּל (yᵉbū'l) *m, w.s.* יְבוּלָם growth, produce, fruit, goods.

יְבוּס (yᵉbū's) *pr.n.*, old name of Jerusalem; *gent.* יְבוּסִי.

יָבוֹשׁ see בּוֹשׁ.

יִבְחָר (yĭbḥā'r); **יָבִין** (yābī'n) *pr.n.m.*

יָבַל (yābă'l) *Hi.* הוֹבִיל, *fut.* יוֹבִיל to lead; to present, to offer. — *Ho.* הוּבַל, *fut.* יוּבַל to be led, conducted, carried.

יָבָל[1] (yābā'l) *m, pl. c.* יִבְלֵי stream, river.

יָבָל[2] (yābā'l) *pr.n.m.*

יַבָּל (yăbbā'l) *adj.*, only *f* יַבֶּלֶת having sores, ulcers.

יֻבַל see יוּבַל.

יִבְלְעָם (yĭblᵉ'ā'm) *pr.n.* of a town in Issachar.

יָבָם (yābā'm) *m, w.s.* יְבָמִי, brother-in-law.

יָבַם (yābă'm) [denom. of יָבָם] *Pi.* יִבֵּם (yĭbbē'm), *inf.* יַבֵּם to fulfil the duty of a brother-in-law, to marry the widow of a brother.

יְבֶמֶת (yᵉbĕ'mĕθ) *f, w.s.* יְבִמְתֵּךְ sister-in-law.

יַבְנְאֵל (yăbnᵉ'ē'l) *pr.n.* of two towns.

יַבְנֶה (yăbnĕ') *pr.n.* of a Philistine town

יִבְנְיָה (yĭbnᵉyā') and **יִבְנִיָּה** (yĭbnĭyyā') *pr.n.m.*

יַבֹּק (yăbbō'k) *pr.n.* of a tributary of the Jordan.

יְבֶרֶכְיָהוּ (yᵉbĕ'rĕḥyā'hū) *pr. n.m.*

יִבְשָׂם (yĭbsā'm) *pr.n.m.*

יָבֵשׁ[1] (yābē's) *inf.* יְבֹשׁ, יְבֹשֶׁת, *fut.* יִיבַשׁ, to be dry, to become dry, to dry up, to be parched, to wither; to be drained. — *Pi.* יִבֵּשׁ, *fut.* יַבֵּשׁ [for יְיַבֵּשׁ] to make dry. — *Hi.* הוֹבִישׁ, *fut.* יוֹבִישׁ, to make dry; *intr.* to become dry.

יָבֵשׁ[2] (yāḇē'š) *adj*., *pl*. יְבֵשִׁים, *f* יְבֵשָׁה dry, parched.

יָבֵשׁ[3] (yāḇē'š) [also יָבֵישׁ] *pr.n*. of a town in Gilead.

יַבָּשָׁה (yăbbāšā') and **יַבֶּשֶׁת** (yăbbĕ'šĕṯ) *f* dry land.

יִגְאָל (yĭg'ā'l) *pr.n.m.*

יָגַב (yāgă'ḇ) to plough; *pt. pl*. יוֹגְבִים ploughmen.

יָגֵב (yāgē'ḇ) *m* arable land.

יָגְבְּהָה (yŏgbᵉhā') *pr.n*. of a town in Gad.

יִגְדַּלְיָהוּ (yĭgdălyā'hū) *pr.n.m.*

יָגָה (yāgā') *Ni*. נוּגָה [for נוּגָה], *pt*. נוּגָה, to be grieved, afflicted. — *Pi*. יִגָּה, *fut*. יַגֶּה [for יְיַגֶּה] to afflict. — *Hi*. הֹגָה, הוֹגָה, *fut*. יוֹגֶה, *pt. w.s.* מוֹגַיִךְ, to afflict, to grieve; to remove.

יָגוֹן (yāgō'n) *m* grief, sorrow.

יָגוֹר (yāgō'r) *adj*. fearing, fearful.

יָגוּר (yāgū'r) *pr.n*. of a place in Judah.

יָגִיעַ[1] (yāgī'aʿ) *adj*., *pl. c*. יְגִיעֵי, wearied, tired.

יְגִיעַ[2] (yāgī'aʿ) *m*, only *c*. יְגִיעַ labour, toil; produce, goods, wealth.

יְגִיעָה (yᵉgīʿā') *f* toil, weariness.

יָגֶל see גָּלָה *Hi.*

יָגְלִי (yŏglī') *pr.n.m*

יָגַע (yāgă'ʿ) *fut*. יִיגַע, יִגַע to be wearied; to toil, to exert oneself. — *Pi*. יִגַּע, *fut*. יְיַגַּע to weary. — *Hi*. הוֹגִיעַ to weary, to importune.

יְגָע (yāgā'ʿ) *m* earnings.

יָגֵעַ (yāgē'aʿ) *adj*., *pl*. יְגֵעִים, weary, exhausted; wearying.

יְגַר (yᵉgă'r) [Chald.] *m* heap of stones.

יָגֹר (yāgō'r) *pf*. יָגֹרְתָּ, יָגֹרְתִּי, to be afraid, to fear.

יָד (yāḏ) *f* [and *m*], *c*. יַד, *w.s.* יָדִי, יָדְךָ, יֶדְכֶם, *du*. יָדַיִם, *c*. יְדֵי, *pl*. יָדוֹת, *c*. יְדוֹת hand; power, strength, assistance; axle, tenon; side; *pl*. turns, times; part, place; monument.

יְדָא see דָּאָה.

יִדְאֲלָה (yĭḏ'ălā') *pr.n*. of a town in Zebulon.

יִדְבָּשׁ (yĭḏbā'š) *pr.n.m.*

יָדַד (yāḏă'ḏ) *pf. pl*. יַדּוּ to cast [lots].

יְדִדוּת (y'ḍīḍū'ϑ) *f* object of love.

יָדָה (yāḍā') *imp. pl.* יְדוּ to throw, cast. — *Pi.* יַדָּה, *inf.* יַדּוֹת, *fut. pl.* וַיַּדּוּ [for וַיְיַדּוּ] to throw, cast. — *Hi.* הוֹדָה, *inf.* הוֹדוֹת, *imp. pl.* הוֹדוּ, *fut.* יוֹדֶה to speak out, to confess; to sing, praise, glorify. — *Hith.* הִתְוַדָּה to confess; to praise.

יִדּוֹ (yīddō'); **יָדוֹן** (yāḍō'n); **יָדוּעַ** (yāḍū'a) *pr.n.m.*

יְדוּתוּן (y'ḍūϑū'n), **יְדִיתוּן** (y'ḍīϑū'n) *pr.n.m.*

יַדַּי (yăddă'y) *pr.n.m.*

יָדִיד (yāḍī'ḍ) *adj., c.* יְדִיד, *pl.* יְדִידִים, *f* יְדִידָה[1], *pl.* יְדִידוֹת, beloved, lovely, pleasant; friend; *f/pl.* lovely things.

יְדִידָה[2] (y'ḍīḍā') *pr.n.f.*

יְדִידְיָה (y'ḍī'ḍ'yā') *pr.n.m.* [= Solomon].

יְדָיָה (y'ḍāyā'); **יְדִיעֲאֵל** (y'ḍī''a'ēl); **יִדְלָף** (yīḍlā'f) *pr.n.m.*

יֶדְכֶם see יָד.

יִדְמוּ see דָּמַם.

יָדַע (yāḍă'') *inf.* יְדֹעַ, דַּעַת, דֵּעָה, *imp.* דַּע, *fut.* יֵדַע, *pt.* יֹדֵעַ, יוֹדֵעַ, *f* יֹדַעַת, *pt. p.* יָדוּעַ to perceive, to understand, to know, to discern; to be acquainted with; to become acquainted with a woman [sexually]. — *Ni.* נוֹדַע, *fut.* יִוָּדַע, *pt.* נוֹדָע to be perceived, known; to make oneself known, to appear. — *Pi.* יִדַּע to cause to know. — *Pu. pt.* מְיֻדָּע to be known, to be familiar. — *Hi.* הוֹדִיעַ, *inf.* הוֹדִיעַ, *imp.* הוֹדַע, הוֹדִיעוּ, *fut.* יוֹדִיעַ, וַיּוֹדַע to cause to know, to let know; to inform, to announce. — *Ho.* הוּדַע [for הוֹדַע], *pt.* מוּדָע, *f* מוּדַעַת to become known. — *Hith. inf.* הִתְוַדַּע to make oneself known, to reveal oneself. — *Po.* יוֹדַע to order, to appoint.

יָדָע (yāḍā''); **יְדַעְיָה** (y'ḍă'yā') *pr.n.m.*

יִדְּעֹנִי (yīḍ'ōnī') *adj., pl.* יִדְּעֹנִים. knowing; *subst.* sorcerer, magician, wizard; prophesying spirit.

יָהּ (yāh) shortened form of יָהוּ, יְהוָֹה.

יָהַב (yāhă'b) only *imp.* הַב, הָבָה, *f* הָבִי, הָבוּ to give; as an exclamation: give! come on!

יְהָב (yᵉhā'b) *m*, *w.s.* יְהָבְךָ, lot, gift, concern.

יָהַד (yāhă'd) *Hith.* הִתְיַהֵד to turn Jew.

יְהֻד (yᵉhū'd) *pr.n.* of a town in Dan.

יֶהְדַּי (yĕhdă'y); **יֵהוּא** (yēhū'); **יְהוֹאָחָז** (yᵉhō''ăḥā'z); **יְהוֹאָשׁ** (yᵉhō'ā's) *pr.n.m.*

יְהוּדָה (yᵉhūdā') *pr.n.m.*, Judah; *gent.* יְהוּדִי, *pl.* יְהוּדִים, *f* יְהוּדִיָּה and יְהוּדִית¹, Judæan, Jew, Jewess, Jewish; *f* in Hebrew language.

יְהוּדִית² (yᵉhūdī'θ) *pr.n.f.*

יְהוָֹה (yᵉhōvā') [with the vowels of אֲדֹנָי] to be pronounced יַהֲוֶה (yăhvĕ'), [meaning the ever-being,] the true God of the Hebrews.

יְהוֹזָבָד (yᵉhō'zābā'd); **יְהוֹחָנָן** (yᵉhō'ḥānā'n); **יְהוֹיָדָע** (yᵉhō'yādā''); **יְהוֹיָכִין** (yᵉhō'yāḥī'n); **יְהוֹיָקִים** (yᵉhō'yākī'm); **יְהוֹיָרִיב** (yᵉhō'yārī'b); **יְהוּכַל** (yᵉhūḥă'l); **יְהוֹנָדָב** (yᵉhō'nādā'b); **יְהוֹנָתָן** (yᵉhō'nāθā'n); **יְהוֹסֵף** (yᵉhōsē'f); **יְהוֹעַדָּה** (yᵉhō''ăddā'); **יְהוֹעַדָּן** (yᵉhō''ăddā'n); **יְהוֹצָדָק** (yᵉhō'ṣādā'k); **יְהוֹרָם** (yᵉhōrā'm); **יְהוֹשֶׁבַע** (yᵉhōsĕ'bă''); **יְהוֹשׁוּעַ** (yᵉhōsū'a''); **יְהוֹשָׁפָט** (yᵉhō'sāfā't) *pr.n.m.*

יְהִי see הָיָה.

יְהֵילִילוּ see יָלַל *Hi.*

יָהִיר (yāhī'r) *adj.* proud, arrogant.

יַהֵל see אָהַל *Pi.*

יְהַלֶּלְאֵל (yᵉhăllĕl'ē'l) *pr.n.m.*

יַהֲלֹם (yă'hălō'm) *m* a precious stone, diamond or emerald.

יַהַץ (yă'hăṣ) or **יַהְצָה** (yă'hṣā) *pr.n.* of a town in Reuben.

יוֹאָב (yō'ā'b); **יוֹאָח** (yō'ā'ḥ); **יוֹאָחָז** (yō''ăḥā'z); **יוֹאֵל** (yō'ē'l); **יוֹאָשׁ** (yō'ā's); **יוֹב** (yōb); **יוֹבָב** (yōbā'b) *pr.n.m.*

יֹבֵל, יוֹבֵל (yōbē'l) *m*, *pl.* יוֹבְלִים, cry of joy, shout, signal, blast of a trumpet; שְׁנַת הַיּוֹבֵל the year of Jubilee, the [50th] year of release.

יוּבָל (yūbā'l) *pr.n.m.*

יוּבַל (yūbă'l) *m* river.

יוֹזָבָד (yō'zābā'd); **יוֹזָכָר** (yō'zāḥā'r); **יוֹחָא** (yōḥā'); **יוֹחָנָן** (yō'ḥānā'n); **יוֹיָדָע** (yō'yādā''); **יוֹיָכִין** (yō'yāḥī'n); **יוֹיָקִים** (yō'yākī'm); **יוֹיָרִיב** (yō'yārī'b); **יוּכַל** (yūḥă'l) *pr.n.m.*

יוֹכֶבֶד (yōǫĕ'ḇĕḏ) *pr.n.f.*

יוּכַל see יָכֹל.

יוֹלֶדֶת see יָלַד.

יוֹם (yōm) *m, du.* יוֹמַיִם, *pl.* יָמִים, *c.* יְמֵי [poetically יְמוֹת] day; *pl.* a number of days, some time, year, life; הַיּוֹם to-day; בַּיּוֹם in the day-time, on the same day; כַּיּוֹם at present, now.

יוֹמָם (yōmā'm) *adv.* by day; יוֹמָם וָלַיְלָה day and night, always.

יָוָן (yāvā'n) *pr.n.m.*, Ionia or Greece; *gent.* יְוָנִי, *pl.* יְוָנִים; also a town in Arabia.

יָוֵן (yāvē'n) *m, c.* יְוַן, mud, mire, dung.

יוֹנָה[1] (yōnā') *f, c.* יוֹנַת, *pl.* יוֹנִים, dove.

יוֹנָה[2] (yōnā') *pr.n.m.*

יוֹנֵק (yōnē'k) *m, pl.* יוֹנְקִים, *f* יוֹנֶקֶת, *pl.* יֹנְקוֹת, sucking child; young twig, shoot.

יוֹנָתָן (yō'nāϑā'n); יוֹסֵף (yōßē'f); יוֹסִפְיָה (yō'ßĭfyā'); יוֹעֵאלָה (yō'ēlā'); יוֹעֵד (yō'ē'd); יוֹעֶזֶר (yō'ĕzĕr); יוֹעָשׁ (yō'ā'š); יוֹצָדָק (yō'ßādā'k) *pr.n.m.*

יוֹצֵר (yōßē'r) *m* fashioner, former, maker, creator, potter.

יוֹקִים (yōkī'm) *pr.n.m.*

יוֹר see יָרָה.

יוֹרָה (yōrā') *pr.n.m.*

יוֹרֶה (yōrĕ') *m* early rain [in autumn].

יוֹרַי (yōrā'y); יוֹרָם (yōrā'm); יוּשַׁב חֶסֶד (yū'šāḇ ǫĕ'ßĕḏ); יוֹשִׁבְיָה (yō'šĭḇyā'); יוֹשָׁה (yōšā'); יוֹשַׁוְיָה (yō'šāvyā'); יוֹשָׁפָט (yō'šāfā't); יוֹתָם (yōϑā'm) *pr.n.m.*

יוֹתֵר (yōϑē'r) *m* remainder, rest, profit; *adv.* more, further; too much; besides.

יוֹתֶרֶת (yōϑĕ'rĕϑ) *f* what is redundant, lobe of the liver.

יַז, יֵז see נָזָה.

יְזִיאֵל (yᵉzī'ē'l); יִזִּיָּה (yĭzzĭyyā'); יָזִיז (yāzī'z); יִזְלִיאָה (yĭzlī'ā'); יְזַנְיָה (yᵉzānyā') *pr.n.m.*

יֶזַע (yĕ'zā') *m* sweat.

יִזְרָח (yĭzrā'ǫ) = אֶזְרָח; יִזְרַחְיָה (yĭzrāǫyā') *pr.n.m.*

יִזְרְעֶאל (yĭzrᵉē'l) [יִזְרְעֶאל] *pr.n.* of towns; *gent.* יִזְרְעֵאלִי, *f* יִזְרְעֵאלִית, יִזְרְעֵלִית; also *pr.n.m.*

יָחַד (yāǫā'ḏ) *fut.* יֵחַד, to be

attached, united.— *Pi. fut.* יַחֵד to unite.

יַחַד (yă'ḥăḍ) *m* oneness, union, communion; *adv.* together, jointly, all alike.

יָחַד see חָדָה.

יַחְדָּו (yăḥdā'v) *adv.* together, with one another, at the same time, jointly.

יַחְדּוֹ (yăḥdō'); יַחְדִּיאֵל (yăḥdī'ēl); יֶחְדְּיָהוּ (yĕḥdᵉyā'hū); יְחַוְאֵל (yᵉḥăvvᵉ'ēl); יַחֲזִיאֵל (yă'ḥᵃzī'ēl); יַחְזְיָה (yăḥzᵉyā'); יְחֶזְקֵאל (yᵉḥĕzkē'l); יְחִזְקִיָּה (yᵉḥīzkīyyā'), יְחִזְקִיָּהוּ (yᵉḥīzkīyyā'hū); יַחְזֵרָה (yăḥzērā'); יְחִיאֵל (yᵉḥī'ēl) *pr.n.m.*

יְחִי see חָיָה.

יָחִיד (yāḥī'ḍ) *adj., pl.* יְחִידִים, *f* יְחִידָה, only, alone, forsaken; *f* [peerless] soul, life.

יְחִיָּה (yᵉḥīyyā') *pr.n.m.*

יָחִיל (yāḥī'l) *adj.* waiting, hoping.

יָחַל (yāḥă'l) *Ni.* נוֹחַל, *fut.* יִיָּחֵל, to wait.— *Pi.* יִחֵל, *imp.* יַחֵל, *fut.* יְיַחֵל, *pt.* מְיַחֵל to wait, hope, expect, to be patient; to cause to hope.— *Hi.* הוֹחִיל, *fut.* יוֹחִיל, נִיּוֹחֵל to wait, to tarry.

יַחְלְאֵל (yăḥlᵉ'ēl) *pr.n.m.*

יָחַם (yāḥă'm) *fut.* יֵחַם, יַחֵם, *pl.* יֶחֱמוּ, to be in heat, to be in the rut, to conceive. — *Pi. pf. f w.s.* יֶחֱמַתְנִי, *inf.* יַחֵם, to be in the rut, to conceive.

יַחְמוּר (yăḥmū'r) *m* a species of deer, buck.

יַחְמַי (yăḥmă'y) *pr.n.m.*

יָחַן see חָנָה.

יָחְנְךָ see חָנַן.

יָחֵף (yāḥē'f) *adj.* barefooted, unshod.

יַחְצְאֵל (yăḥṣᵉ'ēl) *pr.n.m.*

יָחַר (yāḥă'r) *Pi. fut.* יִיחַר [for יְיַחֵר] to delay.

יָחַר see חָרָה.

יַחַשׂ (yă'ḥăs) *m* family, race, genealogy.

יָחַשׂ (yāḥă's) *Hith. pf.* and *inf.* הִתְיַחֵשׂ, to be enrolled in a family register; *inf.* = register.

יַחַת (yă'ḥăϑ) *pr.n.m.*

יַט, יֵט see נָטָה.

יָטַב (yāṭă'ḇ) *fut.* יִיטַב, יֵטַב [once יֵיטַב], to be good, well, beautiful, pleasant, lovely, glad, cheerful. — *Hi.* הֵיטִיב, *inf.* הֵיטֵיב,

הֵיטִיב, הֵיטִב, *imp.* הֵיטִיבָה, *fut.* יֵיטִב, יֵיטֵב, וַיֵּיטֶב, *pt.* מֵיטִיב to do well, to make good, to do good; to make cheerful; to adjust; *inf. adv.* well.

יָטְבָה (yŏtbā'); יָטְבָתָה (yŏtbā'thā); יֻטָּה (yŭttā') *pr.n.* of places.

יְטוּר (yᵉtū'r) *pr.n.m.*

יֵידַע = יֵדַע see יָדַע.

יְיֵלִיל see יָלַל *Hi.*

יַיִן (yă'yĭn) *m, i.p.* יָיִן, *c.* יֵין, *w.s.* יֵינוֹ, wine [made of grapes]; intoxication.

יֵיף see יָפָה.

יַךְ see נָכָה *Hi.*

יְכַבְּדֻנְנִי see כָּבֵד *Pi.*

יָכַח (yāφă'ḥ) *Ni.* נוֹכַח, *fut.* יִוָּכַח, *pt. f* נוֹכַחַת, to dispute with one, to argue; to be convicted, reproved. — *Hi.* הוֹכִחַ, הוֹכַח, *fut.* יוֹכִחַ, יוֹכַח, *pt.* מוֹכִיחַ to decide, judge; to meditate or arbitrate; to reprove, punish, chide. — *Ho.* הוּכַח to be punished. — *Hith.* הִתְוַכַּח to dispute, argue.

יְכִילְיָה (yᵉφī'lᵉyā') *pr.n.f.*

יָכִין (yāφī'n) *pr.n.m., patr.* יָכִינִי; name of a pillar in front of the temple.

יָכֹל (yāφō'l) [יָכוֹל] *pf.* יָכֹלְתִּי, *w.s.* יְכָלְתִּיו (yᵉφŏltī'v), *pl.* יָכְלוּ, *i.p.* יָכֹלוּ, *inf.* יְכֹל, *fut.* [taken from *Ho.*] יוּכַל, נוּכַל, אוּכַל, to be able, capable; to prevail, overcome, master, comprehend.

יְכָלְיָה (yᵉφŏlyā'), יְכָלְיָהוּ (yᵉφŏlyā'hū) *pr.n.f.*

יְכָנְיָה (yᵉφŏnyā'), יְכָנְיָהוּ (yᵉφŏnyā'hū) *pr.n.m.*

יְכַסְיֻמוּ = יְכַסּוּמוֹ see כָּסָה.

יַכְּתוּ, יַכֵּת see כָּתַת *Hi.* and *Ho.*

יָלַד (yālă'd) *inf.* לָדָה, יְלֹד, לֶדֶת, לַת, *w.s.* לִדְתִּי, *fut.* יוֹלֵד, יֵלֵד, וַתֵּלֶד, *pt.* יֹלֵד, יוֹלַדְתְּ, יֹלֶדֶת, *f* יוֹלֵדָה, *pt. p.* יָלוּד to bring forth, to bear; to beget. — *Ni.* נוֹלַד, נוֹלָד, *inf.* הִוָּלֵד, *fut.* יִוָּלֵד, *pt.* נוֹלָד, *pl.* נוֹלָדִים to be born. — *Pi.* יִלֵּד, *inf.* יַלֵּד to bear; to help to bear, to deliver; *pt. f* מְיַלֶּדֶת midwife. — *Pu.* יֻלַּד to be born. — *Hi.* הוֹלִיד, הֹלִיד, *inf.* הוֹלִיד, הֹלִיד, *fut.* יוֹלִיד, וַיּוֹלֶד, *pt.* מוֹלִיד to cause to bear, to beget; to produce, create. — *Ho. inf.*

הֻלֶּדֶת to be born. — *Hith.* הִתְיַלֵּד to cause oneself to be enrolled in a family register.

יֶלֶד (yĕ'lĕḍ) *m, i.p.* יָלֶד, *pl.* יְלָדִים, *c.* יַלְדֵי, יִלְדֵי, one born, male child, son, young one; *pl.* children.

יַלְדָּה (yăldā') *f* girl, maiden.

יַלְדוּת (yălḍū'ϑ) *f* childhood, youth; young men.

יִלּוֹד (yĭllō'ḍ) *m, pl.* יִלֹּדִים, one born.

יָלוֹן (yālō'n) *pr.n.m.*

יָלִיד (yālī'ḍ) *adj., c.* יְלִיד, *pl. c.* יְלִידֵי, born, son, child [born in the house].

יָלַךְ see הָלַךְ.

יָלַל (yālă'l) *Hi.* הֵילִיל, *imp.* הֵילֵל, הֵילִילוּ, *fut.* יְיֵלִיל, יְהֵילִיל, to wail, to lament; to shout triumphantly.

יְלֵל (yᵉlē'l) *m* a howling.

יְלָלָה (yᵉlālā') *f, w.s.* יִלְלָתָהּ, wailing, lamentation.

יַלֶּפֶת (yăllĕ'fĕϑ) *f* an itching scab.

יֶלֶק (yĕ'lĕk) *m* a kind of locust.

יַלְקוּט (yălkū't) *m* shepherd's bag.

יָם (yām) *m, c.* יַם, *w. loc.* יָמָּה ה, *pl.* יַמִּים, sea, lake, the west; large river [Nile, Euphrates]; a laver in the temple-court.

יֵם (yēm) *m,* only *pl.* יֵמִים hot springs.

יְמוּאֵל (yᵉmū'ē'l) *pr.n.m.*

יָמַח see מָחָה.

יְמִימָה (yᵉmīmā') *pr.n.f.*

יָמִין[1] (yāmī'n) *m* and *f, c.* יְמִין [מִימִין, לִימִין, בִּימִין], *w.s.* יְמִינִי, right side, right hand, the south; prosperity.

יָמִין[2] (yāmī'n) *pr.n.m.*; *patr.* יָמִינִי.

יְמִינִי[1] (yᵉmīnī') *adj.* right [as opposed to left].

יְמִינִי[2] (yᵉmīnī') *gent.* of בֶּן יָמִין, Benjaminite.

יִמְלָה, יִמְלָא (yĭmlā') *pr.n.m.*

יַמְלֵךְ (yămlē'ḵ) *pr.n.m.*

יָמַן (yāmă'n) *Hi.* [*denom.* of יָמִין] הֵימִין, *inf.* הֵמִין, *imp. f* הֵימִינִי, *fut.* יֵימִין, *pl.* תֵּאָמִינוּ, *pt.* מֵיְמִין, to turn to the right hand, to use the right hand.

יִמְנָה (yĭmnā') *pr.n.m.*

יְמָנִי (yᵉmānī') *adj., f* יְמָנִית, right.

יִמְנָע (yĭmnā'ᵉ) *pr.n.m.*

יָמַר (yāmă'r) *Hi.* הֵימִיר to change, to exchange. — *Hith.* הִתְיַמֵּר to take one's place [others: to glory].

יֵמַר see מָרַר.

יִמְרָה (yĭmrā') *pr.n.m.*

יְמְרוּ = יֹאמְרוּ see אָמַר.

יָמַשׁ (yāmă'š) *Hi. imp. w.s.* הֲיִמִישֵׁנִי, to let feel or touch.

יָנָה (yānā') *fut.* יִינֶה, *pl. w.s.* נִינֵם [= נִינֶה אוֹתָם], *pt. f* יוֹנָה, to oppress. — *Hi.* הוֹנָה, *pt. w.s.* מוֹנַיִךְ, to oppress, maltreat, overreach, drive away.

יָנוֹחַ (yānō'ªḥ) *pr.n.* of a town in Naphtali.

יָנוּם (yānū'm) *pr.n.* of a place in Judah.

יָנִי see נוא *Hi.*

יַנִּיחַ see נוּחַ *Hi.*

יְנִיקָה (yᵉnĭkā') *f* a sucker, sprout.

יָנַק (yānă'k) *fut.* יִינַק, *pt.* יוֹנֵק, to suck, to enjoy; *pt.* a suckling babe. — *Hi. f* הֵינִיקָה, *inf.* הֵינִיק, *imp. f w.s.* הֵינִקֵהוּ, *fut.* תֵּינִיק, תֵּינַק, וַתֵּינֶק, *pt. f* מֵינֶקֶת, *w.s.* מֵנִקְתּוֹ to suckle; to let enjoy; *pt. f* wet-nurse, nurse.

יַנְשׁוּף (yănšō'f), יַנְשׁוּף (yănšū'f) *m* an unclean bird [owl, heron or ibis].

יַסֵּב, **יִסֹּב** see סָבַב.

יָסַד (yāsă'd) *inf.* יְסֹד, *fut.* יִסַּד [for יִיסַד], *pt.* יֹסֵד, to establish, set, found, build up; to appoint, assign. — *Ni.* נוֹסַד, *inf.* הִוָּסֵד, *fut.* יִוָּסֵד to be founded, settled; to take counsel together. — *Pi.* יִסַּד, *inf.* יַסֵּד, *fut.* יְיַסֵּד, to found, build; to appoint, ordain. — *Pu.* יֻסַּד, *pt.* מְיֻסָּד to be founded. — *Ho. inf.* הוּסַד, *pt.* מוּסָד, to be founded, established.

יְסֻד (yᵉsū'd) *m* foundation, beginning.

יְסוֹד (yᵉsō'd) *m*, *pl.* יְסוֹדִים and יְסֹדוֹת, ground, foundation; *pl.* princes.

יְסוּדָה (yᵉsūdā') *f* foundation.

יָסוּר (yāsū'r) *m*, only *pl. w.s.* יְסוּרַי those who turn away from me.

יִסּוֹר (yĭssō'r) *m* a reprover, blamer.

יָסַךְ (yāsă'ḥ) *fut.* יִיסַךְ to pour.

יִסְכָּה (yĭskā') *pr.n.f.*

יִסְמַכְיָהוּ (yĭsmăḥyā'hū) *pr n.m.*

יָסַף (yāsa'f) *pt. pl.* יֹסְפִים, *Q.* the same as *Hi.* — *Ni.* נוֹסַף, *pt.* נוֹסָף to be added, to be increased; *pt. f/pl.* נוֹסָפוֹת additions. — *Hi.* הוֹסִיף, הֹסִף, *inf.* הוֹסִיף, *fut.* וַיּוֹסֶף, יֹסֵף, יֹסִף, יוֹסִיף, וַיֹּסֶף, וַיֹּאסֶף, *pt.* מוֹסִיף, to add, to increase, to do again, to do further or longer.

יָסַר (yāsa'r) *fut.* יִסֹּר, 1. *sg. w.s.* אֶיסְּרֵם, *pt.* יֹסֵר, to chastise, reprove. — *Ni.* נוֹסַר, *imp.* הִוָּסֵר, *fut.* יִוָּסֵר, to be chastised, to learn reproof, to take warning. — *Pi.* יִסַּר, *inf.* יַסֹּר, יַסֵּר, יַסְּרָה, *imp.* יַסֵּר, *fut.* יְיַסֵּר, to chastise, punish, correct, admonish, instruct. — *Hi. fut.* יַיְסִיר to correct, admonish. — *Nithp.* נִוַּסֵּר, *pl.* נִוַּסְּרוּ, to be warned, instructed.

יָע (yā') *m*, only *pl.* יָעִים shovel.

יַעְבֵּץ (ya'bē'ṣ) *pr.n.* of a place; also *pr.n.m.*

יָעַד[1] (yā'a'd) *fut.* יִיעַד to appoint, to fix [a place or time]; to order [punishment]; to betroth, to give in marriage. — *Ni.* נוֹעַד, *fut.* יִוָּעֵד, *pt.* נוֹעָד, to meet by agreement, to come together, to repair, to gather together. — *Hi.* הוֹעִיד, *fut.* יוֹעִיד, to appoint a place or time, to summon, to cite. — *Ho. pt.* מוּעָד to be fixed, appointed; to be directed.

יָעַד[2] see עוד *Hi.*

יֶעְדּוֹ, יֶעְדִּי (ye'dō', ye'dī') *pr.n.m.*

יָעָה (yā'ā') to snatch or sweep away.

יְעוּאֵל (ye'ū'ē'l); **יְעוּץ** (ye'ū'ṣ); **יָעוּר** (yā'ū'r); **יְעוּשׁ** (ye'ū'š) *pr.n.m.*

יָעוֹר (yā'ō'r) *m*, only *pl.* יְעוֹרִים = יַעַר forest.

יָעַז (yā'a'z) *Ni. pt.* נוֹעָז to be bold, impudent.

יַעֲזִיאֵל (ya'azī'ē'l); **יַעֲזִיָּהוּ** (ya'azyā') *pr.n.m.*

יַעְזֵר, יַעְזֵיר (ya'zē'r) *pr.n.* of a town in Gilead.

יָעַט (yā'a't) to clothe = עָטָה.

יָעַט see עיט.

יָעִיר (yā'ī'r); **יַעְכָּן** (ya'kā'n) *pr.n.m.*

יָעַל (yā'a'l) *Hi.* הוֹעִיל, *fut.* יוֹעִיל, to help, assist, to be of use; to profit.

יָעֵל[1] (yā'ē'l) *m, pl.* יְעֵלִים, chamois, stone-buck.

יָעֵל[2] (yā'ē'l) *pr.n.m.* and *f.*

יַעֲלָה[1] (yă''ălā') *f* chamois.

יַעֲלָה[2] (yă''ălā') *pr.n.m.*

יַעְלָם (yă'lā'm) *pr.n.m.*

יַעַן (yă''ăn) *prep.* because of, on account of; *conj.*, also יַעַן אֲשֶׁר and יַעַן כִּי, although, because, in order that.

יָעֵן (yā'ē'n) *m,* only *pl.* יְעֵנִים ostrich.

יַעֲנָה (yă''ănā') *f* female ostrich.

יַעְנַי (yă'nī') *pr.n.m.*

יְעֹעֵרוּ see עוּר *Pilp.*

יָעֵף[1] (yā'ē'f) *fut.* יִיעַף, יַעַף, to be weary, faint, exhausted.—*Ho. pt.* מֻעָף to be wearied.

יָעֵף[2] (yā'ē'f) *adj., pl.* יְעֵפִים, weary, faint.

יְעָף (y''ā'f) *m* wearisome course.

יָעַץ (yā'ă'ṣ) *fut.* יִיעַץ, *pt.* יוֹעֵץ, יֹעֵץ, *pl.* יוֹעֲצִים, *pt. p.* יָעוּץ, to advise, counsel, admonish; to direct, to resolve, decide.—*Ni.* נוֹעַץ, *fut.* יִוָּעֵץ, *pt.* נוֹעָץ to consult with one another, to counsel together, to be advised. — *Hith. fut.* יִתְיָעֵץ to consult together.

יַעֲקֹב (yă''ăkō'b); יַעֲקֹבָה (yă''ăkō'bā); יַעֲקָן (yă''ăkā'n) *pr.n.m.*

יָעַר see עוּר *Hi.*

יַעַר (yă''ăr) *m, i.p.* יָעַר, *w. loc.* ה יַעְרָה, *w.s.* יַעְרוֹ, *pl.* יְעָרִים, thicket, forest, wood; wild honey, honeycomb.

יַעֲרָה (yă''ărā') *f, c.* יַעְרַת, *pl.* יְעָרוֹת = יַעַר.

יַעְרָה (yă'rā') *pr.n.m.*

יַעֲרֵי אֹרְגִים (yă''ărē' ō'rᵉgī'm) *pr.n.m.*

יְעָרִים *pr.n.* see קִרְיַת יְעָרִים.

יַעֲרֶשְׁיָה (yă''ărĕšyā'); יַעֲשׂוֹ (yă''ăśō'); יַעֲשַׂי (yă''ăśă'y); יַעֲשִׂיאֵל (yă''ăśī'ē'l); יִפְדְיָה (yĭfdᵉyā') *pr.n.m.*

יָפָה (yāfā') *fut.* יִיפֶה, וַיִּיף, to be beautiful, fair.—*Pi.* יִפָּה to beautify, to adorn. — *Polpal.* יְפֵיפָה (yŏfyāfā'), יְפֵיפִיתָ, to be very beautiful.—*Hith.* הִתְיַפָּה to adorn oneself.

יָפֶה (yāfĕ') *adj., c.* יְפֵה, *f* יָפָה, *c.* יְפַת, *pl.* יָפוֹת, *c.* יְפוֹת, יְפֹת beautiful, excellent.

יְפֵה־פִיָּ (yᵉfē' fī') *adj.*, only *f* יְפֵה־פִיָּה, very beautiful.

יָפוֹ (yāfō') *pr.n.* of a sea-port, Joppa or Jaffa.

יָפַח (yāfă'ḥ) *Hith.* הִתְיַפֵּחַ, to pant, to sigh.

יָפֵחַ (yāfē'ᵃḥ) *adj.*, *c.* יְפֵחַ panting, breathing.

יֳפִי (yᵒfī') *m*, *c.* יְפִי, יֳפִי, *i.p.* יֹפִי, *w.s.* יָפְיֵךְ (yŏfyē'ḵ), יָפְיוֹ, beauty, splendour.

יָפִיעַ (yāfī'ăᵉ); יַפְלֵט (yăflē't); יְפֻנֶּה (yᵉfŭnnĕ') *pr.n.m.*

יָפַע (yāfă'ᵉ) *Hi. pf.* and *imp.* הוֹפִיעַ, *fut.* יוֹפִיעַ, יֹפַע, to cause to shine, to give light; to shine, to appear in brightness.

יִפְעָה (yĭfᵉā') *f* beauty, splendour.

יֶפֶת (yĕ'fĕṯ) *pr.n.m.*, *i.p.* יָפֶת.

יִפְתָּח (yĭftā'ḥ) *pr.n.m.*

יִפְתַּח־אֵל (yĭftă'ḥ-ē'l) *pr.n.* of a valley.

יָצָא (yāṣā') *inf.* יָצֹא, צֵאת, *w.s.* צֵאתִי, *imp.* צֵא, צְאָה, צְאִי, צְאוּ, צֵאוּ, *fut.* יֵצֵא, *pt.* יֹצֵא, יוֹצֵא, *pl.* יוֹצְאִים, *c.* יוֹצְאֵי, *f* יוֹצֵאת, יֹצֵת, *pl.* יוֹצְאוֹת, to go out, forth, away, to march out; to come from, to be begotten or born, to grow; to be gone, expended; to rise [of the sun]; to end. — *Hi. pf.* and *inf.* הוֹצִיא, *imp.* הוֹצֵא, *fut.* יוֹצִיא, וַיּוֹצֵא, וַיֹּצֵא, to lead out, forth, away; to produce, to let grow, to cause to appear; to separate; to spread, to announce; to exact [money]. — *Ho.* הוּצָא, *pt. f* מוּצֵאת, to be brought out, to be led forth.

יָצַב (yāṣă'ḇ) [*Ni.*, *Hi.*, *Ho.* taken from נָצַב] *Hith. inf.* and *imp.* הִתְיַצֵּב, *fut.* יִתְיַצֵּב, to take one's stand, to stand forth, to withstand; to hold a position, to stand before one.

יָצַג (yāṣă'g) *Hi.* הִצִּיג, *inf.* הַצֵּג, *imp. pl.* הַצִּיגוּ, *fut.* יַצִּיג, וַיַּצֵּג, *pt.* מַצִּיג, to place, to establish; to leave; to put down. — *Ho. fut.* יֻצַּג to be left.

יִצְהָר[1] (yĭṣhā'r) *m* oil.

יִצְהָר[2] (yĭṣhā'r) *pr.n.m.*

יָצוּעַ (yāṣū'ăᵉ) or יָצִיעַ (yāṣī'ăᵉ) *m* [and *f*], *w.s.* יְצִיעִי.

pl. יְצִיעִים, *c.* יְצִיעֵי, couch, bed; floor, story.

יִצְחָק (yĭßḥā'k) *pr.n.m.*, Isaac.

יִצְטַיָּרוּ see צִיר *Hith.*

יָצִיא (yāßī') *adj.*, *pl. c.* יְצִיאֵי, come forth, born, descended.

יָצַע (yāßă'') *Hi.* הִצִּיעַ, *fut.* יַצִּיעַ, to spread out, to make as a bed.— *Ho. fut.* יֻצַּע to be spread out.

יָצַק (yāßă'k) *inf.* צֶקֶת, *imp.* יְצֹק, צַק, *fut.* יִצֹּק, יִצַק, וַיִּצֹק, *pt. p.* יָצוּק, *pl.* יְצוּקִים, *f* יְצֻקוֹת, to pour, to pour out; to melt, to cast [metals]; to harden; *intr.* to flow out. — *Pi. pt. f* מְיַצֶּקֶת to pour out. — *Hi.* הִצִּיק, *fut.* יַצִּיק, *pt. f* מוּצֶקֶת to pour out; to place, to set. — *Ho.* הוּצַק, *pt.* מוּצָק, *c.* מֻצַּק, to be poured out, to be molten or cast; to be made firm.

יְצֻקָה (y'ßūkā') *f*, *w.s.* יְצֻקָתוֹ, a casting [of metal].

יָצַר¹ (yāßă'r) *fut.* יִצֹר, יִיצַר, יִצַּר, יִיצֶר, יִצֶר, *pt.* יוֹצֵר, יֹצֵר, to form, to fashion, to devise; to produce, create; *pt.* [potter, creator] see יוֹצֵר.—*Ni.* נוֹצַר to be formed or fashioned; to exist. — *Pu.* יֻצַּר to be predestined.—*Ho. fut.* יוּצַר to be formed.

יָצַר² (yāßă'r) *fut.* יֵצַר, to be pressed, to be narrow; to be straitened; to be in trouble or sorrow.

יֵצֶר¹ (yē'ßĕr) *m*, *w.s.* יִצְרוֹ, formation, frame, pattern, image; fiction, thought, device.

יֵצֶר² (yē'ßĕr) *pr.n.m.*

יְצֻר (y'ßū'r) *m*, only *pl.* יְצֻרִים, formation, structure [members].

יִצְרִי (yĭßrī') *pr.n.m.*

יָצַת (yāßă'ϑ) [= צות] *fut.* יִצַּת, *pl.* יִצָּתוּ, to kindle, to set on fire, to burn. — *Ni.* נִצַּת to be kindled, burnt, consumed; to be incensed.— *Hi.* הִצִּית [הִצִּית see צות], once הוֹצִית, *imp. pl. w.s.* הַצִּיתוּהָ, *fut.* יַצִּית, וַיַּצֵּת, *pt.* מַצִּית to kindle, to set on fire, to burn.

יֶקֶב (yĕ'kĕḇ) *m*, *w.s.* יִקְבֶךָ, *pl.* יְקָבִים, *c.* יִקְבֵי, wine-vat, wine-press.

יְקַבְצְאֵל (y'kăḇß''ēl) *pr.n.* of a town in Judah.

יָקַד (yākă'ḏ) *inf.* יְקֹד, *fut*

יֵקַד, יִיקַד, *pt. f* יֹקֶדֶת, *pt. p.* יָקוּד, to glow, burn, blaze. — *Ho. fut.* יוּקַד to be kindled, to burn.

יָקְדְעָם (yŏ'kdᵉʼā'm) *pr.n.* of a town in Judah.

יָקֶה (yākĕ') *pr.n.m.*

יִקְהָה (yĭkhā') or יְקָהָה (yᵉkāhā') *f*, only *c.* יִקְּהַת obedience.

יְקוֹד, יְקֹד (yᵉkō'd) *m* a burning.

יָקוּד (yākū'd) *m* a burning mass.

יְקוּם (yᵉkū'm) *m* substance, being, the living things.

יָקוֹשׁ (yākō's), יָקוּשׁ (yākū's) *m* ensnarer, fowler.

יְקוּתִיאֵל (yᵉkū'θī'ē'l) *pr.n.m.*

יִקַּח, יִקַּח see לָקַח.

יָקְטָן (yŏktā'n) *pr.n.m.*

יָקִים (yākī'm) *pr.n.m.*

יַקִּיר (yăkkī'r) *adj.* dear, valuable.

יְקַמְיָה (yᵉkămyā'); יְקַמְעָם (yᵉkămʼā'm) *pr.n.m.*

יָקְמְעָם (yŏkmᵉʼā'm) *pr.n.* of a town in Ephraim.

יָקְנְעָם (yŏknᵉʼā'm) *pr.n.* of a town in Zebulon.

יָקַע (yākă'ʼ) *fut.* יֵקַע, to remove oneself, to be dislocated, to be alienated. — *Hi.* הוֹקִיעַ, *imp.* הוֹקַע, *fut.* יוֹקִיעַ, to nail to a pale, to impale, crucify, hang. — *Ho. pt.* מוּקָע to be impaled, hanged.

יָקַץ (yākă'ẞ) *fut.* יִיקַץ, יֵקַץ, יִקַץ, וַיִּיקֶץ, וַיִּקַץ, to awake.

יָקַר (yākă'r) *fut.* יִיקַר, יֵיקַר, יֵקַר, to be heavy, precious, dear, costly, esteemed. — *Hi. imp.* הוֹקַר, *fut.* יוֹקִיר, to make precious or rare.

יָקָר (yākā'r) *adj.*, *c.* יְקַר, *pl.* יְקָרִים, *f* יְקָרָה, *c.* יִקְרַת, *pl.* יְקָרוֹת, *c.* יִקְרוֹת, grave, thoughtful; heavy, dear, precious, costly, esteemed, rare, splendid.

יְקָר (yᵉkā'r) *m*, *w.s.* יְקָרוֹ, value, price; preciousness, honour, dignity, splendour.

יִקְרֵהוּ see קָרָה.

יָקֹשׁ (yākō's) *pf. pl.* יָקְשׁוּ, יְקֹשׁוּן, *pt.* יוֹקֵשׁ, to ensnare, to lay snares; *pt.* a fowler. —*Ni.* נוֹקַשׁ, *fut.* יִוָּקֵשׁ, to be snared, caught, ensnared.—*Pu. pt.* יוּקָשׁ [for מְיֻקָּשׁ] to be snared.

יִקֶּשׁ see קָשָׁה.

יָקְשָׁן (yŏksā'n) *pr.n.m.*

יָקְתְאֵל (yŏkϑ'ē'l) *pr.n.* of a town in Judah.

יָרֵא[1] (yārē') *inf.* לְרֹא, יְרֹא, יִרְאָה, *imp.* יְרָא, יְראוּ, *fut.* יִירָא, יִירָא, *pl.* יִירְאוּ, יִרְאוּ, to be afraid, to fear, to reverence. — *Ni.* *fut.* יִוָּרֵא, *pt.* נוֹרָא, *f* נוֹרָאָה, *pl.* נוֹרָאוֹת to be feared, to be dreadful, to be reverenced; *pt.* as a *subst.* wonderful, stupendous deed. — *Pi.* יְרֵא, *inf.* יָרֵא, *pt.* מְיָרֵא, to terrify, to make afraid.

יָרֵא[2] (yārē') *adj.*, *c.* יְרֵא, *pl.* יְרֵאִים, *c.* יִרְאֵי, *f c.* יִרְאַת, fearing, afraid, anxious, timid, reverencing.

יַרְא, יֵרָא see רָאָה.

יִרְאָה (yĭr'ā') *f*, *c.* יִרְאַת, fear, terror, reverence, awe; יִרְאַת יהוה fear of God, piety, religion.

יִרְאוֹן (yĭr'ō'n) *pr.n.* of a town in Naphtali.

יִרְאִיָּה (yĭr'ĭyyā') *pr.n.m.*

יָרֵב (yārē'b) *m* fighter, revenger; title of the Assyrian king.

יָרֵב – יֶאֱרַב see אָרַב.

יְרֻבַּעַל (y'rŭbbā''ăl) *pr.n.m.*, surname of Gideon.

יָרָבְעָם (yā'rŏb'ā'm) *pr.n.m.*, Jeroboam.

יְרֻבֶּשֶׁת (y'rŭbbĕ'šĕϑ) *pr.n.m.* = יְרֻבַּעַל.

יָרַד (yără'd) *inf.* רֶדֶת, יְרֹד, רִדְתָּה, *w.s.* רִדְתִּי, *imp.* רֵד, רְדָה, רְדוּ, רְדִי, רְדָה, *fut.* יֵרֵד, *i.p.* יֵרֵד, וַיֵּרֶד, וַיֵּרַד, *pt.* יוֹרֵד, יֹרֵד, *pl.* יוֹרְדִים, *c.* יוֹרְדֵי, *f* יוֹרֶדֶת, to go, come, flow or fall down, to descend. — *Hi.* הוֹרִיד, *inf.* הוֹרִיד, *imp.* הוֹרֵד, *fut.* יוֹרִיד, וַיּוֹרֶד [וַיֶּרֶד see רָדַד *Hi.*], *pt.* מוֹרִיד, to bring, lead or send down; to throw down, to subdue. — *Ho.* הוּרַד to be led down, to be taken down, to be cast down.

יֶרֶד (yĕ'rĕd) *pr.n.m.*

יַרְדֵּן (yărdē'n) *pr.n.*, the river Jordan.

יָרָה[1] (yārā') *inf.* יָרֹה, יְרוֹת, *imp.* יְרֵה, *fut.* יִירֶה, 1. *pl.* *w.s.* וַנִּירָם, *pt.* יֹרֶה, to cast, to shoot; to lay [a foundation], to found, erect, establish; to shed [water], to irrigate; *pt.* יוֹרֶה early rain. — *Ni.* נוֹרָה to be shot. — *Hi.* הוֹרָה, *fut.* יוֹרֶה, וַיּוֹר [יִרְאוּ for יוֹרוּ], *pt.*

מוֹרֶה, *pl.* מוֹרִים, מוֹרְאִים, to throw, to cast, to shoot, *pt.* archer; to wet, to water; יוֹרֶה – מוֹרֶה early rain.

יָרָה[2] (yārā') *Hi.* הוֹרָה, *inf.* הוֹרֹת, *imp.* הוֹרֵה, *fut.* יוֹרֶה, יֹרֶה, *pt.* מוֹרֶה, *pl. w.s.* מוֹרַי, to show, point out; to teach, instruct; *pt.* teacher, guide.

יָרֵה (yārā'h) *fut. pl.* תִּירְאוּ [or for תִּירָאוּ] to fear, to be afraid.

יְרוּאֵל (yᵉrū'ē'l); **יָרוֹם** (yārō'ᵃḥ) *pr.n.m.*

יָרֹק (yārō'k) *m* green, herb.

יְרוּשָׁא, **יְרוּשָׁה** (yᵉrūšā') *pr.n.f.*

יְרוּשָׁלַיִם, **יְרוּשָׁלַםִ** (yᵉrū'-šālā'yĭm), יְרוּשָׁלֵם (yᵉrū'šā-lē'm), *i.p.* יְרוּשָׁלָיִם, *w. loc.* יְרוּשָׁלַיְמָה ה, *pr.n.*, Jerusalem.

יָרֵחַ (yārē'ᵃḥ) *m* the moon.

יֶרַח[1] (yĕ'răḥ) *m*, *pl.* יְרָחִים, lunar month.

יֶרַח[2] (yĕ'răḥ) *pr.n.m.* of an Arabian tribe.

יְרִיחוֹ, **יְרֵחוֹ** (yᵉrēḥō') and יְרִיחֹה, יְרִיחוֹ (yᵉrĭḥō') *pr.n.*, Jericho.

יְרֹחָם (yᵉrōḥā'm) *pr.n.m.*

יְרַחְמְאֵל (yᵉrăḥmᵉ'ē'l) *pr.n.m.*; *patr.* יְרַחְמְאֵלִי.

יַרְחָע (yărḥā'ᵒ) *pr.n.m.*

יָרַט (yārā't) *fut.* יִירַט, יָרַט, to deliver up; to be pernicious or fatal.

יְרִיאֵל (yᵉrī'ē'l) *pr.n.m.*

יָרִיב[1] (yārī'b) adversary.

יָרִיב[2] (yārī'b); **יְרִיבַי** (yᵉrībā'y); **יְרִיָּה** (yᵉrĭyyā'); **יְרִימוֹת** [יְרֵמוֹת] (yᵉrēmō'th) *pr.n.m.*

יְרִיעָה (yᵉrī'ā') *f*, *pl.* יְרִיעוֹת, curtain, hanging, tent.

יְרִיעוֹת (yᵉrī'ō'th) *pr.n.f.*

יָרֵךְ (yārē'k) *f*, *c.* יֶרֶךְ, *w.s.* יְרֵכִי, *du.* יְרֵכַיִם, thigh; haunch, ham; side; lower end, stem.

יֶרֶךְ see **רכך**.

יַרְכָּה (yărkā') *f*, *w.s.* יַרְכָתוֹ, *du.* יַרְכָתַיִם, *c.* יַרְכְּתֵי, side, hinder side, rear, inmost part, recess.

יַרְמוּת (yărmū'th) *pr.n.* of two towns.

יְרֵמוֹת (yᵉrēmō'th); **יְרֵמַי** (yᵉrē-mā'y); **יִרְמְיָה** (yĭrmᵉyā'), **יִרְמְיָהוּ** (yĭrmᵉyā'hū) *pr.n.m.*

יָרַע (yārā'ᵒ) to be afraid, to tremble.

יִרְפְּאֵל (yĭrp°'ē'l) *pr.n.* of a place in Benjamin.

יָרַק (yārā'**k**) *inf.* יְרֹק, to spit.

יָרָק (yārā'**k**) *m, c.* יְרַק *coll.* greens, herbs, vegetables.

יֶרֶק (yĕ'rĕ**k**) *m* greenness, verdure, foliage.

יֵרָקוֹן (yē'rā**k**ō'n) *m* yellow colour, paleness, withering.

יַרְקוֹן (yăr**k**ō'n) *pr.n.* of a place in Dan.

יָרְקְעָם (yŏr**k**°'ā'm) *pr.n.m.*

יְרַקְרַק (y°rā**k**rā'**k**) *adj., f/pl.* יְרַקְרַקּוֹת greenish, yellowish, yellow like gold.

יָרַשׁ (yārā'š) [יָרֵשׁ] *pf. w.s.* וִירִשְׁתָּהּ, וִירֵשׁוּהָ, *inf.* רֶשֶׁת, *w.s.* רִשְׁתָּהּ, יְרִשְׁנוּ (yŏršē'nū), *imp.* רֵשׁ, רֵשׁ, יְרַשׁ, יְרָשָׁה, *fut.* יִירַשׁ, *pl.* יִרְשׁוּ, *pt.* יוֹרֵשׁ, to seize, to take possession of, to possess, to inherit; to drive away, to take away, to dispossess. — *Ni.* נוֹרַשׁ, *fut.* יִוָּרֵשׁ to be dispossessed, to become poor. — *Pi.* יֵרֵשׁ, *fut.* יְיָרֵשׁ, to occupy, seize, possess. — *Hi.* הוֹרִישׁ, *inf.* הוֹרֵשׁ, הוֹרִישׁ, *fut.* יוֹרִישׁ, וַיּוֹרֶשׁ, *pt.* מוֹרִישׁ, to give in possession; to possess, to dispossess, to expel, to make poor.

יְרֵשָׁה (y°rēšā') and יְרֻשָּׁה (y°rŭššā') *f* possession, inheritance.

יִשְׂחָק = יִצְחָק.

יָשַׂם (yāsā'm) *fut.* יִישַׂם, וַיִּישֶׂם = שׂוּם.

יְשִׂימָאֵל (y°sĭ'mā'ē'l) *pr.n.m.*

יִשְׂרָאֵל (yĭsrā'ē'l) *pr.n.m.*

יִשָּׂשכָר [read יִשָּׂכָר] (yĭssāφā'r) *pr.n.m.*

יֵשׁ (yēš), יֶשׁ־ (yĕš) *m, w.s.* יֶשְׁךָ, יֶשְׁנוֹ, existence, substance, — there is, there are; יֶשׁ־לִי I have; יֶשְׁךָ thou art there.

יָשַׁב (yāšā'b) *inf.* יְשׁוֹב, שֶׁבֶת, *w.s.* שִׁבְתִּי, *imp.* שֵׁב, שְׁבָה, *fut.* יֵשֵׁב, יֵשֶׁב, *pt.* יֹשֵׁב, יוֹשֵׁב, *c.* יֹשְׁבִי, *pl.* יוֹשְׁבִים, *c.* יֹשְׁבֵי, *f* יוֹשֶׁבֶת, יֹשֶׁבֶת, *i.p.* יֹשָׁבֶת, *pl.* יֹשְׁבוֹת, יוֹשְׁבוֹת, to sit, to take a seat, to be seated, to remain, stay, wait; to dwell, to inhabit. — *Ni. pt.* נוֹשָׁב, *f i.p.* נוֹשָׁבֶת to be inhabited. — *Pi.* יִשֵּׁב to pitch a hut. — *Hi.* הוֹשִׁיב, *inf.* הוֹשִׁיב, *imp.* הוֹשֵׁב, *fut.* יוֹשֵׁב, יוֹשִׁיב, *pt.* מוֹשִׁיב, to cause to sit, to cause to dwell, to cause to be inhabited; to marry. — *Ho.* הוּשַׁב to be inhabited, to be made to dwell.

יֶשֶׁבְאָב (yĕ'šĕḇ'ā'ḇ); יֹשֵׁב בַּשֶּׁבֶת (yōšē'ḇ bāššĕ'ḇĕṯ); יִשְׁבַּח (yĭšbā'ḥ); יִשְׁבִּי בְּנֹב (yĭšbī' b'nō'ḇ); יִשְׁבִּי לֶחֶם (yāšū'ḇī lĕ'ḥĕm); יָשֻׁבְעָם (yā'šŏḇ'ā'm); יִשְׁבָּק (yĭšbā'k); יָשְׁבְקָשָׁה (yŏšḇ'kāšā') *pr.n.m.*

יָשׁוּב (yāšū'ḇ) *pr.n.m.*; *patr.* יָשֻׁבִי.

יָשׁוֹד — יָשֹׁד see שָׁדַד.

יִשְׁוָה (yĭšvā'); יִשְׁוִי (yĭšvī'); יְשׁוֹחָיָה (y'šō'ḥāyā'); יֵשׁוּעַ (yēšū'a') *pr.n.m.*

יְשׁוּעָה (y'šū'ā') *f, c.* יְשׁוּעַת, help, deliverance, salvation, victory, welfare.

יֶשַׁח (yĕ'šāḥ) *m* emptiness, hunger.

יִשַּׁח see שָׁחַח *Ni.*

יָשַׁט (yāšā't) *Hi.* הוֹשִׁיט to stretch out.

יִשַׁי (yĭšā'y); יָשִׁיב (yāšī'ḇ), יִשִּׁיָּה (yĭššīyyā'); יִשִּׁיָּהוּ (yĭššīyyā'hū) *pr.n.m.*

יַשִּׁי — יַשִּׁיא see נָשָׁא.

יְשִׁימָה (y'šīmā') *f,* only *pl.* יְשִׁימוֹת, desolation, devastation, destruction.

יְשִׁימוֹן, יְשִׁמֹן (y'šīmō'n) *m* waste, desert.

יָשִׁישׁ (yāšī'š) *m* an old man.

יְשִׁישַׁי (y'šīšā'y) *pr.n.m.*

יָשַׁם (yāšā'm) *fut.* יִישַׁם, יֵשַׁם, to be waste, desolate, deserted.

יָשֹׁם see שָׁמַם.

יִשְׁמָא (yĭšmā'); יִשְׁמָעֵאל (yĭšmā'ē'l) [*patr.* יִשְׁמְעֵאלִי, *pl.* יִשְׁמְעֵאלִים]; יִשְׁמַעְיָה (yĭšma'yā'); יִשְׁמְרַי (yĭšm'rā'y) *pr.n.m.*

יָשַׁן (yāšā'n), יָשֵׁן[1] (yāšē'n) *inf.* יְשׁוֹן, *fut.* יִישַׁן, to fall asleep, to be asleep. — *Pi. fut.* יְיַשְּׁנֵ to lull, to make one sleep.

יָשָׁן (yāšā'n) *adj.*, *f* יְשָׁנָה, old, of the last year.

יָשֵׁן[2] (yāšē'n) *adj.*, *pl.* יְשֵׁנִים, *c.* יְשֵׁנֵי, *f* יְשֵׁנָה, sleeping, dead.

יָשֵׁן[3] (yāšē'n) *pr.n.m.*

יְשָׁנָה (y'šānā') *pr.n.* of a town in Judah.

יָשַׁע (yāšā'') *Ni.* נוֹשַׁע, *imp. pl.* הִוָּשְׁעוּ, *fut.* יִוָּשַׁע, *pt.* נוֹשָׁע, to be delivered, saved, to get help. — *Hi* הוֹשִׁיעַ, *inf.* הוֹשִׁיעַ, הוֹשֵׁעַ, *imp.* הוֹשַׁע, הוֹשִׁיעָה

[הוֹשִׁיעָה־נָּא = Hosanna], *fut.* יוֹשִׁיעַ, יוֹשַׁע, *pt.* מוֹשִׁיעַ, to help, save, deliver.

יֵשַׁע (yē'šă'), יֶשַׁע (yĕ'šă') *m*, *w.s.* יִשְׁעִי, יִשְׁעֲךָ, יִשְׁעֶךָ, help, deliverance, salvation, freedom, welfare.

יִשַׁע see שָׁעָה.

יִשְׁעִי (yĭš'ī'); יְשַׁעְיָה (y'šă'yā'), יְשַׁעְיָהוּ (y'šă'yā'hū) *pr.n.m.*

יָשְׁפֵה (yā'š'fē') or יָשְׁפֶה (yā'š'fĕ') *m* a precious stone, jasper.

יִשְׁפָּה (yĭšpā'); יִשְׁפָּן (yĭšpā'n) *pr.n.m.*

יָשַׁר (yāšā'r) *fut.* יִישַׁר, וַיִּשַׁר, to be straight, to go straight, to be right, convenient, even, tranquil. — *Pi.* יִשֵּׁר, יִשַּׁר, *imp. pl.* יַשְּׁרוּ, *fut.* יְיַשֵּׁר, *pt.* מְיַשֵּׁר, to make straight, even, level; to declare right, to approve. — *Pu. pt.* מְיֻשָּׁר to be made even, to be beaten out flat [metal]. — *Hi.* הוֹשִׁיר, *imp.* הוֹשַׁר, *fut.* יַיְשִׁיר to make straight or even, to look straight on.

יָשָׁר (yāšā'r) *adj.*, *c.* יְשַׁר, *pl.* יְשָׁרִים, *c.* יִשְׁרֵי, *f* יְשָׁרָה, *pl.* יְשָׁרוֹת, straight, even, level; right, upright, just, righteous; pleasing, agreeing.

יֵשֶׁר (yē'šĕr) *pr.n.m.*

יֹשֶׁר (yō'šĕr) *m*, *w.s.* יָשְׁרוֹ (yŏšrō'), straightness, right, truth, duty, honesty.

יְשַׂרְאֵלָה (y'šăr'ē'lā) *pr.n.m.*

יִשְׁרָה (yĭšrā') *f*, *c.* יִשְׁרַת = יֹשֶׁר.

יְשֻׁרוּן (y'šūrū'n) *m* the honest one, the righteous little people [a poetical name for the people of Israel].

יָשֵׁשׁ (yāšē'š) *adj.* old, grey-headed.

יִשְׁתַּחוּ see שָׁחָה *Hith.*

יִשְׁתַּקְשְׁקוּן see שָׁקַק *Hith-palp.*

יָתֵד (yāϑē'd) *f*, *c.* יְתַד, *pl.* יְתֵדוֹת, *c.* יִתְדוֹת, peg, nail, pin; settled condition; prince; spade, shovel.

יָתוֹם (yāϑō'm) *m*, *pl.* יְתוֹמִים, orphan, childless, forsaken.

יְתוּר (y'ϑū'r) *m* what is sought out.

יַתִּיר (yăttī'r) *pr.n.* of a town in Judah.

יִתְכַּס see כָּסָה *Hith.*

יָתַל see תָּלַל.

יִתְלָה (yĭϑlā') *pr.n.* of a place in Dan.

יַתַּמּוּ, יִתְמוֹ, יִתֹּם see תָּמַם.

יִתְמָה (yĭϑmā'); **יַתְנִיאֵל** (yăϑnĭ'ē'l) *pr.n.m.*

יִתְנָן (yĭϑnā'n) *pr.n.* of a town in Judah.

יָתַר (yāϑă'r) *Ni.* נוֹתַר, *fut.* יִוָּתֵר. *pt.* נוֹתָר, *pl.* נוֹתָרִים, *f* נוֹתֶרֶת, *pl.* נוֹתָרוֹת, to be left, to remain; *pt.* remnant, remainder. — *Hi.* הוֹתִיר, *inf.* הוֹתִיר, הוֹתֵר, *imp.* הוֹתֵר, *fut.* יוֹתִיר, יוֹתֵר, וַיּוֹתֵר, to let remain, to leave, to spare; to prefer, to give superiority or abundance.

יֶתֶר[1] (yĕ'ϑĕr) *m, w.s.* יִתְרוֹ, *pl.* יְתָרִים, rope, cord, thread, string; remainder, remnant, rest; abundance, preference, excellence; *adv.* over and above, besides.

יֶתֶר[2] (yĕ'ϑĕr) *pr.n.m.* = יִתְרוֹ; *patr.* יִתְרִי.

יֹתֵר, יֹתֶרֶת see יוֹתֵר, יוֹתֶרֶת.

יִתְרָה (yĭϑrā') *f* abundance, wealth.

יִתְרוֹ (yĭϑrō') *pr.n.m.*

יִתְרוֹן (yĭϑrō'n) *m* preference, gain, profit.

יִתְרָן (yĭϑrā'n); **יִתְרְעָם** (yĭϑrᵉʿā'm); **יְתֵת** (yᵉϑē'ϑ) *pr.n.m.*

כ

כ, ך the eleventh letter of the alphabet, called כַּף [hollow hand, palm]; as a numeral כ = 20, ך = 500.

כְּ prefix, particle of comparison, similarity or proportion; before Sheva כִּ, *w. art.* כַּ, *w.s.* כָּמוֹנִי, כָּמוֹךָ, כָּכֶם, כָּמוֹנוּ, כָּמוֹךְ, כָּמוֹהוּ [כְּמוֹכֶם]. כָּהֵם [כְּמוֹהֶם], כָּהֵנָּה, as, like, as if; at, about [a time], according to, after; before an *inf.* = as, when, if, after.

כָּאַב (kā'ē'b) *fut.* יִכְאַב, *pt.* כּוֹאֵב, *pl.* כּוֹאֲבִים, to feel pain, to feel a pang, to suffer. — *Hi. inf.* הַכְאִיב, *fut.* יַכְאִיב, *pl.* תַּכְאִבוּ, *pt.* מַכְאִב, to cause pain, to make sad, to wound, to spoil.

כְּאֵב (kᵉ'ē'b) *m, w.s.* כְּאֵבִי, pain. sorrow, grief.

כָּאָה (kā'ā') *Ni. pt. c.* נִכְאֵה, to be terrified, humbled, timid, sad. — *Hi.* הִכְאָה, *inf.* הַכְאוֹת to make timid or sad.

כָּאֶה (kā'ě') *adj.*, only *pl.* כָּאִים, troubled, sad, timid.

כָּאַר (kā'ă'r) *pf. pl.* כָּאֲרֵי [for כָּאֲרוּ; or כָּארוּ = כָּרוּ, see כּוּר], to pierce, to dig out.

כַּאֲשֶׁר (kă'ᵃšě'r) *conj.* as, while, where, in order that, so that, when, in so far as [see אֲשֶׁר].

כָּבֵד[1] (kābē'd) *inf.* כְּבֹד, *fut.* יִכְבַּד, to be heavy, weighty, severe, numerous, considerable, honoured, renowned; to be dull. — *Ni.* נִכְבַּד, *inf.* הִכָּבֵד, *fut.* יִכָּבֵד, *pt.* נִכְבָּד, *pl. c.* נִכְבַּדֵּי, *f/pl.* נִכְבָּדוֹת, to be honoured, esteemed; to show oneself great or mighty; to be wealthy, rich. — *Pi.* כִּבֵּד, *inf.* and *imp.* כַּבֵּד, *fut.* יְכַבֵּד. *pt.* מְכַבֵּד to honour; to make heavy, hard, dull. — *Pu. fut.* יְכֻבַּד to be honoured, esteemed. — *Hi.* הִכְבִּיד, *inf.* and *imp.* הַכְבֵּד, *fut.* וַיַּכְבֵּד, *pt.* מַכְבִּיד to make heavy, to oppress; to make dull; to make honoured; to get renown.

כָּבֵד[2] (kābē'd) *adj.*, *c.* כְּבַד, כְּבֶד, *pl.* כְּבֵדִים, *c.* כִּבְדֵי, heavy, weighty, grievous; numerous, great; dull, hardened, awkward.

כָּבֵד[3] (kābē'd) *m*, *w.s.* כְּבֵדִי, the liver.

כָּבֹד (kābō'd) *adj.*, *f* כְּבוּדָּה, splendid, rich; *subst.* riches, possession.

כֹּבֶד (kō'běd) *m* heaviness, weight; multitude; violence.

כְּבֵדֻת (kᵉbēdū'ϑ) *f* difficulty.

כָּבָה (kābā') *fut.* יִכְבֶּה, to be quenched, to go out. — *Pi.* כִּבָּה, *inf.* כַּבּוֹת, *fut.* יְכַבֶּה, to quench, to extinguish.

כָּבוֹד (kābō'd) *m* [*inf.* of כָּבֵד[1]], *c.* כְּבוֹד, כְּבֹד, *w.s.* כְּבוֹדִי, כְּבֹדִי, weight, honour, esteem, glory, majesty; abundance, wealth; *poet.* soul, person.

כָּבוּל (kābū'l) *pr.n.* of a city in Asher; a district of 20 towns in Galilee.

כַּבּוֹן (kăbbō'n) *pr.n.* of a place in Judah.

כַּבִּיר (kăbbī'r) *adj.*, *pl.* כַּבִּירִים, great, mighty.

כְּבִיר (kᵉbī'r) *m* mattress.

כֶּבֶל (kĕ'bĕl) *m*, *pl. c.* כַּבְלֵי, fetter, bond.

כָּבַס (kābă's) *pt.* כּוֹבֵס, to tread, to trample; to wash, to full. — *Pi.* כִּבֶּס and כִּבֵּס, *imp.* כַּבֵּס, *fut.* יְכַבֵּס, *pt.* מְכַבֵּס, to wash, to full, to cleanse. — *Pu.* כֻּבַּס to be washed. — *Hothp.* הֻכַּבֵּס [for הָתְכַּבֵּס] to be washed, purified.

כָּבַר (kābă'r) *Hi.* הִכְבִּיר, *fut.* יַכְבִּיר, *pt.* מַכְבִּיר, to make heavy, to make many; to multiply; *pt.* = fulness, plenty.

כְּבָר[1] (kᵉbā'r) *m* length, extent; *adv.* long ago, already.

כְּבָר[2] (kᵉbā'r) *pr.n.* of a river in Mesopotamia.

כְּבָרָה (kᵉbārā') *f* a sieve.

כִּבְרָה (kĭbrā') *f*, *c.* כִּבְרַת, length, extent; a measure of distance [parasang or 30 stadia].

כֶּבֶשׂ (kĕ'bĕs) *m*, *pl.* כְּבָשִׂים, young sheep, lamb.

כִּבְשָׂה (kĭbsā') *f*, *c.* כִּבְשַׂת, *pl.* כְּבָשׂת, *c.* כִּבְשׂת; also **כַּבְשָׂה** (kăbsā') *f* lamb, young female sheep.

כָּבַשׁ (kābă'š) *inf.* כְּבוֹשׁ, *imp. w.s.* כִּבְשֻׁהָ, *fut.* יִכְבּוֹשׁ, *pt.* כֹּבֵשׁ, to tread down, to trample on, to subdue, to force [a woman]. — *Ni.* נִכְבַּשׁ to be conquered, subdued. — *Pi.* כִּבֵּשׁ to subdue. — *Hi. fut.* יַכְבִּישׁ to subdue.

כֶּבֶשׁ (kĕ'bĕš) *m* footstool.

כִּבְשָׁן (kĭbšā'n) *m* oven, furnace.

כַּד (kăd) *f*, *w.s.* כַּדֵּךְ, *pl.* כַּדִּים, bucket, pail, vessel.

כַּדּוּר (kăddū'r) *m* ball.

כְּדֵי see דַּי.

כַּדְכֹּד (kădkō'd) *m* a precious stone, ruby or carbuncle.

כְּדָרְלָעֹמֶר (kᵉdŏrlāʿō'mĕr) *pr.n.m.*

כֹּה (kō) *adv.* thus, so; here, there, thither; this way, that way.

כָּהָה (kāhā') *inf.* כָּהֹה, *fut.* יִכְהֶה, to be faint, dim, feeble, dull. — *Pi.* כִּהָה, כֵּהָה *intr.* to be faint, pale, dim; to be timid, desponding; *tr.* to rebuke, chide.

כֵּהָה (kēhā') *f* mitigation.

כֵּהֶה (kēhĕ') *adj.*, *f* כֵּהָה, *pl.* כֵּהוֹת, dim, expiring, faint, dull, timid, pale.

כָּהַן (kāhă'n) *Pi.* כִּהֵן, *inf.* כַּהֵן, *w.s.* כַּהֲנוֹ, *fut.* יְכַהֵן, to act as priest, to be a priest, to adorn with priestly dress.

כֹּהֵן (kōhē'n) *m*, *pl.* כֹּהֲנִים, *c.* כֹּהֲנֵי, priest, minister; הַכֹּהֵן הַגָּדוֹל the High Priest.

כְּהֻנָּה (kᵉhŭnnā') *f*, *c.* כְּהֻנַּת, *pl.* כְּהֻנּוֹת, priesthood, priest's office.

כּוּב (kūḇ) *pr.n.* of a southern country [Nubia].

כּוֹבַע (kōḇā'ᵉ) *m*, *i.p.* כּוֹבַע, *c.* כּוֹבַע, helmet.

כָּוָה (kāvā') *Ni.* נִכְוָה, *fut.* יִכָּוֶה to be burned, scorched.

כְּוִיָּה (kᵉvĭyyā') *f* burn, scar.

כּוֹכָב (kōḫā'ḇ) *m*, *c.* כּוֹכַב, *pl.* כּוֹכָבִים, *c.* כּוֹכְבֵי a star; a great prince.

כּוּל (kūl) *pf.* כָּל, to hold, to measure. — *Pilp.* כִּלְכֵּל, *fut.* יְכַלְכֵּל, *pt.* מְכַלְכֵּל to hold, to contain; to bear; to preserve, maintain, support, nourish. — *Pulp.* כָּלְכַּל (kŏlkă'l) to be sustained, nourished. — *Hi.* הֵכִיל, *inf.* הָכִיל, *fut.* יָכִיל to hold, contain; to bear, hold out.

כּוּמָז (kūmā'z) *m* an ornament, gold beads or bracelet.

כּוּן [1] (kūn) *Ni.* נָכוֹן, *imp.* הִכּוֹן, *fut.* יִכּוֹן, *pt.* נָכוֹן, *pl.* נְכוֹנִים, *f* נְכוֹנָה to stand firm, to be established; to be firm, steadfast, faithful, sure, reliable, fixed; to be ready, prepared, determined. — *Pil.* כּוֹנֵן, *imp.* כּוֹנְנָה, *fut.* יְכוֹנֵן, to set up, to make firm, to establish, to build, to make ready, to prepare, to direct. — *Pu.* כּוֹנַן to be made firm, to be formed. — *Hi.* הֵכִין, *inf.* הָכִין, *imp.* הָכֵן, *fut.* יָכִין, וַיָּכֶן to set up, to establish, to found, to prepare, to direct, to aim, to attend to. — *Ho.* הוּכַן, *pt.* מוּכָן to be established, to be made ready, to be set in order. — *Hith.* הִתְכּוֹנֵן, הִכּוֹנֵן, *fut.* יִתְכּוֹנֵן, יִכּוֹנֵן to be set up, to be built; to make oneself ready.

כּוּן[2] (kūn) *pr.n.* of a city in Phenicia.

כַּוָּן (kăvvā'n) *m*, *pl.* כַּוָּנִים, a cake for offerings.

כּוֹס[1] (kōs) *f*, *pl.* כֹּסוֹת, cup, vessel; portion, lot.

כּוֹס[2] (kōs) *m* an unclean bird, owl or pelican.

כּוּר[1] (kūr) to dig out, to pierce; see כָּאַר.

כּוּר[2] (kūr) *m* oven, furnace.

כּוֹר־עָשָׁן (kō'r 'āšā'n) *pr.n.* of a town in Simeon.

כּוֹרֶשׁ *pr.n.m.* see כֹּרֶשׁ.

כּוּשׁ (kūš) *pr.n.m.*; Ethiopia; *gent.* כּוּשִׁי, *pl.* כּוּשִׁים, כֻּשִׁיִּים, Ethiopian.

כּוּשִׁי (kūšī') *pr.n.m.*

כּוּשָׁן (kūšā'n) *pr.n.* = כּוּשׁ Ethiopia.

כּוּשַׁן רִשְׁעָתַיִם (kūšă'n riš-'āthă'yim) *pr.n.m.*

כּוֹשָׁרָה (kō'šārā') *f*, only *pl.* כּוֹשָׁרוֹת, prosperity.

כּוּת (kūth), כּוּתָה (kūthā') *pr.n.* of a city in Babylonia.

כּוֹתֶרֶת see כֹּתֶרֶת.

כָּזַב (kāză'b) *pt.* כֹּזֵב, to lie, to speak falsehood. — *Ni.* נִכְזַב to be found a liar, to be false. — *Pi.* כִּזֵּב, *inf.* כַּזֵּב, *fut.* יְכַזֵּב to lie, to deceive, to be faithless, to be false, to prove untrue. — *Hi. fut.* יַכְזִיב to charge one with a lie.

כָּזָב (kāzā'b) *m*, *pl.* כְּזָבִים, *c.* כִּזְבֵי, a lie, falsehood, deception; idolatry, idol.

כֹּזֵבָא (kō'zēbā') *pr.n.* of a place in Judah.

כָּזְבִּי (kŏzbī') *pr.n.f.*

כְּזִיב (kăzī'b) *pr.n.* of a place in Judah.

כֹּחַ[1], כּוֹחַ (kō'ach) *m*, *w.s.* כֹּחִי, כֹּחֲךָ, strength, power; violence; ability; wealth, riches.

כֹּחַ[2] (kō'ach) *m* a species of lizard.

כָּחַד (kāchă'd) *Ni.* נִכְחַד, *fut.* יִכָּחֵד, *pt. f* נִכְחֶדֶת, *pl.* נִכְחָדוֹת, to hide oneself, to disappear, to be destroyed. — *Pi.* כִּחֵד, *fut.* יְכַחֵד to hide, conceal; to deny, to disown. — *Hi* הִכְחִיד, *inf.* הַכְחִיד, *fut.* יַכְחִיד, וַיַּכְחֵד to hide, conceal, destroy.

כָּחַל (kāchă'l) to paint [the inner sides of the eyelids with stibium].

כָּחַשׁ (kåḥå'š) to decrease, to become lean. — *Ni. fut.* יִכָּחֵשׁ and *Hith. fut.* יִתְכַּחֵשׁ to dissemble oneself, to flatter. — *Pi.* כִּחֵשׁ, *inf.* כַּחֵשׁ, *fut.* יְכַחֵשׁ to feign, to deny; to lie, to deceive [expectation]; to submit oneself, to flatter.

כַּחַשׁ (kå'ḥåš) *m*, *w.s.* כַּחֲשִׁי, *pl.* כְּחָשִׁים, *c.* כַּחֲשֵׁי, lying, deceit, denial, flattery; leanness.

כֶּחָשׁ (kĕḥå'š) *adj.*, only *pl.* כֶּחָשִׁים, lying, false.

כִּי[1] (kī) *m* mark, burn, brand.

כִּי[2] (kī) *conj.* that, so that, because, when, for; כִּי אִם that if, but, nay but, but when, unless, but indeed, certainly.

כִּיד (kīḍ) *m* calamity.

כִּידוֹד (kīḍō'ḍ) *m* spark.

כִּידוֹן[1] (kīḍō'n) *m* spear, javelin.

כִּידוֹן[2] (kīḍō'n) *pr.n.* of a place.

כִּידוֹר (kīḍō'r) *m* war, storming.

כִּיּוּן (kīyyū'n) *pr.n.* of a heathen deity, Saturn.

כִּיֹּר, כִּיּוֹר (kīyyō'r) *m* pot, basin, fire-pan, water-basin.

כִּילַי (kīlå'y), כֵּלַי (kēlå'y) *adj.* niggard, miser, cheat.

כֵּילַף (kēlå'f) *m*, only *pl.* כֵּילַפּוֹת, hammer, axe.

כִּימָה (kīmå') *f* the Pleiades, a group of seven stars.

כִּיס (kīs) *m* purse, bag; cup.

כִּיר (kīr) *m*, only *du.* כִּירַיִם, cooking-pan [with a lid].

כִּישׁוֹר (kīšō'r) *m* a distaff, holding the flax for spinning.

כָּכָה (kå'ḵå) *adv.* so, thus.

כִּכָּר (kīkkå'r) *f*, *c.* כִּכַּר, *du.* כִּכְּרַיִם, *pl.* כִּכָּרִים, *c.* כִּכְּרֵי, and כִּכָּרוֹת, *c.* כִּכְּרוֹת, round, circle, circuit, district; disk, round loaf or cake; round weight, talent [= 3000 shekels].

כֹּל (kōl) *m*, *c.* כָּל־ (kŏl), *w.s.* כֻּלְּכֶם, כֻּלָּנוּ, כֻּלּוֹ, the whole, totality; all, whole, each, every, any; *adv.* wholly.

כָּלָא (kålå') [takes also forms from כָּלָה] *pf. w.s.* כְּלָתְנִי, *inf.* כְּלוֹא, *imp.* כְּלָא, *w.s.* כְּלָאָם, *fut.* יִכְלָא, יִכְלֶה, *pt. p.* כָּלוּא, כָּלֻא, to retain, bar, restrain, close, shut up, hinder. — *Ni. fut.* יִכָּלֵא to be restrained, hindered. — *Pi. inf.* כַּלֵּא = כַּלֵּה see כָּלָה *Pi.*

כֶּלֶא (kĕ'lĕ) *m*, *w.s.* כִּלְאוֹ, *pl.* כְּלָאִים, confinement, prison; *du.* כִּלְאַיִם two different things, two kinds.

כִּלְאָב (kĭl'ā'b) *pr.n.m.*

כָּלֵב (kālē'b) *pr.n.m.*; *patr.* כָּלִבִּי, כְּלוּבַי.

כֶּלֶב (kĕ'lĕb) *m*, *i.p.* כָּלֶב, *pl.* כְּלָבִים, *c.* כַּלְבֵי, a dog; a male prostitute.

כָּלָה[1] (kālā') *inf.* כְּלוֹת, *fut.* יִכְלֶה, יִכֶל, to be completed, finished, ready; to be at an end, to be consumed, destroyed, to vanish. — *Pi.* כִּלָּה, *inf.* כַּלֵּה [כַּלֵּא], כַּלּוֹת, כַּלֹּת, *imp.* כַּלֵּה, *fut.* יְכַלֶּה, וַיְכַל, to complete, finish, end, execute; to cease; to consume, to spend, to destroy. — *Pu.* כֻּלָּה, *fut.* יְכֻלֶּה to be completed, finished [see also כָּלָא].

כָּלָה[2] (kālā') *f* consumption, destruction; עָשָׂה כָלָה to destroy totally; *adv.* totally, entirely.

כָּלֶה (kālĕ') *adj.*, *fpl.* כָּלוֹת, pining [of the eye].

כַּלָּה (kăllā') *f*, *w.s.* כַּלָּתוֹ, *pl.* כַּלּוֹת, כַּלֹּת, bride; daughter-in-law.

כְּלוּא (kᵉlū') *m* = כֶּלֶא prison.

כְּלוּב[1] (kᵉlū'b) *m* basket; cage for birds.

כְּלוּב[2] (kᵉlū'b) *pr.n.m.*

כְּלוּבַי see כָּלֵב.

כְּלוּהַי (kᵉlūhă'y), כְּלוּהוּ (kᵉlūhū') *pr.n.m.*

כְּלוּלָה (kᵉlūlā') *f*, only *pl.* כְּלוּלוֹת, bridal state.

כֶּלַח[1] (kĕ'lăḥ) *pr.n.* of a city in Assyria, to-day Nimrûd.

כֶּלַח[2] (kĕ'lăḥ) *m* vigour, strength.

כְּלִי (kᵉlī') *m*, *i.p.* כֶּלִי, *pl.* כֵּלִים, *c.* כְּלֵי, *w.s.* כֵּלַי, כְּלֵיהֶם, vessel, implement, equipment, baggage; garments; instruments, weapons, armour; boat; seat.

כְּלִיא see כְּלוּא.

כִּלְיָה (kĭlyā') *f*, only *pl.* כְּלָיוֹת, *c.* כִּלְיוֹת, the reins, kidneys; the interior, the inward parts.

כִּלָּיוֹן (kĭllāyō'n) *m*, *c.* כִּלְיוֹן, destruction, pining.

כִּלְיוֹן (kĭlyō'n) *pr.n.m*

כָּלִיל (kālī'l) *adj.*, *c.* כְּלִיל, complete, perfect; *subst.* the whole, complete sacrifice, holocaust.

כַּלְכֹּל (kălkō'l) *pr.n.m.*

כָּלַל (kālă'l) to make perfect.

כָּלַם (kālă'm) *Ni.* נִכְלַם, *inf.* הִכָּלֵם, *fut.* יִכָּלֵם, *pt.* נִכְלָם, to be ashamed, to be insulted, to be disappointed. — *Hi.* הִכְלִים, *inf.* הַכְלִים, *fut.* יַכְלִים, *pt.* מַכְלִים, to reproach, revile, chide; to shame; *intr.* to feel shame. — *Ho.* הָכְלַם to be disappointed; to be hurt.

כִּלְמַד (kĭlmă'd) *pr.n.* of a district in Mesopotamia or Media.

כְּלִמָּה (kelĭmmā') *f*, *c.* כְּלִמַּת, *pl.* כְּלִמּוֹת, reproach, shame, contumely.

כְּלִמּוּת (kelĭmmū'th) *f* reproach, contumely.

כַּלְנֵה (kălnē') *pr.n.* of a city in Babylonia, Ctesiphon.

כַּלְנוֹ (kălnō') *pr.n.* of a city, either = כַּלְנֵה, or in Syria.

כָּמַהּ (kāmă'h) to pine, to long for.

כַּמָּה (kămmā') [— כְּמָה as what?] how great! how long! how many! how often!

כִּמְהָם (kĭmhā'm); **כִּמְהָן** (kĭmhā'n); **כְּמוֹהָם** (kemōhā'm) *pr.n.m.*

כְּמוֹ (kemō') *rel. part.* — כְּ as, like; like as, when, as soon as; thus.

כְּמוֹשׁ (kemō'š) *pr.n.m.* of a Moabitish god.

כַּמּוֹן (kămmō'n) *m* cumin.

כָּמַס (kāmă's) *pt. p.* כָּמֻס, to lay up, to store.

כָּמַר (kāmă'r) *Ni.* נִכְמַר, to be burnt, scorched; to be blackened; to be contracted, to be moved.

כָּמָר (kāmā'r) or **כֹּמֶר** (kō'mĕr) *m*, only *pl.* כְּמָרִים, priest, idol-priest.

כִּמְרִיר (kĭmrī'r) *m*, *pl. c.* כִּמְרִירֵי, obscuration, eclipse [of the sun].

כֵּן[1] (kēn), **כֶּן** (kĕn) *adv.* so, thus, just so, such, so much; לָכֵן therefore, on account of, nevertheless.

כֵּן[2] (kēn) *adj.*, *pl.* כֵּנִים, right, upright, honest; *subst.* the right; *adv.* rightly, honestly.

כֵּן[3] (kēn) *m*, *w.s.* כַּנִּי, base, pedestal, stand; place, station, office.

כָּנָה (kānā') *Pi.* כִּנָּה, *fut.* יְכַנֶּה, to distinguish by a surname or title, to name with honour.

כַּנָּה (kănnā') *f* a shoot, a layer.

כִּנָּה (kĭnnā') *f*, *pl.* כִּנִּים, gnat, stinging-fly.

כַּנֵּה (kănnē') *pr.n.* of a town, probably the same as כַּלְנֵה.

כִּנּוֹר (kĭnnō'r) *m*, *pl.* כִּנֹּרִים, כִּנֹּרוֹת, a harp, lyre.

כַּנְלֹתְךָ — כְּהַנְלֹתְךָ see נָלָה *Hi.*

כִּנָּם (kĭnnā'm) *m* gnat, *coll.* gnats.

כָּנַן (kānă'n) *imp.* כַּנָּה, to protect [but see כַּנָּה].

כְּנָנִי (kᵉnānī'); כְּנַנְיָה (kᵉnăn-yā'); כְּנַנְיָהוּ (kᵉnănyā'hū) *pr.n.m.*

כָּנַס (kānă's) *inf.* כְּנוֹס, *pt.* כֹּנֵס, to collect, heap up; to assemble. — *Pi.* כִּנֵּס, *fut.* יְכַנֵּס to collect, to gather together. — *Hith.* *inf.* הִתְכַּנֵּס to hide oneself, to wrap oneself in.

כָּנַע (kānă'ᵉ) *Ni.* נִכְנַע, *inf.* הִכָּנֵעַ, *fut.* יִכָּנֵעַ, to be humbled, subdued, subjected; to humble oneself, to submit. — *Hi.* הִכְנִיעַ, *fut.* יַכְנִיעַ, יַכְנַע to bow down, humble, subdue.

כִּנְעָה (kᵉnāᵉā') *f*, *w.s.* כִּנְעָתֵךְ, bundle, travelling effects.

כְּנַעַן (kᵉnă'ᵉăn) *pr.n.m.*, Canaan; *gent.* כְּנַעֲנִי, *pl.* כְּנַעֲנִים, Canaanite, Phenician; tradesman, merchant.

כְּנַעֲנָה (kᵉnă'ᵃnā') *pr.n.m.*

כָּנַף (kānă'f) *Ni.* *fut.* יִכָּנֵף, to hide oneself.

כָּנָף (kānā'f) *f*, *c.* כְּנַף, *w.s.* כְּנָפִי, *du.* כְּנָפַיִם, *c.* כַּנְפֵי, *w.s.* כְּנָפֶיךָ, כַּנְפֵיהֶם, *pl. c.* כַּנְפוֹת, wing; *du.* pair of wings; extremity, edge, border, skirt, side, wing of an army; pinnacle, battlement.

כִּנֶּרֶת (kĭnnĕ'rĕϑ) *pr.n.*, *i.p.* כִּנָּרֶת, also כִּנְּרוֹת, כִּנְרוֹת, a city in Naphtali; יָם כִּנֶּרֶת or יָם כִּנְּרוֹת the Lake of Gennezaret.

כְּנָת (kᵉnā'ϑ) *f*, only *pl.* כְּנָוֹת, surname, title; fellow-officer, colleague.

כֵּס (kēß) *m* = כִּסֵּא throne.

כֶּסֶא, כֶּסֶה (kĕ'ßĕ) *m* time of the full moon, festival.

כִּסֵּא (kĭßßē'), כִּסֵּה *m*, *w.s.* כִּסְאִי, כִּסְאֲךָ, כִּסְאוֹ, *pl.* כִּסְאוֹת high seat, chair, throne.

כָּסָה (kāßā') *pt.* כֹּסֶה, *pt. p.* כָּסוּי, *c.* כְּסוּי, to cover, to conceal. — *Ni. inf.* הִכָּסוֹת to be covered. — *Pi.* כִּסָּה, *inf.* כַּסּוֹת, *fut.* יְכַסֶּה, וַיְכַס to cover, conceal, hide; to clothe; to cover sin, to forgive; to keep secret. — *Pu.* כֻּסָּה and כֻּסָּה (kŭßßā'), *fut.* יְכֻסֶּה, *pt.* מְכֻסֶּה, *Hith. fut.* יִתְכַּסֶּה, יִתְכַּס, *pt.* מִתְכַּסֶּה, *pl.* מִתְכַּסִּים, to hide oneself, to wrap oneself up.

כַּסּוּחָה see סוּחָה.

כָּסוּי (kāßū'y) *m*, *c.* כְּסוּי a covering.

כְּסוּת (kᵉßū'ϑ) *f* a covering, veiling, cover, garment.

כָּסַח (kāßă'ḥ) *pt. p.* כָּסוּחַ, *pl.* כְּסוּחִים, *f* כְּסוּחָה, to cut off.

כְּסִיל[1] (kᵉßī'l) *adj.*, *pl.* כְּסִילִים, foolish, a fool, stupid, impious; *pl.* the constellation Orion.

כְּסִיל[2] (kᵉßī'l) *pr.n.* of a place in Judah.

כְּסִילוּת (kᵉßīlū'ϑ) *f* folly.

כָּסַל (kāßă'l) *fut.* יִכְסַל to be foolish.

כֶּסֶל (kĕ'ßĕl) and **כֵּסֶל** (kē'ßĕl) *m*, *w.s.* כִּסְלָם, *pl.* כְּסָלִים, loin, interior; folly; confidence.

כִּסְלָה (kĭßlā') *f* folly; confidence, hope.

כִּסְלֵו (kĭßlē'v) *m* name of the 9th month of the Hebrew year [December to January].

כְּסָלוֹן (kᵉßālō'n) *pr.n.* of a place in Judah.

כִּסְלוֹן (kĭßlō'n) *pr.n.m.*

כְּסֻלּוֹת (kᵉßŭllō'ϑ) and **כִּסְלוֹת־תָּבוֹר** (kĭßlō'ϑ-tāḃō'r) *pr.n.* of a place near Mount Tabor.

כַּסְלֻחִים (kăßlŭḥī'm) *pr.n.* of a people and district in Lower Egypt.

כָּסַם (kāßă'm) *inf.* כָּסוֹם, *fut.* יִכְסֹם to shear.

כֻּסֶּמֶת (kŭßßĕ'mĕϑ) *f* a species of grain, spelt.

כָּסַס (kāßă'ß) *fut.* 2.*pl.* תָּכֹסּוּ, to number, reckon.

כָּסַף (kāßă'f) *fut.* יִכְסֹף, to pine for, to long after. —

Ni. נִכְסַף, *inf.* נִכְסֹף, *pt.* נִכְסָף to turn pale, to be disconcerted; to long after.

כֶּסֶף (kĕ'ßĕf) *m*, *i.p.* כָּסֶף, *w.s.* כַּסְפִּי, *pl.* כְּסָפִים, *w.s.* כַּסְפֵּיהֶם, silver, silver coin, money, shekel.

כָּסִפְיָא (kā'ßĭfyā') *pr.n.* of a place between Babylon and Jerusalem.

כֶּסֶת (kĕ'ßĕϑ) *f*, only *pl.* כְּסָתוֹת, *c.* כִּסְתוֹת, pillow, cushion.

כָּעַס (kā'ă'ß) *inf.* כְּעוֹס, *fut.* יִכְעַס, to be disturbed, fretful, angry. — *Pi.* כִּעֵס to provoke, irritate. — *Hi.* הִכְעִיס, *inf.* הַכְעִיס, *fut.* יַכְעִיס, וַיַּכְעֵס, *pt.* מַכְעִיס, to excite, provoke, vex, grieve.

כַּעַס (kă''ăß) *m*, *w.s.* כַּעְסִי, כַּעַסְךָ, *pl.* כְּעָסִים, sorrow, vexation, anger, provocation, fretfulness.

כַּעַשׂ (kă''ăß) *m*, the same as כַּעַס.

כַּף (kăf) *f*, *w.s.* כַּפִּי, *du.* כַּפַּיִם, *c.* כַּפֵּי, *w.s.* כַּפָּי, *pl.* כַּפּוֹת, the curved or hollow hand, palm, paw, forefoot; sole [of the foot]; pan, dish; handle; twig, branch.

כֵּף (kēf) *m*, only *pl.* כֵּפִים rock, cliff.

כָּפָה (kāfā') *fut.* יִכְפֶּה, to turn aside.

כַּפָּה (kăppā'), כִּפָּה (kĭppā') *f* palm-branch, branch; the high, the noble.

כְּפוֹר (k^e^fō'r) *m* cup, goblet; hoar-frost.

כְּפוֹר see כְּפָרִים.

כָּפִיס (kāfī'ß) *m* cross-beam, rafter.

כְּפִיר (k^e^fī'r) *m*, *pl.* כְּפִירִים, young lion, young hero; village.

כְּפִירָה (k^e^fīrā') *pr.n.* of a city in Benjamin.

כָּפַל (kāfă'l) *pt.* *p.* כָּפוּל to fold together, to double up; *pt. p.* doubled, double. — *Ni.* נִכְפַּל, *fut.* יִכָּפֵל, to be doubled, repeated.

כֶּפֶל (kĕ'fĕl) *m*, *du.* כִּפְלַיִם, a doubling, the double; *adv.* twice.

כָּפַן (kāfă'n) to bend towards.

כָּפָן (kāfā'n) *m* hunger.

כָּפַף (kāfă'f) *inf.* כֹּף [הֲלָכֹף with הֲ *interr.* and לְ], *pt. p.* כָּפוּף to curve, to bend down. — *Ni.* *fut.* 1. *sg.* אִכַּף to bow, to humble oneself.

כָּפַר[1] (kāfă'r) *Pi.* כִּפֶּר, *inf.* and *imp.* כַּפֵּר, *fut.* יְכַפֵּר, to cover, to forgive, expiate, atone for. — *Pu.* כֻּפַּר, *fut.* יְכֻפַּר to be atoned for, to be forgiven, extinguished. — *Hith. fut.* יִתְכַּפֵּר and *Nithp.* נִכַּפֵּר to be forgiven, expiated.

כָּפַר[2] (kāfă'r) [*denom.* from כֹּפֶר] to cover with pitch.

כָּפָר (kāfā'r) *m*, *c.* כְּפַר, *pl.* כְּפָרִים, hamlet, village.

כְּפַר הָעַמּוֹנִי (kᵉfă'r hā'ăm-mōnī') *pr.n.* of a place in Benjamin.

כֹּפֶר (kō'fĕr) *m*, *w.s.* כָּפְרוֹ (kŏfrō'), *pl.* כְּפָרִים village; pitch; cypress-flower; ransom.

כִּפֻּרִים (kĭppūrī'm) *m/pl.* expiation, atonement.

כַּפֹּרֶת (kăppō'rĕϑ) *f* cover, lid of the ark, the propiatory.

כָּפַשׁ (kāfă'š) *Hi.* הִכְפִּישׁ, to press down, to trample down.

כַּפְתֹּר[1], כַּפְתּוֹר (kăftō'r) *m*, *pl.* כַּפְתֹּרִים, capital of a column, ornament [knob, crown] of the candelabrum.

כַּפְתֹּר[2] (kăftō'r) *pr.n.*, *pl.* כַּפְתֹּרִים, Crete [Cappadocia, Cyprus?]; *pl.* Cretans.

כַּר[1] (kăr) *m*, *pl.* כָּרִים, lamb, sheep; battering-ram.

כַּר[2] (kăr) *m*, *pl.* כָּרִים, pasture, meadow; a camel's saddle, litter.

כֹּר (kōr) *m* a measure for dry goods and liquids [= 10 ephahs or baths].

כִּרְבֵּל (kărbă'l) *Pu. pt.* מְכֻרְבָּל to be clothed with.

כָּרָה[1] (kārā') *fut.* יִכְרֶה, to pierce, dig, excavate; to devise. — *Ni. fut.* יִכָּרֶה to be digged.

כָּרָה[2] (kārā') *fut.* יִכְרֶה, to prepare a banquet, to make a feast.

כָּרָה[3] (kārā') *fut.* יִכְרֶה, to buy, purchase; to bargain.

כָּרָה[4] (kārā') *f*, only *pl.* כָּרֹת, כְּרֹת, pit, cistern.

כֵּרָה (kērā') *f* banquet, feast.

כְּרוּב[1] (kᵉrū'b) *m*, *pl.* כְּרוּבִים, כְּרֻבִים, Cherub.

כְּרוּב[2] (kᵉrū'b) *pr.n.* of a place in Babylonia.

כָּרִי (kārī') *m coll.* royal body-guard, executioners [Carians?].

כְּרִית (kᵉrī'ϑ) *pr.n* of a brook.

כְּרִיתֻת (kᵉrīϑū'ϑ) *f*, *pl.* כְּרִיתֻתִים, separation, divorce.

כַּרְכֹּב (kărkō'ḇ) *m*, *w.s.* כַּרְכֻּבּוֹ, border, margin.

כַּרְכֹּם (kărkō'm) *m* Indian saffron.

כַּרְכְּמִישׁ (kărkᵉmī'š) *pr.n.* of a city on the Euphrates, Circesium.

כַּרְכַּס (kărkă's) *pr.n.m.*

כִּרְכָּרֶת (kĭrkă'rĕϑ) *f*, only *pl.* כִּרְכָּרוֹת, fleet camel, dromedary.

כֶּרֶם (kĕ'rĕm) *m*, *i.p.* כָּרֶם, *w.s.* כַּרְמִי, *pl.* כְּרָמִים, *c.* כַּרְמֵי, garden, orchard, vineyard, plantation.

כַּרְמִי (kărmī') *pr.n.m.*

כַּרְמִיל (kărmī'l) *m* carmine, crimson colour and cloth.

כַּרְמֶל (kărmĕ'l) *m* [= כֶּרֶם], *w.s.* כַּרְמִלּוֹ, garden-fruit, garden-grain; as a *pr.n.* Mount Carmel; also a town near the Dead Sea; *gent.* כַּרְמְלִי, *f* כַּרְמְלִית.

כְּרָן (kᵉrā'n) *pr.n.m.*

כִּרְסֵם (kĭrsē'm) *Pi.*, *fut. w.s.* יְכַרְסְמֶנָּה, to browse, to eat off.

כָּרַע (kārā'ʿ) *inf.* כְּרֹעַ, *fut.* יִכְרַע, *pt.* כֹּרֵעַ, *pl.* כֹּרְעִים, *f* כֹּרְעוֹת, to bend [the knees], to kneel down, to sink down, to cower, to writhe in pain. — *Hi.* הִכְרִיעַ, *inf.* הַכְרֵיעַ, *fut.* יַכְרִיעַ, to bow, bend, prostrate, afflict, grieve.

כְּרָע (kārā'ʿ) *f*, only *du.* כְּרָעַיִם, *w.s.* כְּרָעָיו, the legs, the lower parts of the thigh.

כַּרְפַּס (kărpă's) *m* cotton-stuff.

כָּרַר (kārā'r) *Pi. pt.* מְכַרְכֵּר, to turn about, to dance.

כְּרֵשׂ (kᵉrē's) *m* belly, paunch.

כֹּרֶשׁ (kō'rĕš) *pr.n.m.*, Cyrus.

כַּרְשְׁנָא (kăršᵉnā') *pr.n.m.* [Persian].

כָּרַת (kārā'ϑ) *inf.* כְּרֹת, כָּרֹת, *w.s.* כָּרְתִי (kŏrϑī'), *imp.* כְּרֹת, *fut.* יִכְרֹת, *pt.* כֹּרֵת, *pt. p.* כָּרוּת, *f/pl.* כְּרֻתוֹת, to cut, to cut off; to maim, castrate; to root out, to destroy; כָּרַת בְּרִית to make a covenant. — *Ni.* נִכְרַת, *inf.* הִכָּרֵת, *fut.* יִכָּרֵת, to be felled, to be cut off;

to be consumed, exiled, destroyed. — *Pu.* כֹּרַת to be cut off, to be cut down. — *Hi.* הִכְרִית, *inf.* הַכְרִית, *fut.* יַכְרִית, יַכְרֵת to destroy, cut off, withdraw. — *Ho.* הָכְרַת to be cut off, withdrawn.

כְּרֻתוֹת (kᵉrūϑō'ϑ) *f/pl.* hewed beams.

כְּרֵתִי (kᵉrēϑī') *pr.n.m.*, *pl.* כְּרֵתִים, executioner, body-guard of David [Cretans or Philistines come from Crete].

כֶּשֶׂב (kĕ'ßĕḇ) *m*, *pl.* כְּשָׂבִים, and כִּשְׂבָּה (kĭßbā') *f* = כֶּבֶשׂ and כִּבְשָׂה, lamb.

כֶּשֶׂד (kĕ'ßĕd) *pr.n.m.*

כַּשְׂדִּי (kăßdī') *pr.n.*, only *pl.* כַּשְׂדִּיִּם, כַּשְׂדִּים, Chaldeans, astrologers, star-gazers; Chaldæa; *w. loc.* ה כַּשְׂדִּימָה.

כָּשָׂה (kāßā') to be fat.

כַּשִּׁיל (kăššī'l) *m* axe, hoe.

כָּשַׁל (kāšă'l) *inf.* כָּשׁוֹל, *fut.* יִכְשֹׁל, *pt.* כּוֹשֵׁל, *f/pl.* כֹּשְׁלוֹת, to totter, to fail, to stumble, to faint, to fall.—*Ni.* נִכְשַׁל, *fut.* יִכָּשֵׁל, *pt.* נִכְשָׁל to totter, stumble, fall; to become weak. — *Pi. fut.* יְכַשֵּׁל to cause to fall. — *Hi.* הִכְשִׁיל, *inf.* הַכְשִׁיל, *fut.* יַכְשִׁיל to cause to fall, to cause to stumble, to seduce, to lead astray. — *Ho. pt.* מֻכְשָׁל to be overthrown, to be felled.

כִּשָּׁלוֹן (kĭššālō'n) *m* stumbling, fall, ruin.

כָּשַׁף (kāšă'f) *Pi. pt.* מְכַשֵּׁף, *f* מְכַשֵּׁפָה, to mutter magical words or incantations, to practice magic.

כַּשָּׁף (kăššā'f) *m* magician, sorcerer.

כֶּשֶׁף (kĕ'šĕf) *m*, only *pl.* כְּשָׁפִים, incantation, sorcery.

כָּשֵׁר (kāšē'r) *fut.* יִכְשַׁר to be proper, right, pleasing; to thrive, to grow. — *Hi. inf.* הַכְשֵׁיר to give prosperity.

כִּשְׁרוֹן (kĭšrō'n) *m* profit, advantage, success, prosperity.

כָּתַב (kāϑă'ḇ) *inf.* כָּתוֹב, כְּתֹב, *fut.* יִכְתֹּב, *pt.* כֹּתֵב, *pt. p.* כָּתוּב, to write, to inscribe, to write down, to record, to describe, to prescribe.—*Ni.* נִכְתַּב, *fut.* יִכָּתֵב, to be written, inscribed. — *Pi.* כִּתֵּב, *pt.* מְכַתֵּב to write [a decree].

כְּתָב (kᵉϑā'ḇ) *m* writing, copy, book, register, letter, written decree.

כְּתֹבֶת (kᵉϑō'ḇĕϑ) *f* a writing.

כִּתִּים (kĭttī'm) and כִּתִּיִּים (kĭttĭyyī'm) *pr.n.m. pl.*, inhabitants of כֵּת [Cittium], Cyprians, western nations.

כָּתִית (kāϑī'ϑ) *m* fine oil [from pounded olives].

כֹּתֶל (kō'ϑĕl) *m* a wall.

כִּתְלִישׁ (kĭϑlī'š) *pr.n.* of a place in Judah.

כָּתַם (kāϑă'm) *Ni. pt.* נִכְתָּם to be inscribed, to be written.

כֶּתֶם (kĕ'ϑĕm) *m* [fine] gold.

כֻּתֹּנֶת (kŭttō'nĕϑ), כְּתֹנֶת (kᵉϑō'nĕϑ) *f*, *w.s.* כֻּתָּנְתִּי (kŭttŏntī'), *pl.* כֻּתֳּנוֹת, *c.* כָּתְנוֹת (kŏϑnō'ϑ) shirt, tunic.

כָּתֵף (kāϑē'f) *f*, *c.* כֶּתֶף, *du.* כְּתֵפַיִם, *w.s.* כְּתֵפָיו, *pl.* כְּתֵפוֹת, כִּתְפֹת, *c.* כִּתְפוֹת, shoulder, shoulder-blade, side, flank, border; *pl.* shoulder-parts, projections.

כָּתַר (kāϑă'r) *Pi.* כִּתֵּר to surround, besiege; to wait. — *Hi.* הִכְתִּיר, *fut.* יַכְתִּיר to surround; to encompass; to wear as a crown.

כֶּתֶר (kĕ'ϑĕr) *m* crown, diadem.

כֹּתֶרֶת (kōϑĕ'rĕϑ) *f*, *pl.* כֹּתָרוֹת, crown of a column, capital.

כָּתַשׁ (kāϑă'š) *fut.* יִכְתּשׁ to pound, to bruise.

כָּתַת (kāϑă'ϑ) *inf.* כָּתוֹת, *imp.* כֹּת, *pl.* כֹּתּוּ, *fut.* יִכֹּת, *pt. p.* כָּתוּת to hammer, to forge; to beat to pieces, to shatter; to castrate. — *Pi.* כִּתֵּת to hammer; to beat to pieces; to ruin, destroy. — *Pu.* כֻּתַּת to be dashed together. — *Hi.* הֵכַת, *fut. pl. w.s.* וַיַּכְּתוּם to scatter, to rout. — *Ho.* הֻכַּת, *fut.* יֻכַּת to be beaten to pieces, to be broken; to be crushed, to be destroyed.

ל

ל the twelfth letter of the alphabet, called לָמֶד [ox-goad]; as a numeral = 30.

לְ [לָ] prefixed *prep.* to, for, towards, belonging to, in regard to, according to, in;

w.s. לִי, לְךָ [*i.p.* לָךְ], לָךְ, לָכֶנָה, לָכֶם, לָנוּ, לָהּ, לוֹ, לָהֶם [לָהֶמָה, לָמוֹ], לָהֶן, לָהֵנָּה.

לֹא (lō̄) *adv.* of negation, not, no; in questions, expecting affirmative answers: הֲלֹא; בְּלֹא besides, without.

לֹא־דְבָר (lō̄-d^e^ḇā̄'r) *pr.n.* of a place in Gilead.

לֹא עַמִּי (lō̄ 'ămmī') *pr.n.m.*

לֹא רֻחָמָה (lō̄ rŭḥā'mā̄) *pr.n.f.*

לָאָה (lā̄'ā̄') *fut.* וַיֵּלֶא, יִלְאֶה, to be tired, to be wearied, to toil. — *Ni.* נִלְאָה, *pt. f* נִלְאָה to tire oneself, to be tired, weary, exhausted. — *Hi.* הֶלְאָה, *inf.* הַלְאוֹת to make weary, to exhaust, to make impatient.

לֵאָה (lē̄'ā̄') *pr.n.f.*

לָאט (lā̄t) = לָט see לוּט.

לָאַט, **לָאט** see לָט.

לָאַט (lā̄'ă't) to hide, to cover.

לָאֵט (lā̄'ē̄'t) *m*, *w.s.* לְאִטִּי, tarrying, slowness [or derived from אַט, אֵט = privily, noiselessly].

לָאֵל (lā̄'ē̄'l) *pr.n.m.*

לְאֹם (l^e^'ō̄'m) *m*, *w.s.* לְאֻמִּי, *pl.* לְאֻמִּים, לְאוּמִּים, people, nation.

לְאֻמִּים (l^e^'ŭmmī'm) *pr.n.* of an Arabian tribe.

לֵב (lē̄ḇ) *m*, *c.* לֶב־, *w.s.* לִבִּי, *pl.* לִבּוֹת, and לֵבָב (lē̄ḇā̄'ḇ), *c.* לְבַב, *w.s.* לְבָבִי, לְבַבְכֶם. the heart, the centre, the middle.

לְבָאָה (l^e^ḇā̄'ā̄') *f*, only *pl.* לְבָאוֹת, lioness.

לְבָאוֹת (l^e^ḇā̄'ō̄'ϑ) *pr.n.* of a place in Simeon.

לָבַב (lā̄ḇă'ḇ) *Ni.* נִלְבַּב, *fut.* יִלָּבֵב to be intelligent. — *Pi. fut.* יְלַבֵּב to rob the heart, to bewitch; to make cakes [*den.* of לְבִיבָה].

לֵבָב see לֵב.

לְבִבָה see לְבִיבָה.

לְבַד see בַּד.

לַבָּה (lăbbā̄') *f* [= לֶהָבָה], *c.* לַבַּת, flame.

לִבָּה (lĭbbā̄') *f* = לֵב heart.

לְבוֹנָה see לְבֹנָה.

לְבוּשׁ, **לְבֻשׁ** (l^e^ḇū̄'š) *m*, *w.s.* לְבוּשִׁי, לְבוּשְׁכֶן, garment, clothing, wife [?].

לָבַט (lā̄ḇă't) *Ni.* נִלְבַּט, *fut.* יִלָּבֵט, to fall, to be thrown down.

לְבִי (lᵉḅī') *m*, *pl.* לְבָאִם, lion.

לָבִיא (lāḅī') *m* and *f* lion, lioness.

לְבִיָּא (lᵉḅīyyā') *f* lioness.

לְבִיבָה (lᵉḅīḅā') *f*, only *pl.* לְבִבוֹת, cake, pancake.

לְבִים see לוּבִים.

לָבַן (lāḅă'n) *inf.* לְבֹן, *fut.* 1. *pl.* נִלְבְּנָה to make bricks [לְבֵנָה]. — *Hi.* הִלְבִּין, *inf.* לַלְבֵּן [for לְהַלְבִּין], *fut.* יַלְבִּין to be white; to make white, to purify.

לָבָן[1] (lāḅā'n) *adj.*, *c.* לְבֶן, *pl.* לְבָנִים, *f* לְבָנָה, *pl.* לְבָנוֹת, white, bright.

לָבָן[2] (lāḅā'n) *pr.n.m.*; also *pr.n.* of a place in the desert.

לְבָנָה[1] (lᵉḅānā') *f* the moon [the white, the pale].

לְבָנָה[2] (lᵉḅānā') *pr.n.m.*

לְבֵנָה (lᵉḅēnā') *f*, *pl.* לְבֵנִים, *c.* לִבְנֵי, limestone, brick, tile.

לִבְנָה[1] (lĭḅnā') *f* whiteness, transparency.

לִבְנָה[2] (lĭḅnā') *pr.n.* of a town in Judah.

לִבְנֶה (lĭḅnĕ') *m* storax-tree, *perh.* white poplar.

לְבוֹנָה, לְבֹנָה[1] (lᵉḅōnā') *f*, white resin, frankincense.

לְבֹנָה[2] (lᵉḅōnā') *pr.n.* of a place near Shiloh.

לְבָנוֹן (lᵉḅānō'n) *pr.n.*, *w. art.* הַלְּבָנוֹן, the white mountain, Lebanon.

לִבְנִי (lĭḅnī') *pr.n.m.*

לִבְנָת see שִׁיחוֹר.

לָבַשׁ (lāḅă'š), **לָבֵשׁ** (lāḅē'š) *inf.* לְבשׁ, *imp.* לְבַשׁ, *fut.* יִלְבַּשׁ, *pt. p.* לָבוּשׁ, to wrap up, to cover, to put on, to dress or clothe oneself. — *Pu. pt.* מְלֻבָּשׁ to be clothed. — *Hi.* הִלְבִּישׁ, *fut.* יַלְבִּישׁ, יַלְבֵּשׁ, *pt.* מַלְבִּישׁ to clothe.

לְבֻשׁ see לָבוּשׁ.

לֹג (lōg) *m* basin; a measure containing the 12th part of a הִין.

לֹד (lōḍ) *pr.n.* of a town in Benjamin, Lydda.

לִדְבִר (lĭḍbī'r) *pr.n.* of a place in Gilead.

לֵדָה, לֶדֶת see יָלַד.

לַהַב (lă'hăḅ) *m*, *pl.* לְהָבִים, *c.* לַהֲבֵי, flame, lightning; the shining point of a spear; sword-blade.

לֶהָבָה (lĕ'hāḅā'), **לֶהֶבֶת** (lĕhĕ'bĕϑ) *f*, *pl.* לְהָבוֹת, *c.* לַהֲבוֹת = לַהַב.

לְהָבִים (lᵉhāḇī'm) *pr.n. pl.*, an Hamitic people, Libyans.

לַהַג (lă'hăg) *m* meditation, study.

לַהַד (lă'hăḏ) *pr.n.m.*

לָהָה (lāhā') *fut.* וַתֵּלַהּ to be exhausted, to faint.

לָהַהּ (lāhă'h) *Hithpalp. pt.* מִתְלַהְלֵהַּ, to behave foolishly, to be mad.

לָהַט (lāhă't) *pt.* לֹהֵט, *pl.* לֹהֲטִים, to burn, to be furious. — *Pi.* לִהֵט, *fut.* יְלַהֵט to set on fire, to kindle, to consume.

לַהַט (lă'hăt) *m* flame, flashing blade.

לָהָט (lāhā't) *m*, *pl.* לְהָטִים, *c.* לַהֲטֵי, secret art, magic, sorcery.

לָהַם (lāhă'm) *Hith. pt. pl.* מִתְלַהֲמִים what is eaten greedily, dainties; [others: wounding or mysterious words].

לָהֵן (lāhē'n) *adv.* therefore.

לַהֲקָה (lᵉhāḳā') *f*, only *c.* לַהֲקַת, assembly, troop, company.

לוֹ = לֹא [see also לְ].

לוּ, לוּא (lū) *conj.* if, if yet; oh that! oh if!

לוּבִים (lūḇī'm) also לֻבִּים (lŭbbī'm) *pr.n.m.pl.*, Libyans.

לוּד (lūḏ) *pr.n.m.* Lydia, Lydians; לוּדִים a people in Ethiopia.

לָוָה (lāvā') *fut.* יִלְוֶה, *pt.* לֹוֶה, to cleave to, to accompany; to borrow. — *Ni.* נִלְוָה, *fut.* יִלָּוֶה, to join, to attach oneself. — *Hi.* הִלְוָה, *fut.* יַלְוֶה, *pt.* מַלְוֶה to lend.

לוּז[1] (lūz) *fut.* יָלֻז to bend, to turn away. — *Ni. pt.* נָלוֹז to be perverted, perverse, wicked. — *Hi. fut.* יַלִּיז to turn away, to depart.

לוּז[2] (lūz) *m* almond- or nut-tree.

לוּז[3] (lūz) *pr.n.* of a town, afterwards בֵּית־אֵל; *pr.n.* of a Hittite town.

לוּחַ (lū'aḥ) *m*, *pl.* לוּחוֹת, לֻחֹת, table, plate, slab, board, plank; *du.* לֻחֹתַיִם deck of a ship.

לוּחִית (lūḥī'ϑ) *pr.n.* of a place in Moab.

לוֹחֵשׁ (lōḥē's); לוֹט[1] (lōt) לוֹטָן (lōtān) *pr.n.m.*

לוט² (lōṭ) *m* covering, veil.

לוט (lūṭ) *pf.* לָט, *pt.* לוֹט, *pt. p. f* לוּטָה, to cover, hide, conceal. — *Hi. fut.* וַיָּלֶט to cover.

לֵוִי (lēvī') *pr.n.m.*; *patr.* לֵוִי [for לֵוִיִּי], *pl.* לְוִיִּם.

לִוְיָה (lĭvyā') *f* wreath, garland.

לִוְיָתָן (lĭvyāϑā'n) *m* serpent, crocodile, huge sea-monster.

לול (lūl) *m*, only *pl.* לוּלִים winding stairs.

לוּלֵא (lūlē') [= לוּ לֹא], לוּלֵי, *conj.* if not, unless.

לון¹ (lūn), **לין** (līn) *pf.* לָן, *inf.* לוּן, לִין, *imp.* לִין, *fut.* יָלִין, יָלֵן, וַיָּלֶן, *pt.* לָן, to pass the night, to turn in, to stop for the night, to lodge, to abide, to remain, to continue. — *Hi.* הֵלִין, *fut.* יָלִין, to cause to remain over night.—*Hith. fut.* יִתְלוֹנָן to lodge, to stay.

לון² (lūn) *Ni.* נָלוֹן, *fut.* יִלּוֹן, to mutter, to murmur, to be refractory. — *Hi.* הֵלִין, *fut.* וַיַּלֶן, יַלִּין, *pt.* מַלִּין the same as *Ni.*

לוע (lūʿ) *pf. pl.* לָעוּ, וְלָעוּ, *fut.* יָלַע, to swallow down; to talk foolishly.

לוץ (lūṣ) [לִיץ] *pf.* לָץ, *pt.* לֵץ, *pl.* לֵצִים, to mock, deride, scorn. — *Hi.* הֵלִיץ, *fut.* יָלִיץ, *pt.* מֵלִיץ, *pl. c.* מְלִיצֵי, to mock, scorn; to interpret, to meditate. — *Hith.* הִתְלוֹצֵץ to act as a mocker.

לוש¹ (lūš) *inf.* לוּשׁ, *imp. 2. sg.* לוּשִׁי, *fut.* יָלוּשׁ, וַיָּלָשׁ (văyyā'lōš), *pt. f/pl.* לָשׁוֹת, to knead.

לוש² (lūš) *pr.n.m.*

לָזוּת (lāzū'ϑ) *f*, *c.* לְזוּת, perverseness.

לַח (lăḥ) *adj.*, *pl.* לַחִים, moist, fresh, green.

לֵחַ (lē'aḥ) *m*, *w.s.* לֵחֹה, freshness, vigour.

לְחוּם (lᵉḥū'm), **לָחוּם** (lāḥū'm) *m*, *w.s.* לַחְמִי, לְחוּמוֹ, food, nourishment; flesh, body.

לְחִי¹ (lᵉḥī') *f*, *i.p.* לֶחִי, *w.s.* לֶחְיוֹ, *du.* לְחָיַיִם, *c.* לְחָיֵי, chin, cheek; jaw-bone.

לְחִי² (lᵉḥī') *pr.n.* [רָמַת לְחִי] of a place on the border of Philistæa.

לָחַךְ (lāḥă'ḵ) *inf.* לְחֹךְ, to lick, to lick off, to eat off.

— *Pi.* לִחֵךְ, *fut.* יְלַחֵךְ, to lick up, to consume.

לָחַם[1] (lāḥă'm) *imp.* לְחַם, *fut.* יִלְחַם, *pt.* לֹחֵם, *pl.* לֹחֲמִים, to compress, to fight, to make war. — *Ni.* נִלְחַם, *inf.* נִלְחֹם, הִלָּחֵם, *imp.* הִלָּחֵם, *fut.* יִלָּחֵם, יִלָּחֶם, to fight, to make war.

לָחַם[2] (lāḥă'm) *fut.* יִלְחַם, *pt. p.* לָחוּם, *pl. c.* לֹחֲמֵי, to eat, to consume.

לָחֶם (lāḥĕ'm) *m, c.* לְחֶם, war, fight, siege.

לֶחֶם (lĕ'ḥĕm) *m, i.p.* לָחֶם, *w.s.* לַחְמִי, food, grain, wheat, bread, loaf.

לַחְמִי (lăḥmī') *pr.n.m.* = בֵּית הַלַּחְמִי Bethlehemite.

לַחְמָם = לְחָמָם, לְחֹם see חָמַם *inf.*

לַחְמָס (lăḥmā'ß) *pr.n.* of a place in Judah.

לָחַץ (lāḥă'ß) *fut.* יִלְחַץ, *pt.* לֹחֵץ, *pl.* לֹחֲצִים, to press, to crush, to oppress. — *Ni. fut.* יִלָּחֵץ to press oneself.

לַחַץ (lă'ḥăß) *m, i.p.* לָחַץ, *w.s.* לַחֲצֵנוּ, oppression, distress, affliction.

לָחַשׁ (lāḥă'š) *Pi. pt. pl.* מְלַחֲשִׁים, to whisper, to mutter incantations. — *Hith. fut.* יִתְלַחֵשׁ, *pt. pl* מִתְלַחֲשִׁים, to whisper to each other.

לַחַשׁ (lă'ḥăš) *m, i.p.* לָחַשׁ, *pl.* לְחָשִׁים, whisper, murmur, whispered prayer; incantation, charm, spell; amulet.

לְחֹת see לוּחַ.

לָט [לָאט] (lāt) *m* secrecy, secret arts; בַּלָּט secretly.

לֹט (lōt) *m* ladanum, resin of the cistus-plant.

לְטָאָה (lᵉtā'ā') *f* a species of lizard.

לְטוּשִׁם (lᵉtūšī'm) *pr.n.* of an Arabian tribe.

לָטַשׁ (lāṭă's) *inf.* לְטוֹשׁ, *fut.* יִלְטֹשׁ, *pt.* לֹטֵשׁ, to hammer, to forge, to sharpen, to point. — *Pu. pt.* מְלֻטָּשׁ to be whetted, sharpened.

לִיָה (lōyā') *f,* only *pl.* לֹיוֹת, wreath, garland, festoon [in architecture].

לַיִל (lă'yīl) and [*w. loc.* ה] לַיְלָה (lă'ylā) *m, c.* לֵיל, *pl.* לֵילוֹת, night; *adv.* by night.

לִילִית (līlī'θ) *f* night-spectre,

night-spirit, ghost [Lamia, Empusa].

לִין see לוּן.

לִיץ see לוּץ.

לַיִשׁ[1] (lă'yĭš) *m* lion.

לַיִשׁ[2] (lă'yĭš) *pr.n.* of a town, afterwards called דָּן; also *pr.n.m.*

לָכַד (lāꞓă'ḍ) *inf.* לְכֹד, לָכֹד, *imp. w.s.* לָכְדָהּ (lŏꞓḍā'h), *fut.* יִלְכֹּד, *pt.* לֹכֵד, to catch, take, seize; to capture, to conquer; to choose. — *Ni.* נִלְכַּד, *fut.* יִלָּכֵד, *pt.* נִלְכָּד to be taken, caught, captured, conquered, selected. — *Hith.* הִתְלַכֵּד to hold fast together, to become firm.

לֶכֶד (lĕ'ꞓĕḍ) *m* capture.

לְכָה[1], לֵךְ, לֶכֶת see הָלַךְ.

לְכָה[2] = לָךְ, see לְ.

לֵכָה (lēꞓā') *pr.n.* of a place in Judah.

לָכִישׁ (lāꞓī'š) *pr.n.* of a city in the plain of Judah.

לָכֵן see כֵּן.

לֻלָאֹת (lŭ'lā'ō'th) *f/pl.*, *c.* לֻלְאֹת, loop, noose.

לָמַד (lāmă'ḍ) *inf.* לָמוֹד, לְמֹד, *w.s.* לָמְדִי (lŏmdī'), *fut.* יִלְמַד, *pt.p.* לָמוּד, to learn, to study, to be accustomed to. — *Pi.* לִמֵּד, *inf.* and *imp.* לַמֵּד, *fut.* יְלַמֵּד, *pt.* מְלַמֵּד, to teach, instruct, practise, train. — *Pu. pt.* מְלֻמָּד to be taught, to be trained.

לִמּוּד, לִמֻּד (lĭmmū'ḍ) *adj.*, *pl.* לִמּוּדִים, *c.* לִמּוּדֵי, taught, trained, skilled, accustomed; disciple.

לְמוֹ = לְ.

לְמוֹאֵל (lᵉmō'ē'l), לְמוּאֵל (lᵉmū'ē'l) *pr.n.m.*

לִמּוּד see לָמַד.

לֶמֶךְ (lĕ'mĕꞓ) *pr.n.m.*, *i.p.* לָמֶךְ.

לֹעַ (lō'aᵉ) *m* throat.

לָעַב (lāᵉă'b) *Hi. pt.* מַלְעָב to mock at.

לָעַג (lāᵉă'g) *fut.* יִלְעַג, *pt.* לוֹעֵג, to laugh at, to mock, to deride. — *Ni. pt. c.* נִלְעַג to stammer, to speak unintelligibly. — *Hi. fut.* יַלְעִיג, *pt.* מַלְעָג the same as *Qal*.

לַעַג (lă'ᵉăg) *m*, *w.s.* לַעֲגָם, mockery, scorn, blasphemy.

לָעֵג (lāᵉē'g) *adj.*, *pl. c.* לַעֲגֵי, speaking barbarously, stammering; mocker.

לַעְדָּה (lă·dā'); **לַעְדָּן** (lă·dā'n) *pr.n.m.*

לָעוּת see עות.

לָעַז (lā·ă'z) *pt.* לֹעֵז, to stammer, to speak unintelligibly.

לָעַט (lā·ă't) *Hi. imp. w.s.* הַלְעִיטֵנִי, to give to eat.

לַעֲנָה (lă·'anā') *f* a bitter herb, wormwood, bitterness, hard lot, curse.

לַפִּיד (lăppī'd) *m, pl.* לַפִּידִים, torch, flame, lightning.

לַפִּידוֹת (lăppīdō'ϑ) *pr.n.m.*

לִפְנֵי see פָּנֶה.

לִפְנַי (lĭfnă'y) *adj.* interior.

לָפַת (lāfă'ϑ) *fut.* יִלְפֹּת, to bend a bow, to clasp, to embrace. — *Ni. fut.* יִלָּפֵת to turn oneself.

לֵץ (lēß) [see לוץ] *m* mocker.

לָצוֹן (lāßō'n) *m* mockery, derision.

לָצַץ (lāßă'ß) *pt.* לוֹצֵץ, to mock, to deride.

לַקּוּם (lăkkū'm) *pr.n.* of a place in Naphtali.

לָקַח (lākă'ḥ) *inf.* לָקֹחַ, קַחַת, *w.s.* קַחְתִּי, *imp.* קַח, קָחָה, קְחִי, *i.p.* קָח, קְחִי, לְקָחִי, *fut.* יִקַּח, *pt.* לֹקֵחַ, to take, to seize, to lay hold of; to take from, to take away, to capture, to conquer; to accept, receive; to perceive. — *Ni.* נִלְקַח, *inf.* הִלָּקַח, *fut.* יִלָּקַח to be taken, seized; to be taken away. — *Pu.* לֻקַּח, *fut.* יֻקַּח [or *Ho.*] to be taken, to be taken away, to be led away. — *Ho. fut.* יֻקַּח to be brought, to be fetched, to be taken away. — *Hith. pt. f* מִתְלַקַּחַת to contain oneself, to be continuous.

לֶקַח (lĕ'kăḥ) *m, w.s.* לִקְחִי, learning, instruction, doctrine, knowledge.

לִקְחִי (lĭkḥī') *pr.n.m.*

לָקַט (lākă't) *inf.* and *imp.* לְקֹט, *fut.* יִלְקֹט, to prick up, to collect, gather, glean. — *Pi.* לִקֵּט, *inf.* לַקֵּט, *fut.* יְלַקֵּט, *pt.* מְלַקֵּט, the same as *Qal.* — *Pu. fut.* יְלֻקַּט to be gathered. — *Hith. fut.* יִתְלַקֵּט to be gathered, to assemble.

לֶקֶט (lĕ'kĕt) *m* a gleaning.

לָקַק (lākă'k) *fut.* יָלֹק, *pl.* יָלֹקּוּ, to lick, to lap up. — *Pi. pt.* מְלַקֵּק the same as *Qal.*

לָקַשׁ (lāķă'š) *Pi.* לִקֵּשׁ to gather the late fruits.

לֶקֶשׁ (lĕ'ķĕš) *m* after-grass, after-math.

לֵרָא = לִירֹא [לְ and יְרֹא], see יָרֵא.

לָשָׁד (lāšā'd) *m*, *c.* לְשַׁד, *w.s.* לְשַׁדִּי, juice [of life], vigour; sweet cake.

לָשׁוֹן (lāšō'n) *f* and *m*, *c.* לְשׁוֹן, *w.s.* לְשׁוֹנִי, *pl.* לְשֹׁנוֹת, לְשֹׁנֹת, tongue; speech, language; tongue-like bar of gold; flame; tongue of a sea-bay.

לִשְׁכָּה (lĭškā') *f*, *c.* לִשְׁכַּת, *w. loc.* ה לִשְׁכָּתָה, *pl.* לְשָׁכוֹת, *c.* לִשְׁכוֹת, chamber, cell, room, appartment, magazine.

לֶשֶׁם[1] (lĕ'šĕm) *m* a precious stone, opal.

לֶשֶׁם[2] (lĕ'šĕm) *pr.n.* of a town = לַיִשׁ.

לָשַׁן (lāšā'n) *Po. pt.* מְלוֹשֵׁן [מְלָשֶׁן] to slander. — *Hi. fut.* יַלְשֵׁן to slander, calumniate.

לֶשַׁע (lĕ'šă') *i.p.* לָשַׁע, *pr.n.* of a place near the Dead Sea.

לַת = לֶדֶת see יָלַד.

לֶתֶךְ (lĕ'θĕch) *m* a measure for grain.

מ

מ, ם the thirteenth letter of the alphabet, called מֵים [water]; as a numeral מ = 40, ם = 600.

מַאֲבוּס (mă''abū's) *m*, *pl.* *w.s.* מַאֲבֻסֶיהָ, granary.

מְאֹד (m''ō'd) *m*, *w.s.* מְאֹדוֹ, power, strength, force; בְּמְאֹד מְאֹד with all might; עַד מְאֹד to a high degree, very much; *adv.* much, greatly, exceedingly, very.

מֵאָה[1] (mē'ā') *f*, *c.* מְאַת, *du.* מָאתַיִם, *pl.* מֵאוֹת, מְאָיוֹת, a hundred, the hundredth, one per cent, a hundred times; *du.* two hundred; *pl.* hundreds.

מֵאָה[2] (mē'ā') *pr.n.* of a tower in Jerusalem.

מְאוּזָל see אָזַל.

מַאֲוַי (mă''avă'y) *m*, only *pl.* *c.* מַאֲוַיֵּי desire.

מאוּם (mūm) [מוּם], *m*, *w.s.* מוּמָם, defect, spot, stain.

מְאוּמָה (mᵉ'ūmā') [=מָה וּמָה] whatever, anything, something.

מָאוֹס (mā'ō's) *m* refuse, anything despicable [see מָאַס].

מָאוֹר (mā'ō'r) *m*, *c.* מְאוֹר, *pl.* מְאֹרוֹת, מְאֹרִים, a luminous body, light, luminary; candlestick.

מְאוּרָה (mᵉ'ūrā') *f* place of light; cave, hole; eye.

מֹאזֵן (mō'zē'n) *m*, only *du.* מֹאזְנַיִם, *c.* מֹאזְנֵי, pair of scales, balance.

מַאֲכָל (mă''aḉā'l) *m*, *c.* מַאֲכַל, eatables, food, victuals.

מַאֲכֹלֶת (mă''aḉō'lĕϑ) *f* food [fuel].

מַאֲכֶלֶת (mă''aḉĕ'lĕϑ) *f* knife.

מַאֲמָץ (mă''amā'ß) *m*, only *pl.* מַאֲמַצִּים, power, exertion.

מַאֲמָר (mă''amā'r) *m* word, edict.

מָאֵן¹ (mā'ē'n) *Pi.* מֵאֵן, *inf.* מָאֵן, *fut.* יְמָאֵן, to be unwilling, to refuse.

מָאֵן² (mā'ē'n) *adj.* unwilling, refusing.

מֵאֵן (mē'ē'n) *adj.*, only *pl.* מֵאֲנִים = מָאֵן².

מָאַס¹ (mā'ă's) *inf.* מָאוֹס, מָאֹס, *fut.* יִמְאַס, *pt.* מוֹאֵס, to despise, reject, refuse, repudiate. — *Ni.* נִמְאַס, *fut.* יִמָּאֵס, *pt.* נִמְאָס to be despised, rejected.

מָאַס² (mā'ă's) [= מָסַס] *fut.* יִמְאַס to melt, to feel undone. — *Ni.* *fut.* יִמָּאֵס [= יִמַּס] to melt away, to dissolve.

מַאֲפֶה (mă''afĕ') *m* something baked.

מַאֲפֵל (mă''afē'l) *m* darkness.

מַאְפֵּלְיָה (mă'pē'lᵉyā') *f* darkness of יָהּ, utter darkness.

מָאַר (mā'ă'r) *Hi.* הִמְאִיר, *pt.* מַמְאִיר, *f* מַמְאֶרֶת, to hurt, to wound.

מַאֲרָב (mă''arā'ḇ) *m*, *c.* מַאֲרַב, ambush, ambuscade.

מְאֵרָה (mᵉ'ērā') *f* curse.

מֵאֵת = מִן אֵת.

מֵאֲשֶׁר = מִן אֲשֶׁר *conj.* because.

מִבְדָל (mĭḇdā'l) *adj.*, only *f/pl.* מִבְדָּלוֹת, separated, single.

מָבוֹא (māḇō') *m*, *c.* מְבוֹא, *w.s.* מְבֹאוֹ, מְבֹאֶךָ, *pl. c.* מְבוֹאֵי, entrance, act of entering, entry; setting [of the sun], west.

מְבוֹאָה (mᵉḇō'ā') *f*, only *pl.* מְבוֹאוֹת, entry [of the sea], haven.

מְבוּכָה (mᵉḇūḉā') *f* consternation.

מַבּוּל (măbbū'l) *m* flood, deluge.

מְבוּסָה (mᵉḇūsā') *f* a trampling down, subduing.

מַבּוּעַ (măbbū'ă') *m*, *pl. c.* מַבּוּעֵי, fountain, spring.

מְבוּקָה (mᵉḇūkā') *f* emptiness, desolation.

מָבוּשׁ (māḇū's) *m*, only *pl.* מְבוּשִׁים, מְבֻשִׁים, the privy parts, pudenda.

מִבְחוֹר (mĭḇḥō'r) and מִבְחָר¹ (mĭḇḥā'r) *m*, *c.* מִבְחַר, selection, the choicest, best.

מִבְחָר² (mĭḇḥā'r) *pr.n.m.*

מַבָּט (măbbā't) *m*, *w.s.* מֶבָּטָהּ, מַבָּטֵנוּ, expectation, hope.

מִבְטָא (mĭḇtā') *m* rash utterance.

מִבְטָח (mĭḇtā'ḥ) *m*, *c.* מִבְטַח, *w.s.* מִבְטָחִי, מִבְטַחִי, *pl.* מִבְטַחִים, confidence, trust, security, ease, prosperity; object of trust.

מֵבִי = מֵבִיא, see בּוֹא.

מַבְלִיגִית (măḇlīgī'ṯ) *f* a cheering up, cheerfulness.

מִבְנֶה (mĭḇnĕ') *m* building, house.

מְבֻנַּי (mᵉḇŭnnă'y) *pr.n.m.*

מְבַעֲתֶךָ = מְבַעֲתֶתְךָ, see בָּעַת *Pi. pt. f.*

מִבְצָר¹ (mĭḇṣā'r) *m*, *c.* מִבְצַר, *pl.* מִבְצָרִים, מִבְצָרוֹת, *c.* מִבְצְרֵי, fortification, fortress, citadel, fortified city.

מִבְצָר² (mĭḇṣā'r) *pr.n.m.*

מִבְרָח (mĭḇrā'ḥ) *m* flight; a fugitive.

מִבְשָׂם (mĭḇsā'm) *pr.n.m.*

מְבַשְּׁלֹת (mᵉḇăššĕ'lōṯ) *f*, only *pl.* מְבַשְּׁלוֹת, cooking-place, hearth.

מָג (māg) *m* magus, Persian priest.

מַגְבִּישׁ (măgbī's) *pr.n.* of a place.

מִגְבָּלָה (mĭgbālā') *f*, only *pl.* מִגְבָּלוֹת, something twisted, string, cord.

מִגְבָּעָה (mĭgbā'ā') *f*, *pl.* מִגְבָּעֹת, turban, headdress of priests.

מֶגֶד (mĕ'gĕḏ) *m*, *pl.* מְגָדִים, preciousness, precious thing, choice fruit.

מְגִדּוֹ (m^e^gĭddō') *pr.n.* of a city in Issachar.

מַגְדִּיאֵל (măgdī'ē'l) *pr.n.m.*

מִגְדָּל (mĭgdā'l) *m, c.* מִגְדַּל, *pl.* מִגְדָּלִים, מִגְדָּלוֹת, tower, watch tower; pulpit, high stage; raised bank of flowers; מִגְדַּל עֵדֶר tower of the flock, a place near Bethlehem.

מִגְדֹּל, מִגְדּוֹל (mĭgdō'l) *pr.n.* of two towns.

מִגְדָּנָה (mĭgdānā') *f,* only *pl.* מִגְדָּנוֹת, precious things.

מָגוֹג (māgō'g) *pr.n.* of a northern people, Scythians.

מָגוֹר[1] (māgō'r) *m* fear, terror.

מָגוֹר[2] (māgō'r), מָגוּר (māgū'r), *m, c.* מְגוּר, *pl.* מְגוּרִים, *c.* מְגוּרֵי, temporary abode, sojourn; inn, dwelling.

מְגוֹרָה (m^e^gōrā') *f* fear.

מְגוּרָה (m^e^gūrā') *f, pl.* מְגוּרוֹת, fear, object of fear; granary, store-house.

מַגְזֵרָה (măgzērā') *f, pl.* מַגְזֵרוֹת, *c.* מַגְזְרוֹת, axe, hatchet.

מַגָּל (măggā'l) *m* sickle.

מְגִלָּה (m^e^gĭllā') *f, c.* מְגִלַּת, roll, book-roll, volume.

מְגַמָּה (m^e^gămmā') *f, c.* מְגַמַּת troop, crowd.

מָגַן (māgă'n) *Pi.* מִגֵּן, *fut.* יְמַגֵּן, to deliver over, to give, to bestow.

מָגֵן (māgē'n) *m* and *f, w.s.* מָגִנִּי, *pl.* מָגִנִּים, מָגִנּוֹת, *c.* מָגִנֵּי, shield, protection, protector.

מְגִנָּה (m^e^gĭnnā') *f* covering; infatuation, blindness.

מִגְעֶרֶת (mĭg'ĕ'rĕϑ) *f* rebuke, curse.

מַגֵּפָה (măggēfā') *f, c.* מַגֵּפַת, *pl.* מַגֵּפוֹת, blow, plague, pestilence, defeat [in battle].

מַגְפִּיעָשׁ (măgpī'ā'š) *pr.n.m.*

מָגַר (māgă'r) *pt. p.* מָגוּר, to give up, to abandon. — *Pi.* מִגֵּר to cast down.

מְגֵרָה (m^e^gērā') *f, pl.* מְגֵרוֹת, a saw.

מִגְרוֹן (mĭgrō'n) *pr.n.m.* of two towns in Benjamin.

מִגְרָעָה (mĭgrā'ā') *f,* only *pl.* מִגְרָעוֹת, diminution, ledge, rest.

מֶגְרָפָה (mĕgrāfā') *f, pl. c.* מֶגְרְפוֹת, clod of earth.

מִגְרָשׁ (mĭgrā'š) *m, c.* מִגְרַשׁ,

pl. מִגְרְשִׁים, *c.* מִגְרְשֵׁי, מִגְרְשׁוֹת, pasture, common land surrounding towns; area, precincts.

מַד (măḍ) *m*, *w.s.* מַדּוֹ, מִדָּהּ, *pl.* מַדִּים, מִדִּים [מִדִּין], garment, coat; covering, carpet.

מִדְבָּר (mĭḍbā'r) *m*, *c.* מִדְבַּר, *w. loc.* ה מִדְבָּרָה, *w.s.* מִדְבָּרָהּ, pasture, grassland, steppe, desert; mouth, speach [דָּבָר].

מָדַד (māḍă'ḍ) *inf.* מֹד, *fut.* יָמֹד, וַיָּמָד (văyyā'mŏḍ), יָמֹדּוּ, to stretch, to measure, to mete out. — *Ni. fut.* יִמַּד, *pl.* יִמַּדּוּ, to be meted out. — *Pi.* מִדַּד, *fut.* יְמַדֵּד to stretch out, to extend, to measure. — *Po. fut.* יְמוֹדֵד to measure. — *Hith. fut.* יִתְמוֹדֵד to stretch oneself.

מִדָּד (mĭddā'ḍ) *m*, *c.* מִדַּד, the passing away.

מִדָּה (mĭddā') *f*, *c.* מִדַּת, *pl.* מִדּוֹת, extension, length, tallness; dimension; measure; garment, vestment; tribute.

מַדְהֵבָה (măḍhēḇā') *f* a name for Babylon, exactress of gold [others read מַרְהֵבָה oppression].

מַדְוֶה[1] (măḍvĕ') *m*, only *pl. c.* מַדְוֵי garment.

מַדְוֶה[2] (măḍvĕ') *m*, *pl. c.* מַדְוֵי, sickness, disease.

מַדּוּחַ (măddū'ăḥ) *m*, only *pl.* מַדּוּחִים, expulsion.

מָדוֹן[1] (māḍō'n) *m* dispute, quarrel, object of strife.

מָדוֹן[2] (māḍō'n) *m* extension, length.

מָדוֹן[3] (māḍō'n) *pr.n.* of a Phenician town.

מַדּוּעַ (măddū'ă') *adv.* [for מָה יָדוּעַ] why? for what reason?

מְדוּרָה (mᵉḍūrā') *f*, *w.s.* מְדֻרָתָהּ, pile of wood.

מְדוּשָׁה (mᵉḍūšā') *f*, *w.s.* מְדֻשָׁתִי, a thrashing, something thrashed, oppressed.

מִדְחֶה (mĭḍḥĕ') *m* overthrow, fall.

מַדְחֵפָה (măḍḥēfā') *f*, only *pl.* מַדְחֵפֹת, blow, overthrow, ruin.

מָדַי (māḍă'y) *pr.n.*, Media; a Mede, Medes [also מָדִי].

מַדַּי = מָה דַּי what is enough.

מִדֵּי see דַּי.

מִדְיָן (mĭdyā'n) *pr.n.* of an Arabian tribe; *gent.* מִדְיָנִי, *pl.* מִדְיָנִים, *f* מִדְיָנִית.

מִדִּין (mĭddī'n) *pr.n.* of a town in Judah [see also מַד].

מְדִינָה (mᵉdīnā') *f* province, district of jurisdiction.

מְדֹכָה (mᵉdōchā') *f* a mortar.

מַדְמֵן (mădmē'n) *pr.n.* of a town in Moab.

מַדְמַנָּה (mădmănnā') *pr.n.* of a town in Judah.

מַדְמֵנָה[1] (mădmēnā') *f* dung-hill.

מַדְמֵנָה[2] (mădmēnā') *pr.n.* of a town in Benjamin.

מְדָן[1] (mᵉdā'n) *m*, only *pl.* מְדָנִים, contention, strife.

מְדָן[2] (mᵉdā'n) *pr.n.m.*

מְדָנִי (mᵉdānī') *pr.n.m.*, *pl.* מְדָנִים = מִדְיָנִים see מִדְיָן.

מַדָּע (măddā'ᵉ) and מַדַּע (măddā'ᵉ) *m* knowledge, thought.

מֹדָע see מוֹדָע.

מֹדַעַת (mōdă'ᵉăth) see מוֹדַעַת.

מַדְקָרָה (mădkārā') *f*, only *pl. c.* מַדְקְרוֹת, a piercing, wounding.

מַדְרֵגָה (mădrēgā') *f* a stair-like height.

מִדְרָךְ (mĭdrā'ch) *m* a trodden place, foot-hold.

מִדְרָשׁ (mĭdrā'š) *m* inquiry, examination, commentary.

מָה (mā) *pron. interr.* [מַה־, מֶה, מַ־] what? which? anything, something; *adv.* why? how? how! — בַּמָּה wherein? whereby? — לָמָּה wherefore? why? — עַד־מָה till when? — עַל־מָה wherefore?

מָהַהּ (māhă'h) *Hith.* הִתְמַהְמַהּ, *inf.* הִתְמַהְמֵהַּ, *imp. w.s.* הִתְמַהְמְהוּ, to tarry, delay, hesitate.

מְהוּמָה (mᵉhūmā') *f*, *c.* מְהוּמַת confusion, consternation, disturbance, noise.

מְהוּמָן (mᵉhūmā'n) *pr.n.m.*

מְהֵיטַבְאֵל (mᵉhētăb'ē'l) *pr n.f.*; *pr.n.m.*

מָהִיר (māhī'r) *adj.*, *c.* מְהִיר, quick, prompt.

מָהַל (māhă'l) *pt. p.* מָהוּל to cut [wine], to sophisticate.

מַהֲלָךְ (mă'hălā'ch) *m*, *c.* מַהֲלַךְ, way, journey, walk.

מַהֲלֵךְ (mă'hălē'ch) *m*, only *pl.*

מַהֲלָכִים way, access [others: companion, guide].

מַהֲלָל (mă'hᵃlā'l) *m*, *c.* מַהֲלַל praise, approbation.

מַהֲלַלְאֵל (mă'hᵃlăl'ē'l) *pr.n.m.*

מַהֲלֻמָּה (mă'hᵃlŭmmā') *f*, only *pl.* מַהֲלֻמּוֹת blow, stroke.

מַהֲמֹרָה (mă'hᵃmōrā') *f*, only *pl.* מַהֲמֹרוֹת, flood, stream.

מַהְפֵּכָה (măhpēḉā') *f*, *c.* מַהְפֵּכַת, overthrow, destruction, ruin.

מַהְפֶּכֶת (măhpĕ'ḉĕϑ) *f* stock [for culprits].

מָהַר¹ (māhă'r) *inf.* מָהֹר, *fut. w.s.* יִמְהָרֶנָּה, to exchange, to buy.

מָהַר² (māhă'r) to hasten. — *Ni.* נִמְהַר, *pt.* נִמְהָר to be hurried, to be hasty, rash; to be timid. — *Pi.* מִהַר, *inf.* and *imp.* מַהֵר¹, *fut.* יְמַהֵר, *pt.* מְמַהֵר to hasten, to accelerate, to do quickly; *inf. adv.* in haste, quickly; to be expert, skilled.

מַהֵר² (măhē'r) *adj.* hastening, quick.

מֹהַר (mō'hăr) *m* marriage-price.

מְהֵרָה (mᵉhērā') *f* haste, speed; *adv.* quickly, speedily.

מַהֲרַי (mă'hᵃrā'y) *pr.n.m.*

מַהֲתַלָּה (mă'hᵃϑăllā') *f*, only *pl.* מַהֲתַלּוֹת, delusion.

מוֹאָב (mō'ā'ḇ) *pr.n.m.*; *gent.* מוֹאָבִי, *pl.* מוֹאָבִים, *f* מוֹאָבִית, מוֹאֲבִיָּה.

מואל see מול².

מוֹבָא (mōḇā') *m*, *w.s.* מוֹבָאֶךָ, entrance.

מוג (mūg) *inf.* מוג, *fut.* יָמוּג, יָמֹוג, to melt, to tremble, to shake, to fear; to cause to despond. — *Ni.* נָמוֹג, *pt. pl.* נְמוֹגִים, to be dissolved; to tremble, to be afraid or dismayed. — *Pil.* מוֹגֵג, *fut. w.s.* תְּמוֹגְגֶנָּה, תְּמוֹגְגֵנוּ, to cause to dissolve, to soften. — *Hith. fut.* יִתְמוֹגֵג to dissolve, to tremble.

מוד (mūḍ) *Pil. fut.* יְמוֹדֵד, to cause to quake [see מָדַד].

מוֹדַע, מֹדָע (mōḍā'ᵉ) *m* acquaintance, friend.

מוֹדַעַת (mōḍă'ᵉăϑ) *f* — מוֹדָע.

מוט (mūt) *pf.* מָט, *inf.* מוֹט, *fut.* יָמוּט, *pt.* מָט, to waver, totter, quake. —

Ni. נָמוֹט, *fut.* יִמּוֹט to totter, stumble, fall, tremble. — *Hi.* הֵמִיט, *fut.* יָמִיט to cause to totter, to cause to fall, to precipitate. — *Hith.* הִתְמוֹטֵט the same as *Qal.* and *Ni.*

מוֹט (mōt) *m*, *w.s.* מֹטֵהוּ, a tottering, stumbling; carrying-pole, yoke.

מוֹטָה (mōṭā') *f*, *pl.* מוֹטוֹת, pole for carrying, staff, yoke, injustice.

מוּךְ (mūḵ) *fut.* יָמוּךְ, to be reduced, to become poor.

מוּל[1] (mūl) *pf.* מָל, *fut.* וַיָּמָל (văyyā'mǫl), *pt. p.* מוּל, to cut off, to circumcise. *Ni. pf. pl.* נִמֹּלוּ, *inf.* הִמּוֹל, *fut.* יִמּוֹל, *pl.* יִמֹּלוּ, *pt.* נִמּוֹל, to be circumcised, to circumcise oneself. — *Hi. fut.* יָמִיל, *w.s.* אֲמִילַם to cut off, to destroy.

מוּל[2] (mūl), מוֹל, מוֹאל (mōl) *prep.* and *adv.* before, opposite, in front; אֶל־מוּל before, towards; מִמּוּל from before; מִמֻּלִי from before me, near me.

מוֹלָדָה (mō'lādā') *pr.n.* of a town in Judah.

מוֹלֶדֶת (mōlĕ'dĕṯ) *f*, *w.s.* מוֹלַדְתִּי, *pl.* מוֹלְדוֹת, *c.* מוֹלְדוֹת, birth, nativity, descent; offspring, family, countrymen.

מוּלָה (mūlā') *f* circumcision.

מוֹלִיד (mōlī'd) *pr.n.m.*

מוּם (mūm) *m*, *w.s.* מוּמוֹ, spot, stain, defect, fault, disgrace.

מוּמָת see מות *Hi.*

מוּסַב (mūsă'ḇ) *m* circuit [round a house].

מוּסַבָּה (mū'săbbā') *f* [or *pt. Ho.* of סָבַב], only *pl.* מוּסַבּוֹת, fold of a door.

מוֹסָד (mōsā'ḏ) *m*, *pl.* מוֹסָדוֹת, *c.* מוֹסְדֵי, מוֹסְדוֹת, foundation, basis.

מוּסָד (mūsā'ḏ) *m*, *c.* מוּסַד, foundation.

מוּסָדָה (mū'sādā') *f* foundation; decree.

מוּסָךְ (mūsā'ḵ) *m*, *c.* מוּסַךְ, covered passage, corridor.

מוֹסֵר[1] (mōsē'r) *m* [for מֹאסֵר], only *pl.* מוֹסֵרִים, *c.* מוֹסְרֵי, and מוֹסֵרוֹת, *c.* מוֹסְרוֹת, fetter, bond.

מוֹסֵר[2] (mōsē'r) and מוֹסֵרוֹת (mō'sērōṯ), *w. loc.* ה מוֹסֵרָה, *pr.n.* of a station in the desert.

מוּסָר (mūßā'r) *m*, *c.* מוּסַר, chastisement, punishment, correction, instruction, discipline, self-control.

מוֹעָד (mō'ā'd) *m*, *pl.* מוֹעָדִים, assembly, troop.

מוֹעֵד (mō'ē'd) *m*, *w.s.* מוֹעֲדוֹ, *pl.* מוֹעֲדִים, *c.* מוֹעֲדֵי, fixed, appointed time, season, term, epoch, festival time; appointed place; assembly, meeting, congregation, festive gathering; appointment, signal.

מוֹעָדָה (mō''ādā') *f*, only *pl.* מוֹעָדוֹת, festival.

מוּעָדָה (mū''ādā') *f* appointed place, refuge, asylum.

מוּעָף (mū'ā'f) *m* darkness.

מוֹעֵצָה (mō''ēßā') *f*, only *pl.* מוֹעֵצוֹת, *c.* מוֹעֲצוֹת, counsel, resolution, project.

מוּעָקָה (mū''ākā') *f* pressure, burden.

מוּפָּז see פָּזַז *Ho.*

מוֹפֵת (mōfē'ϑ) *m*, *pl.* מוֹפְתִים, *c.* מוֹפְתֵי, wonderful deed, wonder, miraculous sign, prodigy, portent, omen.

מוּץ (mūß) *pt.* מֵץ, to oppress.

מוֹץ, מֹץ (mōß) *m* chaff.

מוֹצָא (mōßā') *m*, *w.s.* מוֹצָאוֹ, *pl. c.* מוֹצָאֵי, a going out, egress; rise [of the sun]; place whence a thing comes or proceeds, spring, mine, gate; utterance, speech, edict.

מוֹצָאָה (mō'ßā'ā') *f*, *pl.* מוֹצָאוֹת, descent; sewer, privy.

מוּצֵאת (mūßē'ϑ) see יָצָא *Ho.*

מוּצָק (mūßā'k) *m* cast metal, the casting of metal.

מוּצַק (mūßă'k) *m*, *i.p.* מוּצָק, narrowness; affliction, distress.

מוּצֶקֶת (mū'ßakā') *f* tube, pipe.

מוּק (mūk) *Hi.* הֵמִיק, *fut.* יָמִיק, to mock, deride.

מוֹקֵד (mōkē'd) *m*, *pl. c.* מוֹקְדֵי, heat, conflagration.

מוֹקְדָה (mō'kᵉdā') *f* hearth, altar [others: fuel].

מוֹקֵשׁ (mōkē'š) *m*, *pl.* מוֹקְשִׁים, *c.* מוֹקְשֵׁי, and מוֹקְשׁוֹת, implement for fowling, hook, snare, noose.

מוֹר see מֹר.

מוּר (mūr) *Ni.* נָמַר, to be changed, to alter oneself.

—*Hi. inf.* הָמִיר, *fut.* יָמִיר, יָמֵר to change, exchange; to alter oneself.

מוֹרָא (mōrā') *m, w.s.* מוֹרָאִי, מוֹרַאֲכֶם, *pl.* מוֹרָאִים, fear, reverence; object of fear; miracle.

מוֹרַג (mōrā'g) *m, pl.* מוֹרַגִּים [מוֹרִיגִים], thrashing-sledge.

מוֹרָד (mōrā'ḍ) *m, c.* מוֹרַד descent, declivity, slope; festoon.

מוֹרָה[1] (mōrā') *m* razor.

מוֹרָה[2] (mōrā') *f* teaching, instruction; or = מוֹרָא fear, terror.

מוֹרֶה[1] (mōrĕ') *m* teacher, guide.

מוֹרֶה[2] (mōrĕ') *m* shooter, archer.

מוֹרֶה[3] (mōrĕ') *pr.n.m.*; אֵלוֹן מוֹרֶה oak or terebinth of Moreh.

מוֹרֶה[4] (mōrĕ') *pt. Hi.* of יָרָה, early rain.

מוֹרָט (mōrā't) for מְמֹרָט [see מָרַט] sharpened, sharp.

מוֹרִיָּה see מֹרִיָּה.

מוֹרָשׁ (mōrā'š) *m, c.* מוֹרַשׁ, *pl. c.* מוֹרָשֵׁי, possession.

מוֹרָשָׁה (mō'rāšā') *f* possession, property.

מוֹרֶשֶׁת גַּת (mōrĕ'šĕϑ gāϑ) *pr.n.* of a place in Judea; *gent.* מוֹרַשְׁתִּי.

מוּשׁ[1] (mūš), *fut.* יָמוּשׁ to give way, to depart; to take away. — *Hi.* הֵמִישׁ, *fut.* יָמִישׁ to take away, to remove; to depart, to give way.

מוּשׁ[2] (mūš) *fut.* יָמוּשׁ, to touch, feel. — *Hi. imp. w.s.* הֲמִישֵׁנִי, *fut.* יָמִישׁ to let touch; to touch, feel.

מוֹשָׁב (mōšā'ḇ) *m, c.* מוֹשַׁב, *w.s.* מוֹשָׁבוֹ, *pl. c.* מוֹשְׁבוֹת, seat; session; dwelling-place; stay, time of abode; inhabitants of a place; site of a town.

מוּשִׁי (mūšī') *pr.n.m.*

מוֹשֶׁכֶת (mōšĕ'ḵĕϑ) *f*, only *pl.* מוֹשְׁכוֹת, rope, fetter.

מוֹשָׁעָה (mō'šā'ā') *f*, only *pl.* מוֹשָׁעוֹת, deliverance, salvation.

מוּת (mūϑ) *pf.* מֵת, מַתִּי, מֵתוּ, *inf.* מוּת, מוֹת, *imp.* מֻת, *fut.* יָמוּת, יָמֹת, וַיָּמָת, (văyyā'mŏϑ), וַיָּמוֹת, *pt.* מֵת, *pl.* מֵתִים, *f* מֵתָה, to die, to wither, to decay, to be dead. — *Pi.* מוֹתֵת, *inf.* מוֹתֵת, *imp. w.s.* מוֹתְתֵנִי,

fut. יְמוֹתֵת, *pt.* מְמוֹתֵת, to kill, to slay. — *Hi.* הֵמִית, *inf.* הָמֵת, הָמִית, *imp. w.s.* הֲמִיתֵנִי, *fut.* יָמִית, וַיָּמֶת, *pt.* מֵמִית, *pl.* מְמִיתִים, to cause to die, to bring to death, to kill, to slay. — *Ho.* הוּמַת, *fut.* יוּמַת, *pt.* מוּמָת to be put to death.

מָוֶת (mā'vĕϑ) *m*, *w. loc.* מָוְתָה ה, *c.* מוֹת, *w.s.* מוֹתִי, *pl.* מוֹתִים, *c.* מוֹתֵי, death, realm of the dead; deadly sickness, pestilence, destruction.

מוֹתָר (mōϑā'r) *m* abundance, excellence, profit.

מִזְבֵּחַ (mĭzbē'aḥ) *m*, *c.* מִזְבַּח, *w.s.* מִזְבְּחִי, מִזְבַּחֲךָ, *pl.* מִזְבְּחוֹת, altar.

מֶזֶג (mĕ'zĕg) *m* mixed wine, spiced wine.

מָזֶה (māzĕ') *adj.*, *pl. c.* מְזֵי, sucked out, exhausted.

מִזָּה (mĭzzā') *pr.n.m.*

מֶזֶו (mĕ'zĕv) or מָזוּ (mā'zū) or מְזָו (mᵉzā'v) *m*, only *pl.* *w.s.* מְזָוֵינוּ, garner.

מְזוּזָה (mᵉzūzā') *f*, *c.* מְזוּזַת, *pl.* מְזוּזוֹת, door-post.

מָזוֹן (māzō'n) *m* food.

מָזוֹר[1] (māzō'r) *m* wound, hurt; a binding up, healing.

מָזוֹר[2] (māzō'r) *m* net, trap.

מֵזַח (mē'zăḥ) *m* girdle; bridle, fetter.

מְזִיחַ (māzī'aḥ) *m*, *c.* מְזִים, girdle.

מַזָּל (măzzā'l) only *pl.* *f* מַזָּלוֹת, wandering stars, planets; or the 12 constellations of the zodiac.

מַזְלֵג (măzlē'g) *m* fork, flesh-hook.

מִזְלָגָה (mĭzlāgā') *f*, only *pl.* מִזְלָגוֹת, fork.

מְזִמָּה (mᵉzĭmmā') *f*, *c.* מְזִמַּת, *pl.* מְזִמּוֹת, meditation, thought, prudence; plan, device, plot, purpose, intrigue, mischief.

מִזְמוֹר (mĭzmō'r) *m* song [for musical accompaniment], psalm.

מַזְמֵרָה (măzmērā') *f*, only *pl.* מַזְמֵרוֹת, vine-knife, pruning-hook.

מְזַמֶּרֶת (mᵉzămmĕ'rĕϑ) *f*, only *pl.* מְזַמְּרוֹת, snuffers.

מִזְעָר (mĭzʿā'r) *m* littleness, fewness; *adv.* little.

מָזָר (māzā'r) *m*, only *pl.* מְזָרִים, northern constellations or winds; the north.

מִזְרֶה (mĭzrĕ') *m* winnowing-shovel.

מַזָּרוֹת (măzzārō'ϑ) only *pl.*, probably = מַזָּלוֹת.

מִזְרָח (mĭzrā'ḥ) *m*, *c.* מִזְרַח, *w. loc.* ה מִזְרָחָה, sunrise, east.

מִזְרָע (mĭzrā'') *m*, *c.* מִזְרַע, sown field.

מִזְרָק (mĭzrā'k) *m*, *pl.* מִזְרָקִים and מִזְרָקוֹת, sprinkling vessel, sprinkler; wine-bowl.

מֵחַ (mē'aḥ) *adj.*, *pl.* מֵחִים, marrowy, fat, wealthy.

מֹחַ (mō'aḥ) *m* marrow.

מָחָא (māḥā') *fut.* יִמְחָא, to strike, to clap [the hands for joy]. — *Pi. inf. w.s.* מַחֲאֲךָ to strike, to clap.

מַחֲבֵא (mă'ḥaḇē') *m* hiding-place.

מַחֲבֹא (mă'ḥaḇō') *m*, only *pl.* מַחֲבֹאִים = מַחֲבֵא.

מַחְבֶּרֶת (măḥbĕ'rĕϑ) *f*, only *pl.* מַחְבְּרוֹת, connecting beam; cramp, hook.

מַחֲבַת (mă'ḥaḇă'ϑ) *f* and *m* frying-pan.

מַחֲגֹרֶת (mă'ḥagō'rĕϑ) *f* a girding, girdle.

מָחָה¹ (māḥā') *inf.* מָחֹה, מְחוֹת, *imp.* מְחֵה, *fut.* יִמְחֶה, *pt.* מֹחֶה to wipe, to wipe off, to blot out; to adjoin, to touch on. — *Ni.* נִמְחָה, *fut.* יִמָּחֶה, יִמַּח, to be wiped out or off, to be removed, effaced, destroyed. — *Pu. pt. pl.* מְמֻחָיִם, to be smeared with fat [but see מָחָה²]. — *Hi.* הִמְחָה, *inf.* לַמְחוֹת [for לְהַמְחוֹת], *fut.* 2. *sg.* תֶּמַח, to wipe off, to put away.

מָחָה² (māḥā') *Pu. pt. pl.* מְמֻחָיִם, to be marrowy or fat; *pt.* fat things taken from the marrow.

מְחוּגָה (meḥūgā') *f* compasses [for drawing a circle].

מָחוֹז (māḥō'z) *m*, *c.* מְחוֹז, coast, haven.

מְחוּיָאֵל (meḥū'yā'ēl), **מְחִיָּאֵל** (meḥĭyyā'ēl) *pr.n.m.*

מַחֲוִים (măḥavī'm) *pr.n.* of an unknown people.

מָחוֹל¹ (māḥō'l) *m* dance, circular dance.

מָחוֹל² (māḥō'l) *pr.n.m.*

מְחֹלָה, **מְחוֹלָה** (meḥōlā') *f*, *pl.* מְחֹלֹת, dance.

מַחֲזֶה (mă'ḥazĕ') *m*, *c.* מַחֲזֵה, vision, sight, apparition.

מֶחֱזָה (mĕ'ḥezā') *f* window, out-look.

מַחֲזִיאוֹת (mă'ḥazī'ō'ϑ) *pr. n.m.*

מְחִי (mᵉḥī') *m* stroke, blow.

מְחִידָא (mᵉḥīdā') *pr.n.m.*

מִחְיָה[1] (mīḥyā') *f* preservation of life, livelihood, victuals.

מִחְיָה[2] (mīḥyā') *f* sign, spot [or wound, scar].

מְחִיר[1] (mᵉḥī'r) *m*, *pl. c.* מְחִירֵי, price, purchase-money, wages.

מְחִיר[2] (mᵉḥī'r) *pr.n.m.*

מַחֲלֶה (mă'ḥalĕ') *m* and מַחֲלָה (mă'ḥalā') *f* sickness.

מַחְלָה (măḥlā') *pr.n.f.*

מְחִלָּה (mᵉḥīllā') *f*, only *pl.* מְחִלּוֹת, hole, cave.

מַחְלוֹן (măḥlō'n); מַחְלִי (măḥlī') *pr.n.m.*

מַחֲלֻיִים (mă'ḥalūyī'm) *m/pl.* sickness, disease.

מַחֲלָף (mă'ḥalā'f) *m*, only *pl.* מַחֲלָפִים, knife.

מַחֲלָפָה (mă'ḥalāfā') *f*, only *pl. c.* מַחְלְפוֹת, braid, plait of hair.

מַחֲלָצָה (mă'ḥalāßā') *f*, only *pl.* מַחֲלָצוֹת, festive garment.

מַחְלְקָה (măḥlᵉkā') *f*, *pl.* מַחְלְקוֹת, smoothness, escape.

מַחֲלֹקֶת (măḥalō'kĕϑ) *f*, *w.s.* מַחֲלֻקְתּוֹ, *pl.* מַחְלְקוֹת, division, class.

מַחֲלַת (mă'ḥală'ϑ) *m* a musical instrument or a mode of performing music.

מָחֲלַת (mā'ḥală'ϑ) [מַחֲלַת] *pr.n.f.*

מְחֹלָתִי (mᵉḥō'lāϑī') *gent.* of אָבֵל מְחוֹלָה.

מַחֲמָאָה (mă'ḥamā'ā') *f*, only *pl.* מַחֲמָאֹת, words smooth as butter, flattery.

מַחְמָד (măḥmā'd) *m*, *c.* מַחְמַד, *pl.* מַחֲמַדִּים, *c.* מַחֲמַדֵּי, desire, delight; darling, a precious, desirable thing; charm, loveliness.

מַחֲמֹד (mă'ḥamō'd) *m*, only *pl.* מַחֲמֹדִּים, precious things.

מַחְמָל (măḥmā'l) *m*, *c.* מַחְמַל, desire.

מַחְמֶצֶת (măḥmĕ'ßĕϑ) *f* something leavened.

מַחֲנֶה (mă'ḥanĕ') *m*, *c.* מַחֲנֵה, *pl.* מַחֲנִים, *c.* מַחֲנֵי and מַחֲנוֹת, *du.* מַחֲנַיִם[1], camp, encampment, army, host, troop; band, station of priests.

מַחֲנֵה־דָן (mă'ḥᵃnē'-dā'n) *pr.n.* of a place.

מַחֲנַיִם[2] (mă'ḥᵃnă'yĭm) *pr.n.* of a town between Gad and Manasseh.

מַחֲנָק (mă'ḥᵃnā'k) *m*, *c.* מַחֲנַק, strangling, strangulation.

מַחֲסֶה (mă'ḥᵃsĕ'), מַחְסֶה (măḥsĕ') *m*, *c.* מַחֲסֵה, *w.s.* מַחֲסִי, refuge, shelter.

מַחְסוֹם (măḥsō'm) *m* muzzle.

מַחְסֹר, מַחְסוֹר (măḥsō'r) *m* want, need, poverty.

מַחְסֵיָה (măḥsēyā') *pr.n.m.*

מָחַץ (māḥă'ẓ) *imp.* מְחַץ, *fut.* יִמְחַץ, to split, to cleave, to crush, to wound; to shake, to dip.

מַחַץ (mă'ḥăẓ) *m* wound.

מַחְצֵב (măḥẓē'b) *m* a hewing [of stones].

מֶחֱצָה (mĕ'ḥᵉẓā') *f* the half.

מַחֲצִת, מַחֲצִית (mă'ḥᵃẓī'ϑ) *f* the half, the middle.

מָחַק (māḥă'k) to pierce, to cut through.

מֶחְקָר (mĕḥkā'r) *m*, only *pl.* *c.* מֶחְקְרֵי, the deepest, the innermost.

מָחָר (māḥā'r) *m* and *adv.* [from אָחַר, what comes after, the future], the next morning, the morrow; to-morrow, later, hereafter.

מַחֲרָאָה (mă'ḥᵃrā'ā') *f*, only *pl.* מַחֲרָאוֹת, privy, sink, cloaca.

מַחֲרֵשָׁה (mă'ḥᵃrēšā') *f*, *w.s.* מַחֲרַשְׁתּוֹ, and מַחֲרֶשֶׁת (mă'ḥᵃrĕ'šĕϑ) *f*, *w.s.* מַחֲרַשְׁתּוֹ, *pl.* מַחֲרֵשׁוֹת, plough-share, coulter, spade, mattock, sickle.

מָחֳרָת (mŏ'ḥᵒrā'ϑ) *f* and *adv.*, also מָחֳרָתָם (mŏ'ḥᵒrāϑā'm) *adv.*, the following day, to-morrow.

מַחְשֹׂף (măḥsō'f) *m* the peeling off, decortication.

מַחֲשָׁבָה (mă'ḥᵃšābā') and מַחֲשֶׁבֶת (mă'ḥᵃšĕ'bĕϑ) *f*, *pl.* מַחֲשָׁבוֹת, *c.* מַחְשְׁבוֹת, thought, intention, purpose, plan, device; skilful work, fortification-work.

מַחְשָׁךְ (măḥšā'ḏ) *m*, *pl.* מַחְשַׁכִּים, *c.* מַחְשַׁכֵּי, darkness, dark place, the realm of the dead.

מַחַת (mă'ḥăϑ) *pr.n.m.*

מַחְתָּה (mǎȼhtā') *f, w.s.* מַחְתָּתוֹ, *pl.* מַחְתּוֹת, מַחְתֹּת, fire-pan, coal-pan, incense-bowl; snuffers.

מְחִתָּה (mᵉȼhǐttā') *f, c.* מְחִתַּת, crushing, destruction, terror, consternation.

מַחְתֶּרֶת (mǎȼhtě'rěϑ) *f* a breaking in, burglary.

מַטְאֲטֵא (mǎt'ᵃtē') *m* broom, besom.

מַטְבֵּחַ (mǎtbē'ᵃȼh) *m* slaughter, massacre.

מַטֶּה (mǎttě') *m, c.* מַטֵּה, *w.s.* מַטֵּהוּ, מַטְּךָ, *pl.* מַטִּים and מַטּוֹת, מַטֹּת, branch, twig; rod, staff, stick, sceptre, spear; stem, tribe.

מַטָּה (mǎ'ttā) *adv.* downwards, down, below, beneath, underneath.

מִטָּה (mǐttā') *f, c.* מִטַּת, *w.s.* מִטָּתִי, *pl.* מִטּוֹת, bed, couch, divan, litter, bier.

מֻטָּה (mŭttā') *f, pl.* מֻטּוֹת, and מֻטֶּה (mŭttě') *m* extension; the warping of justice.

מַטְוֶה (mǎtvě') *m* a spinning, something spun.

מָטִיל (mātī'l) *m, c.* מְטִיל, iron-bar.

מַטְמוֹן, מַטְמֹן (mǎtmō'n) *m, pl.* מַטְמֹנִים, *c.* מַטְמֻנֵי, hidden place, underground, store-house, hid treasure, treasure.

מַטָּע (mǎttā'ᵃ) *m, c.* מַטַּע, *pl. w.s.* מַטָּעַי, a planting, plantation, garden.

מַטְעַם (mǎt'ǎ'm) *m, pl.* מַטְעַמִּים and מַטְעַמּוֹת, dainties, tit-bits.

מִטְפַּחַת (mǐtpǎ'ȼhǎϑ) *f, pl.* מִטְפָּחוֹת, mantle, cloak.

מָטַר (mātǎ'r) *Ni.* נִמְטַר to be rained upon. — *Hi.* הִמְטִיר, *inf.* הַמְטִיר, *fut.* יַמְטֵר, יַמְטִיר, *pt.* מַמְטִיר, to cause to rain, to send down [rain, hail, lightning].

מָטָר (mātā'r) *m, c.* מְטַר, *pl. c.* מִטְרוֹת, rain.

מַטְרֵד (mǎtrē'd) *pr.n.f.*

מַטָּרָה [once מַטָּרָא] (mǎttārā') *f* prison, dungeon; aim, mark.

מַטְרִי (mǎtrī') *pr.n.m.*

מַי (mǎy) *m,* only *pl.* מַיִם, *i.p.* מָיִם, *c.* מֵי and מֵימֵי, *w.s.* מֵימָיו, water; juice, liquid; abundance; danger.

מִי (mī) *pron. interr.* who? which? *indef.* whoever, every one.

מֵידְבָה (mē'dᵉbā') *pr.n.* of a town in Moab.

מֵידָד (mēdā'd) *pr.n.m.*

מֵי זָהָב (mē zāhā'b) *pr.n.m.*

מֵיטָב (mētā'b) *m, c.* מֵיטַב, the best, the choicest.

מִיכָא (mīchā'); מִיכָאֵל (mīchā'ē'l); מִיכָה (mīchā'); מִיכָהוּ (mīchā'hū); מִיכָיָה (mī'chāyā'); מִיכָיְהוּ (mī'chāyā'hū); מִיכָיָהוּ (mīchā'yᵉhū') *pr.n.m.*

מִיכָל (mīchā'l) *m, c.* מִיכַל, brook.

מִיכַל (mīchă'l) *pr.n.f.*

מִיָּמִן, מִיָּמִין (mīyyāmī'n) *pr.n.m.*

מִין (mīn) *m, w.s.* מִינוֹ, *pl. w.s.* מִינֵיהֶם, species, kind.

מֵינֶקֶת (mēnĕ'kĕth) see יָנַק *Hi.*

מֵיפַעַת, מֵפַעַת (mēfă'ᵃăth) *pr.n.* of a town in Reuben.

מִיץ (mīẞ) *m* pressure, squeezing out.

מֵישָׁא (mēšā') *pr.n.m.*

מִישָׁאֵל (mī'šā'ē'l) *pr.n.m.*

מִישׁוֹר, מִישֹׁר (mīšō'r) *m* plain, level land; honesty, righteousness, equity.

מֵישַׁךְ (mēšă'ch); מֵישַׁע (mēšă'ᵉ) or מֵישָׁע (mēšā'ᵉ) *pr.n.m.*

מֵישָׁר (mēšā'r) *m,* only *pl.* מֵישָׁרִים, straightness, evenness; uprightness; righteousness, equity, concord, peace; *adv.* rightly, uprightly.

מֵיתָר (mēthā'r) *m, pl.* מֵיתָרִים, string of a bow; cord of a tent.

מַכְאֹב, מַכְאוֹב (măch'ō'b) *m, pl.* מַכְאֹבִים and מַכְאֹבוֹת, pain, disease, suffering, sorrow, wound.

מַכְבִּיר (măchbī'r) *m* fulness, abundance.

מַכְבֵּנָה (măchbēnā') *pr.n.* of a place.

מַכְבַּנַּי (măchbănnă'y) *pr.n.m.*

מַכְבֵּר (măchbē'r) *m* cloth, mat, coverlet.

מִכְבָּר (mīchbā'r) *m* plaited work, grate.

מַכָּה (măkkā') *f, c.* מַכַּת, *pl.* מַכּוֹת, מַכִּים, blow, stroke, beating, wound, defeat.

מִכְוָה (mīchvā') *f* a burn.

מָכוֹן (māchō'n) *m, c.* מְכוֹן, *w.s.* מְכוֹנִי, *pl.* מְכוֹנִים, stand, place; dwelling place, site, foundation, basis.

מְכֹנָה, מְכוֹנָה[1] (mᵉchōnā') *f,*

w.s. מְכֻנָתָהּ, *pl.* מְכֹנוֹת, place, pedestal, basis.

מְכֹנָה[2] (m'ḍōnā') *pr.n.* of a place in Judah.

מְכוּרָה (m'ḍōrā'), מְכוּרָה (m'ḍūrā') *f* origin, descent.

מָכִי (māḍī') *pr.n.m.*

מָכִיר (māḍī'r) *pr.n.m.*, *patr.* מָכִירִי.

מָכַךְ (māḍă'ḍ) *fut.* יָמֹךְ, וַיָּמֹכּוּ, to sink, to perish. — *Ni. fut.* יִמַּךְ to sink, to go to ruin. — *Ho. pf. pl.* הֻמְּכוּ, to sink, to perish.

מִכְלָה[1] (mĭḍlā') *f*, *pl. c.* מִכְלְאוֹת, sheepfold.

מִכְלָה[2] (mĭḍlā') *f*, *pl.* מִכְלוֹת, completion, perfection.

מִכְלוֹל (mĭḍlō'l) *m*, and מִכְלָל (mĭḍlā'l) *m*, *c.* מִכְלַל, completion, perfection, perfect beauty, splendour.

מַכְלֻלִים (măḍlūlī'm) *m/pl.* perfect things, splendid garments.

מַכֹּלֶת (măkkō'lĕϑ) *f* food.

מִכְמָן (mĭḍmă'n) *m*, only *pl.* מִכְמַנִּים, treasures.

מִכְמָס (mĭḍmā's), מִכְמָשׂ (mĭḍmā's), מִכְמַשׂ (mĭḍmă's) *pr.n.* of a place in Benjamin.

מִכְמָר (mĭḍmā'r) and מִכְמֹר (mĭḍmō'r) *m* a hunter's net.

מִכְמֶרֶת (mĭḍmĕ'rĕϑ) and מִכְמֹרֶת (mĭḍmō'rĕϑ) *f* net, fish-net.

מִכְמָשׂ see מִכְמָס.

מִכְמְתָת (mĭḍm'ϑā'ϑ) *pr.n.* of a town.

מַכְנַדְבַי (măḍnădbă'y) *pr.n.m.*

מִכְנָס (mĭḍnā's) *m*, *du. c.* מִכְנְסֵי trowsers [of the priests].

מֶכֶס (mĕ'ḍĕs) *m* tax, tribute.

מִכְסָה (mĭḍsā') *f*, *c.* מִכְסַת, number, amount, price.

מִכְסֶה (mĭḍsĕ') *m*, *c.* מִכְסֵה, covering, roof.

מְכַסֶּה (m'ḍăssĕ') *m* covering, clothing; the caul [of intestines].

מַכְפֵּלָה (măḍpēlā') *f* doubling; *pr.n.* of a cave near Hebron.

מָכַר (māḍă'r) *inf.* מָכֹר, מְכֹר, *w.s.* מָכְרָהּ (mŏḍrā'h), מָכְרָם, *imp.* מְכֹר, מִכְרָה, *fut.* יִמְכֹּר, *pt.* מוֹכֵר, to sell, to deliver up. — *Ni.* נִמְכַּר, *inf.* הִמָּכֵר, *fut.* יִמָּכֵר, to be sold, to sell oneself; to be given over, abandoned. — *Hith.* הִתְמַכֵּר,

inf. w.s. הִתְמַכֶּרְךָ, to be sold, to sell oneself.

מֶכֶר (mĕ'ḥĕr) *m, w.s.* מִכְרָם, things for sale, ware; price, value; possession.

מַכָּר (măkkā'r) *m, pl.* מַכָּרִים, acquaintance, friend.

מִכְרֶה (mĭḥrĕ') *m, c.* מִכְרֵה, pit.

מְכֵרָה (mᵉḥērā') *f,* only *pl.* מְכֵרֹת, a weapon, sword.

מִכְרִי (mĭḥrī') *pr.n.m.*

מְכֵרָתִי (mᵉḥē'rāṯī') *gent. m,* an inhabitant of an unknown place מְכֵרָה.

מִכְשׁוֹל, מִכְשֹׁל (mĭḥšō'l) *m, pl.* מִכְשֹׁלִים, stumbling block, obstacle, cause of falling or sinning, enticement, offence, scruple.

מַכְשֵׁלָה (măḥšēlā') *f, pl.* מַכְשֵׁלוֹת, fall, ruin; offence.

מִכְתָּב (mĭḥtā'ḇ) *m* a writing; something written, letter, poem, book.

מְכִתָּה (mᵉḥĭttā') *f, w.s.* מְכִתָּתוֹ, a breaking, smashing.

מִכְתָּם (mĭḥtā'm) *m* golden poem or epigram.

מַכְתֵּשׁ[1] (măḥtē's) *m* mortar; hollow, socket of a tooth.

מַכְתֵּשׁ[2] (măḥtē's) *pr.n.* of a place near or in Jerusalem

מָלֵא[1] (mālē') *inf.* מְלֹאת, *imp. pl.* מִלְאוּ, *fut.* יִמְלָא, *pl.* יִמְלְאוּ, *pt.* מָלֵא, *pl.* מְלֵאִים, to be full, to become full; to overflow, to be filled, to be complete; to make full, to fill.— *Ni.* נִמְלָא, *fut.* יִמָּלֵא to be filled, to become full, to be satisfied, to be completed. — *Pi.* מִלֵּא, *inf.* מַלֵּא, מַלְּאוֹת, *imp.* מַלֵּא, *fut.* יְמַלֵּא, *pt.* מְמַלֵּא, *pl.* מְמַלְאִים, to make full, to fill; to satisfy, to complete, to fulfil; to do fully; to fill in or up.— *Pu. pt. pl.* מְמֻלָּאִים, to be filled in, to be set [of gems].— *Hith.* הִתְמַלֵּא to make one another full, to assist each other.

מָלֵא[2] (mālē') *adj., c.* מְלֵא, *pl.* מְלֵאִים, *f* מְלֵאָה, *c.* מְלֵאַתִי, *pl.* מְלֵאוֹת, filling up; full, filled, abundant; strong, pregnant; *subst.* fulness, abundance; *adv.* fully.

מְלוֹא, מְלֹא (mᵉlō') *m, w.s.* מְלוֹאָהּ, fulness, what fills up; multitude.

מְלֵאָה (mᵉlḗʼā') *f*, *w.s.* מְלֵאָתְךָ, fulness, abundance; tithes of grain and wine.

מִלֻּאָה (mĭllūʼā') *f*, *c.* מִלֻּאַת, *pl. w.s.* מִלּוּאֹתָם, a filling in, setting [of gems].

מִלֻּאִים (mĭllūʼī'm) *m/pl.*, *c.* מִלֻּאֵי, installation [of priests], consecration; setting [of stones].

מַלְאָךְ (măl'ā'ḵ) *m*, *c.* מַלְאַךְ, *w.s.* מַלְאָכִי, *pl.* מַלְאָכִים, *c.* מַלְאֲכֵי, messenger, herald; angel; prophet, priest.

מְלָאכָה (mᵉlāḵā')*f*, *c.* מְלֶאכֶת, *w.s.* מְלַאכְתּוֹ, *pl.* מְלָאכוֹת, *c.* מַלְאֲכוֹת, service, errand, business, trade, labour, work, performance; goods gained by labour; cattle.

מַלְאָכוּת (măl'āḵū'ṯ) *f*, *c.* מַלְאֲכוּת, message.

מַלְאָכִי (măl'āḵī') *pr.n.m.*

מַלְאָכִים = מְלָכִים see מֶלֶךְ.

מִלֵּאת (mĭllḗ'ṯ) *f* fulness [of waters], others: the setting of the eye in the eye-hole.

מַלְבּוּשׁ (mălbū's) *m*, *pl. c.* מַלְבּוּשֵׁי, garment, clothes.

מַלְבֵּן (mălbḗ'n) *m* brick-kiln; pavement of bricks.

מִלָּה (mĭllā') *f*, *w.s.* מִלָּתוֹ, *pl.* מִלִּים [מִלִּין], *c.* מִלֵּי, word, speech, matter, thing.

מִלּוֹא (mĭllṓ') *m* a filling up, rampart, bastion, fortress, citadel [in Sichem and Jerusalem].

מַלּוּחַ (măllū'ᵃḥ) *m* a salt-plant, orache [Atriplex halimus] or sea-purslain.

מַלּוּךְ (măllū'ḵ) *pr.n.m.*

מְלוּכָה, **מְלֻכָה** (mᵉlūḵā') *f* dominion, rule, reign.

מָלוֹן (mālṓ'n) *m*, *c.* מְלוֹן, night-quarters, inn, shelter.

מְלוּנָה (mᵉlūnā') *f* night-hut.

מָלַח[1] (mālă'ḥ) *Ni.* נִמְלַח to vanish [like dust].

מָלַח[2] (mālă'ḥ) to salt. — [*denom.* of מֶלַח] *Pu. pt.* מְמֻלָּח to be salted. — *Ho.* הָמְלַח, *inf.* הָמְלֵחַ (hŏmlḗᵃḥ) to be washed with salt-water.

מֶלַח (mĕ'lăḥ) *m* salt, salt-water, sea; יָם הַמֶּלַח the Dead Sea.

מַלָּח (măllā'ḥ) *m*, *pl.* מַלָּחִים, seaman, mariner.

מָלָח (mālā'ḥ) *m*, only *pl.* מְלָחִים rags.

מְלֵחָה (m°lēḥā') *f* salt land, barren land.

מִלְחָמָה (mĭlḥāmā'), מִלְחֶמֶת (mĭlḥĕ'mĕθ) *f*, *w.s.* מִלְחַמְתּוֹ, *pl.* מִלְחָמוֹת, *c.* מִלְחֲמוֹת, war, fight, battle; weapons, victory.

מָלַט (mālă't) *Ni.* נִמְלַט, *inf.* הִמָּלֵט, *fut.* יִמָּלֵט, *pt.* נִמְלָט, to escape, to deliver oneself; to be delivered, saved, freed; to hasten away.—*Pi.* מִלֵּט, *inf.* מַלֵּט, *imp.* מַלְּטָה, *fut.* יְמַלֵּט to deliver, to save; to cause to escape; to escape; to let slip, to lay [eggs]. — *Hi.* הִמְלִיט to deliver, to save; to lay [eggs].—*Hith.* *fut.* יִתְמַלֵּט to escape; to emit [sparks].

מֶלֶט (mĕ'lĕt) *m* mortar, cement.

מְלַטְיָה (m°lăṭyā') *pr.n.m.*

מְלִילָה (m°līlā') *f* an ear [of corn].

מַלִּין see לון *Hi.*

מְלִיצָה (m°līßā') *f* riddle, proverb; satirical song, taunt.

מָלַךְ (mālă'ch) *inf.* מָלֹךְ, מְלֹךְ, *w.s.* מָלְכוֹ (mŏlchō'), *imp.* מְלֹךְ, *fut.* יִמְלֹךְ, *pt.* מֹלֵךְ, to be or become king, to rule, to reign. — *Ni.* *fut.* יִמָּלֵךְ, to consult, to determine. — *Hi.* הִמְלִיךְ, *inf.* הַמְלִיךְ, *fut.* יַמְלִיךְ, וַיַּמְלֵךְ, *pt.* מַמְלִיךְ, to constitute as king, to cause to reign. — *Ho.* הָמְלַךְ to be made king.

מֶלֶךְ (mĕ'lĕch) *m*, *i.p.* מָלֶךְ, *w.s.* מַלְכִּי, *pl.* מְלָכִים, *c.* מַלְכֵי, king, ruler, prince; God; false god, idol-king.

מֹלֶךְ (mō'lĕch) *m* a god of the Phenicians and Ammonites, Moloch.

מַלְכֹּדֶת (mălkō'dĕθ) *f* net, snare.

מַלְכָּה (mălkā') *f*, *c.* מַלְכַּת, *pl.* מְלָכוֹת, queen, princess.

מִלְכָּה (mĭlkā') *pr.n.f.*

מַלְכוּת (mălchū'θ) *f*, *w.s.* מַלְכֻתוֹ, מַלְכוּתוֹ, kingdom, dominion, realm, reign.

מַלְכִּיאֵל (mălkī'ēl); מַלְכִּיָּה (mălkīyyā'), מַלְכִּיָּהוּ (mălkīyyā'hū); מַלְכִּי־צֶדֶק (mălkī-ßĕ'dĕk); מַלְכִּירָם (mălkīrā'm); מַלְכִּישׁוּעַ (mălkīšū'a°) *pr.n.m*

מַלְכָּם (mălkā'm), מִלְכֹּם (mĭlkō'm) *m* a god of the Ammonites = מֹלֶךְ.

מְלֶכֶת (m^elĕ'ȼĕϑ) *f* queen.

מֹלֶכֶת (mōlĕ'ȼĕϑ) *pr.n.f.*

מָלַל[1] (mālă'l) *Pi.* מִלֵּל to speak, to relate, to tell.

מָלַל[2] (mālă'l) *imp.* מֹל, to circumcise. — *Ni.* נָמַל, *fut.* יִמַּל, *pl.* יִמָּלוּ, to be cut off, to be circumcised. — *Po. fut.* יְמוֹלֵל to be cut off. — *Hith. fut.* יִתְמֹלָל to be cut off, to become blunted.

מָלַל[3] (mālă'l) *fut. pl.* יִמָּלוּ to fade, to wither, to decay. — *Po. fut.* יְמוֹלֵל [or from מָלַל[2]] to be withered.

מִלֲלַי (mă'lală'y) *pr.n.m.*

מַלְמַד (mălmă'd) *m* ox-goad.

מָלַץ (mālă'ß) *Ni.* נִמְלַץ to be smooth, pleasant.

מֶלְצַר (mĕlßă'r) *m* overseer, guardian [others: butler].

מָלַק (mālă'k) to break off, to nip off [partly].

מַלְקוֹחַ[1] (mălkō'aȼ) *m* booty.

מַלְקוֹחַ[2] (mălkō'aȼ) *m*, *du. w.s.* מַלְקוֹחָי the jaws, the upper and lower palate.

מַלְקוֹשׁ (mălkō's) *m* late rain [in March and April].

מֶלְקָח (mĕlkā'ȼ), מַלְקָח (mălkā'ȼ) *m*, only *du.* מֶלְקָחַיִם, *w.s.* מֶלְקָחֶיהָ, tongs, snuffers.

מֶלְתָּחָה (mĕltāȼā') *f* a wardrobe, dress-chamber.

מַלְתָּעָה (măltā'ā') *f*, *pl. c.* מַלְתְּעוֹת tooth.

מַמְגֻּרָה (mămgūrā') *f*, only *pl.* מַמְגֻּרוֹת, storehouse, granary.

מֵמַד (mēmă'd) *m*, only *pl. w.s.* מְמַדֶּיהָ, measure, extension.

מְמוּכָן (m^emūȼā'n) *pr.n.m.*

מָמוֹת (māmō'ϑ) *m*, only *pl.* מְמוֹתִים, deaths, painful deaths; the dead, corpses.

מַמְזֵר (mămzē'r) *m* mongrel, bastard.

מִמְכָּר (mĭmkā'r) *m*, *c.* מִמְכַּר, *pl.* מִמְכָּרִים, sale; thing for sale or sold.

מִמְכֶּרֶת (mĭmkĕ'rĕϑ) *f* sale.

מַמְלָכָה (mămlāȼā') *f*, *c.* מַמְלֶכֶת, *w.s.* מַמְלַכְתִּי, *pl.* מַמְלָכוֹת, *c.* מַמְלְכוֹת, kingdom, dominion, reign, realm.

מַמְלָכוּת (mămlāchū'th) *f*, *c.* מַמְלְכוּת = מַמְלָכָה.

מִמְסָךְ (mĭmsā'ch) *m* spiced wine.

מֶמֶר (mĕ'mĕr) *m* bitterness, sorrow.

מַמְרֵא (mămrē') *pr.n.m.*

מַמְרֹר (mămrō'r) *m*, only *pl.* מַמְרֹרִים = מֶמֶר.

מִמְשַׁח (mĭmshă'ch) *m* unction, anointing.

מִמְשָׁל (mĭmshā'l) *m* dominion, rule.

מֶמְשָׁלָה (mĕmshālā') *f*, *c.* מֶמְשֶׁלֶת, *w.s.* מֶמְשַׁלְתּוֹ, *pl. c.* מַמְשְׁלוֹת, dominion, rule, reign.

מִמְשָׁק (mĭmshā'k) *m*, *c.* מִמְשַׁק, possession.

מַמְתַּק (mămtă'k) *m*, only *pl.* מַמְתַּקִּים, sweetness, sweet things.

מָן (mān) *m*, *w.s.* מַנְּךָ, manna.

מֵן[1] (mēn) *m*, *w.s.* מִנֵּהוּ, part, portion.

מֵן[2] (mēn) *m*, *pl.* מִנִּים, strings, a stringed instrument.

מִן (mĭn) *prep.*, before vowels and gutturals מֵ, before other consonants ·מִ, *w.s.* מִמֶּנִּי [מִנִּי], מִמְּךָ, מִמֵּךְ, מִמֶּנּוּ, מִמֶּנָּה, מִמֶּנּוּ, מִכֶּם, מֵהֶם, מִכֶּן, מֵהֵנָּה, from, out of, away from, apart from, part of; since, after; because of; with *adj.* = more than.

מַנְגִּינָה (măngĭnā') *f* song of derision, satire.

מָנָה[1] (mānā') *inf.* מְנוֹת, *imp.* מְנֵה, *fut.* יִמְנֶה, *pt.* מוֹנֶה, to divide, to separate; to number, to count; to appoint, to allot to. — *Ni.* נִמְנָה, *inf.* הִמָּנוֹת, *fut.* יִמָּנֶה, to be numbered, reckoned. — *Pi.* מִנָּה, *imp.* מַן, *fut.* וַיְמַן, to dispose, to appoint; to allot to; to cause, to prepare. — *Pu. pt.* מְמֻנֶּה to be appointed, to be set over.

מָנָה[2] (mānā') *f*, *c.* מְנַת, *pl.* מָנוֹת, part, portion, share, lot.

מָנֶה (mānĕ') *m*, *pl.* מָנִים, a weight, the 60th part of a talent, a hundred-shekel weight; in money value equal to 50 shekels.

מֹנֶה (mōnĕ') *m*, only *pl.* מֹנִים parts, times.

מִנְהָג (minhā'g) *m, c.* מִנְהַג, the driving [of a chariot].

מִנְהָרָה (minhārā') *f,* only *pl.* מִנְהָרוֹת, cleft, dug hole; mountain-recess.

מָנוֹד (mānō'd) *m, c.* מְנוֹד, a shaking of the head.

מָנוֹחַ[1] (mānō'aḥ) *m, pl. w.s.* מְנוּחָיְכִי, rest, repose, resting-place; settlement, providing [by marriage].

מָנוֹחַ[2] (mānō'aḥ) *pr.n.m.*

מְנוּחָה (menūḥā'), מְנֻחָה *f, w.s.* מְנוּחָתִי, *pl.* מְנוּחֹת, rest, repose, peace, ease, quiet dwelling, resting-place; settlement.

מָנוֹן (mānō'n) *m* child; offspring; others: refractory.

מָנוֹס (mānō's) *m, w.s.* מְנוּסִי, flight, escape, refuge.

מְנוּסָה (menūsā') *f, c.* מְנֻסַת = מָנוֹס.

מָנוֹר (mānō'r) *m, c.* מְנוֹר, a weaver's beam.

מְנֹרָה, מְנוֹרָה (menōrā') *f, c.* מְנֹרַת, *pl.* מְנֹרוֹת, candlestick.

מִנְזָר (minzā'r) *m,* only *pl.* מִנְזָרִים, princes; others: troops of mercenaries.

מִנְחָה (minḥā') *f, c.* מִנְחַת, *w.s.* מִנְחָתִי, *pl.* מְנָחוֹת, *c.* מִנְחוֹת, present, gift; tribute; sacrifice [mostly an unbloody one], offering.

מְנֻחוֹת (menūḥō'th) *pr.n.* of a place.

מְנַחֵם (menaḥē'm) *pr.n.m.*

מָנַחַת (māna'ḥath) *pr.n.m.*; also *pr.n.* of a place; *patr.* מָנַחְתִּי.

מְנִי (menī') *pr.n.* of a Babylonian goddess [Venus].

מִנִּי[1], מִנֵּי = מִן.

מִנִּי[2] (minnī') *pr.n.* of a province of Armenia.

מִנִּים see מֵן.

מִנְיָמִין (minyāmī'n) *pr.n.m.* = בִּנְיָמִין.

מִנִּית (minnī'th) *pr.n.* of a city of the Ammonites.

מִנְלֶה (minle') *m,* only *w.s.* מִנְלָם, wealth, riches, property.

מָנַע (māna'') *imp.* מְנַע, *fut.* יִמְנַע, *pt.* מֹנֵעַ, to keep back, to withhold, to bar, to refrain, to refuse. — *Ni.* נִמְנַע, *fut.* יִמָּנַע, to be withheld, to keep oneself back, to be reserved; to be refused.

מַנְעוּל (mănʼŭʼl) *m* bolt, bar, lock.

מַנְעָל (mănʼăʼl) *m* = מַנְעוּל.

מַנְעַם (mănʼăʼm) *m*, only *pl.* מַנְעַמִּים delicious food, dainties.

מְנַעֲנַע (mʼnăʼʼanăʼʼ) *m*, only *pl.* מְנַעַנְעִים, a musical instrument, sistrum, rattle, cymbal.

מְנַקִּית (mʼnăkkīʼϑ) *f*, *pl.* מְנַקִּיּוֹת, a bowl for libation, sprinkling-vessel.

מֵנֶקֶת see יָנַק *Hi.*

מְנַשֶּׁה (mʼnăssĕʼ) *pr.n.m.*

מְנָת (mʼnāʼϑ) *f*, *c.* מְנַת, *pl.* מְנָאוֹת, מְנָיוֹת, part, portion, share.

מָס (măs) *m* a suffering, discouraged one.

מַס (măs) *m*, *pl.* מִסִּים, tribute, tax, bond-service; bond-servant.

מֵסַב (mēsăʼb) *m*, *w.s.* מְסִבּוֹ, *pl.* מְסִבִּים, *c.* מְסִבֵּי circle, environs; *adv.* round about.

מְסִבָּה (mʼsĭbbăʼ) *f*, *pl.* מְסִבּוֹת = מֵסַב.

מַסְגֵּר (măsgēʼr) *m* locksmith; prison.

מִסְגֶּרֶת (mĭsgĕʼrĕϑ) *f*, *w.s.* מִסְגַּרְתּוֹ, *pl.* מִסְגְּרוֹת, enclosure; fortress, stronghold; margin, border, ledge; panel.

מַסַּד (măssăʼd) *m* foundation.

מִסְדְּרוֹן (mĭsdʼrōʼn) *m* portico.

מָסָה (măsăʼ) *Hi.* הִמְסָה, *fut.* יַמְסֶה, וַתֶּמֶס, to cause to melt, to cause to flow, to dissolve, to wet.

מַסָּה[1] (măssăʼ) *f*, *c.* מַסַּת, *pl.* מַסּוֹת, trial, temptation, testing by misfortune.

מַסָּה[2] (măssăʼ) *pr.n.* of a place in the desert.

מִסָּה (mĭssăʼ) *f*, *c.* מִסַּת, amount, proportion, measurement; *adv.* according to measure.

מַסְוֶה (măsvĕʼ) *m* covering, veil.

מְסוּכָה (mʼsŭchăʼ) *f* thorn-hedge.

מַסָּח (măssăʼch) *m* a keeping back; others: a relieving.

מִסְחָר (mĭschăʼr) *m*, *c.* מִסְחַר, trade, traffic.

מָסַךְ (măsăʼch) *inf.* מְסֹךְ to mix, to mingle.

מֶסֶךְ (mĕʼsĕch) *m* mixture, mixed or spiced wine.

מָסָךְ (māsā'ḥ) *m*, *c.* מְסַךְ, curtain, covering.

מְסֻכָּה (m^e^sŭkkā') *f* a covering.

מַסֵּכָה[1] (măssēḥā') *f* = מְסֻכָּה.

מַסֵּכָה[2] (măssēḥā') *f*, *c.* מַסֵּכַת, *pl.* מַסֵּכוֹת, a founding, fusion, cast; cast idol; covenant, league.

מִסְכֵּן (mĭskē'n) *m* poor, wretched.

מִסְכֵּנוּת (mĭskēnū'ϑ) *f* poverty, neediness.

מִסְכְּנֹת (mĭskĕ'nĕϑ) *f*, only *pl.* מִסְכְּנוֹת, store, storehouse, magazine.

מַסֶּכֶת (măssĕ'ḥĕϑ) *f* the warp of a web.

מְסִלָּה (m^e^sĭllā') *f*, *c.* מְסִלַּת, *pl.* מְסִלּוֹת, highway, road, street; course, march; staircase, stairs.

מַסְלוּל (măslū'l) *m* road, way.

מַסְמֵר (măsmē'r) *m*, only *pl.* מַסְמְרִים, nail, pin.

מַסְמֶרֶת (măsmĕ'rĕϑ) *f.* only *pl.* מַסְמְרוֹת, nail.

מָסַס (māsă's) *inf.* מְסֹס, to melt, to dissolve, to perish. — *Ni.* נָמֵס, *fut.* יִמַּס, *pl.* יִמַּסּוּ, יִמָּאסוּ, *pl.* נָמֵסּ, to melt, to dissolve, to perish; to despond, to despair; to be loosened, to become lean. — *Hi.* הֵמֵס to cause to despond, to discourage.

מַסַּע (măssă'ᵉ) *m*, *pl.* מַסָּעִים, *c.* מַסְעֵי, a breaking up, departure, journey, station.

מַסָּע (măssā'ᵉ) *m* stone-quarry, broken and hewn stones; dart.

מִסְעָד (mĭsᵉā'd) *m* balustrade.

מִסְפֵּד (mĭspē'd) *m*, *c.* מִסְפַּד, *w.s.* מִסְפְּדִי, mourning, lamentation.

מִסְפּוֹא (mĭspō') *m* fodder.

מִסְפַּחַת (mĭspă'ḥăϑ) *f* scarf, scab; *pl.* מִסְפָּחוֹת, kerchief, cape, cowl.

מִסְפָּר[1] (mĭspā'r) *m*, *c.* מִסְפַּר, *pl.* *c.* מִסְפְּרֵי, number; countableness, fewness; a telling, narration.

מִסְפָּר[2] (mĭspā'r), **מִסְפֶּרֶת** (mĭspĕ'rĕϑ) *pr.n.m.*

מָסַר (māsă'r) *inf.* מְסֹר (m^e^sŏ'r), to give, to commit. — *Ni.* *fut.* יִמָּסֵר to be given.

מֹסָר (mōsā'r) *m* warning, admonition.

מָסֹרֶת (māsō'reth) *f* obligation, duty.

מִסְתּוֹר (mĭstō'r) *m* hiding-place, refuge.

מַסְתֵּר (măstē'r) *m* a hiding; object of hiding the face.

מִסְתָּר (mĭstā'r) *m*, *pl.* מִסְתָּרִים, hiding-place, hidden place.

מַעְבָד (mă'bā'd) *m*, only *pl.* מַעְבָדִים, doing, work.

מַעֲבֶה (mă''abĕ') *m*, *c.* מַעֲבֵה, density, compactness; mould of clay.

מַעֲבָר (mă''abā'r) *m*, *c.* מַעֲבַר, passing over, stroke, passage; ford, mountain-pass.

מַעְבָּרָה (mă'bārā') *f*, only *pl.* מַעְבָּרוֹת and מַעְבְּרוֹת, *c.* מַעְבְּרוֹת, passage, ford, pass.

מַעְגָּל (mă'gā'l) *m*, *c.* מַעְגַּל, *pl. c.* מַעְגְּלֵי, *w.s.* מַעְגְּלֶיךָ, track, way, way of life; bulwark formed by waggons.

מָעַד (mā'ă'd) *fut.* יִמְעַד, *pt.* מוֹעֵד, to waver, totter. — *Pu. pt. f* מוּעֶדֶת [for מְמוּעֶדֶת] to be made to waver. — *Hi.* הַמְעִיד, *imp.* הַמְעֵד, to cause to waver or tremble.

מַעַדַי (mă''adă'y), מַעַדְיָה (mă''ădyā') *pr.n.m.*

מַעֲדָן (mă''adā'n) *m*, only *pl.* מַעֲדַנִּים, מַעֲדַנִּים, *c.* מַעֲדַנֵּי, and מַעֲדַנּוֹת, delights, dainties, pleasures; *adv.* cheerfully.

מַעֲדַנָּה (mă''adănnā') *f*, only *pl.* מַעֲדַנּוֹת, fetters, group of stars.

מַעְדֵּר (mă'dē'r) *m* weeding-hook.

מֵעֶה (mē'ĕ') *m*, only *pl.* מֵעִים, *c.* מְעֵי and מֵעוֹת, *c.* מְעוֹת, the bowels, the intestines, womb, body, belly; the inmost part, the heart; the sands of the sea.

מָעוֹג, **מָעֹג** (mā'ō'g) *m* bread-cake; לַעֲגֵי מָעוֹג cake-mockers, parasites who earn their bread by jesting.

מָעוֹז, **מָעֹז** (mā'ō'z) *m*, *w.s.* מָעֻזִּי, מָעוּזּוֹ, *pl.* מָעֻזִּים, *w.s.* מָעֻזֶּיהָ [for מָעֻזֶּיהָ], fortress, strong city, protection, defence, refuge.

מָעוֹךְ (mā'ō'kh) *pr.n.m.*

מָעוֹן[1] (mā'ō'n) *m*, *c.* מְעוֹן, habitation, dwelling, habitation of God, refuge, asylum.

מָעוֹן[2] (mā'ō'n) *pr.n.* of a town in Judah; of a temple in Arabia Petræa; *gent.* מְעוּנִים.

מְעוֹנָה (m'ōnā') = מָעוֹן[1].

מְעוֹנֹתַי (m'ō'nōthā'y) *pr.n.m.*

מָעוּף (mā'ū'f) *m*, *c.* מְעוּף, darkness.

מָעוֹר (mā'ō'r) *m*, only *pl.* מְעוֹרִים pudenda.

מָעֹז see מָעוֹז.

מַעֲזְיָה (mă'ăzyā'), מַעַזְיָהוּ (mă'ăzyā'hū) *pr.n.m.*

מָעַט (mā'ă't) *inf.* מְעֹט, *fut.* יִמְעַט, to be or become little, small, few; to be lessened. — *Pi.* מִעֵט to become few. — *Hi.* הִמְעִיט, *fut.* יַמְעִיט, *pt.* מַמְעִיט, to make little or small, to lessen, to diminish, to do or give little.

מְעַט (m'ă't) *m*, *pl.* מְעַטִּים, a little, little, few, a few; *adv.* little, a short time; כִּמְעַט almost, soon; מְעַט מְעַט by little and little, by degrees.

מָעֹט (mā'ō't) *adj.*, only *f* מְעֻטָּה, whetted, sharp.

מַעֲטֶה (mă'ătĕ') *m*, *c.* מַעֲטֵה, garment, covering.

מַעֲטָפָה (mă'ătāfā') *f*, only *pl.* מַעֲטָפוֹת, cloak, mantle.

מָעַי (mā'ī') *pr.n.m.*

מְעִי (m'ī') *m* heap of rubbish, ruins.

מְעִיל (m'ī'l) *m*, *w.s.* מְעִילוֹ, *pl.* מְעִילִים, upper garment, sleeveless robe.

מֵעִים see מֵעֶה.

מַעְיָן (mă'yā'n) *m*, *c.* מַעְיַן and מַעְיְנוֹ, *pl.* מַעְיָנִים, *c.* מַעְיְנֵי, and מַעְיָנוֹת, *c.* מַעְיְנוֹת, place of fountains, spring.

מַעֲכָה (mă'ăchā') *pr.n.* of a city at the foot of Hermon; also *pr.n.m.* and *f.*

מָעַל (mā'ă'l) *inf.* מָעוֹל, מְעָל־ (m'ŏ'l), מְעֹל, *fut.* יִמְעַל and יִמְעֹל, to cover, to veil; to act secretly, faithlessly, to steal.

מַעַל[1] (mă'ăl) *m*, *w.s.* מַעֲלוֹ, faithlessness, treachery.

מַעַל[2] (mă'ăl) *m* what is above, the upper part; *adv.* with *loc.* ה מַעְלָה upwards, forward; מִמַּעַל from above, above; לְמַעְלָה upwards; מִלְּמַעְלָה from above upon.

מֵעַל = מִן עַל.

מֹעַל (mō′′ăl) *m* the lifting up [of hands].

מַעֲלָה (mă′′alā′) *f*, *pl.* מַעֲלוֹת, ascent, the journeying up; rising of the mind, thought; step, degree [of a dial]; in inscriptions of psalms: שִׁיר הַמַּעֲלוֹת song of step-like rythm, or song of ascent to the temple, or song of pilgrimage, song of excellence.

מַעֲלֶה (mă′′alĕ′) *m*, *c.* מַעֲלֵה, ascent, slope, hill; elevated place, platform.

מַעֲלִיל = מַעֲלָל.

מַעֲלָל (mă′′alā′l) *m*, only *pl.* מַעֲלָלִים, *c.* מַעַלְלֵי, deed, action, great deed.

מַעֲמָד (mă′′amā′d) *m*, *c.* מַעֲמַד, station, post.

מָעֳמָד (mŏ′′omā′d) *m* standing-place, footing.

מַעֲמָסָה (mă′′amāsā′) *f* burden, weight.

מַעֲמָק (mă′′amā′k) *m*, only *pl.* מַעֲמַקִּים, *c.* מַעֲמַקֵּי, depth.

מַעַן (mă′′ăn) *m* intention, purpose; *adv.* only לְמַעַן, *w.s.* לְמַעֲנִי, on account of, because, for the sake of, in order that, so that.

מַעֲנָה (mă′′anā′) *f* a furrow's length.

מַעֲנֶה (mă′′anĕ′) *m*, *c.* מַעֲנֵה, answer, reply, hearing; refutation, object, purpose.

מְעֹנָה see מְעוֹנָה.

מַעֲנִית (mă′′anī′ϑ) *f* = מַעֲנָה.

מַעַץ (mă′′ăß) *pr.n.m.*

מַעֲצֵבָה (mă′′aßēbā′) *f* pain, sorrow.

מַעֲצָד (mă′′aßā′d) *m* axe, hatchet.

מַעֲצוֹר (mă′′aßō′r), מַעְצָר (mă′′aßā′r) *m* restraint, hindrance.

מַעֲקֶה (mă′′akĕ′) *m* ledge about a flat roof.

מַעֲקָשׁ (mă′′akā′s) *m*, only *pl.* מַעֲקַשִּׁים, crooked way.

מַעַר (mă′′ăr) *m* nakedness, pudenda; empty or bare space.

מַעֲרָב[1] (mă′′arā′b) *m* occident, west, westward.

מַעֲרָב[2] (mă′′arā′b) *m*, *pl.* מַעֲרָבִים, barter-goods, wares; exchange, barter, market.

מַעֲרָבָה (mă′′arābā′) *f* = מַעֲרָב[1].

מְעָרָה (mᵉʿārā') *f*, *c*. מְעָרַת, *pl*. מְעָרוֹת, cave.

מַעֲרֶה (mă'ʿarĕ') *m*, *c*. מַעֲרֵה, bare place, treeless plain.

מַעֲרִיץ (mă'ʿarī'ß) *m* object of fear [see עָרַץ *Hi.*]

מַעֲרָךְ (mă'ʿarā'ȼ) *m*, only *pl*. *c*. מַעַרְכֵי, arrangement, project.

מַעֲרָכָה (mă'ʿarāȼā') *f* and **מַעֲרֶכֶת** (mă'ʿarĕ'ȼĕϑ) *f*, *pl*. מַעֲרָכוֹת and מַעַרְכוֹת, arrangement, order, pile, row, array, army; a setting forth, exhibition, show.

מַעֲרֹם (mă'ʿarō'm) *m*, only *pl*. מַעֲרֻמִּים, nakedness, naked body.

מַעֲרָצָה (mă'ʿarāßā') *f* sudden terror.

מַעֲרָת (mă'ʿarā'ϑ) *pr.n.* of a place in Judah.

מַעֲשֶׂה (mă'ʿaßĕ') *m*, *c*. מַעֲשֵׂה, *w.s.* מַעֲשֵׂהוּ, *pl*. מַעֲשִׂים, *c*. מַעֲשֵׂי, the doing, executing; activity, action, business; work, deed, production, fabric; property.

מַעֲשַׂי (mă'ʿaßă'y); **מַעֲשֵׂיָה** (mă'ʿaßēyā'), **מַעֲשֵׂיָהוּ** (mă'ʿaßēyā'hū) *pr.n.m.*

מַעֲשֵׂר (mă'ʿaßē'r) *m*, *c*. מַעְשַׂר, *w.s.* מַעַשְׂרוֹ, *pl*. מַעַשְׂרוֹת, the tenth part, the tenth, tithe.

מַעֲשַׁקָּה (mă'ʿašăkkā') *f*, only *pl*. מַעֲשַׁקּוֹת, oppression, exaction.

מֹף (mōf) *pr.n.* of a city in Egypt, Memphis.

מַפְגִּיעַ (măfgī'aʿ) *m* aggressor; asker, mediator [see פָּגַע *Hi.*].

מִפְגָּע (mĭfgā'ʿ) *m* assault, object of attack.

מַפָּח (măppā'ȼh) *m* a breathing out, expiring.

מַפֻּחַ (măppū'aȼh) *m* bellows.

מְפִיבֹשֶׁת (mᵉfībō'šĕϑ) *pr.n.m.*

מֻפִּים (mŭppī'm) *pr.n.m.*

מֵפִיץ (mēfī'ß) *m* hammer, club.

מַפָּל (măppā'l) *m*, *c*. מַפַּל, *pl*. *c*. מַפְּלֵי, chaff; dewlap, flap.

מִפְלָאָה (mĭflā'ā') *f*, only *pl*. *c*. מִפְלְאוֹת, miracle, wonder.

מִפְלַגָּה (mĭflăggā') *f* division, class.

מַפָּלָה (măppālā') *f* and **מַפֵּלָה** (măppēlā') *f* fall, ruins, heap of rubbish.

מִפְלָט (mĭflā't) *m* place of refuge.

מִפְלֶצֶת (mĭflĕ'ßĕϑ) *f* monster, terror, hideous idol.

מִפְלָשׂ (mĭflā's) *m* the poising or floating [of clouds].

מַפֶּלֶת (măppĕ'lĕϑ) *f, w.s.* מַפַּלְתּוֹ, fall, ruin; fallen trunk; corpse, carcass.

מִפְעָל (mĭf'ā'l) *m, pl.* מִפְעָלִים, and מִפְעָלָה (mĭf'ălā') *f, pl. c.* מִפְעֲלוֹת, work, deed.

מֵפַעַת see מֵיפַעַת.

מַפָּץ (măppā'ß) *m* a crushing, smashing.

מַפֵּץ (măppē'ß) *m* hammer.

מִפְקָד (mĭfkā'd) *m, c.* מִפְקַד, numbering, census; arrangement, mandate; appointed place.

מִפְרָץ (mĭfrā'ß) *m, pl.* מִפְרָצִים, incision, inlet, harbour.

מַפְרֶקֶת (măfrĕ'kĕϑ) *f, w.s.* מַפְרַקְתּוֹ, the neck.

מִפְרָשׂ (mĭfrā's) *m, pl. c.* מִפְרְשֵׂי, a spreading out, extension, sail.

מִפְשָׂעָה (mĭfsā'ā') *f* place where the legs fork off, buttocks.

מַפְתֵּחַ (măftē'aḥ) *m* a key.

מִפְתָּח (mĭftā'ḥ) *m* the opening.

מִפְתָּן (mĭftā'n) *m, c.* מִפְתַּן, threshold.

מֵץ = מוֹץ chaff.

מָצָא (māßā') *inf.* מְצֹא, *w.s.* מֹצַאֲכֶם, *imp.* מְצָא, *fut.* יִמְצָא, *pt.* מוֹצֵא, *w.s.* מֹצְאִי, *f* מֹצֵאת, to come to, to reach to, to arrive at, to acquire; to find, to discover; to meet with, to befall. — *Ni.* נִמְצָא, *inf.* הִמָּצֵא, *fut.* יִמָּצֵא, *pt.* נִמְצָא, *f* נִמְצָאָה, to be found, to be met with; to be acquired; to be discovered; to exist. — *Hi.* הִמְצִיא, *fut.* יַמְצִיא, *pt.* מַמְצִיא, to let come, to deliver, to cause to find; to bring, to present.

מַצָּב (măßßā'b) *m, c.* מַצַּב, stand, station, post, garrison, office.

מֻצָּב (mŭßßā'b) *m,* מַצָּבָה (măßßābā') *f,* מִצָּבָה (mĭßßābā') *f* = מַצָּב.

מַצֵּבָה (măßßēbā') *f, c.* מַצֶּבֶת, מַצְּבַת, *w.s.* מַצַּבְתָּהּ,

pl. מַצֵּבוֹת, *c.* מַצְּבוֹת and מַצֵּבֹת, pillar, column, monument, statue [of idols]; stump, trunk.

מְצֹבָיָה (m^eßō'bāyā') *pr.n.* of a place.

מְצָד (m^eßā'd) *m, pl.* מְצָדוֹת, mountain-hold, castle, stronghold, fortress.

מָצָה (māßā') *fut.* וַיִּמֶץ, to suck out, to empty; to press out [moisture]. — *Ni.* נִמְצָה, *fut.* יִמָּצֶה, to be sucked out, to be squeezed out.

מַצָּה[1] (măßßā') *f, pl.* מַצּוֹת, unleavened bread or bread-cake.

מַצָּה[2] (măßßā') *f* contention, quarrel.

מֹצָה (mōßā') *pr.n.* of a place in Benjamin.

מִצְהָלָה (mĭßhālā') *f, pl. c.* מִצְהֲלוֹת, neighing.

מָצוֹד (māßō'd) *m, c.* מְצוֹד, net, capture, gain; fortress.

מָצוּד (māßū'd) *m* net.

מְצוֹדָה (m^eßōdā') *f, pl.* מְצֹדוֹת, fortress, tower, mountain-castle; net.

מְצוּדָה (m^eßūdā') *f, c.* מְצֻדַת, *w.s.* מְצוּדָתִי, *pl.* מְצוּדוֹת = מָצוֹד.

מִצְוָה (mĭßvā') *f, c.* מִצְוַת, *pl.* מִצְוֹת, מִצְוֹוֹת (mĭßvō'ϑ), commandment, precept, law; the due.

מְצוֹלָה (m^eßōlā') *f, pl.* מְצֹלוֹת, and מְצוּלָה (m^eßūlā') *f, pl.* מְצוּלוֹת, מְצֻלוֹת, מְצֻלֹת, depth [of the sea, of water], abyss.

מָצוֹק (māßō'k) *m* pressure, distress, embarrassment.

מָצוּק (māßū'k) *m, pl. c.* מְצֻקֵי, pillar; height, cliff, peak.

מְצוּקָה (m^eßūkā') *f, pl.* מְצוּקוֹת = מָצוֹק.

מָצוֹר[1] (māßō'r) *m, c.* מְצוֹר, straitness, embarrassment, distress; siege; wall, circumvallation, fortification, fortress.

מָצוֹר[2] (māßō'r) *pr.n.* = מִצְרַיִם.

מָצוּר (māßū'r) *m, w.s.* מְצוּרֵךְ = מָצוֹר[1] siege.

מְצוּרָה (m^eßūrā') *f, pl.* מְצֻרוֹת, circumvallation; fortress, fortification.

מַצּוּת (măßßū'ϑ) *f* contention, quarrel, strife.

מֵצַח (mē'ßăch) *m, w.s.* מִצְחוֹ, *pl.* מִצְחוֹת forehead.

מִצְחָה (mĭßchā') *f*, *c.* מִצְחַת. greave, frontlet of the leg.

מְצִלָּה (m'ßĭllā') *f*, *pl.* מְצִלּוֹת, bell.

מְצֻלָּה (m'ßŭllā') *f* shady place; others: tent.

מְצִלֶת (m'ßē'lĕth) *f*, only *du.* מְצִלְתַּיִם, cymbal of two plates.

מִצְנֶפֶת (mĭßnĕ'fĕth) *f* turban [of the high priest or the king]; tiara.

מַצָּע (măßßā'') *m* couch.

מִצְעָד (mĭß'ā'd) *m*, only *pl.* *c.* מִצְעֲדֵי, *w.s.* מִצְעָדָיו, step, walk.

מִצְעָר[1] (mĭß'ā'r) *m* littleness, smallness, fewness, a little while.

מִצְעָר[2] (mĭß'ā'r) *pr.n.* of a hill.

מִצְפָּה (mĭßpā') *pr.n.* of towns in Gilead and Benjamin; a district near Hermon.

מִצְפֶּה[1] (mĭßpĕ') *m*, *c.* מִצְפֵּה, look-out, watch-tower.

מִצְפֶּה[2] (mĭßpĕ') *pr.n.* of several places.

מַצְפֹּן (măßpō'n) *m*, only *pl.* מַצְפֻּנִים, hidden thing, treasure.

מָצַץ (māßă'ß) *fut. pl.* תָּמֹצּוּ, to suck out.

מֵצַר (mēßă'r) *m*, *pl.* מְצָרִים, *c.* מְצָרֵי, straitness, distress.

מִצְרַיִם (mĭßră'yĭm) *pr.n.* *du.*, a son of Ham; [upper and lower] Egypt, Egyptians; *w. loc.* ה מִצְרַיְמָה; *gent.* מִצְרִי, *pl.* מִצְרִים, *f* מִצְרִית, *pl.* מִצְרִיּוֹת, Egyptian.

מַצְרֵף (măßrē'f) *m* crucible.

מַק (măk) *m* rottenness, putridity.

מַקָּבָה (măkkābā') *f* and **מַקֶּבֶת** (măkkĕ'bĕth) *f*, *pl.* מַקָּבוֹת, hammer; fissure in a rock, hole.

מַקֵּדָה (măkkēdā') *pr.n.* of a town in Judah.

מִקְדָּשׁ (mĭkdā'š) *m*, *c.* מִקְדַּשׁ, *pl.* מִקְדָּשִׁים, *c.* מִקְדְּשֵׁי, a holy thing, sanctuary, temple, asylum.

מַקְהֵל (măkhē'l) *m*, only *pl.* מַקְהֵלִים and מַקְהֵלוֹת, assembly, choir.

מִקְוָה (mĭkvā') *f* reservoir.

מִקְוֶה (mĭkvĕ') *m*, *c.* מִקְוֵה, hope, trust; gathering, confluence of water; assembly, troop, company.

מָקוֹם (mākō'm) *m* [and *f*], *c.* מְקוֹם, *pl.* מְקוֹמוֹת, מְקֹמוֹת, stand, place, spot, dwelling-place, abode; מְקוֹם אֲשֶׁר at the place where.

מָקוֹר (mākō'r) *m*, *c.* מְקוֹר, fountain, spring; the female pudenda.

מִקָּח (mĭkkā'ḥ) *m* the taking, receiving.

מִקָּחָה (mĭkkāḥā') *f*, only *pl.* מַקָּחוֹת, saleable things, merchandise.

מִקְטָר (mĭktā'r) *m*, *c.* מִקְטַר, place of incensing.

מִקְטֶרֶת (mĭktē'reṯ) *f* censer.

מַקֵּל (măkkē'l) *m*, *c.* מַקֵּל and מַקַּל, *w.s.* מַקְלוֹ, מַקֶּלְכֶם, *pl.* מַקְלוֹת and מַקְּלוֹת, twig, rod, staff, stick.

מִקְלוֹת (mĭklō'ṯ) *pr.n.m.*

מִקְלָט (mĭklā't) *m* place of refuge, asylum.

מִקְלַעַת (mĭklă'ʿăṯ) *f*, *pl.* מִקְלָעוֹת, *c.* מִקְלְעוֹת, sculptured work, relievo.

מִקְנֶה (mĭknē') *m*, *c.* מִקְנֵה, *w.s.* מִקְנְךָ, מִקְנֶיךָ, acquisition, purchase, possession, property, cattle.

מִקְנָה (mĭknā') *f*, *c.* מִקְנַת, purchase, price, possession, property.

מִקְנֵיָהוּ (mĭknēyā'hū) *pr.n.m.*

מִקְסָם (mĭksā'm) *m* soothsaying, divination.

מָקַץ (mākă'ṣ) *pr.n.* of a place.

מִקְצֹעַ, מִקְצוֹעַ (mĭkṣō'aʿ) *m*, *pl.* מִקְצֹעוֹת and מִקְצוֹעִים, *c.* מִקְצוֹעֵי, angle, corner, nook.

מַקְצֻעָה (măkṣūʿā') *f*, only *pl.* מַקְצֻעוֹת, carving-knife, chisel.

מִקְצָת, מִקְצֹת see קָצָת.

מָקַק (mākă'k) *Ni.* נָמַק, *pl.* נָמַקּוּ, *fut.* יִמַּק, *pt. pl.* נְמַקִּים, to be melted, to be dissolved, to vanish; to flow, to pine away, to perish.

מִקְרָא (mĭkrā') *m*, *pl. c.* מִקְרָאֵי, *w.s.* מִקְרָאֶהָ, a calling together, convocation, assembly, congregation; place of meeting; reading, recital.

מִקְרֶה (mĭkrē') *m*, *c.* מִקְרֵה, *w.s.* מִקְרֶהָ, chance, hap, accident, event, lot.

מְקָרֶה (mᵉkārē') *m* framework.

מְקֵרָה (mᵉkērā') *f* a cooling.

מְקַרְקַר (mᵉkărkă'r) *m* a breaking down, overthrow [or *Pi. pt.* of קוּר].

מִקְשָׁה¹ (mĭkšā') *f* turned or carved work.

מִקְשָׁה² (mĭkšā') *f* field of cucumbers or melons.

מִקְשֶׁה (mĭkšĕ') *m* twisted hair, lock.

מַר¹ (măr) *m* a drop.

מַר² (măr) *adj.*, *i.p.* מָר, *pl.* מָרִים, *c.* מָרֵי, *f* מָרָה [מָרָא], *c.* מָרַת, bitter, sad, embittered, fierce, violent, wild; *subst.* bitterness, sadness.

מֹר, מוֹר (mōr) *m* myrrh.

מָרָא¹ (mārā') *pt. f* מוֹרְאָה, to be obstinate, rebellious. — *Hi. fut.* יַמְרִיא, to flap the wings.

מָרָא² (mārā') *pr.n.f.* [— מָרָה, see מַר²].

מְרֹאדַךְ (mᵉrōdă'ḳ), מְרֹדַךְ *pr.n.* of a Babylonian god, Marduk.

מְרֹאדַךְ בַּלְאֲדָן (mᵉrōdă'ḳ băl'ᵃdā'n) *pr.n.m.* of a king of Babylon.

מַרְאֶה (măr'ĕ') *m*, *c.* מַרְאֵה, *pl. c.* מַרְאֵי, the seeing, sight, appearance, aspect, form; sight, vision.

מַרְאָה (măr'ā') *f*, *pl.* מַרְאוֹת, sight, vision, revelation; mirror.

מֻרְאָה (mŭr'ā') *f* craw, crop of birds.

מְרֹאוֹן (mᵉrō'n) *pr.n.* of a place.

מָרֵאשָׁה (mārēšā'), מָרֵשָׁה *pr.n.* of a fortress in Judah.

מַרְאֶשֶׁת (măr'ĕšĕϑ) and מְרַאֶשֶׁת (mᵉrĕ'šĕϑ) *f*, only *pl. c.* מַרְאֲשׁוֹת, מְרַאֲשׁוֹת, the place of the head; *adv.* at or under the head.

מֵרַב (mērā'ḇ) *pr.n.f.*

מַרְבַד (mărḇă'ḍ) *m*, only *pl.* מַרְבַדִּים, coverlet, carpet.

מַרְבֶּה (mărbĕ') *m*, *c.* מַרְבֵּה, multitude, increase, plenty.

מִרְבָּה (mĭrbā') *f* amplitude, abundance.

מַרְבִּית (mărbī'ϑ) *f* multitude, greatness, the greater part; increase, interest, usury.

מַרְבֵּץ (mărbē'ß) *m*, *c.* מִרְבַץ, resting-place [for animals].

מַרְבֵּק (mărbē'k) *m* stall, fattening-stable.

מַרְגּוֹעַ (mărgō'a•) *m* rest, resting-place.

מַרְגְּלֹת (mărgĕ'lĕϑ) *f*, only *pl. c.* מַרְגְּלוֹת, place of the feet; *adv.* at the feet.

מַרְגֵּמָה (mărgēmā') *f* heap of stones; others: sling, swing [for throwing stones].

מַרְגֵּעָה (mărgē'ā') *f* = מַרְגּוֹעַ.

מָרַד (mārā'd) *inf.* מְרֹד, *fut.* יִמְרֹד, יִמְרָד־, *pt. p.* מָרוּד, to be obstinate, to resist, to disobey, to rebel.

מֶרֶד[1] (mĕ'rĕd) *m* obstinacy, rebellion.

מֶרֶד[2] (mĕ'rĕd) *pr.n.m.*

מַרְדּוּת (mărdū'ϑ) *f* obstinacy, refractoriness.

מֹרְדַךְ see מְרֹאדַךְ.

מָרְדְּכַי (mŏrd'ĕφă'y) *pr.n.m.*

מֻרְדָּף (mŭrdā'f) *m* persecution.

מָרָה[1] (mārā') *inf.* מְרֹא, *pt.* מֹרֶה, *pl.* מֹרִים, to be refractory, rebellious; to rebel, resist, despise. — *Hi.* הִמְרָה, *inf.* לַמְרוֹת [for לְהַמְרוֹת], *fut.* יַמְרֶה, וַיֶּמֶר, *pt. pl.* מַמְרִים, to quarrel, to dispute; to be rebellious, to rebel, resist, offend.

מָרָה[2] (mārā') *pr.n.* of a bitter fountain in the peninsula of Sinai.

מָרָה[3] (mārā') *f*, *du.* מְרָתַיִם double rebellion, i. e. Babylon.

מָרָה (mŏrrā') and מֹרָה (mōrā') *f*, *c.* מֹרַת, bitterness, grief, sorrow.

מָרוּד (mārū'd) *m*, *w.s.* מְרוּדִי, *pl.* מְרוּדִים, expulsion, persecution; one homeless, fugitive.

מֵרוֹז (mērō'z) *pr.n.* of a town in northern Palestine.

מָרוֹחַ (mārō'aḥ) *adj.*, *c.* מְרוֹחַ, bruised, castrated.

מָרוֹם (mārō'm) *m*, *c.* מְרוֹם, *pl.* מְרוֹמִים, *c.* מְרוֹמֵי, height, elevation, high place [heaven]; high rank; excellence; pride; *adv.* proudly; far.

מֵרוֹם (mērō'm) *pr.n.* of a district near the source of the Jordan.

מֵרוֹץ (mērō'ß) *m* and מְרוּצָה[1] (m'rūßā') *f*, *c.* מְרוּצַת, race, running.

מְרוּצָה[2] (m'rūßā') *f* oppression.

מְרוּקִים (m'rūkī'm) *m/pl.* an anointing, cleansing.

מָרוֹת (mārō'ϑ) *pr.n.* of a town in Judah.

מַרְזֵחַ (mărzē'aḥ) *m*, *c.* מַרְזַח, cry, shout, wailing.

מָרַח (māră'ḥ) *fut.* יִמְרַח, to rub, to rub in, to lay on.

מֶרְחָב (mĕrḥā'b) *m*, *pl. c.* מֶרְחֲבֵי, wide place, broad space; enlargement, liberty.

מֶרְחָק (mĕrḥā'k) *m*, *pl.* מֶרְחַקִּים, מֶרְחַקִּים, *c.* מֶרְחַקֵּי, remoteness, far distance, remote country.

מַרְחֶשֶׁת (mărḥĕ'sĕϑ) *f* boiling-pot, kettle.

מָרַט (mārǎ't) *inf.* מָרְטָה (mŏrtā'), *fut.* יִמְרַט, *pt.* מֹרֵט, *pt. p. f* מְרוּטָה, to pluck out [hair]; to whet, sharpen; to wear off [the skin by a burden]. — *Ni.* נִמְרַט to be plucked, to become bald. — *Pu.* מֹרַט, *pt.* מְמֹרָט, to be polished, to be sharpened [see מוֹרָט].

מְרִי (m'rī') *m*, *i.p.* מֶרִי, *w.s.* מֶרְיְךָ, refractoriness, rebellion, perverseness.

מְרִיא (m'rī'') *adj.*, *pl.* מְרִיאִים, fat, fattened; *subst.* fattened beast.

מְרִי בַעַל (m'rī' bă''ăl), מְרִיב בַּעַל (m'rī'b bă''ăl) *pr.n.m.*

מְרִיבָה[1] (m'rībā') *f*, *c.* מְרִיבַת, *pl.* מְרִיבוֹת, contention, quarrel, strife.

מְרִיבָה[2] (m'rībā') *pr.n.* of two fountains.

מְרָיָה (m'rāyā') *pr.n.m.*

מֹרִיָּה (mō'rīyyā') *pr.n.* of a hill in Jerusalem.

מְרָיוֹת (m'rāyō'ϑ) *pr.n.m.*

מִרְיָם (mīryā'm) *pr.n.f.* [Maria].

מְרִירוּת (m'rīrū'ϑ) *f* bitterness, grief.

מְרִירִי (m'rīrī') *adj.* bitter, sharp, poisonous.

מֹרֶךְ (mō'rĕḥ) *m* timidity, fear.

מֶרְכָּב (mĕrkā'b) *m* chariot, chariot-seat.

מֶרְכָּבָה (mĕrkābā') *f*, *c.* מִרְכֶּבֶת, *w.s.* מֶרְכַּבְתּוֹ, *pl.* מַרְכָּבוֹת, *c.* מַרְכְּבוֹת, chariot, war-chariot.

מַרְכֹּלֶת (mărkō'lĕϑ) *f* market, mart.

מִרְמָה (mīrmā') *f*, *pl.* מִרְמוֹת, fraud, falsehood, deceit; ill-gotten wealth.

מְרֵמוֹת (m'rēmō'ϑ) *pr.n.m.*

מִרְמָס (mĭrmā's), מִרְמַס (mĭrmă's) *m*, *c.* מִרְמַס, a treading down, object and place of treading down.

מֵרֹנֹתִי (mērō'nōthī') *pr.n.m.*, inhabitant of the unknown place מֵרֹנוֹת.

מֶרֶס (mĕ'rĕs); מַרְסְנָא (măr-sᵉnā') *pr.n.m.* [both Persian].

מֵרֵעַ (mērē'aᵉ) *m*, *w.s.* מֵרֵעֲךָ, מֵרֵעֵהוּ, *pl.* מֵרֵעִים, friend, companion.

מֵרַע (mērăᵉ) *m* wickedness, evil-doing.

מִרְעֶה (mĭrᵉĕ') *m*, *c.* מִרְעֵה, pasture, fodder.

מַרְעִית (mărᵉī'th) *f* a pasturing, feeding; flock.

מַרְעֲלָה (mărᵉalā') *pr.n.* of a place in Zebulon.

מַרְפֵּא, מַרְפֵּה (mărpē') *m* cure, healing; remedy, health; placidity, softness, calmness.

מִרְפָּשׂ (mĭrpā's) *m* muddled water.

מָרַץ (mārā's) *Ni.* נִמְרַץ, *pt.* נִמְרָץ, *f* נִמְרֶצֶת, to be forcible, violent.— *Hi. fut.* יַמְרִיץ to excite.

מַרְצֵעַ (mărsē'aᵉ) *m* an awl.

מַרְצֶפֶת (mărsĕ'fĕth) *f* pavement.

מָרַק (mārā'k) *imp. pl.* מִרְקוּ, *pt. p.* מָרוּק, to rub, polish, sharpen.—*Pu.* מֹרַק to be scoured.

מָרָק (mārā'k) *m*, *c.* מְרַק, broth, soup.

מֶרְקָח (mĕrkā'ch) *m*, only *pl.* מֶרְקָחִים, aromatic herb.

מֶרְקָחָה (mĕrkāchā') *f* a seasoning, spicing; unguent-pot.

מִרְקַחַת (mĭrkă'chăth) *f* the spicing of unguents; unguent, ointment.

מָרַר (mārā'r) *pf.* מַר, מָרָה, *fut.* יֵמַר to be bitter, to be grieved, embittered. — *Ni.* נָמַר to be changed [see מוּר] — *Pi.* מֵרֵר, *fut.* יְמָרֵר, to make bitter, to embitter; to irritate, provoke. — *Hi.* הֵמַר, *inf.* הָמֵר, *fut.* יַמֵּר, to embitter, to grieve; to weep violently. — *Hith.* הִתְמַרְמַר to be embittered, exasperated.

מָרֹר (mārō'r) *m*, only *pl.* מְרֹרִים bitter herbs.

מְרֵרָה (mᵉrērā') *f* gall.

מְרֹרָה (mᵉrōrā') *f*, *c.* מְרֹרַת,

pl. מְרֹרוֹת, gall, poison, bitter things [unripe grapes].

מְרָרִי (mᵉrārī′) *pr.n.m.*

מָרֵשָׁה (mā′rēšā′) see מָרְ.אֵשָׁה.

מִרְשַׁעַת (mĭršă′ʿă𝔱) *f* wickedness.

מַשָּׂא[1] (măssā′) *m* a carrying, a lifting; burden, load; tribute, present; elevation of the voice, song, utterance, oracle; desire, longing.

מַשָּׂא[2] (măssā′) *pr.n.m.*

מַשָּׂאָה (măssā′ā′) *f* rising smoke, conflagration.

מַשְׂאֵת (măs′ē𝔱) *f*, *c.* מַשְׂאַת, *pl.* מַשְׂאוֹת, a lifting-up; fire-signal; tribute, tax, present; burden; saying, oracle.

מַשָּׂאָה see מַשְׁאָה.

מִשְׂגָּב (mĭsgā′b) *m*, *c.* מִשְׂגַּב, *w.s.* מִשְׂגַּבִּי, height, high place, fortress, refuge, protection.

מְשׂוּכָה, מְשֻׂכָה (mᵉsūchā′), מְשׂוּכָּה *f* thorn-hedge.

מַשּׂוֹר (măssō′r) *m* a saw.

מְשׂוּרָה (mᵉsūrā′) *f* a measure for liquids.

מָשׂוֹשׂ (māsō′s) *m*, *c.* מְשׂוֹשׂ, joy, object of joy.

מִשְׂחָק (mĭsḥā′k) *m* laughter.

מַשְׂטֵמָה (măsṭēmā′) *f* enmity, hostility.

מַשְׂכִּיל (măskī′l) *m* didactic or artful poem [see also שָׂכַל *Hi.*].

מַשְׂכִּית (măskī′𝔱) *f*, *pl.* מַשְׂכִּיּוֹת, image, figure, picture, sculptured work; imagination, thought.

מַשְׂכֹּרֶת (măskō′rĕ𝔱) *f*, *w.s.* מַשְׂכֻּרְתִּי wages, reward.

מַשְׂמֶרֶת see מַסְמֶרֶת.

מִשְׂפָּח (mĭspā′ḥ) *m* bloodshed, murder.

מִשְׂרָה (mĭsrā′) *f* dominion, lordship.

מִשְׂרֶפֶת (mĭsrĕ′fĕ𝔱) *f*, only *pl.* *c.* מִשְׂרְפוֹת, a burning, cremation.

מִשְׂרְפוֹת מַיִם (mĭsrᵉfō′𝔱 mă′yĭm) *pr.n.* of a place near Sidon.

מַשְׂרֵקָה (măsrēkā′) *pr.n.* of a place in Edom.

מַשְׂרֵת (măsrē′𝔱) *m* a pan.

מַשׁ (măš) *pr.n.m.*

מַשָּׁא (măššā′) *m* loan, debt, pledge, usury.

מֵשָׁא (mēšā') *pr.n.* of a place in Arabia.

מַשְׁאָב (mašʼāb) *m*, only *pl.* מַשְׁאַבִּים, draw-well, trough for drawn water.

מַשָּׂאָה (maššāʼā') *f*, *c.* מַשַּׂאת, *pl.* מַשָּׂאוֹת, — מַשָּׂא.

מַשֻּׁאָה (maššūʼā') *f*, only *pl.* מַשֻּׁאוֹת, מַשּׁוּאוֹת, ruin, desolation.

מְשֹׁאָה (mᵉšōʼā') *f* desolation, desolate place.

מִשְׁאָל (mišʼāl) *pr.n.* of a town in Asher.

מִשְׁאָלָה (mišʼālā') *f*, *pl. c.* מִשְׁאֲלוֹת, request, wish.

מִשְׁאֶרֶת (mišʼereṯ) *f*, *w.s.* מִשְׁאַרְתֶּךָ, *pl. c.* מִשְׁאֲרוֹת, kneading-trough.

מִשְׁבֶּצֶת (mišbeṣeṯ) *f*, only *pl. c.* מִשְׁבְּצוֹת, texture, brocade; setting [of precious stones].

מַשְׁבֵּר (mašbēr) *m*, *c.* מִשְׁבַּר, mouth of the womb.

מִשְׁבָּר (mišbār) *m*, *pl.* מִשְׁבָּרִים, *c.* מִשְׁבְּרֵי, breakers, surf, breaking wave.

מִשְׁבָּת (mišbāṯ) *m*, only *pl.* מִשְׁבַּתִּים, cessation, ruin.

מַשְׁגֶּה (mašgē') *m* deceiver, misleader [see שָׁגָה].

מִשְׁגֶּה (mišgē') *m* error, mistake.

מָשָׁה (māšā') to draw out, to save. — *Hi.* הִמְשָׁה, *fut.* יַמְשֶׁה to draw out, to rescue.

מַשֶּׁה (maššē') *m* loan, debt.

מֹשֶׁה (mōšē') *pr.n.m.*

מְשׁוֹאָה see מְשֹׁאָה.

מַשּׁוּאָה see מַשֻּׁאָה.

מְשׁוֹבָב (mᵉšōbāb) *pr.n.m.*

מְשׁוּבָה (mᵉšūbā') *f*, *c.* מְשׁוּבַת, *pl.* מְשׁוּבוֹת, *w.s.* מְשׁוּבֹתֵיכֶם, turning away, apostasy; an apostate.

מְשׁוּגָה (mᵉšūgā') *f* error, mistake.

מָשׁוֹט (māšōṭ) and מִשּׁוֹט (miššōṭ) *m* oar, rudder.

מְשׁוּסָּה (mᵉšūssā') *f* a plundering.

מָשַׁח (māšaḥ) *m*, *inf.* מְשֹׁחַ, מְשֹׁחַ, *w.s.* מָשְׁחוֹ (mošḥō'), מְשָׁחֲךָ, *imp.* מְשַׁח, *fut.* יִמְשַׁח, *pt. pl.* מֹשְׁחִים, *pt. p.* מָשׁוּחַ, *pl.* מְשֻׁחִים, to besmear, to paint; to anoint, to consecrate. — *Ni.* *inf.* הִמָּשַׁח to be anointed.

מִשְׁחָה (mišḥā') *f*, *c.* מִשְׁחַת,

anointing, unction; part, portion.

מָשְׁחָה (mŏšḥā') *f* = מִשְׁחָה.

מַשְׁחִית (măšḥī'ϑ) *m* destruction; ambush, snare, trap; destroyer [see שָׁחַת].

מִשְׁחָר (mĭšḥā'r) *m* dawn, day-blush.

מַשְׁחֵת (măšḥē'ϑ) *m* destruction.

מִשְׁחַת (mĭšḥă'ϑ) *m* disfigurement, defacement.

מָשְׁחָת (mŏšḥā'ϑ) *m* blemish.

מִשְׁטוֹחַ (mĭšṭō'ᵃḥ) *m* and **מִשְׁטָח** (mĭšṭā'ḥ) *m*, *c.* מִשְׁטַח, place for spreading out [nets].

מִשְׁטָר (mĭšṭā'r) *m* dominion, command.

מֶשִׁי (mĕ'šī) *m* silk, silk-stuff.

מְשֵׁיזַבְאֵל (mᵉšē'zăḇ'ē'l) *pr. n.m.*

מָשִׁיחַ (māšī'ᵃḥ) *adj.*, *c.* מְשִׁיחַ, *w.s.* מְשִׁיחִי, besmeared, anointed; an anointed one [priest, king, patriarch]; the Christ, Messiah.

מָשַׁךְ (māšă'ḵ) *inf.* מְשֹׁךְ, *imp.* מְשֹׁךְ, *pl.* מִשְׁכוּ and מָשְׁכוּ (mŏšḵū'), *fut.* יִמְשֹׁךְ, *pt.* מֹשֵׁךְ, to draw, pull; to extend, prolong; to sow; to attract, to take, to cherish, to preserve; to wander, to go. — *Ni.* נִמְשַׁךְ, *fut.* יִמָּשֵׁךְ, to be protracted, delayed. — *Pu.* מְמֻשַּׁךְ, *pt.* מְמֻשָּׁךְ, to be protracted, to be extended, to be tall.

מֶשֶׁךְ[1] (mĕ'šĕḵ) *m* the drawing, sowing; possession.

מֶשֶׁךְ[2] (mĕ'šĕḵ) *pr.n.m.* of a Japhetic people [Moschians] near the Caucasus.

מִשְׁכָּב (mĭškā'ḇ) *m*, *c.* מִשְׁכַּב, *w.s.* מִשְׁכָּבוֹ, *pl. c.* מִשְׁכְּבוֹת and מִשְׁכְּבֵי, the lying [in bed]; couch, bed.

מִשְׁכָּן (mĭškā'n) *m*, *c.* מִשְׁכַּן, *pl.* מִשְׁכָּנוֹת, *c.* מִשְׁכְּנוֹת and מִשְׁכְּנֵי, habitation, dwelling, haunt; hut, tent; tabernacle, sanctuary, temple; grave.

מָשַׁל[1] (māšă'l) *inf.* מָשׁוֹל, מְשֹׁל, -מְשָׁל, *imp.* מְשֹׁל, *fut.* יִמְשֹׁל, *pt.* מֹשֵׁל, מוֹשֵׁל, *f* מֹשְׁלָה, to rule, reign, govern; to rule over, to manage. — *Hi.* הִמְשִׁיל, *fut.* יַמְשִׁיל, to cause to rule.

מָשַׁל² (māšă'l) [*den.* of מָשָׁל] *imp.* מְשֹׁל, *fut.* יִמְשֹׁל, *pt.* מֹשֵׁל, to propose or use a proverb, a parable; *pt.* gnomic poet. — *Ni.* נִמְשַׁל to be comparable, like, similar. — *Pi.* מִשֵּׁל to speak in parables. — *Hi.* הִמְשִׁיל to compare, liken. — *Hith.* הִתְמַשֵּׁל to become like.

מָשָׁל¹ (māšā'l) *m*, *c.* מְשַׁל, *pl.* מְשָׁלִים, *c.* מִשְׁלֵי, comparison, similitude, parable, proverb, saying, gnomic song, satire, by-word.

מָשָׁל² (māšā'l) *pr.n.* of a town.

מְשֹׁל (m'šō'l) *m* by-word, satire.

מֹשֶׁל (mō'šĕl) *m*, *w.s.* מָשְׁלוֹ (mŏšlō') rule, dominion; likeness, similitude.

מִשְׁלָח (mĭšlā'ḥ) *m*, *c.* מִשְׁלַח, place where one is sent; business; possession.

מִשְׁלֹחַ (mĭšlō'aḥ) *m*, *c.* מִשְׁלוֹחַ, a sending; seizure, possession.

מִשְׁלַחַת (mĭšlă'ḥăϑ) *f* sending, troop; dismissal, discharge.

מְשֻׁלָּם (m'šŭllā'm); מְשִׁלֵּמוֹת (m'šĭllēmō'ϑ); מְשֶׁלֶמְיָה (m'šĕ'lĕmyā') *pr.n.m.*

מְשֻׁלֶּמֶת (m'šŭllĕ'mĕϑ) *pr.n.f.*

מְשַׁמָּה (m'šămmā') *f*, *pl.* מְשַׁמּוֹת, desolation, horror.

מִשְׁמָן (mĭšmā'n) *m*, *c.* מִשְׁמַן, *pl.* מִשְׁמַנִּים, *c.* מִשְׁמַנֵּי, fatness, fat or fertile soil; strong warrior.

מִשְׁמַנָּה (mĭšmănnā') *pr.n.m.*

מַשְׁמַנִּים (măšmănnī'm) *m/pl.* fat food, delicacies.

מִשְׁמָע¹ (mĭšmā'ʻ) *m*, *c.* מִשְׁמַע, a hearing, report.

מִשְׁמָע² (mĭšmā'ʻ) *pr.n.m.*

מִשְׁמַעַת (mĭšmă'ʻăϑ) *f*, *w.s.* מִשְׁמַעְתּוֹ, audience, admission at court; obedience; subjects.

מִשְׁמָר (mĭšmā'r) *m*, *c.* מִשְׁמַר, guard, watch, post; prison; a thing to be guarded; usage.

מִשְׁמֶרֶת (mĭšmĕ'rĕϑ) *f*, *w.s.* מִשְׁמַרְתִּי, guard, watch, watch-post, service, duty; keeping, preservation, usage; command, law; fidelity.

מִשְׁנֶה (mĭšnĕ') *m*, *c.* מִשְׁנֵה. *pl.* מִשְׁנִים, repetition, doubling; the double, the second; copy; the second place in rank; the younger, later.

מְשִׁסָּה (m'šĭssā') *f*, *pl.* מְשִׁסּוֹת, plundering, plunder, booty.

מִשְׁעוֹל (mĭš'ō'l) *m* narrow path, hollow way.

מִשְׁעִי (mĭš'ī') *m* cleansing, purity.

מִשְׁעָם (mĭš'ā'm) *pr.n.m.*

מִשְׁעָן (mĭš'ā'n) *m*, *c.* מִשְׁעַן, support, stay, staff.

מַשְׁעֵן (măš'ē'n) *m* and מִשְׁעֶנֶת מַשְׁעֵנָה (măš'ēnā'), (mĭš'ĕ'nĕϑ) *f*, *w.s.* מִשְׁעַנְתִּי = מִשְׁעָן.

מִשְׁפָּחָה (mĭšpāḥā') *f*, *c.* מִשְׁפַּחַת, *w.s.* מִשְׁפַּחְתּוֹ, *pl.* מִשְׁפָּחוֹת, *c.* מִשְׁפְּחוֹת, species, kind, sort, family; race, tribe, people.

מִשְׁפָּט (mĭšpā't) *m*, *c.* מִשְׁפַּט, *w.s.* מִשְׁפָּטִי, *pl.* מִשְׁפָּטִים, *c.* מִשְׁפְּטֵי judgment, sentence; place of judgment; cause, suit; crime, guilt; right, law, rule; the due.

מִשְׁפָּת (mĭšpā'ϑ) *m*, only *du.* מִשְׁפְּתַיִם, fold, pen.

מֶשֶׁק (mĕ'šĕk) *m* possession, heirdom.

מַשָּׁק (măššā'k) *m*, *c.* מַשַּׁק, a running about.

מַשְׁקֶה (măškĕ') *m*, *c.* מַשְׁקֵה, *pl.* מַשְׁקִים, cup-bearer, butler; drink, wine; watered region [see שָׁקָה *Hi.*].

מִשְׁקוֹל (mĭškō'l) *m* weight.

מַשְׁקוֹף (măškō'f) *m* upper beam of a door.

מִשְׁקָל (mĭškā'l) *m*, *c.* מִשְׁקַל, a weighing; weight, value.

מִשְׁקֶלֶת (mĭškĕ'lĕϑ) and מִשְׁקֹלֶת (mĭškō'lĕϑ) *f* plummet, level.

מִשְׁקָע (mĭškā'') *m*, *c.* מִשְׁקַע, a settling; settled and clear water.

מִשְׁרָה (mĭšrā') *f*, *c.* מִשְׁרַת, solution, maceration, drink.

מִשְׁרָעִי (mĭšrā'ī') *pr.n. gent.*, one dwelling at מִשְׁרָע.

מָשַׁשׁ (māšă'š) *fut.* יָמֹשׁ, *w.s.* יְמֻשֵּׁנִי, אֲמֻשְּׁךָ [or from מוּשׁ], to touch, to feel.— *Pi.* מִשֵּׁשׁ, *fut* יְמַשֵּׁשׁ, *pl.* מְמַשֵּׁשׁ, to grope, to explore. — *Hi.* הֵמֵשׁ, *imp.* *w.s.* הֲמִישֵׁנִי, *fut.* יָמֵשׁ, *pl.* יְמִישׁוּן, to touch, to feel; to let touch.

מִשְׁתֶּה (mĭštĕ') *m*, *c.* מִשְׁתֵּה

pl. w.s. מִשְׁתֵּיהֶם, drink, place of drinking; banquet, feast, drinking.

מַתְּ, מַתָּה see מות.

מַת (mă𝑡ʰ) *m*, only *pl.* מְתִים, מְתֵם, *c.* מְתֵי, *w.s.* מְתֶיךָ, men, males.

מֵת (mē𝑡ʰ) *adj.*, *pl.* מֵתִים, *f* מֵתָה, dead [see מות].

מַתְבֵּן (mă𝑡ʰbē'n) *m* heap of straw.

מֶתֶג (mĕ'𝑡ʰĕg) *m. w.s.* מִתְגִּי, bit, curb.

מָתוֹק (mā𝑡ʰō'k) *adj.*, *pl.* מְתוּקִים, *f* מְתוּקָה, sweet; lovely, pleasant; *subst.* sweetness.

מְתוּשָׁאֵל (mᵉ𝑡ʰū'šā'ē'l); מְתוּשֶׁלַח (mᵉ𝑡ʰūšĕ'lăḥ), *i.p.* מְתוּשָׁלַח, *pr.n.m.*

מָתַח (mā𝑡ʰă'ḥ) *fut.* יִמְתַּח, to extend, to stretch out.

מָתַי (mā𝑡ʰă'y) *m* extension of time; *adv.* when?; לְמָתַי and עַד־מָתַי till when? how long?

מַתְכֹּנֶת (mă𝑡ʰkō'nĕ𝑡ʰ) *f*, *w.s.* מַתְכֻּנְתּוֹ, measure; task; proportion.

מַתְּלָאָה = מַה־תְּלָאָה what a weariness [see תְּלָאָה].

מְתַלְּעָה (mᵉ𝑡ʰăllᵉʿā') *f*, only *pl.* מְתַלְּעוֹת [for מַלְתָּעוֹת], tooth.

מְתֹם (mᵉ𝑡ʰō'm) *m* wholeness, completeness; a thing uninjured.

מַתָּן[1] (măttā'n) *m* present, gift.

מַתָּן[2] (măttā'n) *pr.n.m.*

מֹתֶן (mō'𝑡ʰĕn) *m*, only *du.* מָתְנַיִם (mŏ𝑡ʰnă'yĭm), *c.* מָתְנֵי, the loins, the waist.

מַתָּנָה[1] (măttānā') *f*, *c.* מַתְּנַת, *pl.* מַתָּנוֹת, מַתָּנֹת, *c.* מַתְּנוֹת, gift, present; offering, sacrificial gift; bribe.

מַתָּנָה[2] (măttānā') *pr.n.* of a place on the eastern border of Moab.

מַתְנַי (mă𝑡ʰnă'y) *pr.n.m.*

מִתְנִי (mĭ𝑡ʰnī') *pr.n. gent.* one dwelling at the unknown place מֶתֶן or מִתְנָה.

מַתַּנְיָה (măttănyā'), מַתַּנְיָהוּ (măttănyā'hū) *pr.n.m.*

מָתַק (mā𝑡ʰă'k) *pf. w.s.* מְתָקוֹ, *fut.* יִמְתַּק, to enjoy, to relish; to be sweet, to be pleasant. — *Hi.* הִמְתִּיק, *fut.* יַמְתִּיק, to make sweet, pleasant; to become sweet.

מֶתֶק (mĕ'𝑡ʰĕk) *m* and מֹתֶק (mō'𝑡ʰĕk) *m*, *w.s.* מָתְקִי

(mŏϑkī') *m* sweetness, pleasantness.

מִתְקָה (mĭϑkā') *pr.n.* of a station in the wilderness.

מִתְרְדָת (mĭϑrᵉdā'ϑ) *pr.n.m.* [Persian = Mithradates].

מַתָּת (măttā'ϑ) *f*, *c.* מַתַּת, gift, present.

מַתַּתָּה (măttăttā'); מַתִּתְיָה (măttĭϑyā'); מַתִּתְיָהוּ (măttĭϑyā'hū) *pr.n.m.*

נ

נ, ן the fourteenth letter of the alphabet, called נוּן [fish]; as a numeral נ = 50, ן = 700.

נָא[1] (nā) a particle of entreating and inciting: pray! now! oh!

נָא[2] (nā) *adj.* raw, half-cooked.

נֹא (nō) and נֹא־אָמוֹן (nō-āmō'n) *pr.n.* of a city in upper Egypt, Thebes.

נֹאד (nōd) *m*, *pl.* נֹאדוֹת, leather-bag.

נָאָה[1] (nā'ā') *Pil. pf.* נַאֲוָה, נָאוָה, *pl.* נָאווּ, to be convenient, becoming, lovely, pleasant.

נָאָה[2] (nā'ā') *f*, *pl. c.* נְאוֹת, habitation, dwelling, pasture.

נָאוֶה (nāvě') *adj.*, *f* נָאוָה, becoming, comely, lovely.

נֵאוֹתָה see אות *Ni.*

נָאַם (nā'ă'm) *fut.* יִנְאַם, to whisper, to murmur.

נְאֻם (nᵉ'ū'm) *m* [mostly with following יהוה] declaration, utterance, oracle.

נָאַף (nā'ă'f) *inf.* נָאוֹף, *fut.* יִנְאַף, *pt.* נֹאֵף, *f* נֹאֶפֶת, to commit adultery [with]. — *Pi. fut.* יְנָאֵף, יְנַאֵף, *pt.* מְנָאֵף, *pl.* מְנָאֲפִים, to commit adultery or idolatry.

נִאֻף (nĭ'ū'f) *m*, only *pl.* נִאֻפִים, and נַאֲפוּף (nă'ᵃfū'f) *m*, only *pl.* נַאֲפוּפִים, adultery, unchastity.

נָאַץ[1] (nā'ă'ṡ) *fut.* יִנְאַץ, to revile, scorn, despise, reject. — *Pi.* נִאֵץ, *inf.* נָאֵץ [for נַאֵץ], *fut.* יְנָאֵץ, *pt.* מְנָאֵץ, *pl.* מְנָאֲצִים, to despise, contemn, deride, reject. — *Hithpo. pt.* מִנֹּאָץ to be derided, scorned.

נָאַץ[2] (nā'ă'ß) *Hi. fut.* יְנָאֵץ [for יְנָאֵץ] to bloom, to put forth blossoms.

נְאָצָה (nᵉ'āßā') and נֶאָצָה (nĕ''āßā') *f*, only *pl.* נֶאָצוֹת, reviling, contempt.

נָאַק (nā'ă'k) *fut.* יִנְאַק, to cry, groan, wail.

נְאָקָה (nᵉ'ākā') *f, c.* נַאֲקַת, *pl.* נַאֲקוֹת, a groaning, complaining.

נָאַר (nā'ă'r) *Pi.* נִאֵר, נֵאֵר, to despise, reject.

נֹב (nōḅ), נֹבֶה (nō'ḅĕ) *pr.n.* of a town in Benjamin.

נָבָא (nāḅā') *Ni.* נִבָּא, *inf.* הִנָּבֵא, *fut.* יִנָּבֵא, *pt. pl.* נִבְּאִים and נִבָּאִים, to be inspired, to prophesy, to speak or sing as a prophet. — *Hith.* הִתְנַבֵּא, *inf.* הִתְנַבְּאוֹת, *fut.* יִתְנַבֵּא, *pt.* מִתְנַבֵּא, the same as *Ni.*; to rave, to play the madman.

נָבַב (nāḅă'ḅ) *pt. p.* נָבוּב, *c.* נְבוּב, to bore through, to hollow.

נֹבֶה see נֹב.

נְבוֹ (nᵉḅō') *pr.n.* of a mountain; of towns in Reuben and Judah; of a Chaldean god, Hermes or Mercury.

נְבוּאָה (nᵉḅū'ā') *f, c.* נְבוּאַת, prophecy.

נְבוּזַרְאֲדָן (nᵉḅū'zăr'ᵃdā'n) *pr.n.m.*

נְבֻכַדְנֶאצַּר, נְבוּכַדְנֶאצַּר, נְבֻכַדְנֶצַּר (nᵉḅū'ḉădnĕßßă'r), נְבוּכַדְרֶאצַּר (nᵉḅū'ḉădrĕßßă'r) *pr.n.m.* Nebuchadnezzar, king of Babylon.

נְבוּשַׁזְבָּן (nᵉḅū'šăzbā'n) *pr. n.m.*.

נָבוֹת (nāḅō'ϑ) *pr.n.m.*

נָבְזָה = נְבָזָה, see בָּזָה.

נָבַח (nāḅă'ḥ) *inf.* נְבֹחַ, to bark.

נֹבַח (nō'ḅăḥ) *pr.n.* of a town in Gad; *pr.n.m.*

נִבְחַז (nĭḅḥă'z) *pr.n.* of an idol of the Avites [עַוִּים].

נָבַט (nāḅă't) *Pi.* נִבַּט to look. — *Hi.* הִבִּיט, *inf.* הַבִּיט, *imp.* הַבֵּט, הַבִּיט, הַבֶּט־. *fut.* יַבִּיט, יַבֵּט, *pt.* מַבִּיט, to look, to look at, out, about, on; to behold, regard, respect.

נְבָט (nᵉḅā't) *pr.n.m.*

נָבִיא (nāḅī') *m, c.* נְבִיא, *pl.* נְבִיאִים, נְבִאִים, *c.* נְבִיאֵי, prophet, speaker of oracles.

נְבִיאָה (nᵉḅī'ā') *f* prophetess; wife of a prophet.

נְבָיוֹת (nᵉḇāyō'ϑ) *pr.n.m.* of an Arabian tribe.

נֵבֶךְ (nē'ḇĕḵ) *m*, only *pl. c.* נִבְכֵי, spring, fountain.

נָבַל (nāḇă'l), נָבֵל (nāḇē'l), *inf.* נָבֹל, נְבֹל, *fut.* יִבֹּל, יִבּוֹל, *pl.* יִבְּלוּ, *pt.* נֹבֵל, *f* נֹבֶלֶת, to wither, fade, decay; to be worn out, to vanish, to perish; to act foolishly. — *Pi.* נִבֵּל, *fut.* יְנַבֵּל, *pt.* מְנַבֵּל, to esteem lightly, to despise, reject.

נָבָל¹ (nāḇā'l) *adj.*, *pl.* נְבָלִים, *f* נְבָלָה, foolish, unbelieving, irreligious, godless; *subst.* fool, unbeliever.

נָבָל² (nāḇā'l) *pr.n.m.*

נֵבֶל (nē'ḇĕl), נֶבֶל (nĕ'ḇĕl) *m*, *i.p.* נָבֶל, *pl.* נְבָלִים, *c.* נִבְלֵי, leather-bag, vessel, bottle, pitcher; harp.

נְבָלָה (nᵉḇālā') *f* foolishness, wickedness, foul deed, punishment.

נְבֵלָה (nᵉḇēlā') *f*, *c.* נִבְלַת, *w.s.* נִבְלָתִי and נִבְלָתוֹ, corpse, carcass.

נַבְלוּת (năḇlū'ϑ) *f* the parts of shame.

נְבַלָּט (nᵉḇăllā't) *pr.n.* of a town in Benjamin.

נֹבֶלֶת (nōḇĕ'lĕϑ) *f coll.* withering leaves.

נָבַע (nāḇă'') *pt.* נֹבֵעַ, to bubble forth, to rush. — *Hi.* הִבִּיעַ, *fut.* יַבִּיעַ, *pl.* תַּבַּעְנָה, to pour out, to utter, speak, pronounce; to cause to ferment.

נִבְקָה see בָּקַק.

נִבְשָׁן (nĭḇšā'n) *pr.n.* of a town in Judah.

נְגֹאֲלוּ see גָּאַל.

נֶגֶב (nĕ'gĕḇ) *m*, *w. loc.* נֶגְבָּה ה, the south, southern region.

נָגַד (nāgă'd) *Hi.* הִגִּיד, *inf.* הַגֵּד, הַגִּיד [לַגֵּד = לְהַגֵּד], *imp.* הַגֵּד, הַגֶּד־, הַגִּידִי, *fut.* יַגִּיד, וַיַּגֵּד, *pt.* מַגִּיד, to bring forward, to declare, explain, announce; to make known, to betray. — *Ho.* הֻגַּד, *inf.* הֻגֵּד, *fut.* יֻגַּד, to be announced, to be shown.

נֶגֶד (nĕ'gĕd) *m* the front, the visible; *adv.* and *prep.* opposite, in front of, before, in presence of, against, corresponding to; also כְּנֶגֶד, נֶגְדָּה, מִנֶּ׳, לְנֶ׳.

נָגַהּ (nāgă'h) *fut.* יִגַּהּ, to shine, to glitter. — *Hi.*

הִגִּיהַּ, *fut.* יַגִּיהַּ, to cause to shine, to illuminate, to make bright.

נֹגַהּ[1] (nō'găh) *m*, *w.s.* נָגְהָם (nŏghā'm) brightness, splendour, glory.

נֹגַהּ[2] (nō'găh) *pr.n.m.*

נְגֹהָה (n^e^gōhā') *f* brightness, splendour.

נָגַח (nāgă'ḥ) *fut.* יִגַּח, to thrust, to push. — *Pi.* נִגַּח, *fut.* יְנַגַּח, *pt.* מְנַגֵּחַ, to gore, to thrust, to throw down. — *Hith.* הִתְנַגַּח to strike one another, to make war.

נַגָּח (năggā'ḥ) *adj.* wont to gore.

נָגִיד (nāgī'd) *m*, *c.* נְגִיד, נְגִד, *pl.* נְגִידִים, *c.* נְגִידֵי, a high, a noble one, prince, leader, overseer; *pl.* noble things.

נָגַן (nāgă'n) *pt. pl.* נֹגְנִים, to touch the strings. — *Pi.* נִגֵּן, *inf.* נַגֵּן, *fut.* יְנַגֵּן, *pt.* מְנַגֵּן, to harp, to strike the strings.

נָגַע (nāgă'') *inf.* נְגֹעַ, גַּעַת. *imp.* גַּע, *fut.* יִגַּע, *pt.* נֹגֵעַ, *f* נֹגַעַת, *pl.* נֹגְעֹת, *pt. p.* נָגוּעַ, to smite, beat, strike; to punish; to touch; to reach to, to arrive. — *Ni.* *fut.* יִנָּגַע, to be smitten. — *Pi.* *fut.* יְנַגַּע, to smite, to inflict plagues. — *Pu.* נֻגַּע to be smitten. — *Hi.* הִגִּיעַ, *inf.* הַגִּיעַ, הַגַּע, *fut.* יַגִּיעַ, וַיַּגַּע, *pt.* מַגִּיעַ, to cause to touch, to cause to reach; to reach to, to touch; to arrive at, to obtain.

נֶגַע (nĕ'gă') *m*, *w.s.* נִגְעִי, *pl.* נְגָעִים, *c.* נִגְעֵי, blow, stroke, punishment,plague,leprosy, pestilence, plague-spot, scurf.

נָגַף (nāgă'f) *inf.* נְגֹף, נְגֹף, *fut.* יִגֹּף, *pt.* נֹגֵף, to smite, push, thrust, punish. — *Ni.* נִגַּף, *inf.* הִנָּגֵף, *fut.* יִנָּגֵף, *pt.* נִגָּף, to be beaten or routed. — *Hith.* הִתְנַגֵּף to stumble.

נֶגֶף (nĕ'gĕf) *m* a stumbling; plague, punishment.

נָגַר (nāgă'r) *Ni.* נִגַּר, *pt.* נִגָּר, to be poured out, to flow, to be stretched out. — *Hi.* הִגִּיר, *fut.* יַגִּיר, וַיַּגֵּר, to pour out, to pour down; to deliver up, to abandon. — *Ho.* *pt.* מֻגָּר to be poured out.

נָגַשׂ (nāgă's) *fut.* יִגֹּשׂ, יִנְגֹּשׂ,

pt. נֹגֵשׂ, *pl.* נֹגְשִׂים, *c.* נֹגְשֵׂי, to press, urge, drive, exact; *pt.* driver, task-master, exactor.— *Ni.* נִגַּשׂ to be pressed, harassed; to harass one another; to be tired out, wearied.

נָגַשׁ (nāgă'š) *inf.* גֶּשֶׁת, *w.s.* גִּשְׁתּוֹ, *imp.* גַּשׁ, גֶּשׁ־, גְּשׁוּ, *fut.* יִגַּשׁ, to come near, to approach, to touch; to draw near; to stand back. — *Ni.* נִגַּשׁ, *pt.* נִגָּשׁ, to approach; to come near. — *Hi.* הִגִּישׁ, *imp.* הַגִּישָׁה, *fut.* יַגִּישׁ, יַגֵּשׁ, *pt.* מַגִּישׁ, to bring near, to present; to approach. — *Ho.* הֻגַּשׁ, *pt.* מֻגָּשׁ, to be brought near, to be offered. — *Hith.* הִתְנַגֵּשׁ to draw near.

נֵד (nēḍ) *m* heap, wall.

נָדָא (nāḍā') *Hi. fut.* יַדֵּא, to force away, to remove.

נָדַב (nāḍă'ḇ) *fut. w.s.* יִדְּבֶנּוּ, to incite, impel. — *Hith.* הִתְנַדֵּב, to impel oneself, to be willing, to do or give freely.

נָדָב (nāḍā'ḇ) *pr.n.m.*

נְדָבָה (nᵉḍāḇā') *f*, *c.* נִדְבַת, *pl.* נְדָבוֹת, *c.* נִדְבוֹת, willingness; free-will gift; plenty; בִּנְדָבָה spontaneously, voluntarily, freely.

נְדַבְיָה (nᵉḍăḇyā') *pr.n.m.*

נָדַד (nāḍă'ḍ) *fut.* יִדּוֹד, יִדַּד, *pt.* נֹדֵד, to flap the wings, to move about, to flee, to escape. — *Po.* נוֹדֵד to disappear, to fly away.— *Hi. fut. w.s.* יְנִדֻהוּ, to chase, to scare away. — *Ho. fut.* יֻדַּד, *pt.* מֻנָּד, to be scared away; to be thrust away. — *Hith.* הִתְנוֹדֵד, *fut.* יִתְנוֹדֵד [or from נוד], to move to and fro; to flee, to lament.

נְדֻדִים (nᵉḍūḍī'm) *m/pl.* a tossing to and fro [sleeplessness].

נָדָה (nāḍā') *Pi.* נִדָּה, *pt.* מְנַדֶּה, *pl. w.s.* מְנַדֵּיכֶם, to remove, expel.

נֵדֶה (nē'ḍĕ) *m* liberal gift; a whore's wages.

נִדָּה (nĭddā') *f*, *c.* נִדַּת, removal, rejection, abomination, impurity; incest.

נָדַח (nāḍă'ḥ) *inf.* נְדֹחַ, *fut.* יַדַּח, to strike into; to thrust out, to expel.—*Ni. pt.* נִדָּח, *w.s.* נִדָּחוֹ, *pl.* נִדָּחִים, *f* נִדָּחָה, נִדַּחַת, to be thrust out, expelled, banished; to be seduced; *pt.* a fugitive, an outcast. — *Pu. pt.* מְנֻדָּח, to be cast out. — *Hi.* הִדִּיחַ, *inf.* הַדִּיחַ, *imp. w.s.* הַדִּיחֵמוֹ, *fut.* יַדִּיחַ, יַדַּח, to thrust out, drive out, expel, reject; to seduce, to bring down upon. — *Ho. pt.* מֻדָּח to be frightened away.

נָדִיב (nāḏī'ḇ) *adj.*, *c.* נְדִיב, *pl.* נְדִיבִים, *c.* נְדִיבֵי, *f* נְדִיבָה, willing, prompt, generous, liberal; *subst.* a noble, prince, tyrant.

נְדִיבָה (nᵉḏīḇā') *f*, *pl.* נְדִיבוֹת, nobility, honour; noble or generous dealing.

נָדָן (nāḏā'n) *m*, *w.s.* נְדָנָהּ, *pl.* נְדָנִים, sheath [of a sword]; liberal gift.

נָדַף (nāḏă'f) *fut.* יִנְדֹּף, יִדֹּף, *w.s.* תִּדְּפֶנּוּ, to disperse, to drive away, to expel, to beat. — *Ni.* נִדַּף, *inf.* הִנְדֹּף, *pt.* נִדָּף, to be scattered, to be driven about.

נָדַר (nāḏă'r) *inf.* נְדֹר, *imp. pl.* נִדְרוּ, *fut.* יִדֹּר, יִדַּר, *pt.* נֹדֵר, to vow.

נֶדֶר (nĕ'ḏĕr), **נֵדֶר** (nē'ḏĕr) *m*, *w.s.* נִדְרִי, *pl.* נְדָרִים, *c.* נִדְרֵי, a vow, vowed sacrifice.

נֹהַּ (nō'ᵃh) *m* splendour, eminence.

נָהַג (nāhă'g) *imp.* נְהַג, *fut.* יִנְהַג, *pt.* נֹהֵג, *pl.* נֹהֲגִים, to drive on, to drive forward, to lead away, to carry away, to act. — *Pi.* נִהַג, *fut.* יְנַהֵג, to drive, to lead, to carry off; to sigh, to lament.

נָהָה (nāhā') *imp.* נְהֵה, to wail, lament, mourn. — *Ni.* *fut.* יִנָּהֶה, to assemble [others: to lament].

נְהִי (nᵉhī') *m*, *i.p.* נֶהִי, a lament, wail.

נָהַל (nāhă'l) *Pi.* נִהֵל, *fut.* יְנַהֵל, *pt.* מְנַהֵל, to conduct, lead; to provide for, to protect. — *Hith. fut.* יִתְנַהֵל, to walk on.

נַהֲלָל (nă'hᵃlā'l), נַהֲלוֹל[1] (nă'hᵃlō'l) *pr.n.* of a town in Zebulon.

נַהֲלֹל[2] (nă'hᵃlō'l) *m* pasture.

נָהַם (nāhă'm) *fut.* יִנְהֹם, to gnarl, to growl; to roar.

נַהַם (nă'hăm) *m* a growling, roaring.

נְהָמָה (nᵉhāmā') *f*, *c.* נַהֲמַת, the same as נַהַם.

נָהַק (nāhā'k) *fut.* יִנְהַק, to bray; to cry wildly.

נָהַר (nāhā'r) *fut.* יִנְהַר, to flow, to run; to crowd to; to shine, to be cheerful.

נָהָר (nāhā'r) *m*, *c.* נְהַר, *du.* נַהֲרַיִם, *pl.* נְהָרִים and נְהָרוֹת, *c.* נַהֲרֵי, river, stream, current; the Euphrates, the Nile; אֲרַם נַהֲרַיִם Mesopotamia.

נְהָרָה (n^ehārā') *f* light, daylight.

נוּא (nū) *fut. pl.* תְּנוּאוּן, to avert, hinder. — *Hi.* הֵנִיא, *fut.* יָנִי [for יָנִיא], to avert, hinder; to refuse, to frustrate.

נוּב[1] (nūḃ) *fut.* יָנוּב, to bud, sprout, grow, thrive; to utter, to speak. — *Pil. fut.* יְנוֹבֵב to cause to sprout, to produce.

נוֹב, נוּב[2] see נִיב.

נוּד (nūḍ) *pf.* נָד, נֵד, *inf.* and *imp.* נוּד, *fut.* יָנוּד, *pt.* נָד, to move to and fro, to shake, to nod; to rove about, to wander, to flee; to lament, deplore, pity, condole. — *Hi.* הֵנִיד, *inf.* הָנִיד, *fut.* יָנִיד, to cause to wander, to scare away; to nod, to shake. — *Ho. pt.* מֻנָד see נָדַד. — *Hith.* הִתְנוֹדֵד see נָדַד.

נוֹד[1] (nōḍ) *m*, *w.s.* נֹדִי, a wandering about.

נוֹד[2] (nōḍ) *pr.n.* of a country east of Eden.

נוֹדָב (nōḍā'ḃ) *pr.n.m.*

נָוָה[1] (nāvā') *fut.* יִנְוֶה, to dwell, abide, rest.

נָוָה[2] (nāvā') *Hi. fut.* יַנְוֶה, to praise, extol.

נָוָה[3] (nāvā') *f*, *c.* נְוַת, *pl. c.* נְוֹת, the same as נָוֶה[2].

נָוֶה[1] (nāvĕ') *adj.*, *f* נָוָה, *c.* נְוַת, dwelling, abiding; comely, beautiful, lovely; נְוַת בַּיִת the mistress [honour or inhabitant] of the house.

נָוֶה[2] (nāvĕ') *m*, *c.* נְוֵה, *pl.* נָוִים, *c.* נְוֵי, dwelling-place, habitation; pasture.

נוּחַ[1] (nū'ah) *pf.* נָח, נוֹחַ, *inf.* נוּחַ, נֻחַ, *imp.* נוּחַ, *fut.* יָנוּחַ, וַיָּנַח, to settle down, to rest, to lie down, to dwell; to be silent. — *Hi.* הֵנִיחַ, הִנִּיחַ [הִנֵּחַ], *inf.* הָנִיחַ, *imp.* הָנִיחַ, הַנַּח, הַנִּיחָה, *fut.* יָנִיחַ, יַנִּיחַ, וַיַּנַּח, *pt.* מֵנִיחַ, to set or lay down, to lead to rest, to give rest, to leave in quiet; to leave, to let remain; to permit, to place or put, to cast down. — *Ho.* הוּנַח and הֻנִּיחַ, *pt.* מֻנָּח, to be set down or placed, to be left, to be brought to rest.

נוּחַ[2] (nū'aḥ), נֹחַ (nō'aḥ) *m* rest, quiet, resting-place.

נוֹחָה (nōḥā') *pr.n.m.*

נוּט (nūt) *fut.* יָנוּט, to quake.

נְוָיֹת (nᵉvāyō'th) = נָיוֹת *pr.n.*, dwelling of a prophetic school.

נוּם (nūm) *pf.* נָם, *fut.* יָנוּם, to slumber, to fall asleep.

נוּמָה (nūmā') *f* slumber, drowsiness.

נוּן[1] (nūn) *Ni. fut.* יִנּוֹן or *Hi. fut.* יָנִין, to sprout, to spread.

נוּן[2] (nūn) *pr.n.m.*

נוּס (nūs) *pf.* נָס, *inf.* נוֹס, נוּס, *imp.* נוּס, נֻסוּ, *fut.* יָנוּס, וַיָּנָס (vāyyā'nōs), וַיָּנֻס, *pt.* נָס, *pl.* נָסִים, to flee, to move on quickly; to escape. — *Pil.* נוֹסֵס to chase, to drive. — *Hi.* הֵנִיס, *inf.* הָנִיס, *fut.* יָנִיס, to put to flight; to rescue, to save. — *Hith.* הִתְנוֹסֵס to betake oneself to flight.

נוּעַ (nū'aᵉ) *pf.* נָע, *inf.* נוֹעַ, נוּעַ, *fut.* יָנוּעַ, וַיָּנַע, *pt.* נָע, *f/pl.* נָעוֹת, to totter, quake, shake, reel; to move to and fro, to tremble; to wave about, to rove, to wander. — *Ni. fut.* יִנּוֹעַ to be shaken, to be sifted. — *Hi.* הֵנִיעַ, *imp. w.s.* הֲנִיעֵמוֹ, *fut.* יָנִיעַ, יָנַע, *pl.* יְנִיעוּן, to shake, to drive, to move, to set in motion, to drive abroad, to disturb.

נוֹעַדְיָה (nō'ᵃădyā') *pr.n.m.* and *f.*

נוּף (nūf) *Hi.* הֵנִיף, *inf.* הָנִיף, הֲנָפָה, *imp. pl.* הָנִיפוּ, *fut.* יָנִיף, וַיָּנֶף, *pt.* מֵנִיף, *w.s.* מְנִיפוֹ, to cause to move, to shake, to swing, to wave, to move up and down; to wave [a sacrifice], to dedicate; to sprinkle, to moisten. — *Ho.* הוּנַף to be waved. — *Pil. fut.* יְנוֹפֵף, to beckon, to threaten.

נוֹף (nōf) *m* elevation, height.

נוּץ (nūs) *Hi. pf. pl.* הֵנֵצוּ, *fut.* יָנֵאץ, to bloom, to blossom [see נָצַץ].

נוֹצָה (nōsā') *f* wing, pinion.

נוק (nūk) *Hi. fut. w.s.* וַתְּנִיקֵהוּ, to suckle, see יָנַק.

נוש (nūš) *fut.* אָנוּשָׁה, to be ill, sick.

נָזָה (nāzā') *fut.* יִזֶּה, וַיִּז, וַיֵּז, to spirt, to sprinkle. — *Hi.* הִזָּה, *fut.* יַזֶּה, וַיַּז, *pt.* מַזֶּה, to sprinkle; to cause to start, to startle.

נָזִיד (nāzī'd) *m* a cooked dish, mess.

נָזִיר (nāzī'r) *m, c.* נְזִיר, a separate, dedicated one; Nazarite; prince; the unpruned vine.

נָזַל (nāză'l) *fut.* יִזַּל, *pt.* נֹזֵל, *pl.* נֹזְלִים, to flow down, to run down; to overflow, to spread. — *Hi.* הִזִּיל to cause to flow.

נֶזֶם (nĕ'zĕm) *m, w.s.* נִזְמָהּ, *pl.* נְזָמִים, *c.* נִזְמֵי ring [for the nose and ears].

נֵזֶק (nē'zĕk) *m* loss, damage.

נָזַר (nāză'r) *Ni.* נִזַּר, *inf.* הִנָּזֵר, *fut.* יִנָּזֵר, to separate oneself; to abstain; to devote oneself. — *Hi.* הִזִּיר, *inf.* הַזִּיר, *fut.* יַזִּיר, to refrain, restrain; to consecrate; to abstain.

נֵזֶר (nē'zĕr) *m, w.s.* נִזְרוֹ, consecration; consecrated or unshorn head; diadem, crown.

נֹחַ (nō'aḥ) *pr.n.m.*, Noah.

נַחְבִּי (năḥbī') *pr.n.m.*

נָחָה (nāḥā') *imp.* נְחֵה, to guide, to lead. — *Hi.* הִנְחָה, *inf. w.s.* לַנְחֹתָם [for לְהַנְחֹתָם], *fut.* יַנְחֶה, to guide, to lead.

נַחוּם (năḥū'm) *pr.n.m.*

נִחוּם (niḥū'm) *m*, only *pl.* נִחֻמִים, consolation, comfort, compassion.

נָחוֹר (nāḥō'r) *pr.n.m.*

נָחוּשׁ (nāḥū'š) *adj*, *f* נְחוּשָׁה, of copper or bronze; *subst.* copper.

נְחִילָה (n[e]ḥīlā') *f*, only *pl.* נְחִילוֹת [for נְחִלָּה], pipe, flute.

נָחִיר (nāḥī'r) *m*, only *du.* נְחִירַיִם, nostrils.

נָחַל (nāḥă'l) *inf.* נְחֹל, *fut.* יִנְחַל, to seize, to take into possession; to get, to inherit; to take or have for one's own; to give in possession. — *Pi.* נִחַל, *inf.* נַחֵל, to distribute, to allot. — *Hi.* הִנְחִיל, *inf* הַנְחִיל, הַנְחֵל, *fut.* יַנְחִיל, *pt.* מַנְחִיל, to give in possession or inheritance. —

Ho. הָנְחַל to be made to possess. — *Hith.* הִתְנַחֵל to possess for oneself.

נַחַל (nă'ḥăl) *m*, *i.p.* נָחַל, *w. loc.* ה נַחְלָה, *pl.* נְחָלִים, *c.* נַחֲלֵי, *du.* נַחֲלַיִם, brook, stream, torrent; valley, ravine, gorge.

נַחֲלָה (nă'ḥᵃlā') *f*, *c.* נַחֲלַת, *pl.* נְחָלוֹת, possession, property, inheritance.

נַחֲלִיאֵל (nă'ḥᵃlī'ē'l) *pr.n.* of a station in the desert.

נֶחֱלָם (nĕ'ḥᵉlā'm) *pr.n.m.*

נַחֲלָת (nă'ḥᵃlā'ϑ) *f* = נַחֲלָה.

נָחַם (nāḥă'm) *Ni.* נִחַם, *i.p.* נִחָם, *inf.* and *imp.* הִנָּחֵם, *fut.* יִנָּחֵם, *pt.* נִחָם, to have compassion, to pity, to grieve, to be sorry; to comfort oneself; to feel repentance; to take vengeance. — *Pi.* נִחַם, *inf.* נַחֵם, *imp. pl.* נַחֲמוּ, *fut.* יְנַחֵם, *pt.* מְנַחֵם, to comfort, console, pity. — *Pu.* נֻחַם, *fut.* יְנֻחַם, to be comforted. — *Hith.* הִתְנַחֵם to feel compassion, repentance; to comfort oneself; to take revenge.

נַחַם (nă'ḥăm) *pr.n.m.*

נֹחַם (nō'ḥăm) *m* repentance.

נֶחָמָה (nĕ'ḥāmā') *f* consolation, comfort.

נְחֶמְיָה (nᵉḥĕmyā') *pr.n.m.*

נִחֻמִים see חָמַם.

נִחוּמִים (nĭḥūmī'm) see נְחוּם,

נַחְנוּ see אֲנַחְנוּ.

נָחַץ (nāḥă'ẓ) *pt. p.* נָחוּץ, to press, to urge.

נָחַר (nāḥă'r) *Ni. pt. pl.* נֶחֱרִים, see חָרָה.

נַחַר (nă'ḥăr) *m* a snorting.

נַחֲרָה (nă'ḥᵃrā') *f* = נַחַר.

נַחֲרַי (nă'ḥᵃrăy) *pr.n.m.*.

נָחַשׁ (nāḥă's) *Pi.* נִחֵשׁ, *inf.* נַחֵשׁ, *fut.* יְנַחֵשׁ, *pt.* מְנַחֵשׁ, to practice sorcery, to give oracles, to divine, to foretell.

נָחָשׁ[1] (nāḥā's) *m*, *c.* נְחַשׁ, *pl.* נְחָשִׁים, serpent, the constellation of the dragon.

נָחָשׁ[2] (nāḥā's) *pr.n.m.*

נַחַשׁ (nă'ḥăs) *m*, *pl.* נְחָשִׁים, incantation, omen.

נַחְשׁוֹן (năḥsō'n) *pr.n.m.*

נְחֹשֶׁת (nᵉḥō'sĕϑ) *f* and *m*, *w.s.* נְחֻשְׁתִּי (nᵉḥŭstī'), נְחֻשְׁתָּה, *du.* נְחֻשְׁתַּיִם, copper, bronze; fetter; [copper] money.

נְחֻשְׁתָּא (nᵉḥŭstā') *pr.n.f.*

נְחֻשְׁתָּן (nᵉḥŭstā'n) *adj.*

made of copper; the bronze serpent made by Moses.

נָחַת (nāḥă'θ) *fut.* יֵחַת, יִנְחַת, to descend, to come down, to sink. — *Ni.* נִחַת to come down on. — *Pi.* נִחֵת, *imp.* נַחֵת, to press down, to bend [a bow], to level [or to water]. — *Hi. imp.* הַנְחֵת to cause to come down.

נַחַת[1] (nă'ḥăθ) *m* a coming down, descent, rest, repose, ease.

נַחַת[2] (nă'ḥăθ) *pr.n.m.*

נָחֵת (nāḥē'θ) *adj.*, only *pl.* נְחִתִּים, descending.

נְחַת see נָחַת and חָתַת.

נָטָה (nāṭā') *inf.* נְטוֹת, *imp.* נְטֵה, *fut.* יִטֶּה, וַיֵּט, יֵט, *pt.* נֹטֶה, *f* נֹטָה, *pt. p.* נָטוּי, *f* נְטוּיָה, *pl.* נְטוּיוֹת, to stretch, to extend; to stretch out, to spread out; to bend, to bow down, to decline; to turn aside. — *Ni.* נִטָּה, *fut.* יִנָּטֶה, to be stretched, extended. — *Hi.* הִטָּה, *inf.* הַטּוֹת, *imp.* הַטֵּה, הַט, *fut.* יַטֶּה, וַיַּט, *pt.* מַטֶּה, *pl.* מַטִּים, to stretch out, to spread out, to reach; to bow down, to incline; to turn aside, to avert, to turn away; to bend.

נָטִיל (nāṭī'l) *adj.*, only *pl. c.* נְטִילֵי, bearing, laden.

נָטִיעַ (nāṭī'aʿ) *m*, only *pl.* נְטִעִים, a plant.

נְטִיפָה (nᵉṭīfā') *f*, only *pl.* נְטִיפוֹת, pendant for the ear.

נְטִישָׁה (nᵉṭīšā') *f*, only *pl* נְטִישׁוֹת, tendril, twig.

נָטַל (nāṭă'l) *fut.* יִטּוֹל, *pt.* נוֹטֵל, to lift up, to raise. — *Pi. fut.* יְנַטֵּל to take up.

נֵטֶל (nē'ṭĕl) *m* load, burden.

נָטַע (nāṭă'ʿ) *inf.* נְטֹעַ, טַעַת, *imp.* נְטַע, *fut.* יִטַּע, *pt.* נֹטֵעַ, *w. interr.* ה הֲנֹטַע, to set in, to plant; to set up, to establish. — *Ni.* נִטַּע to be planted.

נֶטַע (nĕ'ṭăʿ) *m*, *i.p.* נָטַע, *c.* נְטַע, *w.s.* נִטְעֵךְ, *pl.* נְטָעִים, *c.* נִטְעֵי, the planting, plantation, plant.

נְטִעִים see נָטִיעַ.

נָטַף (nāṭă'f) *fut.* יִטֹּף, to drop, to drip, to flow. — *Hi.* הִטִּיף, *fut.* יַטִּיף, *pt.* מַטִּיף, to cause to drip; to speak, preach, prophesy.

נָטָף (nāṭā'f) *m*, *pl. c.* נִטְפֵי.

drop, aromatic resin [myrrh].

נְטֹפָה (nᵉṭōfā') *pr.n.* of a town near Bethlehem; *gent.* נְטוֹפָתִי.

נָטַר (nāṭa'r) *fut.* יִטֹּר, יִנְטֹר, to keep, to guard, to watch.

נָטַשׁ (nāṭa's) *fut.* יִטֹּשׁ, *pt. p.* נָטוּשׁ, *pl.* נְטוּשִׁים, *f* נְטוּשָׁה, to stretch, to extend, to spread; to scatter; to reject, to leave, to give up, to remit, to allow; to draw [a sword], to brandish. — *Ni.* נִטַּשׁ, *fut.* יִנָּטֵשׁ, to be spread out, to be dispersed, to be loosened. — *Pu.* נֻטַּשׁ to be left, forsaken.

נִי (nī) *m* wailing, lament.

נִיב (nīḇ) *m* fruit, produce; speech [praise].

נֵיבַי (nēḇa'y) *pr.n.m.*

נִיד (nīḏ) *m* consolation, comfort.

נִידָה (nīḏā') *f* abomination; others: banishment.

נָיוֹת see נְוָיֹת.

נִיחֹחַ, נִיחוֹחַ (nīḥō'aḥ) *m*, *pl.* נִיחֹחִים, rest, pleasantness, agreeableness, delight.

נִין (nīn) *m*, *w.s.* נִינִי, offspring, descendant.

נִינְוֵה (nīnᵉvē') *pr.n.* of a city in Assyria, Nineveh.

נִיס (nīs) *m* a fugitive.

נִיסָן (nīsā'n) *m* the first month of the Hebrew year.

נִיצוֹן (nīẓō'n) *m* spark.

נֵיר (nēr) *m* light, lamp.

נִיר¹ (nīr) *imp. pl.* נִירוּ, to make arable, to plough.

נִיר² (nīr) = נֵר.

נִיר³ (nīr) *m* newly broken land, land made arable.

נִירָם see יָרָה.

נֵךְ see נָכָה *Hi.*

נָכָא¹ (nāḵā') *Ni.* נִכָּא, *pl.* נִכְּאוּ, to be beaten.

נָכָא² (nāḵā') and נָכֵא (nāḵē'), *adj.*, *pl.* נְכָאִים, *f* נְכֵאָה, beaten, afflicted, grieved.

נְכֹאת (nᵉḵō'ṯ) *f* powdered spice, an aromatic gum [tragacanth] for censing.

נֶכֶד (ne'ḵeḏ) *m*, *w.s.* נֶכְדִּי, progeny.

נָכָה (nāḵā') *Ni.* נִכָּה to be beaten, slain. — *Pi. inf.* נַכֵּה see *Hi. fut.* — *Pu.* נֻכָּה to be beaten. — *Hi.* הִכָּה, *inf.* הַכֵּה, הַכּוֹת, *imp.*

הַכֵּה, הַךְ, *fut.* יַכֶּה, וַיַּךְ, יַךְ, *pt.* מַכֶּה, *w.s.* מַכְּךָ, *pl.* מַכִּים, to beat, strike, smite, hit, hurt, wound, kill, slay, pierce; to rout, defeat, conquer. — *Ho.* הֻכָּה, הוּכָּה, *fut.* יֻכֶּה, *pt.* מֻכֶּה, *c.* מֻכֵּה, *pl.* מֻכִּים, to be beaten, hit, punished, killed.

נָכֶה (nāɸĕ′) *adj.*, *c.* נְכֵה, smitten, afflicted.

נֵכֶה (nēɸĕ′) *m*, only *pl.* נֵכִים, slanderer.

נְכוֹ, נְכֹה (nᵉɸō′) *pr.n.m.*

נָכוֹן (nāɸō′n) *m* thrashing-floor [*pr.n.*].

נָכֹחַ (nāɸō′ᵃɸ) *adj.*, *w.s.* נְכֹחוֹ, *pl.* נְכֹחִים, *f* נְכֹחָה, *pl.* נְכֹחוֹת, lying ahead, straight on; right, righteous; *subst.* right, justice, righteousness.

נֵכַח (nē′ɸăɸ) *m*, *w.s.* נִכְחוֹ, the front; *prep.* before, in presence of, over against, straight ahead.

נֹכַח (nō′ɸăɸ) = נֵכַח.

נָכַל (nāɸă′l) *pt.* נוֹכֵל, to deal deceitfully, to deceive. — *Pi.* נִכֵּל same as *Qal.* — *Hith.* הִתְנַכֵּל to show oneself cunning, deceitful.

נֵכֶל (nē′ɸĕl) *m*, only *pl. c.* נִכְלֵי, cunning, deceit.

נֶכֶס (nĕ′ɸĕs) *m*, only *pl.* נְכָסִים, riches, wealth.

נָכַר (nāɸă′r) *Ni.* נִכַּר, *fut.* יִנָּכֵר, to feign, to dissemble, to make oneself unknown; to be recognised, known. — *Pi.* נִכַּר, *fut.* יְנַכֵּר, to find strange, not to know; to disdain, to deny, to reject. — *Hi.* הִכִּיר, *inf.* הַכִּיר, הַכֵּר, הַכֶּר־, *imp.* הַכֶּר־, *fut.* יַכִּיר, וַיַּכֵּר, *pt.* מַכִּיר, to find out, to recognise, to regard, to observe, to perceive, to understand; to honour. — *Hith.* הִתְנַכֵּר to feign, to dissemble; to be recognised.

נֵכָר (nēɸā′r) *m*, *c.* נֵכַר, strangeness; strange, foreign land.

נֶכֶר (nĕ′ɸĕr) *m* and **נֹכֶר** (nō′ɸĕr) *m* misfortune, calamity.

נָכְרִי (nŏɸrī′) *adj.*, *pl.* נָכְרִים, *f* נָכְרִיָּה, *pl.* נָכְרִיּוֹת, strange, foreign, alien, unknown.

נְכֹת (nᵉɸō′ϑ) *f*, *w.s.* נְכֹתֹה [for נְכֹתוֹ], only in בֵּית־נְכֹת treasure-house, store-house.

נָלָה (nālā') *Hi. inf. w.s.* כַּנְּלֹתְךָ [for כְּהַנְלוֹתְךָ], to bring to an end.

נִמְבְזֶה (nᵉmĭbzĕ') *adj.* — נִבְזֶה contemptible, vile.

נְמוּאֵל (nᵉmū'ē'l) *pr.n.m.*

נְמָלָה (nᵉmālā') *f, pl.* נְמָלִים, an ant.

נָמַר (nāmă'r) see מור.

נָמֵר (nāmē'r) *m, pl.* נְמֵרִים, leopard, panther.

נִמְרֹד (nĭmrō'd) *pr.n.m.*; אֶרֶץ נ׳ Babylonia.

נִמְרָה (nĭmrā') and נִמְרִים (nĭmrī'm) *pr.n.* of a place.

נִמְשִׁי (nĭmšī') *pr.n.m.*

נֵס (nēs) *m, w.s.* נִסִּי, pole, sign, standard, banner, signal.

נְסִבָּה (nᵉsĭbbā') *f* turn, course.

נָסַג see סוג.

נָסָה (nāsā') *Pi.* נִסָּה, *inf.* נַסּוֹת, נַסֹּת, *imp.* נַס, *fut.* יְנַסֶּה, *pt.* מְנַסֶּה, to try, to put to the proof, to tempt, to attempt.

נְסָה — נָשָׂא, see נָשָׂא.

נָסַח (nāsă'ḥ) *fut.* יִסַּח, to pull out, to root out, to expel, to banish; to pull down. — *Ni.* נִסַּח, *fut.* יִסַּח, to be driven out.

נָסִיךְ (nāsī'ḵ) *m, w.s.* נְסִיכָם, *pl. c.* נְסִיכֵי, *w.s.* נְסִיכֵמוֹ, libation, drink-offering; a cast image; prince, ruler.

נָסַךְ[1] (nāsă'ḵ) *inf.* נְסֹךְ, *fut.* יִסֹּךְ, יַסֵּךְ, to pour out [libations]; to cast [metals]; to appoint, to consecrate. —*Ni.* נִסַּךְ to be appointed. — *Pi. fut.* יְנַסֵּךְ to pour out. — *Hi.* הִסִּיךְ, *inf.* הַסֵּךְ, הַסֵּיךְ, *fut.* יַסִּיךְ, וַיַּסֵּךְ, to pour out [as a libation]. — *Ho. fut.* יֻסַּךְ to be poured out.

נָסַךְ[2] (nāsă'ḵ) *pt. pf.* נְסוּכָה, to knot, weave; to cover, to veil.

נֶסֶךְ (nĕ'sĕḵ), נֵסֶךְ (nē'sĕḵ) *m, w.s.* נִסְכִּי, *pl.* נְסָכִים, *c.* נִסְכֵּי, a pouring out, libation, drink-offering; a molten image.

נִסְמָן see סָמַן.

נָסַס[1] (nāsă's) *pt.* נֹסֵס, to be sick.

נָסַס[2] (nāsă's) *Hith.* הִתְנוֹסֵס, to lift oneself up, to become conspicuous [or to collect round a standard].

נָסַע (nāsă'') *inf.* נְסוֹעַ, נְסֹעַ.

w.s. נָסְעָם (nŏ**s**ʻă'm), *imp.* סַע, סְעוּ, *fut.* יִסַּע, to pull up, to tear out [tent-pins, &c.], to break up [a tent], to move on, to remove, to migrate. — *Ni.* נִסַּע to be torn away. — *Hi.* הִסִּיעַ, *fut.* יַסַּע, יַסִּיעַ, *pt.* מַסִּיעַ, to cause to break up, to lead forth; to remove; to quarry stones.

נָסַק (nā**s**ă'**k**) *fut.* יִסַּק, to rise, to ascend.

נִסְרֹךְ (nĭ**s**rō'ḍ) *pr.n.* of an Assyrian idol.

נֵעָה (nēʻā') *pr.n.* of a place in Zebulon.

נֹעָה (nōʻā') *pr.n.f.*

נְעוּרוֹת (nᵉʻūrō'θ) *f/pl.* and נְעוּרִים (nᵉʻūrī'm) *m/pl.* youth, childhood, boyhood.

נְעִיאֵל (nᵉʻīʼē'l) *pr.n.m.*

נָעִים (nāʻī'm) *adj.*, *c.* נְעִים, *pl.* נְעִימִים, *f* נְעִימָה, *pl.* נְעִימוֹת, lovely, sweet, pleasant, agreeable.

נָעַל[1] (nāʻă'l) *inf.* נְעֹל, *fut.* יִנְעַל, *pt. p.* נָעוּל, *f/pl.* נְעֻלוֹת, to bolt, to bar, to lock up.

נָעַל[2] (nāʻă'l) [*denom.* of נַעַל], *fut.* יִנְעַל, to shoe. — *Hi.* הִנְעִיל to shoe.

נַעַל (năʻʻăl) *m*, *w.s.* נַעֲלִי, *pl.* נְעָלִים, נְעָלוֹת, *c.* נַעֲלֵי, *du.* נַעֲלַיִם, a shoe, sandal.

נָעֵם (nāʻē'm) *fut.* יִנְעַם, *i.p.* יִנְעָם, to be lovely, gracious, charming, pleasant, mild, sweet.

נַעַם (năʻʻăm) *pr.n.m.*

נֹעַם (nōʻʻăm) *m* loveliness, pleasantness, charm; kindness, favour.

נַעֲמָה (năʻʻᵃmā') *pr.n.f.*; *pr.n.* of towns, *gent.* נַעֲמָתִי.

נָעֳמִי (nŏʻʻᵒmī') *pr.n.f.*

נַעֲמָן[1] (năʻʻᵃmā'n) *adj.* lovely, pleasant; *pl.* נַעֲמָנִים loveliness, delight.

נַעֲמָן[2] (năʻʻᵃmā'n) *pr.n.m.*

נַעֲצוּץ (năʻʻᵃ**ṣ**ū'**ṣ**) *m*, *pl.* נַעֲצוּצִים, thorn-bush, thorn-hedge.

נָעַר[1] (nāʻă'r) to growl, to roar.

נָעַר[2] (nāʻă'r) *pt.* נֹעֵר, *pt. p.* נָעוּר, to shake, to stir; to shake out. — *Ni.* נִנְעַר, *fut.* יִנָּעֵר, to shake oneself free from, to get rid of; to be shaken off. — *Pi.* נִעֵר, *fut.* יְנַעֵר, to shake, push, drive away. — *Hith.* הִתְנַעֵר to shake oneself from.

נַעַר[1] (nă'ăr) *m*, *w.s.* נַעֲרוֹ, *pl.* נְעָרִים, *c.* נַעֲרֵי, child, boy, youth; servant; male; maid, girl.

נַעַר[2] (nă'ăr) *m* scattered, straying sheep.

נֹעַר (nō'ăr) *m* boyhood, youth.

נַעֲרָה[1] [נַעֲרָ] (nă'ᵃrā') *f*, *pl.* נְעָרוֹת, *c.* נַעֲרוֹת, girl, maid, young woman, servant.

נַעֲרָה[2] (nă'ᵃrā') *pr.n.f.*; *pr.n.* of a place in Ephraim.

נַעֲרַי (nă'ᵃră'y); נְעַרְיָה (nᵉ'ăryā') *pr.n.m.*

נַעֲרָן (nă'ᵃrā'n) *pr.n.* = נַעֲרָה[2].

נְעֹרֶת (nᵉ'ō'rĕϑ) *f* tow, refuse.

נֹף (nōf) *pr.n.* = מֹף Memphis.

נֶפֶג (nĕ'fĕg) *pr.n.m.*

נָפָה[1] (nāfā') *f*, *c.* נָפַת, sieve.

נָפָה[2] (nāfā') *f*, *c.* נָפַת, *pl.* נָפוֹת, elevation, height, hill.

נְפוּסִים (nᵉfūsī'm) *pr.n.m.*

נָפַח (nāfă'ḥ) *inf.* פַּחַת, *fut.* יִפַּח, *pt.* נֹפֵחַ, *pt. p.* נָפוּחַ, to blow, to breathe; to blow on, up, away; to exhale, to breathe one's last. — *Pu.* נֻפַּח to be blown up [a fire]. — *Hi.* הִפִּיחַ to cause to breathe one's last; to despise, to contemn.

נֹפַח (nō'făḥ) *pr.n.* of a town in Moab.

נָפִיל (nāfī'l) *m*, only *pl.* נְפִלִים, נְפִילִים, giant.

נְפִיסִים = נְפוּסִים.

נָפִישׁ (nāfī's) *pr.n.m.*

נֹפֶךְ (nō'fĕḥ) *m* a precious stone, ruby, carbuncle or garnet.

נָפַל (nāfă'l) *inf.* נְפֹל, *w.s.* נָפְלוֹ (nŏflō'), נִפְלוֹ, *fut.* יִפֹּל, *pt.* נֹפֵל, *f* נֹפֶלֶת, to fall, to fall down, to be prostrate, to drop; to be born; to fall out, to happen, to turn out; to fall away, to sink; to be overthrown, to decay; to settle down, to abide. — *Hi.* הִפִּיל, *inf.* הַנְפִּל, הַפִּיל, *fut.* יַפִּיל, וַיַּפֵּל, *pt.* מַפִּיל, to make fall, to cause to fall, to throw down, to fell, to make the face fall; to lay down, to desist. — *Hith.* הִתְנַפֵּל to cast oneself down; to fall upon, to attack. — *Pil.* נִפְלֵל to fall.

נֵפֶל (nĕ'fĕl), **נֵפֶל** (nē'fĕl) *m* untimely birth, abortion.

נָפַץ (nāfă'ß) *inf.* נָפוֹץ, *pt. p.* נָפוּץ, to be dispersed; *tr.* to scatter, smash, dash to pieces. — *Pi.* נִפֵּץ, *fut.* יְנַפֵּץ, to break or dash to pieces, to shatter, to scatter. — *Pu. pt.* מְנֻפָּץ to be broken, scattered.

נֶפֶץ (nĕ'fĕß) *m* shower of rain, tempest.

נַפֵּץ (năppē'ß) *m* dispersion.

נָפַשׁ (nāfă'š) *Ni.* נִפַּשׁ, *fut.* יִנָּפֵשׁ, to take breath; to be refreshed.

נֶפֶשׁ (nĕ'fĕš) *f, w.s.* נַפְשִׁי, *pl.* נְפָשׁוֹת, *c.* נַפְשׁוֹת, breath, respiration, life; soul, spirit, mind; living being, creature, a person, self.

נֶפֶת (nĕ'fĕϑ) *f* height, hill.

נֹפֶת (nō'fĕϑ) *m* liquid honey.

נַפְתּוּל (năftū'l) *m,* only *pl.* נַפְתּוּלִים, wrestling, fight.

נַפְתֻּחִים (năftŭḥī'm) *pr.n.* the people of middle Egypt.

נַפְתָּלִי (năftālī') *pr.n.m.*

נֵץ (nēß) *m, w.s.* נִצָּהּ, blossom, flower; hawk.

נָצָא (nāßā') *inf.* נְצֹא, to fly, to fly away.

נָצַב (nāßă'b) = יָצַב, *Ni.* נִצַּב, *pt.* נִצָּב, *f* נִצָּבָה, *f* נִצֶּבֶת, to be set up, to be stationed, to station oneself, to stand; to be firm or healthy. — *Hi.* הִצִּיב, *inf.* הַצִּיב, *imp. f* הַצִּבִי, *fut.* יַצִּיב, יַצֵּב, *pt.* מַצִּיב, to set, to place, to erect, to establish. — *Ho.* הֻצַּב, *pt.* מֻצָּב, to be placed. — *Hith.* הִתְיַצֵּב see יָצַב.

נִצָּב (nĭßßā'b) *m* handle, haft; prefect, superior.

נָצָה (nāßā') *fut.* יִצֶּה, to flee; to be waste, to be desolate. — *Ni. fut.* יִנָּצֶה, *pt.* נִצֶּה, *pl.* נִצִּים, to quarrel, to strive; to be wasted, destroyed. — *Hi.* הִצָּה, *inf. w.s.* הַצֹּתוֹ, to quarrel, to strife, to war.

נֹצָה[1] (nōßā') = נוֹצָה.

נֹצָה[2] (nōßā') *f* filth, excrements [in the crop].

נִצָּה (nĭßßā') *f* blossom, flower.

נְצוּרָה (nᵉßūrā') *f* watch, guard.

נְצוּרִים (nᵉßūrī'm) *m/pl.* and **נְצוּרוֹת** (nᵉßūrō'ϑ) *f/pl* guarded, secret places.

נָצַח (nāBă'ḥ) *Pi.* נִצַּח, *inf.* נַצֵּחַ, *pt.* מְנַצֵּחַ, to excel, to be superior; to superintend, to be chief; *pt.* music-master, precentor. — *Ni. pt. f* נִצַּחַת, to endure, to last.

נֶצַח (nĕ'Băḥ), **נֵצַח** (nē'Băḥ) *m, w.s.* נִצְחִי, *pl.* נְצָחִים, splendour, glory, truth, power, firmness, confidence, duration, perpetuity; *adv.* and לָנֶצַח, עַד־נֶצַח always, for ever, till eternity.

נְצִיב[1] (nᵉBī'b) *m, pl.* נְצִיבִים, *c.* נְצִיבֵי, prefect, superior; military post; pillar, column.

נְצִיב[2] (nᵉBī'b) *pr.n.* of a town in Judah.

נְצִיחַ (nᵉBī'aḥ) *pr.n.m.*

נָצִיר (nāBī'r) see נְצוּרִים.

נָצַל (nāBă'l) *Ni.* נִצַּל, *inf.* הִנָּצֵל, *fut.* יִנָּצֵל, to be drawn out, to be delivered, saved; to free oneself. — *Pi.* נִצֵּל, *fut.* יְנַצֵּל, to rob, to plunder; to deliver, to save.—*Hi.* הִצִּיל, *inf.* הַצֵּל, הַצִּיל, *imp.* הַצֵּל, *fut.* יַצִּיל, יַצֵּל, *pt.* מַצִּיל, to tear apart, to pull away, to snatch, to rob; to withdraw, escape; to deliver, to save, to free. — *Ho.* הֻצַּל, *pt.* מֻצָּל, to be drawn out, to be snatched out of. — *Hith.* הִתְנַצֵּל to strip or put off [a garment].

נִצָּן (nĭBBā'n) *m* flower, blossom.

נָצַץ (nāBă'B) *pt.* נֹצֵץ, to glitter, to sparkle. — *Hi.* see נָאַץ[2] *Hi.*

נָצַר (nāBă'r) *imp.* נְצֹר, צוֹר, נִצְרָה, *fut.* יִצֹּר, יִנְצֹר, *pt.* נֹצֵר, *f* נֹצְרָה, *pt. p.* נָצוּר, *f* נְצוּרָה, to observe, behold; to watch, guard, inspect, keep, preserve, protect; to hide; to besiege.

נֵצֶר (nē'Bĕr) *m* sprout, shoot, descendant.

נָצַת see יָצַת.

נָקַב (nākă'b) *inf.* נְקֹב, נָקֹב, *imp.* נָקְבָה (nŏkbā'), *fut.* יִקֹּב, יִנְקֹב, *pt.* נֹקֵב, *pt. p.* נָקוּב, *pl. c.* נְקֻבֵי, to bore, to pierce, to hollow out; to mark, to distinguish, to fix; to curse, to blaspheme. — *Ni.* נִקַּב to be marked, to be called by name.

נֶקֶב[1] (nĕ'kĕb) *m* a bezel for precious stones.

נֶקֶב[2] (nĕ'**k**ĕb) *pr.n.* of a town in Naphtali.

נְקֵבָה (nᵉ**k**ēbā') *f* a female [of men and beasts].

נָקֹד (nā**k**ō'd) *adj.*, *pl.* נְקֻדִּים, *f/pl.* נְקֻדּוֹת, spotted, speckled.

נֹקֵד (nō**k**ē'd) *m* shepherd.

נְקֻדָּה (nᵉ**k**ŭddā') *f*, *pl.* נְקֻדּוֹת, a stud [of silver].

נָקָה (nā**k**ā') *Ni.* נִקָּה, *imp.* הִנָּקֵה, *fut.* יִנָּקֶה, to be pure, guiltless, free from punishment; to be free, empty, evacuated, destroyed. — *Pi.* נִקָּה, *inf.* נַקֵּה, *fut.* יְנַקֶּה, to declare innocent, to let go unpunished, to acquit; to cleanse by punishment.

נִקּוּד (nĭ**kk**ū'd) *m*, only *pl.* נִקֻּדִים, crumb, crust; a kind of cake.

נְקוֹדָא (nᵉ**k**ōdā') *pr.n.m.*

נָקַט see קוט.

נָקִי (nā**k**ī') *adj.*, *c.* נְקִי, *pl.* נְקִיִם, נְקִיִּם, pure, innocent, guiltless, free, quit.

נָקִיא — נָקִי.

נִקָּיוֹן (nĭ**kk**āyō'n) *m*, *c.* נִקְיוֹן, purity, innocence; bareness.

נָקִיק (nā**k**ī'**k**) *m*, *pl. c.* נְקִיקֵי, cleft, crevice.

נָקֵל (nā**k**ē'l) see קָלַל *Ni.*

נָקַם (nā**k**ă'm) *inf.* נְקֹם, נָקוֹם, *fut.* יִקֹּם, *pt.* נֹקֵם, to avenge, to punish, to take vengeance, to revenge on. — *Ni.* נִקַּם, *inf.* הִנָּקֵם, *fut.* יִנָּקֵם, to take revenge, to avenge oneself; to be avenged, punished. — *Pi.* נִקֵּם to avenge. — *Ho. fut.* יֻקַּם to be avenged, punished. — *Hith.* הִתְנַקֵּם to avenge oneself; to be revengeful.

נָקָם (nā**k**ā'm) *m*, *c.* נְקַם, revenge, vengeance, retaliation, punishment.

נְקָמָה (nᵉ**k**āmā') *f*, *c.* נִקְמַת, *pl.* נְקָמוֹת, vengeance, retaliation, punishment; vindictiveness.

נָקַע (nā**k**ă'ʻ) to turn away [*intr.*].

נָקַף[1] (nā**k**ă'f) *Pi.* נִקֵּף, to cut down, to fell; to destroy.

נָקַף[2] (nā**k**ă'f) *fut.* יִנְקֹף, to go round, to move in a circle. — *Hi.* הִקִּיף, *inf.* הַקֵּף, *imp. pl.* הַקִּיפוּ, *fut.* יַקִּיף, *pt.* מַקִּיף, to let go round, to make round, to surround, to draw arround.

נֹ֫קֶף (nō'kĕf) *m* the shaking or beating off [fruits].

נִקְפָּה (nĭkpā') *f* rope [for a girdle].

נָקַר (nākă'r) *inf.* נְקוֹר, *fut.* יִקֹּר, to bore, pierce, hollow out. — *Pi.* נִקֵּר, *fut.* יְנַקֵּר the same as *Qal.* — *Pu.* נֻקַּר to be dug out.

נְקָרָה (nᵉkārā') *f, c.* נִקְרַת, *pl. c.* נִקְרוֹת, a hole, cavern.

נָקַשׁ (nākă'š) *pt.* נוֹקֵשׁ, to snare, ensnare. — *Ni. fut.* יִנָּקֵשׁ to be snared, to be seduced. — *Pi. fut.* יְנַקֵּשׁ to lay a snare. — *Hith. pt.* מִתְנַקֵּשׁ to lay a snare.

נֵר¹ (nēr) *m, w.s.* נֵרִי, *pl.* נֵרוֹת, נֵרֹת, light, lamp; prosperity, instruction.

נֵר² (nēr) *pr.n.m.*

נֵרְגַל (nērgă'l) *pr.n.* of an idol of the Cuthites, the planet Mars.

נֵרְגַל שַׁרְאֶצֶר (nērgă'l săr-'ĕ'ßĕr) *pr.n.m.*

נִרְגָּן (nĭrgā'n) *m* whisperer, slanderer.

נֵרְדְּ (nērd) *m, w.s.* נִרְדִּי, *pl.* נְרָדִים, nard, a fragrant grass.

נֵרִיָּה (nē'rĭyyā') *pr.n.m.*

נָשָׂא (nāßā') *inf.* נָשׂא, נָשׂוֹא, נְשׂא, שְׂאֵת, שֵׂאת, *imp.* שָׂא, נְשָׂא [נְסָה], שְׂאִי, שְׂאוּ, *fut.* יִשָּׂא, *pt.* נֹשֵׂא, *pl.* נֹשְׂאִים, *c.* נֹשְׂאֵי, *f* נֹשֵׂאת, *pl.* נֹשְׂאֹת, *pt. p.* נָשׂוּא, *c.* נְשׂוּא, נְשׂוּי, *pl.* נְשׂוּאִים, to raise, to lift up [the countenance, the eyes, the voice, the soul]; to bear, to carry, to wear; to take, to take away; to accept, to be partial. — *Ni.* נִשָּׂא, *imp.* הִנָּשֵׂא, *fut.* יִנָּשֵׂא, *pt.* נִשָּׂא, *pl. m* נִשָּׂאִים, *f* נִשָּׂאוֹת, to be lifted up, to be raised; to be elevated, extolled, exalted; to be borne, carried, taken away. — *Pi.* נִשֵּׂא, *imp.* נַשֵּׂא, *fut.* יְנַשֵּׂא, to raise, lift up, exalt, heighten; to support, help; to carry off. — *Hi.* הִשִּׂיא to cause to bear; to apply to. — *Hith. fut.* יִתְנַשֵּׂא, יִנַּשֵּׂא, *pt.* מִתְנַשֵּׂא, to raise oneself, to be exalted, to be proud, haughty.

נָשַׂג (nāßă'g) *Hi.* הִשִּׂיג, *inf.* הַשֵּׂג, *fut.* יַשִּׂיג, יַשֵּׂג, *pt.* מַשִּׂיג, to reach, catch, overtake; to attain to, to obtain, to acquire; to bring near.

נְשׂוּאָה (nᵉśū'ā') *f, pl.* נְשׂוּאֹת, idol carried in procession.

נָשִׂיא (nāśī') *m, c.* נְשִׂיא, *pl.* נְשִׂאִים, *c.* נְשִׂיאֵי, an exalted one, prince, king, chief; rising vapour, mist, cloud.

נָשַׂק (nāśa'k) *Ni.* נִשַּׂק to be kindled. — *Hi.* הִשִּׂיק, *fut.* יַשִּׂיק, to kindle, to set on fire.

נָשָׁא[1] (nāšā') *pt.* נֹשֶׁא, נֹשֵׁא, to lend on usury; *pt.* money-lender, creditor. — *Hi. fut.* יַשִּׁיא, to vex like a creditor.

נָשָׁא[2] (nāšā') *inf.* נְשֹׁא see נָשָׁה. — *Ni.* נִשָּׁא to be deceived. — *Hi.* הִשִּׁיא, *fut.* יַשִּׁיא, יַשִּׁא, יַשִּׁי, to lead astray, to mislead, to deceive, to seduce; to surprise, to oppress.

נָשַׁב (nāša'b) to breathe, to blow. — *Hi. fut.* יַשִּׁיב, יַשֵּׁב, to cause to blow; to blow away.

נָשָׁה (nāšā') *inf.* נְשֹׁא [for נְשֹׁה], *pt.* נֹשֶׁה, *pl.* נֹשִׁים, to neglect, to forget; to loan, to lend on usury; *pt.* usurer, creditor. — *Ni. fut.* יִנָּשֶׁה to be forgotten. — *Pi.* נִשָּׁה, *w.s.* נַשַּׁנִי, to cause to forget. — *Hi.* הִשָּׁה, *fut.* יַשֶּׁה, to cause to forget; to lend to.

נָשֶׁה (nāšẹ') *m* sinew, tendon in the thigh, hip-sinew.

נְשִׁי (nᵉšī') *m, w.s.* נִשְׁיֵךְ, debt.

נְשִׁיָּה (nᵉšīyyā') *f* forgetfulness, oblivion.

נָשִׁים see **אִשָּׁה**.

נַשִּׁים see **שָׁמַם**.

נְשִׁיקָה (nᵉšīkā') *f* a kiss.

נָשַׁךְ (nāša'ch) *fut.* יִשֹּׁךְ, יִשַּׁךְ, *pt.* נֹשֵׁךְ, *pt. p.* נָשׁוּךְ, to bite, to vex, to inflict injury. — *Pi.* נִשֵּׁךְ, *fut.* יְנַשֵּׁךְ, to bite, to sting. — *Hi.* הִשִּׁיךְ, *fut.* יַשִּׁיךְ, *pt.* מַשִּׁיךְ, to lend on usury; to impose tribute.

נֶשֶׁךְ (nẹ'šẹch) *m* interest, usury.

נִשְׁכָּה (nīškā') *f* = לִשְׁכָּה, cell, appartment.

נָשַׁל (nāša'l) *imp.* שַׁל, *fut.* יִשַּׁל, to draw off, to pull off; to reject, cast out; *intr.* to fall off, to drop off. — *Pi. fut.* יְנַשֵּׁל to expel, to drive out.

נָשַׁם (nāšă'm) *fut.* 1. *sg.* אֶשֹּׁם, to breathe, to pant.

נְשָׁמָה (nᵉšāmā') *f*, *c.* נִשְׁמַת, *pl.* נְשָׁמוֹת, breath, breathing, panting; breathing being, animal, living soul.

נָשַׁף (nāšă'f) to breathe, to blow.

נֶשֶׁף (nĕ'šĕf) *m* a blowing, cooling; twilight, darkness.

נָשַׁק (nāšă'**k**) *inf.* נְשֹׁק, נְשָׁק־, *imp.* שַׁק, שָׁקָה, *fut.* יִשַּׁק, *pt.* נֹשֵׁק, to kiss; to be attached; to put on, to arm oneself. — *Pi. inf.* נַשֵּׁק, *imp. pl.* נַשְּׁקוּ, *fut.* יְנַשֵּׁק, to kiss. — *Hi.* הִשִּׁיק, *pt. f/pl.* מַשִּׁיקוֹת, to touch, to fit to one another.

נֶשֶׁק (nĕ'šĕ**k**), **נֵשֶׁק** (nē'šĕ**k**) *m*, *i.p.* נָשֶׁק, armour, arms; armoury, arsenal.

נֶשֶׁר (nĕ'šĕr) *m*, *i.p.* נָשֶׁר, *pl.* נְשָׁרִים, *c.* נִשְׁרֵי, eagle, vulture, or other bird of prey.

נָשַׁת (nāšă'ϑ) to be parched, to be dried up. — *Ni.* נִשַּׁת to be dried up, to be drained.

נִשְׁתְּוָן (nĭštᵉvā'n) *m* letter, epistle [Persian].

נָתַח (nāϑă'ḥ) *Pi.* נִתַּח, *fut.* יְנַתַּח, to cut in pieces [flesh].

נֵתַח (nē'ϑăḥ) *m*, *pl.* נְתָחִים, a piece of flesh.

נָתִיב (nāϑī'b) *m*, *c.* נְתִיב, and **נְתִיבָה** (nᵉϑībā') *f*, *pl.* נְתִיבִים, נְתִיבוֹת, trodden way, path.

נָתִין (nāϑī'n) *m*, only *pl.* נְתִינִים, a dedicated one, servant of the temple.

נָתַךְ (nāϑă'ḳ) *fut.* יִתַּךְ, to be poured out, to flow out. — *Ni.* נִתַּךְ, *pt. f* נִתֶּכֶת, to be poured out; to be melted, dissolved. — *Hi.* הִתִּיךְ, *inf.* הַנְתִּיךְ, *fut.* יַתִּיךְ, to pour out, to melt. — *Ho.* יֻתַּךְ to be melted.

נָתַן (nāϑă'n) *pf.* 2. *sg.* נָתַתָּ, נָתַתָּה, תַּתָּה [for נָתַנְתָּ], *inf.* תֵּת, תְּנָה, נְתֹן, נָתֹן, נָתוֹן, *w.s.* תִּתִּי, *imp.* תֵּן, תֶּן־, תְּנָה, *fut.* יִתֵּן, יִתֶּן־, *pt.* נֹתֵן, נוֹתֵן, *pt. p.* נָתוּן, to give, to hand over, to grant, to yield; to allow, permit; to put, place, establish, constitute; to make, render. — *Ni.* נִתַּן, *inf.* הִנָּתֹן, הִנָּתֵן, *fut.* יִנָּתֵן, *pt.* נִתָּן, to be given, to be given over, to be delivered; to be placed; to be reduced. — *Ho.* הֻתַּן, *fut.* יֻתַּן, to be given, put, placed.

נָתָן (nāϑā'n); **נְתַנְאֵל** (nᵉϑăn'ēl); **נְתַנְיָה** (nᵉϑănyā'), **נְתַנְיָהוּ** (nᵉϑănyā'hū); **נְתַן־מֶלֶךְ** (nᵉϑăn mĕ'lĕḵ) *pr.n.m.*

נָתַס (nāϑă's) to tear up, to destroy.

נָתַע (nāϑă'ʻ) *Ni.* נִתַּע to be broken out, to be crushed.

נָתַץ (nāϑă'ṣ) *fut.* יִתֹּץ, to pull down, to break down, to destroy; to knock out [teeth]. — *Ni.* נִתַּץ to be torn down, to be destroyed. — *Pi.* נִתֵּץ, *fut.* יְנַתֵּץ, to break, to smash. — *Pu.* נֻתַּץ to be broken, smashed down. — *Ho. fut.* יֻתַּץ, to be broken up.

נָתַק (nāϑă'k) *fut.* יִתַּק, *pt. p.* נָתוּק, to tear away, to cut off; to castrate. — *Ni.* נִתַּק, *fut.* יִנָּתֵק, to be torn or broken off; to be pulled, torn out; to be torn away, removed. — *Hi.* הִתִּיק, *inf.* הַתִּיק, to push away; to cut off. — *Ho.* הָנְתַּק to be driven away, to be removed.

נֶתֶק (nĕ'ϑĕk) *m* scurf, scab; one affected with the mange.

נָתַר[1] (nāϑă'r) *fut.* יִתַּר, to be startled, to tremble. — *Pi. inf.* נַתֵּר to spring, to leap. — *Hi.* הִתִּיר, *imp.* הַתֵּר, *fut.* יַתֵּר, to cause to tremble.

נָתַר[2] (nāϑă'r) *Hi.* הִתִּיר, *fut.* יַתִּיר, to loose, to untie, to set free.

נֶתֶר (nĕ'ϑĕr) *m* an alkaline salt, natron, potash.

נָתַשׁ (nāϑă'š) *inf.* נְתוֹשׁ, *fut.* יִתּוֹשׁ, to tear out, to root out, to expel, to destroy. — *Ni.* נִתַּשׁ, *fut.* יִנָּתֵשׁ, to be rooted out, to be destroyed; to be dried up. *Ho. fut.* יֻתַּשׁ, to be rooted out.

ס

ס the fifteenth letter of the alphabet, called סָמֶךְ [support]; as a numeral = 60.

סְאָה (sᵉʼā') *f, pl.* סְאִים, *du.* סָאתַיִם, a measure for grain, one third of an Ephah, one thirtieth of a

Kor or Homer; בְּסַאסְּאָה moderately.

סְאוֹן (sᵉ'ō'n) *m* shoe, boot; others: armour.

סָאַן (sā'ă'n) [*denom.* of סְאוֹן], *pt.* סֹאֵן, to put on [shoes], to be shod; to equip oneself.

סַאסְּאָה = סְאָה סְאָה. see סְאָה.

סָבָא[1] (sābā') *fut.* יִסְבָּא, 1. *pl.* נִסְבְּאָה, *pt.* סֹבֵא, *pl.* סֹבְאִים, *pt. p.* סָבוּא, to drink, to quaff, to tipple; to be drunk.

סָבָא[2] (sābā') *m*, only *pl.* סֻבָאִים, drunkard.

סֹבֶא (sō'bĕ) *m* drink, wine; carousal.

סְבָא (sᵉbā') *pr.n.* of a son of Cush, and a people in Ethiopia [Meroe].

סָבַב (sābă'b) *inf.* סֹב, סְבֹב, *imp.* סֹב, *fut.* יָסֹב, *pt.* סוֹבֵב, to go round, to go in a circle, to surround, to encompass, to besiege; to go or turn about; to change; to bring about. — *Ni.* נָסַב, *fut.* יִסֹּב, to turn oneself; to place oneself in a circle; to turn to, to turn about. — *Pi. inf.* סַבֵּב to change, to alter. — *Po.* סוֹבֵב, *fut.* יְסוֹבֵב, יְסֹבֵב, to go about; to encompass; to surround. — *Hi.* הֵסֵב, *inf.* and *imp.* הָסֵב, *fut.* יָסֵב, יַסֵּב, *pt.* מֵסֵב, to cause to turn; to change; to transfer; to bring; to direct, to conduct, to lead about; to surround; to go about. — *Ho.* הוּסַב, *fut.* יוּסַב, *pt.* מוּסָב, *f/pl.* מֻסַבּוֹת, מוּסַבֹּת, to be turned; to be turning, to revolve; to be surrounded; to be changed.

סִבָּה (sĭbbā') *f* a turn, course; divine ordinance.

סָבִיב (sābī'b) *m*, *c.* סְבִיב, *pl.* סְבִיבִים, סְבִיבוֹת, circle, circuit; *pl.* environs, neighbourhood; *adv.* round about.

סְבִיבָה see סָבִיב.

סָבַךְ (sābă'ch) *pt. p.* סָבֻךְ, to interweave, to fold together. — *Pu. fut.* יְסֻבַּךְ, to be interwoven.

סְבָךְ (sᵉbā'ch) *m* and **סֲבֶךְ** (sĕ'bĕch) *m*, *c.* סְבַךְ, *pl. c.* סִבְכֵי, thicket, shrubbery.

סֹבֶךְ (sō'bĕch) *m*, *w.s.* סֻבְּכוֹ, סֻבֳּכוֹ, i. q. סְבָךְ.

סִבְּכַי (sĭbbᵉchă'y) *pr.n.m.*

סָבַל (ßāḇă'l) *inf.* סְבֹל, *fut.* יִסְבֹּל, to bear, to suffer, to carry. — *Pu. pt.* מְסֻבָּל, to be pregnant. — *Hith.* הִסְתַּבֵּל, to be burdensome, to drag along [*intr.*].

סַבָּל (ßăbbā'l) *m* bearer, porter.

סֵבֶל (ßē'ḇĕl) *m* burden, charge.

סֹבֶל (ßō'ḇĕl) *m, w.s.* סֻבֳּלוֹ (ßŭbbºlō'), burden.

סְבָלָה (ßºḇālā') *f*, only *pl. c.* סִבְלוֹת, hard labour, heavy task.

סִבֹּלֶת (ßĭbbō'lĕϑ) Ephraimitic pronunciation of שִׁבֹּלֶת.

סִבְרַיִם (ßĭḇră'yĭm) *pr.n.* of a town in Syria.

סְבָא, סַבְתָּה, סַבְתָּא (ßăḇtā') *pr.n.m.* of a son of Cush, people in southern Arabia.

סַבְתְּכָא (ßăḇtºḵā') *pr.n.m.* of a son of Cush, people east of the Persian gulf.

סָגַד (ßāgă'ḏ) *fut.* יִסְגּוֹד, יִסְגֹּד, to bow down, to fall down, to adore [an idol].

סְגוֹר (ßºgō'r) *m* enclosure; — זָהָב סָגוּר gold kept in a treasury, fine gold; spear or battle-axe.

סִגִּים see סִיג.

סְגֻלָּה (ßºgŭllā') *f* property, possession.

סָגָן (ßāgā'n) *m*, only *pl.* סְגָנִים, prefect, governor, nobleman.

סָגַר (ßāgă'r) *inf.* סְגוֹר, *imp.* סְגֹר, *fut.* יִסְגֹּר, *pt.* סֹגֵר, *f* סֹגֶרֶת, *pt. p.* סָגוּר, to surround, to enclose; to shut, to close, to shut up; זָהָב סָגוּר solid, fine gold [see סְגוֹר]. — *Ni.* נִסְגַּר, *fut.* יִסָּגֵר, to be shut; to be shut up; to shut oneself in. — *Pi.* סִגֵּר, *fut.* יְסַגֵּר, to deliver over, to give up. — *Pu.* סֻגַּר, *pt. f* מְסֻגֶּרֶת, to be shut, to be barred. — *Hi.* הִסְגִּיר, *inf.* הַסְגִּיר, *fut.* יַסְגִּיר, יַסְגֵּר, to shut up or in; to deliver over, to give up to, to abandon.

סַגְרִיר (ßăgrī'r) *m* heavy rain, rain-gush.

סַד (ßăḏ) *m* stocks [for the feet of a culprit].

סָדִין (ßāḏī'n) *m, pl.* סְדִינִים, linen garment, shirt.

סְדֹם (ßºḏō'm) *pr.n.* of a town, Sodom.

סֶדֶר (ßĕ'ḏĕr) *m*, only *pl* סְדָרִים, order, rank, row.

סַהַר (ßă'hăr) *m* roundness.

סֹהַר (ßǫ'hăr) *m* tower, prison.

סוֹא (ßǫ) *pr.n.m.* of an Egyptian king, Sabaco or Sethos.

סוּג[1] (ßūg) *pf.* סָג, *fut.* יָסוּג, *pt. p.* סוּג, to go back, to draw back; to hedge in. — *Ni.* נָסוֹג, *fut.* יִסֹּג, *pt. pl.* נְסוֹגִים, to draw back, to retreat, to turn apostate. — *Hi.* הִסִּיג to put away or back, to remove. — *Ho.* הֻסַּג to be driven back, to be removed.

סוּג[2] (ßūg) *m* dross, refuse.

סוּגַר (ßūgă'r) *m* prison, cage.

סוֹד (ßǫd) *m* a sitting, session, consultation, talk, association, counsel, secret.

סוֹדִי (ßǫdī'); **סוּחַ** (ßū'ach) *pr.n.m.*

סוּחָה (ßūchā') *f* sweepings, filth, dung.

סוּטַי (ßūtă'y) *pr.n.m.*

סוּךְ (ßūch) *pf.* סָךְ, *inf.* סוֹךְ, *fut.* יָסוּךְ [יָסַךְ see יִיסַךְ], to pour out, to anoint; to anoint oneself. — *Hi.* הֵסִיךְ, *fut.* וַיָּסֶךְ, to anoint [oneself].

סְוֵנֵה (ßᵉvēnē') *pr.n.* of an Egyptian town, Syene.

סוּס[1] (ßūß) *m*, *pl.* סוּסִים, *c.* סוּסֵי, horse, war-horse.

סוּס[2] (ßūß) *m* swallow.

סוּסָה (ßūßā') *f* a mare.

סוּסִי (ßūßī') *pr.n.m.*

סוּף[1] (ßūf) *pf.* סָף, *fut.* יָסוּף, to be at an end, to cease, vanish, perish. — *Hi.* הֵסִיף, *fut.* יָסִיף, יָסֵף, to bring to an end, to destroy.

סוּף[2] (ßūf) *m* sea weed, reed, rushes, bulrushes; יַם־סוּף northwestern part of the Red Sea.

סוּף[3] (ßūf) *pr.n.* of a place.

סוֹף (ßǫf) *m* the end, the last.

סוּפָה (ßūfā') *f*, *pl.* סוּפוֹת, tempest, hurricane, whirlwind.

סוּר[1] (ßūr) *pf.* סָר, *inf.* סוֹר, סוּר, *imp.* סוּר, *fut.* יָסוּר, וַיָּסַר, *pt.* סָר, to turn aside, to go away, to recede, to depart, to apostatise; to forsake; to pass away, cease; to turn to, to apply to, to approach, to turn in, to alight. — *Pi.* סוֹרֵר *tr.* to turn aside, to pervert. — *Hi.* הֵסִיר, *inf.* הָסֵר,

הֵסִיר, *imp.* הָסֵר, *fut.* יָסִיר, יָסֵר, וַיָּסַר, *pt.* מֵסִיר, to cause to turn away, to make depart or disappear, to put away, to take away, to remove; to cause to turn to, to let come to.— *Ho.* הוּסַר, *fut.* יוּסַר, *pt.* מוּסָר, to be taken or carried away, to be removed.

סוּר² (sūr) *adj.*, *f* סוּרָה, separated, removed, departed; infidel, rebellious; wild twig of a vine.

סוּר³ (sūr) *pr.n.* of a gate of the temple.

סוּת¹ (sūth) *Hi.* הֵסִית, הִסִּית, *fut.* יָסִית, יַסִּית, וַיָּסֶת, to incite, to stimulate, to urge on, to persuade, to entice, to seduce.

סוּת² (sūth) *f*, *w.s.* סוּתֹה, garment, clothing.

סָחַב (sāchă'b) *inf.* סָחוֹב, סְחֹב, *fut.* יִסְחַב, to draw, drag, trail, pull; to tear to rags.

סְחָבָה (sᵉchābā') *f*, only *pl.* סְחָבוֹת, old, torn clothes, rags.

סָחָה (sāchā') *Pi.* סִחָה to wipe off, to sweep away.

סְחִי (sᵉchī') *m* sweepings, offscouring, dirt.

סָחִישׁ (sāchī'sh) *m* after-growth, what grows spontaneously after reaping.

סָחַף (sāchă'f) *pt.* סֹחֵף, to sweep or wash away. — *Ni.* נִסְחַף to be thrown down, to be prostrate.

סָחַר (sāchă'r) *fut.* יִסְחַר, *pt.* סֹחֵר, *pl.* סֹחֲרִים, *c.* סֹחֲרֵי, *f* סֹחֶרֶת, to go about, to roam about, to traverse [a land]; to go about as a trader; *pt.* trader, merchant, buyer, seller. — *Pilp.* סְחַרְחַר to palpitate, to throb.

סָחָר (sāchā'r) *m*, *c.* סְחַר, trade, traffic; mart; gain.

סַחַר (să'chăr) *m*, *w.s.* סַחְרָהּ, the same as סָחָר.

סֹחֵרָה (sō'chērā') *f* a shield.

סְחֹרָה (sᵉchōrā') *f* trade, traffic; merchants.

סֹחֶרֶת (sōchĕ'rĕth) *f* a kind of red or black marble; see also סַחַר.

סֵט (sēt) *m*, only *pl.* סֵטִים, transgression, error, sin.

סִיג (sīg) *m*, *pl.* סִיגִים, refuse, offal, dross, base metal.

סִיוָן (sîvā'n) *pr.n.m.*, the third month of the Hebrew year [June and July].

סִיחוֹן, סִיחֹן (sîḥō'n) *pr.n.m.*

סִין (sîn) *pr.n.* of a desert near Mount Sinai; *pr.n.* of a town in Egypt, Pelusium.

סִינַי (sînā'y) *pr.n.* of a mountain, Sinai.

סִינִי (sînî') *pr.n.m.* of a son of Canaan, and of a people near Lebanon.

סִינִים (sînî'm) *pr.n.m. pl.*, a people in the far East, the Chinese; אֶרֶץ ס׳ China.

סִיס (sîs) *m* swallow [= סוּס²].

סִיסְרָא (sî'serā') *pr.n.m.*

סִיעָה (sîʿā') or קִיעֲהָא (sî'ʿahā') *pr.n.m.*

סִיר¹ (sîr) *m* [and *f*], *pl.* סִירֹת, סִירוֹת, vessel, pot, bowl, kettle.

סִיר² (sîr) *m*, *pl.* סִירִים, סִירוֹת, thorns, briars; fish-hook.

סָךְ (sāḵ) *m* mass of people, crowd.

סֹךְ (sōḵ) *m*, *w.s.* סֻכּוֹ, סֻכָּה, hut, tent; covert, thicket.

סֻכָּה (sŭkkā') *f*, *c.* סֻכַּת, *pl.* סֻכֹּת, סֻכּוֹת, booth, hut, arbour, tent, house, covert; חַג הַסֻּכּוֹת the feast of tabernacles.

סֻכּוֹת (sŭkkō'th) *pr.n.* of a station in Goshen; *pr.n.* of towns in Gad.

סֻכּוֹת בְּנוֹת (sŭkkō'th benō'th) *pr.n.* of a Babylonian idol [or huts for worshipping it].

סִכּוּת (sîkkū'th) *pr.n.* of a Babylonian deity.

סֻכִּיִּים (sŭkkîyyî'm) *pr.n.* of a people, Troglodytes in Ethiopia.

סָכַךְ (sāḵā'ḵ) *fut.* יָסֹךְ, *pt.* סֹכֵךְ, *pl.* סֹכְכִים, to cover, protect, shelter, hide; to plait, to interweave. — *Hi.* הֵסֵךְ, *inf.* הָסֵךְ, *fut.* יָסֵךְ, וַיָּסֶךְ, *pt.* מֵסִיךְ [for מֵסֵךְ], to cover, protect, shelter, surround, enclose, hedge in; הֵסֵךְ רַגְלָיו to cover one's feet, i. e. to ease one-self. — *Ho.* הוּסַךְ, *fut.* יֻסַךְ, to be covered. — *Pilp.* סִכְסֵךְ to incite, to stir up.

סֹכֵךְ (sōḵē'ḵ) *m* a sheltering roof or covering.

סְכָכָה (seḵāḵā') *pr.n.* of a place in Judah.

סָכַל (sāḵā'l) *Ni.* נִסְכַּל, to

act foolishly, wickedly. — *Pi. imp.* -סַכֵּל, *fut.* יְסַכֵּל, to make foolish, to frustrate. — *Hi.* הִסְכִּיל to commit folly, to act foolishly.

סָכָל (sāḥā'l) *m* fool, foolish.

סֶכֶל (se'ḥel) *m* folly.

סִכְלוּת (siḥlū'th) *f* folly.

סָכַן¹ (sāḥa'n) *fut.* יִסְכֹּן, *pt.* סֹכֵן, *f* סֹכֶנֶת, to be familiar, to manage, to perform, to administer; to do useful service; *pt.* keeper, steward, administrator.—*Hi.* הִסְכִּין, *inf.* הַסְכֵּן, to be familiar, to be accustomed.

סָכַן² (sāḥa'n) *Ni. fut.* יִסָּכֵן, to be endangered, hurt.— *Pu. pt.* מְסֻכָּן to be impoverished, to be poor.

סָכַר¹ (sāḥa'r) *Ni.* נִסְכַּר, *fut.* יִסָּכֵר, to be shut, stopped. — *Pi.* סִכֵּר to deliver, to give up.

סָכַר² (sāḥa'r) = שָׂכַר.

סָכַת (sāḥa'th) *Hi.* הִסְכִּית, *imp.* הַסְכֵּת, to keep silence.

סַל (sal) *m, pl.* סַלִּים, *c.* סַלֵּי, basket.

סָלָא (sālā') *Pu. pt.* מְסֻלָּא, to be weighed.

סִלָּא (sillā') *pr.n.* of a locality [street or highway], or of a town near Jerusalem.

סָלַד (sāla'd) *Pi. fut.* יְסַלֵּד, to exult, to rejoice.

סֶלֶד (se'led) *pr.n.m.*

סָלָה (sālā') to despise, to reject. — *Pi.* סִלָּה same as *Qal.* — *Pu. fut.* יְסֻלֶּה to be weighed [see סָלָא *Pu.*].

סֶלָה (se'lā) *m* a musical term: pause, silence, interlude, elevation of the voice.

סַלּוּא, סָלוּא, סַלּוּ (sallū') *pr.n.m.*

סַלּוֹן (sallō'n), **סִלּוֹן** (sillō'n) *m* thorn.

סָלַח (sāla'ḥ) *inf.* סְלֹחַ, *imp.* סְלַח, *fut.* יִסְלַח, אֶסְלוֹחַ, *pt.* סֹלֵחַ, to forgive, pardon. — *Ni.* נִסְלַח to be forgiven, pardoned.

סַלָּח (sallā'ḥ) *adj.* forgiving, gracious, merciful.

סַלַּי (salla'y) *pr.n.m.*

סְלִיחָה (seliḥā') *f* forgiveness, pardon.

סַלְכָה (salḥā') *pr.n.* of a town in Bashan.

סָלַל (sāla'l) *imp. pl.* סֹלּוּ, *w.s.* סָלּוּהָ (sollū'hā), *fut.* יָסֹל,

pt. p. f סְלוּלָה, to heap up, to pile up, to cast up [earth for making a road]. — *Pilp. imp. w.s.* סַלְסְלֶהָ, to extol, to esteem highly. — *Hith.* הִסְתּוֹלֵל to resist like a barrier.

סֹלְלָה (sō'lᵉlā') *f* mound, wall, rampart.

סֻלָּם (sŭllā'm) *m* ladder, stairs.

סַלְסִלָּה (sălsĭllā') *f*, only *pl.* סַלְסִלּוֹת, basket.

סֶלַע[1] (sĕ'lăᵉ) *m*, *i.p.* סָלַע, *w.s.* סַלְעִי, *pl.* סְלָעִים, rock, cliff.

סֶלַע[2] (sĕ'lăᵉ) *pr.n.* of the chief-town in Idumea, Petra.

סָלְעָם (sălᵉā'm) *m* a kind of eatable winged locust.

סָלַף (sālă'f) *Pi.* סִלֵּף, *fut.* יְסַלֵּף, to pervert, corrupt; to overthrow, destroy.

סֶלֶף (sĕ'lĕf) *m* perversity.

סָלַק (sālă'k) *fut.* 1. *sg.* אֶסַּק or אֶסְלַק, to ascend.

סֹלֶת (sō'lĕϑ) *f* and *m* fine meal, flour.

סַם (săm) *m*, only *pl.* סַמִּים, perfume, aromatics, spices.

סַמְגַּר נְבוֹ (sămgă'r nᵉbū') *pr.n.m.*

סְמָדַר (sᵉmādă'r) *m*, *i.p.* סְמָדָר, bud, blossom [of the vine].

סָמַךְ (sāmă'ф) *imp. w.s.* סָמְכֵנִי (sŏmфē'nī), *fut.* יִסְמֹךְ, *pt.* סוֹמֵךְ, *pl. c.* סֹמְכֵי, *pt. p.* סָמוּךְ, to support, to lean, to press, to lie on, to lay hold of; to prop, to aid, to assist; to draw near. — *Ni.* נִסְמַךְ, *fut.* יִסָּמֵךְ, to be supported, to support oneself.— *Pi. imp.* סַמֵּךְ to support, to refresh.

סְמַכְיָהוּ (sᵉmăфyā'hū) *pr.n.m.*

סֶמֶל (sĕ'mĕl), סֵמֶל (sē'mĕl) *m*, *i.p.* סָמֶל, likeness, image, statue.

סָמַן (sāmă'n) *Ni. pt.* נִסְמָן, to be marked, determined.

סָמַר (sāmă'r) to bristle, to stand on end, to shudder. — *Pi. fut.* יְסַמֵּר, to stand erect.

סָמָר (sāmā'r) *adj.* bristling.

סְנָאָה (sᵉnā'ā') *pr.n.* of a town in Judah.

סַנְבַלַּט (sănbăllă't) *pr.n.m.*

סְנֶה (sᵉnĕ') *m* thorn-bush.

סֶנֶּה (sĕ'nĕ) *pr.n.* of a rock.

סְנוּאָה (s'nū'ā') *pr.n.m.* or *f.*

סַנְוֵר (sănvē'r) *m*, only *pl.* סַנְוֵרִים blindness.

סַנְחֵרִיב (sănchērī'b) *pr.n.m.*

סַנְסַן (sănsă'n) *m*, only *pl.* סַנְסִנִּים, twig of a palm-tree.

סַנְסַנָּה (sănsănnā') *pr.n.* of a town in Judah.

סַנְפִּיר (sănpī'r) *m* fin [of a fish].

סָס (sās) *m* a moth.

סִסְמַי (sĭsmă'y) *pr.n.m.*

סָעַד (sā'ă'd) *inf. w.s.* סַעֲדָהּ, *imp.* סַעֲדָה (sŏ'odā'), *fut.* יִסְעַד, to support, to make firm, to assist, to help, to refresh.

סָעָה (sā'ā') *pt. f* סֹעָה, to rush forth.

סָעִיף[1] (sā'ī'f) *m*, *pl. w.s.* סְעִפֶּיהָ, twig, tender branch.

סָעִיף[2] (sā'ī'f) *m*, *c.* סְעִיף, *pl.* סְעִפִּים, *c.* סְעִפֵּי, cleft, fissure.

סָעַף (sā'ă'f) *Pi. pt.* מְסָעֵף, to cut off boughs.

סֵעֵף (sē'ē'f) *adj.*, *pl.* סֵעֲפִים, wavering in opinion, doubter, sceptic.

סְעַפָּה (s''ăppā') *f*, only *pl.* סְעַפּוֹת, twig, branch.

סְעִפָּה (s''ĭppā') *f*, *pl.* סְעִפִּים, divided opinion, division, party.

סָעַר (sā'ă'r) *fut.* יִסְעַר, *pt.* סֹעֵר, *f* סֹעֲרָה, to storm, rage, to be agitated. — *Ni. fut.* יִסָּעֵר to be moved, to be restless.—*Pi. fut.* 1. *sg.* אֲסָעֵר to toss about. — *Pu.* סֹעַר, *fut.* יְסֹעַר, to be whirled about.

סַעַר (să'ăr) *m*, *i.p.* סָעַר, *w.s.* סַעַרְךָ, storm, tempest, hurricane.

סְעָרָה (s''ārā') *f*, *c.* סַעֲרַת, *pl.* סְעָרוֹת, *c.* סַעֲרוֹת = סַעַר.

סַף[1] (săf) *m*, *i.p.* סָף, *pl.* סִפִּים and סִפּוֹת, basin, bowl.

סַף[2] (săf) *m*, *pl.* סִפִּים, threshold, entrance.

סַף[3] (săf) *pr.n.m.*

סָפַד (săfă'd) *inf.* סְפֹד, *imp. pl.* סִפְדוּ, *fut.* יִסְפֹּד, *pt.* סֹפֵד, to lament, to mourn. — *Ni.* נִסְפַּד, *fut.* יִסָּפֵד, to be lamented.

סָפָה (sāfā') *inf.* סְפוֹת, *imp. pl.* סְפוּ, *fut.* יִסְפֶּה, to take off, to shave; to destroy; *intr.* to perish; to add, to augment. — *Ni.*

נִסְפָּה, *fut.* יִסָּפֶה, *pt.* נִסְפֶּה, to be taken away, to be destroyed, to perish; to be seized. — *Hi. fut.* יַסְפֶּה to collect, to heap up.

סָפַח[1] (ßāfă'ḥ) *imp. w.s.* סְפָחֵנִי, to attach, to associate. — *Ni.* נִסְפַּח to attach oneself. — *Hith. inf.* הִסְתַּפֵּחַ, to join oneself, to adhere to.

סָפַח[2] (ßāfă'ḥ) *Pi. pt.* מְסַפֵּחַ, to pour out. — *Pu. fut.* יְסֻפַּח, to be poured out, to be prostrate.

סַפַּחַת (ßăppă'ḥăϑ) *f* scurf, scab.

סָפִיחַ (ßāfī'aḥ) *m, c.* סְפִיחַ, *pl.* סְפִיחִים, rain, flood; spontaneous growth.

סְפִינָה (ßᵉfīnā') *f* ship.

סַפִּיר (ßăppī'r) *m, pl.* סַפִּירִים, sapphire.

סֵפֶל (ßē'fĕl) *m* bowl, dish, cup.

סָפַן (ßāfă'n) *fut.* יִסְפֹּן, *pt. p.* סָפוּן, סָפֻן, to cover, to roof, to overlay, to wainscot; to preserve.

סִפֻּן (ßĭppū'n) *m* ceiling, wainscoting.

סָפַף (ßāfă'f) *Hith.* הִסְתּוֹפֵף [*denom.* of סַף[2]], to stand at the threshold, to be a door-keeper.

סָפַק[1] (ßāfă'k) *fut.* יִסְפֹּק, to strike, thrust, slap; to clap [the hands]; to punish, to chastise; to fall into.

סָפַק[2] (ßāfă'k) to overflow, to vomit.

סֵפֶק (ßē'fĕk) *m, w.s.* סִפְקוֹ, abundance.

סָפַר (ßāfă'r) *inf.* סְפֹר, *imp.* סְפֹר, *fut.* יִסְפֹּר, *pt.* סֹפֵר, to write; *pt.* writer, scribe, secretary, chancellor; to number, to count, to tell, to measure. — *Ni.* נִסְפַּר, *fut.* יִסָּפֵר, to be numbered. — *Pi.* סִפֵּר, *inf.* and *imp.* סַפֵּר, *fut.* יְסַפֵּר, *pt.* מְסַפֵּר, to count; to tell, relate, narrate, to celebrate, make known, praise; to speak. — *Pu.* סֻפַּר, *fut.* יְסֻפַּר, to be told, recounted.

סֵפֶר (ßē'fĕr) *m, w.s.* סִפְרְךָ, *pl.* סְפָרִים, *c.* סִפְרֵי, a writing, letter, document, bill; book, book-roll.

סְפָר[1] (ßᵉfā'r) *m* a numbering, census.

סְפָר[2] (ßᵉfā'r) *pr.n.* of a town in Hadramaut.

סְפָרַד (s'fără'd) *pr.n.* of a country near the Black-Sea [wrongly Spain].

סִפְרָה (sĭfrā') *f* book or enumeration.

סְפֹרָה (s'fōrā') *f*, only *pl.* סְפֹרוֹת, number, measure, limit.

סְפַרְוַיִם (s'fărvă'yĭm) *pr.n.* of a town and district belonging to Assyria.

סֹפֶרֶת (sōfĕ'rĕth) *pr.n.m.*

סָקַל (sākă'l) *inf.* סָקוֹל, *imp. pl.* סִקְלוּ, *fut.* יִסְקֹל, to stone, to cover with stones. — *Ni. fut.* יִסָּקֵל to be stoned. — *Pi.* סִקֵּל, *imp.* סַקֵּל, *fut.* יְסַקֵּל, to stone, to pelt with stones; to free from stones. — *Pu.* סֻקַּל to be stoned to death.

סַר (săr) *adj.*, *f* סָרָה, ill-humoured, peevish; rebellious.

סָרָב (sārā'b) *adj.*, only *pl.* סָרָבִים, rebellious; rebels [others: thorns].

סַרְגוֹן (sărgō'n) *pr.n.m.*

סֶרֶד (sĕ'rĕd) *pr.n.m.*

סָרָה (sārā') *f* a turning away, apostasy; cessation, remission.

סִרָה (sĭrā') *pr.n.* of a cistern.

סָרַח (sāră'ḥ) *fut.* יִסְרַח, *pt. f* סֹרַחַת, *pt. p.* סָרוּחַ, *intr.* to extend, to spread out; to overhang; to be luxuriant. — *Ni.* נִסְרַח to be poured out, wasted [others: to be corrupt].

סֶרַח (sĕ'răḥ) *m* the overhanging, superfluous part.

סִרְיוֹן (sĭryō'n) *m*, *w.s.* סִרְיֹנוֹ, *pl.* סִרְיֹנִים, coat of mail.

סָרִיס (sārī's) *m*, *c.* סְרִיס, *pl.* סָרִיסִים, *c.* סָרִיסֵי, סְרִיסֵי, a castrated one, eunuch; courtier, minister, chamberlain.

סֶרֶן (sĕ'rĕn) *m*, *pl.* סְרָנִים, *c.* סַרְנֵי, axle; prince [of the Philistines].

סַרְעַפָּה (săr'ăppā') *f* bough, branch.

סָרַף (sāră'f) *Pi. pt.* מְסָרֵף, to burn [a corpse].

סִרְפָּד (sĭrpā'd) *m* a prickly plant, nettle.

סָרַר (sāră'r) *pt.* סוֹרֵר, *pl.* סוֹרְרִים, *f* סֹרֶרֶת, to be refractory, rebellious, to apostatise.

סְתָו (s'thā'v) *m* rainy season, winter.

סְתוּר (s'thū'r) *pr.n.m.*

סָתַם (sāthă'm) *fut.* יִסְתֹּם, *pt. p.* סָתֻם, סָתוּם, to stop up, to close up; to keep secret, to conceal. — *Ni.* נִסְתַּם, to be closed, filled up, repaired. — *Pi.* סִתֵּם, *fut.* יְסַתֵּם, to stop up.

סָתַר (sāthă'r) *Ni.* נִסְתַּר, *fut.* יִסָּתֵר, *pt.* נִסְתָּר, to be hidden, concealed, not known; to hide, cover or protect oneself; to escape. — *Pi. imp. f* סַתְּרִי, to hide, conceal. — *Pu. pt. f* מְסֻתֶּרֶת, to be hidden. — *Hi.* הִסְתִּיר, *inf.* הַסְתֵּר [לַסְתֵּר for לְהַסְתֵּר], *imp.* הַסְתֵּר, *fut.* יַסְתִּיר, יַסְתֵּר. *pt.* מַסְתִּיר, מַסְתֵּר, to hide, conceal, cover; to keep secret, to protect, shelter, save, pardon; to disregard, ignore; to cause to hide. — *Hith.* הִסְתַּתֵּר to hide oneself, to disappear.

סֵתֶר (sē'thĕr) *m, i.p.* סָתֶר, *w.s.* סִתְרִי, *pl.* סְתָרִים, a covering, veil; shelter, hiding place, protection; concealment, secrecy; a secret.

סִתְרָה (sĭthrā') *f* screen, protection.

סִתְרִי (sĭthrī') *pr.n.m.*

ע

ע the sixteenth letter of the alphabet, called עַיִן [eye]; as a numeral = 70.

עָב¹ ('āb) *m, c.* עָב and עַב, *pl.* עָבִים, עָבוֹת, *c.* עָבֵי, density, thicket; darkness, cloud.

עָב² ('āb) *m* a term of architecture: threshold, projecting step.

עֹב ('ōb) *m,* only *pl.* עֻבִּים = עָב².

עָבַד ('ābă'd) *inf.* עֲבֹד, *w.s.* עָבְדָם ('ŏbdā'm), *imp.* עֲבֹד, עִבְדוּ, *fut.* יַעֲבֹד, *pt.* עֹבֵד, *pl.* עֹבְדִים, *c.* עֹבְדֵי, to work, to labour, to toil, to till, to plough; to serve, to work as a slave; to worship. — *Ni.* נֶעֱבַד, *fut.* יֵעָבֵד, to be cultivated; to be served or honoured. — *Pu.* עֻבַּד to be worked. — *Hi.* הֶעֱבִיד, *inf.* הַעֲבִיד, *fut.*

יַעֲבִיד, *pt.* מַעֲבִיד, to cause to work, to make weary, to fatigue; to enslave; to cause to worship. — *Ho.* *fut.* יָעֳבַד (yŏ'ʻobă'd) to be made to serve.

עֶבֶד[1] (ʻĕ'bĕd) *m*, *i.p.* עָבֶד, *w.s.* עַבְדִּי, *pl.* עֲבָדִים, *c.* עַבְדֵי, labourer, servant, slave, bondsman, subject; worshipper.

עֶבֶד[2] (ʻĕ'bĕd) *pr.n.m.*

עַבְדָּא (ʻăbdā'); עַבְדְּאֵל (ʻăbdᵉ'ē'l) *pr.n.m.*

עֹבֵד אֱדֹם (ʻōbē'd ᵉdō'm); עֶבֶד מֶלֶךְ (ʻĕ'bĕd mĕ'lĕch); עֲבֵד נְגוֹ (ʻabē'd nᵉgō') *pr.n.m.*

עֲבֹדָה (ʻabōdā') *f*, *c.* עֲבֹדַת, work, labour, husbandry, service, employment, business; worship, divine service; implements, furniture.

עֲבֻדָּה (ʻabŭddā') *f* service; servants.

עַבְדּוֹן (ʻăbdō'n) *pr.n.m.*; *pr.n.* of a town in Asher.

עַבְדוּת (ʻăbdū'th) *f* servitude, bondage.

עַבְדִּי (ʻăbdī'); עַבְדִּיאֵל (ʻăbdī'ē'l); עֹבַדְיָה (ʻō'bădyā'), עֹבַדְיָהוּ (ʻō'bădyā'hū) *pr.n.m.*

עָבָה[1] (ʻābā') to be fat, thick.

עָבָה[2] (ʻābā') *f*, *pl.* עָבוֹת, see עָב[1].

עֲבוֹט (ʻabō't) *m* pledge.

עָבוּר (ʻābū'r) *m*, *c.* עֲבוּר, end, produce, fruit; בַּעֲבוּר, *w.s.* בַּעֲבוּרִי, בַּעֲבוּרָם, *prep.* and *conj.* in order that, because of, on account of, for the sake of, while.

עָבַט (ʻābă't) *inf.* עֲבֹט, *fut.* יַעֲבֹט, to borrow [upon a pledge], to pledge. — *Pi.* *fut.* יְעַבֵּט, to twist, to make tortuous. — *Hi. inf.* הַעֲבֵט, *fut.* יַעֲבִיט, to lend on a pledge.

עַבְטִיט (ʻăbtī't) *m* a pledging; extorted goods, robbery.

עֲבִי (ʻabī') *m* and עֳבִי (ʻobī') *m*, *w.s.* עָבְיוֹ (ʻŏbyō'), denseness, thickness.

עָבַר (ʻābă'r) *inf.* עֲבוֹר, עֲבֹר, *w.s.* עָבְרִי (ʻŏbrī'), *imp.* עֲבֹר, עִבְרוּ, *fut.* יַעֲבֹר, *pt.* עֹבֵר, עוֹבֵר, *pl.* עֹבְרִים, *c.* עֹבְרֵי, to pass over, to cross, to go over or through; to penetrate, to go beyond, to pass by, to pass along, to travel; to pass away, to disappear; to go forward, to pass on; to transgress; to depart. — *Ni. fut.* יֵעָבֵר to be passed through, to be crossed. — *Pi.* עִבֵּר, *fut.* יְעַבֵּר, to bolt, to shut up; to impregnate. — *Hi.* הֶעֱבִיר, *inf.* הַעֲבִיר, הַעֲבֵר, *imp.* הַעֲבֵר, *fut.* יַעֲבִיר, יַעֲבֵר, *pt.* מַעֲבִיר, *pl.* מַעֲבִירִים, to cause to pass, to cause to cross over, to lead over, to transport, to conduct across; to remove, transfer; to cause to trespass; to let pass through, to lead along or through, to bring. — *Hith.* הִתְעַבֵּר to be irritated, to be wroth, to fall into a passion.

עֵבֶר[1] (ʿē'bĕr) *m*, *w.s.* עֶבְרוֹ, *pl.* עֲבָרִים, *c.* עֶבְרֵי, what is beyond, region or land beyond, river-land, coast-land; the opposite side, flank, side; אֶל־עֵבֶר to beyond, to the other side, across, forwards; מֵעֵבֶר from beyond; עַל־עֵבֶר over against.

עֵבֶר[2] (ʿē'bĕr) *pr.n.m.*

עֲבָרָה (ʿaḇārā') *f*, *pl.* עֲבָרוֹת, *c.* עַבְרוֹת, passage, ford, crossing; ferry-boat.

עֶבְרָה (ʿĕḇrā') *f*, *c.* עֶבְרַת, *pl.* עֲבָרוֹת, *c.* עֶבְרוֹת and עַבְרוֹת, an overflowing, outburst of wrath, fury, pride, haughtiness.

עִבְרִי (ʿIḇrī') *pr.n.m.*, *pl.* עִבְרִיִּים, עִבְרִים, *f* עִבְרִיָּה, *pl.* עִבְרִיּוֹת [*gent.* of עֵבֶר[2]], Hebrew, i. e. emigrant.

עֲבָרִים (ʿaḇārī'm) *pr.n.* of a mountain-range in Moab.

עַבְרֹנָה (ʿăḇrōnā') *pr.n.* of a station near Eziongeber.

עָבַשׁ (ʿāḇă'š) to be shrunk, to die.

עָבַת (ʿāḇă'ϑ) *Pi. fut.* יְעַבְּתָ, to interweave, to complicate.

עָבֹת (ʿāḇō'ϑ) *adj.*, *f* עֲבֻתָּה, interwoven, tangled.

עֲבֹת (ʿaḇō'ϑ) *m* [and *f*], *pl.* עֲבֹתִים, *w.s.* עֲבֹתֵימוֹ, and עֲבֹתֹת, rope, cord, band; braided work, wreath; tangled bough [or = עָבוֹת clouds].

עָגַב (ʿāgă'ḇ) *fut.* יַעְגַּב, *pt.* עֹגֵב, to desire, to dote on, to be inflamed, to lust after.

עֶגֶב (ʿĕ'gĕḇ) *m*, only *pl.* עֲגָבִים, loveliness, charm.

עֲגָבָה ('ᵃgābā') *f*, *w.s.* עֲגָבָתָהּ, lust, impure passion.

עֻגָה ('ūgā') and עֻגָּה ('ŭggā') *f*, *c.* עֻגַת, *pl.* עֻגוֹת, עֻגֹת, round cake or loaf.

עָגוּר ('āgū'r) *m* swallow [or crane].

עָגִיל ('āgī'l) *m*, *pl.* עֲגִילִים, ear-ring, ring.

עָגֹל, **עָגוֹל** ('āgō'l) *adj.*, *f* עֲגֻלָּה, *pl.* עֲגֻלּוֹת, rounded, round.

עֵגֶל ('ē'gĕl) *m*, *w.s.* עֶגְלְךָ, *pl.* עֲגָלִים, *c.* עֶגְלֵי, a calf; calf-image.

עֶגְלָה[1] ('ĕglā') *f*, *c.* עֶגְלַת, *pl.* עֶגְלוֹת, calf, young cow, heifer.

עֶגְלָה[2] ('ĕglā') *pr.n.f.*

עֲגָלָה ('ᵃgālā') *f*, *w.s.* עֶגְלָתוֹ, *pl.* עֲגָלוֹת, *c.* עֶגְלוֹת, cart, waggon, thrashing-sledge, war-chariot.

עֶגְלוֹן ('ĕglō'n) *pr.n.m.*; *pr.n.* of a town in Judah.

עֶגְלַת ('ĕglă'ϑ) *pr.n.* of a place.

עָגַם ('āgă'm) to be grieved, to be sad.

עָגַן ('āgă'n) *Ni.* נֶעֱגַן, *fut.* יֵעָגֵן, to shut oneself up, to be lone.

עַד[1] ('ăḏ), also עָד, *m* duration, advance, perpetuity, eternity; *prep.* and *conj.* during, while, as far as, to [of space and time], till; עַד כִּי, עַד אֲשֶׁר until that; עֲדֵי־עַד till eternity; עוֹלְמֵי עַד eternities of eternity.

עַד[2] ('ăḏ) *m* booty.

עֵד ('ēḏ) *m*, *pl.* עֵדִים, *c.* עֵדֵי, עֵידַי, a witness; proof, testimony; ruler.

עֹד see עוֹד.

עִדֹּא, **עִדּוֹ** ('ĭddō') *pr.n.m.*

עָדָה[1] ('āḏā') *imp.* עֲדֵה, *fut.* יַעְדֶּה, וַיַּעַד, to veil, to cover, to put on, to adorn oneself; to go on, to march along. — *Hi.* הֶעֱדָה, *pt.* מַעֲדֶה, to put off.

עָדָה[2] ('āḏā') *pr.n.f.*

עֵדָה[1] ('ēḏā') *f*, *pl.* עֵדוֹת, female witness; testimony; attestation, prescription.

עֵדָה[2] ('ēḏā') *f*, *c.* עֲדַת, *w.s.* עֲדָתוֹ, *pl.* עֵדוֹת, assembly, meeting, congregation, company; household, family; troop, gang, herd, swarm.

עִדָּה ('ĭddā') *f*, only *pl.* עִדִּים, period, monthly courses.

עֵדוּת (ʽēḏū'ϑ), עֵדֻת *f*, *pl.* עֵדוֹת and עֵדְוֹת (ʽē'dᵉvō'ϑ), testimony, prescription, precept, law; אֲרוֹן הָעֵדֻת ark of the law; אֹהֶל הָעֵדוּת tabernacle of the law.

עֲדִי (ʽᵃḏī') *m*, *i.p.* עֶדִי, *w.s.* עֶדְיֵךְ, *pl.* עֲדָיִים, covering, ornament; trappings, harness [of a horse].

עֲדִיאֵל (ʽᵃḏī'ēl); עֲדָיָה (ʽᵃḏāyā'), עֲדָיָהוּ (ʽᵃḏāyā'hū) *pr.n.m.*

עָדִין[1] (ʽāḏī'n) *adj.*, only *f* עֲדִינָה, delicate, voluptious, luxurious.

עָדִין[2] (ʽāḏī'n); עֲדִינָא (ʽᵃḏīnā'); עֲדִינוֹ (ʽᵃḏīnō') [perh. for עֲדִינוֹן] *pr.n.m.*

עֲדִיתַיִם (ʽᵃḏīϑă'yĭm) *pr.n.* of a town in Judah.

עַדְלַי (ʽădlă'y) *pr.n.m.*

עֲדֻלָּם (ʽᵃḏŭllā'm) *pr.n.* of a town near Bethlehem; *gent.* עֲדֻלָּמִי.

עָדַן (ʽāḏă'n) *Hith.* הִתְעַדֵּן to live voluptuously.

עֵדֶן (ʽē'ḏĕn) *m*, *pl.* עֲדָנִים, loveliness, delight, pleasure; גַּן־עֵדֶן Eden, the garden of Paradise.

עֶדֶן (ʽĕ'ḏĕn) *pr.n.* of a district in Mesopotamia.

עֲדֶן (ʽᵃḏĕ'n), עֲדֶנָּה (ʽᵃḏĕ'nnā') *adv.* till now.

עַדְנָא, עַדְנָה (ʽăḏnā') *pr.n.m.*

עֶדְנָה (ʽĕḏnā') *f* sexual pleasure.

עֲדְעָדָה (ʽăḏʽāḏā') *pr.n.* of a town in Judah.

עָדַף (ʽāḏă'f) *pt.* עֹדֵף, *f* עֹדֶפֶת, to overhang; to remain over, to be more than enough, to be redundant. — *Hi.* הֶעֱדִיף to have in excess.

עָדַר[1] (ʽāḏă'r) *Ni.* נֶעְדַּר, *fut.* יֵעָדֵר, to be missed, to be wanting. — *Pi. fut.* יְעַדֵּר, to let be wanting.

עָדַר[2] (ʽāḏă'r) *inf.* עֲדֹר, *pt.* עֹדֵר, to arrange, to set in order. — *Ni.* נֶעְדַּר, *pt. f* נֶעְדֶּרֶת, to be arranged, to be set in order, to be cultivated.

עֵדֶר[1] (ʽē'ḏĕr) *m*, *w.s.* עֶדְרוֹ, *pl.* עֲדָרִים, *c.* עֶדְרֵי, a herd, flock.

עֵדֶר[2] (ʽē'ḏĕr) *pr.n.* of a town in Judah; *pr.n.m.*

עֵדֶר (ʽĕ'ḏĕr) *i.p.* עָדֶר, *pr.n.m.*

עַדְרִיאֵל (ʽădrī'ēl) *pr.n.m.*

עֲדָשָׁה (ʽᵃḏāšā') *f*, only *pl.* עֲדָשִׁים lentils.

עוּב ('ūḇ) *Hi.* הֵעִיב, *fut.* יָעִיב, to enwrap in clouds, to darken.

עוֹבֵד ('ōḇē'ḏ) *pr.n.m.*

עוֹבָל ('ōḇā'l) *pr.n.* of a people in the south-west of Arabia.

עוּג ('ūg) *fut.* יָעוּג, *w.s.* תְּעֻגֶנָּה, to bake [a cake].

עוֹג ('ōg) *pr.n.m.*

עוּגָב ('ūgā'ḇ), **עֻגָּב** ('ŭggā'ḇ) *m* musical instrument, flute, pipe.

עוֹד, עֹד ('ōḏ) *m* repetition, duration, continuance; *adv.* again, once more; continually, further, longer, still, yet; בְּעוֹד while yet; מֵעוֹד ever since.

עוּד ('ūḏ) *fut.* יָעוּד, to attest, to assure. — *Pi.* עִוֵּד ('ĭvvē'ḏ) to surround; *fut.* יְעוֹדֵד, *pt.* מְעוֹדֵד, to restore, to make firm, to support. — *Hi.* הֵעִיד, *inf.* הָעֵד, *imp.* הָעֵד, *fut.* יָעִיד, יָעֵד, יָעַד, *pt.* מֵעִיד, to make firm; to assure, attest, affirm, to protest, to testify; to be a witness, to take as witness; to adjure, admonish, warn, comfort, punish. — *Ho.* הוּעַד to be testified, announced. — *Hith.* הִתְעוֹדֵד to be established, to stand upright.

עוֹדֵד ('ōḏē'ḏ) *pr.n.m.*

עָוָה ('āvā') to act perversely, to sin. — *Ni.* נַעֲוָה, *pt.* נַעֲוֶה, to be bent, to writhe; to be perverse. — *Pi.* עִוָּה ('ĭvvā') to subvert, to turn upside down, to make impassable. — *Hi.* הֶעֱוָה, *inf.* *w.s.* הַעֲוֹתוֹ (hă'avōṯō') to make crooked, to bend, to pervert, to sin.

עַוָּה ('ăvvā') *f* destruction, ruin.

עִוָּה, עַוָּא ('ĭvvā', 'ăvvā') *pr.n.* of a city in Mesopotamia or Syria; *gent. pl.* עַוִּים.

עָווֹן see עָוֹן.

עוֹז see עֹז.

עוּז ('ūz) *inf.* עוֹז, to flee, to take refuge. — *Hi.* הֵעִיז, *imp.* הָעֵז, הָעִיזוּ, to transport in haste, to save by fleeing; to flee in haste.

עוּזָה see עָזָן.

עֲוִיל ('ăvī'l) *m*, only *pl.* עֲוִילִים, child, boy.

עֲוִיל ('avī'l) *adj.* perverse, insolent, wicked.

עַוִּית ('avī'ṯ) *pr.n.* of a town in Edom.

עוֹל see **עֹל**.

עוּל[1] (ʿūl) *pt.* עָל, *f/pl.* עָלוֹת, to suckle, to give milk.

עוּל[2] (ʿūl) *m*, *w.s.* עוּלָהּ, suckling, infant.

עָוַל (ʿāvā'l) *Pi.* עִוֵּל, *fut.* יְעַוֵּל, *pt.* מְעַוֵּל, to do wrong, to act wickedly.

עַוָּל (ʿăvvā'l) *m* a wicked one, a wrong-doer.

עָוֶל (ʿā'vĕl) *m*, *c.* עֶוֶל, *w.s.* עַוְלוֹ, perverseness, wickedness, dishonesty, wrong.

עַוְלָה (ʿăvlā') *f*, *w. loc.* עַוְלָתָה ה, *pl.* עוֹלֹת – עָוֶל.

עוֹלָה see **עֹלָה** and **עַוְלָה**.

עוֹלֶה (ʿōlĕ') *m* ascent, step.

עוֹלָל (ʿōlā'l) *m*, *pl.* עוֹלָלִים, and **עוֹלֵל** (ʿōlē'l) *m*, *pl.* עוֹלְלִים, *c.* עוֹלְלֵי, child, infant, boy.

עוֹלֵלוֹת see **עֹלֵלוֹת**.

עֹלָם, עוֹלָם (ʿōlā'm) *m*, *w.s.* עֹלָמוֹ, *pl.* עוֹלָמִים, *c.* עוֹלְמֵי, time immemorial, time past, eternity, distant future, duration, everlasting time, life-time; *pl.* ages, endless times.

עוּם (ʿūm) *Ho. fut.* יוּעַם see **עָמַם**.

עוּן (ʿūn) *pf.* עָן, *f* עָנָה, to dwell [or from עָנָה].

עָוֹן, עָווֹן (ʿāvō'n) *m*, *c.* עֲוֹן, *w.s.* עֲוֹנִי, *pl.* עֲוֹנִים, עֲוֹנוֹת, perverseness, sin, guilt, crime; punishment, suffering.

עוֹנָה (ʿōnā') *f* cohabitation; *pl.* עוֹנוֹת = עֲוֹנוֹת see **עָוֹן**.

עִוְעֶה (ʿĭvʿĕ') *m*, only *pl.* עִוְעִים, perverseness, confusion, giddiness.

עוּף (ʿūf) *pf.* עָף, *inf.* עוּף, *fut.* יָעוּף, יָעֹף, וַיָּעָף (văyyā'-ʿŏf), to fly, to flit; to cover, to shelter under the wings; to be overcast, gloomy, dark; to swoon, to faint. — *Pil.* עוֹפֵף, *fut.* יְעוֹפֵף, *pt.* מְעוֹפֵף, to fly about; to brandish [a sword]. — *Hi.* הֵעִיף to cause to fly away. — *Hith.* הִתְעוֹפֵף to fly away, to vanish.

עוֹף (ʿōf) *m* *coll.* what flies, birds, fowl.

עוּץ[1] (ʿūẞ) *imp. pl.* עֻצוּ, to counsel, advise, recommend.

עוּץ[2] (ʿūẞ) *pr.n.m.*; also *pr.n.* of an eastern country.

עוּק (ʿūk) *Hi. fut.* יָעִיק, *pt.* מֵעִיק, to press down.

עוּר ('ūr) *imp.* עוּרִי, עוּרָה, *fut.* יָעוּר, *pt.* עָר, to awake, to be astir, to wake; *tr.* to rouse, to stir up.—*Ni.* נֵעוֹר, *fut.* יֵעוֹר, to be awaked, aroused, to rise. — *Pi.* עוֹרֵר, *imp.* עוֹרְרָה, *fut.* יְעוֹרֵר, to stir up, arouse, excite; to brandish. — *Pilp.* עִרְעֵר, *inf.* עַרְעֵר, *fut. pl.* יְעֹעֵרוּ [for יְעַרְעֵרוּ], to raise [cries]. — *Hi.* הֵעִיר, *inf.* בָּעִיר [for בְּהָעִיר], *fut.* יָעִיר, יָעֵר, to excite, to stir, to waken, to rouse; *intr.* to awake. — *Hith.* הִתְעוֹרֵר to rouse oneself; to exult, to start from joy.

עוֹר ('ǭr) *m*, *w.s.* עוֹרוֹ, עֹרוֹ, *pl.* עוֹרוֹת, עֹרֹת, skin, hide, leather; body, flesh.

עָוֵר ('ăvē'r) [to be blind] *Pi.* עִוֵּר, *fut.* יְעַוֵּר, to make blind, to blind; to bribe.

עִוֵּר ('ĭvvē'r) *adj.*, only *pl. m* עִוְרִים, *f* עִוְרוֹת, blind, blinded; infatuated.

עִוָּרוֹן ('ĭvvārǭ'n) *m* blindness.

עַוֶּרֶת ('ăvvĕ'rĕθ) *f* blindness.

עוּשׁ ('ūš) *imp. pl.* עוּשׁוּ, to hurry up.

עָוַת ('ăvă'θ) *Pi.* עִוֵּת, *inf.* עַוֵּת, *fut.* יְעַוֵּת, to bend, to make crooked, to pervert to falsify, to corrupt, to seduce, to subvert. — *Pu. pt.* מְעֻוָּת, to be crooked, curved. — *Hith.* הִתְעַוֵּת to bend oneself, to stoop.

עוּת ('ūθ) *inf.* עוּת, to succour, help, support.

עַוָּתָה ('ăvvāθā') *f* oppression.

עוּתַי ('ūθă'y) *pr.n.m.*

עַז ('ăz) *adj.*, *i.p.* עָז, *pl.* עַזִּים, *c.* עַזֵּי, *f* עַזָּה, *pl.* עַזּוֹת, strong, powerful, firm; fierce, violent, hard, bold; *subst.* strength, power.

עֵז ('ēz) *f*, *pl.* עִזִּים, goat, she-goat; *pl.* goat's hair; גְּדִי עִזִּים kid of the goats; שְׂעִיר ע׳ buck of the goats.

עֹז, עוֹז ('ǭz) *m*, *c.* עָז־, *w.s.* עֻזִּי, strength, power, might; firmness; violence, boldness; protection, refuge; splendour, glory, praise.

עֻזָּה, עֻזָּא ('ŭzzā') *pr.n.m.*

עֲזָאזֵל ('azāzē'l) *pr.n.* of an evil spirit dwelling in the wilderness.

עָזַב[1] ('āză'ḅ) *inf.* עֲזֹב, עָזוֹב, *w.s.* עָזְבְךָ ('ŏzḅĕ'ḁ), *imp.* עֲזֹב, *fut.* יַעֲזֹב, *pt.* עֹזֵב, *pl.* עֹזְבִים, *c.* עֹזְבֵי, *pt. p.* עָזוּב, *f* עֲזוּבָה, *pl.* עֲזֻבוֹת,

to loosen, to release, to set free, *pt. p.* freed; to leave, forsake, abandon, to leave behind; to omit, to relax. — *Ni.* נֶעֱזַב, *fut.* יֵעָזֵב, *pt.* נֶעֱזָב, to be forsaken, abandoned. — *Pu.* עֻזַּב to be forsaken.

עָזַב[2] (ʻāzăḇ) to build, repair, fortify.

עִזָּבוֹן (ʻĭzzāḇō'n) *m*, only *pl.* עִזְבֹנִים, commerce, traffic, waves.

עַזְבּוּק (ʻăzbū'**k**); **עַזְגָּד** (ʻăzgā'd) *pr.n.m.*

עַזָּה (ʻăzzā') *pr.n.*, *w. loc.* עַזָּתָה ה, Gaza, one of the five Philistine cities; *gent.* עַזָּתִי, *pl.* עַזָּתִים.

עֲזוּבָה[1] (ʻazūḇā') *f*, *c.* עֲזוּבַת, desolations, ruins.

עֲזוּבָה[2] (ʻazūḇā') *pr.n.f.*

עֱזוּז (ʻezū'z) *m*, *w.s.* עֱזוּזוֹ, might, power, strength.

עִזּוּז (ʻĭzzū'z) *adj.* strong, mighty.

עָזַז (ʻāză'z) *inf.* עֲזוֹז, עוֹז, *imp.* עוּזָה, *fut.* יָעוֹז, יָעֹז, to be or become strong, firm, powerful; to be bold, hard [see יָעֹז]. — *Hi.* הֵעֵז to harden, to make bold.

עָזָז (ʻāzā'z); **עֲזַזְיָהוּ** (ʻazăzyā'hū); **עֻזִּי** (ʻŭzzĭ'); **עֻזִּיָּא** (ʻŭzzĭyyā'); **עֻזִּיאֵל** (ʻŭzzĭ'ę'l); **עֻזִּיָּה** (ʻŭzzĭyyā'), **עֻזִּיָּהוּ** (ʻŭzzĭyyā'hū); **עֲזִיזָא** (ʻazĭzā'); **עַזְמָוֶת** (ʻăzmā'vĕϑ); **עַזָּן** (ʻăzzā'n) *pr.n.m.*

עָזְנִיָּה (ʻăznĭyyā') *f* a species of eagle, black eagle.

עָזַק (ʻāză'**k**) *Pi.* *fut.* יְעַזֵּק, to dig up, to till.

עֲזֵקָה (ʻazę**k**ā') *pr.n.* of a town in Judah.

עָזַר (ʻāză'r) *inf.* עֲזֹר, *w.s.* עָזְרֵנִי (ʻŏzrę'nĭ), *imp.* *w.s.* עָזְרֵנִי, *fut.* יַעֲזֹר, *pt.* עֹזֵר, עוֹזֵר, *pl. c.* עֹזְרֵי, *pt. p.* עָזוּר, to help, assist, aid. — *Ni.* נֶעֱזַר to be helped, to obtain help. — *Hi.* *inf.* לַעְזִיר [for לְהַעְזִיר], *pt.* מַעְזִיר, *pl.* מַעְזְרִים, to help.

עֵזֶר[1] (ʻę'zĕr) *m*, *w.s.* עֶזְרִי, help, assistance, helper.

עֵזֶר[2] (ʻę'zĕr); **עֶזֶר** (ʻĕ'zĕr); **עַזּוּר** (ʻăzzū'r); **עֶזְרָא** (ʻĕzrā'); **עֲזַרְאֵל** (ʻazăr'ę'l); **עֶזְרָה** (ʻĕzrā'); **עֶזְרִי** (ʻĕzrĭ'); **עַזְרִיאֵל** (ʻăzrĭ'ę'l); **עֲזַרְיָה** (ʻazăryā'), **עֲזַרְיָהוּ** (ʻazăryā'hū); **עַזְרִיקָם** (ʻăzrĭ**k**ā'm) *pr.n.m.*

עֶזְרָה (ʻĕzrā') and **עֶזְרָת** (ʻĕzrāϑ) *f*, *c.* עֶזְרַת = עֵזֶר[1].

עַזָּתִי see עַזָּה.

עֵט ('ēt) *m* style for engraving letters, writing-tool, pen, reed.

עָטָה¹ ('ātā') *inf.* עָטֹה, *fut.* יַעֲטֶה, וַיַּעַט, *pt.* עֹטֶה, *w.s.* עֹטְךָ, *f* עֹטְיָה, to cover, veil; to wrap, fold up, to put on; to veil oneself. — *Hi.* הֶעֱטָה, *fut.* יַעֲטֶה וַיַּעַט [or from עִיט], *w.s.* יַעְטֵנִי [for יַעֲטֵנִי], to cover.

עָטָה² ('ātā') *Hi.* *fut.* וַיַּעַט, to rush on, to fly at [see עִיט].

עֲטִין ('ᵃtī'n) *m*, only *pl.* עֲטִינָיו, vessel, pail [others: resting-place; vein].

עֲטִישָׁה ('ᵃtīšā')*f* a sneezing.

עֲטַלֵּף ('ᵃtallē'f) *m*, *pl.* עֲטַלֵּפִים, a bat.

עָטַף ('ātā'f) *inf.* עֲטֹף, *fut.* יַעֲטֹף, *pt. p.* עָטוּף, to cover, clothe; to be covered; to languish, to faint, to be exhausted; to hide oneself; to turn to; *pt. p.* weak, exhausted. — *Ni.* *inf.* בְּעָטֵף [for בְּהֵ'], to be exhausted, to faint. — *Hi.* *inf.* בַּעֲטִיף to be weak. — *Hith.* הִתְעַטֵּף to be feeble, to languish, to faint.

עָטַר ('ātā'r) *fut.* יַעְטֹר, *w.s.* תַּעְטְרֶנּוּ, *pt.* עֹטֵר, *pl.* עֹטְרִים, to surround, to encircle, to encompass. — *Pi.* עִטֵּר, *fut. w.s.* תְּעַטְּרֵהוּ, *pt.* מְעַטֵּר, to encircle with a diadem, to crown. — *Hi. pt. f* מַעֲטִירָה to distribute crowns.

עֲטָרָה¹ ('ᵃtārā') *f*, *c.* עֲטֶרֶת, *pl.* עֲטָרוֹת, *c.* עַטְרוֹת, crown, diadem, chaplet.

עֲטָרָה² ('ᵃtārā') *pr.n.f.*

עֲטָרוֹת ('ᵃtārō'ϑ) *pr.n.* of several towns.

עַי ('āy) mostly *w. art.* הָעַי, also עַיָּא, עַיָּה, עַיָּת, *pr.n.* of a town near Bethel.

עִי ('ī) *m*, *pl.* עִיִּים, heap of stones, rubbish, ruin, ruins.

עִיִּים ('īyyī'm) *pr.n.* of a town in Judah; *pr.n.* of a mountain.

עֵיבָל ('ēbā'l) *pr.n.* of a mountain near Shechem.

עִיּוֹן ('īyyō'n) *pr.n.* of a town in Naphtali.

עִיט ('īt) *fut.* וַיַּעַט, to rush on, to fly at [see עָטָה²].

עַיִט ('ā'yit) *m*, *c.* עֵיט, bird of prey; *coll.* birds of prey.

עֵיטָם (ʿēṭā'm) *pr.n.* of a town in Judah.

עֵילוֹם (ʿēlō'm) *m* = עוֹלָם eternity.

עִילַי (ʿīlă'y) *pr.n.m.*

עֵילָם (ʿēlā'm) *pr.n.* of a people and country east of Babylonia [Lusiana]; also *pr.n.* of a place.

עֲיָם (ʿayā'm) *m, c.* עֲיָם [בַּעְיָם], heat, glow.

עַיִן[1] (ʿă'yĭn) *f, c.* עֵין, *w.s.* עֵינִי. *du.* עֵינַיִם, *c.* עֵינֵי, *w.s.* עֵינַי [עֵינֶךָ for עֵינֶיךָ], *pl.* עֲיָנוֹת, *c.* עֵינוֹת, the eye; eye of the mind; look, appearance, sight, face, surface; the sparkling or bead of wine; fountain, spring.

עַיִן[2] (ʿă'yĭn) *pr.n.* of a town in Simeon.

עֵין (ʿēn) in compounds of proper names: ע׳ גֶּדִי; ע׳ דּוֹר or ע׳ דֹאר; ע׳ גַּנִּים; ע׳ מִשְׁפָּט; ע׳ חָצוֹר; ע׳ חַדָּה; ע׳ רִמּוֹן; ע׳ רֹגֵל; ע׳ עֶגְלַיִם; ע׳ תַּפּוּחַ; ע׳ תַּנִּין; ע׳ שֶׁמֶשׁ.

עֵינַיִם (ʿēnă'yĭm) and **עֵינָם** (ʿēnā'm) *pr.n.* of a place in Judah.

עֵינָן (ʿēnā'n) *pr.n.m.*

עָיֵף[1] (ʿāyē'f) to be weary, to languish.

עָיֵף[2] (ʿāyē't) *adj., pl.* עֲיֵפִים, *f* עֲיֵפָה, weary, exhausted, languid, faint.

עֵיפָה[1] (ʿēfā') *f* darkness, obscurity.

עֵיפָה[2] (ʿēfā') *pr.n.* of a tribe of the Midianites.

עֵיפַי (ʿēfă'y) *pr.n.m.*

עִיר[1] (ʿīr) *f, w. loc.* ה עִירָה, *pl.* עָרִים, עֲיָרִים, *w. art.* הֶעָרִים, *c.* עָרֵי, tower, city, town, village, hamlet, capital; עִיר הַתְּמָרִים Jericho.

עִיר[2] (ʿīr) *m* anger, wrath.

עִיר[3] (ʿīr) *m* anguish, distress.

עַיִר (ʿă'yĭr) *m, w.s.* עִירֹה, *pl.* עֲיָרִים, young ass, ass.

עִירָא (ʿīrā'); **עִירָד** (ʿīrā'd); **עִירוּ** (ʿīrū'); **עִירִי** (ʿīrī'); **עִירָם** (ʿīrā'm) *pr.n.m.*

עֵרֹם, עֵירֹם (ʿērō'm) *adj., pl.* עֵירֻמִּים, naked, bare; *subst.* nakedness, bareness.

עַיִשׁ (ʿă'yĭš) *f* a constellation, the Great Bear [or the Pleiades].

עַיָּת = עַי.

עַכְבּוֹר (ʿăḇbō'r) *pr.n.m.*

עַכָּבִישׁ ('ăkkābī'š) *m* spider.

עַכְבָּר ('ăḵbā'r) *m*, *pl. c.* עַכְבְּרֵי, mouse.

עַכּוֹ ('ăkkō') *pr.n.* of a city, Acca or Acre in Phenicia.

עָכוֹר ('āḵō'r) *pr.n.* of a valley near Jericho.

עָכָן ('āḵā'n) *pr.n.m.*

עָכַס ('āḵă's) *Pi.* עִכֵּס, *fut.* יְעַכֵּס, to wear anklets.

עֶכֶס ('ĕ'ḵĕs) *m*, *pl.* עֲכָסִים, fetter, anklet, ankle-band.

עַכְסָה ('ăḵsā') *pr.n.f.*

עָכַר ('āḵă'r) *fut.* יַעְכֹּר, *pt.* עֹכֵר, *pl. c.* עֹכְרֵי, to trouble, to disturb; to afflict, to grieve. — *Ni. pt.* נֶעְכָּר, *f* נֶעְכֶּרֶת, to be troubled, grieved; *pt.* trouble.

עָכָר ('āḵā'r); עָכְרָן ('ŏḵrā'n) *pr.n.m.*

עַכְשׁוּב ('ăḵšū'ḇ) *m* adder, viper.

עַל ('ăl) *m* what is high, the upper part; *prep.* [also עֲלֵי], *w.s.* עָלַי, עָלֶיךָ, עֲלֵיכֶם, on, upon, above, over; on account of; to, unto; towards, near, against, according to, after; in spite of; because of; מֵעַל from above, from upon; מֵעַל לְ over, above.

עֹל, **עוֹל** ('ōl) *m*, *w.s.* עֻלִּי, yoke, servitude.

עֻלָּא ('ŭllā') *pr.n.m.*

עִלֵּג ('ĭllē'g) *adj.*, *pl.* עִלְּגִים, stammering.

עָלָה ('ālā') *inf.* עֲלֹה, עֲלוֹת, עֲלֹת, *imp.* עֲלֵה, עֲלִי, *fut.* יַעֲלֶה, וַיַּעַל, *pt.* עֹלֶה, עוֹלֶה, *pl.* עֹלִים, *f* עֹלָה, *pl.* עֹלוֹת, to ascend, to mount up, to go up, to rise; to grow up; to be lifted up, to be put up. — *Ni.* נַעֲלָה, *inf.* הֵעָלוֹת, *imp. pl.* הֵעָלוּ, *fut.* יֵעָלֶה, to be led up or away; to rise up; to be high, exalted. — *Hi.* הֶעֱלָה, *inf.* הַעֲלוֹת, *imp.* הַעַל, הַעֲלֵה, *fut.* יַעֲלֶה, וַיַּעַל, *pt.* מַעֲלֶה, *c.* מַעֲלֵה, *pl.* מַעֲלִים, *f* מַעֲלָה, to cause to go up, to lead or bring up, to raise, to impose; to take away, to remove; to overlay. — *Ho.* הָעֲלָה to be brought up, offered. — *Hith.* הִתְעַלָּה to be elated, to pride oneself.

עָלֶה ('ālĕ') *m*, *w. art.* הֶעָלֶה, *c.* עֲלֵה, *w.s.* עָלֵהוּ, *pl. c.* עֲלֵי, *coll.* foliage, leaves.

עֹלָה ('ōlā') *f* [עוֹלָה], *c.* עֹלַת, *pl.* עֹלוֹת, burnt-offering, holocaust; ascent, stairs.

עַלְוָה[1] ('ălvā') *f* for עַוְלָה wickedness, wrong.

עַלְוָה[2] ('ălvā') *pr.n.m.*

עֲלוּמִים ('alūmī'm) *m/pl.*, *w.s.* עֲלֻמָיו, youth, time of youth, youthful vigour.

עַלְוָן ('ălvā'n) *pr.n.m.*

עֲלוּקָה ('alūkā') *f* blood-sucking monster, leech, vampire.

עָלַז ('ālă'z) *inf.* עֲלוֹז, *imp. pl.* עִלְזוּ, *fut.* יַעֲלֹז ,יַעֲלֹז, to exult, rejoice.

עָלֵז ('ālē'z) *adj.* rejoicing.

עֲלָטָה ('alātā') *f* darkness.

עֵלִי ('ēlī') *pr.n.m.*

עֱלִי ('elī') *m* a pestle.

עִלִּי ('illī') *adj.*, *f* עִלִּית, *pl.* עִלִּיּוֹת, the upper, the higher.

עֲלִיָּה ('aliyyā') *f* upper room, upper story; the chambers of heaven; ascent, stairs.

עֶלְיוֹן ('ělyō'n) *adj.*, *f* עֶלְיוֹנָה, high, exalted; the most high, supreme [i. e. God].

עַלִּיז ('ăllī'z) *adj.*, *pl.* עַלִּיזִים, *f* עַלִּיזָה, exultant, rejoicing, noisy, proud.

עֲלִיל ('alī'l) *m* crucible [or workshop].

עֲלִילָה ('alīlā') *f*, *pl.* עֲלִילֹת, עֲלִלוֹת, work, deed, exploit.

עֲלִילִיָּה ('alīliyyā') *f* deed.

עֲלִיצוּת ('aliṣū'th) *f* exultation, rejoicing.

עָלַל ('ālă'l) *Poel fut.* יְעוֹלֵל, *pt.* מְעוֹלֵל, to vex, maltreat; to glean, to destroy the remnant; *pt.* child, wanton boy. — *Poal* עוֹלַל to be inflicted. — *Hith.* הִתְעַלֵּל to practise wantonness, to vex, to mock; to be busy, to achieve. — *Hithpo.* הִתְעוֹלֵל to perform, to do [an evil deed].

עֹלֵלוֹת ('ō'lēlō'th) *f/pl.* gleanings; gleaning-time.

עָלַם ('ālă'm) *pt. p.* עָלוּם, *pl.* עֲלֻמִים, to hide, conceal; *pt. p.* secret sin. — *Ni.* נֶעְלַם, *pt.* נֶעֱלָם, to be hidden, concealed, dissembled. — *Hi.* הֶעְלִים, הֶעְלִים, *fut.* יַעְלִים, *pt.* מַעְלִים, to cover, hide, conceal; to darken, to blame. — *Hith.* הִתְעַלֵּם to hide oneself, to withdraw oneself.

עֶלֶם ('ĕ'lĕm) *m*, *i.p.* עָלֶם, a youth, young man.

עַלְמָה ('ălmā') *f*, *pl.* עֲלָמוֹת, maiden, young marriageable woman; עַל־עֲלָמוֹת a musical term: in treble or soprano.

עַלְמוֹן ('ălmō'n) *pr.n.* of a town in Benjamin; *pr.n.* of a station in the desert.

עַלְמוּת ('ălmū'ϑ) – עַל־מוּת – עַל־עֲלָמוֹת, see עַלְמָה.

עָלֶמֶת ('ālĕ'mĕϑ) *pr.n.m.*

עָלַס ('ālă's) *fut.* יַעֲלֹס, to exult, rejoice. — *Ni.* נֶעֱלַס to exult, to wave joyfully.

עָלַע ('ālă'') *Pi.* *fut.* יְעַלַּע, *pl.* יְעַלְעוּ, to suck up.

עָלַף ('ālă'f) *Pu.* עֻלַּף, to be covered; to be overcome, to faint. — *Hith.* הִתְעַלֵּף to cover or veil oneself; to faint.

עֻלְפֶּה ('ŭlpĕ') *m* a mourning, languor; or *adj.* languishing, mourning.

עָלַץ ('ālă'ʙ) *inf.* עֲלֹץ, *fut.* יַעֲלֹץ, 1. *sg.* אֶעֶלְצָה, to exult, rejoice; to show mischievous joy.

עַם ('ām), **עַם** ('ăm) *m* [and *f*], *w. art.* הָעָם, *c.* עַם, *w.s.* עַמִּי, *pl.* עַמִּים, עֲמָמִים, *c.* עַמֵּי, people, nation, tribe, community; common people, men, inhabitants, populace, mankind.

עִם ('ĭm) *prep.*, *w.s.* עִמִּי and עִמָּדִי, עִמְּךָ, עִמּוֹ, עִמָּנוּ, עִמָּכֶם, עִמָּם, with, by, beside, at, near; מֵעִם from with, away from, from away.

עָמַד ('āmă'd) *inf.* עֲמֹד, *w.s.* עָמְדוֹ ('ŏmdō'), *imp.* עֲמֹד, עִמְדִי, *fut.* יַעֲמֹד, *pt.* עֹמֵד, עוֹמֵד, *pl.* עֹמְדִים, *f* עֹמֶדֶת, *pl.* עֹמְדוֹת, to stand, to stand before one, to wait on, to serve; to place oneself; to stay, to continue, to persist, to persevere, to resist; to stand still, to cease; to stand up, to rise, to make one's appearance. — *Hi.* הֶעֱמִיד, *inf.* הַעֲמִיד, *imp.* הַעֲמֵד, *fut.* יַעֲמִיד, יַעֲמֵד, *pt.* מַעֲמִיד, to cause to stand, to set up, to erect, to establish, to appoint, to place, to settle, to raise up, to stir up; to preserve, to maintain. — *Ho.* הָעֳמַד,

fut. יֵעָמֵד, *pt.* מָעֳמָד, to be placed, to stand upright.

עִמָּד (ʿĭmmā'd) *prep.* in עִמָּדִי, see עִם.

עֹמֶד (ʿō'mĕd) *m* a standing, station, platform.

עֶמְדָּה (ʿĕmdā') *f* domicile.

עֻמָּה[1] (ʿŭmmā') *f, c.* עֻמַּת, union, society, junction; *adv.* and *prep.* לְעֻמַּת together with, at, by, near, by the side of, near to, compared with, like as, beside.

עֻמָּה[2] (ʿŭmmā') *pr.n.* of a town in Asher.

עַמּוּד (ʿămmū'd) *m, pl.* עַמּוּדִים, pillar, column; stage, platform.

עַמּוֹן (ʿămmō'n) *pr.n.m.*; *gent.* עַמּוֹנִי, *pl.* עַמּוֹנִים = בְּנֵי עַמּוֹן Ammonites.

עָמוֹס (ʿāmō's); עָמוֹק (ʿāmō'k); עַמִּיאֵל (ʿămmī'ē'l); עַמִּיזָבָד (ʿămmī'zābā'd); עַמִּיהוּד (ʿămmīhū'r); עַמִּינָדָב (ʿămmī'nādā'b) *pr.n.m.*

עָמִיר (ʿāmī'r) *m* bundle, heap of cut grain, swath.

עַמִּישַׁדַּי (ʿămmī'săddă'y) *pr. n.m.*

עָמִית (ʿāmī'th) *f, w.s.* עֲמִיתוֹ, society, fellowship; neighbour, fellow-man.

עָמַל (ʿāmă'l) *fut.* יַעֲמֹל, to labour, to toil.

עָמָל (ʿāmā'l) *m, c.* עֲמַל, *w.s.* עֲמָלִי, labour, toil; gain by labour; trouble, misery, distress, sorrow, suffering; mischief, wrong, oppression.

עָמֵל (ʿāmē'l) *adj., pl.* עֲמֵלִים, labouring, toiling, suffering, wretched; *subst.* workman, labourer.

עֲמָלֵק (ʿamālē'k) *pr.n.m.*; *gent.* עֲמָלֵקִי.

עָמַם (ʿāmă'm) to surpass, to be higher. — *Ho. fut.* יוּעַם to be darkened.

עִמָּנוּאֵל (ʿĭmmā'nū'ē'l) *pr.n.m.*

עָמַס (ʿāmă's) *fut.* יַעֲמֹס, *pt.* עֹמֵס, *pt. p.* עָמוּס, to lift up, to heave; to bear, to carry; to lay upon, to bestow. — *Hi.* הֶעֱמִיס to load upon.

עֲמַסְיָה (ʿamăsyā') *pr.n.m.*

עַמְעָד (ʿămʿā'd) *pr.n.* of a town in Asher.

עָמַק (ʿāmă'k) to be unfathomable, unsearchable. — *Hi.* הֶעֱמִיק, *imp.* הַעֲמֵק,

pt. מַעֲמִיק, to make deep; to do extensively.

עָמֵק (ʿāmē'k) *adj.*, *pl. c.* עִמְקֵי, deep, unintelligible.

עָמֹק (ʿāmō'k) *adj.*, *pl.* עֲמֻקִּים, *f* עֲמֻקָּה, *pl.* עֲמֻקּוֹת, deep, low; mysterious, unsearchable.

עֵמֶק (ʿē'mĕk) *m*, *w.s.* עִמְקְךָ, *pl.* עֲמָקִים, depth, deep plain, valley.

עֵמֶק הָאֵלָה (ʿē'mĕk hā'ēlā') *pr.n.*, terebinth-valley, near Bethlehem.

עֵמֶק הַבָּכָא (ʿē'mĕk hăbbāḏā') *pr.n.*, valley of the balsam-shrub, near Jerusalem.

עֵמֶק הַבְּרָכָה (ʿē'mĕk hăbbᵉrāḏā') *pr.n.*, valley of the praise or blessing, near Tekoah.

עֵמֶק הַמֶּלֶךְ (ʿē'mĕk hămmĕ'lĕḏ) *pr.n.*, the king's valley, i. e. the valley of the Kidron.

עֵמֶק רְפָאִים (ʿē'mĕk rᵉfā'ī'm) *pr.n.*, valley of giants, between Jerusalem and Bethlehem.

עֵמֶק הַשִּׂדִּים (ʿē'mĕk hăßßĭddī'm) *pr.n.*, valley on the site of the Dead Sea.

עֹמֶק (ʿō'mĕk) *m* depth.

עָמַר (ʿāmă'r) *Pi. pt.* מְעַמֵּר, to bind; *pt.* sheaf-binder. — *Hith.* הִתְעַמֵּר to pawn [others: to be harsh or rough].

עֹמֶר[1] (ʿō'mĕr) *m*, *pl.* עֳמָרִים, sheaf, bundle of ears.

עֹמֶר[2] (ʿō'mĕr) *m* a measure for dry goods, 10th part of an Ephah.

עֲמֹרָה (ʿamōrā') *pr.n.* of a town, Gomorrah.

עָמְרִי (ʿŏmrī'); **עַמְרָם** (ʿăm-rā'm) *pr.n.m.*

עָמַשׂ = עָמַס.

עֲמָשָׂה (ʿamāßā'); **עֲמָשַׂי** (ʿamāßă'y); **עֲמַשְׁסַי** (ʿamăšßă'y) *pr.n.m.*

עֲנָב (ʿanā'b) *pr.n.* of a town near Hebron.

עֵנָב (ʿēnā'b) *m*, *pl.* עֲנָבִים, *c.* עִנְּבֵי, *w.s.* עֲנָבֵמוֹ, berry, grape, raisin.

עָנַג (ʿānă'g) *Pu. pt.* מְעֻנָּג, to be delicate, luxurious. — *Hith.* הִתְעַנֵּג to make oneself delicate; to enjoy oneself, to relish; to mock.

עָנֹג (ʿānō'g) *adj.*, *w. art.* הָעָנֹג, *f* עֲנֻגָּה, delicate, effeminate.

עֹנֶג (ʿō'nĕg) *m* delight, enjoyment, joy.

עָנָה¹ (ʿānā') *inf.* עֲנוֹת, *imp.* עֲנֵה, *fut.* יַעֲנֶה, וַיַּעַן, *pt.* עֹנֶה, *w.s.* עֹנֵהוּ, *f* עֹנָה, to reply, to answer, to hear [prayers]; to bear witness; to vindicate oneself; to begin to speak, to begin to sing, to respond in a choir; to declare, announce, reveal. — *Ni.* נַעֲנָה, *fut.* יֵעָנֶה, *pt.* נַעֲנֶה, to be answered, to be heard; to answer. — *Pi.* עִנָּה, *inf.* עַנּוֹת. *imp.* עַנֵּה, to answer in singing, to sing alternately. — *Hi. pt.* מַעֲנֶה to answer, to vouch [others: to cause to sing].

עָנָה² (ʿānā') *inf.* עֲנוֹת, *fut.* יַעֲנֶה, to be bowed down, to be oppressed or depressed, humbled, miserable; to toil, to labour. — *Ni.* נַעֲנָה, *inf.* לֵעָנוֹת [for לְהֵעָנוֹת], *pt.* נַעֲנֶה, *f* נַעֲנָה, to be bowed down, to be afflicted; to humble oneself. — *Pi.* עִנָּה, *inf.* עַנֵּה, עַנֹּת, *fut.* יְעַנֶּה, *pt.* מְעַנֶּה, to bow down, oppress, humble; to maltreat; to force, violate; to afflict oneself, to fast. — *Pu.* עֻנָּה, *inf.* עֻנּוֹת, *fut.* יְעֻנֶּה, *pt.* מְעֻנֶּה, to be maltreated, afflicted, humbled. — *Hi.* הֶעֱנָה, *fut.* יַעֲנֶה, to oppress, humble. — *Hith.* הִתְעַנָּה, *inf.* הִתְעַנּוֹת, to humble oneself, to be afflicted, to suffer.

עֲנָה (ʿanā') *pr.n.m.*

עֹנָה see עוֹנָה.

עָנָו (ʿānā'v) *adj.*, *pl.* עֲנָוִים, *c.* עַנְוֵי, oppressed, humbled, submitting, suffering, patient, pious.

עָנוּב (ʿānū'b) *pr.n.m.*

עֲנָוָה (ʿanāvā') *f*, *w.s.* עַנְוָתְךָ [עַנְוְתְךָ], humility, gentleness, condescension.

עַנְוָה (ʿănvā') *f* = עֲנָוָה.

עָנוֹק = עֲנָק.

עָנוּת (ʿānū'ϑ) *f*, *c.* עֱנוּת, affliction, suffering [others: cry].

עָנִי (ʿānī') *adj.*, *pl.* עֲנִיִּים [עֲנָוִים], *c.* עֲנִיֵּי, oppressed, afflicted, poor, wretched, miserable, helpless; humble, patient, meek.

עֳנִי (ʿonī') *m*, *i.p.* עֹנִי, *w.s.* עָנְיִי (ʿŏnyī'), oppression, affliction, misery, suffering, poverty.

עֻנִּי (ʿŭnnī') ; **עֲנָיָה** (ʿanāyā') *pr.n.m.*

עָנִים (ʿānī'm) *pr.n.* of a town in Judah.

עִנְיָן (ʿĭnyā'n) *m*, *c.* עִנְיַן, toil, work, labour, employment, business; matter, thing, cause.

עָנֵם (ʿānē'm) *pr.n.* of a place in Issachar.

עֲנָמִים (ʿanāmī'm) *pr.n.* of a tribe in Egypt.

עֲנַמֶּלֶךְ (ʿanămmĕ'lĕḱ) *pr.n.m.*; *pr.n.* of a god of the Sepharvites.

עָנַן[1] (ʿānă'n) *Po.* עוֹנֵן, *pt.* מְעוֹנֵן, to act covertly, to practise magic, to soothsay, to divine; *pt.* sorcerer, enchanter.

עָנַן[2] (ʿānă'n) [*den.* of עָנָן] *Pi. inf. w.s.* עַנְנִי, to gather clouds.

עָנָן[1] (ʿānā'n) *m*, *w. art.* הֶעָנָן, *c.* עֲנַן, *pl.* עֲנָנִים, cloud, clouds; crowd, host.

עָנָן[2] (ʿānā'n) *pr.n.m.*

עֲנָנָה (ʿanānā') *f* = עָנָן[1] clouds.

עֲנַנְיָה (ʿanănyā') *pr.n.m.*; *pr.n.* of a place in Benjamin.

עָנָף (ʿānā'f) *m*, *c.* עֲנַף, *pl. c.* עַנְפֵי, sprout, branch, bough.

עָנֵף (ʿānē'f) *adj.*, *f* עֲנֵפָה, full of boughs.

עָנַק (ʿānă'k) *pf. w.s.* עֲנָקַתְמוֹ, to be put round the neck, to deck as a collar. — *Hi.* הֶעֱנִיק, *fut.* יַעֲנִיק, to lay upon the neck, to load, to supply.

עָנָק (ʿānā'k) *m*, *pl.* עֲנָקִים, עֲנָקוֹת, neck-ornament, neck-lace.

עֲנָק (ʿanā'k) *pr.n.m.* of a giant, Anak, and his descendants, *pl.* עֲנָקִים.

עָנֵר (ʿānē'r) *pr.n.m.*; *pr.n.* of a town in Manasseh.

עָנַשׁ (ʿānă's) *inf.* עֲנוֹשׁ, עֲנוֹשׁ, to impose a contribution or fine; to punish. — *Ni.* נֶעֱנַשׁ, *fut.* יֵעָנֵשׁ, to be fined, to be punished.

עֹנֶשׁ (ʿō'nĕs) *m* contribution, fine, punishment.

עֲנָת (ʿanā'ϑ) *pr.n.m.*

עֲנָתוֹת (ʿanāϑō'ϑ) *pr.n.* of a place near Jerusalem in Benjamin; *gent.* עַנְּתֹתִי.

עַנְתֹתִיָּה (ʿănϑōϑīyyā') *pr.n.m*

עָסִים ('āsī'm) *m, c.* עֲסִיס, new wine, must.

עֳפִי ('ofī') *m, pl.* עֳפָאִים, twig, branch, foliage.

עָפַל ('āfă'l) *Pu.* עֻפַּל to be inflated, arrogant. — *Hi. fut.* יַעְפִּיל to act proudly or presumptuously.

עֹפֶל ('ō'fĕl) *m, pl.* עֳפָלִים, *c.* עָפְלֵי ('ŏflē'), hill; הָעֹפֶל an eminence upon Zion; tumor, swelling.

עָפְנִי ('ŏfnī') *pr.n.* of a place in Benjamin.

עַפְעַף ('ăf'ă'f) *m,* only *du.* עַפְעַפַּיִם, *c.* עַפְעַפֵּי, eyelashes, eyelids.

עָפַר ('āfă'r) [*den.* of עָפָר] *Pi.* עִפֵּר to pelt with dust, to bedust.

עָפָר ('āfā'r) *m, w. art.* הֶעָפָר, *c.* עֲפַר, *pl. c.* עַפְרוֹת, dust, dry earth, soil, clay, lump, clod; gold-dust.

עֵפֶר ('ē'fĕr) *pr.n.m.*

עֹפֶר ('ō'fĕr) *m* young deer, roe, gazelle.

עָפְרָה ('ŏfrā') *pr.n.* of towns in Benjamin and Manasseh.

עֶפְרוֹן ('ĕfrō'n) *pr.n.m.*; *pr.n.* of a town in Benjamin; *pr.n.* of a mountain.

עוֹפֶרֶת, עֹפֶרֶת ('ōfĕ'rĕth) *f* lead.

עֵץ ('ēts) *m, w.s.* עֵצְךָ, *pl.* עֵצִים, *c.* עֲצֵי, tree, wood, timber, stake, pole, log, wooden work.

עָצַב ('ātsă'b) *pt. p.* עָצוּב, *f c.* עֲצוּבַת, to afflict, grieve, pain. — *Ni.* נֶעֱצַב, *fut.* יֵעָצֵב, to grieve oneself, to be sorrowful. — *Pi.* עִצֵּב, *fut.* יְעַצֵּב, to form, to shape; to grieve, pain, afflict. — *Hi.* הֶעֱצִיב, *inf.* בְּהַעֲצִיב, *fut.* יַעֲצִיב, to form, fashion, shape; to grieve, offend. — *Hith.* הִתְעַצֵּב to grieve oneself; to be angry.

עָצָב ('ātsā'b) *m,* only *pl.* עֲצַבִּים, *c.* עֲצַבֵּי, image, idol.

עָצֵב ('ātsē'b) *m,* only *pl. c.* עַצְּבֵי, labourer, bondsman.

עֶצֶב ('ĕ'tsĕb) *m, pl.* עֲצָבִים, a thing formed or shaped; earthen vessel; labour, toil, gain; trouble, grievance.

עֹצֶב ('ō'tsĕb) *m, w.s.* עָצְבְּךָ ('ŏtsb'khā'), image, idol; pain, labour, affliction.

עִצָּבוֹן ('ĭtstsābō'n) *m, c.*

עִצָּבוֹן, w.s. עִצְּבוֹנֵךְ, labour, toil; pain.

עַצֶּבֶת (ʿăBBĕ'ḇĕϑ) f, c. עַצְּבַת, pl. c. עַצְּבוֹת, pain, grievance, affliction, sorrow, wound.

עָצָה (ʿāBā') pt. עֹצֶה, to shut, to close.

עָצֶה (ʿāBĕ') m the spine, the back-bone.

עֵצָה (ʿēBā') f, c. עֲצַת, w.s. עֲצָתוֹ, pl. עֵצוֹת, w.s. עֲצֹתֶיךָ, wood [= עֵץ]; counsel, advice; consultation; purpose, project, plan, design; wisdom, deliberation.

עָצוּם (ʿāBū'm) adj., pl. עֲצוּמִים, strong, powerful, mighty, numerous; pl. strong limbs, fangs.

עֶצְיוֹן גֶּבֶר (ʿĕByō'n gĕ'ḇĕr) pr.n. of a seaport on the Elanitic gulf.

עָצַל (ʿāBă'l) Ni. fut. יֵעָצֵל, to be idle, to tarry.

עָצֵל (ʿāBē'l) adj. slothful, sluggard.

עַצְלָה (ʿăBlā') and עַצְלוּת (ʿăBlū'ϑ) f, du. עֲצַלְתַּיִם, sloth.

עָצַם (ʿāBă'm), עָצֵם (ʿāBē'm) inf. w.s. עָצְמוֹ (ʿŏBmō'), fut. יֶעְצַם, יַעֲצֹם, pl. יַעַצְמוּ, pt. עֹצֵם, to be or become firm, strong, powerful, mighty; to shut, to close. — Pi. עִצֵּם, fut. יְעַצֵּם, to close; den. of עֶצֶם: to break or gnaw the bones. — Hi. fut. יַעֲצִים to make strong.

עֶצֶם (ʿĕ'Bĕm) f [and m], w.s. עַצְמִי, pl. עֲצָמִים and עֲצָמוֹת, c. עַצְמוֹת, bone; body, frame; essence, self; the selfsame; בְּעֶצֶם הַיּוֹם הַזֶּה on that very day.

עֹצֶם (ʿō'Bĕm) m, w.s. עָצְמִי (ʿŏBmī'), strength, might; bone, body.

עָצְמָה (ʿŏBmā') f, c. עָצְמַת, strength; multitude.

עַצְמוֹן (ʿăBmō'n) pr.n. of a town.

עַצֻּמוֹת (ʿăBBūmō'ϑ) f/pl. arguments, reasons, proofs.

עֵצֶן (ʿē'Bĕn) m, only in הָעֶצְנוֹ or הָעֶצְנִי, spear [or gent. of pr.n. עֵצֶן].

עָצַר (ʿāBă'r) inf. עֲצֹר, fut. יַעֲצֹר, pt. p. עָצוּר, f עֲצֻרָה, to close, to shut up, to restrain, to stop, to hold back, to retain, to withhold; to rule, prevail, bridle; עָצוּר וְעָזוּב a slave and a freed one. — *Ni.* נֶעֱצַר, *inf.* הֵעָצֵר, *pt.* נֶעֱצָר, to be shut up, restrained, hindered; to be assembled.

עֶצֶר ('ĕ'ßĕr) *m* dominion.

עֹצֶר ('ō'ßĕr) *m* a shutting up; constraint, oppression.

עֲצָרָה ('aßārā') *f*, עֲצֶרֶת ('aßĕ'rĕϑ) *f* assembly, festive assembly, festival.

עָקַב ('ākă'b) *inf.* עָקוֹב, *fut.* יַעְקֹב, to deceive; to take by the heel. — *Pi. fut.* יְעַקֵּב to keep back.

עָקֵב[1] ('ākē'b) *m, c.* עֲקֵב, *w.s.* עֲקֵבוֹ, *pl.* עֲקֵבִים, *c.* עִקְּבֵי and עִקְּבוֹת, heel, hoof; step, foot-print; the rear.

עָקֵב[2] ('ākē'b) [*adj.*] *m, pl. w.s.* עֲקֵבַי, plotter, deceiver, lier-in-wait.

עָקֹב ('ākō'b) *adj.*, *f* עֲקֻבָּה, uneven, hilly; deceitful; showing foot-prints.

עֵקֶב ('ē'kĕb) *m* the end, the last; result, reward; *prep.* and *conj.* on account of, because of, because.

עָקְבָה ('ŏkbā') *f* cunning, deceit.

עָקַד ('ākă'd) *fut.* יַעֲקֹד to bind.

עָקֹד ('ākō'd) *adj.*, *pl.* עֲקֻדִּים, striped, streaky.

עָקָה ('ākā') *f*, *c.* עַקַת, oppression.

עַקּוּב ('ăkkū'b) *pr.n.m.*

עָקַל ('ākă'l) *Pu. pt.* מְעֻקָּל, to be perverted.

עֲקַלְקַל ('akălkă'l) *adj.*, *f/pl.* עֲקַלְקַלּוֹת, crooked, winding.

עֲקַלָּתוֹן ('akăllāϑō'n) *adj.* crooked, winding, tortuous.

עֲקָן ('akā'n) *pr.n.m.*

עָקַר ('ākă'r) *inf.* עָקוֹר to root out. — *Ni.* נֶעֱקַר to be destroyed. — *Pi.* עִקֵּר, *fut.* יְעַקֵּר, to lame, to hamstring.

עָקָר ('ākā'r) *adj.*, *f* עֲקָרָה, *c.* עֲקֶרֶת, barren.

עֵקֶר[1] ('ē'kĕr) *m* a naturalized foreigner.

עֵקֶר[2] ('ē'kĕr) *pr.n.m.*

עַקְרָב ('ăkrā'b) *m, c.* עַקְרַב, *pl.* עַקְרַבִּים, scorpion; a knotted scourge.

עֶקְרוֹן ('ĕkrō'n) *pr.n.* of a Philistine city.

עָקַשׁ ('ākă's) *Ni.* נֶעְקַשׁ to be perverted. — *Pi.* עִקֵּשׁ[1] to pervert, to make crooked. — *Hi. fut. w.s.* יַעְקְשֵׁנִי, to regard as perverse.

עִקֵּשׁ² (ʿĭkkē'š) *adj., pl.* עִקְּשִׁים, *c.* עִקְּשֵׁי, perverted, perverse.

עִקֵּשׁ³ (ʿĭkkē'š) *pr.n.m.*

עִקְּשׁוּת (ʿĭkšū'ϑ) *f* perverseness.

עָר¹ (ʿār) = עִיר; עָר מוֹאָב *pr.n.*, chief town in Moab.

עָר² (ʿār) = צַר enemy, *pl.* עָרִים.

עֵר (ʿēr) *pr.n.m.* [see also עוּר].

עָרַב¹ (ʿāră'ḇ) *fut.* יֶעֱרַב, *w.s.* אֶעֶרְבֶנּוּ, *pt.* עֹרֵב, *pl.* עֹרְבִים, to exchange, to traffic; to pledge, to pawn; to give security, to warrant. — *Hith.* הִתְעָרֵב to intermingle, to have intercourse, to rival.

עָרַב² (ʿāră'ḇ) to be or grow dark, to be obscured. — *Hi. inf.* בְּהַעֲרֵב to do at evening.

עָרֵב¹ (ʿārē'ḇ) *fut.* יֶעֱרַב, to be sweet, pleasant.

עֲרָב (ʿārā'ḇ) *m, pl.* עֲרָבִים, *c.* עַרְבֵי, poplar or willow.

עֲרָב (ʿarā'ḇ), עֲרַב (ʿară'ḇ) *pr.n.* Arabia; *gent.* עֲרָבִי, *pl.* עַרְבִים and עַרְבִיאִים, Arab, Arabian.

עָרֵב² (ʿārē'ḇ) *adj.* sweet, pleasant.

עֵרֶב (ʿē'rĕḇ), עֶרֶב¹ (ʿĕ'rĕḇ) *m* woof, weft; mixed multitude, promiscuous mass of foreigners.

עֶרֶב² (ʿĕ'rĕḇ) *m* and *f, i.p.* עָרֶב, *du.* עַרְבַּיִם, the becoming dark, evening, twilight; בֵּין הָעַרְבַּיִם between the two evenings, at the time of sunset, or between sunset and dark.

עֹרֵב¹ (ʿōrē'ḇ) *m, pl.* עֹרְבִים, raven, crow.

עֹרֵב² (ʿōrē'ḇ) *pr.n.m.*

עָרֹב (ʿārō'ḇ) *m, w. art.* הֶעָרֹב, a stinging insect, dog-fly, gadfly.

עֲרָבָה (ʿarāḇā') *f, w. loc.* ה עֲרָבָתָה, *w.s.* עַרְבָתָהּ, *pl.* עֲרָבוֹת, *c.* עַרְבוֹת, dry land, desert, wilderness, plain.

עֲרֻבָּה (ʿarŭbbā') *f, w.s.* עֲרֻבָּתָם, surety, pawn, pledge.

עֵרָבוֹן (ʿē'rāḇō'n) *m* pledge, warrant-money.

עַרְבָתִי (ʿărḇāϑī') *pr.n.m.* inhabitant of an unknown place עַרְבָה or עֲרָבָה.

עָרַג ('ārā'g) *fut.* יַעֲרֹג, to pant, to long for.

עֲרָד ('arā'd) *pr.n.* of a royal town of the Canaanites; *pr.n.m.*

עָרָה[1] ('ārā') *Pi.* עֵרָה, *inf.* עָרוֹת, *imp. pl.* עָרוּ, *fut.* יְעָרֶה, יְעַר, to uncover; to destroy, demolish; to pour out, to empty. — *Ni. fut.* יֵעָרֶה, to be poured out. — *Hi.* הֶעֱרָה to uncover, to pour out, to give up. — *Hith.* הִתְעָרֶה to uncover oneself, to make oneself naked, to spread oneself.

עָרָה[2] ('ārā') *f*, only *pl.* עָרוֹת, cleared place, meadow.

עֲרוּגָה ('arūgā') *f*, *c.* עֲרוּגַת, *pl.* עֲרוּגוֹת, garden-bed.

עָרוֹד ('ārō'd) *m* wild ass.

עֶרְוָה ('ĕrvā') *f*, *c.* עֶרְוַת, *w.s.* עֶרְוָתְךָ, nakedness, bareness, the pudenda; shame; shameful or foul thing, filthiness.

עָרוֹם, עָרֹם ('ārō'm) *adj.*, *pl.* עֲרֻמִּים, עֲרוּמִּים, *f* עֲרֻמָּה, naked, bared, half-dressed.

עָרוּם ('ārū'm) *adj.*, *pl.* עֲרוּמִים, cunning, sly, crafty.

עֲרוֹעֵר[1] ('arō'ē'r) *m* tree, shrub, heath.

עֲרוֹעֵר[2] ('arō'ē'r), עֲרֹעֵר, *pr.n.* of several towns.

עָרוּץ ('ārū'ß) *m*, *c.* עֲרוּץ, horror [others: fissure].

עֵרִי ('ērī') *pr.n.m.*

עֶרְיָה ('ĕryā') *f* = עֶרְוָה nakedness, bareness.

עֲרִיסָה ('arīßā') *f*, only *pl.* עֲרִיסוֹת, grit, groats; gruel.

עָרִיף ('ārī'f) *m*, only *pl.* עֲרִיפִים, clouds, darkness of clouds.

עָרִיץ ('ārī'ß) *adj.*, *pl.* עָרִיצִים, *c.* עָרִיצֵי, violent, tyrannical; mighty, powerful; tyrant; a mighty one.

עֲרִירִי ('arīrī') *adj.*, *pl.* עֲרִירִים, forsaken, solitary, childless.

עָרַךְ ('āră'ch) *inf.* עָרוֹךְ, עֲרֹךְ, *imp.* עֲרֹךְ, עִרְכָה, *fut.* יַעֲרֹךְ, *pt.* עֹרֵךְ, *pl.* עֹרְכִים, *pt. p.* עָרוּךְ, *f* עֲרוּכָה, *pl.* עֲרֻכוֹת, to set in order, to prepare, to arrange; to draw up for battle, to muster; to compare, to equal, to estimate. — *Hi.* הֶעֱרִיךְ, *fut.* יַעֲרִיךְ, to estimate or value.

עֵרֶךְ ('ē'rĕḵ) *m, w.s.* עֶרְכּוֹ, arrangement, row, pile; preparation; estimation, value, price.

עָרַל ('ārā'l) to cast away as profane. — *Ni. imp.* הֵעָרֵל to show one's foreskin, to bare oneself.

עָרֵל ('ārē'l) *adj., c.* עֲרַל, עָרֵל, *pl.* עֲרֵלִים, *c.* עַרְלֵי, *f* עֲרֵלָה, uncircumcised, unclean, unconsecrated, insensible.

עָרְלָה ('ŏrlā') *f, c.* עָרְלַת, *w.s.* עָרְלָתוֹ, *pl.* עֲרָלוֹת, *c.* עָרְלוֹת ('ŏrlō'ϑ), foreskin; uncleanness, insensibility; unclean fruit.

עָרַם[1] ('ārā'm) *inf.* עָרֹם to be cunning, crafty. — *Hi.* הֶעֱרִים, *fut.* יַעֲרִים, יַעֲרִם, to act craftily, to form a cunning plan; to act prudently.

עָרַם[2] ('ārā'm) *Ni.* נֶעֱרַם, to be heaped up, to be amassed.

עָרֹם see עָרוֹם.

עֹרֶם ('ō'rĕm) *m* cunning; craftiness.

עָרְמָה ('ŏrmā') *f* cunning, craft, prudence.

עֲרֵמָה ('ărēmā') *f, c.* עֲרֵמַת, *pl.* עֲרֵמוֹת, עֲרֵמִים, heap [of grain, of rubbish].

עַרְמוֹן ('ărmō'n) *m* plane-tree, maple.

עֵרָן ('ērā'n) *pr.n.m.*; *patr.* עֵרָנִי.

עַרְעוֹר see עֲרוֹעֵר.

עַרְעָר ('ăr'ā'r) *adj.* naked, bare, forsaken.

עָרַף[1] ('ārā'f) *fut.* יַעֲרֹף, to drop down.

עָרַף[2] ('ārā'f) *pt.* עֹרֵף, to break the neck [of an animal].

עֹרֶף ('ō'rĕf) *m, w.s.* עָרְפִּי ('ŏrpī'), the neck, the nape.

עָרְפָּה ('ŏrpā') *pr.n.f.*

עֲרָפֶל ('ărā'fĕl) *m* darkness, dark clouds.

עָרַץ ('ārā'ʒ) *inf.* עֲרֹץ, *fut.* יַעֲרֹץ, to be afraid, to fear; *tr.* to frighten, to terrify. — *Ni. pt.* נֶעֱרָץ to be fearful, terrible. — *Hi.* הֶעֱרִיץ, *fut.* יַעֲרִיץ, *pt.* מַעֲרִיץ, to fear, to be afraid; *tr.* to inspire fear or awe.

עָרַק (ʿārăʹk) *pt.* עֹרֵק, to gnaw; others: to flee.

עַרְקִי (ʿărkīʹ) *pr.n.m.*

עָרַר (ʿārăʹr) *imp.* עֹרָה, to be naked, bare; to bare oneself. — *Pi.* עוֹרֵר to lay bare, to demolish. — *Pil. inf.* עַרְעֵר, to lay bare. — *Hithpalp.* הִתְעַרְעֵר to be bared or demolished.

עֶרֶשׂ (ʿĕʹrĕs) *f* bedstead, bed, canopy-bed.

עֵשֶׂב (ʿēʹsĕb) *m, w.s.* עֶשְׂבָּם, *pl. c.* עִשְּׂבוֹת, plant, vegetable, herb, greens.

עָשָׂה (ʿāsāʹ) *inf.* עֲשׂה, עֲשׂוֹת, עֲשׂה, עֲשׂוֹ, *imp.* עֲשֵׂה, *fut.* יַעֲשֶׂה, וַיַּעַשׂ, *pt.* עֹשֶׂה, עוֹשֶׂה, *c.* עֹשֵׂה, *pl.* עֹשִׂים, *c.* עֹשֵׂי, *f* עֹשָׂה, *pt. p.* עָשׂוּי, *pl.* עֲשׂוּיִם, *f/pl.* עֲשֻׂיוֹת, to work, labour, toil; to make, to create, construct, build, accomplish; to acquire, earn, procure; to prepare; to offer or sacrifice; to appoint or constitute; to keep, to fulfil. — *Ni.* נַעֲשָׂה, נַעֲשָׂה, *inf.* הֵעָשׂוֹת, *fut.* יֵעָשֶׂה, יֵעָשׂ, *pt.* נַעֲשֶׂה, to be made, done, created, prepared; to happen, to be. — *Pi.* עִשָּׂה to handle, to squeeze. — *Pu.* עֻשָּׂה to be made, created.

עֲשָׂהאֵל (ʿasāʾēʹl) *pr.n.m.*

עֵשָׂו (ʿēsāʹv) *pr.n.m.*

עָשׂוֹר (ʿāsōʹr) *m, w. art.* הֶעָשׂוֹר, the number ten; decad; ten days, tenth day; an instrument with ten strings, decachord.

עֲשִׂיאֵל (ʿasīʾēʹl); **עֲשָׂיָה** (ʿasāyāʹ) *pr.n.m.*

עֲשִׂירִי (ʿasīrīʹ) *adj. num., f* עֲשִׂירִיָּה, עֲשִׂירִית, tenth; *f* the tenth part.

עָשַׂק (ʿāsăʹk) *Hith.* הִתְעַשֵּׂק, to quarrel, to strive.

עֵשֶׂק (ʿēʹsĕk) *pr.n.* of a well near Gerar.

עָשַׂר (ʿāsăʹr) [*den.* of עֶשֶׂר] *fut.* יַעְשֹׂר, to tithe, to take the tenth part. — *Pi. inf.* עַשֵּׂר, *fut.* יְעַשֵּׂר, *pt.* מְעַשֵּׂר, to give or take the tenth part. — *Hi. inf.* לַעְשֵׂר [for לְהַעֲשֵׂר] the same as *Pi.*

עֶשֶׂר (ʿĕʹsĕr) *f, m* עֲשָׂרָה, עֲשֶׂרֶת, *num.* ten; *pl.* עֲשָׂרוֹת decads.

עָשָׂר (ʿāsāʹr) *m, f* עֶשְׂרֵה ten [in compounded numbers from 11 to 19]; *pl.* עֶשְׂרִים *m* and *f* twenty; the twentieth.

עִשָּׂרוֹן ('Issārō'n) *m* the tenth part; a measure for grain and meal [one tenth of an Ephah].

עָשׁ[1] ('āš) *m* a moth.

עָשׁ[2] ('āš) = עַיִשׁ.

עָשׁוֹק ('āšō'k) *m* oppressor.

עָשׁוּק ('āšū'k) *m*, only *pl.* עֲשׁוּקִים, oppression, violence.

עָשׁוֹת ('āšō'ϑ) *adj.* forged, wrought.

עַשְׁוָת ('ăšvā'ϑ) *pr.n.m.*

עָשִׁיר ('āšī'r) *adj.*, *w. art.* הֶעָשִׁיר, *pl.* עֲשִׁירִים, *c.* עֲשִׁירֵי, rich, wealthy; noble, distinguished; proud, violent.

עָשַׁן ('āšā'n) *fut.* יֶעְשַׁן, to smoke, to burn.

עָשֵׁן ('āšē'n) *adj.*, *pl.* עֲשֵׁנִים, smoking.

עָשָׁן ('āšā'n) *m*, *w. art.* הֶעָשָׁן, *c.* עֲשַׁן, smoke, vapour.

עָשַׁק ('āšā'k) *inf.* עֲשֹׁק, *w.s.* עָשְׁקָם ('ŏškā'm), *fut.* יַעֲשֹׁק, *pt.* עֹשֵׁק, *pt. p.* עָשׁוּק, to oppress, maltreat, subjugate; to cheat; to overflow. — *Pu. pt.* מְעֻשָּׁק to be forced, subdued.

עֵשֶׁק ('ē'šĕk) *pr.n.m.*

עֹשֶׁק[1] ('ō'šĕk) *m* oppression, violence; extortion, unjust gain; grievance, distress.

עֹשֶׁק[2] ('ō'šĕk) *pr.n.m.*

עָשְׁקָה ('ŏškā') *f* oppression, distress.

עָשַׁר ('āšā'r) *fut.* יֶעְשַׁר, to be or become rich. — *Hi.* הֶעֱשִׁיר, *fut.* יַעֲשִׁיר, יַעְשִׁר, *w.s.* יַעְשְׁרֶנּוּ, to make rich, to enrich; to acquire wealth, to become rich. — *Hith.* הִתְעַשֵּׁר to feign oneself rich.

עֹשֶׁר ('ō'šĕr) *m*, *w.s.* עָשְׁרוֹ ('ŏšrō'), riches, wealth.

עָשֵׁשׁ ('āšē'š) to become dry, to grow old, to decay, to wither.

עָשַׁת ('āšā'ϑ) *Hith.* הִתְעַשֵּׁת to recollect, to consider.

עֶשֶׁת ('ĕ'šĕϑ) *f* device, artificial work.

עַשְׁתּוּת ('ăštū'ϑ) *f* thought, opinion.

עַשְׁתֵּי עָשָׂר ('ăštē' 'āsā'r), **עַשְׁתֵּי עֶשְׂרֵה** ('ăštē' 'ĕsrē') *num.* eleven, the eleventh.

עֶשְׁתֹּנֶת ('ĕštō'nĕϑ) *f*, only

pl. w.s. עֶשְׁתֹּנֹתָיו, thought, plan.

עַשְׁתֹּרֶת ('ăstō'rĕϑ) *pr.n.f.*, *pl.* עַשְׁתָּרוֹת, *c.* עַשְׁתְּרוֹת, a Phenician goddess, Astarte, also called אֲשֵׁרָה; *pl.* statues or different forms of **A.**; increase of the flock.

עַשְׁתָּרוֹת ('ăstārō'ϑ) *pr.n.*, *c.* עַשְׁתְּרוֹת, a city in Bashan.

עֵת ('ēϑ) *f*, *w.s.* עִתִּי, *pl.* עִתִּים, עִתּוֹת, time, right or proper time, season; *pl.* circumstances, courses of time, occurrences, events.

עֵת קָצִין ('ēϑ kāẓī'n) *pr.n.* of a town in Zebulon, *w. loc.* ה עִתָּה ק׳.

עַתְּ = עַתָּה.

עָתַד ('āϑă'd) *Pi.* עִתֵּד to make ready, to prepare. — *Hith.* הִתְעַתֵּד to be destined, prepared.

עַתָּה ('ăttā') *adv.* now, at present; then, presently, soon.

עָתוּד see עָתִיד.

עַתּוּד ('ăttū'd) *m*, *pl.* עַתּוּדִים he-goat; leader.

עַתַּי ('ăttă'y) *pr.n.m.*

עִתִּי ('ittī') *adj.* opportune, convenient.

עָתִיד ('āϑī'd) *adj.*, *pl.* עֲתִידִים, *f* עֲתִידָה, *pl.* עֲתִידוֹת, עֲתוּדוֹת, ready, prepared, skilful; *f/pl.* future things, future destiny; treasures.

עֲתָיָה ('aϑāyā') *pr.n.m.*

עָתִיק ('āϑī'k) *adj.* splendid, stately.

עַתִּיק ('ăttī'k) *adj.*, *pl.* עַתִּיקִים, removed [from the breast], weaned; old.

עֲתָךְ ('aϑā'ch) *pr.n.* of a town in Judah.

עַתְלַי ('ăϑlă'y) *pr.n.m.*

עֲתַלְיָה ('aϑălyā'), עֲתַלְיָהוּ ('aϑălyā'hū) *pr.n.m.* and *f.*

עָתַם ('āϑă'm) *Ni.* נֶעְתַּם to be burnt, to be parched up.

עָתְנִי ('ŏϑnī'); עָתְנִיאֵל ('ŏϑnī'ē'l) *pr.n.m.*

עָתַק ('āϑă'k) *fut.* יֶעְתַּק, to be removed, to be advanced, to become old; to be released, freed. — *Hi.* הֶעְתִּיק, *fut.* יַעְתִּיק, וַיַּעְתֵּק, to displace, remove, transfer, advance; to take away.

עָתָק ('āϑā'k) *adj.* arrogant, bold, wanton.

עָתֵק (ʿāθē'k) *adj.* old [and good]; solid; splendid.

עָתַר[1] (ʿāθă'r) *fut.* יֶעְתַּר, to pray, to supplicate. — *Ni.* נֶעְתַּר, *inf.* נַעְתּוֹר, *fut.* יֵעָתֵר, to let oneself be entreated, to hear [a prayer]. — *Hi.* הֶעְתִּיר, *imp. pl.* הַעְתִּירוּ, *fut.* יַעְתִּיר, to pray, to supplicate.

עָתַר[2] (ʿāθă'r) *Ni.* נֶעְתַּר to be abundant or plentiful. — *Hi.* הֶעְתִּיר to make abundant, to multiply.

עָתָר (ʿāθā'r) *m, c.* עֲתַר, fragrance, perfume; worshipper, suppliant.

עֶתֶר (ʿĕ'θĕr) *pr.n.* of a town in Simeon.

עֲתֶרֶת (ʿaθĕ'rĕθ) *f* abundance, riches.

פ

פ, ף the seventeenth letter of the alphabet, called פֵּא, פֵּי [= פֶּה mouth]; as a numeral = 80, ף = 800.

פא see פֹּה.

פָּאָה (pāʾā') *Hi. fut.* יַפְאֶה, *w.s.* אַפְאֵיהֶם, to blow away, to scatter.

פֵּאָה (pēʾā') *f, c.* פְּאַת, *pl.* פֵּאֹת, *du.* פְּאָתַיִם, *c.* פַּאֲתֵי, side, quarter, region, district; extremity, border, corner.

פָּאַר (pāʾă'r) *Pi.* פֵּאֵר, *inf.* פָּאֵר, *fut.* יְפָאֵר, to adorn, beautify, glorify; to glean from a fruit-tree [*den.* of פֹּארָה]. — *Hith.* הִתְפָּאֵר to be glorified, to glorify oneself; to boast, to glory; to declare, to speak plainly.

פְּאֵר (pᵉʾē'r) *m, pl.* פְּאֵרִים, *c.* פַּאֲרֵי, head-dress, turban, chaplet, tiara.

פֹּארָה (pōrā') and **פֻּארָה** (pūrā') *f* green branch, bough, top-branch.

פָּארוּר (pārū'r) *m* redness, flush.

פָּארָן (pārā'n) *pr.n.* of a desert.

פַּג (păg) *m,* only *pl.* פַּגִּים, unripe fig.

פִּגּוּל (pĭggū'l) *m, pl.* פִּגֻּלִים, filth, what is putrified, unclean, abominable.

פָּגַע (pāgă'ʿ) *inf.* פְּגֹעַ, *imp.* פְּגַע, *fut.* יִפְגַּע, to meet with, to push against, to strike, to hit, to attack; to entreat; to intercede for, to help; to reach to, to border upon. — *Hi.* הִפְגִּיעַ, *fut.* יַפְגִּיעַ, *pt.* מַפְגִּיעַ, to cause to fall on, to lay upon; to assail; to intercede, to entreat.

פֶּגַע (pĕ'gă') *m* event, chance.

פָּגַר (pāgă'r) *Pi.* פִּגֵּר to be languid, lazy.

פֶּגֶר (pĕ'gĕr) *m, pl.* פְּגָרִים, *c.* פִּגְרֵי, body, corpse, dead body.

פָּגַשׁ (pāgă'š) *fut.* יִפְגֹּשׁ, to fall upon, to attack, to strike, to meet, to come together. — *Ni.* נִפְגַּשׁ to meet one another. — *Pi.* פִּגֵּשׁ, *fut.* יְפַגֵּשׁ, to hit, to meet one another.

פָּדָה (pāḏā') *inf.* פָּדֹה, פְּדוֹת, *imp.* פְּדֵה, *fut.* יִפְדֶּה, *pt.* פּוֹדֶה, *pt. p.* פָּדוּי, to redeem, to ransom, to free; to dismiss, to rescue. — *Ni. fut.* יִפָּדֶה to be redeemed, to be released. — *Hi. pf. w.s.* הֶפְדָּה to cause to be redeemed. — *Ho. inf.* הָפְדֵּה to be redeemed.

פְּדַהְאֵל (pᵉḏăh'ē'l); פְּדָהצוּר (pᵉḏāẞū'r) *pr.n.m.*

פָּדוּי (pāḏū'y) *m,* only *pl.* פְּדוּיִם ransom, redemption.

פָּדוֹן (pāḏō'n) *pr.n.m.*

פְּדֻת, פְּדוּת (pᵉḏū'ϑ) *f* redemption, deliverance; division, separation, interval.

פְּדָיָה (pᵉḏāyā'), פְּדָיָהוּ (pᵉḏāyā'hū) *pr.n.m.*

פִּדְיוֹם (pĭḏyō'm), פִּדְיֹן (pĭḏyō'n) *m* redemption-money.

פַּדָּן (păddā'n) *m, c.* פַּדַּן, *w. loc.* ה פַּדֶּנָה, plain, flat, field; פַּדַּן אֲרָם plain of Syria, i. e. Upper Mesopotamia.

פָּדַע (pāḏă'') *imp.* פְּדַע to deliver, to rescue.

פֶּדֶר (pĕ'ḏĕr) *m* fat, grease.

פֶּה (pĕ) *m, c.* פִּי, *w.s.* פִּי, פִּיךָ, פִּיו and פִּיהוּ, פִּיהָ, פִּיהֶם and פִּימוֹ, *pl.* פִּים and פִּיּוֹת, mouth, bill; opening, entrance; edge, border, side; mouthful, portion; לְפִי, כְּפִי according to; עַל־פִּי in proportion to, according to command or to one's assertion.

פֹּה (pō), פוֹ, *adv.* here, in this place; hither.

פּוּאָה (pŭ'ā') *pr.n.m.*

פּוּג (pūg) *fut.* יָפוּג, וַיָּפָג (văyyā'fŏg), to be cold, chilled, torpid; to be weak. — *Ni.* נָפוֹג, 1. *sg.* נְפוּגֹתִי, to be benumbed, to be without vital force.

פּוּגָה (pūgā') *f* intermission, cessation.

פֻּוָּה (pŭvvā') *pr.n.m.*

פּוּחַ (pū'aḥ) *fut.* יָפוּחַ, to breathe, to blow, to become cool. — *Hi.* הֵפִיחַ, *inf.* הָפֵחַ, *fut.* יָפִיחַ, to breathe or blow through; to blow up; to speak, to utter; to address harshly.

פּוּט (pūt) *pr.n.* of a people in Africa, Libyans.

פּוּטִיאֵל (pū'tī'ēl); פּוֹטִיפַר (pō'tīfă'r); פּוֹטִי פֶרַע (pō'tī fĕ'ră') *pr.n.m.*

פּוֹטֵר (pōtē'r) *m* a breaking out; see פֶּטֶר.

פּוּךְ (pūḥ) *m* antimony; eye-paint; mortar, cement.

פּוֹל (pōl) *m* bean.

פּוּל¹ (pūl) *pr.n.* of an unknown people, perh. the same as פּוּט.

פּוּל² (pūl) *pr.n.m.*

פּוּן (pūn) *fut.* יָפוּן, 1. *sg.* אָפוּנָה, to become weak, helpless.

פּוֹנֶה (pōnĕ') *m* corner [for פִּנָּה].

פּוּנִי (pūnī') *pr.n.m.*, *patr.* of an unknown פּוּן.

פּוּנֹן (pūnō'n) *pr.n.* of a town in Edom.

פּוּעָה (pū'ā') *pr.n.f.*

פּוּץ (pūṣ) *imp. pl.* פֻּצוּ, *fut.* יָפוּץ, *pt. p.* פּוּץ, to scatter, disperse; to be scattered, to be spread out; to overflow. — *Ni.* נָפוֹץ, *pt.* נָפוֹץ, *f* נְפוֹצֶת, to be scattered, dispersed; to disperse oneself. — *Pil.* פּוֹצֵץ to dash in pieces. — *Pilp.* פִּצְפֵּץ to dash to pieces. — *Hi.* הֵפִיץ, *inf.* הָפִיץ, *fut.* יָפִיץ, וַיָּפֶץ, *pt.* מֵפִיץ, to scatter, disperse, destroy; to drive away; to pour forth; to be dispersed. — *Hith.* הִתְפּוֹצֵץ to be dashed to pieces, to be reduced to dust.

פּוּק¹ (pūk) *pf.* פָּק, to waver, to totter. — *Hi. fut.* יָפִיק to be unsteady.

פּוּק² (pūk) *Hi.* הֵפִיק, *fut.* יָפִיק, יָפֵק, *pt. pl.* מְפִיקִים, to let go out, to send forth, to supply; to obtain;

to bring to an end, to carry out.

פּוּקָה (pūkā') *f* stumbling-block.

פּוּר[1] (pūr) *Hi.* הֵפִיר to frustrate; see פָּרַר.

פּוּר[2] (pūr) *m*, *pl.* פּוּרִים, lot; *pl.* the feast of Purim.

פּוּרָה (pūrā') *f* wine-press; a measure for liquids.

פּוֹרָתָא (pō'rāϑā') *pr.n.m.*

פּוּשׁ (pūš) *pf. pl.* פָּשׁוּ, פִּשְׁתֶּם [for פַּשְׁתֶּם], to leap or caper about, to prance, to be proud. — *Ni.* נָפוֹשׁ to be scattered about.

פּוּתִי (pūϑī') *pr.n.m.*

פָּז (pāz) *m* pure gold, refined gold.

פָּזַז[1] (pāză'z) *Ho. pt.* מוּפָז, to be purified, refined.

פָּזַז[2] (pāză'z) *fut.* יָפֹז, to be flexible, supple. — *Pi. pt.* מְפַזֵּז to leap, to dance.

פָּזַר (pāză'r) *pt. p. f.* פְּזוּרָה, to scatter, to lead astray. — *Ni.* נִפְזַר to be scattered. — *Pi.* פִּזֵּר, *fut.* יְפַזֵּר, to scatter, disperse; to distribute largely.

פַּח[1] (păḥ) *m*, *i.p.* פָּח, *pl.* פַּחִים, snare, trap-net; danger, calamity.

פַּח[2] (păḥ) *m*, *pl.* פַּחִים, *c.* פַּחֵי, plate of metal.

פָּחַד (pāḥă'd) *fut.* יִפְחַד, to tremble, to quake, to be afraid; to palpitate with joy. — *Pi. fut.* יְפַחֵד, *pt.* מְפַחֵד, to be afraid, timid, cautious. — *Hi.* הִפְחִיד to make tremble.

פַּחַד[1] (pă'ḥăd) *m*, *i.p.* פָּחַד, *w.s.* פַּחְדּוֹ, fear, terror, awe; object of fear.

פַּחַד[2] (pă'ḥăd) *m*, only *pl.* *w.s.* פַּחֲדָיו, the loins [the testicles].

פַּחְדָּה (păḥdā') *f* fear, terror.

פֶּחָה (pĕḥā') *m*, *c.* פַּחַת, *pl.* פַּחוֹת, *c.* פַּחֲווֹת, [Babylonian or Persian] governor, prefect, pasha.

פָּחַז (pāḥă'z) *pt. pl.* פֹּחֲזִים, to be frivolous, wanton, fickle.

פַּחַז (pă'ḥăz) *m* a boiling over, wantonness.

פַּחֲזוּת (pă'ḥazū'ϑ) *f* boastfulness.

פָּחַח (pāḥă'ḥ) *Hi.* הָפֵחַ, *inf.* הָפֵחַ, to ensnare, to fetter.

פַּחִים (păḥī'm) *m* glow, heat, lightning [or *pl.* of פַּח].

פֶּחָם (pĕḥā'm) *m* live coal.

פַּחַת (pă'ȼhăϑ) *m* [and *f*], *pl.* פְּחָתִים, pit, fissure; destruction.

פַּחַת מוֹאָב (pă'ȼhăϑ mō'ā'ḇ) *pr.n.m.*

פְּחֶתֶת (pᵉȼhĕ'ϑĕϑ) *f* sunken spot [made by the leprosy of garments].

פִּטְדָה (pĭṭḏā') *f* a precious stone, topaz.

פָּטוּר, פְּטוּר, פָּטִיר, see פָּטַר.

פַּטִּישׁ (păṭṭī'š) *m* hammer.

פָּטַר (pāṭă'r) *fut.* יִפְטַר, *pt. p.* פָּטוּר, to split, to break open, to let out; *pt. p.* burst open flower, garland; one set free or made exempt. — *Hi.* הִפְטִיר, *fut.* יַפְטִיר, to gape with the lips in mockery.

פֶּטֶר (pĕ'ṭĕr) *m* a breaking through; what breaks through, first-born.

פִּטְרָה (pĭṭrā') *f* first-born.

פִּי see פֶּה.

פִּי־בֶסֶת (pī ḇĕ'sĕϑ) *pr.n.* of a city in lower Egypt, Bubastis.

פִּיד (pīḏ) *m* misfortune.

פֵּיָה (pēyā') *f*, only *pl.* פֵּיוֹת, edge [= פֶּה].

פִּיָּה (pĭyyā') *f*, *pl.* פִּיּוֹת, see פֶּה.

פִּי־הַחִירֹת (pī hă'ȼhīrō'ϑ) *pr.n.* of a place in Egypt.

פִּיחַ (pī'ᵃȼh) *m* ashes, dust.

פִּיכֹל (pīȼhō'l) *pr.n.m.*

פִּילֶגֶשׁ (pīlĕ'gĕš) and **פִּלֶגֶשׁ** (pĭllĕ'gĕš) *f*, *w.s.* פִּילַגְשׁוֹ, *pl.* פִּלַגְשִׁים, *c.* פִּלַגְשֵׁי, concubine; prostitute.

פִּימָה (pīmā') *f* fat, fatness.

פִּינְחָס (pī'nᵉȼhā's); **פִּינֹן** (pīnō'n) *pr.n.m.*

פִּיפִיּוֹת (pī'fĭyyō'ϑ) *f/pl.* mouths, edges.

פִּיק (pīk) *m* a tottering.

פִּישׁוֹן (pīšō'n) *pr.n.* of a river in Paradise.

פִּיתוֹן (pīϑō'n) *pr.n.m.*

פַּךְ (păȼh) *m* flask, bottle.

פָּכָה (pāȼhā') *Pi. pt.* מְפַכֶּה, to flow out, to drip.

פֹּכֶרֶת הַצְּבָיִים (pōȼhĕ'rĕϑ hăȿȿᵉḇāyī'm) *pr.n.m.*

פָּלָא (pālā') *Ni.* נִפְלָא, *fut.* יִפָּלֵא, *pt. pl.* נִפְלָאִים, *f* נִפְלֵאת, *pl.* נִפְלָאוֹת, *c.* נִפְלְאֹת, נִפְלְאוֹת, to be distinguished, to be singular, extraordinary, wonderful, miraculous, astonishing, hard; *pt. f/pl.* wondrous things, miracles. — *Pi.* פִּלֵּא, *inf.* פַּלֵּא, to separate, to consecrate. — *Hi.* הִפְלִיא, הִפְלָא, הִפְלִא, *inf.* הַפְלִא, הַפְלִיא, *fut.* יַפְלִא, *pt.* מַפְלִא, to make extraordinary, wonderful, to act miraculously, marvellously; to consecrate, to sanctify.— *Hith.* הִתְפַּלֵּא to show oneself extraordinary.

פֶּלֶא (pĕ'lĕ) *m*, *w.s.* פִּלְאֲךָ, *pl.* פְּלָאִים and פְּלָאוֹת, wonder, wonderful thing or deed, miracle.

פִּלְאִי (pĭlī') *adj.*, *f* פִּלְאִיָּה, wonderful.

פְּלָאיָה (pᵉlāyā') *pr.n.m.*

פִּלְאֶסֶר (pĭl'ĕ'sĕr) see תִּגְלַת.

פָּלַג (pālă'g) *Ni.* נִפְלַג to be divided. — *Pi.* פִּלֵּג, *imp.* פַּלֵּג, to divide, to make discordant.

פֶּלֶג¹ (pĕ'lĕg) *m*, *pl.* פְּלָגִים, *c.* פַּלְגֵי, river, brook, stream.

פֶּלֶג² (pĕ'lĕg) *pr.n.m.*

פְּלַגָּה (pᵉlăggā') *f*, only *pl.* פְּלַגּוֹת, division of a family, kindred, clan; brook.

פְּלֻגָּה (pᵉlŭggā') *f* division, class.

פִּלֶּגֶשׁ (pĭllĕ'gĕš) *f* see פִּילֶגֶשׁ.

פְּלָדָה (pᵉlādā') or פַּלְדָּה (păldā') *f*, only *pl.* פְּלָדוֹת, iron, steel [scythes of war-chariots].

פִּלְדָּשׁ (pĭldā'š) *pr.n.m.*

פָּלָה (pālā') *Ni.* נִפְלָה to be separated, singled out, preferred. — *Hi.* הִפְלָה, *imp.* הַפְלֵה, *fut.* יַפְלֶה, to distinguish, to select, to favour.

פַּלּוּא (păllū') *pr.n.m.*

פָּלַח (pālă'ḥ) *pt.* פֹּלֵחַ, to cleave, to plough, to furrow. — *Pi.* פִּלַּח, *fut.* יְפַלַּח, to cleave, to cut in pieces, to let break forth, to bring forth.

פֶּלַח (pĕ'lăḥ) *m* piece, slice, the half; פֶּלַח רֶכֶב the upper mill-stone; פ׳ תַּחְתִּית the lower mill-stone.

פִּלְחָא (pĭlḥā') *pr.n.m.*

פָּלַט (pālă't) to escape. — *Pi.* פִּלֵּט, *inf.* and *imp.* פַּלֵּט, *fut.* יְפַלֵּט, *pt.* מְפַלֵּט, to let escape, to deliver, to let slip forth, to bring forth; *intr.* to escape. — *Hi. fut.* יַפְלִיט, וַיַּפְלֵט, to save, to rescue, to bring into safety.

פָּלֵט (pālē't) *m*, only *pl.* פְּלֵטִים, a fugitive, who has escaped.

פַּלֵּט (păllē't) *m* deliverance.

פֶּלֶט (pĕ'lĕt) *pr.n.m.*

פְּלֵטָה (pᵉlētā') see פְּלֵיטָה.

פַּלְטִי (păltī'); פִּלְטַי (pĭltă'y); פַּלְטִיאֵל (păltī'ē'l); פְּלַטְיָה (pᵉlătyā'), פְּלַטְיָהוּ (pᵉlătyā'-hū); פְּלָיָה (pᵉlāyā') *pr.n.m.*

פְּלִי and פְּלִיא (pᵉlī') *adj.*, *f* פְּלִיאָה, wonderful.

פָּלִיט (pālī't), פָּלֵיט (pālē't) *m*, *pl.* פְּלִיטִים, פְּלֵיטִים, a fugitive, one saved or escaped.

פְּלֵטָה, פְּלֵיטָה (pᵉlētā') *f*, *c.* פְּלֵיטַת, deliverance, escape, remnant.

פָּלִיל (pālī'l) *m*, only *pl.* פְּלִלִים, פְּלִילִים, judge.

פְּלִילָה (pᵉlīlā') *f* judgment, decision of an umpire.

פְּלִילִי (pᵉlīlī') *adj.* judicial; *f* פְּלִילִיָּה judgment.

פֶּלֶךְ (pĕ'lĕch) *m*, *w.s.* פִּלְכּוֹ, circuit, district; staff, stick; spindle.

פָּלַל (pālă'l) *Pi.* פִּלֵּל, *fut.* יְפַלֵּל, to judge, decide, punish; to adjudge; to think. — *Hith.* הִתְפַּלֵּל to act as arbiter or mediator: to pray [to God].

פָּלָל (pālā'l); פְּלַלְיָה (pᵉlălyā') *pr.n.m.*

פַּלְמֹנִי (pălmōnī'), פְּלֹנִי (pᵉlō-nī') *adj. m* such a one, a certain one, an unnamed one.

פָּלַס (pālă's) *Pi.* פִּלֵּס, *fut.* יְפַלֵּס, to make level, to prepare [a path]; to weigh [*den.* of פֶּלֶס].

פֶּלֶס (pĕ'lĕs) *m* a balance.

פָּלַץ (pālă'ts) *Hith.* הִתְפַּלֵּץ to burst, to be shaken, to tremble.

פַּלָּצוּת (păllātsū'th) *f* trembling, terror, horror.

פָּלַשׁ (pālă'sh) *Hith.* הִתְפַּלֵּשׁ to roll oneself.

פְּלֶשֶׁת (pᵉlĕ'shĕth) *pr.n.*, the land of the Philistines, Philistia [hence Palestine].

פְּלִשְׁתִּי (pᵉlĭshtī') *pr.n.m.*, *pl.* פְּלִשְׁתִּיִּים, פְּלִשְׁתִּים, Philistine.

פֶּלֶת (pĕ'lĕth) *pr.n.m.*

פְּלֵתִי (pᵉlēthī') *pr.n.m.* [Philistine, or runner, courier], body-guard of king David, together with כְּרֵתִי.

פֶּן (pĕn) *conj.* that not, lest.

פַּנַּג (pănnă'g) *m* sweet cake.

פָּנָה (pānā') *inf.* פְּנוֹת, פָּנֹה, *imp.* פְּנֵה, *fut.* יִפְנֶה, וַיִּפֶן, וַתֵּפֶן, *pt.* פֹּנֶה, *pl.* פֹּנִים, to turn [*intr.*], to turn to, to turn away; to go, to look. — *Pi.* פִּנָּה, *imp. pl.* פַּנּוּ, to remove, to drive away, to clear. — *Hi.* הִפְנָה, *inf.* הַפְנוֹת, *fut.* וַיֶּפֶן, to turn [*tr.* and *intr.*], to flee. — *Ho.* הָפְנָה to be turned or directed.

פָּנֶה (pānĕ') *m*, only *pl.* פָּנִים, *c.* פְּנֵי, face, countenance, surface, front; appearance, exterior, person; אֶל־פְּנֵי to the front of, before; — אֶת־פְּנֵי before; — לִפְנֵי in sight of, in presence of, before, sooner than; — מִלִּפְנֵי, מִפְּנֵי from before, by reason of; — עַל־פְּנֵי before, over against, upon the surface, over the surface.

פִּנָּה (pĭnnā') *f*, *c.* פִּנַּת, *pl.* פִּנּוֹת, pinnacle, corner, turn; pillar, chief, prince.

פְּנוּאֵל (pᵉnū'ē'l) *pr.n.* of a town beyond the Jordan; *pr.n.m.*

פְּנִי (pᵉnī') *m*, only *pl.* פְּנִיִּים = פְּנִינִים see פָּנִין.

פְּנִיאֵל (pᵉnī'ē'l) = פְּנוּאֵל.

פְּנִימָה (pᵉnī'mā) *adv.* within, in the interior; לִפְנִימָה to within, in the inside of, inwardly; מִפְּנִימָה from within.

פְּנִימִי (pᵉnīmī') *adj.*, *f* פְּנִימִית, interior, inner.

פָּנִין (pānī'n) *m*, only *pl.* פְּנִינִים, coral, pearl.

פְּנִנָּה (pᵉnĭnnā') *pr.n.f.*

פָּנַק (pānă'k) *Pi. pt.* מְפַנֵּק, to fondle, indulge.

פַּס (păs) *m*, only *pl.* פַּסִּים, extremity; כְּתֹנֶת פַּסִּים a long tunic with sleeves [others: a garment with stripes].

פָּסַג (pāsă'g) *Pi. imp. pl.* פַּסְּגוּ, to pass through, to walk through.

פִּסְגָּה (pĭsgā') *pr.n.* of a mountain ridge in Moab.

פִּסָּה (pĭssā') *f*, *c.* פִּסַּת, plenty, abundance.

פָּסַח (pāsă'ḥ) *inf.* פָּסוֹחַ, *fut.* יִפְסַח, *pt. pl.* פֹּסְחִים, to pass through, to pass over, to spare; to halt, to waver [in opinion]. — *Ni. fut.* יִפָּסֵחַ to become lame. — *Pi. fut.* יְפַסֵּחַ to leap, to hobble, to dance.

פֶּסַח (pĕ'săḥ) *m, i.p.* פָּסַח, *pl.* פְּסָחִים, a sparing, exemption; the passover-feast, the paschal lamb.

פָּסֵחַ (pāsē'aḥ) *pr.n.m.*

פִּסֵּחַ (pĭssē'aḥ) *adj., pl.* פִּסְחִים, lame.

פָּסִיל (pāsī'l) *m, only pl.* פְּסִילִים, *c.* פְּסִילֵי, cast or carved image, idol; *pl. pr.n.* of a place.

פָּסַךְ (pāsă'ḵ) *pr.n.m.*

פָּסַל (pāsă'l) *imp.* פְּסֹל, *fut.* יִפְסֹל, to hew, cut, carve.

פֶּסֶל (pĕ'sĕl) *m, i.p.* פָּסֶל, *w.s.* פִּסְלִי, carved or cast idol.

פָּסַס (pāsă's) to cease, to disappear.

פִּסְפָּה (pĭspā') *pr.n.m.*

פָּעָה (pā'ā') *fut.* יִפְעֶה, to groan, to pant.

פָּעוּ (pā'ū') *pr.n.* of a town in Idumea.

פְּעוֹר (pᵉ'ō'r) *pr.n.* of a mountain in Moab; בַּעַל פ׳ a deity worshipped there.

פָּעַל (pā'ă'l) [in poetry = עָשָׂה] *fut.* יִפְעַל, *pt.* פֹּעֵל, *pl. c.* פֹּעֲלֵי, to do, make, form, create, accomplish, prepare.

פֹּעַל (pō''ăl) *m, w.s.* פָּעֳלוֹ (pŏ'olō'), *pl.* פְּעָלִים, work, deed, action, business; product, achievement; gain, wages, reward.

פְּעֻלָּה (pᵉ'ŭllā') *f, c.* פְּעֻלַּת, *pl.* פְּעֻלּוֹת, פְּעֻלֹּת, a doing, performing; wages, reward.

פְּעֻלְּתַי (pᵉ'ŭltī') *pr.n.m.*

פָּעַם (pā'ă'm) *inf., w.s.* פַּעֲמוֹ, to beat, strike, impel. — *Ni.* נִפְעַם, *fut.* יִפָּעֵם, to be moved, stirred. — *Hith.* הִתְפָּעֵם to be agitated.

פַּעַם (pă''ăm) *f* and *m, i.p.* פָּעַם, *pl.* פְּעָמִים, *c.* פַּעֲמֵי, *du.* פַּעֲמַיִם, stroke, anvil; tread, step, pace; with numerals = times, turns; *sing.* once; *du.* twice; הַפַּעַם this time.

פַּעֲמָה (pă''amā') *f, only pl.* פַּעֲמוֹת, [artificial] foot.

פַּעֲמוֹן (pă''amō'n) *m, pl.* פַּעֲמֹנִים, bell, clock.

פַּעְנֵחַ (pă''anē'aḥ) see צָפְנַת־פַּעְנֵחַ.

פָּעַר (pā‛ă'r) to open the mouth, to gape.

פַּעֲרַי (pă‛‛ᵃră'y) *pr.n.m.*

פָּצָה (pāßā') *imp.* פְּצֵה, *fut.* יִפְצֶה, *pt.* פֹּצֶה, to open wide [the mouth]; to deliver, rescue.

פָּצַח (pāßă'ḥ) *imp.* פִּצְחִי, פִּצְחוּ, *fut.* יִפְצַח, to break out into joy, to rejoice. — *Pi.* פִּצֵּחַ, to break in pieces.

פְּצִירָה (pᵉßîrā') *f* bluntness, dulness.

פָּצַל (pāßă'l) *Pi. fut.* יְפַצֵּל to peel off.

פְּצָלָה (pᵉßālā') *f*, only *pl.* פְּצָלוֹת, a peeling, peeled spot.

פָּצַם (pāßă'm) to split, to rend.

פָּצַע (pāßă‛) *inf.* פָּצוֹעַ, *pt. p.* פָּצוּעַ, *c.* פְּצוּעַ, to cut, wound, crush.

פֶּצַע (pĕ'ßă‛) *m*, *i.p.* פָּצַע, *w.s.* פִּצְעִי, *pl.* פְּצָעִים, *c.* פִּצְעֵי, a wound.

פִּצֵּץ (pĭßßē'ß) *pr.n.m.*

פָּצַר (pāßă'r) *fut.* יִפְצַר to press, to urge. — *Hi. inf.* הַפְצַר [for הַפְצֵר] to be obstinate or stubborn; *inf.* obstinacy, rebelliousness.

פָּקַד (pākă'd) *inf.* פְּקֹד, פָּקֹד, *w.s.* פָּקְדִי (pŏkdī'), *imp.* פְּקֹד, *fut.* יִפְקֹד, *pt.* פּוֹקֵד, *pt. p. pl.* פְּקֻדִים, *c.* פְּקוּדֵי, *f* פְּקֻדַּת, to visit, inspect, muster, review, number; to care for; to look for, to miss; to chastise, punish; to cause to inspect, to appoint, to charge with, to entrust; *pt. p.* an officer, overseer. — *Ni.* נִפְקַד, *inf.* הִפָּקֵד, *fut.* יִפָּקֵד, to be visited, punished, mustered, missed; to be set over. — *Pi. pt.* מְפַקֵּד to muster. — *Pu.* פֻּקַּד to be mustered; to be punished; to want. — *Hi.* הִפְקִיד, *imp.* הַפְקֵד, *fut.* יַפְקִיד, וַיַּפְקֵד, to appoint, to set over; to entrust or charge with; to deposit or lay up. — *Ho. pt.* מָפְקָד to be appointed, to be set over; to be punished; to be deposited. — *Hith.* הִתְפַּקֵּד to be mustered, numbered.

פְּקֻדָּה (pᵉkŭddā') *f*, *c.* פְּקֻדַּת, *pl.* פְּקֻדּוֹת, a numbering, mustering, review; visitation, punishment; charge, service, care, watch, office; goods in trust, stores, property.

פִּקָּדוֹן (pĭkkădō'n) *m* goods in trust, deposit.

פְּקִדוּת (pᵉkĭdū'ϑ) *f* oversight, office.

פָּקוּד (păkū'd) *m*, only *pl.* פְּקוּדִים, *c.* פְּקוּדֵי, a numbering, mustering.

פִּקּוּד (pĭkkū'd) *m*, only *pl.* פִּקּוּדִים, *c.* פִּקּוּדֵי, precept, order, command.

פָּקַח (păkă'ḥ) *inf.* פָּקֹחַ, פְּקֹחַ, *imp.* פְּקַח, *fut.* יִפְקַח, *pt.* פֹּקֵחַ, to open [the eyes or ears], to be watchful; to open one's eyes, to make one see.—*Ni.* נִפְקַח, *fut.* יִפָּקַח, to be opened, to get sight or understanding.

פֶּקַח (pĕ'kăḥ) *pr.n.m.*

פִּקֵּחַ (pĭkkē'aḥ) *adj.*, *pl.* פִּקְחִים, open-eyed, seeing, intelligent.

פְּקַחְיָה (pᵉkăḥyā') *pr.n.m.*

פְּקַח־קוֹחַ [פְּקַחְקֹחַ] (pᵉkăḥ kō'aḥ) *m* an opening, loosening, deliverance.

פָּקִיד (păkī'd) *m*, *c.* פְּקִיד, *pl.* פְּקִידִים, officer, overseer, prefect, magistrate, commander.

פֶּקַע (pĕ'kă') *m*, only *pl.* פְּקָעִים, an architectural ornament in the shape of cucumbers or coloquints.

פַּקֻּעָה (păkkū'ā') *f*, only *pl.* פַּקֻּעֹת, gourd, cucumber, pumpkin or coloquint.

פַּר (păr) *m*, *i.p.* פָּר, *pl.* פָּרִים, a bull, young bullock; victim, offering.

פָּרָא (pārā') *Hi.* *fut.* יַפְרִיא, to bring forth, to bear fruit.

פֶּרֶא (pĕ'rĕ) *m*, *pl.* פְּרָאִים, wild ass, culan.

פִּרְאָם (pĭr'ā'm) *pr.n.m.*

פַּרְבָּר (părbā'r) and **פַּרְוָר** (părvā'r) *m*, *pl.* פַּרְוָרִים, portico on the western side of the temple-building, open summer house; others: suburb.

פָּרַד (pără'd) to spread out. — *Ni.* נִפְרַד, *inf.* and *imp.* הִפָּרֵד, *fut.* יִפָּרֵד, *pt.* נִפְרָד, to be parted, divided, separated, scattered; *pt.* going one's own way, whimsical.— *Pi.* *fut.* יְפָרֵד to separate oneself, to go aside. — *Pu.* *pt.* מְפֹרָד to be separated, isolated. —

Hi. הִפְרִיד, *inf.* הַפְרִיד, *fut.* יַפְרִיד, to separate, divide, disperse.—*Hith.* הִתְפָּרֵד to be dispersed, to separate oneself.

פֶּרֶד (pĕ'rĕd) *m*, *w.s.* פִּרְדּוֹ, *pl.* פְּרָדִים, *c.* פִּרְדֵי, a mule.

פִּרְדָּה (pĭrdā') *f*, *c.* פִּרְדַּת, she-mule.

פְּרֻדָּה (p^e^rŭddā') *f*, only *pl.* פְּרֻדוֹת, seed-corn, grains.

פַּרְדֵּס (părdē's) *m*, *pl.* פַּרְדֵּסִים, park, pleasure-garden; hence Paradise [Persian].

פָּרָה[1] (pārā') *imp.* פְּרוּ, פְּרֵה, *fut.* יִפְרֶה, *pt.* פֹּרֶה, *f* פֹּרִיָּה, פֹּרָת, to break forth, to be fertile, to bear fruit; to bring forth [children].—*Hi.* הִפְרָה, *fut.* יַפְרֶה, וַיֶּפֶר, *pt.* *w.s.* מַפְרְךָ, to make fruitful.

פָּרָה[2] (pārā') *f* young cow, heifer.

פָּרָה[3] (pārā') *pr.n.* of a town in Benjamin.

פֵּרָה (pērā') *f*, only *pl.* פֵּרוֹת, mouse or rat.

פֶּרֶה see פֶּרֶא.

פֻּרָה (pūrā'); פְּרוּדָא (p^e^rūdā') *pr.n.m.*

פְּרוּזִי see פְּרָזִי.

פָּרוּחַ (pārū'ach) *pr.n.m.*

פַּרְוַיִם (părvă'yĭm) *pr.n.* of a gold-region.

פַּרְוָר see פַּרְבָּר.

פָּרוּר (pārū'r) *m* pot, kettle.

פֶּרֶז (pĕ'rĕz) or **פָּרָז** (pārā'z) *m*, only *pl.* פְּרָזִים, ruler, chief, leader; others: populace, country-people, crowd.

פְּרָזָה (p^e^rāzā') *f*, only *pl.* פְּרָזוֹת open country.

פְּרָזוֹן (p^e^rāzō'n) *m*, *w.s.* פִּרְזוֹנוֹ, open country, peasantry; others: ruler, leader.

פְּרָזִי (p^e^rāzī') *adj.* living in the open country, country-man, peasant.

פְּרִזִּי (p^e^rĭzzī') *pr.n.m.* of a Canaanitish tribe.

פָּרַח (pārăch) *inf.* פְּרֹחַ, *fut.* יִפְרַח, *pt.* פֹּרֵחַ, *f* פֹּרַחַת, to burst forth, to sprout, to blossom; to break out; to thrive, prosper; to fly.—*Hi.* הִפְרִיחַ, *fut.* יַפְרִיחַ, to cause to blossom; *intr.* to blossom, flourish, thrive.

פֶּרַח (pĕ'răch) *m*, *w.s.* פִּרְחָם, *pl.* פְּרָחִים, sprout, blossom; blossom-shaped ornament.

פִּרְחָה (pĭrḥā') *f* brood, rabble, mob.

פָּרַט (pārăṭ) *pt.* פֹּרֵט, to sing foolishly.

פֶּרֶט (pĕ'rĕṭ) *m* single berry [fallen off in the vintage].

פְּרִי (peri') *m*, *i.p.* פֶּרִי, *w.s.* פִּרְיוֹ, fruit; offspring; result, consequence.

פְּרִידָא (peridā') *pr.n.m.*

פָּרִיץ (pārī'ṣ) *adj.*, *c.* פְּרִיץ, *pl.* פָּרִיצִים, *c.* פָּרִיצֵי, violent, wild; tyrant, robber, oppressor.

פֶּרֶךְ (pĕ'rĕḥ) *m* oppression.

פָּרֹכֶת (pārō'ḥĕth) and פַּרֹכֶת (părō'ḥĕth) *f* curtain [before the holy of holies].

פָּרַם (pārăm) *fut.* יִפְרֹם, to rend, to tear.

פַּרְמַשְׁתָּא (părmăštā') *pr.n.m.* [Persian].

פַּרְנָךְ (părnā'ḥ) *pr.n.m.* [Persian].

פָּרַס¹ (pārăs) *inf.* פָּרֹס, *fut.* יִפְרֹס, to break [bread], to distribute. — *Hi.* הִפְרִיס, *pt.* מַפְרִיס, *f* מַפְרֶסֶת, to cleave, divide [the hoof], to have a cloven hoof.

פָּרַס² (pārăs) *pr.n.* of a country, Persia, *i.p.* פָּרָס; *gent.* פַּרְסִי.

פֶּרֶס (pĕ'rĕs) *m*, *pl. c.* פַּרְסֵי, hoof, cloven foot, claw; a species of eagle.

פַּרְסָה (părsā') *f*, *pl.* פְּרָסוֹת, *c.* פַּרְסוֹת, hoof, claw, cloven foot.

פָּרַע (pārăʿ) *inf.* פְּרֹעַ, *fut.* יִפְרַע, *pt. p.* פָּרֻעַ, to loosen, dismiss, absolve; to make bare; to reject; to lead, to be at the head. — *Ni.* *fut.* יִפָּרַע to be unruly. — *Hi.* הִפְרִיעַ, *fut.* יַפְרִיעַ, to make unruly; to free [from work].

פֶּרַע¹ (pĕ'răʿ) *m*, only *pl.* פְּרָעוֹת, *c.* פַּרְעוֹת, leader, prince.

פֶּרַע² (pĕ'răʿ) *m* the hair.

פַּרְעֹה (părʿō') *m* title of the kings of Egypt, Pharaoh.

פַּרְעֹשׁ¹ (părʿō'š) *m* a stinging insect, flea.

פַּרְעֹשׁ² (părʿō'š) *pr.n.m.*

פִּרְעָתוֹן (pĭrʿāthō'n) *pr.n.* of a town in Ephraim.

פַּרְפַּר (părpă'r) *pr.n.* of a river near Damascus.

פָּרַץ (pārăṣ) *inf.* פָּרֹץ, פְּרֹץ,

fut. יִפְרֹץ, *pt.* פֹּרֵץ, to break, to demolish, to tear down, to make a breach, to scatter; *intr.* to rush upon, to spread; to increase, to overflow. — *Ni. pt.* נִפְרָץ to be spread, diffused, to be common. — *Pu. pt. f* מְפֹרֶצֶת to be broken down. — *Hith.* הִתְפָּרֵץ to separate oneself, to run away.

פֶּרֶץ[1] (pĕ'rĕß) *m, i.p.* פָּרֶץ, *pl.* פְּרָצִים, *c.* פִּרְצֵי, breach, gap, fissure; a breaking through, attack, defeat.

פֶּרֶץ[2] (pĕ'rĕß) *pr.n.m.*; *patr.* פַּרְצִי.

פִּרְצָה (părßā') *f*, only *pl.* פְּרָצוֹת, breach.

פָּרַק (pāră'k) *fut.* יִפְרֹק, *pt.* פֹּרֵק, to break off, to tear to pieces; to tear away, to deliver, to set free. — *Pi.* פֵּרֵק, *imp. pl.* פָּרְקוּ, *fut.* יְפָרֵק, *pt.* מְפָרֵק, to tear off, to break to pieces. — *Hith.* הִתְפָּרֵק to be broken; to tear off from oneself.

פָּרָק (pārā'k) *m*, *c.* פְּרַק, lump, bit; others: broth, soup.

פֶּרֶק (pĕ'rĕk) *m* violence, murder; cross-way, fork.

פָּרַר (pāră'r) *inf.* פּוֹר, to break in pieces, to crush. — *Hi.* הֵפֵר, הָפֵר, *inf.* and *imp.* הָפֵר, *fut.* יָפֵר, יָפִיר, וַיָּפֶר, *pt.* מֵפֵר, to break, dissolve, violate; to frustrate, annihilate, annul. — *Ho. fut.* יֻפַר to be dissolved, destroyed. — *Po.* פּוֹרֵר to cleave, to divide. — *Pilp.* פִּרְפֵּר to crush, to shatter. — *Hith.* הִתְפּוֹרֵר to be torn asunder, to be shaken.

פָּרַשׂ (pāră'ß) *fut.* יִפְרֹשׂ, *pt.* פֹּרֵשׂ, *pl.* פֹּרְשִׂים, *c.* פֹּרְשֵׂי, *pt. p. f* פְּרוּשָׂה, *pl.* פְּרוּשׂוֹת, to divide, to break in pieces, to distribute; to spread out, to expand. — *Ni. fut.* יִפָּרֵשׂ to be dispersed, scattered. — *Pi.* פֵּרֵשׂ, *inf.* פָּרֵשׂ, *w.s.* פָּרֶשְׂכֶם, *fut.* יְפָרֵשׂ, to spread out, to scatter.

פָּרַשׁ (pāră's) *inf.* פְּרֹשׁ, to divide, to distinguish, to declare distinctly. — *Ni.* נִפְרָשׁ to be dispersed, scattered. — *Pu.* פֹּרַשׁ, *pt.* מְפֹרָשׁ, to be declared distinctly; *pt.* distinctly, plainly. — *Hi. fut.* יַפְרִשׁ to sting, to wound.

פָּרָשׁ (pārā'š) *m*, *pl.* פָּרָשִׁים, horse [for riding and war-chariots]; rider, horseman.

פֶּרֶשׁ[1] (pĕ'rĕš) *m*, *w.s.* פִּרְשׁוֹ, excrement, dung.

פֶּרֶשׁ[2] (pĕ'rĕš) *pr.n.m.*

פַּרְשֶׁגֶן (păršĕ'gĕn) *m* transcript, copy [Persian].

פַּרְשְׁדוֹן (păršᵉdō'n) *m*, *w. loc.* פַּרְשְׁדֹנָה ה, fork between the legs; others evacuation of excrements [פֶּרֶשׁ1], or flat roof.

פָּרָשָׁה (pārāšā') *f*, *c.* פָּרָשַׁת, distinct declaration, explanation.

פַּרְשֵׁז (păršē'z) to spread out.

פַּרְשַׁנְדָּתָא (păršăndā'ϑā) *pr.n.m.* [Persian].

פְּרָת (pᵉrā'ϑ) or נְהַר־פְּרָת, *pr.n.*, the river Euphrates.

פֹּרָת (pōrā'ϑ) *f* fruit-tree.

פָּשָׂה (pāsā') *inf.* פָּשֹׂה, *fut.* יִפְשֶׂה, to spread.

פָּשַׂע (pāsă'ᵉ) *fut.* 1. *sg.* אֶפְשְׂעָה, to stride, to advance, to rush upon.

פֶּשַׂע (pĕ'săᵉ) *m* step, stride.

פָּשַׂק (pāsă'k) *pt.* פּוֹשֵׂק, to open wide [the lips]. — *Pi. fut.* יְפַשֵּׂק to spread out [the feet].

פַּשׁ (păš) *m* folly, haughtiness.

פָּשַׁח (pāšă'ḥ) *Pi. fut.* יְפַשֵּׁחַ, to tear in pieces.

פָּשַׁט (pāšă't) *imp.* פְּשֹׁט, *fut.* יִפְשֹׁט, יִפְשַׁט, *intr.* to spread out, to roam about; to put off, to lay aside, to strip. — *Pi.* פִּשֵּׁט, *inf.* פַּשֵּׁט, to strip, spoil, plunder. — *Hi.* הִפְשִׁיט, *inf.* הַפְשֵׁט, *fut.* יַפְשִׁיט, to cause to put off; to strip off, to take off; to flay. — *Hith.* הִתְפַּשֵּׁט to strip oneself.

פָּשַׁע (pāšă'ᵉ) *inf.* פְּשֹׁעַ, *fut.* יִפְשַׁע, *pt.* פֹּשֵׁעַ, *pl.* פֹּשְׁעִים, to sin, to transgress, to rebel, to be refractory. — *Ni. pt.* נִפְשָׁע, to be offended.

פֶּשַׁע (pĕ'šăᵉ) *m*, *i.p.* פָּשַׁע, *w.s.* פִּשְׁעִי, *pl.* פְּשָׁעִים, *c.* פִּשְׁעֵי, transgression, sin, wickedness, faithlessness, apostasy; sin-offering; punishment for sin.

פֵּשֶׁר (pē'šĕr) *m* explanation, interpretation.

פֵּשֶׁת (pē'šĕϑ) *f*, *w.s.* פִּשְׁתִּי, *pl.* פִּשְׁתִּים, *c.* פִּשְׁתֵּי, flax, linen.

פִּשְׁתָּה (pĭštā') *f* = פֵּשֶׁת.

פַּת (păϑ) *f, w.s.* פִּתִּי, *pl.* פִּתִּים, *c.* פִּתּוֹת, lump, piece, bit, morsel.

פֹּת (pōϑ) *m, w.s.* פָּתְהֶן (pŏϑhĕ'n), *pl.* פֹּתוֹת, opening; hole in which a door-hinge moves; female pudenda.

פְּתָאיִם see פְּתִי.

פִּתְאֹם (pĭϑ'ō'm) *adv.* suddenly, in a moment.

פַּתְבַּג (păϑbă'g) *m, w.s.* פַּתְבָּגוֹ, food, dainties.

פִּתְגָּם (pĭϑgā'm) *m* word, sentence, edict.

פָּתָה (pāϑā') *fut.* יִפְתֶּה, וַיֵּפְתְּ, *pt.* פֹּתֶה, to open; *intr.* to be open; to be open-hearted, susceptible, accessible, simple; to be open to seduction. — *Ni.* נִפְתָּה, *fut.* 1. *sg.* אֶפָּת, to be easily persuaded, enticed, seduced. — *Pi.* פִּתָּה, *inf.* פַּתֹּת, *imp. f s.* פַּתִּי, *fut.* יְפַתֶּה, to persuade, entice, seduce, deceive.—*Pu.* פֻּתָּה, *fut.* יְפֻתֶּה, to be persuaded, deceived. — *Hi. fut.* יַפְתְּ to make wide.

פְּתוּאֵל (pᵉϑū'ē'l) *pr.n.m.*

פִּתּוּחַ (pĭttū'aḥ) *m, w.s.* פִּתֻּחָהּ, *pl.* פִּתּוּחִים, *c.* פִּתּוּחֵי, engraving, sculpture.

פְּתוֹר (pᵉϑō'r) *pr.n.* of a town on the Euphrates.

פְּתוֹת see פַּת.

פָּתַח (pāϑă'ḥ) *inf.* פָּתוֹחַ, פְּתֹחַ, *imp.* פְּתַח, פִּתְחוּ, *fut.* יִפְתַּח, *pt.* פֹּתֵחַ, *pt. p. f* פְּתוּחָה, to open, to throw open, to uncover; to release; to begin; to surrender. — *Ni.* נִפְתַּח, *inf.* הִפָּתֵחַ, *fut.* יִפָּתַח, יִפָּתֵחַ, to be opened, to be loosed, to be released or set free. — *Pi.* פִּתַּח, *inf.* פַּתֵּחַ, *fut.* יְפַתַּח, יְפַתֵּחַ, *pt.* מְפַתֵּחַ, to open, to loose, to untie, to set free; to plough; to engrave, carve, hew; to open oneself. — *Pu. pt.* מְפֻתָּח to be engraved. — *Hith.* הִתְפַּתַּח to loosen for oneself [fetters].

פֶּתַח (pĕ'ϑăḥ) *m, i.p.* פָּתַח, *w. loc.* פֶּתְחָה ה, *w.s.* פִּתְחִי, *pl.* פְּתָחִים, *c.* פִּתְחֵי, opening, entrance, door, gate; *adv.* at the door.

פֵּתַח (pē'ϑăḥ) *m* opening, explanation, insight.

פִּתָּחוֹן (pĭttāḥō'n) *m, c* פִּתְחוֹן, the opening.

פְּתַחְיָה (pᵉϑăḥyā') *pr.n.m.*

פְּתִי (pᵉϑî') *m*, *i.p.* פֶּתִי, *pl.* פְּתָאִים, פְּתָיִים, simplicity, folly; *adj.* simple, foolish, credulous.

פְּתִיגִיל (pᵉϑîgî'l) *m* festive garment, mantle.

פְּתַיּוּת (pᵉϑăyyū'ϑ) *f* simplicity, folly.

פְּתִיחָה (pᵉϑîḥā') *f*, only *pl.* פְּתִחוֹת, drawn sword.

פָּתִיל (pāϑî'l) *m*, *c.* פְּתִיל, *pl.* פְּתִילִים, thread, cord.

פָּתַל (pāϑă'l) to twist. — *Ni.* נִפְתַּל, *pt.* נִפְתָּל, to be twisted, to wrestle; to be tortuous, perverse, crafty. *Hith.* הִתְפַּתֵּל to show oneself cunning, perverse, crafty.

פְּתַלְתֹּל (pᵉϑăltō'l) *adj.* twisted, tortuous, crafty, perverse.

פִּתֹם (pîϑō'm) *pr.n.* of a town in Goshen.

פֶּתֶן (pĕ'ϑĕn) *m*, *i.p.* פָּתֶן, *pl.* פְּתָנִים, poisonous snake, adder, viper.

פֶּתַע (pĕ'ϑă') *m* the opening of the eyes, moment, wink, twinkling; *adv.* suddenly.

פָּתַר (pāϑă'r) *inf.* פְּתֹר, *fut.* יִפְתֹּר, *pt.* פּוֹתֵר, פֹּתֵר, to explain, to interpret.

פִּתְרֹן, פִּתְרוֹן (pîϑrō'n) *m*, *pl.* פִּתְרֹנִים, explanation, interpretation.

פַּתְרוֹס (păϑrō's) *pr.n.* of a southern country, upper Egypt; *gent. pl.* פַּתְרֻסִים.

פַּרְשֶׁגֶן = פַּתְשֶׁגֶן.

פָּתַת (pāϑă'ϑ) to break.

צ

צ, ץ the eighteenth letter of the alphabet, called צָדֵי [fishing-hook]; as a numeral צ = 90, ץ = 900.

צֵא, צֵאת see יָצָא.

צֵאָה (ʙē'ā') *f*, *c.* צֵאַת, excrements, dung.

צֹאָה (ʙō'ā'), צוֹאָה, *f*, *c.* צֹאַת, *w.s.* צֹאָתָם, excrements, dung, filth.

צֹאִי (ʙō'î'), צוֹאִי, *adj.*, only *pl.* צֹאִים, filthy, dirty.

צֶאֱל (ʙĕ''ĕl) *m*, only *pl.* צֶאֱלִים, lotus-shrub, lotus-tree.

צֹאן (ʙōn) *f* [also *m*], *coll.*

w.s. צֹאנְךָ, צֹאנֵנוּ, צֹאנִי, small cattle, sheep and goats; flock, troop.

צַאֲנָן (Ṣa'ᵃnā'n) *pr.n.* of a town in Judah.

צֶאֱצָא (Ṣĕ'ĕṣā') *m*, only *pl.* צֶאֱצָאִים, *c.* צֶאֱצָאֵי, produce, shoot, issue, offspring, children.

צָב (Ṣāb) *m*, *pl.* צַבִּים, litter, sedan-chair, covered wagon; a species of lizard.

צָבָא[1] (Ṣābā') *inf.* צְבֹא, *fut.* יִצְבָּא, *pt.* צֹבֵא, *pl.* צֹבְאִים, *f* צֹבְאוֹת, to do military service, to collect and go forth for war; to do temple service. — *Hi. pt.* מַצְבִּא to levy for military service,

צָבָא[2] (Ṣābā') *m* [also *f*], *c.* צְבָא, *w.s.* צְבָאֲךָ, צְבָאוֹ [צְבָאָיו], *pl.* צְבָאוֹת, *c.* צִבְאוֹת, host, army, troop; host of heaven [angels or stars]; יהוה צְבָאוֹת the Lord of the heavenly hosts; military service, warfare, campaign; heavy service, hardship, calamity, temple service.

צְבֹאִים (Ṣᵉbō'ī'm) *pr.n.* of a place in the valley of Siddim.

צֹבֵבָה (Ṣō'bēbā') *pr.n.f.*

צָבָה (Ṣābā') *pt.* צֹבֶה to swell; = צָבָא[1] to go forth to war. — *Hi.* הַצְבָּה, *inf. w.* ל לַצְבּוֹת to cause to swell.

צָבֶה (Ṣābĕ') *adj.* swelling, swollen.

צָבוּעַ (Ṣābū'aᵃ) *m* hyena.

צִבּוּר (Ṣibbū'r) *m*, only *pl.* צִבֻּרִים, a heap.

צָבַט (Ṣābă't) *fut.* יִצְבֹּט, to reach out to [others: to bind together].

צְבִי[1] (Ṣᵉbī') *m*, *i.p.* צֶבִי, ornament, splendour, glory, beauty.

צְבִי[2] (Ṣᵉbī') *f*, *pl.* צְבָיִם, צְבָאִים, צְבָאוֹת, צְבָיִים, gazelle, antelope.

צִבְיָא (Ṣibyā'), צִבְיָה *pr.n.f.*

צְבִיָּה (Ṣᵉbiyyā') *f* female gazelle.

צְבִיִם, צְבִיִּים see צְבֹאִים.

צֶבַע (Ṣĕ'bă') *m*, only *pl.* צְבָעִים, party-coloured or dyed garment.

צִבְעוֹן (Ṣib'ō'n) *pr.n.m.*

צְבֹעִים (Ṣᵉbō'ī'm) *pr.n.* of a place and valley in Benjamin.

צָבַר (Ṣāḇă'r) *fut.* יִצְבֹּר, to heap up, to collect.

צִבְּרִים see צִבּוּר.

צֶבֶת (Ṣĕ'ḇĕṯ) *m*, only *pl.* צְבָתִים, bundle of ears, sheaf.

צַד (Ṣăḍ) *m*, *w.s.* צִדּוֹ, *w. loc.* צִדָּה ה, *pl.* צִדִּים, *c.* צִדֵּי, side, turning; מִצַּד at the side; עַל־צַד on the side, i. e. upon the arms; לְצִדִּים at the sides [as cumbersome adversaries].

צְדָד (Ṣăḍā'ḍ) or צְדָד, only *w. loc.* צְדָדָה ה (Ṣᵉḍā'ḍā) a town in northern Palestine.

צָדָה (Ṣāḍā') *pt.* צֹדֶה, to look after, to lie in wait for. — *Ni.* נִצְדָּה to be laid waste, to be destroyed.

צֵדָה see צֵידָה.

צָדוֹק (Ṣāḍō'k) *pr.n.m.*

צְדִיָּה (Ṣᵉḍĭyyā') *f* intention, purpose.

צִדִּים (Ṣĭddī'm) *pr.n.* of a town in Naphtali.

צַדִּיק (Ṣăddī'k) *adj.*, only *pl.* צַדִּיקִים, just, righteous, honest, right.

צֵדֹנִית [from צֵדֹנִי] see צִידוֹנִי.

צָדַק (Ṣāḍă'k) *fut.* יִצְדַּק to be right, straight, just, true, upright, righteous; to be in the right. — *Ni.* נִצְדַּק to be justified, to be restored. — *Pi.* צִדֵּק, *inf.* צַדֶּקֶת, to justify, to declare righteous. — *Hi.* הִצְדִּיק, *inf.* הַצְדִּיק, *imp. pl.* הַצְדִּיקוּ, *fut.* יַצְדִּיק, *pt.* מַצְדִּיק, to justify, to make righteous, to declare innocent, to absolve, to approve of. — *Hith. fut.* יִצְטַדָּק to justify oneself.

צֶדֶק (Ṣĕ'ḍĕk) *m*, *w.s.* צִדְקִי, straightness,justness,right, justice, honesty.

צְדָקָה (Ṣᵉḍākā') *f*, *c.* צִדְקַת, *w.s.* צִדְקָתִי, *pl.* צְדָקוֹת, *c.* צִדְקוֹת, divine and human right, claim, justice, righteousness, justness, faithfulness, piety, mercy, mildness.

צִדְקִיָּה (Ṣĭḍkĭyyā'), צִדְקִיָּהוּ *pr.n.m.*

צַדֶּקֶת see צָדַק *Pi.*

צָהַב (Ṣāhă'ḇ) *Ho. pt.* מֻצְהָב, to be shining, glittering.

צָהֹב (Ṣāhō'ḇ) *adj.* yellow like gold.

צָהַל (Ṣāhă'l) *imp. f* צַהֲלִי, *fut.* יִצְהַל, to cry, rejoice exult; to neigh. — *Pi. imp. f* צַהֲלִי [or *Q.*] to make shrill. — *Hi. inf.* הַצְהִיל to make bright, to cause to shine.

צָהַר (Ɓāhă'r) *Hi. fut.* יַצְהִירוּ, to press out oil.

צֹהַר (Ɓō'hăr) *f* opening for light, window.

צָהֳרַיִם (Ɓŏ'hºră'yĭm), צָהֳרָיִם *du. f* [of צֹהַר] two lights, double light [between forenoon and afternoon, or intensively full light], midday, clear day; בַּצָּהֳרָיִם suddenly, unexpectedly.

צַו (Ɓăv), צָו (Ɓāv) *m* statute, law, precept; צַו לָצָו precept to precept [*prob.* imitation of childish babble].

צַוָּאר (Ɓăvvā'r) *m, c.* צַוַּאר, *w.s.* צַוָּארוֹ, *pl.* צַוָּארִים, *c.* צַוְּארֵי, the neck, the nape.

צַוֶּארֶת (Ɓăvvĕ'rĕϑ) *f*, only *pl. w.s.* צַוְּארֹתֵיכֶם = צַוָּאר.

צוֹבָא, **צוֹבָה** (Ɓōḇā') *pr.n.* of an Aramæan kingdom [אֲרַם צוֹבָה].

צוּד (Ɓūḍ) *pf.* and *pt.* צָד, *inf.* צֹד, צוּד, *imp.* צוּדָה, *fut.* יָצוּד, to hunt, to catch, to seize, to fish, to waylay. — *Pi.* צוֹדֵד to catch, to waylay. — *Hith.* הִצְטַיֵּד see צִיד.

צָוָה (Ɓāvā') *Pi.* צִוָּה, *inf.* צַוֹּת, *imp.* צַוֵּה, צַו, צַוּוּ, *fut.* יְצַוֶּה, יְצַו, וַיְצַו, *pt.* מְצַוֶּה, *c.* מְצַוֵּה, *w.s.* מְצַוְּךָ, *f* מְצַוָּה, to constitute, to make firm, to establish, appoint, arrange; to command, charge, ordain. — *Pu.* צֻוָּה, *fut.* יְצֻוֶּה, to be commanded.

צָוַח (Ɓāvă'ɧ) *fut.* יִצְוָחוּ, to cry out, to shout with joy.

צְוָחָה (Ɓ'vāɧā') *f, c.* צִוְחַת, shout of joy or sorrow.

צוּלָה (Ɓūlā') *f* depth of water, abyss.

צוּם (Ɓūm) *pf.* and *pt.* צָם, *inf.* צוֹם, *fut.* יָצוּם, וַיָּצָם (văyyā'Ɓŏm) to fast.

צוֹם (Ɓōm) *m, w.s.* צֹמְכֶם, *pl.* צוֹמוֹת, a fasting.

צוֹעַר see צֹעַר.

צוּעָר (Ɓū'ā'r) *pr.n.m.*

צוּף[1] (Ɓūf) *pf.* צָף, to flow, to flow over. — *Hi.* הֵצִיף, *fut.* וַיָּצֶף, to cause to flow, to cause to float.

צוּף[2] (Ɓūf) *m, pl.* צוּפִים, honey-comb.

צוּף[3] (**ß**ụ̄f) *pr.n.m.*; *pr.n.* of a district in Benjamin.

צוֹפַח (**ß**ụ̄fă'ḥ) *pr.n.m.*

צוֹפִים (**ß**ọ̄fị̄'m) see רָמָתַיִם.

צוֹפַר (**ß**ọ̄fă'r) *pr.n.m.*

צוּץ (**ß**ụ̄**ß**) *pf.* צָץ, to shine, to bloom. — *Hi. fut.* יָצִיץ, *pt.* מֵצִיץ, to shine, to glitter; to bloom.

צוּק[1] (**ß**ụ̄k) *Hi.* הֵצִיק, *fut.* יָצִיק, *pt.* מֵצִיק, to straiten, to confine, to press hard, to urge, to oppress, to besiege. — *Ho. pt.* see מוּצָק.

צוּק[2] (**ß**ụ̄k) = יָצַק, *pf. pl.* צָקוּ = צָקוּן, *fut.* יָצוּק, to pour out; to place, to set.

צוֹק (**ß**ọ̄k) *m* narrowness, oppression.

צוּקָה (**ß**ụ̄kā') *f* = צוֹק.

צוּר[1] (**ß**ụ̄r) *pf.* and *pt.* צָר, *inf.* and *imp.* צוּר, *fut.* יָצוּר, וַיָּצַר, to bind together, to straiten, to invest, besiege, assail, attack; to press, to instigate; to cut, form, shape.

צוּר[2] (**ß**ụ̄r) *m, w.s.* צוּרִי, *pl.* צוּרִים, צֻרִים, stone, rock, refuge, protection; sharpness, edge; form, shape.

צוּר[3] (**ß**ụ̄r) *pr.n.m.*

צוֹר, צֹר (**ß**ọ̄r) *pr.n.* of a city in Phenicia, Tyrus; *gent.* צֹרִי.

צַוָּר see צַוָּאר.

צוּרָה (**ß**ụ̄rā') *f/pl.* צוּרוֹת, form, shape; stone, rock.

צַוְּרוֹן (**ß**ăvvārọ̄'n) *m*, only *pl. w.s.* צַוְּרֹנָיִךְ, neck-chain, neck-lace.

צוּרִיאֵל (**ß**ụ̄rị̄'ē'l) *pr.n.m.*

צוּרִישַׁדַּי (**ß**ụ̄rị̄'šăddă'y) *pr. n.m.*

צות (**ß**ụ̄ϑ) = יָצַת. — *Hi. fut. w.s.* אֲצִיתֶנָּה, to kindle, to set on fire.

צַח (**ß**ăḥ) *adj.*, *f/pl.* צַחוֹת, dazzling white, sunlit, bright, clear, hot.

צִחֶה (**ß**ịḥĕ') *adj.*, *c.* צְחֵה, dry.

צָחַח (**ß**āḥă'ḥ) to shine, to be dazzling white.

צְחִיחַ (**ß**āḥị̄'aḥ) *m*, *c.* צְחִיחַ, dryness, nakedness.

צְחִיחָה (**ß**ᵉḥị̄ḥā') *f* sunburnt, parched or waste land.

צְחִיחִי (**ß**ᵉḥị̄ḥị̄') *m*, only *pl.* צְחִיחִים, sunburnt [parched places].

צַחֲנָה (**ß**ă'ḥ^anā') *f* stench, bad smell.

צַחְצָחָה (**ß**ăḥ**ß**āḥā') *f*, only *pl.* צַחְצָחוֹת, = צְחִיחָה.

צָחַק (**ß**āḥă'**k**) *fut.* יִצְחַק, to laugh. — *Pi. inf.* צַחֵק, *fut.* יְצַחֵק, *pt.* מְצַחֵק, to laugh repeatedly, to jest, to caress.

צְחֹק (**ß**^eḥō'**k**) *m* laughter, mockery.

צַחַר (**ß**ă'ḥăr) *m* dazzling whiteness.

צָחֹר (**ß**āḥō'r) *adj.*, *f/pl.* צְחֹרוֹת, white, spotted with white.

צֹחַר (**ß**ō'ḥăr) *pr.n.m.*

צִי (**ß**ī) *m*, *pl.* צִים, צִיִּים, צִיּוֹת, dryness, dry desert; ship, boat.

צִיבָא (**ß**ībā') *pr.n.m.*

צִיד (**ß**īḍ) *Hith.* הִצְטַיֵּד [*denom.* of צַיִד] to provide oneself with food.

צַיִד (**ß**ă'yīḍ) *m*, *i.p.* צָיִד, *c.* צֵיד, *w.s.* צֵידוֹ, chase, hunting; game, venison; food, nourishment, provision.

צַיָּד (**ß**ăyyā'ḍ) *m* hunter.

צֵידָה, צֵדָה (**ß**ēḍā') *f* food, nourishment, provision [for travelling].

צִידֹן, צִידוֹן (**ß**īḍō'n) *pr.n.m.*; *pr.n.* of a city in Phenicia, Sidon.

צִידוֹנִי (**ß**ī'ḍōnī') *pr.n.m.* [*gent.* of צִידוֹן], *pl.* צִידֹנִים, צִדֹנִים, צִידֹנִין, *f* צִידֹנִית, *pl.* צִדֹנִיֹּת, Sidonian.

צִיָּה (**ß**īyyā') *f*, *pl.* צִיּוֹת, dryness, desert, steppe.

צָיוֹן (**ß**āyō'n) *m* dryness, desert.

צִיּוֹן (**ß**īyyō'n) *pr.n.* of the south-western hill of Jerusalem, Sion, with the temple-building, the holy mountain of God; poetically = Jerusalem; בַּת צִיּוֹן the inhabitants of Jerusalem, the Jewish people; בְּנוֹת צ׳ the women of Jerusalem.

צִיּוּן (**ß**īyyū'n) *m* erected stone, pillar, monument [on sepulchres], waymark.

צִיִּי (**ß**īyyī') *adj.*, only *pl.* צִיִּים, dwelling in the desert, nomad, wild beast or bird of the steppe; see also צִי.

צִין see צִן.

צִינֹק (**ß**īnō'**k**) *m* confinement, prison [others: pillory].

צִיעֹר (Bî'ọ'r) *pr.n.* of a place in Judah.

צִיף see צוּף[3].

צִיץ[1] (Bîß) *m, pl.* צִיצִים, צִצִּים, gold plate, diadem; blossom, flower; festoon, ornament [in architecture]; wing.

צִיץ[2] (Bîß) *pr.n.* of a place.

צִיצָה (Bîßā') *f, c.* צִיצַת, a flower.

צִיצִת (Bîßî'ϑ) *f* forelock; tassel, fringe.

צִיקְלַג see צִקְלַג.

צִיר[1] (Bîr) *Hith.* הִצְטַיֵּר, to go as a messenger, to set off.

צִיר[2] (Bîr) *m, pl.* צִירִים, *c.* צִירֵי, hinge of a door; pain, labour in childbirth; messenger; form, shape, idol.

צֵל (Bēl) *m, w.s.* צִלִּי, צִלְלוֹ, *pl.* צְלָלִים, *c.* צִלְלֵי, shadow; protection, shelter; transitoriness.

צָלָה (Bālā') *inf.* צְלוֹת, *fut.* יִצְלֶה, to roast.

צִלָּה (Bîllā') *pr.n.f.*

צְלוּל (Bᵉlū'l) [also צְלִיל] *m* round cake.

צָלַח (Bālă'ḥ) *fut.* יִצְלַח, to pass through, to get on, to thrive, to succeed, to fall upon, to come over. — *Hi.* הִצְלִיחַ, *imp.* הַצְלַח, הַצְלִיחָה, *fut.* יַצְלִיחַ, וַיַּצְלַח, *pt.* מַצְלִיחַ, to bring to an end, to cause to thrive, to lead to success; to be successful or blessed.

צְלָחָה (Bᵉ'lāḥā') *f,* only *pl.* צְלָחוֹת, a dish, bowl.

צְלֹחִית (Bᵉlōḥî'ϑ) *f* and צַלַּחַת (Băllă'ḥăϑ) *f* = צְלָחָה.

צָלִי (Bālî') *m, c.* צְלִי, something roasted, roasted meat.

צָלַל[1] (Bālă'l) *fut.* 3. *pl. f* תְּצִלֶּינָה, תִּצַּלְנָה [or *Hi.*], to sound, to tinkle, to tingle, to clatter, to quiver.

צָלַל[2] (Bālă'l) to sink, to plunge.

צָלַל[3] (Bālă'l) to give shadow, to become overshadowed. — *Hi. pt.* מֵצַל to shade, to give shadow.

צְלָלִים, צִלְלוֹ see צֵל.

צֶלֶם (Bĕ'lĕm) *m, w.s.* צַלְמוֹ, *pl.* צְלָמִים, *c.* צַלְמֵי, image, likeness, idol; shade, phantom, nothingness.

צַלְמוֹן[1] (Bălmō'n) *adj.* shady, dark; darkness.

צַלְמוֹן[2] (Bălmō'n) *pr.n.m.*

צַלְמָוֶת (ʙălmā'vĕϑ) *f* [either for צֵל מָוֶת shadow of death, or = צַלְמוּת] deep darkness, terror.

צַלְמֹנָה (ʙălmōnā') *pr.n.* of a station in the desert.

צַלְמֻנָּע (ʙălmŭnnā'') *pr.n.m.*

צָלַע (ʙālă'') *pt.* צֹלֵעַ, *f* צֹלֵעָה, to be sprained in the hip, to halt, to be lame.

צֵלָע[1] (ʙēlā'') *f*, *c.* צֶלַע, צֶלַע, *pl.* צְלָעִים, צְלָעוֹת, *c.* צַלְעוֹת, rib; side, wing of a building, side-chamber, leaf of a folding door, slope of a mountain; board, beam.

צֵלָע[2] (ʙēlā'') *pr.n.* of a town in Benjamin.

צֶלַע[1] (ʙĕ'lă') *f*, *w.s.* צַלְעִי, a falling, fall.

צֶלַע[2] (ʙĕ'lă') *f* side, slope, flank.

צָלָף (ʙālā'f) *pr.n.m.*

צְלָפְחָד (ʙ'lŏfḥā'd) *pr.n.m.*

צֶלְצַח (ʙĕlʙă'ḥ) *pr.n.* of a town in Benjamin.

צְלָצַל (ʙ'lāʙă'l) *m*, *i.p.* צְלָצָל, *c.* צִלְצַל, *pl.* צֶלְצְלִים, *c.* צִלְצְלֵי, a whirring; whirring insect, cricket, grasshopper; cymbal, fishing spear, harpoon.

צֶלֶק (ʙĕ'lĕk) *pr.n.m.*

צִלְּתַי (ʙĭll'ϑă'y) *pr.n.m.*.

צָמֵא[1] (ʙāmē') *pf.* צָמֵת, צָמֵתִי, *fut.* יִצְמָא, to gape, to thirst.

צָמֵא[2] (ʙāmē') *adj.*, *pl.* צְמֵאִים, *f* צְמֵאָה, thirsty, dry.

צָמָא (ʙāmā') *m*, *w.s.* צְמָאִי, thirst.

צִמְאָה (ʙĭm'ā') *f* thirst, desire.

צִמָּאוֹן (ʙĭmmā'ō'n) *m* thirsty, parched, arid land.

צָמַד (ʙāmă'd) *Ni. fut.* יִצָּמֵד, to be attached, to be devoted, to serve. — *Pu. pt. f i.p.* מְצֻמֶּדֶת to be bound, to be fastened. — *Hi. fut.* יַצְמִיד to knot, to contrive, to devise.

צֶמֶד (ʙĕ'mĕd) *m*, *w.s.* צִמְדּוֹ, *pl.* צְמָדִים, *c.* צִמְדֵּי, a pair, a yoke; a measure for land.

צַמָּה (ʙămmā') *f*, *w.s.* צַמָּתֵךְ, a veil [others: net-cap].

צִמּוּק (ʙĭmmū'k) *m* cake of dried grapes, pressed raisins.

צָמַח (ßāmă'ḥ) *fut.* יִצְמַח, *pt.* צֹמֵחַ, *fpl.* צֹמְחוֹת, to sprout forth, to spring up, to grow, to turn out. — *Pi.* צִמַּח, *inf.* צַמֵּחַ, *fut.* יְצַמַּח, to sprout, to grow. — *Hi.* הִצְמִיחַ, *fut.* יַצְמִיחַ, וַיַּצְמַח, to cause to sprout, to let grow, to give offspring.

צֶמַח (ße'măḥ) *m, w.s.* צִמְחָהּ, a sprout, fruit, descendant; the Messiah.

צָמִיד (ßāmī'd) *m, pl.* צְמִידִים, bracelet; cover, lid.

צַמִּים (ßămmī'm) *m* noose, snare; perdition.

צְמִיתֻת (ßᵉmīθū'θ) *f* destruction, extinction.

צָמַק (ßāmă'k) to be dried up.

צֶמֶר (ße'mĕr) *m, i.p.* צָמֶר, *w.s.* צַמְרִי, wool.

צְמָרִי (ßᵉmārī') *pr.n.m.* of a Canaanitish people.

צְמָרַיִם (ßᵉmārắyīm) *pr.n.* of a town in Benjamin.

צַמֶּרֶת (ßămme'rĕθ) *f, w.s.* צַמַּרְתּוֹ, foliage, branch of a tree.

צָמַת (ßāmă'θ) to extirpate. — *Ni.* נִצְמַת to be destroyed, to become extinct, to vanish. — *Pi.* צִמֵּת, *pl. w.s.* צִמְּתֻתוּנִי [צִמְּתוּנִי], to destroy, to extirpate. — *Hi.* הִצְמִית, *imp. w.s.* הַצְמִיתֵם, *fut.* יַצְמִית, *pt.* מַצְמִית, to destroy, to annihilate.

צִן, צִין (ßīn) *pr.n.* of a district in southern Canaan, *w. loc.* ה צִנָה.

צֵן (ßēn) *m,* only *pl.* צְנִים, thorn, thorn-hedge.

צֹנֶא (ßōnē'), **צֹנֶה** (ßōnĕ') *f* = צֹאן.

צִנָּה (ßĭnnā') *f, c.* צִנַּת, *pl.* צִנּוֹת, cold; thorn, fishing hook; shield.

צָנוֹף, צָנוּף see צָנִיף.

צִנּוֹר (ßĭnnō'r) *m, pl.* צִנּוֹרִים, conduit, canal, waterfall.

צָנַח (ßānă'ḥ) *fut.* יִצְנַח, to descend, to sink, to penetrate.

צָנִין (ßānī'n) *m,* only *pl.* צְנִינִים, thorn, prick.

צָנִיף (ßānī'f) *m, c.* צְנִיף, *pl.* צְנִיפוֹת, headdress, turban, tiara, diadem.

צָנַם (ßānă'm) only *pt. p. f/pl.* צְנֻמוֹת dry, hard, barren.

צָנַע (ßānă'ʿ) *pt. p.* צָנוּעַ, to be humble, modest. — *Hi.*

inf. הַצְנֵעַ to behave humbly or modestly.

צָנַף (Bānă'f) *inf.* צָנוֹף, *fut.* יִצְנֹף, to wrap, to roll around or together.

צְנֵפָה (Bᵉnēfā') *f* ball.

צִנְצֶנֶת (BĭnBĕ'nĕϑ) *f* basket.

צַנְתֶּרֶת (Băntĕ'rĕϑ) *f, pl.* צַנְתְּרוֹת, tube or pipe of an oil-vessel.

צָעַד (Bā'ă'd) *inf. w.s.* צַעְדְּךָ, *fut.* יִצְעַד, to step, to stride, to pace, to march, to mount. — *Hi. fut.* יַצְעִיד to cause to step, to drive.

צַעַד (Bă''ăd) *m, w.s.* צַעֲדִי, *pl.* צְעָדִים, step, pace.

צְעָדָה (Bᵉ'ādā') *f, pl.* צְעָדוֹת, step, pace, march; step-chain [a foot-ornament of women].

צָעָה (Bā'ā') *pt.* צֹעֶה, *pl.* צֹעִים, *f* צֹעָה, to bend downward, to incline; to be bent [by fetters]; to lie down; to walk proudly [for צָעַד]. — *Pi.* צֵעָה to bend down, to incline.

צָעוֹר = צָעִיר.

צָעִיף (Bā'ī'f) *m, w.s.* צְעִיפָהּ, a veil.

צָעִיר[1] (Bā'ī'r) *adj., w.s.* צְעִירוֹ, *pl.* צְעִירִים, *f* צְעִירָה, small, mean, little; weak, humble; young, younger.

צָעִיר[2] (Bā'ī'r) *pr.n.* of a place on the way to Edom; *w. loc.* ה צְעִירָה.

צְעִירָה (Bᵉ'īrā') *f* youngness, age of youth.

צָעַן (Bā'ă'n) *fut.* יִצְעַן to migrate, to wander.

צֹעַן (Bō''ăn) *pr.n.* of a city in Egypt, Tanis.

צַעֲנַנִּים (Bă''ănănnī'm) *pr.n.* of a town in Naphtali.

צַעֲצֻעַ (Bă''aBū'a') *m*, only *pl.* צַעֲצֻעִים, sculptor's work, carving.

צָעַק (Bā'ă'k) *inf.* צְעֹק, צָעֹק, *fut.* יִצְעַק, *pt.* צֹעֵק, *pl.* צֹעֲקִים, *f* צֹעֶקֶת, to cry out, to call out, to complaint, to cry for help. — *Ni.* נִצְעַק, *fut.* יִצָּעֵק, to be called together. — *Pi. pt.* מְצַעֵק to cry aloud. — *Hi. fut.* וַיַּצְעֵק to call together.

צְעָקָה (Bᵉ'āḳā') *f, c.* צַעֲקַת, *w.s.* צַעֲקָתוֹ, a crying, cry.

צָעַר (Bā'ă'r) *fut.* יִצְעַר, to be or become small, mean, despised.

צֹעַר, צוֹעַר (Bō''ăr) *pr.n.* of

a town south east of the Dead Sea.

צָפַד (Ṣāfă'd) to be attached, to cling to.

צָפָה¹ (Ṣāfā') *inf.* צְפֹה, *fut.* יִצְפֶּה, יִצֶף, *pt.* צֹפֶה, *pl.* צֹפִים, צוֹפִים, *f* צֹפִיָּה, *pl.* צֹפוֹת, to look, to view, to regard, to watch, to look out sharply; to expect, to select; *pt.* a seer, prophet, watchman.—*Pi.* צִפָּה, *fut.* יְצַפֶּה, *pt.* מְצַפֶּה, to look out sharply, to watch, to observe.

צָפָה² (Ṣāfā') *inf.* צְפֹה to spread. — *Pi.* צִפָּה, *fut.* יְצַפֶּה, וַיְצַף, to cover, to overlay. — *Pu. pt. pl.* מְצֻפִּים, to be overlaid.

צָפָה³ (Ṣāfā') *f* inundation.

צְפוֹ (Ṣ'fō') *pr.n.m.*

צִפּוּי (Ṣippū'y) *m* an overlaying, coating.

צָפוֹן¹ (Ṣāfō'n) *f* and *m*, *w. loc.* ה צָפוֹנָה, *c.* צְפוֹן, hidden region, the north, the northern side, northern land or people, north wind, northern heaven.

צָפוֹן² (Ṣāfō'n) *pr.n.* of a town in Gad.

צְפוֹנִי (Ṣ'fōnī') *adj.* coming from the north; see also צִפְיוֹן.

צָפוּעַ see צָפִיעַ.

צִפּוֹר¹, **צִפֹּר** (Ṣippō'r) *f* and *m*, *pl.* צִפֳּרִים, a [small] bird, birds.

צִפּוֹר² (Ṣippō'r) *pr.n.m.*

צַפַּחַת (Ṣăppă'chăth) *f* pitcher, jug, flask.

צְפִי = צְפוֹ.

צִפִּיָּה (Ṣippīyyā') *f* watch-tower.

צִפְיוֹן (Ṣifyō'n) *pr.n.m.*; *patr.* צְפוֹנִי.

צַפִּיחִית (Ṣăppīchī'th) *f* cake, flat bread.

צָפִין = צָפוּן [hidden, i. e. treasure], see צָפַן.

צָפִיעַ (Ṣāfī'a') *m*, only *pl.* צְפִיעִים, excrements of beasts, dung.

צְפִיעָה (Ṣ'fī'ā') *f*, only *pl.* צְפִיעוֹת, shoot, sprout.

צָפִיר (Ṣāfī'r) *m*, *c.* צְפִיר, he-goat.

צְפִירָה (Ṣ'fīrā') *f*, *c.* צְפִירַת, circlet, diadem, crown; cycle of time, turn of fate.

צָפִית (Ṣāfī'th) *f* watch, guard [others: carpet, mat, or horoscope].

צָפַן (Ȼāfă'n) *fut.* יִצְפֹּן, *pt. p.* צָפוּן [צָפִין], to cover, conceal, hide; to lay in, to treasure up, to hoard, to preserve; *pt. p.* hidden treasure; to lie in wait. — *Ni.* נִצְפַּן to be hidden, to be unknown; to be preserved or destined for. — *Hi. inf. w.s.* הַצְפִּינוֹ, *fut.* יַצְפִּין, to hide, conceal; to lie in wait.

צְפַנְיָה (Ȼᵉfănyā'), צְפַנְיָהוּ (Ȼᵉfănyā'hū) *pr.n.m.*

צָפְנַת פַּעְנֵחַ (Ȼā'fᵉnă'ϑ pă'nē'ᵃḥ) *pr.n.m.*, Egyptian surname of Joseph.

צֶפַע (Ȼĕ'fă') and צִפְעֹנִי (Ȼĭf'ōnī') *m* a poisonous serpent, basilisk, viper.

צָפַף (Ȼāfă'f) *Pilp. fut.* יְצַפְצֵף, *pt.* מְצַפְצֵף, *pl.* מְצַפְצְפִים, to chirp, to twitter, to whisper.

צַפְצָפָה (ȻăfȻāfā') *f* a willow.

צָפַר (Ȼāfă'r) *fut.* יִצְפֹּר to turn oneself, to turn away.

צְפַרְדֵּעַ (Ȼᵉfărdē'ᵃ') *f* and [in *pl.*] *m*, *pl.* צְפַרְדְּעִים, a frog.

צִפֹּרָה (Ȼĭppōrā') *pr.n.f.*

צִפֹּרֶן (Ȼĭppō'rĕn) *m*, *pl. w.s.* צִפָּרְנֶיהָ, nail of a finger; diamond-pointed style.

צֶפֶת (Ȼĕ'fĕϑ) *m* capital of a column.

צְפַת (Ȼᵉfă'ϑ) *pr.n.* of a Canaanitish town; the same as חָרְמָה.

צְפָתָה (Ȼᵉfā'ϑā) *pr.n.* of a valley in Judah.

צִצִּים see צִיץ.

צַק see יָצַק.

צִקְלַג (Ȼĭklă'g), צִקְלָג, צִיקְלַג, *pr.n.* of a town in Simeon.

צִקָּלוֹן (Ȼĭkkālō'n) *m*, *w.s.* צִקְלֹנוֹ, a sack, bag, knapsack.

צֶקֶת see יָצַק.

צַר[1] (Ȼăr), צָר (Ȼār) *m*, *w.s.* צָרִי, *pl.* צָרִים, *c.* צָרֵי, oppressor, persecutor, adversary, enemy; straitness, distress, embarrassment, danger, trouble.

צַר[2] (Ȼăr) *adj.*, *f* צָרָה, narrow, straitened.

צַר[3] (Ȼăr) *m* = צוּר stone.

צֵר (Ȼēr) *pr.n.* of a town in Naphtali.

צֹר[1] (Ȼōr) [= צוּר] *m*, *pl.* צֻרִים, stone, rock, sharp flint [knife].

צֹר[2] (Bọr) — צוֹר.

צָרַב (Bārǎ'ḇ) *Ni.* נִצְרַב to be burnt.

צָרֵב (Bārẹ'ḇ) *adj.*, *f* צָרֶבֶת, burning, scorching.

צָרֶבֶת (Bārĕ'ḇĕϑ) *f* a burn, mark caused by fire.

צְרֵדָה (Bᵉrẹḍā') *pr.n.* of a town in Ephraim, *w. loc.* צְרֵדָתָה ה.

צָרָה (Bārā') *f*, *c.* צָרַת, *w. loc.* צָרָתָה ה, *w.s.* צָרָתִי, *pl.* צָרוֹת, *c.* צָרוֹת, a female adversary or rival; straitness, distress; anguish.

צְרוּיָה, צְרֻיָה (Bᵉrūyā') *pr.n.f.*

צְרוּעָה (Bᵉrūʻā') *pr.n.f.*

צְרוֹר[1] (Bᵉrọ'r) see צְרֹר.

צְרוֹר[2] (Bᵉrọ'r) *pr.n.m.*

צָרַח (Bārǎ'ḥ) to cry, to shriek. — *Hi. fut.* יַצְרִיחַ to shout, to raise a war-cry.

צֹרִי (Bọrī') *pr.n.m.* Tyrian, *gent.* of צֹר = צוֹר.

צֳרִי (Borī'), צְרִי[1] (Bᵉrī') *m*, *i.p.* צֹרִי, balsam, resin of the mastix-tree.

צְרִי[2] (Bᵉrī') *pr.n.m.* = יִצְרִי.

צְרִיחַ (Bᵉrī'aḥ) *m*, *pl.* צְרִיחִים, hole, vault, cellar [others: watch-tower].

צֹרֶךְ (Bọ'rĕḵ) *m*, *w.s.* צָרְכֶּךָ (Bŏrkĕ'ḵā) need, necessity.

צָרַע (Bārǎ'ʻ) *pt. p.* צָרוּעַ, to plague, to strike with leprosy; *pt. p.* a leper. — *Pu. pt.* מְצֹרָע, *f* מְצֹרַעַת, to be struck with leprosy, to be leprous.

צִרְעָה (Bĭrʻā') *f coll.* wasps, hornets.

צָרְעָה (Bŏrʻā') *pr.n.* of a town in Judah; *gent.* צָרְעִי and צָרְעָתִי.

צָרַעַת (Bārǎ'ʻǎϑ) *f*, *w.s.* צָרַעְתּוֹ, leprosy [of men, garments and houses].

צָרַף (Bārǎ'f) *inf.* צָרוֹף, צְרֹף, צְרָף־, *imp.* צָרְפָה (Bŏrfā'), צְרוֹפָה, *fut.* יִצְרֹף, *pt.* צֹרֵף, צוֹרֵף, *pt. p.* צָרוּף, *f* צְרוּפָה, to smelt, to refine, to test, to prove; *pt.* smelter, goldsmith.

צֹרְפִי (Bọ'rᵉfī') *pr.n.m.*

צָרְפַת (Bā'rᵉfǎ'ϑ) *pr.n.* of a Phenician town near Sidon, Sarepta.

צָרַר (Bārǎ'r) *pf.* also צַר, *inf.* צָרוֹר, צְרֹר, *imp.* צוֹר, צֹר, *fut.* יָצֹר, וַיֵּצֶר, *pt.* צֹרֵר, צוֹרֵר, *pl.* צֹרְרִים,

צָרִים, *pt. p.* צָרוּר, *f* צְרוּרָה, *pl.* צְרֻרֹת, to bind in, to press in or together, to compress, to wrap up; to enclose, to straiten, to persecute, to treat with enmity; *intr.* to be straitened, pressed, narrow, distressed, to be in anguish or sorrow. — *Pu. pt. pl.* מְצֹרָרִים to be bound together. — *Hi.* הֵצַר, *inf.* הָצֵר, *fut.* יָצֵר, יָצֵר, *pt. f* מְצֵרָה, to straiten, to press upon, to distress, to besiege.

צְרוֹר, צְרֹר (ẞ'rō'r) *m* bundle, bag; pebble, flint.

צְרֵדָה = צְרֵרָה.

צֶרֶת (ẞĕ'rĕϑ) *pr.n.m.*

צֶרֶת הַשַּׁחַר (ẞĕ'rĕϑ hăššă'-ḥăr) *pr.n.* of a town in Reuben.

צָרְתָן (ẞā'r'ϑā'n) *pr.n.* of a town near the Jordan, *w. loc.* ה צָרְתָנָה.

ק

ק the nineteenth letter of the alphabet, called קוֹף [back of the head]; as a numeral = 100.

קֵא (kē) *m, w.s.* קִאוֹ, vomit.

קָאַת (kā'ă'ϑ), קָאָת *f, c.* קְאַת, pelican [heron].

קַב (kăḇ) *m* a measure for dry goods, 1/6 of a סְאָה.

קָבַב (kāḇă'ḇ) *inf.* קֹב, *imp.* קָבָה־קֹב, *w.s.* קָבְנוֹ, *fut.* יִקֹּב, *w.s.* תִּקָּבֶנּוּ, to curse, to blaspheme.

קֵבָה (kēḇā') *f* the antestomach of ruminants.

קֹבָה (kōḇā') *f, w.s.* קֳבָתָהּ, female pudenda.

קֻבָּה (kŭbbā') *f* vaulted tent [sleeping apartment].

קִבּוּץ (kĭbbū'ẞ) *m, pl. w.s.* קִבּוּצַיִךְ, heap, gathering, crowd.

קְבוּרָה (k'ḇūrā') *f, c.* קְבֻרַת, *w.s.* קְבֻרָתוֹ, interment, sepulture; grave, sepulchre.

קָבַל (kāḇă'l) *Pi.* קִבֵּל, *imp.* קַבֵּל, *fut.* יְקַבֵּל, to take, receive, accept; to admit, adopt. — *Hi. pt.* מַקְבִּיל, *f/pl.* מַקְבִּילוֹת, to stand over against.

קֹבֶל (kō'ḇĕl) or קְבֹל (k'ḇō'l) *m, c.* קָבָל־ (koḇŏ'l), *w.s.* קָבְלִי (kŏ'ḇolī'), front; *prep.*

in front, in the presence of; battering-ram.

קָבַע (kābă'') *fut.* יִקְבַּע, *pt.* קֹבֵעַ, *pl.* קֹבְעִים, to withhold, to defraud, to rob.

קֻבַּעַת (kŭbbă''ăϑ) *f* cup, chalice, bell of a flower.

קָבַץ (kābă'ß) *imp.* קְבֹץ, קִבְצוּ, *fut.* יִקְבֹּץ, to grasp, to gather, to assemble. — *Ni.* נִקְבַּץ, *inf.* and *imp.* הִקָּבֵץ, *fut.* יִקָּבֵץ, *pt.* נִקְבָּץ, to be gathered, collected, assembled, to gather oneself.—*Pi.* קַבֵּץ, *inf.* and *imp.* קַבֵּץ, *fut.* יְקַבֵּץ, *pt.* מְקַבֵּץ, to seize, to take, to take up, to gather in, to collect. — *Pu.* קֻבַּץ to be gathered. — *Hith.* הִתְקַבֵּץ to gather oneself, to assemble.

קַבְצְאֵל see יְקַבְצְאֵל.

קְבֻצָה (k'bŭßā') *f* collection, heap.

קִבְצַיִם (kĭbßă'yĭm) *pr.n.* of a town in Ephraim.

קָבַר (kābă'r) *inf.* קְבֹר, קָבוֹר, *imp.* קְבֹר, *fut.* יִקְבֹּר, *pt.* קֹבֵר, קוֹבֵר, *pt. p.* קָבוּר, to bury, to inter. — *Ni.* נִקְבַּר, *fut.* יִקָּבֵר, to be buried. — *Pi. inf.* קַבֵּר, *fut.* יְקַבֵּר, *pt.* מְקַבֵּר, to bury [many]. — *Pu.* קֻבַּר to be buried.

קֶבֶר (kĕ'bĕr) *m*, *i.p.* קָבֶר, *w.s.* קִבְרִי, *pl.* קְבָרִים, קְבָרוֹת, *c.* קִבְרֵי, קִבְרוֹת, grave, sepulchre.

קִבְרוֹת הַתַּאֲוָה (kĭbrō'ϑ hăttă''avā') *pr.n.* of a place in the desert [graves of lust].

קָדַד (kādă'd) *fut.* יִקֹּד, *pl.* יִקְּדוּ, *intr.* to incline, to bend, to bow down.

קִדָּה (kĭddā') *f* cassia, cinnamon.

קָדוּם (kādū'm) *m*, only *pl.* קְדוּמִים, time of old, ancient days.

קָדוֹשׁ, קָדֹשׁ (kādō's) *adj.*, *c.* קְדֹשׁ, קְדוֹשׁ, *w.s.* קְדֹשִׁי, *pl.* קְדוֹשִׁים, selected, pure, holy, sacred, consecrated, pious; *m* sanctuary, the holy one, i. e. God, angel.

קָדַח (kādă'ḥ) *inf.* קְדֹחַ, *pt. pl. c.* קֹדְחֵי, *intr.* to burn, to glow; *tr.* to kindle, to burn.

קַדַּחַת (kăddă'ḥăϑ) *f* hot fever.

קָדִים (kādī'm) *m*, *w. loc.* קָדִימָה ה, what is in front, the east, east side, eastern wind.

קָדַם (kādă'm) *Pi.* קִדֵּם, *imp.* קַדְּמָה, *fut.* יְקַדֵּם, to go before, to anticipate, to be beforehand, to be or do early, to advance, to meet, to encounter. — *Hi. fut.* יַקְדִּים to be beforehand, to encounter.

קֶדֶם (kĕ'dĕm), קֵדֶם (kē'dĕm) *m, w. loc.* ה קֵדְמָה, what is in front, *adv.* before; the east, eastern lands, primitive or ancient state, things of old.

קַדְמָה (kădmā') *f, c.* קַדְמַת, *w.s.* קַדְמָתָהּ, origin, primitive state; *adv.* before.

קֵדְמָה (kē'dᵉmā') *pr.n.m.*

קִדְמָה (kĭdmā') *f, c.* קִדְמַת, *prep.* before, on the east of.

קַדְמוֹן (kădmō'n) *adj., f* קַדְמוֹנָה, eastern.

קְדֵמוֹת (kᵉdēmō'ϑ) *pr.n.* of a town in Reuben.

קַדְמִיאֵל (kŏdmī'ē'l) *pr.n.m.*

קַדְמוֹנִי, קַדְמֹנִי[1] (kădmōnī') *adj., pl.* קַדְמֹנִים, *f* קַדְמֹנִית, *pl.* קַדְמֹנִיּוֹת, eastern; former, primitive, primeval, ancient, past.

קַדְמֹנִי[2] (kădmōnī') *pr.n.* of a Canaanitish people.

קָדְקֹד (kŏdkō'd) *m, w.s.* קָדְקֳדוֹ, קָדְקֳדוֹ, crown of the head, vertex.

קָדַר (kādă'r) *pt.* קֹדֵר, קוֹדֵר, to be turbid, soiled, dark, gloomy; to wear mourning-dress, to mourn. — *Hi.* הִקְדִּיר, *fut.* יַקְדִּיר, to darken, to obscure; to cause to mourn. — *Hith.* הִתְקַדֵּר to grow dark.

קֵדָר (kēdā'r) *pr.n.m.*

קִדְרוֹן (kĭdrō'n) *pr.n.* of a brook between Jerusalem and the mount of Olives.

קַדְרוּת (kădrū'ϑ) *f* darkness, obscurity.

קָדַשׁ (kādă's) *fut.* יִקְדַּשׁ, to be selected, to be pure, holy, sacred, consecrated, devoted. — *Ni.* נִקְדַּשׁ, *inf. w.s.* הִקָּדְשִׁי, *fut.* יִקָּדֵשׁ, to be regarded as holy, to show oneself holy, to be consecrated. — *Pi.* קִדֵּשׁ, *inf.* and *imp.* קַדֵּשׁ, *fut.* יְקַדֵּשׁ, *pt.* מְקַדֵּשׁ, to select, to seclude; to consecrate, to declare holy. — *Pu. pt.* מְקֻדָּשׁ to be consecrated. — *Hi.* הִקְדִּישׁ, *inf.* הַקְדֵּשׁ,

הִקְדִּישׁ, *fut.* יַקְדִּישׁ, *pt.* מַקְדִּישׁ, to treat as holy, to declare holy, to consecrate, to hallow.— *Hith.* הִתְקַדֵּשׁ to purify oneself, to show oneself holy, to be consecrated or celebrated.

קָדֵשׁ[1] (kādē'š) *adj.*, *pl.* קְדֵשִׁים, *f* קְדֵשָׁה, a consecrated or devoted one, a prostitute, priest or priestess of Astarte.

קָדֵשׁ[2] (kādē'š) *pr.n.* of a place on the way to Egypt.

קֶדֶשׁ (kĕ'dĕš) *pr.n.* of several towns; *w. loc.* קֶדְשָׁה ,קֶדְשָׁה ה.

קֹדֶשׁ (kō'dĕš) *m, w.s.* קָדְשִׁי (kŏdšī'), *pl.* קָדָשִׁים ,קֳדָשִׁים (kŏ'dāšī'm), קָדְשֵׁי (kŏdšē'), holiness, sanctity; a holy or consecrated thing, sanctuary, temple; קֹדֶשׁ הַקֳּדָשִׁים a most holy thing, the holy of holies.

קָהָה (kāhā') *fut.* יִקְהֶה, to become blunt. — *Pi.* קֵהָה to make blunt.

קָהַל (kāhă'l) *Ni.* נִקְהַל, *inf.* הִקָּהֵל, *fut.* יִקָּהֵל, to be assembled or congregated. — *Hi.* הִקְהִיל, *inf.* הַקְהִיל, *imp.* הַקְהֵל, *fut.* יַקְהִיל, יַקְהֵל, to convoke, to call together.

קָהָל (kāhā'l) *m, c.* קְהַל, *w.s.* קְהָלְךָ, convocation, congregation, assembly, crowd, multitude; the Hebrew communion.

קְהֵלָה (kᵉhēlā') *pr.n.* of a station in the desert; *w. loc.* קְהֵלָתָה ה.

קְהִלָּה (kᵉhĭllā') *f, c.* קְהִלַּת, assembly.

קֹהֶלֶת (kōhĕ'lĕϑ) *m* [and *f*] the preaching Wisdom [a surname of Solomon].

קְהָת (kᵉhā'ϑ) *pr.n.m.*

קָו (kāv), **קַו** (kăv) *m, w.s.* קַוָּם, line, measuring-line; chord, string; rule, norm, order.

קוֹא (kū) *pf.* קָא to vomit, to reject. — *Hi.* הֵקִיא, *fut.* וַיָּקֵא, the same as *Q.*

קוֹבַע (kōbă'ᵉ) *m* helmet.

קָוָה (kāvā') *pt.* קֹוֶה, *pl. c.* קֹוֵי, to hope, to be confident, to trust. — *Ni.* נִקְוָה, *fut.* יִקָּוֶה, to be gathered together, to be joined, to meet.— *Pi.* קִוָּה, *inf.* קַוֹּה, קַוֵּה, *imp.* קַוֵּה,

fut. יְקַוֶּה, וַיְקַו, to wait for, to hope, to expect, to lie in wait for.

קָוֶה (kāvĕ') *m* = קָו.

קוֹחַ see פְּקַח־קוֹחַ.

קוּט (kūt) *pf.* קָט, *fut.* יָקוּט, to loathe, to have a disgust.—*Ni.* נָקוֹט and *Hith.* *fut.* יִתְקוֹטֵט the same as *Q.*

קוֹל (kōl) *m, w.s.* קוֹלִי, *pl.* קוֹלוֹת, קֹלֹת, קֹלוֹת, voice, cry, call, sound, noise, rumour, thunder.

קוֹלָיָה (kō'lāyā') *pr.n.m.*

קוּם (kūm) *pf.* קָם, *inf.* קוּם, קוֹם, *imp.* קוּם, קֻם, קוּמָה, קוּמִי, *fut.* יָקוּם, יָקֻם, יָקֹם, וַיָּקָם (văyyā'kŏm), *pt.* קָם, *pl.* קָמִים, *c.* קָמֵי, to rise up, to arise, to stand up, to appear, to rise against; to exist, subsist, endure, remain. — *Pi.* קִיֵּם, *inf.* קַיֵּם, *fut.* יְקַיֵּם and יְקוֹמֵם, to establish, to confirm, to preserve in life; to fulfil; to rebuild; to rise up against. — *Hi.* הֵקִים, *inf.* הָקֵים, הָקֵם, הָקִים, *imp.* הָקֵם, *fut.* יָקִים, יָקֵם, וַיָּקֶם, *pt.* מֵקִים, *pl. c.* מְקִימֵי, to cause to stand up, to raise up, to establish, to stir up, to rouse; to appoint, to confirm, to preserve, to stop, to calm.—*Ho.* הוּקַם, הֻקַם to be established, appointed.—*Hith.* הִתְקוֹמֵם to stand up against, to resist, to be hostile.

קוֹמָה, קֹמָה (kōmā') *f, c.* קוֹמַת, *w.s.* קוֹמָתוֹ, height, tallness, stature.

קוֹמְמִיּוּת (kō'mᵉmīyyū'ϑ) *f; adv.* upright.

קוֹן see קִין.

קוֹעַ (kō'aᵉ) *m* a noble, prince.

קוֹף (kōf) *m, pl.* קוֹפִים, קֹפִים, ape, monkey.

קוּץ (kūß) *pf.* קָץ, *fut.* יָקוּץ, וַיָּקָץ (văyyā'kŏß), to loathe, to have a disgust, to feel displeasure, horror, fear.—*Hith.* הֵקִיץ, *fut.* יָקִיץ, to terrify, to alarm.

קוֹץ[1] (kōß) *m, pl.* קֹצִים, *c.* קוֹצֵי, thorn, thornbush.

קוֹץ[2] (kōß) *pr.n.m.*

קְוֻצָּה (kᵉvŭßßā') *f,* only *pl.* קְוֻצּוֹת, lock of hair, curl, ringlet.

קַו־קָו (kăv-kā'v) *m* order, might, power.

קוּר[1] (kūr) *pf.* קָר to dig,

to dig up. — *Pi.* [or from קָבַר] קַרְקַר, *inf.* קַרְקַר, *pt.* מְקַרְקַר, to evert, undermine, destroy.— *Hi.* הֵקִיר to cause to spring [water], to cause to gush.

קוּר[2] (**kūr**) *m*, only *pl. c.* קוּרֵי, web, thread of a spider.

קוֹרָה (**kōrā'**) *f*, *w.s.* קוֹרָתִי, *pl.* קֹרוֹת, a beam; shelter, house.

קוֹשׁ (**kōš**) *fut. pl.* יְקֹשׁוּן (**y'kōšū'n**), to lay snares.

קוּשָׁיָהוּ (**kū'šāyā'hū**) *pr.n.m.*

קַח, קַחַת see לָקַח.

קַט (**kat**) *adv.* only.

קֶטֶב (**kĕ'tĕb**) *m*, *i.p.* קָטֶב, and קֹטֶב (**kō'tĕb**) *m*, *w.s.* קָטָבְךָ (**kŏ'tŏbᵽā'**), destruction, defeat, plague.

קְטוֹרָה (**k'tōrā'**) *f* incense.

קְטוּרָה (**k'tūrā'**) *pr.n.f.*

קָטַט (**kātă't**) *fut.* יָקוֹט, to cut off; to be cut off.

קָטַל (**kātă'l**) *fut.* יִקְטֹל, to kill, to slay.

קֶטֶל (**kĕ'tĕl**) *m* murder, slaughter.

קָטֹן[1] (**kātō'n**) *pf.* קָטֹנְתִּי, *fut.* יִקְטַן, to be small, little, indifferent — *Hi.* הִקְטִין to make small.

קָטֹן[2] (**kātō'n**) *adj.*, *c.* קְטֹן, small, little, insignificant; young, younger, youngest.

קָטָן (**kātā'n**) *adj.*, *pl.* קְטַנִּים, *c.* קְטַנֵּי, *f* קְטַנָּה, *pl.* קְטַנּוֹת = קָטֹן[2].

קֹטֶן (**kō'tĕn**) *m*, *w.s.* קָטְנִי (**kŏtnī'**) smallness; the little finger.

קָטַף (**kātă'f**) *fut.* יִקְטֹף, *pt. pl.* קֹטְפִים, to pluck off, to pull off. — *Ni. fut.* יִקָּטֵף to be plucked off.

קָטַר[1] (**kātă'r**) *Pi.* קִטֵּר, *inf.* קַטֵּר, *fut.* יְקַטֵּר, *pt.* מְקַטֵּר, to kindle, to burn incense; to sacrifice; *pt. f/pl.* מְקַטְּרוֹת altars for incense. — *Pu. pt. f* מְקֻטֶּרֶת to be censed, to give fragrance. — *Hi.* הִקְטִיר, *inf.* הַקְטִיר, הַקְטֵר, *imp.* הַקְטֵר, *fut.* יַקְטִיר, יַקְטֵר, to kindle, to burn incense, to sacrifice. — *Ho. fut.* יָקְטַר, *pt.* מֻקְטָר, to be offered, to be burnt as incense.

קָטַר[2] (**kātă'r**) *pt. p. f/pl.* קְטֻרוֹת, to shut, to enclose.

קִטְרוֹן (**kĭtrō'n**) *pr.n.* of a place in Zebulon.

קְטֹרֶת (k^etō'rĕϑ) *f*, *w.s.* קְטָרְתִּי (k^etŏrtī'), incense, offering of incense, fat parts of a sacrifice.

קַטָּת (kăttā'ϑ) *pr.n.* = קִטְרוֹן.

קִיא[1] (kī) [קוא] *Hi.* הֵקִיא, *fut.* יָקִיא, וַיָּקֵא see קוא.

קִיא[2] (kī) *m*, *w.s.* קִיאוֹ, vomit.

קִיָה = קוא, קִיא[1].

קִיטוֹר (kītō'r) *m* smoke, mist.

קִים (kīm) *m* uprising, enmity; adversaries.

קִימָה (kīmā') *f* the rising up.

קִין (kīn) [קון] *Pi.* קוֹנֵן, *fut.* יְקוֹנֵן, *pt. f/pl.* מְקוֹנְנוֹת, to mourn, to wail.

קַיִן[1] (kă'yĭn) *m*, *w.s.* קֵינוֹ, edge, point, lance, spear.

קַיִן[2] (kă'yĭn) *pr.n.m.*; *pr.n.* of a tribe in southern Canaan; *gent.* קֵינִי, קֵנִי, קִינִי Kenite; *pr.n.* of a town in Judah.

קִינָה[1] (kīnā') *f*, *pl.* קִינוֹת, קִינִים, complaint, wailing, dirge, elegy.

קִינָה[2] (kīnā') *pr.n.* of a town in Judah.

קֵינִי see קַיִן[2].

קֵינָן (kēnā'n) *pr.n.m.*

קִיץ[1] (kīß) *pf.* קָץ to pass the summer [קַיִץ].

קִיץ[2] (kīß) *Hi.* הֵקִיץ, *inf.* הָקִיץ, *imp.* הָקִיצָה, *fut.* יָקִיץ, to stir, to awake, to rise, to be active.

קַיִץ (kă'yĭß) *m*, *i.p.* קָיִץ, *w.s.* קֵיצֵךְ, summer, warm season, summer fruit [figs], fruit harvest.

קִיצוֹן (kīßō'n) *adj.*, *f* קִיצוֹנָה, the last, the extreme.

קִיקָיוֹן (kī'kāyō'n) *m* ricinus-plant [others: gourd].

קִיקָלוֹן (kī'kālō'n) *m* shame, ignominy.

קִיר[1] (kīr) *m*, *pl.* קִירוֹת, wall [of a house- or town]; rampart, fortress, walled town; in *pr.n.* קִ׳ מוֹאָב קִ׳ חֲרֶשֶׂת, קִ׳ חֶרֶשׂ.

קִיר[2] (kīr) *pr.n.* of a district in Assyria.

קֵירֹס (kērō's) *pr.n.m.*

קִישׁ (kīš) *pr.n.m.*

קִישׁוֹן (kīšō'n) *pr.n.* of a brook in the plain of Jezreel.

קִישִׁי = קוּשָׁיָהוּ.

קַל (kăl) *adj.*, *pl.* קַלִּים, *f* קַלָּה, light, swift, fleet: runner, swift horse.

קל see קוֹל.

קָלַהּ (kālă'h) *Ni. fut. pl.* יִקָּלְהוּ [miswritten for יִקָּהֲלוּ] to be called together.

קָלָה[1] (kālā') *pt. p.* קָלוּי, to roast, to parch, to burn. — *Ni. pt.* נִקְלֶה to be burnt; *pt.* inflammation, fever.

קָלָה[2] (kālā') *Ni.* נִקְלָה, *pt.* נִקְלֶה, to be despised, reviled. — *Hi. pt.* מַקְלֶה to despise, to esteem lightly.

קָלוֹן (kālō'n) *m, c.* קְלוֹן, shame, disgrace, ignominy; shameful nakedness.

קַלַּחַת (kăllă'ḥăth) *f* pot, kettle.

קָלַט (kālă't) *pt. p.* קָלוּט, to contract, to shorten; *pt. p.* a dwarf.

קָלִי (kālī'), קָלִיא *m* roasted grain.

קַלַּי (kăllă'y); קְלָיָה (kelāyā'); קְלִיטָא (k'līṭā') *pr.n.m.*

קָלַל (kālă'l) *fut.* יֵקַל, *pl.* יֵקַלּוּ, to be small, light, swift, to be lessened, despised. — *Ni.* נָקַל, נָקֵל, *fut. pl.* יֵקַלּוּ, to be small, little, insignificant, light, easy, swift. — *Pi.* קִלֵּל, *inf.* קַלֵּל, *fut.* יְקַלֵּל, *pt.* מְקַלֵּל, *w.s.* מְקַלְלֵנִי, *pl.* מְקַלְלִים, to esteem lightly, to revile, to curse. — *Pu. fut.* יְקֻלַּל, *pt.* מְקֻלָּל, to be cursed. — *Hi.* הֵקַל, *w.s.* הֱקִלֻּנִי, *inf.* and *imp.* הָקֵל, *fut.* יָקֵל, to make light or easy, to lessen; to esteem lightly, to despise, to bring into contempt. — *Pilp.* קִלְקֵל, קִלְקַל *tr.* to shake; to sharpen. — *Hithpalp.* הִתְקַלְקֵל to be moved or shaken.

קָלָל (kālā'l) *adj.* smooth, polished, shining.

קְלָלָה (k'lālā') *f, c.* קִלְלַת, *w.s.* קִלְלָתוֹ, *pl.* קְלָלוֹת, reviling, reproach, curse, malediction.

קָלַס (kālă's) *Pi.* קִלֵּס, *inf.* קַלֵּס, to mock, to scoff at. — *Hith.* הִתְקַלֵּס the same as *Pi.*

קֶלֶס (kĕ'lĕs) *m* mockery, scorn, derision.

קַלָּסָה (kăllāsā') *f* = קֶלֶס.

קָלַע[1] (kālă'') *pt.* קֹלֵעַ, to swing, to hurl with a sling; to expel. — *Pi. fut.* יְקַלַּע, to swing, to sling.

קָלַע[2] (**k**ālă'ʻ) to engrave, to carve.

קֶלַע[1] (**k**ĕ'lăʻ) *m*, *i.p.* קָלַע, *w.s.* קַלְעוֹ, a sling.

קֶלַע[2] (**k**ĕ'lăʻ) *m*, only *pl.* קְלָעִים, *c.* קַלְעֵי, curtain, a hanging, covering.

קַלָּע (**k**ăllāʻ) *m* a slinger.

קְלֹקֵל (**k**ᵉlōkē'l) *adj.* good-for-nothing, vile, mean.

קִלְּשׁוֹן (**k**ĭllᵉšō'n) *m* point; שְׁלֹשׁ ק' trident, three-pronged fork.

קָמָה (**k**āmā') *f*, *c.* קָמַת, *pl.* קָמוֹת, standing corn, grain in the stalk.

קְמוּאֵל (**k**ᵉmū'ē'l) *pr.n.m.*

קָמוֹן (**k**āmō'n) *pr.n.* of a town in Gilead.

קִמּוֹשׁ (**k**ĭmmō'š), קִימוֹשׁ *m* thorn, thistle, nettle, weed.

קֶמַח (**k**ĕ'măḥ) *m* meal, bruised grain.

קָמַט (**k**āmă't) *fut.* יִקְמֹט, to make wrinkled [others: to seize]. — *Pu.* קֻמַּט to be snatched away.

קָמַל (**k**āmă'l) *pf.* *pl.* *i.p.* קָמֵלוּ, to wither, to pine away.

קָמַץ (**k**āmă'ß) to press together, to grasp.

קֹמֶץ (**k**ō'mĕß) *m*, *w.s.* קֻמְצוֹ, *pl.* קְמָצִים, a handful, a grasp; bundle of ears; לִקְמָצִים abundantly.

קִמָּשׁוֹן (**k**ĭmmāšō'n) *m*, only *pl.* קִמְּשׁוֹנִים = קִמּוֹשׁ.

קֵן (**k**ēn) *m*, *w.s.* קִנּוֹ, *pl.* קִנִּים, a nest, young birds; habitation, chamber, cell.

קָנָא (**k**ānā') *Pi.* קִנֵּא, *inf.* קַנֵּא, *w.s.* קַנְאוֹ, קַנְאוֹתוֹ, *fut.* יְקַנֵּא, *pt.* מְקַנֵּא, to be jealous or envious; to be zealous for; to excite jealousy or envy. — *Hi.* *fut.* יַקְנִיא to make jealous.

קַנָּא (**k**ănnā') *m* a jealous one.

קִנְאָה (**k**ĭn'ā') *f*, *c.* קִנְאַת, *w.s.* קִנְאָתִי, *pl.* קְנָאוֹת, zeal, jealousy, envy, anger.

קָנָה[1] (**k**ānā') *inf.* קָנֹה, קְנוֹ, קְנוֹת, קְנֹה, *imp.* קְנֵה, *fut.* יִקְנֶה, וַיִּקֶן, *pt.* קֹנֶה, *c.* קֹנֵה, *pl.* קֹנִים, to procure, to acquire, to purchase, to gain, to create, to possess, to redeem. — *Ni.* *fut.* יִקָּנֶה to be bought. — *Hi.* הִקְנָה to buy [as a slave].

קָנָה[2] (**k**ānā') *pr.n.* of a brook between Ephraim

and Manasseh; *pr.n.* of a town in Asher.

קָנֶה (kānĕ') *m*, *c.* קְנֵה, *pl.* קָנִים, *c.* קְנֵי, reed, cane, stalk; sweet cane or calamus; measuring rod, a measure of six ells; balance-beam, balance; bone of the upper arm; shaft of a candelabrum.

קַנּוֹא (kănnō') *adj.* zealous, jealous.

קְנַז (kᵉnă'z) *pr.n.m.*; *patr.* קְנִזִּי.

קִנְיָן (kĭnyā'n) *m*, *c.* קִנְיַן, *w.s.* קִנְיָנוֹ, purchase, acquisition; possession, wealth; what is acquired or created.

קִנָּמוֹן (kĭnnāmō'n) *m*, *c.* קִנְּמָן (kĭnmŏ'n), cinnamon.

קָנַן (kānă'n) *Pi.* קִנֵּן, *fut.* יְקַנֵּן, to build a nest, to nestle. — *Pu.* קֻנַּן to be nestled.

קֶנֶץ (kĕ'nĕs) *m*, only *pl. c.* קִנְצֵי, hunting-net.

קְנָת (kᵉnā'ϑ) *pr.n.* of a town in the Hauran.

קָסַם (kāsă'm) *inf.* קְסֹם, *imp* קָסֳמִי (kŏ'somī'), קְסוּמִי, *fut* יִקְסֹם, *pt.* קֹסֵם, *pl.* קֹסְמִים, to cut, to divide; to draw lots; to divine, to prophesy, to conjure up.

קֶסֶם (kĕ'sĕm) *m*, *pl.* קְסָמִים, decision, divination, oracle; reward of divination.

קֶסֶת (kĕ'sĕϑ) *f* vessel, bowl, ink-stand.

קְעִילָה ,קְעִלָה (kᵉ'īlā') *pr.n.* of a town in Judah.

קַעֲקַע (kă''akă'') *m* cut or mark on the skin, tattoo.

קְעָרָה (kᵉ'ārā') *f*, *c.* קַעֲרַת, *pl.* קְעָרוֹת, *c.* קַעֲרוֹת, bowl, dish.

קָפָא (kāfā') *fut.* יִקְפָּא, *pt. pl.* קֹפְאִים, to be contracted; to coagulate, to congeal. — *Ni. fut.* יִקָּפֵא to be withdrawn. — *Hi.* הִקְפִּיא, *fut.* יַקְפִּיא, to cause to coagulate.

קִפָּאוֹן (kĭppā'ō'n) *m* congelation, frost.

קָפַד (kāfă'd) *Pi.* קִפֵּד to roll up.

קִפֹּד ,קִפּוֹד (kĭppō'd) *m* hedgehog.

קְפָדָה (kᵉfā'dā) *f* horror, destruction.

קִפּוֹז (kĭppō'z) *m* arrow-snake.

קָפַץ (kāfă's) *fut.* יִקְפֹּץ, to

close, to shut [the mouth], to shut up [compassion]. —*Ni. fut.* יִקָּפֵץ to be drawn together, to die. — *Pi. pt.* מְקַפֵּץ to spring, to leap.

קֵץ (kēẞ) *m, w.s.* קִצִּי, a cutting, end, limit, extremity, fulfilment, death, destruction; מִקֵּץ after.

קָצַב (kāẞă'b) *fut.* יִקְצֹב to cut off, to shear.

קֶצֶב (kĕ'ẞĕb) *m, pl. c.* קִצְבֵי, a cutting, shape, form; end, extremity.

קָצָה[1] (kāẞā') *inf.* קְצוֹת, to cut off; to finish, to decide. — *Pi.* קִצָּה, *inf.* קַצּוֹת, *pt.* מְקַצֶּה, to cut off, to take away. — *Hi.* הִקְצָה, *inf.* הִקְצוֹת, to scrape off.

קָצָה[2] (kāẞā') *f, pl.* קְצוֹת, *c.* קְצוֹת, extremity, end, border, compass, the whole.

קָצֶה (kāẞĕ') *m, c.* קְצֵה, *w.s.* קָצֵהוּ, *pl. c.* קְצֵי, the same as קָצָה[2]; מִקְצֵה at the end of, after, from all sides.

קֵצֶה (kē'ẞĕ) *m* end; אֵין קֵצֶה לְ there is no end to.

קְצָו (k'ẞā'v) or **קָצוּ** (kāẞū') *m.* only *pl. c.* קַצְוֵי, end.

קַצְוָה (kăẞvā') *f, pl. w.s.* קַצְוֹתָיו = קְצָת.

קֶצַח (kĕ'ẞăch) *m* black cumin.

קָצִין (kāẞī'n) *m, c.* קְצִין, *pl. c.* קְצִינֵי, judge, magistrate, military leader, general.

קְצִיעָה[1] (k'ẞī'ā') *f, pl.* קְצִיעוֹת, cassia, an aromatic bark like cinnamon.

קְצִיעָה[2] (k'ẞī'ā') *pr.n..f.*

קָצִיר (kāẞī'r) *m, c.* קְצִיר, *w.s.* קְצִירוֹ, *pl. w.s.* קְצִירֶיהָ, a cutting, reaping, harvest; harvest-time, cut grain; cut off bough, branch; reaper.

קָצַע (kāẞă'') *Pu. pt. f/pl. c.* מְקֻצְעֹת, to be made into angles, to be cornered. *Hi. fut.* יַקְצִיעַ to scrape off.—*Ho. pt. f/pl.* מְהֻקְצָעוֹת the same as *Pu.*

קָצַף (kāẞă'f) *inf.* קְצֹף, *fut.* יִקְצֹף, to be angry, to fly into a passion. — *Hi. inf* הַקְצִיף, *fut.* יַקְצִיף, to provoke to anger. — *Hith.* הִתְקַצֵּף the same as *Q.*

קֶצֶף (kĕ'ẞĕf) *m, i.p.* קָצֶף, *w.s.* קִצְפִּי, anger, wrath, fury, strife, quarrel; fragment of wood, chip.

קְצָפָה (**k**ᵉ**B**āfā') *f* broken off bough, chip-wood.

קָצַץ (**k**ā**B**ă'**B**) *pt. p.* קָצוּץ, to cut off, to clip off, to trim. — *Pi.* קִצֵּץ, קִצַּץ, *fut.* יְקַצֵּץ, to cut or hew off, to cut through. — *Pu. pt.* מְקֻצָּץ to be cut off.

קָצַר (**k**ā**B**ă'r) *inf.* קְצֹר, *w.s.* קְצָרְכֶם, *imp. pl.* קִצְרוּ, *fut.* יִקְצֹר, *pt.* קֹצֵר, קוֹצֵר, *pl.* קֹצְרִים, to cut, to mow, to reap; *pt.* reaper. — *intr. inf.* קָצוֹר, *fut.* יִקְצַר, to be cut, shortened, lessened; to be short, impatient, unable. — *Pi.* קִצֵּר to shorten. — *Hi.* הִקְצִיר to reap; to shorten.

קָצֵר (**k**ā**B**ē'r) *adj.*, *c.* קְצַר, *pl. c.* קִצְרֵי, short; קְצַר יָד short in the hand, powerless.

קֹצֶר (**k**ō'**B**ĕr) *m* shortness; ק׳ רוּחַ impatience.

קְצָת (**k**ᵉ**B**ā'ϑ) *f*, קְצָוֹת (**k**ᵉ**B**āvō'ϑ) end, extremity; the whole.

קַר (**k**ăr) *adj.*, *pl.* קָרִים, cold, cool, quiet.

קִר (**k**īr) — קִיר.

קֹר (**k**ōr) *m* coldness, cold.

קָרָא[1] (**k**ārā') *inf.* קְרֹא, קְרֹאות, *w.s.* קָרְאִי (**k**ŏr'ī'), *imp.* קְרָא, קִרְאוּ, *fut.* יִקְרָא, *pt.* קֹרֵא, קוֹרֵא, *pl.* קֹרְאִים, *c.* קֹרְאֵי, *pt. p.* קָרוּא, *pl.* קְרוּאִים, to cry, to call aloud, to roar; to proclaim, pronounce, preach; to call, to summon, to invite; to implore; to call together, to appoint; to praise, celebrate; to call by name, to name; to read aloud, to recite. — *Ni.* נִקְרָא, *fut.* יִקָּרֵא, *pt.* נִקְרָא, *pl.* נִקְרָאִים, to be called, summoned, named; to be read. — *Pu.* קֹרָא, *pt. w.s.* מְקֹרָאִי, to be called, named.

קָרָא[2] (**k**ārā') *fut.* יִקְרָא, *pt. f/pl.* קֹרְאת, to meet, to happen, to occur, to befall. — *Ni.* נִקְרָא, *inf.* נִקְרֹא, *fut.* יִקָּרֵא, to encounter, meet, happen, to be met with. — *Hi. fut.* יַקְרֵא to cause to happen, to let befall.

קֹרֵא[1] (**k**ōrē') *m* partridge.

קֹרֵא[2] (**k**ōrē') *pr.n.m.*

קְרָאת (**k**ᵉrā'ϑ) [*inf.* of קָרָא²], only in לִקְרָאת

adv., *w.s.* לִקְרָאתִי, in an encounter, in a meeting, over against, opposite to.

קָרַב (**k**ārǎ'b), קָרֵב[1] (**k**ārē'b), *inf.* קְרֹב, קְרוֹב, קָרְבָה (**k**ǒrbā'), *imp.* קְרַב, קִרְבָה, קִרְבוּ, *fut.* יִקְרַב, to approach, to draw near, to appear [before God], to come near, to advance. — *Ni.* נִקְרַב to come near.— *Pi.* קֵרֵב, *imp.* קָרֵב, *fut.* יְקָרֵב, to bring near, to admit; *intr.* to be very near. — *Hi.* הִקְרִיב, *inf.* הַקְרִיב, *imp.* הַקְרֵב, *fut.* יַקְרִיב, וַיַּקְרֵב, *pt.* מַקְרִיב, to cause to come near, to bring near, to admit, to give access; to offer, to present a gift; *intr.* to draw near, to be near.

קָרֵב[2] (**k**ārē'b) *adj.* drawing-near, approaching.

קְרָב (**k**ᵉrā'b) *m* collision, battle, war.

קֶרֶב (**k**ě'rěb) *m*, *w.s.* קִרְבּוֹ, *pl. w.s.* קְרָבַי, the interior, the midst, bowels, intestines, cavity of the belly, the heart, the mind, the centre; בְּקֶרֶב in the midst, among; מִקֶּרֶב from the midst, from away.

קְרָבָה (**k**ᵉrābā') *f*, *c.* קִרְבַת, *pl.* קְרָבוֹת, the approaching, nearness; war.

קָרְבָּן (**k**ǒrbā'n), קֻרְבָּן (**k**ǔr-bā'n) *m*, *c.* קָרְבַּן, *pl. w.s.* קָרְבְּנֵיהֶם, offering, present, sacrificial gift.

קַרְדֹּם (**k**ārdō'm) *m*, *w.s.* קַרְדֻּמּוֹ, *pl.* קַרְדֻּמִּים and קַרְדֻּמּוֹת, an axe.

קָרָה[1] (**k**ārā') *fut.* יִקְרֶה, וַיִּקֶר, *pt. f/pl.* קֹרֹת, to encounter, to meet, to happen, to befall, to occur. — *Ni.* נִקְרָה, *fut.* יִקָּרֶה, וַיִּקָּר, to encounter, to meet with, to hit upon; to be at a place by chance.—*Pi. inf.* קָרוֹת, *pt.* מְקָרֶה, to join or cross beams, to build. — *Hi.* הִקְרָה, *imp.* הַקְרֵה, to cause to meet, to let happen; to build [others: to choose convenient places for].

קָרָה[2] (**k**ārā') *f* cold.

קָרֶה (**k**ārě') *m*, *c.* קְרֵה, accident, occurrence.

קָרֹב, קָרוֹב (**k**ārō'b) *adj.*, *w.s.* קְרוֹבוֹ, *pl.* קְרוֹבִים, קְרֹבִים, *f* קְרוֹבָה, near, nigh, neighbouring, immediate, at hand, lately near relation, kinsman, neighbour.

קָרַח (kārā'ch) *imp.* קָרְחִי (kŏrchī'), *fut.* יִקְרַח, to shear, to make bald. — *Ni.* נִקְרַח to be shorn bald. — *Hi.* הִקְרִיחַ to make bald.

קָרֵחַ (kārē'ach) *pr.n.m.*

קֵרֵחַ (kērē'ach) *m* a bald-head.

קֶרַח (kĕ'rāch) *m*, *w.s.* קַרְחוֹ, cold, chilliness; ice; crystal.

קֹרַח[1] (kō'rāch) *m*, *w.s.* קָרְחוֹ (kŏrchō'), hail, ice.

קֹרַח[2] (kō'rāch) *pr.n.m.*; *patr.* קָרְחִי (kŏrchī'), *pl.* קָרְחִים.

קָרְחָה (kŏrchā') *f*, *w.s.* קָרְחָתֵךְ, baldness [of the back head].

קָרַחַת (kārā'chāth) *f*, *w.s.* קָרַחְתּוֹ, baldness.

קְרִי (k'rī') *m*, *i.p.* קֶרִי, hostile encounter.

קָרִיא (kārī') *adj.*, *pl. c.* קְרִיאֵי, called, selected.

קְרִיאָה (k'rī'ā') *f* proclamation.

קִרְיָה (kĭryā') *f*, *c.* קִרְיַת, town, city [poetically for עִיר]; קִרְיַת in many compounds of proper names, e. g. ק׳ אַרְבַּע, ק׳ יְעָרִים, ק׳ סֵפֶר.

קְרִיּוֹת (k'rĭyyō'th) *pr.n.* of towns in Judah and in Moab.

קִרְיָתַיִם (kĭryāthā'yĭm) *pr.n.* of a town in Reuben.

קָרַם (kārā'm) *fut.* יִקְרַם, to overlay, to cover.

קָרַן (kārā'n) to beam, to shine, to cast forth rays. — *Hi. pt.* מַקְרִן to put forth or have horns.

קֶרֶן (kĕ'rĕn) *f*, *i.p.* קָרֶן, *w.s.* קַרְנִי, *du.* קַרְנַיִם, *c.* קַרְנֵי, *pl.* קְרָנוֹת, *c.* קַרְנוֹת, a horn, horn-vessel, oil-horn; horn for blowing; point, corner; peak; ray of light; might, power, strength, dignity.

קֶרֶן הַפּוּךְ (kĕ'rĕn hăppū'ch) *pr.n.f.* [paint-horn].

קָרַס (kārā's) *pt.* קֹרֵס, to bend, to writhe, to sink down.

קֶרֶס (kĕ'rĕs) *m*, only *pl.* קְרָסִים, *c.* קַרְסֵי, bend, hook.

קֵרֹס = קֵירֹס *pr.n.m.*

קַרְסֹל (kărsō'l) *m*, only *du.* *w.s.* קַרְסֻלָּי, knuckle, ankle.

קָרַע (kārā'') *inf.* קְרֹעַ, *imp.* *pl.* קִרְעוּ, *fut.* יִקְרַע, *pt.* קֹרֵעַ, *pt. p.* קָרוּעַ, *pl.* קְרֻעִים,

c. קִרְעֵי, to tear to pieces, to rend, to tear away; to tear open, to open, to widen; to slander. — *Ni.* *fut.* יִקָּרֵעַ, יִקָּרַע, *pt.* נִקְרָע, to be torn to pieces, to be rent.

קֶרַע (**k**ĕ'ră•) *m*, only *pl.* קְרָעִים, piece, rag, tatter.

קָרַץ (**k**ără'ß) *fut.* יִקְרֹץ, *pt.* קֹרֵץ, to press together, to bite [the lips], to wink. — *Pu.* קֹרַץ to be pinched off, to be nipped off.

קֶרֶץ (**k**ĕ'rĕß) *m* gadfly [others: destruction].

קַרְקַע[1] (**k**ărkă'•) *m* ground, soil, floor, pavement, ceiling; bottom.

קַרְקַע[2] (**k**ărkă'•) *pr.n.* of a town in Judah.

קַרְקֹר (**k**ărkō'r) *pr.n.* of a town beyond the Jordan.

קָרַר (**k**ără'r) *Pi. inf.* קַרְקַר, *pt.* מְקַרְקַר, to pull down, to destroy [or from קוּר].

קֶרֶשׁ (**k**ĕ'rĕš) *m*, *i.p.* קָרֶשׁ, *w.s.* קַרְשֵׁךְ, *pl.* קְרָשִׁים, *c.* קַרְשֵׁי, board, plank; rowing-bench [others: pannelling, deck].

קֶרֶת (**k**ĕ'rĕϑ) *f* city, town.

קַרְתָּה (**k**ărtā') *pr.n.* of a town in Zebulon.

קַרְתָּן (**k**ărtā'n) *pr.n.* of a town in Naphtali.

קָשָׂה (**k**āßā'), קַשְׂוָה (**k**ăßvā') or קְשָׂת (**k**ᵉßā'ϑ) *f*, *pl.* קְשָׂוֹת (**k**ᵉßāvō'ϑ), *c.* קְשׂוֹת, vessel, can, jug.

קְשִׂיטָה (**k**ᵉßītā') *f* something weighed, a piece of money, coin worth 4 shekels.

קַשְׂקֶשֶׂת (**k**ăß**k**ĕ'ßĕϑ) *f*, *pl.* קַשְׂקַשִּׂים, קַשְׂקְשׂוֹת, *c.* קַשְׂקְשׂוֹת, scale [of a fish, of a harness].

קַשׁ (**k**ăš) *m* straw, stubble, chaff.

קִשֻּׁא (**k**ĭššū') *m*, only *pl.* קִשֻּׁאִים, cucumber.

קָשַׁב (**k**āšă'b) *fut.* יִקְשַׁב, to listen, to hearken. — *Hi.* הִקְשִׁיב, *inf.* הַקְשִׁיב, *imp.* הַקְשִׁיבָה, הַקְשֵׁב, *fut.* יַקְשִׁיב, יַקְשֵׁב, to attend, listen, hearken; to make attentive.

קֶשֶׁב (**k**ĕ'šĕb) *m* attention, listening.

קַשָּׁב (**k**ăššā'b) *adj.*, *f* קַשֶּׁבֶת, attentive.

קַשָּׁב (**k**ășšū'ḅ) *adj.*, *f/pl.* קַשֻּׁבוֹת, attentive.

קָשָׁה (**k**ąšą') *fut.* יִקְשֶׁה, וַיִּקֶשׁ, to be hard, heavy, harsh, severe, difficult. — *Ni. pt.* נִקְשֶׁה to be oppressed, depressed. — *Pi. fut.* יְקַשֶּׁה, וַתְּקַשׁ, to make hard, to labour. — *Hi.* הִקְשָׁה, *inf.* הַקְשׁוֹת, *fut.* יַקְשֶׁה, וַיַּקֶשׁ, *pt.* מַקְשֶׁה, to harden, to make heavy or difficult.

קָשֶׁה (**k**ąšę') *adj.*, *c.* קְשֵׁה, קָשִׁים, *f* קָשָׁה, *c.* קְשַׁת, *pl.* קָשׁוֹת, hard, difficult, severe, unfeeling, cruel; inflexible, obstinate; unfortunate, melancholy; strong, violent.

קָשַׁח (**k**ąšą'ȟ) *Hi.* הִקְשִׁיחַ, *fut.* יַקְשִׁיחַ, to harden; to treat harshly.

קֹשְׁטְ (**k**ǫšt), קֹשֶׁט (**k**ǫ'šęt) *m* faithfulness; justness, truth.

קְשִׁי (**k**'šī') *m* hardness, obduration.

קִשְׁיוֹן (**k**ĭšyǭ'n) *pr.n.* of a town in Issachar.

קָשַׁר (**k**ąšą'r) *fut.* יִקְשֹׁר, *pt.* קֹשֵׁר, *pt. p.* קָשׁוּר, *pl* קְשֻׁרִים, *f* קְשׁוּרָה, to bind, to tie; to join in conspiracy, to conspire; *pt.* conspirator; *pt. p.* bound, strong, firm. — *Ni.* נִקְשַׁר, *fut.* יִקָּשֵׁר, to be bound together, to be attached; to be finished. — *Pi.* קִשֵּׁר, *fut.* 2. *f/sg. w.s.* תְּקַשְּׁרִים, to bind, to unite; to bind about. — *Pu. pt. f/pl.* מְקֻשָּׁרוֹת to be strong. — *Hith.* הִתְקַשֵּׁר to conspire.

קֶשֶׁר (**k**ę'šęr) *m*, *i.p.* קָשֶׁר, *w.s.* קִשְׁרוֹ, conspiracy, rebellion.

קִשֻּׁר (**k**ĭššū'r) *m*, only *pl.* קִשֻּׁרִים, girdle.

קָשַׁשׁ (**k**ąšą'š) *imp. pl.* קֹשׁוּ (**k**ǫ'ššū) to collect oneself. — *Po. inf.* קֹשֵׁשׁ, *pt.* מְקֹשֵׁשׁ, *f* מְקֹשֶׁשֶׁת, to gather straw or wood. — *Hith.* הִתְקוֹשֵׁשׁ to collect oneself, to make up one's mind.

קֶשֶׁת (**k**ę'šęϑ) *f* [also *m*], *i.p.* קָשֶׁת, *w.s.* קַשְׁתִּי, *pl.* קְשָׁתוֹת, *c.* קַשְּׁתוֹת, a bow [for shooting], rainbow; power, strength.

קַשָּׁת (**k**ășšą'ϑ) *m* bowman, archer.

ר

ר the twentieth letter of the alphabet, called רֵישׁ [head]; as a numeral = 200.

רָאָה[1] (rā'ā') *inf.* רָאֹה, רָאוֹת, רְאֹה, רְאוֹת, *w.s.* רְאוֹתִי, רְאֹתִי, *imp.* רְאֵה, רְאִי, רְאוּ, *fut.* יִרְאֶה, יֵרֶא, וַיַּרְא, 1. *sg.* אֶרְאֶה, אֵרֶה, *pt.* רֹאֶה, *c.* רֹאֵה, *w.s.* רֹאִי, *pl.* רֹאִים, *c.* רֹאֵי, *f* רֹאָה, *pl.* רֹאוֹת, *pt. p.* רָאוּי, *f/pl.* רְאֻיוֹת, to see, to look, to look at, to view, to inspect, regard, perceive; to feel, understand, learn; to live to see, to enjoy.—*Ni.* נִרְאָה, *inf.* הֵרָאֹה, הֵרָאוֹת [לֵרָאוֹת for לְהֵ'], *imp.* הֵרָאֵה, *fut.* יֵרָאֶה, יֵרָא, *pt.* נִרְאֶה, to be seen; to show oneself, to appear, to reveal oneself; to be shown. — *Pu.* רֻאָה to be seen. — *Hi.* הֶרְאָה, הִרְאָה, *inf.* הַרְאוֹת, *imp.* הַרְאֵה, *fut.* יַרְאֶה, וַיַּרְא, *pt.* מַרְאֶה, to make seeing, to cause to see, to show; to make one feel or know; to cause to enjoy. — *Ho.* הָרְאָה, *pt.* מָרְאֶה, to be made to see, to be shown anything. — *Hith.* הִתְרָאָה to look at one another.

רָאָה[2] (rā'ā') *f* a bird of prey [for דָּאָה].

רָאֶה (rā'ĕ') *adj.*, *c.* רְאֵה, seeing.

רֹאֶה[1] (rō'ĕ') *m* [*pt.* of רָאָה[1]], *pl.* רֹאִים, seer, prophet; vision, oracle.

רֹאֶה[2] (rō'ĕ') *pr.n.m.*

רְאוּבֵן (rᵉ'ūbē'n) *pr.n.m.*, Reuben.

רַאֲוָה (rā''ᵃvā') *f*, *inf.* of רָאָה[1], a seeing, spectacle.

רְאוּמָה (rᵉ'ūmā') *pr.n.f.*

רְאוּת (rᵉ'ū'ϑ) *f* sight, seeing.

רְאִי (rᵉ'ī') *m* mirror.

רֳאִי (ro'ī') *m*, *i.p.* רֹאִי, sight, vision, appearance, spectacle, warning example.

רְאָיָה (rᵉ'āyā') *pr.n.m.*

רְאֵים, רְאֵם (rᵉ'ē'm), רֵם (rēm) *m*, *pl.* רְאֵמִים, רֵמִים, a wild animal, antelope, buffalo, unicorn.

רְאִית (rᵉ'ī'ϑ) = **רְאוֹת**, see רָאָה[1].

רָאמוֹת, רָמֹת (rāmō'ϑ) *pr.n.* of a town in Gilead

רָאמָה (rāmā') *f*, *c.* רָאמַת, *pl.* רָאמוֹת, height; coral.

רֹאשׁ¹ (rōš) *m*, *w.s.* רֹאשִׁי, *pl.* רָאשִׁים [for רְאָשִׁים], רֹאשִׁים, *c.* רָאשֵׁי, the head, person; chief, leader, prince; chief town; point, top, first rank, the best; the total; multitude, band, troop; the beginning; a poisonous plant, poppy, poison.

רֹאשׁ² (rōš) *pr.n.* of a Scythian people, Russians; *pr.n.m.*

רִאשָׁה (rīšā') *f* top, head; הָאֶבֶן הָרִאשָׁה corner-stone, key-stone.

רִישׁוֹן, רִאשֹׁן, רִאשׁוֹן (rīšō'n) *adj.*, *pl.* רִאשׁוֹנִים, *f* רִאשׁוֹנָה, רִאשֹׁנָה, *pl.* רִאשֹׁנוֹת, the first, foremost, chief, former, earlier, preceding, ancient; *adv.* first, before, sooner, formerly.

רִאשֹׁנִי (rīšōnī') *adj.*, only *f* רִאשֹׁנִית, = רִאשׁוֹן.

רֵשִׁית, רֵאשִׁית (rēšī'ϑ) *f* beginning, commencement, origin, former state, the first, the best, firstling.

רְאֶשֶׁת (rĕ'šĕϑ) *f*, only *pl.* *c.* רַאֲשׁוֹתַי, the place of the head, see מְרַאֲשֹׁת.

רַב (rab) *adj.*, *i.p.* רָב, *pl.* רַבִּים, *f* רַבָּה, *c.* רַבַּת, *pl.* רַבּוֹת, much, numerous, many, abundant, sufficient, great, strong, mighty; chief, head, leader, master; *adv.* much, enough, abundantly.

רֹב (rōb) *m*, *c.* רֹב, רָב־, *w.s.* רֻבְּכֶם, *pl. c.* רֻבֵּי, multitude, number, largeness, greatness, fulness, totality; לָרֹב in multitude, abundantly; מֵרֹב for multitude.

רָבַב¹ (rābă'b) *pf. pl.* רַבּוּ, *i.p.* רָבּוּ, *inf.* רֹב, to be or become many, numerous, abundant. — *Pu. pt. f/pl.* מְרֻבָּבוֹת to be multiplied by myriads [רְבָבָה].

רָבַב² (rābă'b) *pf.* רַב, *pl.* רֹבּוּ, to throw, to shoot, to sling.

רְבָבָה (rᵉbābā') *f*, *pl.* רְבָבוֹת, *c.* רִבְבוֹת, great multitude, ten thousand, myriad.

רָבַד (rābă'd) to spread, to prepare a bed.

רָבָה (rābā') *inf.* רְבוֹת, *imp.* רְבֵה, *fut.* יִרְבֶּה, יִרֶב, יֶרֶב, *pt.* רֹבֶה, to be or become many, to increase, to multiply; to be or become large, great, mighty. — *Pi.* רִבָּה, *imp.* רַבֵּה [for רַבֵּה], to make many, to get much, to bring up [children]. — *Hi.* הִרְבָּה, *inf.* הַרְבֵּה, הַרְבָּה, הַרְבֵּה, הַרְבּוֹת, *imp.* הַרְבֵּה, *fut.* יַרְבֶּה, וַיֶּרֶב, *pt.* מַרְבֶּה, *pl.* מַרְבִּים, to make many or great, to multiply, to increase, to do abundantly, to have or give much; *inf.* הַרְבֵּה as an *adv.* much, greatly, abundantly.

רֹבֶה (rōbĕ') *m* shooter, archer [or becoming great, *pt.* of רָבָה].

רַבָּה (răbbā') *f* the great, the chief one; *pr.n.* of the chief town of the Ammonites, רַבַּת בְּנֵי עַמּוֹן.

רִבּוֹ, רִבּוֹא (rĭbbō') *f, du.* רִבֹּתַיִם, *pl.* רִבֹּאוֹת, רִבְּאוֹת, רִבּוֹת, ten thousand, myriad = רְבָבָה.

רָבִיב (rābī'b) *m*, only *pl.* רְבִבִים, רְבִיבִים, abundant rain, shower.

רָבִיד (rābīd) *m*, *e.* רָבַד, collar, neck-chain.

רְבִיעִי (rᵉbīʼī') *adj. num.*, *pl.* רְבִיעִים, רְבִעִים, *f* רְבִיעִית, fourth, fourth part, fourth generation.

רַבִּית (răbbī'ϑ) *pr.n.* of a town in Issachar.

רָבַךְ (rābă'ch) *Ho. pt. f* מֻרְבֶּכֶת, to be mixed, mingled.

רִבְלָה (rĭblā') *pr.n.* of a city in Syria.

רַב־סָרִיס (răb sārī's) *pr.n.m.* [see סָרִיס].

רָבַע[1] (rābă'ʻ) *inf. w.s.* רִבְעִי, to lie down, to lie with. — *Hi. fut.* תַּרְבִּיעַ to cause to gender.

רָבַע[2] (rābă'ʻ) *pt. p.* רָבוּעַ, *pl.* רְבֻעִים, to have four sides; *pt. p.* square, four-sided. — *Pu. pt.* מְרֻבָּע to be made four-sided or square.

רֶבַע[1] (rĕ'băʻ) *m* the fourth part, fourth side [for רִבְעִי see רָבַע[1]].

רֶבַע[2] (rĕ'băʻ) *pr.n.m.*

רִבֵּעַ (rĭbbē'aʻ) *m*, only *pl.* רִבֵּעִים, descendent of the fourth generation, great-grandchild.

רֹבַע (rō'băʻ) *m* = רֶבַע.

רָבַץ (rābă'ß) *fut.* יִרְבַּץ, *pt.*

רָבַץ, pl. רָבְצִים, f רֹבֶצֶת, to lie down, to couch, to rest, to repose; to lie in wait, to lurk.—*Hi.* הִרְבִּיץ, *fut.* יַרְבִּיץ, *pt.* מַרְבִּיץ, to cause to lie down, to lay.

רֵבֶץ (rĕ'bĕẓ) *m*, *w.s.* רִבְצָהּ, a couching, resting-place.

רִבְקָה (rĭbkā') *pr.n.f.*, Rebekah.

רַבְשָׁקֵה (răbshākē') *m* title of an Assyrian dignitary [cup-bearer or general].

רֶגֶב (rĕ'gĕb) or רֵגֶב (rē'gĕb) *m*, only *pl.* רְגָבִים, *c.* רִגְבֵי, a clod.

רָגַז (rāgă'z) or רָגֵז (rāgē'z) *imp.* רְגָזָה, רִגְזוּ, *fut.* יִרְגַּז, to be in a trouble, to be stirred, moved, excited; to tremble, to quake. — *Hi.* הִרְגִּיז, *fut.* יַרְגִּיז, *pt.* מַרְגִּיז, *tr.* to stir, move, agitate, to cause to tremble. — *Hith.* הִתְרַגֵּז to be agitated, to rage.

רַגָּז (răggā'z) *adj.* trembling.

רֹגֶז (rō'gĕz) *m*, *w.s.* רָגְזֶךָ (rŏgzĕ'chā), agitation, excitement, rage, tumult, disquiet.

רָגְזָה (rŏgzā') *f* a trembling, quaking.

רָגַל (rāgă'l) *pt.* רֹגֵל, to use one's feet, to wander about; to slander; to full. — *Pi.* רִגֵּל, *inf.* רַגֵּל, *w.s.* רַגְּלָהּ, *fut.* יְרַגֵּל, *pt. pl.* מְרַגְּלִים, to wander about as a slanderer, as a spy; *pt.* a scout or spy.—*Tiph.* תִּרְגַּלְ [= *Hi.*] to teach to walk, to lead [a child].

רֶגֶל (rĕ'gĕl) *f*, *i.p.* רָגֶל, *w.s.* רַגְלִי, *du.* רַגְלַיִם, *c.* רַגְלֵי, *pl.* רְגָלִים, foot, leg, step, tread; *du.* also pudenda; *pl.* steps, turns, times, שָׁלֹשׁ רְגָלִים three times, thrice.

רֹגֵל (rōgē'l) *m* fuller; in *pr.n.* עֵין רֹגֵל a fountain near Jerusalem.

רַגְלִי (răglī') *m*, *pl.* רַגְלִים, footman, pedestrian, foot-soldier.

רֹגְלִים (rō'gelī'm) *pr.n.* of a place in Gilead.

רָגַם (rāgă'm) *inf.* רָגוֹם, רְגוֹם, *fut. pl.* יִרְגְּמוּ, to heap stones upon, to stone.

רֶגֶם (rĕ'gĕm); רֶגֶם מֶלֶךְ (rĕ'gĕm mĕ'lĕch) *pr.n.m.*

רִגְמָה (rĭgmā') *f*, *w.s.* רִגְמָתָם, heap, crowd.

רָגַן (rāgă'n) *pt. pl.* רֹגְנִים,

to murmur, **to** revolt. — *Ni. fut.* יֵרָגֵן to murmur, to rebel.

רָגַע¹ (rāgă'ᵉ) *pt.* רֹגַע, to set in motion, to cause to tremble, to terrify; to contract oneself. — *Hi.* הִרְגִּיעַ, *fut.* יַרְגִּיעַ, to cause to move, **to** wink with the eye, to do in a moment.

רָגַע² (rāgă'ᵉ) *Ni. imp. f* הֵרָגְעִי, to rest. — *Hi.* הִרְגִּיעַ, *fut.* יַרְגִּיעַ, to cause to **rest**, to settle, to establish.

רָגֵעַ (rāgē'aᵉ) *adj.* living quietly, quiet.

רֶגַע (rĕ'găᵉ) *m, i.p.* רָגַע, *pl.* רְגָעִים, a winking, wink, moment, time, turn; *adv.* suddenly, for a moment, quickly.

רָגַשׁ (rāgă's) **to be** noisy, to rage.

רֶגֶשׁ (rĕ'gĕs) *m* noisy crowd.

רִגְשָׁה (rĭgšā') *f, c.* רִגְשַׁת = רֶגֶשׁ.

רָדַד (rāḍă'ḍ) *inf.* רֹד, רָד־, רַד, *pt.* רֹדֵד, to tread down, to subdue. — *Hi. fut.* וַיָּרֶד to extend, to overlay [with metal].

רָדָה¹ (rāḍā') *inf.* רְדוֹת, *imp.* רְדֵה, *pl.* רְדוּ, *fut.* יִרְדֶּה, וַיֵּרְדְּ. *pt.* רֹדֶה, *w.s.* רֹדֵם, *pl.* רֹדִים, to tread down, to subdue, to oppress; to rule, to sway. — *Pi. fut.* יְרַד [or from יָרַד] to cause to rule, to subdue. — *Hi. fut.* יַרְדְּ to tread down, to subdue.

רָדָה² (rāḍā') *fut.* יִרְדֶּה, to take, to seize.

רַדַּי (răddă'y) *pr.n.m.*

רָדִיד (rāḍī'ḍ) *m, w.s.* רְדִידִי, *pl.* רְדִידִים, thin, wide covering, **veil**, female garment.

רָדַם (rāḍă'm) *Ni. fut.* יֵרָדֵם, *pt.* נִרְדָּם, to lie in a deep sleep, to be stupified, stunned, senseless, motionless.

רָדַף (rāḍă'f) *inf.* רָדוֹף, רְדֹף, *w.s.* רָדְפִי (rŏḍfī'), *imp.* רְדֹף, *fut.* יִרְדֹּף, *pt.* רֹדֵף, רוֹדֵף, *pl.* רֹדְפִים, *c.* רֹדְפֵי, to run after, to pursue, to follow; to strive after; to chase, to drive away. — *Ni.* נִרְדַּף, *pt.* נִרְדָּף, to be pursued; *pt.* what is driven away, the past. — *Pi. fut.* יְרַדֵּף, יְרַדֵּף [or = יִרְדֹּף *Q.*], *pt.* מְרַדֵּף, to follow, to pursue, to strive after. — *Pu.* רֻדַּף to be chased. — *Hi.* הִרְדִּיף to pursue eagerly. — *Ho. pt.* see מֻרְדָּף.

רָהַב (rāhă'b) *fut.* יִרְהַב, to rage, to urge, to importune. — *Hi.* הִרְהִיב, *fut.* יַרְהִיב, to excite; to make courageous.

רָהָב (rā'hāb) *adj., pl.* רְהָבִים, proud, defiant.

רַהַב (ră'hăb) *m, i.p.* רָהַב, rage, violence, noise, defiance; a sea-monster [crocodile, symbolizing Egypt].

רֹהַב (rō'hăb) *m, w.s.* רָהְבָּם (rŏhbā'm), pride, insolence, boasting.

רָהְגָּה (rŏhgā') *pr.n.m.*

רָהָה (rāhā') *fut.* יִרְהֶה, to tremble, to fear.

רַהַט (ră'hăt) *m,* only *pl.* רְהָטִים, watering-trough; lock of hair.

רוֹב see רֹב.

רוּב see רִיב.

רוּד (rūd) *pf.* רָד, to ramble, to rove about, to neglect [God]. — *Hi.* הֵרִיד, *fut.* יָרִיד, to ramble, to rove, to be restless.

רָוָה (rāvā') *fut.* יִרְוֶה, *pl.* יִרְוְיֻן, to overflow, to drink copiously, to be debauched, to enjoy. — *Pi.* רִוָּה, *imp.* רַוֵּה, *fut.* יְרַוֶּה, *w.s.* אֲרַיָּוֵךְ, to be soaked, to be sated, to be drunk; *tr.* to water, to drench, to satiate, to moisten. — *Hi.* הִרְוָה, *pt.* מַרְוֶה, to water, refresh, satiate.

רָוֶה (rāvĕ') *adj., f* רָוָה, watered, satiated with drink.

רָוַח (rāvă'ḥ) *fut.* יִרְוַח, to be extended, to be wide or easy. — *Pu. pt.* מְרֻוָּח to be spacious, airy.

רֶוַח (rĕ'văḥ) *m* room, space; relief.

רוּחַ[1] (rū'aḥ) *Hi. inf.* הָרִיחַ, *w.s.* הֲרִיחוֹ, *fut.* יָרִיחַ, יָרַח, וַיָּרַח, to smell [*tr.*], to scent, to enjoy the odour.

רוּחַ[2] (rū'aḥ) *f, w.s.* רוּחִי, *pl.* רוּחוֹת, breath, wind, air, breeze, blowing; animal life, spirit, ghost, soul, mind, intellect, passion.

רְוָחָה (rĕvāḥā') *f* relief, ease, breathing.

רְוָיָה (rĕvāyā') *f* an overflowing, abundance.

רוּם[1] (rūm) *pf.* רָם, *inf.* רוּם, רֻם, רוּם, *imp.* רוּמָה, *fut.* יָרוּם, יָרֹם, וַיָּרָם (vǎyyā'-rŏm), *pt.* רָם, *f* רָמָה, to be or become high, elevated, exalted, lofty, glorious, mighty, proud.—*Pi.* רוֹמֵם, *imp.* רוֹמְמוּ, *fut.* יְרוֹמֵם, *pt.* מְרוֹמֵם, to make high, to raise, to bring up, to make grow, to exalt, to celebrate. — *Pu.* *fut.* יְרוֹמַם, *pt.* מְרוֹמָם, to be raised, exalted.—*Hi.* הֵרִים, *inf.* הָרִים, *imp.* הָרֵם, *fut.* יָרִים, וַיָּרֶם, *pt.* מֵרִים, *pl. c.* מְרִימֵי, to make high, to raise, to lift up, to exalt, to elevate; to take away, to receive; to offer, to present [a sacrifice].—*Ho.* הוּרַם, *fut.* יוּרַם, to be offered; to be taken away. — *Hith.* הִתְרוֹמֵם, *fut.* 1. *sg.* אֶרוֹמָם, to raise or exalt oneself.

רוּם[2], **רֻם** (rūm) *m* height; pride, haughtiness.

רוֹם (rōm) *m* height.

רוֹמָה (rōmā') *f* haughtiness, pride; *adv.* proudly.

רוּמָה (rūmā') *pr.n.* of a place.

רוֹמָם (rōmā'm) *m, pl.* רוֹמְמוֹת, exaltation, praise; hymn.

רוֹמֵמוּת (rō'mēmū'θ) *f* a rising up; majesty.

רון (rūn) *Hith.* *pt.* מִתְרוֹנֵן, to be overpowerd, intoxicated [but see רָנַן].

רוּעַ (rū'ª) *Pu.* *fut.* יְרֹעַע, to be shouted with joy. — *Hi.* הֵרִיעַ, הֵרַע, *inf.* הָרִיעַ, *imp. pl.* הָרִיעוּ, *fut.* יָרִיעַ, וַיָּרַע, *pt. pl.* מְרִיעִים, to shout with joy, to cry, to raise a cry, to be noisy, to lament.— *Hith.* הִתְרוֹעֵעַ to shout with joy.

רוּף (rūf) *Pu.* *fut.* יְרוֹפַף, to be shaken, to quake.

רוּץ (rūß) *pf.* רָץ, *inf.* רוּץ, *imp.* רוּץ, רֻץ, *fut.* יָרוּץ, יָרֹץ, וַיָּרָץ (vǎyyā'rŏß), *pt.* רָץ, *pl.* רָצִים [רָצִין], to run, to hasten, to rush; *pt.* runner, courier, royal messenger, body-guard. — *Pi.* *fut.* יְרוֹצֵץ to run fast. — *Hi.* הֵרִיץ, *imp.* הָרֵץ, *fut.* יָרִיץ, to cause to run, to bring quickly, to chase away, to accelerate.

רוּק (rūk) *Hi.* הֵרִיק, *inf.* הָרִיק, *fut.* יָרִיק, וַיָּרֶק, *pt.* מֵרִיק, *pl.* מְרִיקִים, to empty, to pour out, to draw [a sword], to lead to battle. — *Ho.* הוּבַק to be poured out.

רוּר (rūr) *pf.* רָר, to let flow out [spittle &c.].

רוֹשׁ (rōš) *m* poppy, poison, see רֹאשׁ.

רוּשׁ (rūš) *pf.* רָשׁ, *pt.* רָשׁ [רָאשׁ], to be poor, needy; *pt.* a poor one, beggar. — *Hith.* הִתְרוֹשֵׁשׁ, to feign oneself poor.

רוּת (rūϑ) *pr.n.f.*

רָזָה (rāzā') to make thin or lean. — *Ni. fut.* יֵרָזֶה to become lean.

רָזֶה (rāzē') *adj.*, *f* רָזָה, lean, meagre.

רָזוֹן[1] (rāzō'n) *m* leanness, consumption

רָזוֹן[2] (rāzō'n) *m* prince.

רְזוֹן (rᵉzō'n) *pr.n.m.* of a king of Damascus.

רָזִי (rāzī') *m* consumption, destruction; רָזִי־לִי woe to me!

רָזַם (rāză'm) *fut.* יִרְזְמוּן, to move the eyes, to wink.

רֹזֵן (rōzē'n) [*pt.* of רָזַן], only *pl.* רוֹזְנִים, רֹזְנִים, prince, ruler.

רָחַב (rāḥă'b) to be wide, spacious, to be wide opened. — *Ni. pt.* נִרְחָב to be wide, spacious. — *Hi.* הִרְחִיב, *inf.* הַרְחִיב, *imp.* הַרְחֶב־, הַרְחִיבִי, *fut.* יַרְחִיב, to make wide, broad, spacious, to open wide; to extend, enlarge, expand; to relieve, to deliver.

רָחָב[1] (rāḥā'b) *adj.*, *c.* רְחַב, *pl. c.* רַחֲבֵי, *f* רְחָבָה, *c.* רַחֲבַת, wide, spacious, broad, large; puffed up, haughty; *subst.* ambition, pride.

רָחָב[2] (rāḥā'b) *pr.n.f.*, Rahab.

רַחַב (ră'ḥăb) *m*, *pl. c.* רַחֲבֵי, breadth, width, extension.

רֹחַב (rō'ḥăb) *m*, *w.s.* רָחְבּוֹ (rŏḥbō'), breadth, extent, comprehensiveness.

רְחֹב[1], **רְחוֹב** (rᵉḥō'b) *m*, *w.s.* רְחֹבָהּ, *pl.* רְחֹבוֹת, wide space, broad way, street, roomy place, court, forum.

רְחֹב[2] (rᵉḥō'b) *pr.n.m.*; *pr.n.* of a town in Asher.

רְחָבָה (rᵉḥābā') [see רָחָב[1]] *f* roominess, freedom.

רְחֹבוֹת (rᵉḥōbō'ϑ) *pr.n.* of a well; ר׳ עִיר a suburb of Nineveh; ר׳ הַנָּהָר a town near the Euphrates.

רְחַבְיָה (rĕhăbyā') or רְחַבְיָהוּ (rĕhăbyā'hū) *pr.n.m.*

רְחַבְעָם (rĕhăb'ā'm) *pr.n.m.*, Rehoboam.

רֵחֶה (rēhĕ') *adj.* grinding; *m* millstone, only *du.* רֵחַיִם the two grind-stones, hand-mill.

רַחוּם (răhū'm) *adj.* merciful, compassionate.

רָחוֹק (rāhō'k) *adj.*, *pl.* רְחֹקִים, רְחוֹקִים, *f* רְחוֹקָה, *pl.* רְחֹקוֹת, far, distant, remote [of place and time]; unattainable, precious; *subst.* distance, future, past; מֵרָחוֹק from afar.

רָחִיט (rāhī't) *m*, *pl.* רְחִיטִים, frame-work, panelling.

רֵחַיִם see רֵחֶה.

רָחֵל¹ (rāhē'l) *f*, *pl.* רְחֵלִים, female lamb, sheep, ewe.

רָחֵל² (rāhē'l) *pr.n.f.*, Rachel.

רָחַם (rāhă'm) *fut.* *w.s.* אֶרְחָמְךָ (ĕrhŏmhā'), to love. — *Pi.* רִחַם, *inf.* רַחֵם, *fut.* יְרַחֵם, *pt.* מְרַחֵם, to have compassion, pity, tenderness, love. — *Pu.* רֻחַם, *fut.* יְרֻחַם, to meet with compassion or mercy.

רָחָם (rāhā'm) *m* a vulture.

רַחַם¹ (ră'hăm) *m*, *i.p.* רָחַם, *pl.* רַחֲמִים, *c.* רַחֲמֵי, a womb, a maiden; *pl.* the bowels; compassion, mercy, sympathy, tenderness, pity.

רַחַם² (ră'hăm) *pr.n.m.*

רֶחֶם (rĕ'hĕm) *m*, *i.p.* רָחֶם, *w.s.* רַחְמָהּ, the womb, the mother's womb.

רַחֲמָה (ră'hamā') *f*, *du.* רַחֲמָתַיִם, woman, maiden.

רַחֲמָנִי (ră'hamānī') *adj.*, *f* רַחֲמָנִית, *pl.* רַחֲמָנִיּוֹת, merciful, compassionate.

רָחַף (rāhă'f) to quake, to tremble. — *Pi.* *fut.* יְרַחֵף, *pt.* *f* מְרַחֶפֶת, to brood, to hover over.

רָחַץ (rāhă'ß) *inf.* רְחֹץ, רָחְצָה (rŏhßā'), *imp.* רְחַץ, רַחֲצוּ, *fut.* יִרְחַץ, *pt.* *f* רֹחֶצֶת, *pl.* רֹחֲצוֹת, to wash, to rinse; to wash away; to wash oneself, to bathe. — *Pu.* רֻחַץ to be washed. — *Hith.* הִתְרַחֵץ to wash oneself.

רַחַץ (ră'hăß) *m*, *w.s.* רַחְצִי, a washing.

רַחְצָה (răhßā') *f* a washing, watering-place.

רָחַק (rāhă'k) *inf.* רְחֹק, *imp.*

רָחֲקִי, *fut.* יִרְחַק, to be far, distant, remote; to remove oneself, to be away.— *Ni. fut.* יֵרָחֵק to be removed. — *Pi.* רִחַק, *fut.* יְרַחֵק, to remove far away. — *Hi.* הִרְחִיק, *inf.* הַרְחֵק, הַרְחִיק, *fut.* יַרְחִיק, to remove, to put far away; *intr.* to be far off; *inf. adv.* far, away, distant.

רָחֵק (rāḥē'k) *adj.*, *pl. w.s.* רְחֵקֶיךָ, departing from, removing.

רָחַשׁ (rāḥă's) to boil over, to pour forth.

רַחַת (ră'ḥăϑ) *f* fan, winnowing-shovel.

רָטַב (rāṭă'ḇ) *fut.* יִרְטַב, to be moist or juicy.

רָטֹב (rāṭō'ḇ) *adj.* juicy, succulent, fresh.

רָטָה (rāṭā') *fut. w.s.* יִרְטֵנִי, see יָרַט.

רֶטֶט (rĕ'ṭĕṭ) *m* terror.

רֻטֲפַשׁ (rū'ṭafă's) a *Pu.*, to become fresh or green again.

רָטַשׁ (rāṭă's) *Pi.* רִטֵּשׁ, *fut.* יְרַטֵּשׁ, to dash to pieces, to prostrate. — *Pu.* רֻטַּשׁ, *fut.* יְרֻטַּשׁ, to be dashed in pieces [to the ground].

רִי (rī) *m* rushing water, watering.

רִיב[1] (rīḇ) *pf.* רָב, *inf.* רִיב, רֹב, רוֹב, *imp.* רִיב, *fut.* יָרִיב, יָרֶב־, יָרֹב, וַיָּרֶב, *pt.* רָב, to quarrel, to strive, to contend, to plead; *pt.* pleader, defender, adversary. — *Hi. pt.* מֵרִיב, *pl. c.* מְרִיבֵי, the same as *Q.*

רִיב[2], **רִב** (rīḇ) *m*, *w.s.* רִיבִי, *pl.* רִיבִים, *c.* רִיבֵי, quarrel, strife, contention, feud, dispute, judicial cause, suit, litigation, plea.

רִיבַי (rīḇă'y) *pr.n.m.*

רִיחַ see רוּחַ.

רֵיחַ (rē'aḥ) *m*, *w.s.* רֵיחֲנוּ, exhalation, scent, smell, fragrance.

רֵים see **רְאֵם**.

רֵיעַ see רֵעַ.

רִיפוֹת, רִפוֹת (rīfō'ϑ) *f/pl.* pounded corn, grits.

רִיפַת (rīfă'ϑ) *pr.n.* of a Japhetic people on the Black Sea, Cimmerians.

רִיק (rīk) *adj.* empty, vain; *subst.* emptiness, vain thing; *adv.* in vain, to no purpose.

רֵיק, רֵק (rēk) *adj.*, *pl.*

רֵיקִים, רֵקִים, *f* רֵיקָה, *pl.* רֵקוֹת, empty, void, vain, wanton, hungry, idle, worthless.

רֵיקָם (rēkā'm) *adv.* emptily, in vain, vainly, without cause or effect.

רִיר (rīr) *m*, *w.s.* רִירוֹ, spittle, slime.

רֵישׁ, **רֵאשׁ** (rēš) and רִישׁ (rīš) *m* poverty.

רִישׁוֹן see רִאשׁוֹן.

רַךְ (răḳ) *adj.*, *pl.* רַכִּים, *f* רַכָּה, *pl.* רַכּוֹת, tender, delicate, weak, soft, flattering, timid.

רֹךְ (rōḳ) *m* softness, delicacy.

רָכַב (rāḳă'ḇ) *inf.* רְכֹב, *imp.* רְכַב, *fut.* יִרְכַּב, *pt.* רֹכֵב, *w.s.* רֹכְבוֹ, *pl.* רֹכְבִים, *f* רֹכֶבֶת, to ride, to drive.— *Hi.* הִרְכִּיב, *imp.* הַרְכֵּב, *fut.* יַרְכֵּב, יַרְכִּיב, to cause to ride, to cause to drive, to convey, to let rest, to subdue.

רֶכֶב (rĕ'ḳĕḇ) *m*, *i.p.* רָכֶב, *w.s.* רִכְבּוֹ, *pl. c.* רִכְבֵי, mostly *coll.*, vehicle, waggon, chariot, war-chariot, train of waggons, horses, riding-horses and horsemen; the upper mill-stone [the runner or rider].

רַכָּב (răkkā'ḇ) *m* horseman, driver, charioteer.

רֵכָב (rēḳā'ḇ) *pr.n.m.*; *patr.* רֵכָבִי.

רִכְבָּה (rĭḳbā') *f* a riding.

רֵכָה (rēḳā') *pr.n.* of an unknown place.

רְכוּב (rᵉḳū'ḇ) *m* vehicle, waggon.

רְכֻשׁ, **רְכוּשׁ** (rᵉḳū'š) *m*, *w.s.* רְכֻשׁוֹ, property, goods, chattle, moveable and landed property.

רָכִיל (rāḳī'l) *m* a going about, trafficking, slander.

רָכַךְ (rāḳă'ḳ) *pf.* רַךְ, *fut.* [or *Ni.*] יֵרַךְ, to be thin, weak, delicate, soft, timid. — *Pu.* רֻכַּךְ to be softened. — *Hi.* הֵרַךְ to make timid.

רָכַל (rāḳă'l) *pt.* רֹכֵל, *pl.* רֹכְלִים, *f* רֹכֶלֶת, to go about as a trader, as a slanderer.

רָכָל (rāḳā'l) *pr.n.* of a town in Judah.

רְכֻלָּה (rᵉḳŭllā') *f*, *w.s.* רְכֻלָּתֵךְ, trade, traffic.

רָכַס (rāḳă's) *fut.* יִרְכְּסוּ, to tie together, to bind on.

רֶכֶס (rĕ'ḳĕs) *m*, only *pl.*

רְכָסִים, hill, mountain-ridge.

רֹכֶס (rōʹḳĕs) *m*, only *pl. c.* רֻכְסֵי, troop, band, conspiracy.

רָכַשׁ (rāḳăʹš) to bring together, to collect, to acquire.

רֶכֶשׁ (rĕʹḳĕš) *m*, *i.p.* רָכֶשׁ, swift horse, courser [*coll.*].

רָם[1] (rām) see רוּם *pt.*

רָם[2] (rām) *pr.n.m.*

רָמָה[1] (rāmāʹ) *pt.* רֹמֶה, *c.* רֹמֵה, *pl. c.* רֹמֵי, to cast down, to shoot; *pt.* shooter, archer. — *Pi.* רִמָּה, *inf.* רַמּוֹת, to cast down, to deceive, to betray.

רָמָה[2] (rāmāʹ) *f*, *c.* רָמַת, [sacred] height, elevation.

רָמָה[3] (rāmāʹ) *w. loc.* ה רָמָתָה, *pr.n.* of towns in Benjamin, Ephraim, &c.; *gent.* רָמָתִי; ר׳ לְחִי, רָמַת לֶחִי, *i.p.* [height of the jaw-bone] a locality in the mountains of Judah.

רִמָּה (rĭmmāʹ) *f coll.* worms; wormhole, rottenness.

רִמּוֹן[1] (rĭmmōʹn) *m*, *w.s.* רִמֹּנִי, *pl.* רִמֹּנִים ,רִמּוֹנִים, *c.* רִמּוֹנֵי, pomegranate [tree and fruit]; an ornament in architecture, artificial pomegranate apple.

רִמּוֹן[2] (rĭmmōʹn) *pr.n.m.* of a Syrian deity; *pr.n.* of several towns.

רָמוֹת (rāmōʹϑ) *pr.n.* of towns in Gilead and Simeon.

רָמוּת (rāmūʹϑ) *f* heap of corpses.

רֹמַח (rōʹmăḥ) *m*, *pl.* רְמָחִים, *c.* רָמְחֵי (rŏmḥēʹ), lance, spear.

רַמְיָה (rămyāʹ) *pr.n.m.*

רְמִיָּה (rᵉmĭyyāʹ) *f* a slackening, remissness, sloth; deceit, fraud.

רַמִּים = אֲרַמִּים.

רַמָּךְ (rămmāʹḳ) *f*, *pl.* רַמָּכִים, a mare [others: stud].

רְמַלְיָהוּ (rᵉmălyāʹhū) *pr.n.m.*

רָמַם[1] (rāmăʹm) *inf.* רֹם, *fut.* יֵרֹם, to creep, to swarm [others: to be rotten].

רָמַם[2] (rāmăʹm) *pf. pl.* רֹמּוּ, רוֹמּוּ, *pt. f* רוֹמֵמָה, to be high, to be lifted up.— *Ni.* *imp. pl.* הֵרֹמּוּ, *fut. pl.* יֵרֹמּוּ, to lift up oneself. — *Hith.* הִתְרוֹמֵם see רוּם.

רֹמַמְתִּי־עֶזֶר (rōmăʹmtī-ʿĕʹzĕr) *pr.n.m.*

רָמַס (rāmăʹs) *inf.* רְמֹס, *fut.*

יִרְמֹס, *pt.* רֹמֵס, to tread, to tread down, to trample on, to profane. — *Ni. fut.* יֵרָמֵס to be trodden down.

רָמַשׂ (rāmă's) *fut.* יִרְמֹשׂ, *pt.* רֹמֵשׂ, *f* רֹמֶשֶׂת, to move, to creep, to crawl, to swarm with.

רֶמֶשׂ (rĕ'mĕs) *m coll.* what moves and creeps, small animals, reptiles, insects.

רֶמֶת (rĕ'mĕϑ) *pr.n.* of a town in Issachar.

רָמָתַיִם (rā'māϑă'yĭm) *pr.n.* [*du.* = double height] of a town; ר׳ צוֹפִים the dwelling place of Samuel, Arimathea.

רֹן (rōn) *m, pl. c.* רָנֵּי (rŏnnē'), shout, rejoicing, song of joy.

רָנָה (rānā') *fut.* יִרְנֶה, to whiz, to clank.

רִנָּה[1] (rĭnnā') *f, w.s.* רִנָּתִי, rejoicing, exultation, shout of joy; lamentation.

רִנָּה[2] (rĭnnā') *pr.n.m.*

רָנַן (rānă'n) *inf.* רֹן, *imp. f* רָנִּי (rŏnnī'), *pl.* רָנּוּ, *fut.* יָרֹן [יָרוּן] to cry aloud, to shout with joy, to rejoice; to lament, to wail. — *Pi.* רִנֵּן, *inf.* רַנֵּן, *imp. pl.* רַנְּנוּ, *fut.* יְרַנֵּן, to rejoice, to shout with joy, to sing praise to. — *Pu. fut.* יְרֻנַּן to be shouted for joy. — *Hi. imp. pl.* הַרְנִינוּ, *fut.* יַרְנִין, to cause to shout with joy; to rejoice. — *Hi. pt.* מִתְרוֹנֵן [or from רון] to rejoice.

רְנָנָה (rᵉnānā') *f, c.* רִנְנַת, *pl.* רְנָנוֹת, shout, joyful cry; *pl.* רְנָנִים female ostriches.

רִסָּה (rĭssā') *pr.n.* of a station in the desert.

רָסִיס (rāsī's) *m,* only *pl.* רְסִיסִים, ruins; drops [of dew].

רֶסֶן[1] (rĕ'sĕn) *m, w.s.* רִסְנוֹ, bridle, curb, bit-mouth; the teeth, the jaws.

רֶסֶן[2] (rĕ'sĕn) *pr.n.* of a city in Assyria [annexed to Nineveh].

רָסַס (rāsă's) *inf.* רֹס, to moisten, to wet.

רַע (rắ') *adj., i.p.* רָע, *pl.* רָעִים, *f* רָעָה, *c.* רָעַת, *pl.* רָעוֹת, bad, wicked, evil, mischievous, malignant, noxious, hurtful, unpleasant, hideous, unhappy; *subst.* an evil.

wickedness, wrong, mischief, misfortune, adversity.

רֵעַ[1] (rē'a) *m*, *w.s.* רֵעֲךָ, רֵעִי, רֵעֵהוּ, *pl.* רֵעִים, *c.* רֵעֵי, friend, companion, fellow, associate, neighbour; see also אִישׁ.

רֵעַ[2] (rē'a) *m*, *w.s.* רֵעִי, *pl.* רֵעִים, thought, desire.

רֵעַ[3] (rē'a) *m*, *w.s.* רֵעֹה, רֵעוֹ, noise, thunder.

רֹעַ, **רוֹעַ** (rō'a) *m* badness, wickedness, wretchedness.

רָעֵב[1] (rāʿēb) *fut.* יִרְעַב, to hunger, to suffer hunger. — *Hi.* הִרְעִיב, *fut.* יַרְעִיב, to cause to hunger, to let famish.

רָעֵב[2] (rāʿēb) *adj.*, *pl.* רְעֵבִים, *f* רְעֵבָה, hungry, famished, exhausted.

רָעָב (rāʿāb) *m*, *w.s.* רְעָבָם, hunger, famine, scarcity.

רְעָבוֹן (reʿābōn) *m*, *c.* רַעֲבוֹן = רָעָב.

רָעַד (rāʿad) *fut.* יִרְעַד, to quake, to tremble. — *Hi.* הִרְעִיד, *pt.* מַרְעִיד, to tremble, to shake.

רַעַד (raʿad) *m* and רְעָדָה (reʿādā) *f* trembling, terror.

רָעָה[1] (rāʿā) *inf.* רְעוֹת, *imp.* רְעֵה, *fut.* יִרְעֶה, יִרְעַ, *pt.* רֹעֶה, *c.* רֹעֵה, *w.s.* רֹעִי, *pl.* רֹעִים, *c.* רֹעֵי, *f* רֹעָה, to feed a flock, to lead to a pasture-ground, to conduct, to guide, govern, protect; *pt.* a shepherd; *intr.* to feed, to consume. — *Hi. fut.* יַרְעֶה, to pasture, to cause to feed.

רָעָה[2] (rāʿā) *fut.* יִרְעֶה, *pt.* רֹעֶה, to like, to be fond of, to delight in, to associate with. — *Pi.* רֵעָה to choose for a companion. — *Hith. fut.* יִתְרָע to associate oneself.

רָעָה[3] (rāʿā) *f* [see רַע], *c.* רָעַת, *pl.* רָעוֹת, evil, badness, suffering, misfortune, destruction, wickedness.

רֵעָה (rēʿā) *f* a female friend or companion.

רֵעֶה (rēʿe) *m*, *c.* רֵעֵה, *w.s.* רֵעֶיךָ [*sg.*], friend, companion.

רֹעֶה (rōʿe) *m* shepherd, see רָעָה[1].

רֹעָה (rōʿā) *f* a breaking, bursting.

רְעוּ (reʿū) *pr.n.m.*

רְעוּאֵל (reʿūēl) *pr.n.m.*

רְעוּת (reʿūth) *f*, *w.s.* רְעוּתָהּ,

female friend or companion; after אִשָּׁה = the other; delight, desire.

רְעִי (r'ī') m pasture.

רֵעִי (rēʻī') pr.n.m.

רֹעִי (rōʻī') m shepherd, = רֹעֶה.

רַעְיָה (răʻyā') f, pl. w.s. רַעְיֹתַי, female friend, one beloved.

רַעְיוֹן (răʻyō'n) m thought, meditation, desire.

רָעַל (rāʻă'l) Ho. הָרְעַל, to be brandished.

רַעַל (ră''ăl) m a reeling, staggering [from intoxication].

רְעָלָה (r'ʻālā') f, only pl. רְעָלוֹת, veil.

רְעֵלָיָה (r'ʻē'lāyā') pr.n.m.

רָעַם (rāʻă'm) fut. יִרְעַם, to tremble, to quake; to rage, to be agitated, to roar. — Hi. הִרְעִים, inf. w.s. הַרְעִימָה, fut. יַרְעֵם ,יַרְעִים, to cause to roar, to thunder; to provoke to anger, to offend.

רַעַם (ră''ăm) m, w.s. רַעַמְךָ, thunder, rage, roaring.

רַעְמָה[1] (răʻmā') f a trembling, quivering.

רַעְמָה[2] (răʻmā') pr.n.m. of a Cushite; also his tribe and country.

רַעֲמְיָה (ră''ămyā') pr.n.m. = רְעֵלָיָה.

רַעְמְסֵס (răʻm'ßē'ß) and רַעַמְסֵס (ră''ămßē'ß) pr.n. of a city in Egypt, Raamses in Goshen.

רָעַן (rāʻă'n) Pil. רַעֲנַן [or adj.] to be or become green.

רַעֲנָן (ră''anā'n) adj., pl. רַעֲנַנִּים, f רַעֲנָנָה, green, succulent, fresh.

רָעַע[1] (rāʻă'') pf. רַע, inf. רַע, רֹעַ, רֹעָה, fut. יָרֹעַ, to break, to dash in pieces, to shatter; to be broken. — Hi. inf. הָרֵעַ, fut. יָרֵעַ, to break to pieces, to destroy. — Hith. הִתְרוֹעַע to be shaken violently, to be broken to pieces, to perish.

רָעַע[2] (rāʻă'') pf. רַע, inf. רֹעַ, imp. pl. רֹעוּ, fut. יֵרַע, וַיֵּרַע, to be bad, evil, angry, sorrowful, sullen, envious, wicked, displeasing. — Hi. הֵרַע, הֵרֵעַ, inf. הָרֵעַ, הָרַע, fut. יָרֵעַ, יָרַע, pt. מֵרַע, i.p. מֵרָע, pl. מְרֵעִים, to do evil, to act badly, wickedly, to make bad or evil.

רָעַף (rā'ă'f) *fut.* יִרְעַף, to drop, to drip, to distil. — *Hi. imp. pl.* הַרְעִיפוּ to let drop.

רָעַץ (rā'ă'ß) *fut.* יִרְעַץ, to break to pieces, to oppress, to vex.

רָעַשׁ (rā'ă's) *fut.* יִרְעַשׁ, to be agitated, to tremble, quake, wave. — *Ni.* נִרְעַשׁ to quake. — *Hi.* הִרְעִישׁ, *fut.* יַרְעִישׁ, *pt.* מַרְעִישׁ, to cause to quake, to shake, to terrify, to cause to leap.

רַעַשׁ (ră''ăs) *m* agitation, violent motion, earthquake, noise, uproar.

רָפָא[1] (rāfā') *inf.* רָפוֹא, *imp.* רְפָא, רְפָה, *fut.* יִרְפָּא, *pt.* רֹפֵא, *pl.* רֹפְאִים, to bind [a wound], to heal, cure, restore, mend, help; to comfort. — *Ni.* נִרְפָּא, *inf.* הֵרָפֵא, *fut.* יֵרָפֵא, to be healed, cured, restored, mended. — *Pi.* רִפֵּא, *inf.* רַפֹּא, *fut.* יְרַפֵּא, to heal, to make sound, to restore; to cause to heal. — *Hith. inf.* הִתְרַפֵּא to cause oneself to be healed, to get healed.

רָפָא[2] (rāfā') *pr.n.m.* of the founder of a race of giants.

רְפֻאָה (rᵉfū'ā') *f*, only *pl.* רְפֻאוֹת, medicine, physic.

רִפְאוּת (rĭf'ū'ϑ) *f* a healing.

רְפָאִים[1] (rᵉfā'ī'm) *pl. m* [*patr.* of רָפָא[2]] giants, Rephaites, the descendants of Rapha.

רְפָאִים[2] (rᵉfā'ī'm) *pl. m* [*sg.* רָפֶה] the dead, the departed, departed spirits, shades.

רְפָאֵל (rᵉfā'ē'l) *pr.n.m.* Rafael.

רָפַד (rāfă'd) *fut.* יִרְפַּד, to stretch out. — *Pi.* רִפֵּד to spread; to support, refresh.

רָפָה[1] (rāfā') = רָפָא[1].

רָפָה[2] (rāfā') *fut.* יִרְפֶּה, יִרֶף, to be slack, weak, feeble; to desist, to sink, to despond. — *Ni. pt.* נִרְפֶּה to be remiss or lazy. — *Pi.* רִפָּה, *pt.* מְרַפֶּה, to loosen, to slacken, to let fall. — *Hi.* הִרְפָּה, *imp.* הַרְפֵּה, הֶרֶף, *fut.* יַרְפֶּה, to slacken, to desist, to withdraw, to let alone, to abandon, to leave off. — *Hith.* הִתְרַפָּה to show oneself lazy, indolent.

רָפָה³ (rāfā') *m* = רְפָא׳.

רָפֶה (rāfĕ') *adj.*, *c.* רְפֵה, *f/pl.* רָפוֹת, slack, feeble, faint-hearted.

רָפוּא (rāfū') *pr.n.m.*

רִפוֹת see רִיפוֹת.

רֶפַח (rĕ'făḥ) *pr.n.m.*

רְפִידָה (r'fīdā') *f* couch, back of a litter.

רְפִידִים (r'fīdī'm) *pr.n.* of a station in the desert.

רְפָיָה (r'fāyā') *pr.n.m.*

רִפְיוֹן (rĭfyō'n) *m* slackness, despondency.

רָפַס, **רָפַשׂ** (rāfă's) *fut.* יִרְפֹּשׂ, to trample, to make muddy. — *Ni.* נִרְפַּשׂ to be muddy. — *Hith.* הִתְרַפֵּס to prostrate or humble oneself.

רַפְסֹדָה (răfsōdā') *f*, only *pl.* רַפְסֹדוֹת, a float or raft.

רָפַק (rāfă'k) *Hith.* הִתְרַפֵּק, to lean oneself, to rest upon.

רֶפֶשׁ (rĕ'fĕš) *m* mud, slime.

רֶפֶת (rĕ'fĕθ) *m*, only *pl.* רְפָתִים, stable for cattle.

רָץ see רוּץ.

רַץ (răß) *m*, *pl.* *c.* רַצֵּי, a piece.

רָצָא (rāßā') *inf.* רָצוֹא — רוּץ to run.

רָצַד (rāßă'd) *Pi.* *fut.* יְרַצֵּד, to observe with jealousy.

רָצָה (rāßā') *inf.* רְצוֹת, *imp.* רְצֵה, *fut.* יִרְצֶה, וַיִּרֶץ, *pt.* רֹצֶה, רוֹצֶה, *pt. p.* רָצוּי, *c.* רְצוּי, to take pleasure in, to be pleased, to delight, to like, to love, to be fond of, to be kind, gracious, propitious, to receive graciously; to be pleasing or agreeable; to be taken for payment, to be paid.—*Pi.* *fut.* יְרַצֶּה to seek favour, to appease. — *Hi.* הִרְצָה to pay off. — *Hith.* הִתְרַצָּה to show oneself pleasing.

רָצוֹן (rāßō'n) *m*, *c.* רְצוֹן, *w.s.* רְצֹנוֹ, רְצוֹנוֹ, good will, inclination, pleasure, delight, favour, grace, kindness, wilfulness.

רָצַח (rāßă'ḥ) *inf.* רְצֹחַ, *fut.* יִרְצַח, *pt.* רֹצֵחַ, to kill, murder, slay. — *Ni.* *fut.* יֵרָצֵחַ to be murdered. — *Pi.* *fut.* יְרַצֵּחַ to kill, to murder, to destroy, to crush. — *Pu.* *fut.* יְרֻצַּח (y'rŭßßă'ḥ) to be crushed [probably for יְרַצַּח *Pi.*].

רֶצַח (rĕ'ßăḥ) *m* a crushing; cry, outburst of the voice.

רִצְיָא (rĭßyā') *pr.n.m.*

רְצִין (r^eßī'n) *pr.n.* of a Syrian king.

רָצַע (rāßă'') to pierce, to perforate.

רָצַף (rāßă'f) *pt. p.* רָצוּף, to arrange, to tessellate.

רֶצֶף¹ (rĕ'ßĕf) *m* glowing stone [others: burning coal].

רֶצֶף² (rĕ'ßĕf) *pr.n.* of a town in Syria, near the Euphrates.

רִצְפָּה¹ (rĭßpā') *f* hot stone, burning coal.

רִצְפָּה² (rĭßpā') *pr.n.f.*

רִצְפָה (rĭ'ßefā') *f, c.* רִצְפַת, tessellated pavement.

רָצַץ (rāßă'ß) *pf.* רַץ, *fut.* יָרוּץ [for יָרֹץ], יָרֻץ, *pt.* רוֹצֵץ, *f/pl.* רוֹצְצוֹת, *pt. p.* רָצוּץ, *pl.* רְצוּצִים, to break, to crack, to crush, to bruise, to oppress; *intr.* to be broken, to be feeble. — *Ni.* נָרוֹץ to be broken, bruised, destroyed. — *Pi.* רִצֵּץ, *fut.* יְרַצֵּץ and יְרוֹצֵץ, to break through, to dash, to oppress. — *Hi. fut.* וַתָּרֶץ to dash to pieces, to crush. — *Hith.* הִתְרוֹצֵץ to dash against one another.

רַק (răk) *adj., f* רַקָּה, *pl.* רַקּוֹת, thin, lean; *adv.* only, solely, except, nothing but.

רֵק see רִיק.

רֹק (rōk) *m, w.s.* רֻקּוֹ, spittle.

רָקַב (rākă'b) *fut.* יִרְקַב, to be rotten, to decay.

רָקָב (rākā'b) *m* rottenness, caries, decay.

רִקָּבוֹן (rĭkkābō'n) *m* = רָקָב.

רָקַד (rākă'd) *inf.* רְקֹד, *fut. pl.* יִרְקְדוּ, to move up and down, to leap, to jump, to start. — *Pi.* רִקֵּד, *fut.* יְרַקֵּד, *pt.* מְרַקֵּד, to leap, jump, dance. — *Hi. fut.* יַרְקִיד to cause to leap.

רַקָּה (răkkā') *f, w.s.* רַקָּתוֹ, thin spot, temples, cheek.

רַקּוֹן (răkkō'n) *pr.n.* of a town in Dan.

רִקּוּחַ (rĭkkū'aḥ) *m,* only *pl.* רִקֻּחִים, an anointing, unguent.

רָקַח (rākă'ḥ) *fut.* יִרְקַח, *pt.* רֹקֵחַ, to mix, to spice, to season, to perfume, to make unguents. — *Pu. pt.*

מְרֻקָּח to be mixed or spiced. — *Hi. imp.* הַרְקַח to spice, to season.

רֶקַח (rĕ'**k**ăḥ) *m* spice.

רֹקַח (rō'**k**ăḥ) *m* spice, perfume.

רַקָּח (răkkā'ḥ) *m* mixer of nnguents.

רַקָּחָה (răkkāḥā') *f* a female mixer of unguents.

רָקִיעַ (rāki'a') *m*, *c.* רְקִיעַ, vault of heaven, firmament, sky; pavement, floor.

רָקִיק (rāki'k) *m* thin cake for offering.

רָקַם (rākă'm) *pt.* רֹקֵם, to delineate, design, variegate; *pt.* embroiderer. — *Pu.* רֻקַּם to be shaped or formed curiously.

רֶקֶם (rĕ'kĕm) *pr.n.* of a town in Benjamin; *pr.n.m.*

רִקְמָה (rikmā') *f*, *w.s.* רִקְמָתָם, *du.* רִקְמָתַיִם, *pl.* רְקָמוֹת, embroidery, variegated work or garment, party-coloured work.

רָקַע (rākă'') *inf.* and *imp.* רְקַע, *fut.* יִרְקַע, *pt.* רֹקֵעַ, *c.* רֹקַע, רוֹקַע, to stamp, to beat, to expand, to crush. — *Pi.* רִקַּע, *fut.* יְרַקַּע, to hammer out, to overlay. — *Pu. pt.* מְרֻקָּע to be beaten out. — *Hi. fut.* יַרְקִיעַ to stretch out, to extend.

רִקֻּעַ (rikkū'a') *m*, only *pl.* *c.* רִקֻּעֵי, plate, beaten-out metal.

רָקַק (rākă'k) *fut.* יָרֹק, to spit.

רַקַּת (răkkă'ϑ) *pr.n.* of a town in Naphtali.

רָשׁ (rāš) *pt.* of רוּשׁ.

רַשׁ, **רֵשׁ** see יָבֵשׁ.

רִשְׁיוֹן (rišyō'n) *m* permission.

רֵשִׁית see רֵאשִׁית.

רָשַׁם (rāšă'm) *pt. p.* רָשׁוּם, to write down.

רָשַׁע (rāšă'') *fut.* יִרְשַׁע, to be godless, wicked, lawless, fractious, guilty. — *Hi.* הִרְשִׁיעַ, *inf.* הַרְשִׁיעַ, *fut.* יַרְשִׁיעַ, *pt.* מַרְשִׁיעַ, to convict, to declare guilty, to condemn, to overcome; to act wickedly, mischievously.

רָשָׁע (rāšā'') *adj.*, *pl.* רְשָׁעִים, *c.* רִשְׁעֵי, *f* רְשָׁעָה, godless, sinful, wicked, lawless, vicious, unrighteous, guilty; sinner, oppressor, apostate.

רֶשַׁע (rĕ'să') *m*, *w.s.* רִשְׁעוֹ, *pl.* רְשָׁעִים, godlessness, wickedness, unrighteousness, lawlessness, injustice, unlawful gain.

רִשְׁעָה (rĭš'ā') *f*, *w.s.* רִשְׁעָתוֹ, *du.* רִשְׁעָתַיִם, wickedness, wicked deed.

רֶשֶׁף[1] (rĕ'sĕf) *m*, *pl.* רְשָׁפִים, *c.* רִשְׁפֵי, spark, flash, flame, lightning; fever, plague, pestilence.

רֶשֶׁף[2] (rĕ'sĕf) *pr.n.m.*

רָשַׁשׁ (rāšă'š) *Pi. fut.* יְרוֹשֵׁשׁ, to waste, to destroy.— *Pu.* רֻשַּׁשׁ to be destroyed.

רֶשֶׁת[1] (rĕ'sĕϑ) *f*, *w.s.* רִשְׁתִּי, a net for fishing or fowling; net-work.

רֶשֶׁת[2] see יָרַשׁ.

רַתּוֹק (răttō'k) *m* and **רַתּוּקָה** (răttūkā') *f*, *pl.* רַתּוּקוֹת, a chain.

רָתַח (rāϑă'ḥ) *Pi. imp.* רַתַּח, to make seethe, to boil [*tr.*]. — *Pu.* רֻתַּח to boil [*intr.*], to be agitated. — *Hi. fut.* יַרְתִּיחַ the same as *Pi.*

רֶתַח (rĕ'ϑăḥ) *m* a seething.

רָתַם (rāϑă'm) *imp.* רְתֹם, to bind fast, to harness.

רֹתֶם (rō'ϑĕm) *m*, *pl.* רְתָמִים, broom-plant.

רִתְמָה (rĭϑmā') *pr.n.* of a station in the desert.

רָתַק (rāϑă'k) *Ni. fut.* יֵרָתֵק, to be unchained [perh. for יִנָּתֵק to be broken]. — *Pu.* רֻתַּק to be bound.

רְתֻקָה (rᵉϑūkā') *f*, only *pl.* רְתֻקוֹת, a chain.

רְתֵת (rᵉϑē'ϑ) *m* terror.

שׁ

שׂ with **שׁ** the twenty-first letter of the alphabet, called שִׂין = שִׁין [tooth]; as a numeral = 300.

שָׂא, **שְׂאֵת** see נָשָׂא.

שְׂאֹר (sᵉ'ō'r) *m* ferment, leaven.

שְׂאֵת (sᵉ'ē'ϑ) *f*, *w.s.* שְׂאֵתִי, a lifting up [of the head and face = cheerfulness]; elevation, majesty; scab, pimple.

שְׂבָךְ (săbă'ḥ) *m*, *pl.* שְׂבָכִים, lattice-work.

שְׂבָכָה (s'bāchā') *f*, *pl.* שְׂבָכוֹת, net, lattice, lattice-work, window.

שְׂבָם (s'bā'm) or שִׂבְמָה (sĭbmā') *pr.n.* of a place in Reuben, near Heshbon.

שָׂבַע (sābă''), שָׂבֵעַ (sābē'a') *inf.* שָׂבֹעַ, שְׂבֹעַ, *fut.* יִשְׂבַּע, to be full, filled, satiated, satisfied; to have abundance, to be surfeited or tired.—*Pi.* שִׂבַּע, *inf. w.s.* שַׂבְּעֵנוּ, to satiate, to satisfy. — *Hi.* הִשְׂבִּיעַ, *inf.* הַשְׂבִּיעַ, *fut.* יַשְׂבִּיעַ, *pt.* מַשְׂבִּיעַ, the same as *Pi.*

שָׂבָע (sābā'') *m* satiety, abundance.

שָׂבֵעַ (sābē'a') *adj.*, *c.* שְׂבַע, *pl.* שְׂבֵעִים, satiated, satisfied, full, having abundantly.

שֹׂבַע (sŏ'bă') *m*, *w.s.* שָׂבְעֲךָ (sŏb'ă'chā) — שָׂבָע.

שִׂבְעָה (sĭb'ā') and שָׂבְעָה (sŏb'ā') *f* satiety, fulness.

שָׂבַר (sābă'r) *Pi.* שִׂבֵּר, *fut.* יְשַׂבֵּר, to wait, expect, hope, wish, to look for.

שֵׂבֶר (sē'bĕr) *m*, *w.s.* שִׂבְרִי, expectation, hope.

שָׂגָא ,שָׂגָה (sāgā') *fut.* יִשְׂגֶּה, to grow, to become large. — *Hi.* הִשְׂגִּיא, *pl.* הִשְׂגּוּ, *fut.* יַשְׂגִּיא, *pt.* מַשְׂגִּיא, to let grow, to make great, to magnify, to praise.

שָׂגַב (sāgă'b) to be steep, high, strong; to ascend, to be extolled. — *Ni.* נִשְׂגַּב, *pt.* נִשְׂגָּב, *f* נִשְׂגָּבָה, to be steep, high, lofty, strong, safe, exalted, unsearchable. — *Pi.* שִׂגֵּב, *fut.* יְשַׂגֵּב, to make high, mighty, to raise, to protest, to make safe.—*Pu. fut.* יְשֻׂגַּב to be protected.—*Hi. fut.* יַשְׂגִּיב to act nobly, to protect.

שָׂגָה see שָׂגָא.

שְׂגוּב (s'gū'b) *pr.n.m.*

שַׂגִּיא (săggī') *adj.* high, great, mighty.

שִׂגְשֵׂג see שׂוּג.

שָׂדַד (sādă'd) *Pi.* שִׂדֵּד, *fut.* יְשַׂדֵּד, to plough repeatedly, to harrow.

שָׂדֶה (sādĕ') *m*, *c.* שְׂדֵה, *w.s.* שָׂדְךָ, שָׂדֵהוּ, שָׂדָהּ, *pl.* שָׂדוֹת, *c.* שְׂדוֹת, שְׂדֵי, a plain, field, open or cultivated field, piece or parcel of land, open country, territory, district.

שָׂדַי (sādă'y) *m*, *i.p.* שָׂדָי, poetical form for שָׂדֶה.

שִׂדִּים (sĭddī'm) *pr.n. pl.* in עֵמֶק הַשִּׂדִּים valley of the fields, the valley of Sodom.

שְׂדֵרָה (sᵉdērā') *f*, only *pl.* שְׂדֵרוֹת, שְׂדֵרֹת, row, rank, file.

שֶׂה (sĕ) *m* and *f* [also זֶה], *c.* שֵׂה, *w.s.* שֵׂיוֹ, שֵׂיֵהוּ, a [young] sheep or goat.

שָׂהֵד (sāhē'd) *m*, *w.s.* שָׂהֲדִי [שַׂהֲדִי or שָׂהֲדִי] a witness.

שָׂהֲדוּתָא (sā'hᵃdūϑā') [Chald.] testimony.

שַׂהֲרֹון (să'hᵃrō'n) *m*, only *pl.* שַׂהֲרֹנִים, little moon, crescent, a neck-ornament of men and beasts.

שׂוֹא¹ see נָשָׂא [*Q. inf.*].

שׂוֹא² (sō) *m*, only *pl. w.s.* שֹׂאֵיכֶם, tumult, destruction.

שׂוֹבֶךְ (sō'bĕch) *m* thicket, entwined branches.

שׂוּג¹ (sūg) = סוּג¹.

שׂוּג² (sūg) *Pilp.* [שִׂגְשֵׂג] *fut.* יְשַׂגְשֵׂג, to hedge in, to fence in.

שׂוּחַ (sū'ᵃch) *inf.* שׂוּחַ, to meditate, see שִׂיחַ.

שׂוּט (sūt) *pt.* שָׂט, only *pl.* *c.* שָׂטֵי, to turn aside [*intr.*].

שׂוּךְ (sūch) *pt.* שָׂךְ, to entwine, interweave, to hedge or fence in. — *Pi. fut.* יְשׂוֹכֵךְ to twist, plait, weave.

שׂוֹךְ (sōch) *m*, *w.s.* שׂוֹכֹה, and שׂוֹכָה (sōchā') *f*, *c.* שׂוֹכַת, twig, branch.

שׂוֹכוֹ, שֹׂכֹה, שׂוֹכֹה (sōchō') *pr.n.* of two towns in Judah [in the mountains and in the plain].

שׂוֹכָתִי (sū'chāϑī') *pr.n.m.*, only *pl.* שׂוֹכָתִים, *gent.* of an unknown place שׂוֹכָה.

שׂוּם (sūm), **שִׂים** (sīm) *pf.* שָׂם, *inf.* שׂוּם, שׂוֹם, שִׂים, *imp.* שִׂים, *fut.* יָשׂוּם, יָשִׂים, וַיָּשֶׂם, יָשֵׂם, יָשִׂם, *pt.* שָׂם, *pl.* שָׂמִים, *pt. p.* שִׂים, *f* שִׂימָה, שׂוּמָה, to set, to establish, erect, plant, put, to set down, to lay in, to make, to constitute, to appoint.—*Hi. imp.* הָשִׂימִי, *pt.* מֵשִׂים, to set, to turn, to lay in.—*Ho. fut.* יוּשַׂם [וַיּוּשַׂם for וַיִּישֶׂם] to be put or set.

שׂוּר¹ (sūr) *fut.* וַיָּשַׂר, (văyyā'sŏr), to saw; to contend or strive; to rule, govern.

שׂוּר² (sūr) = סוּר, *inf. w.s.* שׂוּרִי, to go away, to depart.

שׁוֹרָה (šōrā') *f* row, order.

שׂוֹרֵק (šōrē'k) *pr.n.* of a valley, see שֹׂרֵק.

שׂוּשׂ (šūš), שִׂישׂ (šīš), *pf.* שָׂשׂ, *inf.* שׂוּשׂ, שׂוֹשׂ, *imp.* שִׂישׂ, *fut.* יָשׂוּשׂ, יָשִׂישׂ, *pt.* שָׂשׂ, to leap, to rejoice, exult, to be glad.

שֵׂחַ (šē'ᵃḥ) *m* thought, meditation.

שָׂחָה (šāḥā') *inf.* שְׂחוֹת, *pt.* שֹׂחֶה, to swim. — *Hi. fut.* יַשְׂחֶה to make swim, to drench.

שָׂחוּ (šā'ḥū) *m* a swimming.

שְׂחוֹק, שְׂחֹק (šᵉḥō'k) *m* laughter, joy; jest; scorn, object of scorn.

שָׂחַט (šāḥa't) *fut.* יִשְׂחַט, to press out.

שָׂחַק (šāḥa'k) *inf.* שְׂחוֹק, שְׂחֹק, *fut.* יִשְׂחַק, to laugh, to laugh at, to smile at, to scorn. — *Pi.* שִׂחֵק, *inf.* שַׂחֵק, *fut.* יְשַׂחֵק, *pt.* מְשַׂחֵק, to jest, play, dance, to sport, to make merry. — *Hi. pt.* מַשְׂחִיק to mock, deride.

שְׂחֹק see שְׂחוֹק.

שֵׂט (šēt) *m*, only *pl.* שֵׂטִים, transgression [others: transgressor, unjust judge].

שָׂטָה (šatā') *fut.* יִשְׂטֶה, וַיֵּשְׂטְ, to deviate, to be faithless.

שָׂטַם (šāta'm) *fut.* יִשְׂטֹם, to treat as an enemy, to hate, to persecute, to attack.

שָׂטַן (šāta'n) *inf. w.s.* שִׂטְנוֹ, *fut. w.s.* יִשְׂטְנוּנִי, *pt.* שֹׂטֵן, *pl. c.* שֹׂטְנֵי = שָׂטַם; *pt.* accuser, adversary.

שָׂטָן (šātā'n) *m* adversary, opponent, accuser, enemy, Satan [הַשָּׂטָן].

שִׂטְנָה[1] (šītnā') *f* accusation.

שִׂטְנָה[2] (šītnā') *pr.n.* of a well near Gerar.

שִׂיא (šī) *m* height, elevation.

שִׂיאוֹן (šī'ō'n) *pr.n.* of a town in Issachar.

שִׂיאֹן (šī'ō'n) *pr.n.*, Hebrew name of mount Hermon.

שִׂיב (šīḇ) [or שׂוּב] *pf.* and *pt.* שָׂב, to become grey, to have grey hair.

שֵׂיב (šēḇ) *m* [or שַׂיִב], *w.s.* שֵׂיבוֹ, and שֵׂיבָה (šēḇā') *f*, *c.* שֵׂיבַת, *w.s.* שֵׂיבָתִי, grey hair, old age; old man.

שִׂיג (šīg) [= סִיג] *m* a going away, privacy.

שִׂיד[1] (sîd) *pf.* שַׂדְתָּ, to cover with lime, to plaster.

שִׂיד[2] (sîd) *m* lime, gypsum.

שֵׂיו, שְׂיֵהוּ see שֶׂה.

שִׂיחַ[1] (sî'ach) [שׂוּחַ], *pf.* שָׂח, שָׂח, *inf.* שִׂיחַ, *imp.* שִׂיחַ, *fut.* יָשִׂיחַ, to meditate, to muse; to speak, to talk; to sing, to complain. — *Pi.* *fut.* יְשׂוֹחֵחַ to meditate, to consider.

שִׂיחַ[2] (sî'ach) *m*, *w.s.* שִׂיחִי, meditation, thought; speech, talk, complaint.

שִׂיחַ[3] (sî'ach) *m*, *pl.* שִׂיחִים, שִׂיחִם, shrub, bush.

שִׂיחָה (sîchā') *f*, *w.s.* שִׂיחָתִי, meditation, devotion.

שִׂים see שׂוּם.

שֵׂךְ (sēch) *m*, only *pl.* שִׂכִּים, thorn.

שֹׂךְ (sōch) *m*, *w.s.* שֻׂכּוֹ, enclosure.

שֻׂכָּה (sŭkkā') *f* sharp weapon.

שֵׂכוּ (sē'chū) *pr.n.* of a locality near Ramah.

שֶׂכְוִי (sĕchvî') *m* insight, mind [others: meteor or watchman, i. e. cock].

שְׂכִיָּה (s'chîyyā') *f*, only *pl.* שְׂכִיּוֹת, show, sight, show-work, precious things [others: flag].

שָׂכְיָה (sŏchyā') *pr.n.m.* [or שָׂבְיָה].

שַׂכִּין (săkkî'n) *m* a knife.

שָׂכִיר (sāchî'r) *m* journeyman, day-labourer, hireling.

שְׂכִירָה (s'chîrā') *f* a hiring.

שָׂכַךְ (sāchă'ch) to cover, to protect, = סָכַךְ.

שָׂכַל[1] (sāchă'l) to have insight, to act prudently.— *Pi.* שִׂכֵּל to do [lay hands] purposely. — *Hi.* הִשְׂכִּיל, *inf.* הַשְׂכֵּל, הַשְׂכִּיל, *imp.* *pl.* הַשְׂכִּילוּ, *fut.* יַשְׂכִּיל, יַשְׂכֵּל, *pt.* מַשְׂכִּיל [which see], to look at, to behold, to pay attention to; to have insight, intelligence, understanding; to act prudently, to have success; to teach; *inf.* insight, prudence, wisdom; *pt.* prudent, intelligent, wise, pious.

שָׂכַל[2] (sāchă'l) *Pi.* שִׂכֵּל, to twist, to lay cross-wise [but see שָׂכַל[1] *Pi.*].

שֶׂכֶל (sĕ'chĕl), שֵׂכֶל (sē'chĕl) *m*, *i.p.* שָׂכֶל, *w.s.* שִׂכְלוֹ, intelligence, prudence, insight, cunning, success.

שִׂכְלוּת (sĭḵlū'θ) *f* = סִכְלוּת folly.

שָׂכַר (sāḵā'r) *inf.* שָׂכוֹר, שְׂכֹר, *fut.* יִשְׂכֹּר, *pt.* שֹׂכֵר [סֹכֵר], to hire, to buy, to bribe.—*Ni.* נִשְׂכַּר and *Hith.* הִשְׂתַּכֵּר to be hired, to hire oneself out.

שָׂכָר[1] (sāḵā'r) *m, c.* שְׂכַר, *w.s.* שְׂכָרִי, hire, wages, payment, fare, reward.

שָׂכָר[2] (sāḵā'r) *pr.n.m.*

שֶׂכֶר (sĕ'ḵĕr) *m* hire, wages.

שְׂלָו (s'lā'v) *f, pl.* שַׂלְוִים, quail [also *coll.*].

שַׂלְמָה[1] (sălmā') *f* [=שִׂמְלָה], *c.* שַׂלְמַת, *pl.* שְׂלָמוֹת, *c.* שַׂלְמוֹת, garment, dress, mantle.

שַׂלְמָה[2] (sălmā') or שַׂלְמוֹן (sălmō'n) *pr.n.m.*

שַׂלְמַי (sălmă'y) *pr.n.m.*

שְׂמֹאל, שְׂמֹאול (s'mō'l) *m, w.s.* שְׂמֹאלוֹ, left side, left hand, northern side, north.

שִׂמְאֵל (sĭm'ē'l), שָׂמַל (sāmă'l) *Hi.* הִשְׂמִיל, הִשְׂמְאִיל, *inf.* and *imp.* הַשְׂמִיל, *fut.* יַשְׂמְאִיל, *pt.* מַשְׂמְאִל, to take the left side, to turn to the left, to use the left hand.

שְׂמָלִי, שְׂמָאלִי (s'mālī') *adj., f* שְׂמָאלִית, left, to the left, northward.

שָׂמַח (sāmă'ḥ), שָׂמֵחַ[1] (sāmē'aḥ) *inf.* שְׂמֹחַ, *imp.* שְׂמַח, *pl.* שִׂמְחוּ, *fut.* יִשְׂמַח, to be glad, cheerful, joyful, merry, to rejoice.—*Pi.* שִׂמַּח, *inf.* and *imp.* שַׂמֵּחַ, שַׂמַּח, *fut.* יְשַׂמַּח, to make joyful, to gladden, to cheer. — *Hi.* הִשְׂמִיחַ to make glad.

שָׂמֵחַ[2] (sāmē'aḥ) *adj., pl.* שְׂמֵחִים, *c.* שִׂמְחֵי, שְׂמֵחֵי, glad, joyful, cheerful, rejoicing.

שִׂמְחָה (sĭmḥā') *f, c.* שִׂמְחַת, *w.s.* שִׂמְחָתִי, *pl.* שְׂמָחוֹת, joy, gladness, rejoicing, feast, banquet.

שְׂמִיכָה (s'mīḵā') *f* covering, carpet.

שִׂמְלָה (sĭmlā') *f, c.* שִׂמְלַת, *w.s.* שִׂמְלָתוֹ, *pl.* שְׂמָלוֹת, *c.* שִׂמְלוֹת, garment, dress, mantle, cloak.

שַׂמְלָה (sămlā') *pr.n.m.*

שַׂמְלַי (sămlă'y) *pr.n.m.*

שְׂמָמִית (s'māmī'θ) *f* a poisonous lizard.

שָׂנֵא (sānē') *inf.* שְׂנֹא, שְׂנֹא, *imp.* שִׂנְאוּ, *fut.* יִשְׂנָא, *pt*

שְׂנֵא, שׂוֹנֵא, *w.s.* שְׂנָאוֹ, *pl.* שְׂנֵאִים, *c.* שׂנְאֵי, *w.s.* שְׂנְאַי, *pt. p.* שָׂנוּא, *pl. c.* שְׂנֻאֵי, *f* שְׂנוּאָה, to hate; *pt.* hater, enemy. — *Ni.* נִשְׂנָא, *fut.* יִשָּׂנֵא, to be hated. — *Pi. pt.* מְשַׂנֵּא to hate violently.

שִׂנְאָה (sĭn'ā') *f* hatred, enmity.

שָׂנִיא (sānī') *adj.*, only *f* שְׂנִיאָה, hated.

שְׂנִיר (sᵉnī'r) *pr.n.* of mount Hermon among the Amorites.

שָׂעִיר[1], שָׂעִר (sāʻī'r) *c.* שְׂעִיר, *pl.* שְׂעִירִים, *f* שְׂעִירָה, *pl.* שְׂעִרֹת, *adj.* hairy, shaggy, rough; *subst.* buck, he-goat; hairy demon, satyr.

שָׂעִיר[2] (sāʻī'r) *m*, *pl.* שְׂעִירִים, shower of rain.

שֵׂעִיר (sēʻī'r) *pr.n.* of a mountainous and wooded district in Edom, and people therein; *pr.n.* of a mountain in Judah.

שְׂעִירָה[1] (sᵉʻīrā') *f* [see שָׂעִיר[1]] a she-goat.

שְׂעִירָה[2] (sᵉʻīrā') *pr.n.* of a place in Ephraim, *w. loc.* ה שְׂעִירָתָה

שָׂעֵף (sāʻē'f) *m*, only *pl.* שְׂעִפִּים, *c.* שְׂעִפַּי, thought.

שָׂעַר[1] (sāʻă'r) *fut.* יִשְׂעַר, to rage, to be agitated.—*Ni.* נִשְׂעַר to storm, to rage.—*Pi. fut.* יְשָׂעֵר to sweep away, to carry away in storm. — *Hith.* הִשְׂתָּעֵר to rush on, to assail.

שָׂעַר[2] (sāʻă'r) *imp.* שַׂעֲרוּ, *fut.* יִשְׂעַר, to shudder, to fear.

שַׂעַר (săʻ"ăr) *m* a shuddering; storm, tempest.

שֵׂעָר (sēʻā'r) *m*, *c.* שְׂעַר, שַׂעַר, *w.s.* שְׂעָרוֹ, hair [a single one and *coll.*].

שָׂעִר see שָׂעִיר[1].

שְׂעָרָה (sᵉʻārā') *f* storm, tempest.

שַׂעֲרָה (săʻ"arā') *f*, *c.* שַׂעֲרַת, *w.s.* שַׂעֲרָתוֹ, *pl.* שַׂעֲרוֹת hair [a single one and *coll.*].

שְׂעֹרָה (sᵉʻōrā') *f*, *pl.* שְׂעֹרִים, barley, *pl.* grains of barley.

שְׂעֹרִים (sᵉʻōrī'm) *pr.n.m.*

שָׂפָה (sāfā') *f*, *c.* שְׂפַת, *w.s.* שְׂפָתִי, *du.* שְׂפָתַיִם, *c.* שִׂפְתֵי, *w.s.* שְׂפָתַי, שְׂפָתָמוֹ, *pl. c.* שִׂפְתוֹת, lip, mouth, speech, language; border, edge.

שָׂפַח (săfă'ḥ) *Pi.* שִׂפַּח, to make bald or scabby.

שָׂפָם (săfā'm) *m*, *w.s.* שְׂפָמוֹ, beard, mustache.

שָׂפַן (săfă'n) *pt. p. pl. c.* שְׂפֻנֵי, to hide, to conceal.

שָׂפַק[1] (săfă'k) *fut.* יִשְׂפֹּק, to suffice.

שָׂפַק[2] (săfă'k) *fut.* יִשְׂפֹּק, to strike or clap [hands]. — *Hi. fut.* יַשְׂפִּיק to conclude a covenant [by striking hands].

שֶׂפֶק (sĕ'fĕk) *m*, *w.s.* שִׂפְקוֹ, stroke,chastisement[others: scorn or abundance].

שַׂק (săk) *m*, *i.p.* שָׂק, *w.s.* שַׂקִּי, *pl.* שַׂקִּים, *c.* שַׂקֵּי, coarse stuff, sack cloth, sack, mourning dress.

שָׂקַד (săkă'd) *Ni.* נִשְׂקַד, to be bound, to be harnessed.

שָׂקַר (săkă'r) *Pi. pt. f/pl.* מְשַׂקְּרוֹת, to let glance [the eyes] impudently or coquettishly.

שַׂר (săr) *m*, *i.p.* שָׂר, *pl.* שָׂרִים, *c.* שָׂרֵי, master, head, chief, commander, ruler, prefect, leader, noble, prince.

שָׂרַג (sără'g) *Pu. fut.* יְשֹׂרַג (yᵉsŏră'g), to be twisted together, to be strong. — *Hith.* הִשְׂתָּרֵג to be interwoven.

שָׂרַד (sără'd) to flee, to escape.

שְׂרָד (sᵉrā'd) *m* plaited or twisted work.

שֶׂרֶד (sĕ'rĕd) *m* awl, stylus, red-pencil.

שָׂרָה[1] (sără') to strive, to contend.

שָׂרָה[2] (sără') *f*, *pl.* שָׂרוֹת, *w.s.* שָׂרוֹתֶיהָ, princess, lady.

שָׂרָה[3] (sără') *pr.n.f.*; also שָׂרַי (sără'y).

שְׂרוּג (sᵉrū'g) *pr.n.m.*

שְׂרוֹךְ (sᵉrō'ch) *m* thong [for shoes and sandals].

שְׂרוּקִים see שָׂרֹק.

שֶׂרַח (sĕ'răch) *pr.n.f.*

שָׂרַט (sără't) *inf.* שָׂרוֹט, *fut.* יִשְׂרֹט, to cut, to make incisions. — *Ni. fut.* יִשָּׂרֵט to be lacerated, to be hurt.

שֶׂרֶט (sĕ'rĕt) *m* and שָׂרֶטֶת (sărĕ'tĕth) *f* incision.

שָׂרִיג (sări'g) *m*, only *pl.* שָׂרִיגִם, שָׂרִיגִים, shoot of vine.

שָׂרִיד (sări'd) *m*, *pl.* שְׂרִידִים, *c.* שְׂרִידֵי, fugitive, survivor, one escaped, remnant.

שְׂרָיָה (ß°rāyā') and שְׂרָיָהוּ (ß°rāyā'hū) *pr.n.m.*

שִׂרְיוֹן, שִׂרְיֹן (ßĭryō'n) *pr.n.* of mount Hermon among the Sidonians.

שָׂרִיק (ßārī'k) *adj.*, *f/pl.* שְׂרִיקוֹת, combed, heckled.

שָׂרַךְ (ßără'ch) *Pi. pt. f* מְשָׂרֶכֶת, to complicate, to entangle.

שַׂרְסְכִים (ßărß°chī'm) *pr.n.m.* [= chief of the eunuchs].

שָׂרַע (ßără'°) *pt. p.* שָׂרוּעַ, to extend, to have a lengthened limb. — *Hith.* הִשְׂתָּרֵעַ to stretch oneself out.

שַׂרְעַף (ßăr°ă'f) *m*, only *pl. w.s.* שַׂרְעַפַּי, thought, meditation.

שָׂרַף (ßără'f) *inf.* שְׂרֹף, שָׂרוֹף, *w.s.* שָׂרְפוֹ (ßŏrfō'), *fut.* יִשְׂרֹף, *pt.* שֹׂרֵף, *pl.* שֹׂרְפִים, *pt. p.* שָׂרוּף, *pl.* שְׂרֻפִים, *f* שְׂרוּפָה, שְׂרֻפָה, *pl.* שְׂרֻפוֹת, to burn [*tr.*], to destroy by fire. — *Ni.* נִשְׂרַף, *fut.* יִשָּׂרֵף, to be burnt. — *Pu.* שֹׂרַף to be burnt.

שָׂרָף (ßārā'f) *m*, *pl.* שְׂרָפִים, poisonous serpent; *pl.* winged angels [properly the noble, the high].

שְׂרֵפָה (ß°rēfā') *f*, *c.* שְׂרֵפַת, a burning, conflagration.

שָׂרֹק (ßārō'k) *adj.*, *pl.* שְׂרֻקִּים, red, fox-coloured; *pl.* שְׂרוּקִּים vines with red grapes.

שֹׂרֵק¹, שׂוֹרֵק (ßōrē'k) *m* and שֹׂרֵקָה (ßō'rēkā') *f* a superior kind of vine producing red wine.

שֹׂרֵק² (ßōrē'k) *pr.n.* of a valley between Ascalon and Gaza, see שׂוֹרֵק.

שָׂרַר (ßără'r) *fut. pl.* יָשֹׂרוּ, *pt.* שֹׂרֵר, to rule, govern. — *Hith.* הִשְׂתָּרֵר to make oneself ruler.

שָׂשׂוֹן (ßāßō'n) *m*, *c.* שְׂשׂוֹן, joy.

שֵׂת see שְׂאֵת.

שָׂתַם (ßāϑă'm) to close, stop, hinder.

שָׂתַר (ßāϑă'r) *Ni. fut.* יִשָּׂתֵר, to break forth.

שׁ

שׁ with **שׁ** the twenty-first letter of the alphabet, called שִׁין [tooth]; as a numeral = 300.

שֶׁ, שַׁ [with dagesh following], שָׁ, שְׁ = אֲשֶׁר, an abbreviation used as a prefix.

שׁא (šō) *m, pl. w.s.* שְׁאֵיהֶם, destruction.

שָׁאַב (šā'ă'b) *inf.* שְׁאֹב, *fut.* יִשְׁאַב, *pt.* שֹׁאֵב, *pl. c.* שֹׁאֲבֵי, *f/pl.* שֹׁאֲבוֹת, to draw [water].

שָׁאַג (šā'ă'g) *inf.* שָׁאֹג, *fut.* יִשְׁאַג, *pt.* שֹׁאֵג, שׁוֹאֵג, *pl.* שֹׁאֲגִים, to roar, groan.

שְׁאָגָה (šᵉ'āgā') *f, c.* שַׁאֲגַת, *w.s.* שַׁאֲגָתִי, *pl. w.s.* שַׁאֲגֹתַי, a roaring, groaning.

שָׁאָה[1] (šā'ā') *Ni. fut.* יִשָּׁאֶה, to rush, to rage, to be noisy.

שָׁאָה[2] (šā'ā') to become desolate. — *Ni. fut.* יִשָּׁאֶה to be laid waste.—*Hi. inf.* לְהַשְׁוֹת, הַשְׁאוֹת, to lay waste.

שָׁאָה[3] (šā'ā') = שָׁעָה, *Hith. pt. c.* מִשְׁתָּאֵה, to behold, to gaze at.

שֹׁאָה see שׁוֹאָה.

שַׁאֲוָה (šă''avā') = שׁוֹאָה.

שְׁאֹל, שְׁאוֹל (šᵉ'ō'l) *f, w. loc.* ה שְׁאוֹלָה, depth, abyss, nether world, realm of the dead, Hades.

שָׁאוּל (šā'ū'l) *pr.n.m.*, Saul; *patr.* שָׁאוּלִי.

שָׁאוֹן (šā'ō'n) *m, c.* שְׁאוֹן, *w.s.* שְׁאוֹנָהּ, noise, tumult, roar, rush, desolation, destruction.

שְׁאָט (šᵉ'ā't) *m, w.s.* שָׁאטְךָ, contempt.

שְׁאִיָּה (šᵉ'ĭyyā') *f* destruction, ruins.

שָׁאַל (šā'ă'l), **שָׁאֵל** (šā'ē'l) *inf.* שְׁאֹל, שָׁאוֹל, שְׁאָלָה, *imp.* שְׁאַל, שַׁאֲלוּ, *fut.* יִשְׁאַל, *pt.* שֹׁאֵל, *pl.* שֹׁאֲלִים, *f* שֹׁאֶלֶת, *pt. p.* שָׁאוּל, to ask, inquire, require, demand, entreat, beg, borrow. — *Ni.* נִשְׁאַל, *inf.* נִשְׁאֹל, to ask for oneself. — *Pi.* שִׁאֵל, *fut.* יְשָׁאֵל, to beg [as a beggar]; to question.— *Hi.* הִשְׁאִיל, *fut.* יַשְׁאִיל, to grant, to lend.

שְׁאָל (šᵉ'ā'l) *pr.n.m.*

שְׁאֵלָה (šᵉ'ēlā') *f, w.s.* שְׁאֵלָתִי, שֵׁלָתֵךְ, שֶׁאֱלָתָם, request, petition; a thing obtained by entreaty.

שְׁאָלָה (šᵉ'ālā) *f* request; or for שְׁאוֹלָה.

שְׁאַלְתִּיאֵל (šᵉ'altī'ē'l) *pr.n.m.*

שָׁאַן (šā'ă'n) *Pi.* שַׁאֲנַן, to be or live quietly, tranquilly, at ease.

שַׁאֲנָן (šă''ănā'n) *adj., w.s.* שַׁאֲנַנְךָ, *pl.* שַׁאֲנַנִּים, *f* שַׁאֲנַנָּה, *pl.* שַׁאֲנַנּוֹת, quiet, tranquil, peaceful, easy, secure, prosperous, proud; *subst.* pride.

שְׁאֵם — שֹׁסֵם, see שָׁסַם.

שָׁאַף (šā'ă'f) *inf.* שָׁאוֹף, *fut.* יִשְׁאַף, *pt.* שֹׁאֵף, *pl.* שֹׁאֲפִים, to blow, breathe, pant, snort, snuff; to be eager or greedy.

שָׁאַר (šā'ă'r) to be left, to remain. — *Ni.* נִשְׁאַר, *fut.* יִשָּׁאֵר, *pt.* נִשְׁאָר, *pl.* נִשְׁאָרִים, *f* נִשְׁאָרָה, *c.* נִשְׁאֶרֶת, to be left, to remain, to survive. — *Hi.* הִשְׁאִיר, *fut.* יַשְׁאִיר, to let remain, to leave, to keep over; to be left.

שְׁאָר (šᵉ'ā'r) *m* rest, remnant, remainder.

שְׁאָר יָשׁוּב (šᵉ'ā'r yāšū'b) *pr.n.m.*

שְׁאֵר (šᵉ'ē'r) *m, w.s.* שְׁאֵרִי, flesh; food; blood-relation.

שַׁאֲרָה (šă''ărā') *f* blood-relationship.

שֶׁאֱרָה (šĕ''erā') *pr.n.f.*

שְׁאֵרִית (šᵉ'ērī'th) *f, w.s.* שְׁאֵרִיתְךָ, remainder, remnant, residue, survivors.

שֵׁאת (šēth) *f* destruction, ruin.

שְׁבָא (šᵉbā') *pr.n.* of an Arabian tribe; *gent. pl.* שְׁבָאִים; *pr.n.m.*

שָׁבָב (šābā'b) *m*, only *pl.* שְׁבָבִים, fragment, little piece.

שָׁבָה (šābā'), *inf.* שְׁבוֹת, *imp.* שְׁבֵה, *fut.* יִשְׁבֶּה, *pt.* שֹׁבֶה, *pl.* שֹׁבִים, *w.s.* שֹׁבֵינוּ, *pt. p.* שָׁבוּי, *pl.* שְׁבוּיִם, *f/pl.* שְׁבֻיוֹת, to lead away, to carry off, to hold captive, to lead into captivity or exile. — *Ni.* נִשְׁבָּה to be led away, to be held captive.

שְׁבוֹ (šᵉbō') *m* a precious stone, agate.

שְׁבוּאֵל (šᵉbū'ē'l) *pr.n.m.*

שָׁבוּל — שְׁבִיל.

שָׁבוּעַ (šāḇū'a') *m*, *c.* שְׁבוּעַ, *du.* שְׁבֻעַיִם, *pl.* שָׁבֻעִים, שָׁבֻעוֹת, *c.* שְׁבֻעוֹת, seven days, a week, sennight; a heptad, period of seven weeks or years; חַג שָׁבֻעוֹת festival of the seven weeks, pentecost; חַג שְׁבֻעוֹת יָמִים the Passover.

שְׁבֻעָה, שְׁבוּעָה (š'ḇū'ā') *f*, *c.* שְׁבוּעַת, *w.s.* שְׁבֻעָתִי, *pl.* שְׁבֻעוֹת, oath, swearing; curse.

שְׁבוּת (š'ḇū'ϑ), **שְׁבִית** (š'ḇī'ϑ) *f* captivity, captives; misery, affliction.

שָׁבַח[1] (šāḇă'ḥ) *Pi.* שִׁבַּח, *imp.* שַׁבְּחִי, *fut.* יְשַׁבַּח, *pt.* שַׁבֵּחַ [for מְשַׁבֵּחַ], to praise. to glorify. — *Hith.* *inf.* הִשְׁתַּבֵּחַ to praise oneself, to boast.

שָׁבַח[2] (šāḇă'ḥ) *Pi.* *fut.* יְשַׁבַּח, to still, calm, soothe. — *Hi.* *pt.* מַשְׁבִּיחַ the same as *Pi.*

שֵׁבֶט (šē'ḇĕt) or **שֶׁבֶט** (šĕ'ḇĕt) *m* [and *f*], *w.s.* שִׁבְטְךָ, *pl.* שְׁבָטִים, *c.* שִׁבְטֵי, stick, staff, rod, thrashing-stick; ruler's staff, sceptre; stem, tribe, division; lance, spear.

שְׁבָט (š'ḇā't) *m* eleventh month of the Hebrew year [February to March].

שְׁבִי (š'ḇī') *m*, *i.p.* שֶׁבִי, *w.s.* שֶׁבְיְךָ, שִׁבְיוֹ, a leading away, captivity, exile; captives.

שָׁבִי (šāḇī') *adj.*, only *f* שְׁבִיָּה, led away, captive.

שֹׁבַי (šōḇă'y); **שֹׁבִי** (šōḇī') *pr.n.m.*

שָׁבִיב (šāḇī'ḇ) *m*, *c.* שְׁבִיב, flame.

שִׁבְיָה (šĭḇyā') *f* captivity, captives.

שֹׁבְיָה (šŏḇyā') *pr.n.m.* [also שָׂכְיָה].

שָׁבִיל (šāḇī'l) *m*, only *pl.* *c.* שְׁבִילֵי, שְׁבוּלֵי, *w.s.* שְׁבִילֶיךָ, path, way.

שָׁבִיס (šāḇī's) *m*, only *pl.* שְׁבִיסִים, net-work, or little suns used as a head-dress.

שְׁבִעִי, שְׁבִיעִי (š'ḇī'ī') *adj. num.*, *f* שְׁבִיעִית, שְׁבִעִת, שְׁבִעִת, שְׁבִעִית, the seventh.

שְׁבִית (š'ḇī'ϑ) *f* = שְׁבוּת, captivity, captives.

שֹׁבֶל (šō'ḇĕl) *m* train [of a robe].

שַׁבְּלוּל (šăḇlū'l) *m* a snail.

שִׁבֹּלֶת (šĭbbō'lĕϑ) *f*, *pl.*

שִׁבֳּלִים, *c.* שִׁבֳּלֵי, ear [of corn], point, branch; stream, water-course.

שֶׁבְנָא, **שֶׁבְנָה** (šĕḇnā') *pr.n.m.*

שְׁבַנְיָה (šᵉḇănyā'), שְׁבַנְיָהוּ (šᵉḇănyā'hū) *pr.n.m.*

שָׁבַע (šāḇă'') *Ni.* נִשְׁבַּע, *inf.* הִשָּׁבֵעַ, הִשָּׁבַע, *imp.* הִשָּׁבְעָה, *fut.* יִשָּׁבֵעַ, יִשָּׁבַע, *pt.* נִשְׁבָּע, *pl.* נִשְׁבָּעִים, *f* נִשְׁבָּעוֹת, to swear, to confirm with an oath, to swear to.—*Hi.* הִשְׁבִּיעַ, *inf.* הַשְׁבֵּעַ, הַשְׁבִּיעַ, *fut.* יַשְׁבִּיעַ, *pt.* מַשְׁבִּיעַ, to cause to swear, to bind by an oath; to adjure.

שֶׁבַע (šĕ'ḇă') *num. f, c.* שְׁבַע, and *m* שִׁבְעָה, *c.* שִׁבְעַת, *w.s.* שִׁבְעָתָם, seven, seven times, sevenfold; *du.* שִׁבְעָתַיִם seven times, sevenfold; *pl.* שִׁבְעִים seventy.

שִׁבְעָה (šīḇ'ā') *pr.n.* of a well; see also שֶׁבַע.

שִׁבְעָנָה (šīḇ'ā'nā) = שִׁבְעָה seven.

שָׁבַץ (šāḇă'ṣ) *Pi.* שִׁבֵּץ, to weave after a checkered pattern. — *Pu. pt.* מְשֻׁבָּץ to be set [precious stones in gold].

שָׁבָץ (šāḇā'ṣ) *m* confusion, giddiness [others: cramp].

שָׁבַר[1] (šāḇă'r) *inf.* שְׁבֹר, שָׁבֹר, *w.s.* שִׁבְרִי, *fut.* יִשְׁבֹּר, *pt.* שֹׁבֵר, *pt. p.* שָׁבוּר, to break in pieces, to rend, to tear in pieces; to break, destroy, hurt, quench [thirst]. — *Ni.* נִשְׁבַּר, *inf.* הִשָּׁבֵר, *fut.* יִשָּׁבֵר, *pt.* נִשְׁבָּר, *pl. c.* נִשְׁבְּרֵי, *f* נִשְׁבָּרָה, to be broken, to be wrecked or foundered, to be injured, maimed, destroyed, to be torn in pieces; to be broken by penitence. — *Pi.* שִׁבֵּר, שַׁבֵּר, *inf.* שַׁבֵּר, *fut.* יְשַׁבֵּר, *pt.* מְשַׁבֵּר, to shiver, wreck, crush, smash.—*Hi. fut.* יַשְׁבִּיר to cause to break forth, to open [the womb].

שָׁבַר[2] (šāḇă'r) *inf.* שְׁבֹר, *imp. pl.* שִׁבְרוּ, *fut.* יִשְׁבֹּר, *pt.* שֹׁבֵר, *pl.* שֹׁבְרִים, to buy grain or food. — *Hi. fut.* יַשְׁבִּיר, *pt.* מַשְׁבִּיר, to sell grain.

שֶׁבֶר[1] (šĕ'ḇĕr), שֵׁבֶר (šē'ḇĕr) *m, i.p.* שָׁבֶר, *w.s.* שִׁבְרוֹ, *pl.* שְׁבָרִים, a breaking, shattering, breach, fracture, destruction, misfortune, injury; interpretation, solution.

שֶׁבֶר[2] (šĕ'bĕr) *m*, *w.s.* שִׁבְרוֹ, grain, corn.

שִׁבָּרוֹן (šĭbbārō'n) *m*, *c.* שִׁבְרוֹן, a breaking, pain, destruction.

שְׁבָרִים (šᵉbārī'm) *pr.n.* of a locality between Ai and Jericho [or *m/pl.* quarries].

שָׁבַת (šābă'ϑ) *fut.* יִשְׁבֹּת, יִשְׁבַּת, to desist, to cease, to rest, to come to an end; to keep the sabbath or sacred day.—*Ni.* נִשְׁבַּת to be ended, to cease. — *Hi.* הִשְׁבִּית, *inf.* הַשְׁבִּית, *imp. pl.* הַשְׁבִּיתוּ, *fut.* יַשְׁבִּית, יַשְׁבֵּת, to cause to rest, to let rest, to bring to an end, to abolish, remove, destroy.

שֶׁבֶת[1] (šĕ'bĕϑ) *m*, *i.p.* שָׁבֶת, *w.s.* שִׁבְתּוֹ, rest, cessation, inactivity [from שָׁבַת].

שֶׁבֶת[2] (šĕ'bĕϑ) *f* a sitting, dwelling, seat, place [from יָשַׁב].

שַׁבָּת (šăbbā'ϑ) *f* and *m*, *c.* שַׁבַּת, *w.s.* שַׁבַּתּוֹ, *pl.* שַׁבָּתוֹת, *c.* שַׁבְּתוֹת, day of rest, holy seventh day, sabbath; week, sacred seventh year, sabbath-year.

שַׁבָּתוֹן (šăbbāϑō'n) *m* sacred time of rest, sabbath.

שַׁבְּתַי (šăbbᵉϑă'y); **שָׁגֵא** (šāgē') *pr.n.m.*

שָׁגַג (šāgă'g) *inf.*, *w.s.* שַׁגָּם, *pt.* שֹׁגֵג, to err, to transgress.

שְׁגָגָה (šᵉgāgā') *f*, *w.s.* שִׁגְגָתוֹ, error, mistake, unconscious sin, transgression.

שָׁגָה (šāgā') *fut.* יִשְׁגֶּה, *pt.* שֹׁגֶה, *pl.* שׁוֹגִים, to waver, to wander, to go astray, to err, to transgress.—*Hi.* הִשְׁגָּה, *fut.* יַשְׁגֶּה, *pt.* מַשְׁגֶּה, to lead astray, to seduce.

שָׁגַח (šāgă'ḥ) *Hi.* הִשְׁגִּיחַ, *fut.* יַשְׁגִּיחַ, *pt.* מַשְׁגִּיחַ, to see, to look, to view, to gaze at.

שְׁגִיאָה (šᵉgī'ā) *f*, *pl.* שְׁגִיאוֹת, error, transgression.

שִׁגָּיוֹן (šĭggāyō'n) *m*, *pl.* שִׁגְיֹנוֹת, enthusiastic song, hymn, dithyramb.

שָׁגַל (šāgă'l) *fut.* יִשְׁגַּל, to be rutty, to lie with. — *Ni. fut.* תִּשָּׁגַל to be lain with, to be ravished.—*Pu.* שֻׁגַּל the same as *Ni.*

שֵׁגָל (šēgā'l) *f* paramour, consort of an oriental king, favourite wife.

שָׁגַע (šāgă'') *Pu. pt.* מְשֻׁגָּע, *pl.* מְשֻׁגָּעִים, to be in a frenzy, to rave, to be mad. — *Hith.* הִשְׁתַּגֵּעַ, *pt.* מִשְׁתַּגֵּעַ, to feign oneself mad, to play the madman.

שִׁגָּעוֹן (šĭggā'ō'n) *m* a raving, madness.

שֶׁגֶר (šĕ'gĕr) *m, c.* שְׁגַר, what is brought forth, a young one, fetus.

שַׁד (šăḍ) *m, du.* שָׁדַיִם, *c.* שְׁדֵי, *w.s.* שָׁדַי, שְׁדֵיהֶן, a woman's breast, pap, teat, bosom.

שֵׁד (šēḍ) *m,* only *pl.* שֵׁדִים, wicked demon, idol.

שֹׁד[1] (šōḍ) *m,* = שַׁד a mother's breast.

שֹׁד[2] (šōḍ) *m* violence, severity, oppression, destruction, ruin.

שָׁדַד (šāḍă'ḍ) *inf.* שָׁדוֹד, שְׁדוֹד, שֹׁד, *fut.* יָשֹׁד, *pt.* שׁוֹדֵד, *pt. p.* שָׁדוּד, *f* שְׁדוּדָה, to be violent, to use violence, to oppress, rob, destroy, ravage, plunder. — *Ni.* נָשַׁד to be laid waste. — *Pi.* שִׁדֵּד, *fut.* יְשַׁדֵּד, *pt.* מְשַׁדֵּד, to oppress, to ruin. — *Pu.* שֻׁדַּד and שֻׁדַּד (šŭddă'ḍ) to be laid waste, ruined, destroyed. — *Ho. fut.* יוּשַׁד to be destroyed.

שִׁדָּה (šĭddā') *f, pl.* שִׁדּוֹת, mistress, wife.

שַׁדַּי (šăddă'y) *m* [*adj.*] mighty, powerful, almighty [אֵל שַׁדַּי].

שְׁדֵיאוּר (šᵉḍē'ū'r) *pr.n.m.*

שַׁדִּין (šăddī'n) composed of שׁ [= אֲשֶׁר] and דִּין, that there is a judgment.

שְׁדֵמָה (šᵉḍēmā') *f, pl.* שְׁדֵמוֹת, *c.* שַׁדְמוֹת, שַׁדְמֹת, field, cornfield, vineyard.

שָׁדַף (šāḍā'f) *pt. p. f/pl.* שְׁדוּפֹת, שְׁדֻפוֹת, to parch, to scorch, to blast.

שְׁדֵפָה (šᵉḍēfā') *f* a scorching; = שְׁדֵמָה.

שִׁדָּפוֹן (šĭddāfō'n) *m* a scorching, blasting, blight.

שֹׁהַם[1] (šō'hăm) *m* a precious stone [onyx, beryl, or chrysopras].

שֹׁהַם[2] (šō'hăm) *pr.n.m.*

שָׁו = שָׁוְא.

שָׁוְא (šāv') *m* nothingness, vanity, inanity; falsehood, lying, vainness, sin, wickedness, calamity.

שָׁוְא (šᵉvā') *pr.n.m.*

שׁוֹא (šō) *m, pl. w.s.* שֹׁאֵיהֶם, and שׁוֹאָה (šō'ā') *f, c.* שֹׁאַת, a roaring, crashing, tumult, storm, tempest, destruction, desolation, ruin.

שׁוּב (šūb) *pf.* שָׁב, *inf.* שׁוֹב, שֹׁב, שׁוּב, *imp.* שׁוּב, שֵׁב, *fut.* יָשׁוּב, יָשֹׁב, וַיָּשָׁב (vāyyā'šōb), *pt.* שָׁב, *pl.* שָׁבִים, *c.* שָׁבֵי, *intr.* to turn [oneself], to return, to come back, to turn round, to turn about; to be converted, to turn to, to turn from; to be restored; *tr.* to restore; to do repeatedly, to repeat. — *Pil. pf.* and *inf.* שׁוֹבֵב, *fut.* יְשׁוֹבֵב, *pt.* מְשׁוֹבֵב, *tr.* to turn, to cause to return, to lead back, to seduce; to convert, restore, refresh.—*Pul.* שׁוֹבַב, *pt. f* מְשׁוֹבֶבֶת, to be turned aside. — *Hi.* הֵשִׁיב, *inf.* הָשֵׁב, הָשִׁיב, *imp.* הָשֵׁב, הָשִׁיבָה, *fut.* יָשִׁיב, יָשֵׁב, וַיָּשֶׁב, *pt.* מֵשִׁיב, *pl.* מְשִׁיבִים, *c.* מְשִׁיבֵי, *f c.* מְשִׁיבַת, *tr.* to turn about, away, at, to, upon; to draw, bring, drive or lead back; to give back, restore, return; to answer; to recall, revoke; to render, to offer. — *Ho.* הוּשַׁב, *fut.* יוּשַׁב, *pt.* מוּשָׁב, to be brought or given back.

שׁוּבָאֵל (šū'bā'ē'l) *pr.n.m.* = שְׁבוּאֵל.

שׁוֹבָב[1] (šōbā'b) *adj., pl.* שׁוֹבָבִים, turning away, rebellious, apostate.

שׁוֹבָב[2] (šōbā'b) *pr.n.m.*

שׁוֹבֵב (šōbē'b) *adj., f* שׁוֹבֵבָה, = שׁוֹבָב[1].

שׁוּבָה (šūbā') *f* return, conversion.

שׁוֹבַךְ (šōbă'ch) = שׁוֹפַךְ; שׁוֹבָל (šōbā'l); שׁוֹבֵק (šōbē'k) *pr.n.m.*

שׁוֹד see שֹׁד, שׁוּד see שָׁדַד,

שָׁוָה (šāvā') *fut.* יִשְׁוֶה, *pt.* שֹׁוֶה, to be like, equal, comparable, fit, convenient, enough. — *Pi.* שִׁוָּה, *fut.* יְשַׁוֶּה, *pt.* מְשַׁוֶּה, *tr* make even, to level, to calm; to set, put, place, lay. — *Hi. fut.* יַשְׁוֶה, to liken, to compare.— *Ni.* [mixed with *Hith.*] נִשְׁתָּוָה to be like, to resemble.

שָׁוֵה[1] (šāvē') *m* plain, level country.

שָׁוֵה[2] (šāvē') *pr.n.* of a valley near Jerusalem, called the king's valley.

שׁוּחַ[1] (šū'aḥ) *pf.* שַׁח, *fut.* יָשׁוּחַ, to sink, to be bowed down, to be dejected. — *Hi. fut.* יָשִׁיחַ to become depressed.

שׁוּחַ[2] (šū'aḥ) *pr.n.m.*; *patr.* and *gent.* שׁוּחִי.

שׁוּחָה[1] (šūḥā') *f* depression, depth, pit.

שׁוּחָה[2] (šūḥā') *pr.n.m.* = חוּשָׁה.

שׁוּחָם (šūḥā'm) *pr.n.m.* = חֻשִׁים.

שׁוּט (šūt) *imp.* שׁוּט, *fut.* יָשׁוּט, *pt.* שָׁט, שָׁאט, *pl.* שָׁאטִים, to go about, to rove, to move, to row; to treat with contempt, to despise.

שׁוֹט (šōt) *m, pl.* שׁוֹטִים, a scourge, whip; punishment.

שׁוּל (šūl) *m* train of a robe, skirt, edge.

שׁוֹלָל (šōlā'l) *adj.* stripped, barefoot, captive.

שׁוּלַמִּית (šū'lămmī'ϑ) *pr.n.f.* [or *gent.* of a place שׁוּלֵם = שׁוּנַמִּית, see שׁוּנֵם].

שׁוּם (šūm) *m*, only *pl.* שׁוּמִים, garlic.

שׁוּנִי (šūnī') *pr.n.m.*

שׁוּנֵם (šūnē'm) *pr.n.* of a town in Issachar; *gent.* שׁוּנַמִּי, *f* שׁוּנַמִּית.

שָׁוַע (šāvă'ʻ) *Pi.* שִׁוַּע, *inf. w.s.* שַׁוְּעִי, *fut.* יְשַׁוַּע, יְשַׁוֵּעַ, *pt.* מְשַׁוֵּעַ, to cry for help.

שֶׁוַע (šĕ'vă') *m, w.s.* שַׁוְעִי, cry for help.

שׁוֹעַ[1] (šō'aʻ) *adj.* rich, noble, liberal, generous.

שׁוֹעַ[2] (šō'aʻ) *m* and שׁוּעַ[1] (šū'aʻ) *m* = שֶׁוַע cry for help.

שׁוּעַ[2] (šū'aʻ) *m* wealth.

שׁוּעַ[3] (šū'aʻ); שׁוּעָא (šūʻā') *pr.n.m.*

שַׁוְעָה (šăvʻā') *f, c.* שַׁוְעַת, *w.s.* שַׁוְעָתִי, cry for help.

שׁוּעָל[1] (šūʻā'l) *m, pl.* שׁוּעָלִים, שֻׁעָלִים, fox, jackal.

שׁוּעָל[2] (šūʻā'l) *pr.n.* of a district in Benjamin; *pr. n.m.*

שׁוֹעֵר, **שֹׁעֵר** (šōʻē'r) *m, pl.* שׁוֹעֲרִים, porter, doorkeeper.

שׁוּף (šūf) *fut.* יָשׁוּף, *w.s.* יְשׁוּפֶנּוּ, to bruise, to crush; to pierce, to bite; to cover, to veil.

שׁוֹפָךְ (šọfā'ḥ) *pr.n.m.* = שׁוֹבָךְ.

שׁוֹפָמִי see שְׁפוּפָם.

שׁוֹפָן (šọfā'n) in עַטְרוֹת שׁ׳ *pr.n.* of a town.

שׁוֹפָר (šọfā'r) *m*, *c.* שׁוֹפַר, *pl.* שׁוֹפָרוֹת, *c.* שׁוֹפְרוֹת, trumpet, horn.

שׁוּק[1] (šūk) *Pil. fut.* יְשׁוֹקֵק, to cause to overflow, to give abundance. — *Hi.* הֵשִׁיק to overflow, to run over.

שׁוּק[2] (šūk) *m*, *pl.* שְׁוָקִים, way, street.

שׁוֹק (šọk) *f*, *du.* שׁוֹקַיִם, *c.* שׁוֹקֵי, leg, lower part of the leg, hind leg, fore-leg.

שׁוֹר (šọr) *m*, *w.s.* שׁוֹרִי, *pl.* שְׁוָרִים, head of cattle, ox, bull, cow, calf.

שׁוּר[1] (šūr) *fut.* יָשׁוּר, to go, wander, travel; to look round, to view; to look after, to lie in wait.

שׁוּר[2] (šūr) see שִׁיר[1].

שׁוּר[3] (šūr) *m*, *pl. w.s.* שׁוּרַי = שׁוֹרֵר.

שׁוּר[4] (šūr) *m*, *pl.* שׁוּרוֹת [once שָׁרוֹת], a wall.

שׁוּר[5] (šūr) *pr.n.* of a place and desert near the Red Sea.

שׁוֹרֵר (šọrẹ'r) *m* [for מְשׁוֹרֵר *pt. Pil.* of שׁוּר[1]] a lier in wait, lurker.

שׁוֹשָׁן (šọšā'n) *m*, שׁוּשַׁן (šūšā'n) *m*, *pl.* שׁוֹשַׁנִּים, lily [flower and ornament]; *pl.* musical instruments or melodies or choirs.

שׁוּשַׁן[2] (šūšā'n), שֻׁשַׁן *pr.n.* of a Persian city, Susa.

שׁוֹשַׁנָּה (šọ'šānnā') *f* lily.

שׁוֹשַׁק see שִׁישַׁק.

שׁוּת see שִׁית.

שׁוּתֶלַח (šūϑẹ'lāḥ) *pr.n.m.*; *patr.* שֻׁתַלְחִי.

שָׁזַף (šāzā'f) to scorch, singe, burn; to look on, to scan.

שָׁזַר (šāzā'r) *Ho. pt.* מָשְׁזָר, to be spun or twisted.

שַׁח (šāḥ) *adj.* depressed, dejected.

שָׁחַד (šāḥā'd) *imp.* שִׁחֲדוּ, *fut.* יִשְׁחֹד, to give a present or a bribe.

שֹׁחַד (šọ'ḥād) *m* gift, present, bribe.

שָׁחָה (šāḥā') *imp. f* שְׁחִי, to bow, to sink down. — — *Hi. fut.* יַשְׁחֶה to depress. — *Hith.* הִשְׁתַּחֲוָה, *inf.* הִשְׁתַּחֲוֹת, *imp.* הִשְׁתַּחֲוֵה, *fut.* יִשְׁתַּחֲוֶה, יִשְׁתַּחוּ, *pl.*

יִשְׁתַּחֲוּוּ, *pt.* מִשְׁתַּחֲוֶה, *pl.* מִשְׁתַּחֲוִים, to bow down, to prostrate oneself, to worship, to adore.

שְׁחוֹר (šʼḥō'r) *m* blackness.

שְׁחוּת (šāḥū'ϑ) *f* pit.

שָׁחַח (šāḥă'ḥ) *pf.* שַׁח, *inf.* שְׁחוֹחַ, *fut.* יָשֹׁחַ, *pl.* יָשֹׁחוּ, to crouch, to sink down; to be bowed, depressed. — *Ni. fut.* יִשַּׁח to be bowed down, depressed, to be low [in the voice]. — *Hi.* הֵשַׁח to depress, to make low. — *Hith. fut.* יִשְׁתּוֹחֵחַ, יִשְׁתּוֹחַח, to be bowed down, depressed.

שָׁחַט (šāḥă'ṭ) *inf.* שְׁחֹט, שְׁחוֹט, *imp. pl.* שַׁחֲטוּ, *fut.* יִשְׁחַט, *pt.* שֹׁחֵט, שׁוֹחֵט, *pl. c.* שֹׁחֲטֵי, *pt. p.* שָׁחוּט, to kill, to slaughter, to massacre, to murder; to hammer out, to beat thin, to sharpen. — *Ni.* נִשְׁחַט, *fut.* יִשָּׁחֵט, to be killed, slaughtered.

שַׁחֲטָה (šă'ḥᵃṭā') *f* [*inf.* of שָׁחַט for שַׁחַת] corruption.

שְׁחִיטָה (šʼḥīṭā') *f* a killing, slaughter.

שְׁחִין (šʼḥī'n) *m* inflammation, ulcer, carbuncle, elephantiasis.

שָׁחִיס (šāḥī's) = סָחִישׁ after-growth.

שָׁחִיף (šāḥī'f) *m, c.* שְׁחִיף, thin board.

שָׁחִית (šāḥī'ϑ) *f,* only *pl.* שְׁחִיתוֹת, pit.

שַׁחַל (šă'ḥăl) *m* lion.

שְׁחֵלֶת (šʼḥē'lĕϑ) *f* a shell, an odoriferous muscle.

שַׁחַף (šă'ḥăf) *m* an unclean bird, sea-mew.

שַׁחֶפֶת (šăḥĕ'fĕϑ) *f* leanness, consumption.

שַׁחַץ (šă'ḥăẞ) *m* pride, self-reliance.

שַׁחֲצִים (šă'ḥᵃẞī'm) *pr.n.* of a place in Issachar.

שָׁחַק (šāḥă'k) *fut.* יִשְׁחַק, to rub, to pulverise; to defeat, to rout; to wear out, to hollow out.

שַׁחַק (šă'ḥăk) *m, pl.* שְׁחָקִים, dust; thin cloud; vault of heaven, sky.

שָׁחַר (šāḥă'r) *pt.* שֹׁחֵר, to be black; to seek early, to strive after, to desire. — *Pi.* שִׁחֵר, *inf.* שַׁחֵר, *fut.* יְשַׁחֵר, *pt.* מְשַׁחֵר, to seek, to search, to desire; to charm away.

שַׁחַר (šă'ḥăr) *m*, *i.p.* שָׁחַר, *w.s.* שַׁחְרָהּ, the dawn, day-break, early light; בֶּן־שׁ׳ son of the dawn, the morning star, Lucifer.

שָׁחֹר, שָׁחוֹר (šāḥō'r) *adj.*, *pl.* שְׁחֹרִים, *f* שְׁחֹרָה, *pl.* שְׁחֹרוֹת, black, sunburnt, swarthy.

שִׁחֹר see שִׁיחוֹר.

שַׁחֲרוּת (šă'ḥarū'ϑ) *f* dawn [of life = youth]; others: blackness of hair.

שְׁחַרְחֹר (šeḥărḥō'r) *adj.*, *f* שְׁחַרְחֹרֶת, dark, swarthy.

שְׁחַרְיָה (šeḥăryā'); שַׁחֲרַיִם (šă'ḥarā'yĭm) *pr.n.m.*

שָׁחַת (šāḥă'ϑ) *Ni.* נִשְׁחַת, *fut.* יִשָּׁחֵת, to be spoiled, corrupted, marred. — *Pi.* שִׁחֵת, *inf.* and *imp.* שַׁחֵת, to corrupt, destroy, violate, injure, wound, devastate; to act perversely, to be wicked. — *Hi.* הִשְׁחִית, *inf.* הַשְׁחִית, הַשְׁחֵת, *fut.* יַשְׁחִית, *pt.* מַשְׁחִית, to destroy, kill, ruin, corrupt, mar, injure; *pt.* see מַשְׁחִית.

שַׁחַת[1] (šă'ḥăϑ) *f*, *i.p.* שָׁחַת, pit, pit-fall; water-pit, cistern; grave.

שַׁחַת[2] (šă'ḥăϑ) *m* destruction, ruin, corruption.

שִׁטָּה (šĭttā') *f*, *pl.* שִׁטִּים, acacia tree.

שָׁטַח (šāṭă'ḥ) *inf.* שָׁטוֹחַ, *fut.* יִשְׁטַח, *pt.* שֹׁטֵחַ, to expand, spread out. — *Pi.* שִׁטַּח to stretch out.

שֹׁטֵט (šōṭē't) *m* = שֹׁט scourge.

שִׁטִּים (šĭttī'm) *pr.n.* of a place and valley in Moab, opposite Jericho.

שָׁטַף (šāṭă'f) *fut.* יִשְׁטֹף, *pt.* שֹׁטֵף, שׁוֹטֵף, to flow, to rush or pour out abundantly; *tr.* to overflow, wash away, to drown, to overwhelm; to wash, rinse. — *Ni.* *fut.* יִשָּׁטֵף to be overwhelmed; to be washed. — *Pu.* שֻׁטַּף to be rinsed.

שֶׁטֶף (šĕ'ṭĕf), שֵׁטֶף (šē'ṭĕf) *m* an outpouring, gush, inundation, flood.

שָׁטַר (šāṭă'r) *pt.* שֹׁטֵר, *pl.* שֹׁטְרִים, *c.* שֹׁטְרֵי, to write; *pt.* writer, scribe, officer, overseer, prefect, magistrate.

שִׁטְרַי (šĭtrā'y) *pr.n.m.*

שַׁי (šăy) *m* gift, present, tribute.

שִׁיאֹן (šī'ō'n) *pr.n.* of a town in Issachar.

שִׁיבָה[1] (šībā') *f*, *c.* שִׁיבַת, return; returning people.

שִׁיבָה[2] (šībā') *f*, *w.s.* שִׁיבָתוֹ, a dwelling, abiding, stay.

שָׁיָה (šāyā') *fut.* תֶּשִׁי, to forget, neglect.

שְׁיָה (šᵉyā') *pr.n.m.* = שְׁוָא.

שִׁיזָא (šīzā') *pr.n.m.*

שִׁיחָה (šīḥā') *f*, *pl.* שִׁיחוֹת, pit.

שִׁחֹר, שִׁיחֹר, שִׁיחוֹר (šī-ḥō'r) *pr.n.* of the Nile; *pr.n.* = נַחַל מִצְרַיִם brook between Canaan and Egypt.

שִׁיחֹר לִבְנָת (šīḥō'r lībnā'θ) *pr.n.* of a brook in Asher.

שַׁיִט (šă'yīt) *m* oar, rudder; = שׁוֹט scourge.

שִׁלֹו, שִׁלֹה, שִׁילוֹ, שִׁילֹה (šīlō') *pr.n.* of a town in Ephraim; *gent.* שִׁילֹנִי, שִׁלֹנִי.

שֵׁילָל (šēlā'l) *adj.* stripped, bare, barefoot.

שִׁלֹנִי, שִׁילֹנִי see שִׁילֹה and שֵׁלָה[2].

שִׁימוֹן (šīmō'n) *pr.n.m.*

שַׁיִן (šă'yīn) *m*, only *pl. w.s.* שֵׁינֵיהֶם, urine.

שִׁיר[1] (šīr), **שׁוּר** (šūr) *pf.* שָׁר, *inf.* and *imp.* שׁוּר, שִׁיר, *fut.* יָשִׁיר, יָשׁוּר, יָשֹׁר, וַיָּשַׁר, *pt.* שָׁר, *pl.* שָׁרִים, *f* שָׁרוֹת, to sing, praise, celebrate; *pt.* singer. — *Pil.* שׁוֹרֵר, *fut.* יְשׁוֹרֵר, *pt.* מְשׁוֹרֵר, *pl.* מְשֹׁורְרִים, to sing, to resound; *pt.* singer. — *Ho. fut.* יוּשַׁר to be sung.

שִׁיר[2] (šīr) *m*, *w.s.* שִׁירְךָ, שִׁירָה, *pl.* שִׁירִים, singing, song, hymn, poem; שׁ׳ הַשִּׁירִים the song of songs, the Song of Solomon.

שִׁירָה (šīrā') *f*, *c.* שִׁירַת, *pl.* שִׁירוֹת = שִׁיר.

שַׁיִשׁ (šă'yīš) *m* white marble, alabaster.

שִׁישָׁא (šīšā') *pr.n.m.* = שְׁרָיָה.

שִׁישַׁק (šīšă'k) *pr.n.m.* of a king of Egypt, Sheshenk or Sesonchis.

שִׁית[1] (šīθ), **שׁוּת** (šūθ) *pf.* שָׁת, שַׁתָּה [for שָׁתָה], *inf.* שׁוּת, שִׁית, *imp.* שִׁית, *fut.* יָשִׁית, יָשֵׁת, וַיָּשֶׁת, to set, place, lay, put, establish, appoint, direct, constitute, make, produce. — *Ho. fut.* יוּשַׁת to be laid upon.

שִׁית[2] (šīθ) *m* dress, garment.

שַׁיִת (šă'yĭϑ) *m*, *i.p.* שָׁיִת, *w.s.* שִׁיתוֹ, thorn, thorn hedge.

שָׁכַב (šāϕă'ḇ) *inf.* שְׁכֹב, שְׁכַב, *imp.* שְׁכַב, שִׁכְבָה, *fut.* יִשְׁכַּב, *pt.* שֹׁכֵב, *pl.* שֹׁכְבִים, *f* שֹׁכֶבֶת, to lie down, to lie, to rest, to sleep, to lie dead; to lie with, to sleep with.—*Ni.* *fut.* תִּשָּׁכַבְנָה, to be lain with.—*Pu.* שֻׁכַּב the same as *Ni.* — *Hi.* הִשְׁכִּיב, *inf.* הַשְׁכֵּב, *fut.* יַשְׁכִּיב, to lay or set down, to prostrate; to incline or pour out [a vessel]. — *Ho.* *imp.* הָשְׁכְּבָה, *pt.* מֻשְׁכָּב, to be laid, prostrated.

שְׁכָבָה (š'ϕāḇā') *f*, *c.* שִׁכְבַת, a pouring out, effusion, emission.

שְׁכֹבֶת (š'ϕō'ḇĕϑ) *f* emission [of seed]; others: a lying down.

שָׁכָה (šāϕā') *Hi.* *pt.* *pl.* מַשְׁכִּים, to be mad, voluptuous.

שְׁכוֹל (š'ϕō'l) *m* childlessness, abandonment.

שַׁכּוּל (šăkkū'l) *adj.*, *f* שַׁכֻּלָה, *pl.* שַׁכֻּלוֹת, bereaved of children, childless.

שִׁכּוֹר, **שִׁכֹּר** (šĭkkō'r) *adj.*, *pl.* שִׁכּוֹרִים, *c.* שִׁכֹּרֵי, *f* שִׁכֹּרָה, drunk, intoxicated.

שָׁכַח (šāϕă'ḥ), שָׁכֵחַ[1] (šāϕē'aḥ) *imp.* *f* שִׁכְחִי, *fut.* יִשְׁכַּח, *pt.* שֹׁכֵחַ, *pl.* *c.* שֹׁכְחֵי, to forget, forsake. — *Ni.* נִשְׁכַּח, *fut.* יִשָּׁכַח, יִשָּׁכֵחַ, *pt.* נִשְׁכָּח, *f* נִשְׁכָּחָה, נִשְׁכַּחַת, to be forgotten, forsaken. — *Pi.* שִׁכַּח and *Hi.* *inf.* הַשְׁכִּיחַ to cause to forget. — *Hith.* הִשְׁתַּכַּח to be forgotten.

שָׁכֵחַ[2] (šāϕē'aḥ) *adj.*, *pl.* שְׁכֵחִים, *c.* שְׁכֵחֵי, forgetting, forgotten.

שְׁכַיָה (šŏϕyā') *pr.n.m.*

שָׁכַךְ (šāϕă'ϕ) *inf.* שַׁךְ, שֹׁךְ, *fut.* יָשֹׁךְ, *pl.* יָשֹׁכּוּ, to decrease, to subside; to crouch.—*Hi.* הֵשֵׁךְ to still, to calm.

שָׁכֹל (šāϕō'l) *pf.* 1. *sg.* שָׁכֹלְתִּי, *i.p.* שָׁכָלְתִּי, *fut.* יִשְׁכַּל, *pt.* *p.* *f* שְׁכוּלָה, to be or become childless; *pt.* *p.* childless, forsaken. — *Pi.* שִׁכֵּל, *fut.* יְשַׁכֵּל, *pt.* *f* מְשַׁכֶּלֶת, מְשַׁכֵּלָה, to make childless, to bereave of children, to cause abortion; to miscarry; to be barren.

— *Hi. pt.* מַשְׁכִּיל to make childless, to miscarry.

שִׁכֻּלִים (šĭkkūlī'm) *m/pl., w.s.* שִׁכֻּלַיִךְ, childlessness.

שָׁכַם (šāḏă'm) *Hi.* הִשְׁכִּים, *inf.* הַשְׁכֵּם, הַשְׁכִּים, *imp.* הַשְׁכֵּם, *fut.* יַשְׁכִּים, יַשְׁכֵּם, *pt.* מַשְׁכִּים [*prop.* to load on the shoulders early], to rise early, to do a thing early in the morning.

שְׁכֶם¹ (šᵉḏĕ'm) *m, i.p.* שֶׁכֶם, *w.s.* שִׁכְמוֹ, back, neck, shoulder; tract of land, shoulder of a mountain.

שְׁכֶם² (šᵉḏĕ'm) *pr.n.* of a city in Ephraim, Shechem; *w. loc.* ה שְׁכֶמָה.

שֶׁכֶם (šĕ'ḏĕm) *pr.n.m.*; *patr.* שִׁכְמִי.

שִׁכְמָה (šĭḏmā') *f* — שְׁכֶם¹.

שָׁכַן (šāḏă'n), **שָׁכֵן¹** (šāḏē'n) *inf.* שְׁכֹן, *w.s.* שָׁכְנִי (šŏḏnī'), *imp.* שְׁכֹן, *fut.* יִשְׁכֹּן, יִשְׁכּוֹן, *pt.* שֹׁכֵן, *pl.* שֹׁכְנִים, *pt. p. m/pl. c.* שְׁכוּנֵי, to settle down, to lie down, to rest, to abide, remain, dwell, inhabit, possess; *pt. p.* settled down, dwelling. — *Pi.* שִׁכֵּן, *inf.* שַׁכֵּן, *fut.* יְשַׁכֵּן, to cause to dwell, to set up. — *Hi.* הִשְׁכִּין, *fut.* יַשְׁכֵּן, יַשְׁכִּין, to cause to dwell, to lay down.

שָׁכֵן² (šāḏē'n) *adj., c.* שְׁכַן, *w.s.* שְׁכֵנוֹ, *pl.* שְׁכֵנִים, *f* שְׁכֵנָה, *w.s.* שְׁכֶנְתָּהּ, *pl.* שְׁכֵנוֹת, dwelling, abiding; inhabitant, neighbour.

שֶׁכֶן (šĕ'ḏĕn) *m, w.s.* שִׁכְנוֹ, a dwelling.

שְׁכַנְיָה (šᵉḏănyā'), **שְׁכַנְיָהוּ** (šᵉḏănyā'hū) *pr.n.m.*

שָׁכַר (šāḏă'r) *inf.* שָׁכְרָה (šŏḏrā'), *fut.* יִשְׁכַּר, *pt. p. f c.* שְׁכֻרַת, to drink [wine], to be drunk, intoxicated; *pt. p.* drunken. — *Pi.* שִׁכֵּר, *inf.* שַׁכֵּר, *fut.* יְשַׁכֵּר, *pt. f* מְשַׁכֶּרֶת, to make drunk, to intoxicate. — *Hi.* הִשְׁכִּיר, *fut.* יַשְׁכִּיר, the same as *Pi.* — *Hith. fut.* 2. *sg. f* תִּשְׁתַּכָּרִין to behave like a drunken one.

שֵׁכָר (šēḏā'r) *m* strong, intoxicating drink [wine, mead, &c.].

שִׁכֹּר see שִׁכּוֹר.

שִׁכָּרוֹן¹ (šĭkkārō'n) *m* drunkenness.

שִׁכָּרוֹן² (šĭkkārō'n) *pr.n.* of a town in Judah.

שַׁל (šăl) *m* transgression, fault, crime.

שֶׁל (šĕl) a particle denoting relation, composed of שֶׁ [= אֲשֶׁר] and לְ; בְּשֶׁל because of, on account of, בְּשֶׁלִּי because of me; בְּשֶׁלְּמִי on whose account?

שַׁלְאֲנָן (šăl'ănā'n) *adj.* tranquil, quiet.

שָׁלַב (šālă'b) *Pu.* שֻׁלַּב, *pt.* *f/pl.* מְשֻׁלָּבֹת, to be jointed or fitted together.

שָׁלָב (šālā'b) *m*, only *pl.* שְׁלַבִּים, connecting piece, joint-ledge.

שָׁלַג (šālă'g) *Hi. fut.* יַשְׁלֵג, to produce snow, to snow.

שֶׁלֶג (šĕ'lĕg) *m*, *i.p.* שָׁלֶג, snow.

שָׁלָה¹ (šālā'), שָׁלֵו (šālă'v) *fut. pl.* יִשְׁלָיוּ, to be quiet, tranquil, at ease. — *Ni.* *fut.* יִשָּׁלֶה to be secure, negligent. — *Hi. fut.* יַשְׁלֶה to deceive, seduce.

שָׁלָה² (šālā') *fut.* יֵשֶׁל, to draw out.

שֵׁלָה¹ (šēlā') = שְׁאֵלָה.

שֵׁלָה² (šēlā') *pr.n.m.*; *patr.* שֵׁלָנִי, שִׁלֹנִי.

שִׁלֹה see שִׁילֹה.

שַׁלְהֶבֶת (šălhĕ'bĕth) *f* flame; שַׁלְהֶבֶתְיָה flame of יָהּ.

שָׁלֵו, שָׁלֵו¹ see שָׁלָה¹.

שָׁלֵו² (šālē'v) *adj.*, *pl. c.* שַׁלְוֵי, quiet, tranquil, contented; forgetful, careless.

שֶׁלֶו (šĕ'lĕv) *m*, *w.s.* שַׁלְוִי, tranquillity, ease.

שַׁלְוָה (šălvā') *f* tranquillity, security, rest, carelessness; בְּשׁ׳ unexpectedly.

שִׁלּוּחַ (šĭllū'ăch) *m*, only *pl.* שִׁלּוּחִים, dismission, repudiation [of a wife]; bill of divorce; dowry.

שָׁלוֹם (šālō'm) *m*, *c.* שְׁלוֹם, *w.s.* שְׁלוֹמִי, *pl.* שְׁלוֹמִים, health, welfare, good condition, success, comfort; peace, salvation; *adj.* well, peaceful, secure, whole.

שַׁלּוּם, שַׁלֻּם (šăllū'm) *pr.n.m.*

שִׁלּוּם, שִׁלֻּם (šĭllū'm) *m*, *pl.* שִׁלּוּמִים, requital.

שַׁלּוּן (šăllū'n) *pr.n.m.*

שָׁלוֹשׁ see שָׁלֹשׁ.

שָׁלַח (šālă'ch) *inf.* שְׁלֹחַ, שְׁלֹחַ, שָׁלְחָה, שְׁלֹחַ, *imp.* שְׁלַח, שְׁלַח, *fut.* יִשְׁלַח, *pt.* שֹׁלֵחַ, *w.s.* שֹׁלַחֲךָ, *pt. p.* שָׁלוּחַ, *f* שְׁלוּחָה, to stretch out, to extend, to send, to send away, to withdraw; to send word; *pt. p.* stretched out, tall [others: let loose, roaming at large]. — *Ni. inf.* נִשְׁלוֹחַ to be sent. — *Pi.* שִׁלַּח, *inf.* שַׁלַּח, שַׁלֵּחַ, *w.s.* שַׁלְּחוֹ, *imp.* שַׁלַּח, *fut.* יְשַׁלַּח, *pt.* מְשַׁלֵּחַ, to send away or forth, to despatch; to dismiss, to set free; to cast, to shoot; to let down; to expel, reject; to stretch out. — *Pu.* שֻׁלַּח, *fut.* יְשֻׁלַּח, *pt.* מְשֻׁלָּח, to be sent, to be sent away, dismissed, to be let free; to be scared, abandoned, forsaken. — *Hi.* הִשְׁלִיחַ, *inf.* הַשְׁלִיחַ, *pt.* מַשְׁלִיחַ, to send.

שֶׁלַח[1] (šĕ'lăḥ) *m* missile, javelin; **sprout,** shoot, child.

שֶׁלַח[2] (šĕ'lăḥ) *pr.n.m.*

שִׁלֹחַ (šīlō'aḥ) *pr.n.* of a pond and aqueduct on the south-east of Jerusalem, Shiloah.

שְׁלֻחָה (šᵉlūḥā') *f*, only *pl.* שְׁלֻחוֹת, shoot, sprout.

שִׁלְחִי (šīlḥī') *pr.n.m.*

שִׁלְחִים (šīlḥī'm) *pr.n.* of a town in Judah.

שֻׁלְחָן (šŭlḥā'n) *m*, *c.* שֻׁלְחַן, *w.s.* שֻׁלְחָנִי, *pl.* שֻׁלְחָנוֹת, what is spread out, mat, table; table of God, altar; שֻׁ׳ הַמַּעֲרֶכֶת, שֻׁ׳ הַפָּנִים table of the shewbread.

שָׁלַט (šālă't) *inf.* שְׁלוֹט, *fut.* יִשְׁלֹט, to rule, to have dominion over. — *Hi. fut.* יַשְׁלִיט־, תַּשְׁלֶט, to give power, to permit, to let rule.

שֶׁלֶט (šĕ'lĕt) *m*, *pl.* שְׁלָטִים, *c.* שִׁלְטֵי, a shield.

שִׁלְטוֹן (šīltō'n) *adj.* having power [others: *m* power].

שַׁלֶּטֶת (šallĕ'tĕth) see שַׁלִּיט.

שְׁלִי (šᵉlī') *m*, *i.p.* שֶׁלִי, rest, quiet.

שִׁלְיָה (šīlyā') *f*, *w.s.* שִׁלְיָתָהּ, after-birth.

שָׁלֵיו see שָׁלֵו[2].

שַׁלִּיט (šallī't) *adj.*, *pl.* שַׁלִּיטִים, *f* שַׁלֶּטֶת, having power, imperious; a ruler, magistrate.

שָׁלִישׁ. שָׁלִשׁ (šālī'š) *m*, *pl.* שָׁלִישִׁים, third part, a dry-measure [1/3 ephah]; *adv.* by measure, abundantly; *pl.* a musical instrument, triangle or trichord; a hero, chariot-warrior.

שְׁלִישִׁי, שְׁלִשִׁי (šᵉlīšī') *adj.*

num. m, pl. שְׁלִשִׁים, *f* שְׁלִישִׁת, שְׁלִשִׁיָּה, שְׁלִישִׁיָּה, the third, third part, third time, third day, third story.

שָׁלַךְ (šālă'ḏ) *Hi.* הִשְׁלִיךְ, *inf.* הַשְׁלֵךְ, הַשְׁלִיךְ, *imp.* הַשְׁלֵךְ, הַשְׁלִיכוּ, *fut.* יַשְׁלִיךְ, יַשְׁלֵךְ, *pt.* מַשְׁלִיךְ, *pl. c.* מַשְׁלִיכֵי, to throw, to cast, to cast off, away, down; to overthrow, to expel, reject.— *Ho.* הָשְׁלַךְ, הָשְׁלֵךְ, *fut.* יָשְׁלַךְ, *pt.* מֻשְׁלָךְ, *f* מֻשְׁלֶכֶת, to be thrown, to be cast out or down, to be destroyed.

שָׁלָךְ (šālā'ḏ) *m* a pelican.

שַׁלֶּכֶת¹ (šăllĕ'ḏĕϑ) *f* the felling [of a tree].

שַׁלֶּכֶת² (šăllĕ'ḏĕϑ) *pr.n.* of a gate leading to the temple.

שָׁלַל (šālă'l) *inf.* שְׁלֹל, שֹׁל, *fut. pl.* תָּשֹׁלּוּ, *pt.* שֹׁלֵל, to draw out, to plunder, to rob. — *Ni. fut.* יִשַּׁל to fall off [fruits], or from נָשַׁל. — *Hith.* הִשְׁתּוֹלֵל to be plundered, to become a prey.

שָׁלָל (šālā'l) *m, c.* שְׁלַל, *w.s.* שְׁלָלְכֶם, booty, spoil, gain.

שָׁלַם (šālă'm), שָׁלֵם¹ (šālē'm) *fut.* יִשְׁלַם, *pt.* שָׁלֵם, *w.s.* שְׁלֵמִי, *pt. p. pl. c.* שְׁלֻמֵי, to be whole, uninjured, safe and sound, peaceful, friendly. — *Pi.* שִׁלֵּם, *inf.* שַׁלֵּם, *w.s.* שַׁלְּמִי, *imp.* שַׁלֵּם, שַׁלְּמִי, *fut.* יְשַׁלֵּם, *pt.* מְשַׁלֵּם, *pl. c.* מְשַׁלְּמֵי, to complete, to restore, to give back, repay, requite, reward.. — *Pu.* שֻׁלַּם, *fut.* יְשֻׁלַּם, *pt.* מְשֻׁלָּם, to be paid, repaid, requited, rewarded; to be at friendship. — *Hi.* הִשְׁלִים, *fut.* יַשְׁלִם, יַשְׁלֵם, יַשְׁלִים, to complete, perform, finish; to make or have peace; to submit. — *Ho.* הָשְׁלַם to be a friend.

שָׁלֵם² (šālē'm) *adj., pl.* שְׁלֵמִים, *f* שְׁלֵמָה, *pl.* שְׁלֵמוֹת, whole, complete, uninjured, unhewn; peaceful, friendly.

שָׁלֵם³ (šālē'm) *pr.n.* of a city = יְרוּשָׁלַםִ.

שַׁלֻם see שָׁלוֹם.

שֶׁלֶם (šĕ'lĕm) *m, pl.* שְׁלָמִים, *c.* שַׁלְמֵי, requital, thanks; *pl.* mostly after זֶבַח thank-offering, peace-offering.

שִׁלֵּם[1] (šĭllē'm) *m* requital, recompense.

שִׁלֵּם[2] (šĭllē'm) *pr.n.m.*

שִׁלֹּם see שָׁלוֹם.

שִׁלֻּמָה (šĭllūmā') *f, c.* שִׁלֻּמַת, requital, punishment.

שְׁלֹמֹה (šelōmō') *pr.n.m.*, Solomon.

שְׁלֹמִי (šelōmī'); שְׁלֻמִיאֵל (šelū'mī'ēl); שֶׁלֶמְיָהוּ (šĕ'lĕm-yā'hū) *pr.n.m.*

שְׁלֹמִית (šelōmī'ϑ) *pr.n.f.* and *m.*

שַׁלְמַן (šălmă'n), שַׁלְמַנְאֶסֶר (šălmăn'ĕ'sĕr) *pr.n.m.* of an Assyrian king.

שַׁלְמֹן (šălmō'n) *m*, only *pl.* שַׁלְמֹנִים, gift, bribe.

שָׁלַף (šālă'f) *imp.* שְׁלֹף, *fut.* יִשְׁלֹף, *pt.* שֹׁלֵף, *pt. p. f* שְׁלוּפָה, to draw out, to pull off.

שֶׁלֶף (šĕ'lĕf) *pr.n.m.*, son of Joktan, a tribe in southern Arabia.

שָׁלַשׁ (šālă'š) *Pi.* שִׁלֵּשׁ, *imp.* שַׁלֵּשׁ, *fut.* יְשַׁלֵּשׁ, to divide into three parts, to do for the third time, on the third day.— *Pu. pt.* מְשֻׁלָּשׁ, *f* מְשֻׁלֶּשֶׁת, *pl.* מְשֻׁלָּשׁוֹת, to be threefold, to be three years old.

שָׁלוֹשׁ, שָׁלֹשׁ (šālō'š) *num. f*, *c.* שְׁלֹשׁ, *m* שְׁלוֹשָׁה, שְׁלֹשָׁה, *c.* שְׁלֹשֶׁת, three; *pl.* שְׁלֹשִׁים thirty, the thirtieth.

שִׁלֵּשׁ (šĭllē'š) *m*, only *pl.* שִׁלֵּשִׁים, descendants in the third generation, great grand-children.

שֵׁלֶשׁ (šē'lĕš); שִׁלְשָׁה (šĭlšā') *pr.n.m.*

שָׁלִשָׁה (šā'lĭšā') *pr.n.* of a district near the mountains of Ephraim.

שִׁלְשׁוֹם, שִׁלְשֹׁם (šĭlšō'm) *adv.* three days ago, the day before yesterday, formerly.

שְׁאַלְתִּיאֵל — שַׁלְתִּיאֵל.

שָׁם (šām) *adv.* there, then, *w. loc.* ה שָׁמָּה thither, hither; אֲשֶׁר־שָׁם where; מִשָּׁם thence, since; אֲשֶׁר מִשָּׁם whence.

שֵׁם[1] (šēm) *m, w.s.* שְׁמִי, שְׁמוֹ [שְׁמֵהוּ], *pl.* שֵׁמוֹת, *c.* שְׁמוֹת, sign, memorial, token; name, fame, renown; שֵׁם יָהּ the name, essence, honour of God.

שֵׁם[2] (šēm) *pr.n.m.*

שַׁמָּא (šămmā'); שֶׁמְאֵבֶר (šĕm'ē'bĕr); שִׁמְאָה (šĭm'ā'); שַׁמְגַּר (šămgă'r) *pr.n.m.*

שָׁמַד (šāmă'd) *Ni.* נִשְׁמַד, *inf.* הִשָּׁמֵד, *fut.* יִשָּׁמֵד, to be laid waste, to be destroyed, annihilated; *inf.* destruction. — *Hi.* הִשְׁמִיד, *inf.* הַשְׁמֵד, הַשְׁמִיד [לַשְׁמִד for לְהַשְׁמִיד], *imp.* הַשְׁמֵד, *fut.* יַשְׁמִיד, יַשְׁמֵד, to destroy, to waste, to extirpate.

שַׁמָּה[1] (šămmā') *f, pl.* שַׁמּוֹת, astonishment, horror; desolation, ruin.

שַׁמָּה[2] (šămmā'); שְׁמוּאֵל (šᵉmū'ē'l) Samuel, *pr.n.m.*

שְׁמוּעָה, שְׁמֻעָה (šᵉmū'ā') *f, c.* שְׁמֻעַת, *pl.* שְׁמֻעוֹת, a hearing, something heard, report, news, announcement, message, instruction.

שָׁמוּר (šāmū'r) *pr.n.m.*

שָׁמַט (šāmă't) *imp. pl.* שִׁמְטוּ, *fut.* יִשְׁמֹט, to throw, cast, fling; to neglect, to let lie unused, untilled; to leave [work]. — *Ni.* נִשְׁמַט to be cast or hurled down. — *Hi. fut.* יַשְׁמֵט to release, to let loose.

שְׁמִטָּה (šᵉmĭttā') *f* remission, release; שְׁנַת הַשׁ׳ year of release, sabbath-year.

שַׁמַּי (šămmă'y); שְׁמִידָע (šᵉmĭdā''), *patr.* שְׁמִידָעִי, *pr.n.m.*

שָׁמַיִם (šāmă'yĭm) *pl. m, i.p.* שָׁמָיִם, *w. loc.* ה שָׁמַיְמָה, *c.* שְׁמֵי, *w.s.* שָׁמֶיךָ, height, heaven, sky.

שְׁמִינִי (šᵉmĭnī') *adj. num. m, f* שְׁמִינִית, the eighth; *f* the octave [in music].

שָׁמִיר[1] (šāmī'r) *m, w.s.* שְׁמִירוֹ, thorn, thorn-bush; diamond.

שָׁמִיר[2] (šāmī'r) *pr.n.* of a town in Judah; *pr.n.m.*

שְׁמִירָמוֹת (šᵉmī'rāmō'ϑ) *pr. n.m.*

שָׁמַם (šāmă'm), שָׁמֵם (šāmē'm), *imp.* שֹׁם, *fut.* יִשֹּׁם, יִשֹּׁם, יֵשַׁם, יֵישַׁם, *pt.* [or *Po.*] שׁוֹמֵם, שֹׁמֵם, *pl.* שׁוֹמֵמִים, *f* שׁוֹמֵמָה, *pl.* שׁוֹמֵמוֹת, *c.* שְׁמָמוֹת, to be astonished, stupefied; to be desolate, waste, solitary, depopulated. — *Ni.* נָשַׁם, *pt. f* נְשַׁמָּה, *pl.* נְשַׁמּוֹת, the same as *Q.* — *Po. pt.* מְשׁוֹמֵם to be astonished, stunned; to destroy, to lay waste. — *Hi.* הֵשַׁם, *pl.* הֵשַׁמּוּ, *inf.* הַשְׁמֵם, *fut.* יָשֵׁם, יַשִּׁים, *pt.* מַשְׁמִים, to be astonished; to lay waste, destroy. — *Ho.* הָשַּׁם (hŏššā'm) the same as *Q.* — *Hith.* הִשְׁתּוֹמֵם to be astonished, benumbed; to despair, to ruin oneself.

שָׁמֵם (šāmē'm) *adj.* waste, desolate.

שְׁמָמָה (šᵉmāmā') *f, pl. c.* שִׁמְמוֹת, שְׁמָמוֹת, astonishment, horror, desolation, devastation.

שִׁמֲמָה (šĭ'mᵃmā') = שְׁמָמָה.

שִׁמָּמוֹן (šĭmmāmō'n) *m* astonishment, stupor.

שָׁמַן (šāmā'n) *fut.* יִשְׁמַן, to be or become fat. — *Hi.* הִשְׁמִין, *inf.* הַשְׁמֵן, *fut.* יַשְׁמִין, to make fat, unfeeling; to become fat.

שָׁמֵן (šāmē'n) *adj., f* שְׁמֵנָה, fat, stout, fertile, rich.

שָׁמָן (šāmā'n) *m,* only *pl.* שְׁמַנִּים, *c.* שְׁמַנֵּי, fatness, fertility, fat or rich soil.

שֶׁמֶן (šĕ'mĕn) *m, i.p.* שָׁמֶן, *w.s.* שַׁמְנִי, *pl.* שְׁמָנִים, fatness, fat, fat food; fertility, strength; oil, ointment.

שְׁמֹנֶה, **שְׁמוֹנֶה** (šᵉmōnĕ') *num. f, m* שְׁמֹנָה, *c.* שְׁמֹנַת, eight; *pl.* שְׁמֹנִים, שְׁמוֹנִים, eighty.

שָׁמַע (šāmă'ᵃ), שָׁמֵעַ (šāmē'aᵃ) *inf.* שָׁמוֹעַ, שְׁמוֹעַ, שְׁמֹעַ, *imp.* שְׁמַע, שִׁמְעָה, *fut.* יִשְׁמַע, *pt.* שֹׁמֵעַ, שׁוֹמֵעַ, שָׁמֵעַ, *w.s.* שֹׁמְעוֹ, *pl.* שֹׁמְעִים, *f* שֹׁמַעַת, to hear, to lend an ear to, to listen, to attend; to understand, to obey. — *Ni.* נִשְׁמַע, *inf.* הִשָּׁמַע, *fut.* יִשָּׁמַע, *pt.* נִשְׁמָע, *f* נִשְׁמַעַת, to be heard, to be listened to; to obey; to be understood. — *Pi.* שִׁמַּע, *fut.* יְשַׁמַּע, to make hear, to call. — *Hi.* הִשְׁמִיעַ, *inf.* הַשְׁמִיעַ [לַשְׁמִעַ for לְהַשְׁמִיעַ], *imp.* הַשְׁמִיעוּ, *fut.* יַשְׁמִיעַ, יַשְׁמַע, *pt.* מַשְׁמִיעַ, to cause to hear, to make heard; to sound, call, cry, sing, announce, summon.

שָׁמָע (šāmā'ᵃ) *pr.n.m.*

שֵׁמַע (šē'măᵃ) *m, i.p.* שָׁמַע, *w.s.* שִׁמְעִי, a hearing, sound, report, fame, account, announcement.

שֶׁמַע (šĕ'măᵃ) *pr.n.m.*

שְׁמָע (šᵉmā'ᵃ) *pr.n.* of a town in Judah.

שֵׁמַע (šē'mă') *m*, *w.s.* שָׁמְעוֹ (šŏm'ō') report, rumour.

שִׁמְעָא, שִׁמְעָה (šĭm'ā'), *patr.* שִׁמְעָתִי, *pl.* שִׁמְעָתִים; שְׁמָעָה (š'mā'ā'); שִׁמְעוֹן (šĭm'ō'n); שִׁמְעִי (šĭm'ī'); שְׁמַעְיָה (š'mă'yā'), שְׁמַעְיָהוּ (š'mă'yā'hū) *pr.n.m.*

שִׁמְעָת (šĭm'ā'ϑ) *pr.n.f.*

שֶׁמֶץ (šĕ'mĕß), שֵׁמֶץ (šē'-mĕß) *m* and שִׁמְצָה (šĭmßā') *f* whisper, a whispering, mocking, mischievous joy.

שָׁמַר (šāmă'r) *inf.* שְׁמֹר, *imp.* שְׁמֹר, שִׁמְרָה, *fut.* יִשְׁמֹר, *pt.* שֹׁמֵר, שׁוֹמֵר, *pl.* שֹׁמְרִים, *c.* שֹׁמְרֵי, *pt. p.* שָׁמוּר, *f* שְׁמֻרָה, to watch, to keep, to guard, to retain; to observe, regard, attend. — *Ni.* נִשְׁמַר, *imp.* הִשָּׁמֶר, הִשָּׁמֵר, *fut.* יִשָּׁמֵר, to be kept, guarded; to take heed, to beware. — *Pi. pt.* מְשַׁמֵּר, to honour, to worship.— *Hith.* הִשְׁתַּמֵּר to take heed; to observe, to keep.

שָׁמָר (šāmā'r) or שֶׁמֶר[1] (šĕ'mĕr) *m*, only *pl.* שְׁמָרִים, dregs, lees; old wine.

שֶׁמֶר[2] (šĕ'mĕr) *pr.n.m.*

שִׁמֻּר (šĭmmū'r) *m*, only *pl.* שִׁמֻּרִים, observance, celebration.

שֹׁמֵר[1] (šōmē'r) *m* keeper, watch, see שָׁמַר *Q. pt.*

שֹׁמֵר[2] (šōmē'r) *pr.n.m.* and *f.*

שְׁמֻרָה (š'mūrā') *f*, only *pl.* שְׁמֻרוֹת, eyelid.

שָׁמְרָה (šŏmrā') *f* watch, guard.

שִׁמְרוֹן (šĭmrō'n) *pr.n.m.*, *patr.* שִׁמְרֹנִי; *pr.n.* of a town in northern Canaan.

שֹׁמְרוֹן (šō'm'rō'n) *pr.n.f.* of the chief city in the kingdom of Israel, Samaria; the kingdom itself.

שִׁמְרִי (šĭmrī'); שְׁמַרְיָה (š'-măryā'), שְׁמַרְיָהוּ (š'măryā'hū); שִׁמְרָת (šĭmrā'ϑ) *pr.n.m.*

שִׁמְרִית (šĭmrī'ϑ) *pr.n.f.*

שֶׁמֶשׁ (šĕ'mĕš) *m* and *f*; *i.p.* שָׁמֶשׁ, *w.s.* שִׁמְשֵׁךְ, *pl.* *w.s.* שִׁמְשֹׁתַיִךְ, the sun, sunlight, daylight; *pl.* battlements, pinnacles.

שִׁמְשׁוֹן (šĭmšō'n) Samson; שִׁמְשַׁי (šĭmšă'y); שַׁמְשְׁרַי (šămš'ră'y) *pr.n.m.*

שֻׁמָתִי (šū'māϑī') *pr.n.m.*, *patr.* of an unknown שֻׁמָה.

שֵׁן[1] (šēn) *m* and *f*, *c.* שֶׁן־, *w.s.* שִׁנּוֹ, *du.* שִׁנַּיִם, *c.* שִׁנֵּי,

pl. שִׁנַּיִם, tooth; elephant's tooth, ivory; point of a rock, peak; point of a fork.

שֵׁן[2] (šēn) *pr.n.* of a place.

שָׁנָא see שָׁנָה[1].

שֵׁנָא — שֵׁנָה sleep.

שִׁנְאָב (šĭn'ā'b); **שֶׁנְאַצַּר** (šĕn'ăbbă'r) *pr.n.m.*

שִׁנְאָן (šĭn'ā'n) *m* repetition.

שָׁנָה[1], also שָׁנָא (šānā'), *inf.* שְׁנוֹת, *imp. pl.* שְׁנוּ, *fut.* יִשְׁנֶה, יִשְׁנֶא, *pt.* שֹׁנֶה, *pl.* שׁוֹנִים, *f* שֹׁנוֹת, to double, to do again, to repeat; to be different, to change. — *Ni. inf.* הִשָּׁנוֹת to be repeated. — *Pi.* שִׁנָּה, שִׁנָּא, *inf.* שַׁנּוֹת, *fut.* יְשַׁנֶּה, *pt.* מְשַׁנֶּה, to change [*tr.*], to alter, to pervert, to transfer. — *Pu.* שֻׁנָּא to be changed, improved. — *Hith.* הִשְׁתַּנָּה to disguise oneself.

שָׁנָה[2] (šānā') *f*, *c.* שְׁנַת, *du.* שְׁנָתַיִם, *pl.* שָׁנִים, *c.* שְׁנֵי, *pl.* שָׁנוֹת, *c.* שְׁנוֹת [repetition] year.

שֵׁנָה (šēnā') *f*, *c.* שְׁנַת, *w.s.* שְׁנָתִי, *pl.* שֵׁנוֹת, sleep.

שֶׁנְהַבִּים (šĕnhăbbī'm) *pl. m* ivory.

שָׁנִי (šānī') *m*, *c.* שְׁנִי, *pl.* שָׁנִים, crimson colour, crimson-coloured stuff.

שֵׁנִי (šēnī') *adj. num. m*, *pl.* שֵׁנִים, *f* שֵׁנִית, the second, the other; *f* a second time.

שְׁנַיִם (šᵉnă'yĭm) *num. du. m*, *i.p.* שְׁנָיִם, *c.* שְׁנֵי, *f* שְׁתַּיִם (štă'yĭm), *c.* שְׁתֵּי, two, both, a pair.

שְׁנֵים עָשָׂר (šᵉnē'm 'āsā'r), שְׁנֵי עָשָׂר, *num. m*, *f* שְׁתֵּים עֶשְׂרֵה, twelve, the twelfth.

שְׁנִינָה (šᵉnīnā') *f* sharp word, mockery.

שְׂנִיר — שְׂנִיר.

שָׁנַן (šānă'n) *pt. p.* שָׁנוּן, to sharpen, to point. — *Pi.* שִׁנֵּן to enforce, inculcate. — *Hith.* הִשְׁתּוֹנֵן to be stung, pierced, vexed.

שָׁנַס (šānă's) *Pi. fut.* יְשַׁנֵּס, to gird.

שִׁנְעָר (šĭn'ā'r) *pr.n.m.*, Babylonia.

שְׁנָת (šᵉnā'ϑ) *f* = שֵׁנָה sleep.

שָׁסָה (šāsā') *fut.* יִשְׁסֶה, *pt.* שֹׁסֶה, *w.s.* שֹׁסֵהוּ, *pl.* שֹׁסִים, *c.* שֹׁסֵי, *pt. p.* שָׁסוּי, to plunder, rob, spoil. — *Po.* שׁוֹסֵה, 1. *sg.* שׁוֹשֵׂתִי [for שׁוֹסַתִי], the same as *Q.*

שָׁסַס (šāsă's) — שָׁסָה, *fut. pl.* יָשֹׁסּוּ, *pt.* שֹׁאֵס [for שֹׁסֵס], to plunder, to rob. — *Ni. fut. pl.* יִשַּׁסּוּ to be plundered.

שָׁסַע (šāsă'') *pt.* שֹׁסֵעַ, שֹׁסַע, *f* שֹׁסַעַת, *pt. p.* שָׁסוּעַ, *f* שְׁסוּעָה, to split, to cleave. — *Pi.* שִׁסַּע, *inf.* שַׁסַּע, *fut.* יְשַׁסַּע, to tear asunder, to tear to pieces; to chide.

שֶׁסַע (šĕ'să') *m* cleft, fissure.

שָׁסַף (šāsă'f) *Pi. fut.* יְשַׁסֵּף, to cut in pieces, to chop up

שָׁעָה (šā'ā') *imp.* שְׁעֵה, שְׁעוּ, *fut.* יִשְׁעֶה, יִשַׁע, to look, to look about, at, upon; to observe, regard; to look away from. — *Hi. imp.* הָשַׁע to look away from. — *Hith. fut.* יִשְׁתַּע to look about, to look at one another.

שְׁעָטָה (š''ătā') *f, c.* שַׁעֲטַת, a stamping, tramping.

שַׁעַטְנֵז (šă''ătnē'z) *m* cloth woven of different threads, wool and linen mixed.

שֹׁעַל (šō''ăl) *m, w.s.* שָׁעֳלוֹ (šŏ''olō'), *pl.* שְׁעָלִים, *c.* שַׁעֲלֵי, the hollow of the hand, a handful.

שַׁעַלְבִּים (šă''ălbī'm) *pr.n.* of a town in Dan; *gent.* שַׁעַלְבֹנִי.

שַׁעֲלִים (šă''ălī'm) *pr.n.* of a district in Benjamin.

שָׁעַן (šā'ă'n) *Ni.* נִשְׁעַן, *inf.* הִשָּׁעֵן, *imp. pl.* הִשָּׁעֲנוּ, to lean or support oneself, to rest on, to rely on; to adjoin, to lie near.

שָׁעַע [1] (šā'ă'') *imp. pl.* שֹׁעוּ, to be besmeared [on the eyes], to be blind. — *Hi. imp.* הָשַׁע to besmear, to blind. — *Hith. imp.* הִשְׁתַּעַשְׁעוּ to be besmeared, blinded.

שָׁעַע [2] (šā'ă'') *Pilp.* שִׁעֲשַׁע, *fut. pl.* יְשַׁעַשְׁעוּ, to make glad, to delight, to caress; to play, to amuse oneself. — *Polp. fut. pl.* תְּשָׁעֳשָׁעוּ (t'šŏ''ošā''ū) to be caressed. — *Hith. fut.* יִשְׁתַּעֲשַׁע, to delight in.

שַׁעַף (šă''ăf) *pr.n.m.*

שָׁעַר (šā'ă'r) to think, to estimate.

שַׁעַר [1] (šă''ăr) *m* and *f, i.p.* שָׁעַר, *w. loc.* ה שַׁעְרָה, *du.* שַׁעֲרַיִם, *pl.* שְׁעָרִים, *c.* שַׁעֲרֵי, gate, entrance, forum.

שַׁעַר[2] (šă''ăr) *m*, *pl.* שְׁעָרִים, measure.

שֹׁעָר (šọ'ā'r) *adj.*, only *pl.* שֹׁעָרִים, horrid, harsh, bad.

שֹׁעָר see שׁוֹעָר.

שַׁעֲרוּר (šă''ərū'r) *adj.*, only *f* שַׁעֲרוּרָה, horrible; a horrible thing.

שַׁעֲרוּרִי (šă''ərūrī') *adj.*, only *f* שַׁעֲרוּרִיָּה, horrible.

שְׁעַרְיָה (šᵉ'ăryā') *pr.n.m.*

שַׁעֲרַיִם (šă''ərā'yīm) *pr.n.* of towns in Judah and Simeon.

שַׁעַשְׁגַז (šă''ăšgă'z) *pr.n.m.* [Persian].

שַׁעֲשֻׁעַ (šă''ašŭ'a') *m*, only *pl.* שַׁעֲשׁוּעִים, שַׁעֲשֻׁעִים, delight, enjoyment, pleasure.

שָׁפָה[1] (šāfā') *Ni. pt.* נִשְׁפֶּה, to be bald, bare. — *Pu.* שֻׁפָּה to be bared.

שָׁפָה[2] (šāfā') *f*, only *pl. c.* שְׁפוֹת, cheese.

שְׁפוֹ (šᵉfọ') *pr.n.m.*

שְׁפוֹט (šᵉfọ't) *m*, *pl.* שְׁפוּטִים, judgment, punishment.

שְׁפוּפָם (šᵉfūfā'm), שְׁפוּפָן (šᵉfūfā'n) *pr.n.m.*

שִׁפְחָה (šīfḥā') *f*, *c.* שִׁפְחַת, *w.s.* שִׁפְחָתִי, *pl.* שְׁפָחוֹת, *c.* שִׁפְחוֹת, female servant, maid-servant.

שָׁפַט (šāfă't) *inf.* שָׁפוֹט, שְׁפֹט, *imp.* שְׁפֹט, שָׁפְטָה (šọftā'), שִׁפְטוּ, *fut.* יִשְׁפֹּט, *pt.* שֹׁפֵט, שׁוֹפֵט, *pl.* שֹׁפְטִים, *c.* שֹׁפְטֵי, to decide, to judge, to administer right, to vindicate, condemn, punish; to govern, to rule; *pt.* judge, magistrate, ruler. — *Ni.* נִשְׁפַּט, *inf.* הִשָּׁפֵט, *fut.* יִשָּׁפֵט, to be judged, condemned; to go to law, to plead. — *Po. pt.* מְשֹׁפֵט, *w.s.* מְשֹׁפְטִי, to judge.

שָׁפָט (šāfā't) *pr.n.m.*

שֶׁפֶט (šĕ'fĕt) *m*, only *pl.* שְׁפָטִים, judgment, punishment.

שְׁפַטְיָה (šᵉfătyā'), שְׁפַטְיָהוּ (šᵉfătyā'hū); שִׁפְטָן (šīftā'n) *pr.n.m.*

שְׁפִי[1] (šᵉfī') *m*, *i.p.* שֶׁפִי, *pl.* שְׁפָיִם, שְׁפָיִים, baldness, bareness, bare place.

שְׁפִי[2] (šᵉfī') = שְׁפוֹ; שֻׁפִּים (šŭppī'm) *pr.n.m.*

שְׁפִיפֹן (šᵉfīfọ'n) *m* a species of serpent.

שָׁפִיר (šāfī'r) *pr.n.* of a town.

שָׁפַךְ (šāfă'ḵ) *inf.* שְׁפֹךְ,

imp. שְׁפוֹךְ, שְׁפֹךְ, *fut.* יִשְׁפֹּךְ, *pt.* שֹׁפֵךְ, *pt. p.* שָׁפוּךְ, to pour, to pour out, to shed, to spill; to throw or cast out or up. — *Ni.* נִשְׁפַּךְ, *inf.* הִשָּׁפֵךְ, *fut.* יִשָּׁפֵךְ, to be poured out, to be shed; to be lavished. — *Pu.* שֻׁפַּךְ to be poured out, to slip. — *Hith.* הִשְׁתַּפֵּךְ to be poured out, to pour oneself out.

שֶׁפֶךְ (šĕ'fĕch) *m* place for pouring out.

שָׁפְכָה (šŏfcha') *m* a man's privy member.

שָׁפֵל (šafē'l) *inf.* שְׁפַל, *fut.* יִשְׁפַּל, to sink, to be felled, to be or become low, humbled, subdued. — *Hi.* הִשְׁפִּיל, *inf.* הַשְׁפִּיל, *fut.* יַשְׁפִּיל, *pt.* מַשְׁפִּיל, to make low, to fell, to humble, to overthrow.

שָׁפָל (šafa'l) *adj., c.* שְׁפַל, *pl.* שְׁפָלִים, *f* שְׁפָלָה, low, humble, depressed.

שֵׁפֶל (šē'fĕl) *m, w.s.* שִׁפְלֵנוּ, lowness, low state.

שִׁפְלָה (šifla') *f* = שֵׁפֶל.

שְׁפֵלָה (šᵉfēla') *f w.s.* שְׁפֵלָתָהּ, depression, low land, plain; tract of land between Joppa and Gaza.

שִׁפְלוּת (šiflū'ϑ) *f* the sinking of lands, laziness.

שְׁפָם (šafa'm) *pr.n.m.*

שְׁפָם (šᵉfa'm); **שִׁפְמוֹת** (šifmō'ϑ) *pr.n.* of towns; *gent.* שִׁפְמִי.

שָׁפָן[1] (šafa'n) *m, pl.* שְׁפַנִּים, a rodent, marmot or rabbit.

שָׁפָן[2] (šafa'n) *pr.n.m.*

שֶׁפַע (šĕ'fa') and **שִׁפְעָה** (šif'a') *f, c.* שִׁפְעַת, abundance, plenty, multitude.

שִׁפְעִי (šif'ī) *pr.n.m.*

שָׁפַר (šafē'r) to shine; to be pleasant, agreeable.

שֶׁפֶר[1] (šĕ'fĕr) *m* and **שִׁפְרָה**[1] (šifra') *f* brightness, beauty.

שֶׁפֶר[2] (šĕ'fĕr) *pr.n.* of a mountain in the Arabian desert.

שִׁפְרָה[2] (šifra') *pr.n.f.*

שַׁפְרִיר (šafrī'r) *m* adornment, canopy or carpet of a throne.

שָׁפַת (šafa'ϑ) *imp.* שְׁפֹת, *fut.* יִשְׁפֹּת, to place, to set, to put; to give.

שְׁפָת (šafa'ϑ) *m,* only *du.* שְׁפַתַּיִם, pegs, hooks; enclosure, fold.

שֶׁצֶף (šę'ßęf) *m* an overflowing, effusion.

שָׁקַד (šąkă'd) *inf.* שְׁקֹד, *fut.* יִשְׁקֹד, *pt.* שֹׁקֵד, *pl. c.* שֹׁקְדֵי, to be awake, to watch, to be watchful; to lie in wait, to lurk. — *Pu. pt.* מְשֻׁקָּד [*denom.* of שָׁקֵד] to be almond-shaped.

שָׁקֵד (šąkē'd) *m*, *pl.* שְׁקֵדִים, almond-tree, almond.

שָׁקָה (šąką') *Pu. pt.* יְשֻׁקֶּה, to be moistened. — *Hi.* הִשְׁקָה, *inf.* הַשְׁקוֹת, *imp.* הַשְׁקֵה, *fut.* יַשְׁקֶה, וַיַּשְׁקְ, *pt.* מַשְׁקֶה, *c.* מַשְׁקֵה, *pl.* מַשְׁקִים, to give to drink, to water; *pt.* cupbearer, butler [see מַשְׁקֶה].

שִׁקּוּי (šikkū'y) *m*, only *pl.* *w.s.* שִׁקּוּיָי, שִׁקֻּוָי, drink, refreshment.

שִׁקּוּץ, שִׁקֻּץ (šikkū'ß) *m*, *pl.* שִׁקּוּצִים, abomination, disgust; idol.

שָׁקַט (šąkă't) *fut.* יִשְׁקֹט, יִשְׁקוֹט, *pt.* שֹׁקֵט, to rest, to lie quiet, to be undisturbed, unmolested, inactive. — *Hi. inf.* הַשְׁקִיט, הַשְׁקֵט, *imp.* הַשְׁקֵט, to give rest, to quiet, to calm; to keep quiet; *inf.* rest, quiet.

שֶׁקֶט (šę'kęt) *m* rest, quiet.

שָׁקַל (šąkă'l) *inf.* שָׁקוֹל, שְׁקוֹל, *fut.* יִשְׁקֹל, יִשְׁקוֹל, *pt.* שֹׁקֵל, to poise, to weigh, to weigh to; to estimate, to try. — *Ni.* נִשְׁקַל to be weighed.

שֶׁקֶל (šę'kęl) *m*, *pl.* שְׁקָלִים, *c.* שִׁקְלֵי, weight, definite weight, unit of weight; the standard coin, shekel [a silver shekel equal to 20 גֵּרָה, 50 shekels = 1 mine or 100 drachms].

שִׁקְמָה (šikmą') *f*, only *pl.* שִׁקְמִים and שִׁקְמוֹת, sycamore-tree.

שָׁקַע (šąkă'') *fut.* יִשְׁקַע, to sink down, to subside; to burn down. — *Ni.* נִשְׁקַע the same as *Q.* — *Hi.* הִשְׁקִיעַ, *fut.* יַשְׁקִיעַ, to cause to sink or subside; to press down.

שְׁקַעֲרוּרָה (šekă''arūrą') *f*, only *pl.* שְׁקַעֲרוּרוֹת, depression, hollow.

שָׁקַף (šąkă'f) [*Q.* perh. *pt. p.* שָׁקוּף, *pl.* שְׁקֻפִים, framed] *Ni.* נִשְׁקַף, *pt.* נִשְׁקָף, to look out, down, forth; to be visible. — *Hi.*

הִשְׁקִיף, *fut.* יַשְׁקִיף, יַשְׁקֵף, to look at, down, through.

שֶׁקֶף (šǫ'kǫf) *m*, *i.p.* שָׁקֶף, beam, frame-work, timber-work.

שָׁקֻף (šąkǫ'f) *m*, only *pl.* שְׁקֻפִים [= שֶׁקֶף] work of crossed beams.

שָׁקַץ (šąkă'ß) *Pi.* שִׁקֵּץ, *inf.* שַׁקֵּץ, *fut.* יְשַׁקֵּץ, to make unclean, loathsome; to detest, reject.

שֶׁקֶץ (šǫ'kǫß) *m* abomination, loathing; abominable, unclean things.

שָׁקַק (šąkă'k) *fut.* יָשֹׁק, *pt.* שׁוֹקֵק, *f* שׁוֹקֵקָה, to move to and fro, to run about, to roam; to be greedy, to thirst.—*Hith.* הִשְׁתַּקְשֵׁק to run along.

שָׁקַר (šąkă'r) *fut.* יִשְׁקֹר, to lie, to deceive.—*Pi.* שִׁקֵּר, *fut.* יְשַׁקֵּר, to lie, to deceive, to act falsely.

שֶׁקֶר (šǫ'kǫr) *m*, *i.p.* שָׁקֶר, *pl.* שְׁקָרִים, *c.* שִׁקְרֵי, a lie, falsehood, fraud, deceit; deceitful, vain, unreliable thing; *adv.* in vain.

שֹׁקֶת (šǫ'kǫϑ) [שֶׁקֶת] *f*, *pl.* שְׁקָתוֹת, watering-trough.

שֹׁר (šǫr) *m*, *w.s.* שָׁרֵךְ (šǫrrẹ'ch) navel, navel cord.

שַׂר־אֶצֶר (šăr'ǫ'ßǫr) *pr.n.m.*

שָׁרָב (šąrą'b) *m* mirage [a phenomenon in deserts].

שֵׁרֵבְיָה (šẹ'rẹbyą') *pr.n.m.*

שַׁרְבִיט (šărbi't) *m* sceptre.

שָׁרָה[1] (šąrą') *Pi.* שָׁרָה, to loose, to free.

שָׁרָה[2] (šąrą') *f*, only *pl.* שָׁרוֹת, caravan; also = שׁוּר[4].

שֵׁרָה (šẹrą') *f*, only *pl.* שֵׁרוֹת, chain, bracelet.

שָׁרוּחֶן (šąrūchǫ'n) *pr.n.* of a town in Simeon.

שָׁרוֹן (šąrǫ'n) *pr.n.* of the level sea-coast from mount Carmel to Joppa.

שְׁרוּקָה = שְׁרִיקָה.

שָׁרוֹת see שָׁרָה[2] and שׁוּר[4].

שֵׁרוּת (šẹrū'ϑ) *f* beginning.

שִׁרְטַי = שִׁטְרַי *pr.n.m.*

שָׁרַי (šąră'y) *pr.n.m.*

שִׁרְיָה (širyą') *f*, שִׁרְיוֹן, שִׁרְיֹן (širyǫ'n), שִׁרְיָן (širyą'n) *m*, *pl.* שִׁרְיֹנִים, שִׁרְיֹנוֹת, coat of mail.

שְׁרִיקָה (šriką') *f*, only *pl.* שְׁרִיקוֹת, a hissing, scorn; piping, whistling.

שָׂרִיר (sărī'r) *m*, only *pl.* שְׂרִירָיו, sinew, muscle.

שְׁרִירוּת (šᵉrīrū'ϑ) *f* firmness, strength; obduration, obstinacy.

שֵׁרִית — שְׁאֵרִית.

שְׁרֵמָה (šᵉrēmā') *f*, only *pl.* שְׁרֵמוֹת [perh. for שְׁדֵמוֹת], plain, field.

שָׁרַץ (šără'ß) *imp. pl.* שִׁרְצוּ, *fut.* יִשְׁרֹץ, *pt.* שֹׁרֵץ, to creep, to crawl, to swarm, to multiply.

שֶׁרֶץ (šĕ'rĕß) *m coll.* creeping animals, reptiles, small water animals.

שָׁרַק (šără'k) *fut.* יִשְׁרֹק, to hiss, to pipe, to whistle, to hiss at, to mock.

שְׁרֵקָה (šᵉrēkā') *f* a hissing, scorn.

שָׁרָר (šără'r) *pr.n.m.*

שָׁרַשׁ (šără'š) *Pi.* שֵׁרֵשׁ, to root out. — *Pu.* שֹׁרַשׁ to be rooted out, to be rooted. — *Po.* שׁוֹרֵשׁ to strike root. — *Hi. fut.* יַשְׁרֵשׁ, *pt.* מַשְׁרִישׁ, to strike root, to thrive.

שֹׁרֶשׁ (šŏ'rĕš) *m*, *w.s.* שָׁרְשֶׁךָ (šŏršĕ'ϕ), *pl.* שָׁרָשִׁים (šŏ'rāšī'm), *c.* שָׁרְשֵׁי, root, basis, bottom, race, abode, origin; shoot, sprout, descendant.

שַׁרְשָׁה (šăršā') *f*, only *pl.* *c.* שַׁרְשׁוֹת, chain.

שַׁרְשְׁרָה (šăršᵉrā') *f*, only *pl.* שַׁרְשְׁרוֹת, chain.

שָׁרַת (šără'ϑ) *Pi.* שֵׁרֵת, *inf.* שָׁרֵת, *fut.* יְשָׁרֵת, יְשָׁרֶת, *pt.* מְשָׁרֵת, *w.s.* מְשָׁרְתוֹ, *pl.* מְשָׁרְתִים, *c.* מְשָׁרְתֵי, *f* מְשָׁרַת, to serve, to attend or wait on, to do service [as a priest]; *pt.* servant, minister, attendant.

שָׁשָׁה see שָׁסָה.

שֵׁשׁ¹ (šēš) *num. f*, *m* שִׁשָּׁה, *c.* שֵׁשֶׁת, six; *pl.* שִׁשִּׁים sixty.

שֵׁשׁ² (šēš) *m* = שַׁיִשׁ white marble, alabaster; byssus, white linen or cotton.

שִׁשֵּׁא (šăšā') *Pi.* שִׁשֵּׁא, to lead.

שֵׁשְׁבַּצַּר (šēšbăßßă'r) *pr.n.m.*

שָׁשָׁה (šăšā') *Pi.* שִׁשָּׁה, to divide into six parts.

שָׁשַׁי (šăšă'y); **שֵׁשַׁי** (šēšă'y) *pr.n.m.*

שֵׁשִׁי = שֵׁשׁ².

שִׁשִּׁי (šīššī') *adj. num. m*, *f* שִׁשִּׁית, the sixth, sixth part.

שֵׁשַׁךְ (šēšă'ch) *pr.n.* of a city = Babylon.

שֶׁשֻּׁם = אֲשֶׁר שָׁם.

שֵׁשָׁן (šēšā'n); **שָׁשַׁק** (šāšă'k) *pr.n.m.*

שָׁשֵׁר (šāšē'r) *m, i.p.* שָׁשַׁר, red colour, cinnabar, vermilion.

שָׁת (šāϑ) *m*, only *pl.* שָׁתוֹת, *w.s.* שָׁתֹתֶיהָ, pillar, column; prince, statesman.

שֵׁת[1] (šēϑ) *m, pl. w.s.* שְׁתוֹתֵיהֶם, the buttocks.

שֵׁת[2] (šēϑ) *f* = שְׁאֵת noise, tumult.

שֵׁת[3] (šēϑ) *pr.n.m.*

שָׁתָה (šāϑā') *inf.* שָׁתֹה, שְׁתוֹ, שְׁתֹת, שְׁתוֹת, *imp.* שְׁתֵה, *fut.* יִשְׁתֶּה, יֵשְׁתְּ, וַיֵּשְׁתְּ, *pl.* יִשְׁתָּיוּן, *pt.* שֹׁתֶה, *pl.* שֹׁתִים, *c.* שֹׁתֵי, *f* שֹׁתָה, to drink, to enjoy to undergo. — *Ni. fut.* יִשָּׁתֶה to be drunk. — *Hi.* הִשְׁקָה from שָׁקָה.

שְׁתִי[1] (šᵉϑī') *m* a drinking, carousing.

שְׁתִי[2] (šᵉϑī') *m* the warp of the weaver.

שְׁתִיָּה (šᵉϑīyyā') *f* = שְׁתִי[1].

שָׁתִיל (šāϑī'l) *m* plant, shoot.

שְׁתַּיִם see שְׁנַיִם.

שָׁתַל (šāϑă'l) *fut.* יִשְׁתֹּל, *pt. p.* שָׁתוּל, *pl.* שְׁתוּלִים, to set, to plant.

שָׁתַם (šāϑă'm) *pt. p. c.* שְׁתֻם, to close [others: to open].

שָׁתַן (šāϑă'n) *Hi.* הִשְׁתִּין, *pt.* מַשְׁתִּין [*denom.* of שַׁיִן], to make water, to piss.

שָׁתַק (šāϑă'k) *fut.* יִשְׁתֹּק, to cease, to rest.

שֵׁתָר (šēϑā'r) *pr.n.m.* [Persian].

שְׁתַר בּוֹזְנַי (šᵉϑă'r ḃōzᵉnă'y) *pr.n.m.* [Persian].

שָׁתַת (šāϑă'ϑ) *pf.* שַׁתּ, to set, put, place. — *Ni.* נִשַׁת to subside, to be dried up; but see נָשַׁת.

ת

ת the twenty-second letter of the alphabet, called תָּו [sign, mark, cross]; as a numeral = 400.

תָּא (tā) *m, pl.* תָּאִים, *c.* תָּאֵי, chamber, room.

תָּאַב[1] (tā'ă'ḃ) to desire, to long for.

תָּאַב[2] (tā'ă'b) *Pi. pt.* מְתָאֵב, to detest, abominate.

תַּאֲבָה (tă''abā') *f* desire, longing.

תָּאָה[1] (tā'ā') *Pi. fut.* יְתָאֶה, *pl.* יְתָאוּ, to measure out, to determine.

תָּאָה[2] (tā'ā') *f, pl.* תָּאוֹת = תָּא.

תְּאוֹ (tᵉ'ō') *m* mountain-goat, antelope, gazelle.

תַּאֲוָה[1] (tă''avā') *f, c.* תַּאֲוַת, *w.s.* תַּאֲוָתִי, desire, longing, wish, lust, charm, delight; desirable or pleasant things.

תַּאֲוָה[2] (tă''avā') *f* boundary, limit.

תַּאֲלָה (tă''alā') *f* curse.

תָּאַם (tā'ă'm) *pt. pl.* תֹּאֲמִם, תּוֹאֲמִים, to be double, to be paired. — *Hi.* הִתְאִים, *pt. f/pl.* מַתְאִימוֹת, to bear twins.

תָּאָם (tā'ā'm) *m*, only *pl.* תַּמִּים [תְּאֹמִים], pair, couple.

תְּאֹם (tā'ō'm) *m, pl.* תְּאוֹמִים, תּוֹמִים, *c.* תְּאוֹמֵי, תְּאֳמֵי, twin.

תַּאֲנָה (tă''anā') *f* rut, copulation.

תְּאֵנָה (tᵉ'ēnā') *f, w.s.* תְּאֵנָתִי, *pl.* תְּאֵנִים, *c.* תְּאֵנֵי, fig-tree, fig.

תֹּאֲנָה (tō''anā') *f* occasion.

תַּאֲנִיָּה (tă''aniyyā') *f* sorrow, grief.

תְּאֻנִים (tᵉ'ŭnī'm) *pl. m* toil, labour.

תַּאֲנַת שִׁלֹה (tă''ană'ṯ šīlō') *pr.n.* of a town in Ephraim.

תָּאַר (tā'ă'r) to go round, to compass. — *Pi. fut. w.s.* יְתָאֲרֵהוּ to delineate. — *Pu. pt.* מְתֹאָר, to be turned, extended.

תֹּאַר (tō''ăr) *m, w.s.* תָּאֳרוֹ, תֹּאֲרוֹ, outline, form, figure.

תַּאְרֵעַ (tă'rē'a') *pr.n.m.*

תְּאַשּׁוּר (tᵉ'ăššū'r) *m* a kind of tall cedar or cypress, sherbin-cedar.

תֵּבָה (tēbā') *f, c.* תֵּבַת, chest, box; ark, boat.

תְּבוּאָה (tᵉbū'ā') *f, c.* תְּבוּאַת, *w.s.* תְּבוּאָתוֹ, *pl.* תְּבוּאֹת, produce, fruit, increase, gain, profit, result.

תְּבוּנָה (tᵉbūnā') *f, w.s.* תְּבוּנָתוֹ, תְּבוּנָם, *pl.* תְּבוּנוֹת, insight, prudence, understanding, intelligence.

תְּבוּסָה (tᵉbūsā') *f* a treading down, destruction.

תָּבוֹר (tābō'r) *pr.n.* of a mountain in Galilee; of a town in Zebulon; of an oak in Benjamin.

תֵּבֵל (tēbē'l) *f* the earth, the inhabited earth, the world.

תֶּבֶל (tĕ'bĕl) *m* pollution, profanation.

תֵּבֵל see תּוּבַל.

תַּבְלִית (tăblī'ϑ) *f* consumption, destruction.

תְּבַלֻּל (tᵉbăllū'l) *adj.* bleared or spotted [in the eye].

תֶּבֶן (tĕ'bĕn) *m* straw, chaff.

תִּבְנִי (tĭbnī') *pr.n.m.*

תַּבְנִית (tăbnī'ϑ) *f*, *w.s.* תַּבְנִיתוֹ, pattern, model for building, likeness.

תַּבְעֵרָה (tăbʿērā') *pr.n.* of a station in the desert.

תֵּבֵץ (tēbē'ʒ) *pr.n.* of a town near Shechem.

תִּגְלַת פִּלְאֶסֶר (tĭglă'ϑ pĭlʾĕ'sĕr) *pr.n.m.* [also פִּלֶסֶר, פִּלְנְאֶסֶר, פִּלְנֶסֶר].

תַּגְמוּל (tăgmū'l) *m* benefit.

תִּגְרָה (tĭgrā') *f*, *c.* תִּגְרַת, strife, dispute, quarrel.

תֹּגַרְמָה (tōgărmā') *pr.n.* of a northern people and country, Armenians.

תִּדְהָר (tĭdhā'r) *m* a kind of tree [elm, plane or yew-tree].

תַּדְמֹר (tădmō'r) *pr.n.* of a city in the Syrian desert between Damascus and the Euphrates, Palmyra.

תִּדְעָל (tĭdʿā'l) *pr.n.m.*

תֹּהוּ (tō'hū) *m* desolateness, wasteness, desolation, desert, emptiness, nothingness; *adv.* in vain.

תְּהֹם, תְּהוֹם (tᵉhō'm) *m* and *f*, *pl.* תְּהֹמוֹת, a roaring, water-chaos, deep, abyss, ocean.

תְּהִלָּה (tᵉhĭllā') *f*, *c.* תְּהִלַּת, *w.s.* תְּהִלָּתִי, *pl.* תְּהִלּוֹת, תְּהִלֹּת [תְּהִלִּים in the title of the book of Psalms], praise, song of praise, hymn, psalm.

תָּהֳלָה (tŏ'hºlā') *f* mistake, sin.

תַּהֲלוּכָה (tă'hªlūkā') *f* procession.

תַּהְפּוּכָה (tăhpūkā') *f*, only *pl.* תַּהְפֻּכוֹת, perverseness, falsehood.

תָּו (tāv) *m* sign, mark, cross.

תּוֹא — **תְּאוֹ** gazelle or antelope.

תּוֹאֵם see תְּאָם.

תּוּבַל (tūbă'l); תּוּבַל קַיִן (tūbă'l kă'yĭn) *pr.n.m.*

תּוּגָה (tūgā') *f*, *c.* תּוּגַת, sorrow, grief.

תּוֹדָה (tōdā') *f*, *c.* תּוֹדַת, *pl.* תּוֹדוֹת, confession, avowal; thanks, thanks-giving; a choir of singers.

תָּוָה (tāvā') *Pi. fut.* וַיְתָו, to make signs, to scratch, to scribble. — *Hi.* הִתְוָה to make a sign; to provoke, to grieve.

תּוֹחַ (tō'ach) *pr.n.m.*

תּוֹחֶלֶת (tōchĕ'lĕth) *f*, *w.s.* תּוֹחַלְתִּי, expectation, hope.

תָּוֶךְ (tā'vĕch) *m*, *c.* תּוֹךְ, *w.s.* תּוֹכִי, the middle, centre; within, between; מִתּוֹךְ out of the midst; אֶל־תּוֹךְ into the midst.

תּוֹךְ see תֹּךְ.

תּוֹכֵחָה (tō'chēchā') *f*, *pl.* תּוֹכֵחוֹת, chastisement, punishment.

תּוֹכַחַת (tōcha'chăth) *f*, *w.s.* תּוֹכַחְתִּי, *pl.* תּוֹכָחוֹת, justification, pleading, defence; correction, chastisement, punishment.

תּוּכִּיִּים see תֻּכִּיִּים.

תּוֹלַד (tōlă'd) *pr.n.* of a town in Simeon.

תּוֹלֶדֶת (tōlĕ'dĕth) *f*, only *pl.* *c.* תּוֹלְדוֹת, תֹּלְדֹת, *w.s.* תֹּלְדֹתָם, birth, generation, origin, descent, lineage, family register, genealogy.

תּוֹלָל (tōlā'l) *m*, *pl.* *w.s.* תּוֹלָלֵינוּ, robber, tormenter.

תּוֹלָע[1] (tōlā'') *m*, *pl.* תּוֹלָעִים, worm, insect, vermin, the coccus worm.

תּוֹלָע[2] (tōlā'') *pr.n.m.*

תּוֹלֵעָה (tō'lē'ā'), תּוֹלַעַת (tōlă''ăth) *f*, *w.s.* תּוֹלַעְתָּם = תּוֹלָע[1].

תּוֹמִיךְ see תָּמַךְ.

תּוֹמִים see תָּאֹם.

תּוֹעֵבָה (tō'ēbā') *f*, *c.* תּוֹעֲבַת, *pl.* תּוֹעֵבוֹת, *c.* תּוֹעֲבוֹת, abomination, abominable thing, idolatry, idols.

תּוֹעָה (tō'ā') *f* error, apostasy; damage, misfortune.

תּוֹעָפָה (tō''āfā') *f*, only *pl.* תּוֹעָפוֹת, *c.* תּוֹעֲפוֹת, height, point, peak; perfection.

תּוֹצָאָה (tō'ßā'ā') *f*, only *pl.* תּוֹצָאוֹת, *c.* תּוֹצְאוֹת, issue, outlet, gate, fountain, escape.

תּוּר (tūr) *pf.* תָּר, *inf.* תּוּר,

fut. יָתוּר, *pt. pl.* תָּרִים, to go about as a spy or scout, as a merchant, to search, explore, investigate.—*Hi.* הֵתִיר, *fut.* יָתִיר, וַיָּתַר, to cause to spy out, to lead about, to guide; to spy out.

תּוֹר[1], **תֹּר** (tōr) *m*, *w.s.* תּוֹרְךָ, *pl.* תּוֹרִים, turtle-dove.

תּוֹר[2] (tōr) *m* row, order, turn, manner.

תּוֹרָה (tōrā') *f*, *c.* תּוֹרַת, *w.s.* תּוֹרָתִי, *pl.* תּוֹרוֹת, תּוֹרֹת, instruction, regulation, direction, precept, doctrine, law; manner, arrangement.

תּוֹשָׁב (tōšā'ḇ) *m*, *c.* תּוֹשַׁב, *pl.* תּוֹשָׁבִים, *c.* תּוֹשָׁבֵי, settler, inhabitant, foreigner, alien.

תֻּשִׁיָּה, תּוּשִׁיָּה (tūšiyyā') *f* help, support, salvation; insight, wisdom, understanding.

תּוֹתָח (tōθā'ḥ) *m* bludgeon, club.

תַּזְנוּת (tăznū'θ) *f* whoredom, fornication, idolatry.

תַּחְבֻּלָה, תַּחְבּוּלָה (tăḥbūlā') *f*, only *pl.* תַּחְבּוּלוֹת, guidance, management, craft, cunning.

תֹּחוּ (tō'ḥū) *pr.n.m*

תַּחְכְּמֹנִי (tăḥkᵉmōnī') *pr.n.m.* [*patr.* or *gent.*] one belonging to a family or place תַּחְכְּמֹן.

תְּחִלָּה (tᵉḥillā') *f*, *c.* תְּחִלַּת, beginning, commencement.

תַּחֲלוּא (tă'ḥᵃlū') *m*, only *pl.* תַּחֲלֻאִים, תַּחֲלוּאִים, sickness. disease.

תַּחְמָס (tăḥmā's) *m* an unclean bird [male ostrich, owl or swallow].

תַּחַן (tă'ḥăn) *pr.n.m.*; *patr* תַּחֲנִי.

תְּחִנָּה[1] (tᵉḥinnā') *f*, *c.* תְּחִנַּת, *w.s.* תְּחִנָּתִי, *pl.* תְּחִנּוֹת, mercy, favour, compassion; prayer, entreaty.

תְּחִנָּה[2] (tᵉḥinnā') *pr.n.m.*

תַּחֲנָה (tă'ḥᵃnā') *f*, only *pl.* *w.s.* תַּחֲנֹתִי, camp, encampment.

תַּחֲנוּן [tă'ḥᵃnū'n] *m*, only *pl.* תַּחֲנוּנִים, תַּחֲנוּנוֹת, prayer, supplication.

תַּחְפַּנְחֵס (tăḥpănḥē's), תְּחַפְנְחֵס (tᵉḥăfnᵉḥē's) *pr.n.* of a city in Egypt.

תַּחְפְּנֵיס (tăḥpᵉnē's) *pr.n.f.* of an Egyptian queen.

תַּחְרָא (tăḥrā') *m* coat of mail.

תַּחְרֵעַ (tăḥrē'a') *pr.n.m.*

תַּחַשׁ (tă'ḥăš) *m*, *i.p.* תָּחַשׁ, *pl.* תְּחָשִׁים, an unknown animal [seal, dolphin, badger, marten].

תַּחַת[1] (tă'ḥăth) *f*, *i.p.* תָּחַת, the under part; *pl. w.s.* תַּחְתַּי, תַּחְתָּיו, *adv.* and *prep.* under, beneath, below, at the feet of, down, instead of, in place of; מִתַּחַת from under.

תַּחַת[2] (tă'ḥăth) *pr.n.* of a station in the desert; *pr.n.m.*

תַּחְתּוֹן (tăḥtō'n) *adj.*, *f* תַּחְתּוֹנָה, the lower.

תַּחְתִּי (tăḥtī') *adj.*, *pl.* תַּחְתִּיִּם, *f* תַּחְתִּיָּה, תַּחְתִּית, *pl.* תַּחְתִּיּוֹת, the lower, the lowest; the lowest part, nether world.

תִּיז (tīz) *Hi.* הֵתַז, to cut off.

תִּיכוֹן (tīḥō'n) *adj.*, *f* תִּיכוֹנָה, the middle, the midst.

תִּילוֹן (tīlō'n) *pr.n.m.*

תֵּימָא, **תֵּמָא** (tēmā') *pr.n.m.* [people and country in northern Arabia].

תֵּימָן[1] (tēmā'n) *m*, *w. loc.* תֵּימָנָה ה, south, south-side, south wind.

תֵּימָן[2] (tēmā'n) *pr.n.m.*; *pr.n.* of a district in Edom; *gent.* תֵּימָנִי.

תֵּימְנִי (tē'mᵉnī') *pr.n.m.*

תִּימָרָה (tī'mārā') *f*, only *pl. c.* תִּימְרוֹת, column, pillar.

תִּיצִי (tīṣī') *pr.n.m.* [*gent.* of תִּיץ].

תִּירֹשׁ, **תִּירוֹשׁ** (tīrō'š) *m*, *w.s.* תִּירוֹשִׁי, must, unfermented wine, juice of the grape.

תִּירְיָא (tīrᵉyā') *pr.n.m.*

תִּירָס (tīrā's) *pr.n.m.* a northern people, Thracians, Scythians or Tyrrhenes.

תַּיִשׁ (tă'yĭš) *m*, *pl.* תְּיָשִׁים, he-goat.

תּוֹךְ, **תֹּךְ** (tōḥ) *m* oppression, violence.

תָּכָה (tāḥā') *Pu.* תֻּכָּה to be encamped.

תְּכוּנָה (tᵉḥūnā') *f*, *w.s.* תְּכוּנָתוֹ, arrangement, furniture; place, dwelling.

תֻּכִּי (tŭkkī') *m*, only *pl.* תּוּכִּיִּים, תֻּכִּיִּים, peacock.

תָּכָךְ (tāḥā'ḥ) *m*, only *pl.* תְּכָכִים = תֹּךְ.

תִּכְלָה (tĭḥlā') *f* perfection.

תַּכְלִית (tăḵlī'ϑ) *f* perfection, completeness, end, limit.

תְּכֵלֶת (tᵉḵē'lĕϑ) *f* purple, purple blue or violet, purple dye, purple stuff.

תָּכַן (tāḵă'n) *pt.* תֹּכֵן, to try, to test. — *Ni.* נִתְכַּן, *fut.* יִתָּכֵן, to be poised, adjusted, to be right. — *Pi.* תִּכֵּן to weigh, to determine, to measure, to test. — *Pu. pt.* מְתֻכָּן to be weighed.

תֹּכֶן[1] (tō'ḵĕn) *m* measure, task, day's work.

תֹּכֶן[2] (tō'ḵĕn) *pr.n.* of a town in Simeon.

תָּכְנִית (tŏḵnī'ϑ) *f* arrangement, plan, proportion.

תַּכְרִיךְ (tăḵrī'ḵ) *m* wide garment, mantle.

תֵּל (tēl) *m, w.s.* תִּלָּם, mound, heap; in *pr.n.* of places: תֵּל אָבִיב, תֵּל חַרְשָׁא, תֵּל מֶלַח, towns in Mesopotamia.

תָּלָא see תָּלָה.

תְּלָאָה (tᵉlā'ā') *f* hardship, weariness, distress.

תַּלְאוּבָה (tăl'ūḇā') *f* drought.

תְּלַשָּׂר, תְּלַאשָּׂר (tᵉlăssā'r) *pr.n.* of an Assyrian province in western Mesopotamia.

תִּלְבֹּשֶׁת (tĭlbō'sĕϑ) *f* garment.

תָּלָה, תָּלָא (tālā') *fut.* יִתְלֶה, *pt. p.* תָּלוּי, *pl.* תְּלוּאִים, to hang, to hang up, to bend, to be inclined. — *Ni. fut.* יִתָּלֶה to be hanged. — *Pi.* תִּלָּה to hang.

תְּלוּנָּה (tᵉlūnā') *f,* only *pl.* תְּלֻנּוֹת, תְּלוּנוֹת, murmuring, refractoriness.

תֶּלַח (tĕ'lăḥ) *pr.n.m.*

תְּלִי (tᵉlī') *m, w.s.* תֶּלְיְךָ, quiver.

תָּלַל (tālă'l) *pt. p* תָּלוּל [high], to heighten. — *Hi.* הֵתֵל, הֵתֶל, *inf.* הָתֵל, *fut.* יְהָתֵל [or from הָתַל *Pi.* for יְהַתֵּל] to deceive, cheat, deride, mock.

תֶּלֶם (tĕ'lĕm) *m, pl.* תְּלָמִים, *c.* תַּלְמֵי, furrow, ridge along a furrow.

תַּלְמַי (tălmă'y) *pr.n.m.*

תַּלְמִיד (tălmī'd) *m* disciple.

תָּלַע (tālă'ʻ) *Pu. pt.* מְתֻלָּע, to be clothed in crimson.

תַּלְפִּית (tălpī'ϑ) *f,* only *pl.* תַּלְפִּיּוֹת, height, terrace.

תַּלְתַּלִּים (tăltăllī'm) *pl. m*

twisted or waving boughs [locks of hair].

תָּם (tām) *adj.*, *f* תַּמָּה, whole, complete, perfect, simple, pious, innocent, sincere, mild.

תֹּם (tōm) *m*, *c.* תָּם־ (tŏm), *w.s.* תֻּמִּי, *pl.* תֻּמִּים, wholeness, completeness, perfection, integrity, soundness, simplicity, innocence; *pl.* see אוּרִים.

תָּמַהּ (tāmă'h) *imp. pl.* תְּמָהוּ, *fut.* יִתְמַהּ, to be astonished, amazed, terrified. — *Hith.* הִתַּמַּהּ to be astonished.

תֻּמָּה (tŭmmā') *f* integrity, innocence.

תִּמָּהוֹן (tĭmmāhō'n) *m*, *c.* תִּמְהוֹן, astonishment, amazement, terror.

תַּמּוּז (tămmū'z) *pr.n.* of a Syro-Phenician god, Adonis.

תְּמוֹל (tᵉmō'l) *adv.* = אֶתְמוֹל, yesterday, formerly.

תְּמוּנָה (tᵉmūnā') *f*, *c.* תְּמוּנַת, *w.s.* תְּמוּנָתְךָ, a fashioning, form, shape, image.

תְּמוּרָה (tᵉmūrā') *f* exchange, compensation, wages.

תְּמוּתָה (tᵉmūϑā') *f* a dying, death.

תֶּמַח (tĕ'măḥ) *pr.n.m.*

תָּמִיד (tāmī'd) *m* duration, extension, continuance; *adv.* continually.

תָּמִים (tāmī'm) *adj.*, *c.* תְּמִים, *pl.* תְּמִימִים, *c.* תְּמִימֵי, *f* תְּמִימָה, whole, complete, perfect, faultless, blameless, innocent, simple, upright, honest; *subst.* honesty, integrity, truth.

תַּמִּים = תְּאֹמִים see תְּאֹם.

תָּמַךְ (tāmă'ḥ) *inf.* תְּמֹךְ, תָּמֹךְ, *fut.* יִתְמֹךְ, *pt.* תֹּמֵךְ, תּוֹמֵךְ, תּוֹמִיךְ, to take, to hold, to support, to maintain. — *Ni. fut.* יִתָּמֵךְ to be seized, to be held.

תָּמַם (tāmă'm) *pf.* תַּם, *inf.* תֹּם, תֹּם־, *w.s.* תֻּמּוֹ, *fut.* יִתֹּם, 1. *sg.* אֵיתַם, *pl.* יִתַּמּוּ [or *Ni.*], יִתָּמוּ, to be completed, finished, ended, to be ready, whole; to be consumed, to be gone, to perish; to be innocent, blameless; *tr.* to make whole, to complete, to finish. — *Ni.* see *Q. fut.* — *Hi.* הֵתַם, *inf. w.s.* הֲתִימְךָ, *fut.* יַתֵּם, to complete, to finish, to make full, ready, perfect; to cause to cease;

to pay off. — *Hith.* הִתַּמֵּם to act honestly.

תִּמְנָה (tĭmnā') *pr.n.* of towns in Judah and Dan; *w. loc.* ה תִּמְנָתָה; *gent.* תִּמְנִי.

תִּמְנָע (tĭmnā'") *pr.n.m.*

תִּמְנַת חֶרֶס (tĭmnă'ϑ ḥĕ'rĕs) [תִּמְנַת סֶרַח] *pr.n.* of a town in Ephraim.

תֶּמֶס (tĕ'mĕs) *m* a melting, dissolving.

תָּמָר[1] (tāmā'r) *m, pl.* תְּמָרִים, palm-tree, date-palm.

תָּמָר[2] (tāmā'r) *pr.n..f.*; *pr.n.* of a town in the south of Palestine.

תֹּמֶר (tō'mĕr) *m* palm-tree; pillar.

תִּמֹּרָה (tĭmmōrā') *f, pl.* תִּמֹּרִים and תִּמֹּרוֹת, palm-like ornament in architecture.

תַּמְרוּק (tămrū'k) *m,* only *pl.* תַּמְרוּקִים [תַּמְרִיקִים], cleansing, ointment, remedy.

תַּמְרוּר (tămrū'r) *m,* only *pl.* תַּמְרוּרִים, bitterness; pillar, way-post.

תַּן (tăn) *m,* only *pl.* תַּנִּים [תַּנִּין], howling animal, jackal.

תָּנָה[1] (tānā') *fut.* יִתְנֶה, to bestow, to hire. — *Hi.* הִתְנָה the same as *Q.*

תָּנָה[2] (tānā') *Pi. inf.* תַּנּוֹת, *fut.* יְתַנֶּה, to sing, to praise.

תַּנָּה (tănnā') *f,* only *pl.* תַּנּוֹת, a dwelling.

תְּנוּאָה (tᵉnū'ā') *f, w.s.* תְּנוּאָתִי, alienation, estrangement, enmity.

תְּנוּבָה (tᵉnūbā') *f, c.* תְּנוּבַת, *w.s.* תְּנוּבָתִי, produce, fruit.

תְּנוּךְ (tᵉnū'ch) *m,* only *c.* תְּנוּךְ, point, tip of the ear.

תְּנוּמָה (tᵉnūmā') *f, pl.* תְּנוּמוֹת, slumber, sleepiness.

תְּנוּפָה (tᵉnūfā') *f, c.* תְּנוּפַת, *pl.* תְּנוּפוֹת, the moving to and fro, waving [of a sacrifice], consecration; movement, tumult, excitement.

תַּנּוּר (tănnū'r) *m, pl.* תַּנּוּרִים, oven, furnace.

תַּנְחוּם (tănḥū'm) *m,* only *pl.* תַּנְחוּמִים, consolation, comfort, compassion.

תַּנְחוּמָה (tănḥūmā') *f,* only *pl.* תַּנְחוּמוֹת, = תַּנְחוּם.

תַּנְחֻמֶת (tănḥū'mĕϑ) *pr.n.m.*

תַּנִּים (tănnī'm), תַּנִּין (tănnī'n) *m* [*sing.*], *pl.* תַּנִּינִים, great water-animal, whale, shark, crocodile, serpent, sea-monster.

תִּנְשֶׁמֶת (tĭnsĕ'mĕϑ) *f*, an unclean water-animal, lizard, chameleon; a bird, owl or pelican.

תָּעַב (tā'ă'b) *Ni.* נִתְעַב, *pt.* נִתְעָב, to be abominable, abhorred. — *Pi.* תִּעֵב, *fut.* יְתָעֵב, יְתַעֵב, *pt.* מְתַעֵב, to abhor, refuse, reject; to make one abhor or abhorred. — *Hi.* הִתְעִיב, *fut.* יַתְעֵב, to act abominably.

תָּעָה (tā'ā') *inf.* תְּעוֹת, *fut.* יִתְעֶה, תֵּתַע, *pt.* תֹּעֶה, *pl. c.* תֹּעֵי, to err, to wander; to stray, to go astray; to reel, to be giddy. — *Ni.* נִתְעָה, *inf.* הִתָּעוֹת, to stagger about, to reel; to be deceived. — *Hi.* הִתְעָה, *fut.* יַתְעֶה, יֶתַע, *pt.* מַתְעֶה, *pl.* מַתְעִים, to cause to wander, to lead astray, to seduce; to go astray, to err.

תֹּעוּ (tō'ū) *pr.n.m.*

תְּעוּדָה (tᵉ'ūdā') *f* law, statute, custom; announcement.

תְּעָלָה (tᵉālā') *f*, *c.* תְּעָלַת, *pl.* תְּעָלוֹת, ditch, channel, aqueduct, conduit; plaster, bandage.

תַּעֲלוּל (tă'ᵃlū'l) *m*, only *pl.* תַּעֲלוּלִים, petulancy, wantonness; a wanton boy; tricks, misfortune.

תַּעֲלֻמָה (tă'ᵃlūmā') *f*, *pl.* תַּעֲלֻמוֹת, hidden thing, secret.

תַּעֲנוּג (tă'ᵃnū'g) *m*, *pl.* תַּעֲנוּגִים, תַּעֲנֻגוֹת, good cheer, pleasure, delight, sexual gratification.

תַּעֲנִית (tă'ᵃnī'ϑ) *f* a fasting.

תַּעֲנָךְ (tă'ᵃnā'ꝃ) *pr.n.* of a Canaanitish town, belonging to Manasseh.

תָּעַע (tā'ā') *Pil. pt.* מְתַעְתֵּעַ, to mock. — *Hith. pt. pl* מִתַּעְתְּעִים to mock.

תְּעֻפָה see עוּף *Q. fut.*

תַּעֲצֻמָה (tă'ᵃẞūmā') *f*, only *pl.* תַּעֲצֻמוֹת, forces, strength.

תַּעַר (tă'ăr) *m* knife, razor, pen-knife; sheath of a sword.

תַּעֲרֻבָה (tă'ᵃrūbā') *f*, *pl.* תַּעֲרֻבוֹת, suretyship, surety, pledge.

תַּעְתֻּעַ (tă'tū'a) *m*, only *pl.* תַּעְתֻּעִים, mockery.

תֹּף (tōf) *m*, *pl.* תֻּפִּים, hand-drum; hollow of a gem, bezel.

תִּפְאָרָה (tĭf'ārā') and **תִּפְאֶרֶת** (tĭf'ĕrĕth) *f*, *w.s.* תִּפְאַרְתִּי, splendour, beauty, magnificence, ornament, honour, glory, boast.

תַּפּוּחַ[1] (tăppū'aḥ) *m*, *pl.* תַּפּוּחִים, *c.* תַּפּוּחֵי, apple, apple-tree.

תַּפּוּחַ[2] (tăppū'aḥ) *pr.n.* of towns in Judah and Ephraim; *pr.n.m.*

תְּפוּצָה (t'fūṣā') *f*, only *pl.* תְּפוּצוֹת, dispersion.

תֻּפִין (tŭfī'n) *m*, only *pl. c.* תֻּפִינֵי, a baking, cooking, or something baked, cooked.

תָּפַל (tāfă'l) *Hith.* הִתַּפָּל = הִתְפַּתָּל, see פָּתַל *Hith.*

תָּפֵל (tāfē'l) *m* something insipid, unsavoury; mortar, whitewash.

תֹּפֶל (tō'fĕl) *pr.n.* of a place in the desert.

תִּפְלָה (tĭflā') *f* insipidity, absurdity.

תְּפִלָּה (t'fĭllā') *f*, *c.* תְּפִלַּת, *w.s.* תְּפִלָּתִי, *pl.* תְּפִלּוֹת, prayer, supplication, hymn, psalm.

תִּפְלֶצֶת (tĭflĕ'ṣĕth) *f*, *w.s.* תִּפְלַצְתְּךָ, fear, terror.

תִּפְסַח (tĭfsă'ḥ) *pr.n.* of a city on the Euphrates, Thapsacus.

תָּפַף (tāfă'f) *pt. f/pl.* תּוֹפְפוֹת, to beat [the drum]. — *Po.* תּוֹפֵף, *pt. f/pl.* מְתוֹפְפוֹת, to beat, to strike.

תָּפַר (tāfă'r) *inf.* תְּפוֹר, *fut.* יִתְפֹּר, to sew together. — *Pi. pt. f/pl.* מְתַפְּרוֹת the same as *Q.*

תָּפַשׂ (tāfă's) *inf.* תָּפְשׂ, תְּפֹשׂ, *w.s.* תָּפְשְׂכֶם, *imp. pl.* תִּפְשׂוּ, *fut.* יִתְפֹּשׂ, *pt.* תֹּפֵשׂ, to seize, to lay hold of, to catch, to hold, to hold fast, to handle. — *Ni.* נִתְפַּשׂ, *inf.* הִתָּפֵשׂ, *fut.* יִתָּפֵשׂ, to be taken, seized, caught, captured. — *Pi. fut.* יְתַפֵּשׂ to hold fast.

תֹּפֶת (tō'fĕth) *f* abomination; altar-place of Moloch in the valley of the sons of Hinnom.

תָּפְתֶּה (tŏftĕ') *m* a burning-place for corpses.

תִּקְוָה[1] (tĭkvā') *f*, *w.s.* תִּקְוָתִי, cord; hope, expectation.

תִּקְוָה[2] (tĭkvā') *pr.n.m.*

תְּקוּמָה (t'kūmā') *f* a standing.

תְּקוֹמֵם (t'kōmē'm) *m, pl. w.s.* תְּקוֹמְמֶיךָ, adversary.

תָּקוֹעַ (tākō'a') *m* trumpet, horn.

תְּקוֹעַ (t'kō'a') *pr.n.* of a town near Bethlehem.

תְּקוּפָה (t'kūfā') *f, c.* תְּקוּפַת, *pl.* תְּקוּפוֹת, a circuit, lapse.

תַּקִּיף (tākkī'f) *adj.* strong, mighty.

תָּקַן (tākă'n) *inf.* תְּקֹן, to be straight.—*Pi. fut.* יְתַקֵּן to make straight, to arrange.

תָּקַע (tākă'') *inf.* תְּקֹעַ, תָּקוֹעַ, *imp. pl.* תִּקְעוּ, *fut.* יִתְקַע, *pt.* תֹּקֵעַ, *pl.* תֹּקְעִים, to strike, to beat, to drive in, to fix; to thrust, to blow [a horn].—*Ni.* נִתְקַע, *fut.* יִתָּקַע, to be struck; to be blown.

תֵּקַע (tĕ'kă') *m* a blowing, blast.

תָּקַף (tākă'f) *fut.* יִתְקֹף, to overwhelm, assail, attack.

תֹּקֶף (tō'kĕf) *m, w.s.* תָּקְפּוֹ (tŏkfō'), might, power.

תֹּר see תּוֹר.

תַּרְאֲלָה (tăr'alā') *pr.n.* of a place in Benjamin.

תַּרְבּוּת (tărbū'θ) *f* increase, progeny.

תַּרְבִּית (tărbī'θ) *f* increase, usury, interest.

תַּרְדֵּמָה (tărdēmā') *f, c.* תַּרְדֵּמַת, deep sleep; sleepiness, lethargy.

תִּרְהָקָה (tĭrhākā') *pr.n.m.* of a king of Ethiopia or Egypt.

תְּרוּמָה (t'rūmā') *f, c.* תְּרוּמַת, *w.s.* תְּרוּמָתִי, *pl.* תְּרוּמוֹת, oblation, gift, present, offering, tribute, contribution; heave-offering.

תְּרוּמִי (t'rūmī') *adj., f* תְּרוּמִיָּה, belonging to a heave-offering [תְּרוּמָה].

תְּרוּעָה (t'rū'ā') *f* noise, shout, cries, loud sound, war-cry, sound of the trumpet

תְּרוּפָה (t'rūfā') *f* a healing, medicine.

תִּרְזָה (tĭrzā') *f* a kind of oak.

תֶּרַח (tĕ'răḥ) *pr.n.m.*; *pr.n.* of a station in the desert.

תִּרְחֲנָה (tĭrḥanā') *pr.n.m.*

תָּרְמָה (tŏrmā') *f* cunning, deceit.

תַּרְמוּת (tărmū'θ) and **תַּרְמִית** (tărmī'θ) *f* = תָּרְמָה.

תֹּרֶן (tō'rĕn) *m, w.s.* תָּרְנָם (tŏrnā'm) mast of a ship, flag-staff.

תַּרְעֵלָה (tăr'ĕlā') *f* a reeling, staggering, drunkenness.

תְּרָף (tārā'f) *m*, only *pl.* תְּרָפִים, household gods, Penates.

תִּרְצָה (tĭrẓā') *pr.n.* of a royal city in the kingdom of Israel.

תֶּרֶשׁ (tĕ'rĕsh) *pr.n.m.* [Persian].

תַּרְשִׁישׁ[1] (tărshī'sh) *pr.n.m.*; *pr.n.* of a city in Spain, Tarsis or Tartessus.

תַּרְשִׁישׁ[2] (tărshī'sh) *m* a precious stone, chrysolite or topaze.

תִּרְשָׁתָא (tĭrshā'thā) *m* title of Persian governors.

תַּרְתָּן (tărtān) *m* title of an Assyrian dignitary, general or fieldmarshal.

תַּרְתָּק (tărtā'k) *pr.n.* of an idol of the Avites.

תְּשׂוּמֶה (t'sūmā') *f*, *c.* תְּשׂוּמֶת, a thing deposited as a pledge.

תְּשֻׁאָה (t'shū'ā') *f*, only *pl.* תְּשֻׁאוֹת, noise, tumult, shout, crashing.

תִּשְׁבִּי (tĭshbī') *pr.n.m.*, *gent.* of תִּשְׁבֶּה a town in Naphtali.

תַּשְׁבֵּץ (tăshbē'ẓ) *m* checker-work, checker-cloth.

תְּשׁוּבָה (t'shūbā')*f*, *c.* תְּשׁוּבַת, *pl.* תְּשׁוּבוֹת, return; reply, answer.

תְּשֻׁוָּה (t'shŭvvā') = תְּשׁוּאָה, תְּשֻׁאָה.

תְּשׁוּעָה (t'shū'ā') *f*, *c.* תְּשׁוּעַת, help, assistance, deliverance, salvation.

תְּשׁוּקָה (t'shūkā') *f*, *w.s.* תְּשׁוּקָתֵךְ, longing, desire.

תְּשׁוּרָה (t'shūrā') *f* gift, present.

תְּשִׁיעִי (t'shī'ī') *adj. num. m*, *f* תְּשִׁיעִית, the ninth.

תֵּשַׁע (tē'shă') *num. f*, *c.* תְּשַׁע, *m* תִּשְׁעָה, *c.* תִּשְׁעַת, nine; *pl.* תִּשְׁעִים ninety.

תַּתְּנַי (tăthnă'y) *pr.n.m.* [Persian].

Conjugation Tables.

CONTENTS

I. Verbum

	Qal	*Niphal*	*Piel*
Pf. sg. 3 m.	קָטַל	נִקְטַל	קִטֵּל (קִטַּל)
f.	קָֽטְלָה	נִקְטְלָה	קִטְּלָה
2 m.	קָטַלְתָּ	נִקְטַלְתָּ	קִטַּלְתָּ
f.	קָטַלְתְּ	נִקְטַלְתְּ	קִטַּלְתְּ
1	קָטַלְתִּי	נִקְטַלְתִּי	קִטַּלְתִּי
pl. 3	קָֽטְלוּ	נִקְטְלוּ	קִטְּלוּ
2 m.	קְטַלְתֶּם	נִקְטַלְתֶּם	קִטַּלְתֶּם
f.	קְטַלְתֶּן	נִקְטַלְתֶּן	קִטַּלְתֶּן
1	קָטַלְנוּ	נִקְטַלְנוּ	קִטַּלְנוּ
Inf. abs.	קָטוֹל	הִקָּטֹל, נִקְטֹל	קַטֵּל, קַטֹּל
constr.	קְטֹל	הִקָּטֵל	קַטֵּל
Impt. sg. 2 m.	קְטֹל	הִקָּטֵל	קַטֵּל
f.	קִטְלִי	הִקָּֽטְלִי	קַטְּלִי
pl. 2 m.	קִטְלוּ	הִקָּֽטְלוּ	קַטְּלוּ
f.	קְטֹלְנָה	הִקָּטַלְנָה	קַטֵּלְנָה

firmum.

Pual	*Hithpael*	*Hiphil*	*Hophal*
קֻטַּל	הִתְקַטֵּל	הִקְטִיל	הָקְטַל
קֻטְּלָה	הִתְקַטְּלָה	הִקְטִילָה	הָקְטְלָה
קֻטַּלְתָּ	הִתְקַטַּלְתָּ	הִקְטַלְתָּ	הָקְטַלְתָּ
קֻטַּלְתְּ	הִתְקַטַּלְתְּ	הִקְטַלְתְּ	הָקְטַלְתְּ
קֻטַּלְתִּי	הִתְקַטַּלְתִּי	הִקְטַלְתִּי	הָקְטַלְתִּי
קֻטְּלוּ	הִתְקַטְּלוּ	הִקְטִילוּ	הָקְטְלוּ
קֻטַּלְתֶּם	הִתְקַטַּלְתֶּם	הִקְטַלְתֶּם	הָקְטַלְתֶּם
קֻטַּלְתֶּן	הִתְקַטַּלְתֶּן	הִקְטַלְתֶּן	הָקְטַלְתֶּן
קֻטַּלְנוּ	הִתְקַטַּלְנוּ	הִקְטַלְנוּ	הָקְטַלְנוּ
קֻטֹּל	הִתְקַטֵּל	הַקְטֵל	הָקְטֵל
—	הִתְקַטֵּל	הַקְטִיל	—
—	הִתְקַטֵּל	הַקְטֵל	—
—	הִתְקַטְּלִי	הַקְטִילִי	—
—	הִתְקַטְּלוּ	הַקְטִילוּ	—
—	הִתְקַטֵּלְנָה	הַקְטֵלְנָה	—

	Qal	*Niphal*	*Piel*
Fut. sg. 3 m.	יִקְטֹל	יִקָּטֵל	יְקַטֵּל
f.	תִּקְטֹל	תִּקָּטֵל	תְּקַטֵּל
2 *m.*	תִּקְטֹל	תִּקָּטֵל	תְּקַטֵּל
f.	תִּקְטְלִי	תִּקָּטְלִי	תְּקַטְּלִי
1	אֶקְטֹל	אֶקָּטֵל	אֲקַטֵּל
pl 3 *m.*	יִקְטְלוּ	יִקָּטְלוּ	יְקַטְּלוּ
f.	תִּקְטֹלְנָה	תִּקָּטַלְנָה	תְּקַטֵּלְנָה
2 *m.*	תִּקְטְלוּ	תִּקָּטְלוּ	תְּקַטְּלוּ
f.	תִּקְטֹלְנָה	תִּקָּטַלְנָה	תְּקַטֵּלְנָה
1	נִקְטֹל	נִקָּטֵל	נְקַטֵּל
Cohort.	אֶקְטְלָה	אֶקָּטְלָה	אֲקַטְּלָה
Juss.	—	—	—
Part.	קֹטֵל	נִקְטָל	מְקַטֵּל
Pt. pass.	קָטוּל	—	—

Pual	Hithpael	Hiphil	Hophal
יְקֻטַּל	יִתְקַטֵּל	יַקְטִיל	יָקְטַל
תְּקֻטַּל	תִּתְקַטֵּל	תַּקְטִיל	תָּקְטַל
תְּקֻטַּל	תִּתְקַטֵּל	תַּקְטִיל	תָּקְטַל
תְּקֻטְּלִי	תִּתְקַטְּלִי	תַּקְטִילִי	תָּקְטְלִי
אֲקֻטַּל	אֶתְקַטֵּל	אַקְטִיל	אָקְטַל
יְקֻטְּלוּ	יִתְקַטְּלוּ	יַקְטִילוּ	יָקְטְלוּ
תְּקֻטַּלְנָה	תִּתְקַטֵּלְנָה	תַּקְטֵלְנָה	תָּקְטַלְנָה
תְּקֻטְּלוּ	תִּתְקַטְּלוּ	תַּקְטִילוּ	תָּקְטְלוּ
תְּקֻטַּלְנָה	תִּתְקַטֵּלְנָה	תַּקְטֵלְנָה	תָּקְטַלְנָה
נְקֻטַּל	נִתְקַטֵּל	נַקְטִיל	נָקְטַל
—	אֶתְקַטְּלָה	אַקְטִילָה	—
—	—	יַקְטֵל	—
מְקֻטָּל	מִתְקַטֵּל	מַקְטִיל	מָקְטָל
—	—	—	—

	Qal med. e & o.		Qal i. p.	
Pf. sg. 3 *m.*	כָּבֵד	קָטֹן	קָטֵל	
f.	כָּבְדָה	קָטְנָה	קָטֵלָה	כָּבֵדָה
2 *m.*	כָּבַדְתָּ	קָטֹנְתָּ	קָטָלְתָּ	
f.	כָּבַדְתְּ	קָטֹנְתְּ	קָטָלְתְּ	
1	כָּבַדְתִּי	קָטֹנְתִּי	קָטָלְתִּי	
pl. 3	כָּבְדוּ	קָטְנוּ	קָטֵלוּ	כָּבֵדוּ
2 *m.*	כְּבַדְתֶּם	קְטָנְתֶּם	—	
f.	כְּבַדְתֶּן	קְטָנְתֶּן	—	
1	כָּבַדְנוּ	קָטֹנּוּ	קָטָלְנוּ	
Inf. abs.	(כָּבוֹד)	—	—	—
constr.	(כְּבֹד, כְּבַד)	—	—	—
Impt. sg. 2 *m.*	כְּבַד	—	—	כְּבָד
f.	כִּבְדִי	—	קְטֹלִי	כְּבֵדִי

pl. 2 *m.*	כִּבְדוּ	—	קִטְלוּ	כָּבֳדוּ
f.	כִּבַדְנָה	—	—	כָּבֳדְנָה
Fut. sg. 3 *m.*	יִכְבַּד	יִקְטַן	—	יְכָבֵד
f.	תִּכְבַּד	—	—	u. s. w.
2 *m.*	תִּכְבַּד	—	—	
f.	תִּכְבְּדִי	—	תִּקְטְלִי	
1	אֶכְבַּד	—	—	
pl. 3 *m.*	יִכְבְּדוּ	—	יִקְטְלוּ	
f.	תִּכְבַּדְנָה	—	—	
2 *m.*	תִּכְבְּדוּ	—	תִּקְטְלוּ	
f.	תִּכְבַּדְנָה	—	—	
1	נִכְבַּד	—	—	
Cohort.	אֶכְבְּדָה	—		
Juss.	—	—		
Part.	כָּבֵד	קָטֹן		
Pt. pass.	—	—		

II. Verbum

	sg. 3 m.	3 f.
Pf. sg. 3 m.	קְטָלָהוּ, קְטָלוֹ	קְטָלָהּ
f.	קְטָלַתְהוּ, קְטָלַתּוּ	קְטָלַתָּהּ
2 m.	קְטַלְתָּהוּ, קְטַלְתּוֹ	קְטַלְתָּהּ
f. } ***1***	קְטַלְתִּיהוּ, קְטַלְתִּיו	קְטַלְתִּיהָ
pl. 3	קְטָלוּהוּ	קְטָלוּהָ
2	קְטַלְתּוּהוּ	קְטַלְתּוּהָ
1	קְטַלְנוּהוּ	קְטַלְנוּהָ
Inf.	קָטְלוֹ	קָטְלָהּ
Impt. sg.	קָטְלֵהוּ	קָטְלֶהָ, קָטְלָהּ
pl.	קִטְלוּהוּ	קִטְלוּהָ
Fut. sg. 3 m.	יִקְטְלֵהוּ	יִקְטְלֶהָ, יִקְטְלָהּ
with ן	יִקְטְלֶנּוּ	יִקְטְלֶנָּה
pl. 3 m.	יִקְטְלוּהוּ	יִקְטְלוּהָ
Pi. pf. sg. 3 m.	קִטְּלוֹ	קִטְּלָהּ
Hi. " " "	הִקְטִילוֹ	הִקְטִילָהּ

cum suffixis.

2 m.	*2 f.*	*1*
קְטָלְךָ	קְטָלֵךְ	קְטָלַנִי
קְטָלַתְךָ	קְטָלָתֶךְ	קְטָלַתְנִי
—	—	קְטַלְתַּנִי
—	—	קְטַלְתִּינִי
קְטַלְתִּיךָ	קְטַלְתִּיךְ	—
קְטָלוּךָ	קְטָלוּךְ	קְטָלוּנִי
—	—	קְטַלְתּוּנִי
קְטַלְנוּךָ	קְטַלְנוּךְ	—
קָטְלְךָ, קְטָלְךָ	קָטְלֵךְ	קָטְלִי, קָטְלַנִי
—	—	קָטְלַנִי
—	—	קִטְלוּנִי
יִקְטָלְךָ	יִקְטְלַךְ	יִקְטְלַנִי
יִקְטְלֶךָּ	—	יִקְטְלֶנִּי
יִקְטְלוּךָ	יִקְטְלוּךְ	יִקְטְלוּנִי
קִטְּלְךָ	קִטְּלֵךְ	קִטְּלַנִי
הִקְטִילְךָ	הִקְטִילֵךְ	הִקְטִילַנִי

	pl. 3 m.	3 f.	2 m.	1
***Pf.* sg. 3 m.**	קְטָלָם	קְטָלָן	(קְטַלְכֶם)	קְטָלָנוּ
f.	קְטָלַתַם	קְטָלַתַן	—	קְטָלַתְנוּ
2 m.	קְטַלְתָּם	קְטַלְתָּן	—	קְטַלְתָּנוּ
f.	קְטַלְתִּים	קְטַלְתִּין	—	קְטַלְתִּינוּ
1	קְטַלְתִּים	קְטַלְתִּין	קְטַלְתִּיכֶם	—
***pl.* 3**	קְטָלוּם	קְטָלוּן	—	קְטָלוּנוּ
2	קְטַלְתּוּם	קְטַלְתּוּן	—	קְטַלְתּוּנוּ
1	קְטַלְנוּם	קְטַלְנוּן	קְטַלְנוּכֶם	—
Inf.	קָטְלָם	קָטְלָן	קָטְלְכֶם, קָטָלְכֶם	קָטְלֵנוּ
***Impt.* sg.**	קָטְלֵם	—	—	קָטְלֵנוּ
pl.	קִטְלוּם	—	—	קִטְלוּנוּ
***Fut.* sg. 3 m.**	יִקְטְלֵם	יִקְטְלֵן	יִקְטָלְכֶם	יִקְטְלֵנוּ
with ן	—	—	—	יִקְטְלֶנּוּ
pl. 3 m.	יִקְטְלוּם	יִקְטְלוּן	יִקְטְלוּכֶם	יִקְטְלוּנוּ
Pi pf. sg. 3 m.	קִטְּלָם	קִטְּלָן	קִטֶּלְכֶם	קִטְּלָנוּ
Hi.	[illegible]	[illegible]	[illegible]	[illegible]

III. Verba primae gutturalis.

	Qal	*Niphal*	*Hiphil*	*Hophal*
***Pf.** sg.* **3 m.**	עָמַד	נֶעֱמַד	הֶעֱמִיד	הָעֳמַד
f.	עָמְדָה	נֶעֶמְדָה	הֶעֱמִידָה	הָעָמְדָה
2 m.	עָמַדְתָּ	נֶעֱמַדְתָּ	הֶעֱמַדְתָּ	הָעֳמַדְתָּ
pl. 2 m.	עֲמַדְתֶּם	נֶעֱמַדְתֶּם	הֶעֱמַדְתֶּם	הָעֳמַדְתֶּם
***Inf.** abs.*	עָמוֹד	נַעֲמוֹד	הַעֲמֵד	הָעֳמֵד
constr.	עֲמֹד	הֵעָמֵד	הַעֲמִיד	(הָעֳמַד)
***Impt.** sg.* **m.**	עֲמֹד	הֵעָמֵד	הַעֲמֵד	—
f.	עִמְדִי	הֵעָמְדִי	הַעֲמִידִי	—
***Fut.**sg.3m.*	יַעֲמֹד	יֵעָמֵד	יַעֲמִיד	יָעֳמַד
2 f.	תַּעַמְדִי	תֵּעָמְדִי	תַּעֲמִידִי	תָּעָמְדִי
1	אֶעֱמֹד	אֵעָמֵד	אַעֲמִיד	אָעֳמַד
Part.	עֹמֵד, עָמוּד	נֶעֱמָד	מַעֲמִיד	מָעֳמָד

IV. Verba mediae

	Qal	*Niphal*
Pf. sg. 3 m.	שָׁחַט	נִשְׁחַט
f.	שָֽׁחֲטָה	נִשְׁחֲטָה
pl. 3	שָֽׁחֲטוּ	נִשְׁחַטוּ
Inf. abs.	שָׁחוֹט	נִשְׁחוֹט
constr.	שְׁחֹט	הִשָּׁחַט
Impt. sg. m.	שְׁחַט	הִשָּׁחַט
f.	שַׁחֲטִי	הִשָּׁחֲטִי
pl. f.	שְׁחַטְנָה	הִשָּׁחַטְנָה
Fut. sg. 3 m.	יִשְׁחַט	ישָּׁחַט
2 f.	תִּשְׁחֲטִי	תִּשָּׁחֲטִי
pl. 3 f.	תִּשְׁחַטְנָה	תִּשָּׁחַטְנָה

gutturalis.

Piel	*Pual*	*Hithpael*
בֵּרַךְ	בֹּרַךְ	הִתְבָּרַךְ
בֵּרְכָה	בֹּרְכָה	הִתְבָּֽרֲכָה
בֵּרְכוּ	בֹּרְכוּ	הִתְבֵּֽרֲכוּ
בָּרַךְ	—	—
בָּרַךְ	—	הִתְבָּרַךְ
בָּרַךְ	—	הִתְבָּרַךְ
בָּֽרֲכִי	—	הִתְבָּֽרֲכִי
בָּרַכְנָה	—	הִתְבָּרַכְנָה
יְבָרַךְ	יְבֹרַךְ	יִתְבָּרַךְ
תְּבָֽרֲכִי	תְּבֹרְכִי	תִּתְבָּֽרֲכִי
תְּבָרַכְנָה	תְּבֹרַכְנָה	תִּתְבָּרַכְנָה

V. Verba tertiae

	Qal	*Niphal*	*Piel*
Pf. sg. 3 m.	שָׁלַח	נִשְׁלַח	שִׁלַּח
f,	שָֽׁלְחָה	נִשְׁלְחָה	שִׁלְּחָה
2 m.	שָׁלַחְתָּ	נִשְׁלַחְתָּ	שִׁלַּחְתָּ
f.	שָׁלַחַתְּ	נִשְׁלַחַתְּ	שִׁלַּחַתְּ
Inf. abs.	שָׁלוֹחַ	נִשְׁלֹחַ	שַׁלֵּחַ
constr.	שְׁלֹחַ	הִשָּׁלַח	שַׁלַּח
Impt. sg. m.	שְׁלַח	הִשָּׁלַח	שַׁלַּח
f.	שִׁלְחִי	הִשָּׁלְחִי	שַׁלְּחִי
pl. f.	שְׁלַחְנָה	הִשָּׁלַחְנָה	שַׁלַּחְנָה
Fut.sg.3m.	יִשְׁלַח	יִשָּׁלַח	יְשַׁלַּח
2 f.	תִּשְׁלְחִי	תִּשָּׁלְחִי	תְּשַׁלְּחִי
pl. 3 f.	תִּשְׁלַחְנָה	תִּשָּׁלַחְנָה	תְּשַׁלַּחְנָה
Part.	שָׁלוּחַ,שֹׁלֵחַ	נִשְׁלָח	מְשַׁלֵּחַ

gutturalis.

Pual	*Hiphil*	*Hophal*	*Hithpael*
שֻׁלַּח	הִשְׁלִיחַ	הָשְׁלַח	הִשְׁתַּלַּח
שֻׁלְּחָה	הִשְׁלִיחָה	הָשְׁלְחָה	הִשְׁתַּלְּחָה
שֻׁלַּחְתָּ	הִשְׁלַחְתָּ	הָשְׁלַחְתָּ	הִשְׁתַּלַּחְתָּ
שֻׁלַּחַתְּ	הִשְׁלַחַתְּ	הָשְׁלַחַתְּ	הִשְׁתַּלַּחַתְּ
—	הַשְׁלֵחַ	—	—
—	הַשְׁלִיחַ	—	הִשְׁתַּלַּח
—	הַשְׁלַח	—	הִשְׁתַּלַּח
—	הַשְׁלִיחִי	—	הִשְׁתַּלְּחִי
—	הַשְׁלַחְנָה	—	הִשְׁתַּלַּחְנָה
יְשֻׁלַּח	יַשְׁלִיחַ	יָשְׁלַח	יִשְׁתַּלַּח
תְּשֻׁלְּחִי	תַּשְׁלִיחִי	תָּשְׁלְחִי	תִּשְׁתַּלְּחִי
תְּשֻׁלַּחְנָה	תַּשְׁלַחְנָה	תָּשְׁלַחְנָה	תִּשְׁתַּלַּחְנָה
מְשֻׁלָּח	מַשְׁלִיחַ	מָשְׁלָח	מִשְׁתַּלַּחַ

VI. Verba ע"ע.

	Qal		*Niphal*	*Hiphil*
Pf. sg. 3 m.	סַב		נָסַב	הֵסַב
f.	סַבָּה		נָסַבָּה	הֵסַבָּה
2 m.	סַבּוֹתָ		נְסַבּוֹתָ	הֲסִבּוֹתָ
Inf. abs.	סָבוֹב		הִסּוֹב	הָסֵב
constr.	סֹב		הִסֵּב	הָסֵב
Impt. sg. m.	סֹב		הִסֵּב	הָסֵב
f.	סֹבִּי		הִסַּבִּי	הָסֵבִּי
pl. f.	סֻבֶּינָה		הִסַּבֶּינָה	הֲסִבֶּינָה
Fut. sg. 3 m.	יִסֹב	יסֹּב	יִסַּב	יָסֵב
2 f.	תָּסֹבִּי	תִּסֹּבִי	תִּסַּבִּי	תָּסֵבִּי
pl. 3 f.	תְּסֻבֶּינָה	תִּסֹּבְנָה	תִּסַּבֶּינָה	תְּסִבֶּינָה
Part.	סֹבֵב, סָבוּב		נָסָב	מֵסֵב

Hophal	*Poel*	*Poal*
הוּסַב	סוֹבֵב	סוֹבַב
הוּסָבָּה	סוֹבְבָה	סוֹבְבָה
הוּסַבּוֹתָ	סוֹבַבְתָּ	סוֹבַבְתָּ
—	סוֹבֵב	סוֹבַב
הוּסַב	סוֹבֵב	—
—	סוֹבֵב	—
—	סוֹבֱבִי	—
—	סוֹבֵבְנָה	—
יוּסַב	יְסוֹבֵב	יְסוֹבַב
תּוּסָבִּי	תְּסוֹבֱבִי	תְּסוֹבֲבִי
תּוּסַבֶּינָה	תְּסוֹבֵבְנָה	תְּסוֹבַבְנָה
מוּסָב	מְסוֹבֵב	מְסוֹבָב

VII. Verba פ"ן.

	Qal	
Pf. sg. 3 m.	נָפַל	נָגַשׁ
Inf. abs.	נָפוֹל	נָגוֹשׁ
constr.	נְפֹל	גֶּשֶׁת
Impt. sg. m.	נְפֹל	גַּשׁ
f.	נִפְלִי	גְּשִׁי
pl. f.	נְפֹלְנָה	גַּשְׁנָה
Fut.sg.3m.	יִפֹּל	יִגַּשׁ
2 f.	תִּפְּלִי	תִּגְּשִׁי
pl. 3 f.	תִּפֹּלְנָה	תִּגַּשְׁנָה
Part.		נָגוּשׁ, נִגָּשׁ

Niphal	*Hiphil*	*Hophal*
נִגַּשׁ	הִגִּישׁ	הָגַּשׁ
הִנָּגשׁ	הַגֵּשׁ	הָגֵּשׁ
הִנָּגֵשׁ	הַגִּישׁ	הָגַּשׁ
הִנָּגֵשׁ	הַגֵּשׁ	—
u. s. w.	הַגִּישִׁי	—
	הַגֵּשְׁנָה	—
יִנָּגֵשׁ	יַגִּישׁ	יֻגַּשׁ
תִּנָּגְשִׁי	תַּגִּישִׁי	תֻּגְּשִׁי
תִּנָּגַשְׁנָה	תַּגֵּשְׁנָה	תֻּגַּשְׁנָה
נִגָּשׁ	מַגִּישׁ	מֻגָּשׁ

	VIII. Verba פ״א.	IX. Verba פ״י	
	Qal	*Qal*	*Hifil*
Pf. sg. 3 m.	אָכַל	יָטַב	הֵיטִיב
f.	אָכְלָה	&c.	הֵיטִיבָה
pl. 2 m.	אֲכַלְתֶּם		הֵיטַבְתֶּם
Inf. abs.	אָכוֹל	יָטוֹב	הֵיטֵב
c.	אֱכֹל, אֲכֹל	יְטֹב	הֵיטִיב
Impt. sg. m.	אֱכֹל	(יְטַב	הֵיטֵב
f.	אִכְלִי	(יִטְבִי	הֵיטִיבִי
Fut. sg. 3m.	יֹאכַל (יֹאכֵל)	יִיטַב	יֵיטִיב
1	אֹכַל	אִיטַב	אֵיטִיב
pl. 3 f.	תֹּאכַלְנָה	תִּיטַבְנָה	תֵּיטֵבְנָה
Part.	*regular*	*regular*	מֵיטִיב

X. Verba פ״ו.

	Qal	*Nifal*	*Hifil*	*Hofal*
Pf. sg. 3 m.	יָשַׁב	נוֹשַׁב	הוֹשִׁיב	הוּשַׁב
f.	יָשְׁבָה	נוֹשְׁבָה	הוֹשִׁיבָה	הוּשְׁבָה
Inf. a.	יָשׁוֹב	—	הוֹשֵׁב	—
c.	שֶׁבֶת	הִוָּשֵׁב	הוֹשִׁיב	הוּשַׁב
Impt. sg. m.	שֵׁב	הִוָּשֵׁב	הוֹשֵׁב	—
f.	שְׁבִי	הִוָּשְׁבִי	הוֹשִׁיבִי	—
pl. f.	שֵׁבְנָה	הִוָּשַׁבְנָה	הוֹשֵׁבְנָה	—
Fut.sg.3m.	יֵשֵׁב	יִוָּשֵׁב	יוֹשִׁיב	יוּשַׁב
2 f.	תֵּשְׁבִי	תִּוָּשְׁבִי	תּוֹשִׁיבִי	תּוּשְׁבִי
pl. 3 f.	תֵּשַׁבְנָה	תִּוָּשַׁבְנָה	תּוֹשֵׁבְנָה	תּוּשַׁבְנָה
Part.	יָשׁוּב, יֹשֵׁב	נוֹשָׁב	מוֹשִׁיב	מוּשָׁב

XI. Verba ע״ו.

	Qal	Niphal	Hiphil	Hophal
Pf. sg. 3 m.	קָם	נָקוֹם	הֵקִים	הוּקַם
f.	קָֽמָה	נָקֽוֹמָה	הֵקִֽימָה	הוּקְמָה
2 m.	קַמְתָּ	נְקוּמוֹתָ	הֲקִימוֹתָ	הוּקַמְתָּ
pl. 2 m.	קַמְתֶּם	נְקוּמוֹתֶם	הֲקִימוֹתֶם	הוּקַמְתֶּם
Inf. a.	קוֹם	הִקּוֹם	הָקֵם	—
c.	קוּם	הִקּוֹם	הָקִים	הוּקַם
Impt. sg. m.	קוּם	הִקּוֹם	הָקֵם	—
f.	קֽוּמִי	הִקּֽוֹמִי	הָקִֽימִי	—
pl. f.	קֹֽמְנָה	הִקֹּֽמְנָה	הָקֵֽמְנָה	—
Fut. sg. 3 m.	יָקוּם	יִקּוֹם	יָקִים	יוּקַם
2 f.	תָּקֽוּמִי	תִּקּֽוֹמִי	תָּקִֽימִי	תּוּקְמִי
pl. 3 f.	תְּקוּמֶֽינָה	(תִּקֹּֽמְנָה)	תָּקֵֽמְנָה	תּוּקַֽמְנָה
Juss.	יָקֹם		יָקֵם	
Fut. conv.	וַיָּֽקָם		וַיָּֽקֶם	
Part.	קוּם, קָם	נָקוֹם	מֵקִים	מוּקָם

XII. Verba ע"י.

Piel	*Pual*	*Qal*		*Niphal*
קוֹמֵם	קוֹמַם	בָּן	בִּין	נָבוֹן
קוֹמְמָה	קוֹמְמָה	בָּנָה	בִּינָה	נָבוֹנָה
קוֹמַמְתָּ	קוֹמַמְתָּ	בַּנְתָּ	בִּינוֹתָ	נְבוּנוֹתָ
קוֹמַמְתֶּם	קוֹמַמְתֶּם	בַּנְתֶּם	בִּינוֹתֶם	נְבוּנוֹתֶם
—	—		בֹּן	הִבּוֹן
קוֹמֵם	קוֹמַם		בִּין	הִבּוֹן
קוֹמֵם	—		בִּין	הִבּוֹן
קוֹמְמִי	—		בִּינִי	הִבּוֹנִי
קוֹמֵמְנָה	—		—	—
יְקוֹמֵם	יְקוֹמַם		יָבִין	יִבּוֹן
תְּקוֹמְמִי	תְּקוֹמְמִי		תָּבִינִי	תִּבּוֹנִי
תְּקוֹמֵמְנָה	תְּקוֹמַמְנָה		תְּבִינֶינָה	—
			יָבֵן	—
			וַיָּבֶן	--
מְקוֹמֵם	מְקוֹמָם		בּוֹן, בָּן	נָבוֹן

XIII. Verba ל״א.

	Qal	*Niphal*	*Piel*
Pf. sg. 3 m.	מָצָא	נִמְצָא	מִצֵּא
f.	מָֽצְאָה	נִמְצְאָה	מִצְּאָה
2 m.	מָצָאתָ	נִמְצֵאתָ	מִצֵּאתָ
pl. 2 m.	מְצָאתֶם	נִמְצֵאתֶם	מִצֵּאתֶם
Inf. abs.	מָצוֹא	נִמְצֹא	מַצֹּא
constr.	מְצֹא	הִמָּצֵא	מַצֵּא
Impt. sg. m.	מְצָא	הִמָּצֵא	מַצֵּא
f.	מִצְאִי	הִמָּצְאִי	מַצְּאִי
pl. f.	מְצֶאנָה	הִמָּצֶאנָה	מַצֶּאנָה
Fut.sg.3m.	יִמְצָא	יִמָּצֵא	יְמַצֵּא
2 f.	תִּמְצְאִי	תִּמָּצְאִי	תְּמַצְּאִי
pl 3 f.	תִּמְצֶאנָה	תִּמָּצֶאנָה	תְּמַצֶּאנָה
Part.	מָצוּא, מֹצֵא	נִמְצָא	מְמַצֵּא

Pual	*Hithpael*	*Hiphil*	*Hophal*
מֻצָּא	הִתְמַצֵּא	הִמְצִיא	הָמְצָא (הֻמְצָא)
מֻצְּאָה	הִתְמַצְּאָה	הִמְצִיאָה	הָמְצְאָה
מֻצֵּאתָ	הִתְמַצֵּאתָ	הִמְצֵאתָ	הָמְצֵאתָ
מֻצֵּאתֶם	הִתְמַצֵּאתֶם	הִמְצֵאתֶם	הָמְצֵאתֶם
—	—	הַמְצֵא	—
—	הִתְמַצֵּא	הַמְצִיא	הָמְצָא
—	הִתְמַצֵּא	הַמְצֵא	—
—	הִתְמַצְּאִי	הַמְצִיאִי	—
—	הִתְמַצֶּאנָה	הַמְצֶאנָה	—
יְמֻצָּא	יִתְמַצֵּא	יַמְצִיא	יָמְצָא
תְּמֻצְּאִי	תִּתְמַצְּאִי	תַּמְצִיאִי	תָּמְצְאִי
תְּמֻצֶּאנָח	תִּתְמַצֶּאנָה	תַּמְצֶאנָה	תָּמְצֶאנָה
מְמֻצָּא	מִתְמַצֵּא	מַמְצִיא	מָמְצָא

XIV. Verba ל״ה.

	Qal	*Niphal*	*Piel*
Pf. sg. 3 m.	גָּלָה	נִגְלָה	גִּלָּה
f.	גָּֽלְתָה	נִגְלְתָה	גִּלְּתָה
2 m.	גָּלִיתָ	נִגְלֵיתָ (לִיתָ)	גִּלֵּיתָ, גִּלִּיתָ
pl. 3	גָּלוּ	נִגְלוּ	גִּלּוּ
2 m.	גְּלִיתֶם	נִגְלֵיתֶם	גִּלֵּיתֶם
Inf. abs.	גָּלֹה	נִגְלֹה	גַּלֹּה, גַּלֵּה
constr.	גְּלוֹת	הִגָּלוֹת	גַּלּוֹת
Fut.sg. m.	גְּלֵה	הִגָּלֵה	גַּלֵּה
f.	גְּלִי	הִגָּלִי	גַּלִּי
pl. f.	גְּלֶינָה	הִגָּלֶינָה	גַּלֶּינָה
Fut.sg.3m.	יִגְלֶה	יִגָּלֶה	יְגַלֶּה
2 f.	תִּגְלִי	תִּגָּלִי	תְּגַלִּי
pl. 3 f.	תִּגְלֶינָה	תִּגָּלֶינָה	תְּגַלֶּינָה
Impf. ap.	יִגֶל	יִגָּל	יְגַל
Part.	גֹּלֶה (*f.* גֹּלָה)	נִגְלֶה	מְגַלֶּה
„ *p.*	גָּלוּי		

Pual	*Hithpael*	*Hiphil*	*Hophal*
גֻּלָּה	הִתְגַּלָּה	הִגְלָה	הָגְלָה
גֻּלְּתָה	הִתְגַּלְּתָה	הִגְלְתָה	הָגְלְתָה
גֻּלֵּיתָ	הִתְגַּלֵּיתָ	הִגְלֵיתָ, לִיתָ	הָגְלֵיתָ
גֻּלּוּ	הִתְגַּלּוּ	הִגְלוּ	הָגְלוּ
גֻּלֵּיתֶם	הִתְגַּלֵּיתֶם	הִגְלֵיתֶם	הָגְלֵיתֶם
—	—	הַגְלֵה	הָגְלֵה
גֻּלּוֹת	הִתְגַּלּוֹת	הַגְלוֹת	הָגְלוֹת
—	הִתְגַּלֵּה	הַגְלֵה	—
—	הִתְגַּלִּי	הַגְלִי	—
—	הִתְגַּלֶּינָה	הַגְלֶינָה	—
יְגֻלֶּה	יִתְגַּלֶּה	יַגְלֶה	יָגְלֶה
תְּגֻלִּי	תִּתְגַּלִּי	תַּגְלִי	תָּגְלִי
תְּגֻלֶּינָה	תִּתְגַּלֶּינָה	תַּגְלֶינָה	תָּגְלֶינָה
—	יִתְגַּל	יֶגֶל	—
מְגֻלֶּה	מִתְגַּלֶּה	מַגְלֶה	מָגְלֶה

Modern Hebrew Conjugation Tables.

הָפְעַל Hof'al	הִפְעִיל Hif'il	הִתְפַּעֵל Hitpa'él	פֻּעַל Pu'al	
הָכְתֵּב	הַכְתֵּב	הִתְכַּתֵּב		
–	לְהַכְתִּיב	לְהִתְכַּתֵּב		
מָכְתָּב מָכְתֶּבֶת מָכְתָּבִים מָכְתָּבוֹת	מַכְתִּיב מַכְתִּיבָה מַכְתִּיבִים מַכְתִּיבוֹת	מִתְכַּתֵּב מִתְכַּתֶּבֶת מִתְכַּתְּבִים מִתְכַּתְּבוֹת	מְכֻתָּב מְכֻתֶּבֶת מְכֻתָּבִים מְכֻתָּבוֹת	

לוּחוֹת הַפְּעָלִים

א. גִּזְרַת הַשְּׁלֵמִים

בִּנְיָן			קַל Kal	נִפְעַל Nif'al	פִּעֵל Pi'él
שֹׁרֶשׁ			כתב		
מָקוֹר			כָּתוֹב	נִכְתּוֹב	כַּתֵּב
שֵׁם הַפֹּעַל עִם ל׳			לִכְתֹּב	לְהִכָּתֵב	לְכַתֵּב
הֹוֶה	יָחִיד	ז׳ *m*	אֲנִי, אַתָּה, הוּא כּוֹתֵב	נִכְתָּב	מְכַתֵּב
		נ׳ *f*	אֲנִי, אַתְּ, הִיא כּוֹתֶבֶת	נִכְתֶּבֶת	מְכַתֶּבֶת
	רַבִּים	ז׳ *m*	אָנוּ, אַתֶּם, הֵם כּוֹתְבִים	נִכְתָּבִים	מְכַתְּבִים
		נ׳ *f*	אָנוּ, אַתֶּן, הֵן כּוֹתְבוֹת	נִכְתָּבוֹת	מְכַתְּבוֹת

כֻּתַּבְתִּי	הִתְכַּתַּבְתִּי	הִכְתַּבְתִּי	הֻכְתַּבְתִּי
כֻּתַּבְתָּ	הִתְכַּתַּבְתָּ	הִכְתַּבְתָּ	הֻכְתַּבְתָּ
כֻּתַּבְתְּ	הִתְכַּתַּבְתְּ	הִכְתַּבְתְּ	הֻכְתַּבְתְּ
כֻּתַּב	הִתְכַּתֵּב	הִכְתִּיב	הֻכְתַּב
כֻּתְּבָה	הִתְכַּתְּבָה	הִכְתִּיבָה	הֻכְתְּבָה
כֻּתַּבְנוּ	הִתְכַּתַּבְנוּ	הִכְתַּבְנוּ	הֻכְתַּבְנוּ
כֻּתַּבְתֶּם(ן)	הִתְכַּתַּבְתֶּם(ן)	הִכְתַּבְתֶּם(ן)	הֻכְתַּבְתֶּם(ן)
כֻּתְּבוּ	הִתְכַּתְּבוּ	הִכְתִּיבוּ	הֻכְתְּבוּ
אֲכֻתַּב	אֶתְכַּתֵּב	אַכְתִּיב	אֻכְתַּב
תְּכֻתַּב	תִּתְכַּתֵּב	תַּכְתִּיב	תֻּכְתַּב
תְּכֻתְּבִי	תִּתְכַּתְּבִי	תַּכְתִּיבִי	תֻּכְתְּבִי
יְכֻתַּב	יִתְכַּתֵּב	יַכְתִּיב	יֻכְתַּב
תְּכֻתַּב	תִּתְכַּתֵּב	תַּכְתִּיב	תֻּכְתַּב
נְכֻתַּב	נִתְכַּתֵּב	נַכְתִּיב	נֻכְתַּב
תְּכֻתְּבוּ	תִּתְכַּתְּבוּ	תַּכְתִּיבוּ	תֻּכְתְּבוּ
יְכֻתְּבוּ	יִתְכַּתְּבוּ	יַכְתִּיבוּ	יֻכְתְּבוּ
(תְּכֻתַּבְנָה)	(תִּתְכַּתֵּבְנָה)	(תַּכְתֵּבְנָה)	(תֻּכְתַּבְנָה)
–	הִתְכַּתֵּב	הַכְתֵּב	–
–	הִתְכַּתְּבִי	הַכְתִּיבִי	–
–	הִתְכַּתְּבוּ	הַכְתִּיבוּ	–

כִּתַּבְתִּי	נִכְתַּבְתִּי		כָּתַבְתִּי	1	עָבַר
כִּתַּבְתָּ	נִכְתַּבְתָּ		כָּתַבְתָּ	2 *m*	
כִּתַּבְתְּ	נִכְתַּבְתְּ		כָּתַבְתְּ	2 *f*	יָחִיד
כִּתֵּב	נִכְתַּב		כָּתַב	3 *m*	
כִּתְּבָה	נִכְתְּבָה		כָּתְבָה	3 *f*	
כִּתַּבְנוּ	נִכְתַּבְנוּ		כָּתַבְנוּ	1	
כִּתַּבְתֶּם(ן)	נִכְתַּבְתֶּם(ן)		כְּתַבְתֶּם(ן)	2 Plural	רַבִּים
כִּתְּבוּ	נִכְתְּבוּ		כָּתְבוּ	3	
			משקל		עָתִיד
		ef'al אֶפְעַל	ef'ol אֶפְעֹל		
אֲכַתֵּב	אֶכָּתֵב	אֶרְכַּב	אֶכְתֹּב	1	יָחִיד
תְּכַתֵּב	תִּכָּתֵב	תִּרְכַּב	תִּכְתֹּב	2 *m*	
תְּכַתְּבִי	תִּכָּתְבִי	תִּרְכְּבִי	תִּכְתְּבִי	2 *f*	
יְכַתֵּב	יִכָּתֵב	יִרְכַּב	יִכְתֹּב	3 *m*	
תְּכַתֵּב	תִּכָּתֵב	תִּרְכַּב	תִּכְתֹּב	3 *f*	
נְכַתֵּב	נִכָּתֵב	נִרְכַּב	נִכְתֹּב	1	רַבִּים
תְּכַתְּבוּ	תִּכָּתְבוּ	תִּרְכְּבוּ	תִּכְתְּבוּ	2 *m*	
יְכַתְּבוּ	יִכָּתְבוּ	יִרְכְּבוּ	יִכְתְּבוּ	3 *m*	
(תְּכַתֵּבְנָה)	(תִּכָּתֵבְנָה)	(תִּרְכַּבְנָה)	(תִּכְתֹּבְנָה)	2, 3 *f*	
כַּתֵּב	הִכָּתֵב		כְּתֹב	יָחִיד ז׳	צִוּוּי
כַּתְּבִי	הִכָּתְבִי		כִּתְבִי	Sing. נ׳	
כַּתְּבוּ	הִכָּתְבוּ		כִּתְבוּ	רַבִּים	

הוֶה	עָתִיד	צִווּי
יוֹשֵׁב יוֹשֶׁבֶת יוֹדֵעַ יוֹדַעַת	אֵשֵׁב אֵדַע	שֵׁב! שְׁבִי! דַּע! דְּעִי!
נוֹפֵל נוֹפֶלֶת	אֶפֹּל יִפֹּל	נְפֹל! נִפְלִי!
אוֹכֵל אוֹכֶלֶת	אֹכַל יֹאכַל	אֱכֹל! אִכְלִי!
יוֹנֵק יוֹנֶקֶת	אִינַק יִינַק	יְנַק! יִנְקִי!
קָם קָמָה	אָקוּם יָקוּם	קוּם! קוּמִי!
שָׁר שָׁרָה	אָשִׁיר יָשִׁיר	שִׁיר! שִׁירִי!
קוֹרֵא קוֹרֵאת	אֶקְרָא יִקְרָא	קְרָא! קִרְאִי!
בּוֹנֶה בּוֹנָה	אֶבְנֶה יִבְנֶה	בְּנֵה! בְּנִי!
סַב (סוֹבֵב) סַבָּה	אָסֹב יָסֹב	סֹב! סֹבִּי!

ב. גְּזָרוֹת הַחֲסֵרִים, הַנָּחִים וְהַכְּפוּלִים

בִּנְיָן	גִּזְרָה	הַפֹּעַל	מָקוֹר	שֵׁם הַפֹּעַל עִם ל׳	עָבָר
פָּעַל Kal	חַסְרֵי פ״י(1	ישב ידע	יָשׁוֹב יָדוֹעַ	לָשֶׁבֶת לָדַעַת	יָשַׁב יָדַע
	חַסְרֵי פ״נ(2	נפל	נָפוֹל	לִנְפֹּל, לִפֹּל	נָפַל
	נָחֵי פ״א(3	אכל	אָכוֹל	לֶאֱכֹל	אָכַל
	נָחֵי פ״י(4	ינק	יָנוֹק	לִינֹק	יָנַק
	נָחֵי ע״ו(5	קום	קוֹם	לָקוּם	קָם
	נָחֵי ע״י(6	שיר	שִׁיר	לָשִׁיר	שָׁר
	נָחֵי ל״א(7	קרא	קָרוֹא	לִקְרֹא	קָרָא
	נָחֵי ל״ה(8	בנה	בָּנֹה	לִבְנוֹת	בָּנָה
	כְּפוּלִים(9	סבב	סָבוֹב	לָסֹב	סָבַב

נוֹסַד	נוֹסֶדֶת	אֶוָּסֵד	יִוָּסֵד	הִוָּסֵד!	הִוָּסְדִי!
נִצַּל	נִצֶּלֶת	אֶנָּצֵל	יִנָּצֵל	הִנָּצֵל!	הִנָּצְלִי!
נֶאֱכַל	נֶאֱכֶלֶת	אֵאָכֵל	יֵאָכֵל	הֵאָכֵל!	הֵאָכְלִי!
נוֹסַר	נוֹסֶרֶת	אִוָּסֵר	יִוָּסֵר	הִוָּסֵר!	הִוָּסְרִי!
נָכוֹן	נְכוֹנָה	אֶכּוֹן	יִכּוֹן	הִכּוֹן!	הִכּוֹנִי!
נָבוֹן	נְבוֹנָה	אֶבּוֹן	יִבּוֹן	הִבּוֹן!	הִבּוֹנִי!
נִמְלָא	נִמְלֵאת	אֶמָּלֵא	יִמָּלֵא	הִמָּלֵא!	הִמָּלְאִי!
נִבְנָה	נִבְנֵית	אֶבָּנֶה	יִבָּנֶה	הִבָּנֶה!	הִבָּנִי!
נָסַב	נְסַבָּה	אֶסַּב	יִסַּב	הִסַּב!	הִסַּבִּי!
מְיֻשַּׁב	מְיֻשֶּׁבֶת	אֲיֻשַּׁב	יְיֻשַּׁב	יַשֵּׁב!	יַשְּׁבִי!
מְנַצֵּל	מְנַצֶּלֶת	אֲנַצֵּל	יְנַצֵּל	נַצֵּל!	נַצְּלִי!
מְאַכֵּל	מְאַכֶּלֶת	אֲאַכֵּל	יְאַכֵּל	אַכֵּל!	אַכְּלִי!
מְיַסֵּר	מְיַסֶּרֶת	אֲיַסֵּר	יְיַסֵּר	יַסֵּר!	יַסְּרִי!
מְכוֹנֵן	מְכוֹנֶנֶת	אֲכוֹנֵן	יְכוֹנֵן	כּוֹנֵן!	כּוֹנְנִי!
מְבוֹנֵן	מְבוֹנֶנֶת	אֲבוֹנֵן	יְבוֹנֵן	בּוֹנֵן!	בּוֹנְנִי!
מְמַלֵּא	מְמַלֵּאת	אֲמַלֵּא	יְמַלֵּא	מַלֵּא!	מַלְּאִי!
מְבַנֶּה	מְבַנָּה	אֲבַנֶּה	יְבַנֶּה	בַּנֵּה!	בַּנִּי!
מְסוֹבֵב	מְסוֹבֶבֶת	אֲסוֹבֵב	יְסוֹבֵב	סוֹבֵב!	סוֹבְבִי!

נִפְעַל Nif'al	חֲסְרֵי פ״י	יסד	הִוָּסֵד	לְהִוָּסֵד	נוֹסַד
	חֲסְרֵי פ״נ	נצל	נִצּוֹל	לְהִנָּצֵל	נִצַּל
	נָחֵי פ״א	אכל	נֶאֱכֹל	לְהֵאָכֵל	נֶאֱכַל
	נָחֵי פ״י	יסר	הִוָּסֵר	לְהִוָּסֵר	נוֹסַר
	נָחֵי ע״ו	כון	נָכוֹן	לְהִכּוֹן	נָכוֹן
	נָחֵי ע״י	בין	נָבוֹן	לְהִבּוֹן	נָבוֹן
	נָחֵי ל״א	מלא	נִמְלֹא	לְהִמָּלֵא	נִמְלָא
	נָחֵי ל״ה	בנה	נִבְנֹה	לְהִבָּנוֹת	נִבְנָה
	כְּפוּלִים	סבב	הִסֹּב	לְהִסֵּב	נָסַב
פִּעֵל Pi'él	חֲסְרֵי פ״י	ישב	יַשֵּׁב	לְיַשֵּׁב	יִשֵּׁב
	חֲסְרֵי פ״נ	נצל	נַצֵּל	לְנַצֵּל	נִצֵּל
	נָחֵי פ״א	אכל	אַכֵּל	לְאַכֵּל	אִכֵּל
	נָחֵי פ״י	יסר	יַסֵּר	לְיַסֵּר	יִסֵּר
	נחי ע״ו	כון	כּוֹנֵן	לְכוֹנֵן	כּוֹנֵן
	נָחֵי ע״י	בין	בּוֹנֵן	לְבוֹנֵן	בּוֹנֵן
	נָחֵי ל״א	מלא	מַלֵּא	לְמַלֵּא	מִלֵּא
	נָחֵי ל״ה	בנה	בַּנֵּה	לְבַנּוֹת	בִּנָּה
	כְּפוּלִים	סבב	סוֹבֵב	לְסוֹבֵב	סוֹבֵב

עָבַר	הֹוֶה	עָתִיד	צִוּוּי
יֻשַּׁב	מְיֻשָּׁב מְיֻשֶּׁבֶת	אֲיֻשַּׁב יְיֻשַּׁב	
נֻצַּל	מְנֻצָּל מְנֻצֶּלֶת	אֲנֻצַּל יְנֻצַּל	
אֻכַּל	מְאֻכָּל מְאֻכֶּלֶת	אֲאֻכַּל יְאֻכַּל	
יֻסַּר	מְיֻסָּר מְיֻסֶּרֶת	אֲיֻסַּר יְיֻסַּר	
כּוֹנַן	מְכוֹנָן מְכוֹנֶנֶת	אֲכוֹנַן יְכוֹנַן	–
בּוֹנַן	מְבוֹנָן מְבוֹנֶנֶת	אֲבוֹנַן יְבוֹנַן	
מֻלָּא	מְמֻלָּא מְמֻלֵּאת	אֲמֻלָּא יְמֻלָּא	
בֻּנָּה	מְבֻנֶּה מְבֻנָּה	אֲבֻנֶּה יְבֻנֶּה	
סוֹבַב	מְסוֹבָב מְסוֹבְבָה	אֲסוֹבַב יְסוֹבַב	
הִתְיַשֵּׁב	מִתְיַשֵּׁב ־שֶׁבֶת	אֶתְיַשֵּׁב יִתְיַשֵּׁב	הִתְיַשֵּׁב!
הִתְנַצֵּל	מִתְנַצֵּל ־צֶּלֶת	אֶתְנַצֵּל יִתְנַצֵּל	הִתְנַצֵּל!
הִתְאַכֵּל	מִתְאַכֵּל ־כֶּלֶת	אֶתְאַכֵּל יִתְאַכֵּל	הִתְאַכֵּל!
הִתְיַסֵּר	מִתְיַסֵּר ־סֶּרֶת	אֶתְיַסֵּר יִתְיַסֵּר	הִתְיַסֵּר!
הִתְקוֹמֵם	מִתְקוֹמֵם ־מֶמֶת	אֶתְקוֹמֵם יִתְקוֹמֵם	הִתְקוֹמֵם!
הִתְבּוֹנֵן	מִתְבּוֹנֵן ־נֶנֶת	אֶתְבּוֹנֵן יִתְבּוֹנֵן	הִתְבּוֹנֵן!
הִתְמַלֵּא	מִתְמַלֵּא ־לֵּאת	אֶתְמַלֵּא יִתְמַלֵּא	הִתְמַלֵּא!
הִתְגַּלָּה	מִתְגַּלֶּה ־גַּלָּה	אֶתְגַּלֶּה יִתְגַּלֶּה	הִתְגַּלֵּה!
הִסְתּוֹבֵב	מִסְתּוֹבֵב ־בֶבֶת	אֶסְתּוֹבֵב יִסְתּוֹבֵב	הִסְתּוֹבֵב!

בִּנְיָן	גִּזְרָה	הַפֹּעַל	מָקוֹר	שֵׁם הַפֹּעַל עִם ל׳
פֻּעַל Pu'al	חַסְרֵי פ״י	ישב	יֻשּׁוֹב	
	חַסְרֵי פ״נ	נצל	נֻצּוֹל	
	נָחֵי פ״א	אכל	אֻכּוֹל	
	נָחֵי פ״י	יסר	יֻסּוֹר	–
	נָחֵי ע״ו	כון	כּוֹנוֹן	
	נָחֵי ע״י	בין	בּוֹנוֹן	
	נָחֵי ל״א	מלא	מֻלֹּא	
	נָחֵי ל״ה	בנה	בֻּנֹּה	
	כְּפוּלִים	סבב	סוֹבוֹב	
הִתְפָּעֵל Hitpa'él	חַסְרֵי פ״י	ישב	הִתְיַשֵּׁב	לְהִתְיַשֵּׁב
	חַסְרֵי פ״נ	נצל	הִתְנַצֵּל	לְהִתְנַצֵּל
	נָחֵי פ״א	אכל	הִתְאַכֵּל	לְהִתְאַכֵּל
	נָחֵי פ״י	יסר	הִתְיַסֵּר	לְהִתְיַסֵּר
	נָחֵי ע״ו	קום	הִתְקוֹמֵם	לְהִתְקוֹמֵם
	נָחֵי ע״י	בין	הִתְבּוֹנֵן	לְהִתְבּוֹנֵן
	נָחֵי ל״א	מלא	הִתְמַלֵּא	לְהִתְמַלֵּא
	נָחֵי ל״ה	גלה	הִתְגַּלֵּה	לְהִתְגַּלּוֹת
	כְּפוּלִים	סבב	הִסְתּוֹבֵב	לְהִסְתּוֹבֵב

הוֹשִׁיב	מוֹשִׁיב	־בָה	אוֹשִׁיב	יוֹשִׁיב	הוֹשֵׁב!
הִצִּיל	מַצִּיל	מַצֶּלֶת	אַצִּיל	יַצִּיל	הַצֵּל!
הֶאֱכִיל	מַאֲכִיל	־לָה	אַאֲכִיל	יַאֲכִיל	הַאֲכֵל!
הוֹרִישׁ	מוֹרִישׁ	־שָׁה	אוֹרִישׁ	יוֹרִישׁ	הוֹרֵשׁ!
הֵקִים	מֵקִים	מְקִימָה	אָקִים	יָקִים	הָקֵם!
הֵבִין	מֵבִין	מְבִינָה	אָבִין	יָבִין	הָבֵן!
הִמְצִיא	מַמְצִיא	־צִיאָה	אַמְצִיא	יַמְצִיא	הַמְצֵא!
הִגְלָה	מַגְלֶה	־לָה	אַגְלֶה	יַגְלֶה	הַגְלֵה!
הֵסֵב	מֵסֵב	מְסִבָּה	אָסֵב	יָסֵב	הָסֵב!
הוּשַׁב	מוּשָׁב	־בָה	אוּשַׁב	יוּשַׁב	
הׇצַּל	מׇצָּל	־לָה	אׇצַּל	יׇצַּל	
הׇאֳכַל	מׇאֳכָל	־כֶלֶת	אׇאֳכַל	יׇאֳכַל	
הוּרָשׁ	מוּרָשׁ	־רָשָׁה	אוּרַשׁ	יוּרַשׁ	
הוּקַם	מוּקָם	־קָמָה	אוּקַם	יוּקַם	
הוּבַן	מוּבָן	־בֶנֶת	אוּבַן	יוּבַן	
הׇמְצָא	מׇמְצָא	־צֵאת	אׇמְצָא	יׇמְצָא	
הׇגְלָה	מׇגְלֶה	־לָה	אׇגְלֶה	יׇגְלֶה	
הוּסַב	מוּסַב	־סַבָּה	אוּסַב	יוּסַב	

הִפְעִיל Hif'il	חַסְרֵי פ״י	ישב	הוֹשַׁב	לְהוֹשִׁיב
	חַסְרֵי פ״נ	נצל	הַצֵּל	לְהַצִּיל
	נָחֵי פ״א	אכל	הַאֲכֵל	לְהַאֲכִיל
	נָחֵי פ״י	ירש	הוֹרֵשׁ	לְהוֹרִישׁ
	נָחֵי ע״ו	קום	הָקֵם	לְהָקִים
	נָחֵי ע״י	בין	הָבֵן	לְהָבִין
	נָחֵי ל״א	מצא	הַמְצֵא	לְהַמְצִיא
	נָחֵי ל״ה	גלה	הַגְלֵה	לְהַגְלוֹת
	כְּפוּלִים	סבב	הָסֵב	לְהָסֵב
הָפְעַל Hof'al	חַסְרֵי פ״י	ישב		
	חַסְרֵי פ״נ	נצל		
	נָחֵי פ״א	אכל		
	נָחֵי פ״י	ירש		
	נָחֵי ע״ו	קום		
	נָחֵי ע״י	בין		
	נָחֵי ל״א	מצא		
	נָחֵי ל״ה	גלה		
	כְּפוּלִים	סבב		

Notes

Notes

Notes